THE LAW OF CONFLICTS AND OF INTERNATIONAL ECONOMIC RELATIONS

FERENC MÁDL AND LAJOS VÉKÁS

THE LAW OF CONFLICTS AND OF INTERNATIONAL ECONOMIC RELATIONS

AKADÉMIAI KIADÓ, BUDAPEST

Authors
Ferenc Mádl: Introduction, Chapters VIII–XIX, XXV–XXVI, XXIX, XXXIV–XXXVII
Lajos Vékás: Chapters I–VII, XX–XXIV, XXVII–XXVIII, XXX–XXXIII

This book is published with the financial assistance of the Loránd Eötvös University, Budapest

This book is the English version of the fourth Hungarian edition
Nemzetközi magánjog és nemzetközi gazdasági kapcsolatok joga
published by Nemzeti Tankönyvkiadó, Budapest 1997

Translated by

MIHÁLY KOCSIS

Translation revised by

ALLAN TATHAM

First English edition 1987
Second enlarged and revised English edition 1998

ISBN 963 05 7525 6

Published by Akadémiai Kiadó, H-1117 Budapest, Prielle Kornélia u. 19–35

Printed in Hungary
by Akadémiai Nyomda, Martonvásár

PREFACE

This book presents a broad view of the Hungarian as well as the international systems of institutions through which the myriad of international personal activities and economic relations are currently conducted. In more recent years, these systems have undergone important developments, none so dramatic and revolutionary as those experienced by the system transformation and change of regime in the former centrally-controlled socialist economies of Central and Eastern Europe. Above all, the greatest changes were wrought through and in the law. According to the principles of the market economy, much had to be reconstructed: the legal system, the ownership structure, companies and other models of economic association, tax and investment policy, the rules on foreign investments, the conditions for a properly-functioning banking and credit system, together with the realignment in foreign economic relations occasioned by internal and external factors. The cooperation between these newly-refounded market economies and large international organisations, such as GATT, WTO, IMF, IBRD, EBRD, EU, EFTA etc. therefore required a new legal and commercial reorientation. Future enlargement of the EU to include Central and East European States, has also brought challenges for the law, no less than the transformation of GATT into the WTO, truly the world's pre-eminent international economic organisation. All these innovations have provoked profound changes in the way in which the legal systems of Hungary and international society regulate such matters. This work reflects those changes along with all the functioning laws and legal institutions and thus seeks to be regarded as an indispensible tool for the purposes of education, scientific research, international lawmaking, and assisting persons and entities, both private and public, domestic and foreign, in their understanding of this complex and fascinating field of study.

Budapest, March 15, 1998

The Authors

PREFACE

[illegible]

CONTENTS

INTRODUCTION

ON THE LEGAL REGULATION OF INTERNATIONAL PERSONAL AND ECONOMIC TRANSACTIONS IN GENERAL

§1. THE LEGAL REGULATION OF INTERNATIONAL PERSONAL AND ECONOMIC TRANSACTIONS – AS DISCUSSED IN THIS BOOK

This book covers two branches of jurisprudence or areas of law, namely private international law and the law of international economic relations. In our exposition both are assigned relative independence, with *the systematic totality of private international law and the main elements of the law of international economic relations* discussed in their mutual complementarity and disciplinary complexity. The principal reasons for this approach, as will be theoretically explained in §2 below, are the following.

1. Personal and (external) economic transactions are expressed and served by law, both historically and especially at present, in a way leading to strong complexity as seen either in relation to the branch of law or in respect of the mode of regulation, notably in the spheres of (a) domestic substantive law; (b) substantive and procedural law of international origin (civil law, law of civil procedure, family law, labour law, administrative law, to refer but to the key areas); (c) internal private international law (law of conflicts); and (d) private international law of international origin.

2. In this context, private international law was originally no more than a body of conflict rules and, although this term was later extended to include (at least in part) the substantive civil-law rules of international origin, regulation remained hardly ascertainable in its complexity.

3. The authors have adopted an approach that meets the need for our subject to be discussed, as fully as can be, in all its aspects. This necessitated devising a rational system in which to grasp the vast body of legal material in terms of both "legal field" and discipline so as to satisfy the desiderata of presenting complex regulation.

The authors are convinced of the need (on which they hope to be borne out by the following exposition) for systemizing in some way not only the traditional private international law, but also the law of international economic relations with an overall view of its main elements. Since the compass of this work naturally forbids a full-length treatment of the law of international economic relations, while the law of international personal and economic transactions was deemed advisable to be presented in its complexity, the authors have chosen (a) to consider the full range of private international law and, (b) relying on its system for a general framework of discussion, (c) to cover to the extent possible the sets of rules and problems concerning international economic relations.

§2. ON THE SUBSTANCE OF AND THE LINK BETWEEN PRIVATE INTERNATIONAL LAW AND THE LAW OF INTERNATIONAL ECONOMIC RELATIONS

1. Facts point to the existence of disorder in the domain of private international law, which appears damaging to teaching and research and hence, ultimately, to practice itself in the longer run. Indeed, there is something lying at the root of it, a phenomenon called *the revolt of facts* (as the situation is referred to in international literature). What is implied, then, in this revolt? What scientific attempts have been made to stop the revolt? What kind of solution can be offered here in Hungary?

(a) Any revolt is against some traditional order. In short, facts in our case revolt against two things: *the traditional concept of private international law and its tendency* to embrace the new elements of the law of international personal and economic transactions as well. They revolt against the absolute rule of the concept which was formulated in the most classical way by Savigny in Volume VIII of his *System des heutigen Römischen Rechts*. That volume is entitled *Territorial and Temporal Rule of Laws and Regulations over Legal Relationships*, the very formulation indicating that private international law is a law of conflicts destined to resolve conflicts caused by legal relationships extending beyond national boundaries (since internal laws do not) and also coming within the ambit of "foreign" laws. The law resolves such conflicts by the aid of reference rules, the system of which is called private international law. However, many things have come to pass since Savigny's time. What is beyond the realm of conflict rules? Again, what is revolted against is the traditional separation by branch of law or by the inertial tendency of such systematization to keep new relationships within the bounds of "this or that" traditional branch of law.

(b) *And what are the facts that have come to revolt*? First, the number of legal relationships with international elements is several times greater than that obtaining in Savigny's day. The *quantitative growth* is tremendous. Secondly, these relationships, particularly in the sphere of the external economy, are *qualitatively different* from those which were known in the reign of traditional private international law, when the classical institutions of private international law were basically limited to traditional legal relationships between natural persons. What are the qualitatively new aspects? They include contracts covering large-scale cooperative operations and interlinking for long periods of time the economic, technological, productive and commercial activities of enterprises; foreign investment projects, international leasing and international corporations; special transfers of technology involving not only sale of patents, but establishment by the other party of a plant operating on a new technology; expansion of direct economic operations by the State in the domain of economic relations (consider the Adria Oil Pipelines or, in Western Europe, Eurofima, Eurochemie and other projects or undertakings in which the State acting as *quasi iure gestionis* is directly involved); coordination of the economic policies of States in numerous aspects of European integration; replacement of CMEA by effective bilateral systems of regulation; emergence of global systems of regulation (GATT/WTO, IMF, goods exchange agreements etc.); spread of new systems of payments (export credits, credit guarantees, export credit insurance, letters of credit, etc.); and several other types of transactions and legal relationships that are essentially new in comparison to the classical period of the full-scale development of private international law.

The *mode of regulation* is a third element in the revolt of facts. Regulation by substantive law becomes increasingly dominant in addition to the law of conflicts and, very importantly, this area is heavily invaded by norms of administrative law and public international law. Today almost every branch of the entire legal system is involved in the play of a mechanism which might be called the "law of international economic relations". This is of particular relevance because the active role of the State in this domain can be observed in the application of norms that are in the nature of public law.

The *greater diversity of legislative sources* is a further element in the revolt of facts. The sources of law comprise not only the internal law of conflicts, and the unification of international substantive law, but also, among others, the international agreements on integration or the legal norms constructed by organs of integration. Consider further the type of legislative sources like the United Nations Charter of Economic Rights and Duties of States, the ECE norms in the nature of customary law, the UNCTAD decisions of a normative character influencing the international economic relations of States, including Hungary, or GATT/WTO as a special and complex source of law because, on the one hand, it is destined to govern and influence economic policy decisions by States and, on the other, it contains concrete institutions of commercial law.

The essence therefore consists in the incomparably greater number of legal relationships involved, in the appearance of different types of new legal relationships, in a notable change in the mode and level of regulation, with great prominence given to goal-oriented regulation (including the emergence of a system of complex regulation on the active guiding role of the State, and the necessity to think in terms of such a system). These facts and demands of development do not fit into the framework of private international law or the branches of law as traditionally separated, and call for new forms and systems of regulation.

2. The second question concerns the *solutions generated by the revolt of facts in different countries*.

(a) A few words should be said of the *common law* in the first place. The common law adheres to the *principle of omnis definitio in iure civile periculosa* (avoiding theoretical notions and thorough systematization based on principles) so characteristic of the classical Roman law. This is why the common law is unfamiliar with the kind of structure which, marking the European legal systems, came about historically as a result of thinking in terms of Justinian's principles, forms and systems and which represents the systematic and conceptual approach of dividing the law into branches in which we "live and move". Hence the types of system created by the revolt of facts in contradistinction to private international law has caused no particular problem in the common law literature. It is simply under the approaches of functionalism and pragmatism that monographs were and are written and that branches of study have developed on different questions of international economic relations, bearing titles such as the "common law of Atlantic areas", the "European law", the "law of international economic organizations", the "law of economic competition" in international economic relations and so on. Private international law was kept within its classical framework everywhere, serving basically as the law of conflicts, and no attempt was made to incorporate into this branch of law the legal material affected by the revolt of facts.

(b) *Continental jurisprudence*, which historically traces the form system of its subject-matter to the systemized post-classical Roman law, represents a world of thinking in terms of systems and principles, thus claiming credit for the positive aspects that derive from the inner laws of legal science seeking to elevate knowledge to notion and to systemize it. This is surely a higher degree of cognition in comparison to an absence of such phenomenon in the province of generalizations. European learning is known to have been characterized initially by an effort to fit the said developments into the framework of private international law by inserting sets of appendices related to public law, substantive private law, private international law, administrative law and the law of integration. This method held sway for a while, but by now been abandoned, and private international law has slipped back into its classical domain. The above-mentioned facts of international economic relations called for new systems based on pragmatic approaches such as "international commercial law", "law of international economic organizations" and others. Nevertheless, most monographs seek for some sort of systematization, even in the context of pragmatic tendencies and functionalism. Here, too, functionalism is understood to embrace the totality of legal devices necessary for the workings of a given sector of the economy and to subordinate the system thereto. Theories are nonetheless drafted to elevate things to the level of theoretical generalizations, to provide conceptualistic explanations of a particular sectoral unit. It would take up too much time to analyze all the monographs of this character. To give an example, in his work entitled *The Law of the European Economic Community,*

Ipsen wishes to translate the legal mechanism of the EEC into a system as understood in Europe, theorizing along this line: The law governing the economic integration of Western Europe includes a complex, centripetal, coherent body of legal material which, by its nature as a branch of law, is a kind of mutation of internal economic law; this in turn is nothing other than the totality of civil-law institutions regulating commodity relations, plus the norms of public law grafted onto those institutions and transmitting State "interventionism", the latter being specific tools of economic policy applied to govern, influence and delimit the sphere of civil law at the enterprise level and blending into an admixture of specialized economic law. Integration is nothing more than the elevation of this process from the national to the Community level (*Entnationalisierung*). It follows that, speaking in terms of branches of law, Community law is nothing more than economic law thus elevated to the Community level, a so-called European economic law in which organizational and administrative elements are closely built on the civil-law or commercial-law material. The result is a coherent, self-contained field of law which, presupposed by each of its components, is able to function only in such a unity from the viewpoint of State direction, performance by the State of its economic function, and civil-law practice alike. On the theoretical plane, all this presents the contours of a claim for, and the confines of, an appropriate discipline of the same denomination. Theorizations along this and similar lines as well as switching back to general categories of earlier periods and to general problems of systematization can also be found in the pragmatic "systems" of Western Europe. The facts in this field may be said to have provoked a disintegration of the traditional system of legislative branches in the legal literature of Western countries: where a theory has been devised it postulates such disintegration or "simply" follows the road of pragmatism and functionalism, sometimes even in the "personal union" of "unprincipled" conceptual approaches to theoretical systematization on the one hand and to pragmatism on the other. In his theoretical writings Schmitthoff, for example, upheld Rabel's doctrine of the *lex mercatoria*, which is nothing more than a theoretically well-definable system of the law framed by international legislation and practice to govern international trade (originally a system of civil law). Yet there is no trace of such theorization in his textbook called *The Law of International Trade*, which simply offers a pragmatic treatment of the entire legal mechanism of England's foreign trade law, from customs tariffs through authorization by the State of contractual transactions to everything of relevance to foreign trade and the related function of legislation.

(c) The laws of the *countries in Central and Eastern Europe* similarly form part, *mutatis mutandis* of course, of the process we have called the revolt of facts. With the demise of "real socialism" and of CMEA, theoretical devices and proposed disciplines like the "law of socialist economic integration" or the "(socialist) international economic law" have naturally become of curio value in legal history. However, the painstaking theoretical efforts concerning the nature of private international law as a branch of law and the extent to which the broader concept of private international law was able to cover the said facts (substantive law and areas belonging to other branches of law) as well as the quests for new avenues have also made Hungarian thinking on private international law open to the new systems of rules evolved by the modern world (see §2 in the second Hungarian edition of this book).

(d) It may be stated *as a general conclusion* that, first, the ferment and the search for a way out have been set in train throughout the world; second, private international law has meanwhile undergone a kind of metamorphosis in which it may more or less regain its classical stature, and, third, complexity has grown into an essential and decisive criterion in the exploration of new avenues. Systems have also emerged seeking conceptual justification and terming the legal material covered by the given concept as a complex branch of law or even as a traditional branch of law. All this goes to show, moreover, that a new systematization is of topical interest and that the efforts we have outlined are reflective of an actual social need.

In a study published in *Encyclopedia Moderna,* Heisenberg describes the advance of sciences as a method by which science first perceives new facts within the existing systems and then examines and elevates them into notions, and when they grow in number it tests them against the conceptual elements and the systematic whole of the old system and, as the next step, gives them a general expression, transcribing them into a new system, into a new theory. By doing so science serves progress in a given field with adequate means of responding to reality. It seems that, as regards the problems of international economic relations under consideration, we find ourselves in this state, and even in a more advanced phase, of scientific development.

3. In searching for our answer (for more than ten years now: see §2 (3) in the first Hungarian edition of this book), we have proceeded basically from this consideration: *a theory of systematization must be a device for a clear reflection of two decisive factors of reality.*

The first factor is the characteristic novelty of the regulation of international economic relations, which is marked by the presence of two interdependent elements: (i) that of the State or power, the set of State power and administrative relationships transmitted by public law in the regulation of international economic relations; and (ii) that of the enterprise, the enterprise level, or the sphere of commodity relations expressed and governed by private law, the science of civil law. *This is a fact of a certain legal symbiosis of public and private law* which today determines the character of legal regulation in the sphere of international economic relations.

The other decisive factor to be reflected by a modern theory of systematization is *the relatively independent nature of law*; it is a self-contained system governed by an inner logic of its own, the substance lying in the method of regulation concerning internal delimitation and arrangement, in transcribing, as it were, reality – the various economic sectors or the economy itself – into a system of legal regulation, which is only possible if regard is also had to its inner logic. If this were not the case, expressing reality in its totality or, e.g., by economic sectors with their corresponding branches of law would result either in an amorphous mass of rules unsuited to perform its function or in as many reflections and angles of refraction as there are economic sectors, knowing the proper course of action to be taken in the intricacies of regulation.

Moreover, systematization should meet the *didactic-methodological requirement* of creating a rational order in the processes of our thinking and, in particular, of our teaching and learning.

What follows from these requirements for an adequate reflection?

(i) First of all, *private international law is, even by these criteria, a clearly independent branch of law, in the sense of a classical law of conflicts*. Its subject-matter is the underlying reality: the economic relationships of the subjects at civil law, combined with personal relationships, which come under the regulation of substantive law, a regulatory system tailored to the juxtaposition of equal parties. This system carries the fabric of private international law rules, which employ the remitting method, relying on indirect regulation, wherein lies a distinctive feature marking this system off sharply from other regulatory systems. This is a closed system, being a hierarchical unity of norms, general and special, mutually interrelated and one presupposing the other, with the rules of the general part encompassing the whole special part, and, like coefficients, always acting in common with the rules in brackets, meaning that the general norms are congruous with those of the special part, but do not go beyond the bounds of the law of conflicts. Thus what we have is a branch of law giving an optimal expression of reality, with a known purpose to serve, a known degree of efficiency, and a known field of optimal applicability.

It is a different matter that unresolved problems of systematization abound even in private international law of the classical approach, as is pointed out in the criticism of the first edition (Bán) and is also evidenced by the debate (covered by Király) that followed upon the second Hungarian edition of this book. In connection with this "domestic" problem of private international law, we refer to Chapter I on the Concept of Private International Law, but the argument here is about a different point.

(ii) Notably, our question now is whether or not the large amount of legal material governing international economic relations and thus *remaining outside* the scope of private international law, no matter how broadly yet classically understood and of whatever structure, constitutes a branch of law. It must be said that it does not, although, as previously remarked, one of the components to be reflected is regulatory interdependence prevalent in the branch covered. Yet, let us accept here the theoretical hypothesis that certain legal material is transmuted into a branch of law by the closed nature of the general and special parts. If the language and term "branch of law" are taken to mean this phenomenon, then they should not be used to designate a dissimilar phenomenon. Once the meaning of the term "element" has been clarified, a "compound" cannot also be said to be an element, lest we should confuse what is clear and lose sight of the fundamental requirement of scientific cognition, any more than it is advisable for the complex legal material under consideration (the elements of which mingle and thereby become a compound, a new quality) to be called a branch of law, even for practical purposes.

Nor should the two be confused conceptually on the practical plane. In practice, too, one should always be aware of applying a concrete rule of civil law in order to achieve this or that practical end, or of settling a concrete legal relationship by employing an administrative norm as a direct command of the State, because an unambiguous solution of the particular case can be expected from it alone.

(iii) Well, we ourselves have said that the legal material in question *has taken on a new quality*. This quality, however, is not that of a branch of law but one in the sense that a compound is a new quality and not an element.

We shall now anticipate the thesis, the conception formed of the question contemplated, that *the law of international economic relations is the totality of rules which, given their weight, function and regulative peculiarities, constitute a coherent, relatively independent field of law and, in terms of legal science, an independent discipline*. The designation "law of international economic relations" will henceforward be used in its technical sense, as a technical term. So far as this designation or definition is concerned, it is a descriptive and explanatory expression of a concept. It is difficult to find a term that is linguistically more clearly expressive of the concept of this legal field. The situation would be simpler if, for example, the Hungarian words *ág* (branch) and *ágazat* (a major branch carrying several smaller branches) had sharply different meanings. According to the explanatory dictionary of the Hungarian language, *ág* is a stronger branch growing from the trunk of a tree, while *ágazat* is the totality of smaller branches carried by a major branch. So it might be said that the law of international economic relations is a *jogágazat* (a ramification of law), because it is the totality of those offshoots of the legal system which share the quality denoting the regulation of international economic relations. Yet the difference between these two designations has become blurred in legal literature. One might also say "international economic law" and understand it to mean, as it actually should in the following discussion, the law of international economic relations; it would be a simpler, "more accepted" term, but for many legal writers its meaning is "reserved" for dealing with systems of economic rules purely administrative in nature. Its use with a different meaning for our present purposes would but increase the existing confusion.

(iv) As regards now the nature of the *law of international economic relations* as a coherent, relatively independent, complex field of law, it *can be viewed from both a normative and a disciplinary angle*.

Viewed *from the normative angle*, the following aspects may be mentioned. First, there is a considerable quantity of norms which simply cannot be encompassed by private international law. Second, this body of legal material has no shelter or at least is not cultivated in sufficient depth in any branch of law, even in administrative law or in public international law. Third, it has a homogeneous subject-matter – property and economic relations – overlain with purely public-law mechanisms designed to ensure the proper functioning thereof. Fourth, the peculiarity of its regulation, namely the combined presence of foreign elements, substantive-law rules and conflicts norms, serves as a cohesive block inasmuch as the law of conflicts has a role, though not decisive, to play in the law of international economic relations; another sign of cohesiveness in such regulation is, as mentioned before, the symbiotic presence of State and enterprise, or public-law and civil-law elements, power and administrative relationships and commodity relations, which today determine the character of the regulation. Fifth, this normative material is held together by its purpose and function, by a certain legal guidance, which calls for a complex approach in shaping the pattern of international economic relations; in other words, both the legislator and the judge must be familiar with the entire repertory of legal devices in their guidance of these relations. Sixth, certain general principles have assumed a normative form in the domain of international economic relations and, like a general part or a coefficient, embrace (though in varying degrees of intensity) this field of law, thereby acting upon it as a cementing force.

Viewed *from the disciplinary angle*, it may be stated that, first, legal disciplines have never been wholly confined to the traditional branches of law and that, second, this discipline has abundant normative material to draw upon. Third, this discipline is suitable for relative delimitation, as is the legal material forming its subject-matter. Fourth, the economic laws governing the development of international economic relations and the law-governed features of the relevant body of rules cannot be examined and described except in a complex disciplinary approach. This alone renders it possible to conduct inquiries, in accordance with scientific requirements, into the general problems of the applied legal mechanism as a whole and to devise a workable system of related norms. Moreover, rational and modern solutions concerning the different institutions can also be achieved under this complex disciplinary approach alone.

4. An important question (even with regard to the vitality of the above theoretical conception) is *whether the concrete elements of this legal field and discipline can be* grasped and *built into a worthwhile coherent system. It seems that they can.*

(a) In short, there would be a *general part* in the law of international economic relations.

(i) The general part would have a *theoretical section* concerned with the description and inquiry into the general problems related to the development and system of the law of international economic relations.

(ii) The next section of the general part would be concerned with the *sources of law*: internal law, multilateral and bilateral treaties, norms formulated by organs of integration (their role and characteristics), and other relevant international sources (like *Incoterms,* policy statements and recommendations of UNCTAD, etc.).

(iii) The third section of the general part would be represented by the *principles* guiding international economic relations. Some of them take on political and international forms at esoteric heights, others appear specifically in the form of civil law, and still others bear the character of administrative law or are of a mixed nature. Such are, among others, the principles of equal treatment and non-discrimination. Among the principles embodied in international instruments (e.g. the United Nations Charter of Economic Rights and Duties of States, GATT, the Helsinki Final Act) mention may be made of the rule of law in international relations, sovereignty over national wealth, fair and equitable treatment of capital invested abroad, most-favoured-nation status, anti-dumping rules, reciprocity, sovereign equality of States, membership treatment within the legal mechanism of integration, etc. These principles have each assumed a normative form in the various sources of law. So there is no particular need to look for a comprehensive system of principles: it is at hand, and it embraces, in an indirect or less direct form, the entire legal material, or a significant part thereof, which has a bearing on international economic relations.

(b) The subject of international economic relations and the mass of relevant norms could be treated in either the general or the special part. Leaving aside now the theoretical aspects, the subjects of law could form the first section of the *special part*.

(i) The *subjects* of the law of international economic relations appear on two planes. The first plane is that of the State or of public law, including at the level of internal law the organs of State direction, from parliament down to any authority or agency with a say in the shaping of international economic relations and, at the level of public international law, the intergovernmental organizations that play a role in moulding the shape of international economic relations, such as the United Nations, UNCTAD, ECE or GATT/WTO and IMF or the European Union. The second plane is that of enterprises: domestic companies (also) engaged in external economic activities and various forms of international economic associations. This is, then, the realm of subjects.

(ii) The domain of *contracts* includes in the first place all classical types of contract which by reason of their special features are deemed to be foreign trade contracts. In addition, it is necessary to deal with those sections of interstate trade agreements, consular conventions and goods exchange agreements which have a direct and decisive influence to bear on the development of economic relations, such as multilateral and bilateral treaties of a general nature, interstate agreements relating to concrete transactions, in short, treaties by which the State directs the external economy of the country or influences and determines, in accordance with its economic policy objectives, the economic processes channelled through the civil-law mechanism. Furthermore, the institutions and instruments used by the State to direct and influence the movement of foreign trade contracts "from within" – such as the system of licensing, credits and customs, all incentives and disincentives by which the State subjects the conclusion of concrete foreign trade contracts to a specific system of catalysts – should likewise be discussed in connection with contracts, even though they do not fall within the category of contracts.

(iii) The *law of payments* is, of course, concerned chiefly with the civil-law forms of payment, from bills of exchange, cheques, collection of commercial papers, letters of credit, commercial letters of credit and so on to certain elements of foreign exchange law, which likewise act upon the operation of civil-law institutions.

(iv) Finally, the set of problems concerning *legal disputes* is an essential component of the special part. The settlement of legal disputes in the field of international economic relations has traditionally been regarded as belonging to the domain of private international law. Even if we separate it now from the traditional field of private international law, disputes will naturally arise in the realm of private international law as well. Here, however, prominence would be given to arbitration as the main form for the settlement of disputes arising out of international economic relations. A very important issue is the question of how to deal with State immunity as an aspect of jurisdiction under present-day conditions.

5. In summing up the statements on the law of international economic relations the following points may be noted.

The large number of norms regulating international economic processes, their weight and character assume a new quality even in quantitative aspects and their role in directing the external economy (i.e. their directive function); the increasingly legal nature of the legal instruments used; the symbiotic presence and mutual dependence of the various instruments of a legal nature; and the inherent need of the means of legal regulation in order to make it function in a rational and consistent order – all these combine to demand and indeed warrant the large complex regulatory system in question to be considered in keeping with what it actually embodies, notably as a complex independent field of law and as an independent scientific discipline.

This would be the outline picture of the law sketched of international economic relations, while private international law is fundamentally related to civil law or, in the broader sense, to the science of civil law, being a conflicts law expression thereof.

Let us add in conclusion that the purpose of this survey has been, in part, to provide an outline of a clearer theoretical system and, in part, to formulate certain practical tasks some of which are of interest to, say, university education. What we have anticipated in the Introduction follows clearly from the foregoing: the concept of private international law as broadly understood at present (that it seeks to include the aforementioned new forms of regulation as well) should be abandoned, and both private international law and the law of international economic relations should receive emphasis, appropriate to their role and independence, even in education. This book has been written in pursuit of this end.

TITLE 1

GENERAL PROBLEMS OF PRIVATE INTERNATIONAL LAW

CHAPTER I

THE CONCEPT OF PRIVATE INTERNATIONAL LAW

§3. FACTS OF PRIVATE INTERNATIONAL LAW

1. By way of introduction, let us take three cases as examples to illustrate our proposition.

Case One: a lady bent on marriage

H. K. and J. M. (both Hungarian nationals) were married on 14 May 1941. In December 1942 J. M. was sent to the front and in summer 1943 his wife received official notice that he had "disappeared, presumably fallen in action on 29 June". No proceedings to declare him dead took place. In 1944 H. K. went to Austria, where she met and married G. v. M., a German national, who died, also at the front, on 16 April 1945. In September 1946 H. K. married T. W., a British subject, while in Austria. On 18 December 1950 the English High Court granted a final decree of divorce on the ground that H. K., after deserting her husband without cause, had been living separate from him for more than three years. Meanwhile, in September 1947, H. K. married A. I., an Egyptian national, in England. In 1960, H. K. petitioned the competent West German authorities for a war-widow's pension following on from the death of her second husband G. v. M. The validity of the marriage with G. v. M. is an essential prerequisite, but the validity of any of the subsequent marriages a bar, to a favourable judgment. *The question is this*: the law of which country (countries) is to govern the formal and material validity of each marriage? Should regard be had to the place of the ceremony, the nationality of the husbands, and the fact that H. K. has changed her nationality twice? (On the concrete problems involved, see §98.)

Case Two: a Trabant car and a shepherd dog

P. Z., a Hungarian national, spent his holidays in Spain in 1976. On 30 June, at a coastal resort, the shepherd dog of a Swedish tourist suddenly jumped in front of P. Z.'s car, damaging it. The car was driven by a Spanish national at a speed exceeding the limit of 30 km per hour. P. Z. had an insurance policy with a French company. *The question is this:* under the law of which country is P. Z.'s claim for damages to be decided? This case, too, has connections with several legal systems: the owner suffering the damage is a Hungarian, the person causing the damage is a Swede, the person possibly contributing to the damage by speeding is a Spaniard, the place of the damage is Spain, the place where the result of the damage (e.g. loss of wages) occurred is Hungary, and the seat of the insurance company is in France. (On the concrete set of problems, see §§63–64.)

Case Three: a Canadian uncle

E. J. was born in Budapest, went to England in 1938 and, during the war, to Canada and died as a British subject in 1975, in the Province of Quebec. His estate consisted of a share in jointly held immovable property situated in Hungary, of movables in Canada and of a considerable amount of cash held at a New York-based bank. E. J. died intestate and all his relatives lived in Hungary. *The question is this:* the law of which country is to be applied to the estate? Is inheritance governed by the law of the decedent's nationality or last domicile, or the law of the place where the assets of the estate were situate (and if so, the place of each asset separately)? (On the concrete set of problems, see §§94–95.)

2. A feature common to these cases is that their elements point beyond the bounds of a single legal system, having *links with the laws of several States* at a time, one element being related to a given system of law and another to a different one, thus creating a set of relationships of an international character. To give an example, the subjects at law in a given relationship have different nationalities, are domiciled in different States, their actions take place and the consequences thereof occur in different States, or the assets involved are to be found in various States, etc.

Another feature is that the participants in these relationships, though international in character, are *not States as sovereigns*, exercising public power in the territories concerned, but mainly nationals of different States or their organizations (natural and legal persons), and that the State, even if participating in such relationships, does not act as a sovereign vested with public power. To give an example, if a State is named beneficiary in a will concerning an estate situated abroad, the State participates in that relationship not as the subject of sovereignty, but, just as in domestic, non-international relationships of a similar nature, enjoys a legal status equal with natural and legal persons. (For a fuller treatment of the special status of the State in private international law, see §34.)

In determining the legal nature of relationships as illustrated by the above examples the first question to decide is the law of which State among those involved in a particular relationship should apply. *In principle the choice is between two or more legal systems*, between the laws of two or more States competing, as it were, for applicability. This problem is styled by jurisprudence as *conflict of laws* (the term of Latin origin being *collision* of laws.)

The relationships which have substantive connections with the legal systems of several States, without State sovereignty playing a direct role in them, are called facts of private international law and constitute the subject-matter thereof.

3. There is an immense variety of relationships (facts) constituting the subject-matter of private international law: proprietary relations (involving property, contracts, torts and inheritance) occurring in international economic transactions (*primarily foreign trade*); numerous facts of an international character in which *personal and proprietary elements* are organically intertwined (labour relations, relations connected with intellectual property); and relations in which *personal* aspects are paramount (family relations). Thus, as regards their substantive features, a wide variety of social relations enter the domain of private international law. Among others, international contracts of sale or licence concluded by a foreign trade company (with a foreign partner), labour contracts with foreigners, marriage with an alien, or adoption of an alien child are all deemed to be facts of private international law. A feature common to these relations, underlying essential differences in content, is the *foreign element* which makes it necessary to determine the applicable system of law.

From the foregoing it follows, however, that foreign element cases which are more closely connected with State sovereignty *do not belong* to the subject-matter of private international law. Thus, for instance, the foreign aspects of the law of nationality, the problems of double taxation, or the international ramifications of criminal law remain outside the scope of private international law even though they affect citizens or legal persons. Relations of this category *belong to (public) international law or the law of international economic relations, or* constitute the subject-matter of *international political law, international monetary law or international criminal law.*

In summary, the subject-matter of private international law may be stated as consisting of foreign element cases which, in the domestic field, are regulated chiefly by civil law, family law and labour law under the Hungarian legal system (cf. §8).

§4. JUSTIFICATION FOR THE CONSIDERATION OF FOREIGN LAW

The question is rightly asked why, and on what ground, the forum (court, arbitral tribunal, notary public, etc.) takes cognizance of the law of another country (having a substantial connection with a particular case), indeed, why does it not apply its own law without further consideration? To put it more precisely, why is the forum also subordinated to the law of another State? These questions are easy to answer: the forum has to consider the law of a foreign State because it is required by the law of its own State to do so.

The real problem is rather this: why does the State or the sovereign allow and even order its fora to take account of the statutory provisions of another State or sovereign as well?

An answer to this question, *pivotal to private international law*, has been attempted by jurisprudence in all ages. Differing in smaller or larger measure, the answers given are usually adequate reflections of the general legal conceptions and, directly or indirectly, of the economic, political and ideological conditions prevailing in a particular period. These conceptions will be considered in the chapter on the historical evolution of the theory of private international law (see §§10–11).

Suffice it to state here that the *law of the forum*, i.e. of the State of the court (arbitral tribunal, notary public, etc.) dealing with cases, is geared to the domestic conditions of its own State and rather often *has little* or no *direct contact with private law cases possessing foreign elements*. For this reason, proper adjudication of matters with relevant foreign connections requires the application of the legal system showing the closest link with the given facts, namely the application of a particular foreign law to certain cases. Ultimately it is in order to ensure the most appropriate decision that the State must admit the rules of a foreign sovereign to consideration by its own fora, which must therefore consider and eventually apply a foreign law. This is the underlying cause, the *leitmotiv*, behind the special legal consideration given to private international law cases. All this is, of course, conditional on *States' mutual recognition of and respect for each other's laws* (see item 1 in §9).

§5. INDIRECT AND DIRECT REGULATIONS

Legal development has evolved *two* methods of dealing with facts of private international law, and both are applied side by side. Distinction is made between *indirect* and *direct* regulation by law according to the adopted approach, the way of regulating facts.

1. Indirect regulation is spoken of when a fact of private international law is regulated in two phases, *with the help of rules established on two planes*.

The first-plane rules relate to the selection of the legal systems that may, in principle, be taken into consideration, and to the *choice* of the applicable law, determining which of the competing systems of law is to be looked for arriving at the decision of a concrete case. Accordingly the function of these rules is to resolve the conflict of competing legal systems, to give a guide to the applicable law, to refer to the norms governing the case. These rules are therefore called *conflict rules*, which designate nothing but the applicable system of law, neither determining the substance of private international law cases nor providing any guidance as to the rights and duties of the subjects of a particular legal relationship. Thus, given their nature and character, the conflict rules are always *remitting norms*. If, for instance, the Austrian partner of a Hungarian firm is in default in performing a leasing contract and the dispute between the parties is submitted to a court or an arbitral tribunal, the conflict rules will determine the law governing the case (the Hungarian or the Austrian law, or perhaps a third system of law), but only this and not the concrete consequences of the breach of contract (right of withdrawal, claim for damages, etc.).

The rules designed for the actual solution of a given relationship are found on the *second plane* of indirect regulation and are called *positive rules* as contrasted with conflict rules. They serve to determine the rights and obligations of the subjects of the legal relationship involved. If in our example the conflict rules of the State of the proceeding court (arbitral tribunal) refer to, say, Austrian law, then the positive rules of the applicable Austrian civil law will govern the concrete sanction in respect of the seller's default.

As can be seen, the indirect regulation of private international law facts consists of two phases:

(a) selection of the applicable law according to the *conflict rule*;

(b) solution of the particular legal relationship according to the *positive rules* of the applicable system of law.

2. The *direct* regulation of private international law facts means that the legal norms are directly applied, as in the case of domestic facts with no foreign connection, to the solution of the legal relationship on its merits, determining the rights and obligations of the parties. There is no intermediate phase of regulation, nor is one necessary, and there is no selection and designation of the applicable system of law. Thus the norms of direct regulation bear no conflict-rule character, *they are not conflict rules, but ones directly establishing the legal effects of private international law facts.*

The international character of these facts (their links with two or more legal systems) implies, however, that the direct regulation of such legal relationships is only possible through common (or uniform) legislation by the States (two or more States) concerned, primarily by means of international (bilateral or multilateral) agreements. Confronted with such cases, the States involved try to accommodate their economic interests, moral values, legal traditions, etc. and to resolve, by a common act of legislation, the conflict between their legal systems in a particular area. The direct regulation of private-law relations between States is illustrated by the Vienna Convention of 1980 on International Sale of Goods (see Sect. A of Chapter XXII).

Examples of international treaties concluded for the direct regulation of certain private-law relations between States are found in all periods. Moreover, States maintaining closer personal and economic relations (e.g. the Italian city-states of the Middle Ages) may be said to have made definite attempts to have their most important private law conflicts (conflicts between substantive and procedural laws) regulated directly by treaties. (An Agreement concluded in 1227 between Venice and Bologna, for instance, concerning the mutual recognition and enforcement of judgments testifies to a practice of codification that is still a noteworthy source of experience.)

Direct regulation of private international law facts, however, has never been comprehensive. *Neither can* regulation through international agreements *be exhaustive*, either in respect of State parties or of conflict problems in international property and personal relations. Full-scale regulation would necessitate a web of private international law treaties (or international codes) which, if at all possible, is as yet far from becoming a reality in the context of economic, political and other conditions. And we have not yet mentioned that achieving a degree of harmonization between the large number of interstate treaties, eliminating, or, to the extent possible, solving the contradictions or conflicts between agreements gives rise to no small problems even at the present time (see Majoros' book in the List of Sources).

3. These circumstances explain why once it was recognized that private-law relations with essential foreign elements cannot always be governed exclusively by internal legal rules (see §9), *indirect* (and hence more complicated) solutions for such relations by the application of conflict norms *became the more common approach.*

Although the past hundred years, especially the post-World War Two period, has seen a sharp increase in international agreements of a private-law nature, with *direct regulation of private international law facts receiving great emphasis* as regards the number of both agreements and State parties and, in particular, the practical weight of the problems covered, *the significance of indirect regulation (under the law of conflicts) has not diminished.* Both the indirect and direct methods of regulating facts of private international law are therefore employed even today. (For the principles governing the application of law with parallel reliance on both approaches, see item 2 in Sect. B of §12.)

§6. THE CONCEPT AND NATURE OF PRIVATE INTERNATIONAL LAW

1. The *concept of this branch of law* can be defined by determining the subject-matter of private international relations and the method of their regulation.

In our view, private international law is the totality of legal norms which govern indirectly (as conflicts norms) civil-law (property and connected non-property) as well as family and labour relations (i.e. private-law relations in the broader sense) containing foreign elements and having no direct link to State sovereignty.

The branch-of-law unity of private international law as conflicts law is usually unquestioned from within but there are two relatively recent *points of uncertainty* in this respect as well.

(a) One concerns the *homogeneity of the subject-matter* of regulation and is closely related to differentiation in the legal system, which is manifested mainly in the separation (full or partial) from private law of family law and labour law.

We believe that *these concerns can be safely removed.* There is no Chinese wall between proprietary and non-proprietary relations, and their close interrelationships and linkages are also amply evidenced by the post-World War Two development of Hungarian law: for example, negation of the commodity nature of labour relations has proved illusory. This is indicated in a similar manner by the development of the advanced civil-law systems, which, perhaps with no great theoretical "trumpeting", tend towards achieving a degree of at least relative independence, as is clearly the case with family law and labour law. For all their relatively objective foundations, the branch-of-law boundaries already appear much too variable by themselves to serve as a base of comparison, positive or negative, for any new branch of law. Similarly, the fact that the *method* of regulation plays such a fundamental role in the delimitation of the law of conflicts is explained by the normative peculiarities of conflicts rules (see §15): the distance between conflicts norms and the everyday relations constituting the subject-matter of regulation turns the method of regulation into a determinative factor of a branch of law.

(b) Again, it is this *absolute homogeneity* of the law of conflicts that may serve as a starting point for determining the systematic status of the *treaty-made law of conflicts* (conflict rules created by international treaties or agreements: see Chapter III), *another point of uncertainty,* which tends to break the unity of this branch of law. This has hitherto proved to be a very close link capable of preventing the law of conflicts from splitting into a domestic and a treaty-made law of conflicts.

However, one should not disregard the special features of this legal material which are derived from its international treaty origin, for they raise questions of relevance not only in public international law (or in constitutional law), but are also markedly manifest in the problematic of the law of conflicts, strictly so called.

Science has long neglected studying the separate questions of the *treaty-made private law of conflicts.* Writings of recent years being of a high academic standard give partly different weight to the specifics of the treaty-made private law of conflicts: while Kropholler *(Internationales Einheitsrecht)* places emphasis on a few special traits (classification, connecting factors, *renvoi,* "preliminary question", *ordre public*), Majoros claims that the treaty-made private law of conflicts differs essentially from the autonomous law of conflicts.

We maintain that the two fields show differences and occasionally even essential divergences *within their unity.* Thus, on the whole, *the national (autonomous) and the treaty-made private law of conflicts are invariably held together by the basically identical method of regulation as the chief cohesive force.*

2. As we have noted in the Introduction (§2), recent decades have also witnessed the spread of a *broader* concept of private international law which includes the direct rules governing facts of private international law. Formerly, this concept was understood by legal science and textbooks *alike* to comprise only the direct rules (conflict norms), and the majority of authorities on this discipline continue to define private international law in this narrower sense. The foregoing is evidence that we share this same view.

We are of the opinion that the methodological homogeneity, as discussed above, of conflict norms governing international relations of daily life prevents incorporation of the conflict norms and substantive rules of private international law into one and the same branch of law. Despite the identity of their regulative functions and the near-congruent similarity of the everyday relations regulated, the two fields of law are too incongruous to fit into one branch of law, because *their methods and inner logic are* far too *dissimilar.* (This statement of ours holds true both for the international treaty sources, currently seen as preponderant, of substantive private international law and for the national norms comparatively smaller in number.)

In order to substantiate our view, let us refer to an important aspect regarding the reason for as well as the purpose and role of arranging legal norms into separate branches of law: the *raison d'être* of delimiting branches of law lies in the possibilities of exploring and scientifically investigating the specific law-governed features of the legal norms created by the different branches of law (and at the same time relatively separated from the rest of such norms). Consequently, there is neither cause nor possibility for including in a single branch of law such legal fields as have no identical law-governed features despite the common purpose of regulation. And, at least for us, the conflict norms and the substantive rules of private international law show no such common features.

The deceptive appearance tending towards the opposite train of thought and alluding to the essential unity of the two methods of regulation is created by the identity of everyday relations to be regulated (apparently by that of the subject-matter of regulation). Anyone believing in this illusion might rightly ask the seemingly disarming question of wherein can lie so great a difference between, e.g., a contract of sale dispute eventually settled by the law of conflicts and one decided by the rules of substantive private international law. Indeed, there is no difference between the two contracts, but there are many in their legal regulation, for whereas the rules of substantive law actually decide the issue of law arising in connection with the contract, the conflict rules are by themselves incapable of settling the problem (see §5) but rather serve to designate the applicable substantive law only. It, therefore, seems to us, that this difference in legal regulation is sc fundamental as to *preclude any branch-of-law unity.*

3. It appears necessary to point out on this score that *branch of law* is basically and primarily a *scientific* category: the totality, consciously consolidated

and artificially separated from other sets of norms of the legal system, of the rules of law governing a roughly homogeneous subject-matter and employing a homogeneous method of regulation.

We understand the scientific character of the category to mean that the rationale of incorporating legal norms into branches of law lies primarily in exploring, analyzing and studying the common law-governed features of norms belonging together according to the aforementioned criteria. All this is to be done, of course, to meet the requirements of legislation, law enforcement and teaching rather than to serve as an end in itself, conceived under the false slogan of "science for science's sake". Thus, classification by branch of law is far from being an absolute but is an arrangement of legal norms that is valid within certain limits (is apt to perform specific functions only).

The relative validity of the system of branches of law is also manifested in the need for legislation, more particularly for law enforcement and even for education to step, *a fortiori*, over the branch-of-law barriers at every turn. Branch-of-law codes are still drafted to comprise sets of coherent norms based on identical principles, yet legal norms do not appear in this or that branch of law but, disregarding the boundaries thereof, are aimed at a complex regulation of different facts of daily life. Law enforcement becomes essentially divorced from the classification of legal material by branch of law. And, finally, we also believe it would be ill-advised to overemphasize the branch-of-law approach in the teaching of law. While it appears correct to form teaching the fundamentals of the legal system in an arrangement by branch of law, including the special principles, methodological peculiarities, basic institutions, etc. of the various branches of law, we see merit in the idea of presenting that part of the legal material which is ripe for teaching in a functional arrangement that would eventually break the branch-of-law boundaries. For that matter, our present work is also intended to provide an instance of this endeavour.

4. In this connection the reader may rightly ask whether a branch-of-law concept separating the legal material covered by indirect and direct regulation of private international law facts is not outdated and "aristocratic". We are convinced that it is not, unless the very organizing principle should itself be outdated. The case may further be stated for the latter, notably the anachronism of arranging legal material by branch of law. Eörsi, for example, concludes his work on the fundamental questions concerning the structure of the legal system (1977) with this Dodonian oracle: "Whether all this amounts to an orderly retreat of an outdated branch-of-law concept to a new line of defence or is a skirmish preparatory to a new arrangement based on branches of law is for the future to decide". In our view, full rejection of systematization by branch of law would be a course at least as ill conceived as an exaggeration of the pigeonholing approach. Branches of law should continue to be assigned a role with a good sense of proportion even if actual developments do not always fit into or transgress established frameworks as in the case of direct regulation of private international law facts. Nor will private international law as a branch of law be

a "loser" from its failure to encompass the directly regulatory norms of substantive law along with the law of conflicts or, more accurately, though at its worst, from direct regulation (by substantive law) encroaching upon its domain. Yet that is "the way of the world", which everybody may look on as something positive or negative according to his conviction (or taste).

5. Thus far we have left an important question unanswered. Where, in view of the above considerations, is the place of the rules of substantive private international law? This question cannot be evaded, if only for the reason that, despite its exaggerative formulation, Eörsi's concern (1977) is fed by correct perceptions: "Separation of conflicts law as a branch of law would throw the field of direct regulation into a no-man's land inside and outside the economy".

We cannot counteract this objection even by saying that the law of international economic relations stands ready to occupy areas of direct regulation within the economy. In keeping with our approach this would not be an accurate answer for no other reason than the one that the law of international economic relations is not a branch of law and that any rule of law must have a permanent place in a branch of law, a legal discipline serving merely as a temporary "abode", not to mention that the extra-economic legal material, would have no shelter even in that case.

This leaves us with only *two* options (*tertium non datur*) since we cannot advocate the concept of a uniform private international law being a single branch of law (that of conflicts law and substantive law): the rules of substantive private international law should either be incorporated into the pertinent substantive laws (private law, civil law, family law, labour law) or constitute a separate body of rules, an independent branch of national origin (e.g. the special rules of Hungarian civil law applied to external economic relations) the first option would provide the better solution, partly because the number of those rules is negligible for the time being, partly because as with other rules of domestic substantive law, they can only be applied with the help of conflicts law to facts of private international law.

6. As regards the branch-of-law status of *treaty-made* substantive private international law, we should refer to the fact that in Western literature there is a growing tendency to incorporate international agreements of a private-law nature (both substantive law and the law of conflicts), arranging and analyzing them by scientific methods, in a separate field of law called *international uniform law (droit uniforme international; internationales Einheitsrecht),* (see Kropholler: *Internationales Einheitsrecht).*

Under this approach, the rules governing facts of private international law may be arranged in three groups: internal conflict rules, international agreements on the law of conflicts, and international agreements on substantive law. The last two groups would form part of the international uniform law, and the first would constitute the material of private international law. The concept, scope and principles of the international uniform law cannot yet be considered to have taken final shape, so they will not be treated here at any great length.

An unquestionable advantage of this conception seems to be in having due regard to the traits of international agreements of a private-law nature and their divergences from purely internal law. Combined treatment of international agreements on substantive law and the law of conflicts is less convincing, while full separation of the national and international conflict norms is not opportune despite the differences between them.

We maintain that, precisely because of the said theoretical weaknesses of the "uniform law", consideration should be given to arranging the rules of the treaty-made substantive private international law in a separate branch of law, for the peculiarity of their source marks them off from internal norms, while their subject-matter separates them from other international agreements.

At the same time, since we consider the international element of the subject-matter of regulation and the direct nature of regulation to be the determinant features in both groups of substantive private international rules (i.e. those embodied both in international treaties and in domestic law), a systematization in which the rules of substantive private international law would, regardless of their source, be arranged in a single branch of law likewise appears to be defensible.

Accordingly, a branch-of-law system of the legal field under discussion would be structured as follows:

(a) *private international law of conflicts*, with basically autonomous (national) norms and partly with treaty-made norms also exhibiting distinctive features of their own;

(b) *substantive private international law*,

(i) with treaty-made norms, or

(ii) with treaty-made and national norms.

In the case of variant (b) (ii) the norms of internal (national) substantive law governing international facts would be incorporated into the pertinent branches of law (civil law, family law, labour law).

7. After having discussed the theoretically substantiated branch-of-law arrangement of the subject-matter of the present work we should state again that our book – overstepping in the didactically necessary measure the boundaries of the theoretically justified system – keeps in view the direct regulation of private international law facts in addition to the material of conflict norms and makes an attempt at presenting and critically analyzing the major international agreements on private law and the rules of internal substantive law which cover international elements. The theoretical foundation of and practical justifications for this approach have been more fully discussed in §§1–2.

At the same time, in discussing this complex approach transgressing branch-of-law boundaries, we should remember that the features of the two methods of regulation are as well discernible in matters of detail. The peculiarities of indirect regulation through conflict norms raise a legion of special problems related to legal policy, theory and dogma, a host of unsettled questions which in the case of direct regulation do not emerge at all or, at least, appear in a quite different form. These special problems concerning conflict rules will be summed up under Title 2 (The Conflict Rule and Its Application), whereas indirect regulation (by the law of conflicts) and direct regulation (by international agreements on substantive law) will henceforward be discussed side by side in accordance with the nature of our subject.

§7. ON THE NAME OF "PRIVATE INTERNATIONAL LAW"

The term "private international law" gained currency during the last century. It was first used by the American Joseph Story in his now classical book published in 1834, and it then found favour in the Old World as well. This name is still commonly accepted to designate the subject, although in the generally held view it is *open to objection* concerning its use to describe the solution of private international law cases by means of conflict norms (viz. precisely the field of law which is traditionally considered homologous).

The decisive majority of conflict rules, of course, are *not of international origin*, but are exclusive products of national legislation, as are, for instance, the rules of (domestic) civil law. Cases where a conflict rule becomes part of internal law pursuant to an international agreement can still be regarded as exceptions. Yet there is no question that the *subject-matter* of conflict rules is *international* by reason of the foreign elements contained in the facts (relations of daily life) under their control. The name "private international law" is still less objectionable where facts of private international law are directly regulated by international agreement.

For these considerations and owing largely to the firm hold of traditions, the phrase still holds the field and can be said to be dominant in spite of the recurrent controversies and because of the even less felicitous terms proposed to replace it. In addition, this designation is not misleading but conveys a clear and unambiguous content for the specialist.

It may be noted that the phrase "law of conflicts" is equally used to denote private international law in its narrower sense, to refer to the problems of indirect regulation. However it cannot be reserved for the indirect regulation of private international law facts (viz. the *international* law of conflicts) because the law of conflicts reaches other legal relations of daily life, such as administrative law or procedural law, not to mention other conflict rules of a different (non-international) nature, such as *intertemporal* rules (breaking through the temporal scope of applicability) and *interterritorial* rules (resolving conflicts between statutory provisions of state territories with no separate systems of law or of component States of a federation). The term "conflict of laws" is similarly widespread, mainly in the Anglo-Saxon systems of law ("law of the conflicts of laws"), and is used by Story himself in the title of his book referred to above (*Commentaries on the Conflict of Laws*).

§8. THE RELATIONSHIP OF PRIVATE INTERNATIONAL LAW TO OTHER PARTS OF THE LEGAL SYSTEM

1. As has been stated in connection with determining the subject-matter of private international law, the facts of private international law have no direct link to the element of State sovereignty. The relations arising between States as sovereigns (or between international organizations treated as such) belong to the domain of *public international law.*

Despite the clear line of demarcation, public international law is connected with private international law in several respects, of which we single out only two for their theoretical and practical relevance.

From the theoretical point of view it is essential to note that, according to the dominant view, the obligations of States concerning the mutual recognition of legal systems – their willingness to apply, under specified conditions and within certain limits (see item 2 in §11), foreign law to facts of private international law – stem from public international law. In this sense, therefore, private international law has its roots in public international custom.

It should be emphasized, moreover, that the principles of public international law governing international agreements (conclusion of treaties, interpretation, etc.) also apply, *mutatis mutandis* (not exclusively but with allowance for peculiar traits), to agreements of a private-law nature concerning substantive law and the law of conflicts. This interrelationship is acquiring increasing practical relevance in view of the fact that the sources of private international law include a growing number of international agreements (see item 2 in Sect. B of §12).

2. In addition, private international law or some of the problems under its control have close links with other fields and rules of the legal system.

(a) The provisions of the *Constitution*, or the general principles of our social order emphatically expressed in them, play a fundamental role in determining the extent to which foreign law is to be applied and in defining the concept of "public policy" (see §24).

(b) Nationality is, as will be seen, a frequently employed factor in determining the law applicable to facts of private international law. The *rules on nationality* are therefore closely linked to private international law. Yet most systems of law treat these provisions separately from private international law (the Hungarian legal system has arranged them in public law). An exception is provided by French law, which regulates the questions of nationality (*nationalité*) in the *Code civil.* It is related to this fact (and to the curricular requirements at the end of the last century) that most of the French textbooks and manuals conceive of the law of nationality as forming part of private international law.

(c) Similarly, the rules on foreign exchange control are closely connected with some facts of private international law (chiefly foreign property claims). As regards their systematic arrangement, they are outside the scope of private international law but their application to the legal solution of property relations of an international character is rather frequent and significant (see §80). It should be stressed that the rules on foreign exchange control are normally of a peremptory character, meaning that they are of mandatory application to facts of private international law, overriding a possibly different foreign law (see §24).

3. Separate mention should be made of the "special" rules on foreigners (natural and legal persons), called the "law of foreigners" (*condition des étrangers; Fremdenrecht*), which encompass the statutory provisions governing the domestic status of foreigners in a manner different from the rules relating to nationals. In most systems of law, including the Hungarian, this field of law falls outside the scope of private international law. The laws (e.g. French law) which discuss, in respect to both education and scientific studies, the most important provisions on foreigners within the ambit of private international law may be regarded as exceptions. (For practical considerations, we shall follow suit in Chapter XIII.)

A significant part of the legal material governing the domestic status of foreigners (rules relating to police control and other administrative provisions, aspects of procedural and criminal law, etc.) is farther from private international law. From the viewpoint of private international law, attention is deserved mainly for the regulations which contain special provisions, mostly of an administrative nature, concerning the family status and property rights of foreigners (see §§47–48).

Today the overwhelming majority of States, including Hungary, proceed from the principle of equal treatment with nationals in providing for the acquisition of rights by and the legal protection of foreigners and stateless persons. It was not until the French revolution that this idea of equality started to force its way and to gain prevalence, with smaller or greater setbacks. Of course, this principle is still broken by certain *exceptions* in all States because their political and economic interests require certain limits to the acquisition of rights by foreigners in some areas (e.g. immovable property). Among the relevant rules of Hungarian law, special reference should be made, in view of their significance, to the provisions on the acquisition of immovable property by foreigners (which are currently being considered for review).

The rules on the status of foreigners are, by their nature, not of a conflict type, of a remitting character, but are positive norms laying down direct provisions. According to the prevalent view, they are applied even if a fact of private international law is otherwise subject to a foreign law (see §§44–45).

4. Private international law cases with foreign elements raise special problems not only for substantive law but also for *procedural law*. May a domestic court (arbitral tribunal, notary public or other authority) try a given case, i.e. does it possess *jurisdiction* over the matter? Is a foreign plaintiff under the obligation to deposit a security for the costs of litigation, or does he enjoy any benefit in connection with such costs? Does a foreign party have capacity to sue and to be sued? In which cases are foreign judgments recognizable and en-

forceable? The *international law of civil procedure* is concerned with these and similar questions.

In several systems of law, the international law of civil procedure is treated and discussed by jurisprudence separately from private international law despite a number of rather close interconnections between the two areas of law. Yet certain problems are almost inseparable. Therefore, Anglo-Saxon and French manuals on private international law, for instance, include an inquiry into questions of jurisdiction and, not infrequently, of recognition of foreign judgment. (The relationship between substantive and procedural law is totally different in common law.)

While not discussing here questions concerning the theoretical boundaries (interconnections and divergences) of the two fields of law (private international law and international law of civil procedure), this book will cover jurisdiction, some important problems of procedural law, and the recognition and enforcement of foreign judgments (see Chapters XXXV to XXXVII). This is required by the close tie-up between the two areas and by the fact that the related aspects are also covered by detailed provisions of the Code of Private International Law (Law-Decree No. 13 of 1979).

Also inseparable from the conflict rules for the facts of private international law is the question, which may also be said to pertain to the law of civil procedure, as to whether the judge should ascertain *ex officio* the relevant provisions of the applicable foreign law or, in other words, whether the maxim of *iura novit curia* obtains with respect to the foreign law as well (see §23).

CHAPTER II

A SHORT HISTORY OF THE SCIENCE OF PRIVATE INTERNATIONAL LAW

§9. HISTORICAL PRECONDITIONS FOR THE EMERGENCE OF PRIVATE INTERNATIONAL LAW FACTS

1. (a) The facts of private international law originate in and are generated by *international economic and personal transactions.* Their emergence is conditional first and foremost on the relative spread of the *international exchange of commodities*, on the mass appearance of commodity relations cutting across national boundaries. This stage of development presupposes a higher level and considerable role of commodity relations. It is thus understandable that in the history of legal development private international law appears later and is by far predated by the rise of, say (domestic) private law.

(b) The international (i.e. transboundary) spread of commodity-related and personal transactions does not, even in other aspects, lead necessarily and directly to the appearance of private international law. Other types of methods can also be employed to settle legal issues arising out of international transactions bearing a private character. Ancient Rome (Hamza, 1982), for instance, created special judicial fora (primarily the institution of *praetor peregrinus* and mixed courts) to deal with property disputes between non-Romans ("aliens") and between them and Romans. The *praetor peregrinus* applied to such disputes the rules of a special law based on *naturalis ratio* and called *ius gentium*, or the "law of the peoples", which phrase, coined by Cicero, was designed to express the maxims of law common to civilized mankind. Indeed, it is an admirable product of Roman private law, which owed its existence to an active and fertile interaction with the governing law of Roman citizens (*ius civile*). Developing along this path, Roman law furnished a solid and effective basis for its buoyant international economic transactions without giving rise to conflict problems (as to the law of which party was to be applied by the forum of Rome). Some sources indicate, however, that this line of legal thought was not entirely unfamiliar to the Romans. Yet the general solution was offered by the *us gentium*, a very ingenious approach, behind which we find the theory that full recognition of laws of other peoples and their application to legal disputes to which a Roman was also a party would have been alien to the Roman way of legal thinking, no less than application of the law of Roman citizens (*ius civile*) was unthinkable in matters affecting aliens.

This does not mean that Rome totally disregarded the law of other peoples. On the contrary, Rome was definitely tolerant of local laws. According to incomplete sources, matters of family status and succession in relations between non-Romans, for instance, were governed by their domestic laws. This can be explained among others, by the fact that while in respect of economic transactions Roman private law was generally far superior to the contemporary laws of other peoples, that was not always and necessarily the case with respect to personal law, family law and the law of inheritance.

Roman law offers a good example to show that the emergence of private international law as we understand it today was also conditional on the *need for the States (law enforcement agencies) of the participants in international transactions to recognize in principle the equality of each other's laws and to be ready to apply them in principle*.

(c) With these conditions otherwise prevailing, however, there is naturally no need for private international law when the participants in international economic and personal transactions are citizens of different States but their States apply identical (or nearly identical) laws. The private laws of the *ancient Greek city-states*, for instance, bore so great a resemblance as ordinarily to leave no room for any international conflict of laws.

Of course, there were exceptions, too: a contract made between the laws of the two city-states to the effect that the consequences of wrongful acts were to be determined by the court of the wrongdoer's domicile (according to its own law, the *lex fori*). A similar situation prevailed in the Middle Ages with respect to matrimonial law which was under the control of *canon law* in a large part of Europe. As can be seen, the rise of private international law *presupposes the existence of essential differences between the legal systems of States*.

In summary, we should name *three basic preconditions* for the emergence of private international law:

– advanced and regular commodity exchange, economic and personal transactions, coupled with

– States recognizing the equality of each other's laws and

– having different systems of private law.

2. Taken together, these conditions become prevalent only during a relatively late period. After the fall of the Roman Empire, during the successive waves of the great migrations, relations of commodity exchange had perforce suffered great setbacks; for many centuries one could not even speak of regular international commodity exchange. Nor was it possible therefore for a socio-economic demand for private international law to emerge, although *legal particularism* was at its height.

The early Middle Ages were dominated by the so-called personal law (*principle of personality*), with the legal status of persons determined by the tribes to which they belonged (domination of tribal laws). With the spread of the feudal structure of society, ground was gained by the *territoriality* principle under which the legal relationships of individuals were generally determined, not by their allegiance to a community or group, but by their stay on the territory of feudal lords (domination of territorial laws). The operation of both the personality and territoriality principles involved contacts with countless systems of law differing among themselves to a greater or lesser extent.

Still, given the relatively low level of development of commodity exchange, commodity relations were not of a great volume, frequency and significance to create an awareness of conflict-of-law problems or to dictate a real need for private international law.

The *development* of jurisprudence, *of legal thinking* was an added prerequisite for such a demand. For that matter, science has always played, down to our time, an outstanding role in the history of private international law. The principles and tenets of private international law were being developed and refined in legal practice and, above all, in science up to the 19th century. In fact, one cannot speak of written law in this field before the last century, and science has since retained its great importance in the development of private international law. This special influence justifies placing the focus of our historical survey on the development of the *science* of private international law (Gutzwiller, 1977).

§10. THE PERIODS OF THE "STATUTE THEORY"

1. The conditions for the rise of private international law as we now understand the term were ripening first in the city-states of *northern Italy from the 11th and 12th centuries* onwards. By that time there had emerged in these cities a significant segment of the class of craftsmen and merchants who had promoted commodity relations to a considerable degree. The growth of commodity and money relations had in turn raised serious demands on the law. In its first phase private law developed through customary law, primarily by drawing upon the rediscovered Roman law, but written sources of law had appeared somewhat earlier, from the middle of the 11th century. The laws of cities were called *statutes* (*statuta*). The various cities, such as Genoa, Parma, Milan, Bologna, Modena, Venice, Florence, Siena and Pisa, had all framed municipal laws of their own showing individual variations even on essential questions. The rapid growth of trade flows between cities had led, on the one hand, to mutual recognition of one another and, on the other, to increasingly frequent conflicts between systems of law, or statutes. By the second half of the 12th century there had practically *emerged all the conditions for the birth of private international law* in the city-states: regular commodity-related and personal transactions attended by a growing frequency of conflicts between the diverse statutes of city-

states recognizing each other's legal systems. The facts of private international law were at hand, and it only remained to devise the means of dealing with them.

This task was assumed by jurisprudence: the credit for this proposition goes to the *Glossators*, the first generation of medieval legal scholars. This school of thought in the late 12th and the 13th centuries had its centre in *Bologna*, and its most eminent exponents were Azo, Aldricus, Hugolinus and, chiefly, Accursius. These scholars, who were in close contact with practice, were trying, by adding explanatory notes or glossae (after which they were named) to the tenets of the Justinian Roman law (*Corpus Juris*), to devise appropriate legal means of promoting commodity relations and, among other things, solving cases of private international law.

As early as the end of the 12th century *Aldricus* pointed out that in case of conflicts between statutes the judge should apply the law which "seems stronger and more useful", that is to say, not necessarily the law of the forum (*lex fori*), which may be said to have been of general application in that period. Development in this direction was naturally a slow process. In his comprehensive *Glossa Ordinaria,* Accursius had to emphasize, as many as 70 years later, that "to a Bolognese sued in Modena the statutes of Modena cannot be applied because a citizen of Bologna is not subjected to their rules". (Twenty years earlier he himself had held it necessary to "follow the law and the statutes of the place of litigation".)

Thus, on the one hand, the Glossators were *cognizant of the problem of conflicts between statutes* and, on the other, they elaborated the principle that *the statute of every city was binding on the inhabitants only of the given city* and did not extend to those of other cities. In this way they were trying to break the prevalence of the *lex fori*. In addition to their general results possessing a theoretical value, the Glossators explored and solved several concrete partial problems of conflict between statutes, laying down principles (connecting factors, as we would say today) by which to determine the law applicable to cases of private international law (e.g. the statutes of the place of contracting shall extend and apply to the legal appraisal of contracts).

The method of settling spatial conflicts between municipal laws in northern Italy, by fixing the scope of application of statutes under the logical approach of scholasticism is usually called the *statute theory*. The first centuries of private international law, down to the 19th century, were essentially dominated by this approach and doctrine, which were employed in fixing the spatial limits, first, of the statutes of the Italian city-states, then, of the customary laws (*coutumes*) of the various French territories and, finally, of the legal systems of the more or less sovereign States in modern times. In the course of time, this method became naturally much more refined and polished, it evolved new principles and grew into a system, but always retained what was its core and substance: speculative definition of the scope of application of a given rule of law, logical determination of the province of each legal norm. The theory of statutes accordingly takes each law (statute, *coutume*, *lex*) as its point of departure and is always concerned with determining its scope of application by ascertaining its provisions and hence its applicability to this or that fact or relationship. The method of the statute theory relies on the content of the law for determining its spatial limits, marking out the range of legal relations by interpreting the content of the legal norm concerned.

2. The method invented by the Glossators to deal with cases of private international law was further refined by the Italian jurists, the so-called *Commentators* (post-Glossators) of the 14th and 15th centuries, who developed it into a general and systemized theory. The methodological substance which the Glossators had discovered was reduced to an integral system in the systematic treatises by the commentators. It is for this reason and in this sense that the scholars of that age can rightly be held to have been the first to give a theoretical summation of the statute doctrine, *virtually to have founded the theory of statutes.*

Among the commentators there are two prominent scholars, both working in the 14th century: Bartolus de Saxoferrato, professor at Bologna, and Baldus de Ubaldis, his disciple.

(a) Bartolus is known to have been the first to take a complex approach to the spatial conflict-of-law problems, and in his commentaries on the *Corpus Juris* he devoted an independent study to them. He set out his conception in his quest for answers to two basic questions:

– whether a statute was applicable to an alien staying within the State, and

– whether it was to govern facts occurring outside the territory of the legislator.

In advancing his arguments Bartolus tried to find solutions for a great many cases of private international law involving real rights, contractual, delictual and inheritance problems alike. He formulated principles that are practically accepted even today: the statute of the place of contracting shall govern the extrinsic and intrinsic incidents of the contract; the consequences of default and negligence in performance shall be subject to the statute of the place of performance as stipulated in the contract, etc.

In elaborating his tenets by a method typical of the statute theory Bartolus based himself on the assumption that each rule of law, each normative provision has a limited applicability inherent in its content, which allows for a range of cases under its control to be correctly or adequately defined. In his use of this method he relied (as did most of the later exponents) of the statute theory, on the grammatical and logical analysis of the statutes.

The *trichotomy of statutes* was also his idea. On the basis of this distinction he classified each statute according to whether it concerned persons (personal statutes, or *statuta personalia*), immovables (real statutes, or *statuta realia*) or acts (mixed statutes, or *statuta mixta*), domiciled, situated or done respectively within the given territory. A statute was personal if it applied to e.g. the disposing capacity of persons domiciled in the territory of the legislator. A statute was real if it applied to the right of ownership in immovables, and was therefore held to govern things situated in the given territory. A mixed statute was usually one that concerned contracts, and was applied if the contractual act (formation or performance of a contract) was done (or was to be done) within the territorial scope of the relevant norm. In the later history of the statute theory this classification, evidently of a simplifying nature, assumed paramount importance although in its pure form it was never applicable in practice.

(b) We know of two studies by Baldus on the conflict of laws. His conception was strongly influenced by the ideas of his master, Bartolus, but his exposition thereof and some of his achievements testify to originality of thought. He can be considered to have refined the theory of statutes, having set up several new tenets and having shed more light, if only in rough outline, to bear on the said categories of statutes.

It may be stated in summary that the Glossators and the Commentators created a point of departure for private international law by recognizing and formulating the fundamental problems and offering a device for their solution. The essence of their method (determination of the field of application of statutory rules by relying on scholasticism) remained a decisive weapon used for centuries by proponents of the theory of private international law.

3. It was *in French territories*, besides the cities of northern Italy, that commerce acquired its initial impetus, being based on the resurgence of commodity and money relations, particularly by economic and personal transactions cutting across the boundaries of territorial jurisdiction, while the legal particularism of medieval France proved to be a highly fertile ground for the frequent occurrence of private international law cases. The northern territories were under the control of customary laws (*coutumes*) differing among themselves, while the sources of law in the south were constituted by various written compilations following Roman private law. Thus it is understandable that the problem of private international law appeared rather early. From the second part of the 13th century, private international law was taught in Toulouse and Orléans besides Bologna, whereas at the Sorbonne related expertises had been prepared much earlier. Still, in the era of Glossators and Commentators, northern Italy was the centre of legal science.

The French science of private international law really came to the fore *from the 16th century onwards*. Its exponents carried on the method of the Italian school of Glossators and Commentators and *developed further the theory of statutes*. The starting point remained the same: they sought to determine the applicability of statutes on the basis of their contents. Among the French scholars on the law of conflicts in the 16th century were two eminent jurists, Dumoulin and d'Argentré, with strong personalities holding opposing views, following and supporting different political goals.

(a) Charles Dumoulin made a lasting contribution to legal science primarily by his scientific commentaries on the customary law of Paris and by his comparative analysis of French customary laws. On the political plane he advocated a strong central royal power against secular and ecclesiastical potentates, while in the legal field he stood for the unity of French customary laws (and at the same time against Roman law). His views on private international law served these same goals, and he therefore wanted to leave a wider scope for the operation of mixed and personal statutes as against real statutes, which were more favourable to the feudal forces relying on territorial particularism. Thus, for instance, in a disquisition (for which he had already gained celebrity in his youth), he removed the assets subject to the matrimonial property law from the scope of operation of the *lex situs* (the real statutes governing immovable property) and brought them under the law of the (first) common domicile of the spouses.

On essential issues he did not depart from the conceptions of his Italian predecessors. Recent historical research (Gamillscheg, 1955) may be said to have disproved the earlier established view which gave credit to Dumoulin for laying the theoretical foundation for the choice of law by the parties, or the autonomy of the will of the parties (see §62). His influence however was considerably felt chiefly on the French statutists of the 18th century.

(b) As against Dumoulin, Bertrand d'Argentré was a highly qualified sponsor of feudal particularism, of legal fragmentation. While the Glossators and Commentators and even Dumoulin invoked the famous initial provisions of Justinian's *Corpus Juris* ("*Cunctos populos...*") as a pretext for setting forth their views on the spatial conflict of laws, d'Argentré summed up his tenets in his commentaries on the customary law of Brittany, his native land.

In accordance with his pro-feudal posture he (unlike Dumoulin) wanted to extend the operation of real statutes and therefore he included in this group of laws any enactments – statutory rules on contract, matrimonial property, intestate succession and wills alike – which related in any form to immovables. He classified as personal statutes only the laws "basically covering personal status or the legal incidents of the person (majority, parental authority, guardianship, etc.) and having no bearing on immovable property".

The main value of his work, his chief scientific achievement, should be seen in his placing the known trichotomy of statutes on a clear and solid basis. This classification, the first signs of which can be associated with the Commentators, was developed by him into a truly closed body of doctrine, thus surpassing the numerous attempts at systematization which accompanied the statute theory over the centuries and which grew into a confused maze of concepts and created serious legal uncertainty. His outstanding role is further shown by the acceptance of his teachings by most of the succeeding statutists. On the other hand, his clearly pro-feudal political views, favouring the extension of the operation of real statutes, found fewer followers.

It should be stressed in summary that the *French* school of statute theory bears the imprint primarily of the debate about the strictly territorial operation of laws.

4. In the second half of the 17th century the theory of private international law was developed further, chiefly *in Holland* (now the Netherlands and North-

ern Belgium), which was rapidly advancing on the road of bourgeois development and militantly defending the independence of its provinces against an external world that was still largely under feudal sway. The prominent Dutch jurists of this period are Ulrich Huber and Paul and Johannes Voet (father and son).

The idea of international and territorial independence had by that time been cast in a theoretical-ideological mould through the doctrine of State sovereignty espoused by the Frenchman Bodin (1576). The advocacy of independence supported by the theory of *sovereignty*, the emphasis placed on the significance of territorial and, with it, legal integrity was also strongly reflected in the Dutch jurists' conception of private international law. They accepted d'Argentré's tenets on the strict territoriality of laws, but made them serve their own political ends.

The particular importance of their theory derives from the fact that they were the first to raise clearly the question as to the ground on which foreign law is to be applied at all. This problem had not arisen before in the theory of private international law, for which we may assign various reasons. In the formal aspect, the statutists of earlier periods did not think of a justification for the application of foreign law because their doctrine had established only external limits to the operation of laws, failing to look at the other aspect of the matter, viz. the domestic operation of foreign law and its limitations. Behind the logical reasoning so characteristic of the entire method of the statute theory, however, one should be cognizant of the explanation *in merito* that the conflicting laws of cities or territories were seen, consciously or unconsciously, by the Italian and French statutists as embodying differences within a kind of unity. To these jurists, mutual recognition of alien laws was made practically self-evident, in addition to the identical precepts of the Christian religion and the surviving idea of Roman imperial law, by medieval Roman law (the so-called common law), which had a mostly uniform application, along with the different laws, of Italian cities, or by the central royal power prevailing behind the various provincial laws of France.

The situation was quite different for the Dutch jurists of the 17th century. They did not find it natural for the fora of their sovereign State to apply the law of another sovereign, especially when they had to emphasize and advocate the sovereignty of their country *vis-à-vis* that State, as in the case of the Holy Roman emperor. So they did not recognize any legal obligation to apply foreign law but worked out a theory, formulating the principle of comity (*comitas gentium*), the idea of international courtesy, to support the case for occasional application of foreign law. They regarded reciprocity as the main criterion and inner motive of comity or, in other words, they approached this fine-sounding and abstract-like notion in a basically pragmatic way. The principle of "reciprocal courtesy" was nevertheless capable of easing the rigidity of their starting point, the doctrine of strict territoriality.

In other questions of private international law the Dutch school, too, based itself on the *doctrine of statutes* and was chiefly under the strong influence of d'Argentré. An essential change of outlook and a marked advance should nonetheless be seen in the fact that (apart from several partial results) the Dutch writers, ignoring the earlier concept, did *not* view the problems arising from the facts of private international law *in the context of a single legal system,* but also considered the laws of the other States concerned in seeking to define the scope of operation of a particular law. The difference in approach is related to the fact that it was in that period, and hence in the works of Dutch scholars, that the conflict-of-law problem no longer concerned conflicts between the statutes of cities and the customary laws of provinces but conflicts *between the legal systems of sovereign States*. Interestingly, the *universality* – in a sense the supranational character – of the private international law of conflicts, which had been a matter of course in the earlier centuries of the statute theory, held steadily despite the arguments of the Dutch school and was to start declining only in the national works of codification during the 19th century (see item 4 in §11).

In sum, in the light of its achievements the *Dutch school* can rightly be regarded as having *formulated decisive theoretical tenets which set the stage for the disappearance of the statute theory* and the emergence of modern private international law. Its impact (chiefly in the first part of the 19th century) was not negligible on the Continent (being readily perceivable even in Savigny's work) and was particularly noteworthy in *Anglo-Saxon* learning.

5. *In England* the unified law, the so-called common law, which relied on the central royal power, had arisen early (essentially by the 13th century) and, advancing along a different path from legal development in Italy or France or even the German provinces, headed off conflicts of interterritorial laws, thus eliminating the need for the statute theory of the Middle Ages. At the same time, application of foreign law and recognition of foreign judgments were resisted by the English courts down to the 17th century.

So private international law may, in effect, be said to have acquired impetus under the influence of Huber and other Dutch scholars, practically as late as the middle of the 18th century. The jurists (chiefly from Scotland) who had studied at Dutch universities relied on the theories prevailing there for seeking an appropriate basis for a just solution of private international law cases that were growing in number (in the meantime England had developed into the leading mercantile nation of the world!). They favoured the idea of comity (*comitas gentium*) in particular to break the general application of domestic law, the *lex fori*.

This doctrine (just as several other tenets of the Dutch school) was also accepted by Joseph Story, the first prominent scholar of private international law *in the United States*, but his deservedly world famous *Commentaries*, published in 1834, actually pointed beyond the theory of statutes and were, in point of fact, a milestone *heralding a new era* in science. Story arranged his enormous material (analyzing around 500 cases, half English, half American), not by type of statute, but by subject-matter (disposing capacity, marriage, divorce, contracts, movables, immovables, etc.) (Kegel, 1979, 1988).

§11. THE THEORETICAL FOUNDATION OF MODERN PRIVATE INTERNATIONAL LAW

(A)

1. By the early *19th century* the facts of private international law had begun to grow *more numerous.*

During its more than 500 years of development the theory of statutes had produced *some fundamental tenets in crystallized form*: legal relationships involving immovables are governed by the *lex situs*, the formal requirements of contract are subject to the law of the place of contracting, etc. For quite some time there had been a consensus of opinion concerning these principles, which had even been incorporated into the codes of private international law around the turn of the century (the Prussian *Allgemeines Landrecht* of 1794, the French *Code Civil* of 1804 and the Austrian *ABGB* of 1811).

On the whole, however, the theory of private international law had shown a rather *incoherent picture*. The three categories of statutes, as established earlier, lacked sufficient flexibility and could not offer a workable guide to the solution of more intricate borderline questions. The method of the statute theory, that of determining the field of operation of laws by a mere logical approach from the content of rules, became *less and less capable* of meeting the needs of increased economic and personal transactions. The quest for just solutions to the growing number of private international law cases called for a new method, a new theory.

A comprehensive critique of private international law resting on the theory of statutes was offered by Carl Georg von Wächter, Professor at Tübingen, in his studies published in 1841–42. In his sharp-witted, deeply penetrating analysis, relying in many respects on the teachings of the Dutch school, he disclosed the weaknesses of the centuries-old method but he was also unable to afford a persuasive, positive counter-proposition.

2. A *decisive turn* in the theory of private international law was brought about by the works of Friedrich Carl von Savigny, another German jurist of the last century.

The leading personality of the historical school of law, Savigny covered the problems in the general part of contemporary private law (sources of law, legal relationships, control of law over legal relationships) in a united theoretical system (*System des heutigen Römischen Rechts*) and set out his comprehensive views on the private law of conflicts in the last part, published in 1849, of his eight-volume encyclopaedic work.

(a) We must refer in the first place to a fundamental *change of approach* in Savigny's theory of private international law (which he elaborated as an organic part of his general concept of law and legal relationships). Unlike the approach of the statutists in previous periods, his concern is not with the spatial limits of the control of law, with the territorial scope of the legal systems, but with the consideration of *legal relationships*. Thus his starting point is not the norm itself but the legal relationship. His approach is from a reverse angle: he inquired not into what facts are covered and governed by a norm, but into the norm to which a fact is subjected, *under which a legal relationship is to be considered*. This change of approach was of *paramount significance* in his day. By way of illustration it will perhaps suffice to note that Savigny's new starting point, or his reserve approach to the subject, made it possible at once to abandon the trichotomy of statutes (personal, real and mixed), a product of the statute theory that had become rigid and had practically ended in deadlock, and to devise an approach to facts of private international law that appeared *more appropriate from the angle of legal policy*.

In the development of legal science there is usually a conceptual background even to the most revolutionary innovation, even theories of epochal significance have intellectual sources to draw upon, a circumstance which, however, in no way detracts from the exceptional merits of the outstanding representatives of creative human thinking. Savigny's path to surpassing the theory of statutes had been paved primarily by the aforesaid critique of Wächter, while he had Story to follow in his approach to reducing substantive private law to a new system.

(b) Savigny also proceeded in part from the concept of Story and the Dutch school in his *justification for the application of foreign law*, but he made the idea of *comitas* leave the door wide open for the application of foreign law in all cases where "*so required by the intrinsic substance and the need of the individual legal relationship*". According to Savigny, the application of foreign law should be postulated, not by the grace of sovereign States, but much more by mutual understanding, by an awareness of the desired goal that "facts of private international law should be subject to expectedly uniform decisions, irrespective of the State of the proceeding court". To States living in a "community of laws" (*Rechtsgemeinschaft*) it should, in principle, be a matter of indifference whether the law applied is the domestic law or the law of another State belonging to such a community, as is proposed by Savigny's rather Utopian thesis of international law. What matters is that legal relationships should be decided under the appropriate law (domestic or foreign).

(c) As regards the determination of applicable law, Savigny holds it necessary to choose for every legal relationship the system of law "to which in its proper nature it belongs", to which it is subjected, in which it has its "*seat*" (*Sitz*). For identifying this principle, selecting the connecting factors for the diverse legal relationships, Savigny relied on a profound and detailed analysis, partly accepting earlier rules, partly formulating new ones. The "seat" decisive to the selection of the applicable law was, to him, identified by the characteristic *spatial bearings* of the given legal relationship: the law of the person's domicile is applicable to legal and disposing capacity; the *lex situs* governs both movables and immovables; contracts are subject to the law of the place of performance and to the autonomy of the parties; and so on (for contracts see §82).

(d) Savigny's theory of private international law and his concrete theses deduced from it have exercised an extraordinary influence on posterity: science and practice (legislation as well as law enforcement), accepting, discussing or rejecting them, are still under their powerful impact. Several of his propositions (e.g. the doctrine of *Sitz*, or the idea that the essential incidents of legal relationships can always be localized) have not withstood all tests of criticisms by posterity, while time has simply passed over some of his other views. Unfortunately, his idea based on the legal community of nations favouring the application of foreign law and thereby facilitating the uniform adjudication of private international law cases, independently of the place of the forum, has also failed time and again in the arena of international politics motivated as it is by more material considerations. Nevertheless, the tribute paid by the scientific world to the creative genius of Savigny, even today is more than mere reverence (Gutzwiller, 1923; Neuhaus, 1949, 1982).

3. Among the scholars who rendered great services to laying the foundations of modern private international law, we cannot fail to mention the name of the Italian Pasquale Stanislao Mancini along with Story and Savigny (Jayme, 1980). A leading scholar and politician in the struggle for the unity of Italy, he created a school of private international law by stating (for the first time in 1851) that public international law should be founded on nations (not necessarily on States), with *recognition for every nation of the right to independence. Nationhood in turn is,* in his view, *the principal determinant of individuals.* Exercising great influence chiefly in Italy and France, the Italian school of private international law identified itself with, and worked out theoretically, this political demand or tenet of public international law. According to its principal thesis, the test of personal law shall be *nationality rather than domicile.*

Under the influence of the ideas of the French enlightenment (Montesquieu) and particularly after the rise of nation States, the nation concept evoked sharper and sharper echoes and was even codified in Napoleon's *Code Civil* (para. 3 of Art. 3 reading: "French nationals shall, even if they are abroad, be subject to the laws governing the status and capacity of persons"). Yet, the nationality principle became pervasive under the influence of the Italian school, for, among others, Savigny – not to mention the protagonists of the statute theory – was still firmly of the view that the law of domicile was the normative system most characteristic of persons. On the other hand, the majority of States in the European continent (Italy, France, Germany and, among many others, Hungary) followed the principle of the Italian school and adopted the law of nationality as the law applicable to the status of persons. (For the "competition" between the law of nationality and the law of domicile as well as for the background thereto, see §29.)

The Italian school, following the Mancinian theory, claims lasting credit chiefly for the elaboration of the principle of party autonomy concerning choice of law [(see §82) as an important tenet of the modern private law of conflicts (Jayme, 1980)].

4. (a) By the second half of the 19th century answers had been given to the *fundamental questions* of the private law of conflicts, such as those concerning the reasons for the consideration of foreign law in deciding facts of private international law, the theoretical ground on which foreign law is applied at all, the limits to the acceptance of foreign law, or the possible variants of connecting factors governing the commonest legal relationships. *Thus the foundations of classical private international law had been laid by the middle of the last century.*

More detailed formulations by *individual States* of the conflict rules have appeared *in the form of national codifications* from the 19th century (the Prussian *Landrecht*, the French *Code Civil*, the Austrian *AGBG*, the Saxon *BGB*, the Italian *Codice civile* of 1865, etc.). At the same time, the private international law of conflicts has gradually lost its universal character, which prevailed during the centuries of the statute theory, while national regulation of private international law has perforce resulted in greater or smaller divergences between the sets of positive rules. Hence, attainment of a practicable degree of *harmonization* between the diverse national laws on conflicts, their *unification* through international agreements, again became a concern of the past hundred years. The idea of harmonization likewise originated in Mancini; the paucity of results in the unification effort (if only on regional scales) is to be ascribed, not to flaws of the lofty idea, but to the complexity of the problem and the practical difficulties arising therefrom.

Another essential feature of development over the past hundred years is the disclosure of *dogmatic problems* in the private law of conflicts and the attempts at their solution (classification, remission and transmission, etc.). (See Chapters V and VI.)

(b) Thus it may be stated in summary that over the past hundred years the science of the private law of conflicts has undergone a twofold *process of specialization* on the foundations laid down by it up to the middle of the last century: it has become specialized partly in the form of research into the national laws on conflicts, partly through in-depth analyses of essential matters of detail.

This is not to say that the *fundamental issues* in this field of science are not raised *time and again* or that the methods of research are not being refined. The question concerning the ground upon which, and the reasons why, foreign law is applied, is mooted especially by *Anglo-Saxon* jurisprudence from time to time. Again, the peculiar world of *common law* produces theory upon theory as to the criteria by which the judge is to choose the applicable law (domestic or foreign). This problem is posed day after day by conflicts between the rather diverse State laws of the United States of America.

No wonder that recent decades have seen several theories appear in American learning seeking to relax and renew the system of traditional connecting factors and to promote more equitable decisions on the merits of cases (Cavers, Currie, Ehrenzweig, Leflar, von Mehren, Trautman, etc.). These views are illustrative of the requirements of changed conditions (e.g. in the law of damages), are often accurate in pointing out the frailties of the continental approach based on Savigny's theory, and rightly emphasize the significance of moving closer to reality, while the positive propositions are often vague and contradictory (see item 3 in §15). These problems as well as theoretical innovations are also reflected in numerous solutions offered by the *Restatement* of 1971, a special "private bill", which brings influence to bear on judicial practice in most component States of the United States of America.

The tempests in American practice and science have not remained without influence on the European continent more bound by classical traditions (Joerges, Siehr, etc.). Following upon initially extreme views (swings between almost wholesale rejection of the existing system of private international law and its virtually unconditional apologetics), *theory in Europe* has produced balanced assessments and even summations capable of forming a synthesis (Vicher, Keller–Siehr, Kropholler, Lorenz, Schurig, etc.), while the legislator has sought, mostly with cautious restraint yet with firm resolve, to draw upon the theoretical achievements in the codification of private international law, as is illustrated by the Codes of Austria (1978), Hungary (1979), Yugoslavia (1982), West Germany (1986) and Switzerland (1987), or the European Community Convention on the Law applicable to Contractual Obligations (1980), dealing with the conflicts law of contract.

(B)

Questions are rightly asked as to

– which factors gave rise to the ferment in private international law as outlined above (items 1and 2);

– which characteristics of the traditional private international law were objects of the aforementioned criticisms (item 3).

1. In seeking to determine the causes which led to the "crisis" of private international law and placed it at the heart of enduring and heated debates, we must delve deep into the fundamental changes in *economic and social conditions* when investigating the various factors.

(a) The past hundred or so years regarded as spanning the period of evolution and development in modern private international law are marked by the unparalleled pace of technical-technological progress, historically significant social reforms, victorious and defeated revolutions, wars and world wars, which have all generated qualitative changes. The enormous growth of economic and personal transactions between States as the life-blood of private international law, world trade, external economic relations, international companies, worldwide tourism and millions of migrant workers are incidents of this process which we merely signal here (without seeking to be exhaustive), but which are symbolic of each and every real socio-economic challenge to private international law. Even if we leave aside the developments (multinational corporations, large-volume foreign trade contracts, etc.) which have perhaps outgrown the traditional framework of private international law in all aspects and have called for totally new legal solutions, the social changes which private international law has had to face and respond to are of a vast range and carry almost unpredictable implications.

Even if we emphasize that the practice and science of codifying and applying private international law are far from those bogged down in Savigny's theory and time, as some overreactive critics claim they have, we cannot but wonder why the explosion of criticism – by way of reaction to the said social challenge (ultimately resulting in a kind of negation) – did not occur before the second part of this century.

(b) It is an unquestionable fact that the drift of social change has also gathered speed from the 1950s and 1960s, qualitatively switching into a new gear, yet the reaction of private international law was marked by a striking time-lag. To illustrate this lag, which may even be said to be qualitative, in the fields of substantive law and private international law, it will perhaps suffice to give two examples concerning the evolution of *tortious* liability and the attitude towards modern developments in respect of *contracts* in the two fields of law.

As is known, technological advance (mass use of machinery in production and transport) became a source of social conflicts (industrial and traffic accidents) from the middle of the last century. Substantive private law reacted swiftly and radically to those conflicts, introducing ("reviving") the objective liability for damage, which by the last third of the 19th century had openly broken through the frameworks of liability based on culpability as formulated in the *Code Civil*, and has since increasingly encroached upon its domain. All these developments reached only private international law 100 years later, from the 1950s. It would be true to say, that the law of tortious liability has since become a most inflammable "hotbed" of the revolution in the law of conflicts (see §84).

Similarly, it was with a considerable time-lag that private international law responded to the social changes which have put the substantive law of contracts to the test of time and again since the turn of the century. To highlight but one partial problem, it was not until very recently that questions of standard contracts entered the law of conflicts.

(c) The main cause for the belated response of private international law to socio-economic changes is to be found primarily in the remitting character and *abstract* formulation of conflict norms (§15). While the *social sensitivity of remitting rules* and is low, their *threshold of economic and social sensitiveness* is high, they are reached by the impulses of social conditions mainly through substantive law and, therefore, changes in private international law are also usually preceded by changes in substantive law. So the examples taken from the fields of the law of tortious liability and the law of contracts are by no means particular but definitely typical.

However, this explanation would be incomplete without mentioning that the need for conflict rules to be socially sensitive has arisen only in the past half century. True, it was for similar considerations that, as far back as the turn of the century, Franz Kahn, a most original scholar of this discipline, strongly underlined the significance of developing and refining the connecting factors, for which Rabel and his school disclosed, by the middle of our century, the manifold possibilities offered by *comparative law*. It was not until after World War Two that the "interest-oriented" approach started to pervade the science of private international law (and even then only science, barely practice and least of all legislation!). This occurred at a time when the contradictions generated by the lagging behind of this branch of law were also coming to the surface in the judicial practice of the United States, followed by the elementary volcanic eruptions which were about to overwhelm the entire fabric of traditional private international law.

Thus, in the face of the mid-century socio-economic acceleration, private international law found itself in a rather *underdeveloped state* despite its numerous results and significant achievements; it was unprepared to respond to challenges and, when weighed, was found wanting in many respects. Yet there is one point to make clear: the criticisms, however justified, were mistaken in the "diagnosis of the crisis" as they underestimated the possibilities for the development of private international law and its potential for further advance. In the heat of passions they overlooked the relative youth of this branch of law, the fact that modern private international law, which can be said to date only from the period beginning with Savigny in any case, has a history of barely 150 years, not too long a period for a branch of law like the international law of conflicts which was destined to solve complicated tasks by means of great complexity.

2. Let us now consider at some length the reasons, peculiarities and incapabilities which provoke the *criticisms* addressed to private international law.

It is not even easy to review the flood of criticisms during the past decades, marked as they are, for good measure, by a great deal of overlap, repetition and contradiction. This is one reason why we do not pretend to be exhaustive, especially not from the extensive point of view: we do not wish to draw up a catalogue of the authors holding critical views, but (following Schurig, 1980) shall attempt a *synthesis of the* lasting *kernel* of the countless critical theories.

(a) *World of preconceptions.* A notable part of criticisms is levelled in principle at the indirect method of private international law and at the two-phase selection of law and questions as against the suitability of the *overcomplicated set of notions* used by conflicts law to satisfy the increased demands of present-day international economic and personal transactions.

A few general institutions of private international law have come under particularly vigorous criticism. In this critical views concerning conflicts law rules will be applied in practice when the real reasons for concrete decisions are intended to be glossed over, when the judge is reluctant to state the actual motives of a judgment and therefore invokes a general principle. It is noteworthy that such criticisms, which originally appeared in US literature, have also received a considerable and even favourable response from European authors much more bound by tradition.

(b) *Social insensitivity.* It is similarly on principle that the modernity and operability of private international law are questioned by criticisms which object to the social insensitivity of its solutions and would expect its instruments to achieve social justice in a direct way.

According to these views, modern private international law fails to rise to the challenges chiefly because of its inability to transmit the application of those norms which possess a public-law character, and which today play an irreplaceable role in accommodating private interests, just as in harmonizing private and public interests. The tendency of private law to become a "public law", or its tendency to "socialization", is irreversible, as protection of the economically weaker party is a social demand which calls for a private international law based on new principles. Hence the need for private international law to renew its foundations, to embrace "social values", to become "politicized", etc.

(c) *Deficit of material justice.* The need to assert material justice is a general aspect in the focus of criticisms of the private international law of conflicts, which claim that private international law cannot indulge in the luxury of confining itself to designating the applicable system of law, however adequate, while turning a blind eye, with elegant indifference, to the requirement for *in merito* decisions to contain material justice.

While the so-called justice of private international law (ensuring the predictability of the legal system to be applied, selecting the law most appropriate to a particular set of facts, ensuring the international harmony of decisions, etc.) is an extremely important goal, it cannot replace the *postulate of material justice* for decisions *in merito*. The impressive principle of the theoretical equality of legal systems and the tolerance and openness manifested therein cannot allow us to forget about a grave imperfection of the traditional private international law, namely its inability to secure a corrective except in the case of a most striking injustice of an *in merito* decision and *a posteriori*. The value-judgment expressed in *ordre public* (see §24) is basically reflective, as well as in other aspects, of the scale of values of the forum, while the facts of a case may likewise show substantive links to a system of law with a different orientation in the selection of value.

For all these reasons, the criticisms, of which we present here the main arguments only, demand a private international law which will itself pursue the foremost aim of asserting material justice. The system of axiomatic connecting factors is blind to this fundamental requirement, which it is hardly capable of satisfying, as is claimed by critics, who demand a total renewal and state that a new private international law will have to accord primacy to the postulate of material legal justice; the parties going to law can hardly be satisfied by the reasoning that the law to be applied to their dispute was foreseeable (predictability, legal certainty), and that any forum would have applied the same law (international harmony of decisions), if at the same time the decision on the merits of the case is inequitable and even unjust.

(d) *Indifference of legal policy.* The critical remarks blaming the private international law of conflicts for its inability to affirm duly the interests of its own legal order or the legal policy objectives of another State involved are not of a recent vintage. Important legal policy interests of the State vanish in the private international criteria of justice, in the quest for the most adequate system of law.

This is why the exponents of these views want to see a private international law in which selection of the applicable law would be based on comparison of the interests of the States involved.

(e) *International fact v. national law.* According to its critics, the private international law of conflicts is beset by one of its greatest flaws in inevitably giving a distorted solution, even in the case of selecting the most appropriate law, by reason of imparting to an international fact (one having links to several legal systems) a national character (sub-ordinating it to the law of a single State), thereby disregarding the most important feature of the private international law fact, its *international* character, which is thus caused to blend into the national law. The (indirect) solution by conflicts law necessarily treats even the most international fact as a purely internal legal case controlled by the legal system of a single State, which often leads to unsatisfactory results.

Therefore, with even the best national law as selected by conflicts law being unable to respect duly the international character of private international law facts, there is a need for special *norms of substantive law* (wedded not only to facts of domestic roots) to have the peculiarity of those facts properly considered. Best equipped to decide "absolutely international legal relations" ("*relations juridiques absolument internationales*") are special rules of substantive law tailored to the specific traits of private international law facts ("*IPR-Sachnormen*", "*règles de droit international privé matériel*").

No one has ever deemed total regulation by substantive law either possible or necessary, and even critics stress, with more or less vigour, the methodological pluralism of solutions for facts of private international law, yet increasing emphasis is being laid on the need for regulation by substantive law.

3. A striking lesson drawn from the study of recent theories consists of the fact that the vast *majority* of them, while sharply criticizing the existing private international law, do not flatly reject the indirect method of using remitting rules to determine the applicable law, but essentially *retain the two-phase method*, with some change proposed only in its technique.

It is worth distinguishing three basic types of the reform proposals accepting the indirect method of selecting the appropriate law, the traditional point of departure in this sense.

(a) As far back as the last century, the concept of a private international law based on a system of "*unilateralistic*", or exclusively *unilateral choice-of-law rules* (see item 2 in §14) was supported by eminent scholars (chiefly Schnell, Neumann and Niedner) who espoused this method basically for considerations of public international law. We maintain that mutual respect for the sovereignty of States precludes the possibility of conflict rules fixing the scope of operation of the substantive law of other States, which every State may do exclusively in respect of its own law.

The modern exponents of a private international law based on a system of unilateral conflict rules (Niboyet, Sohn, Pilenko, Quadri) have elaborated unilateralism as an alternative to present-day private international law favouring as it does multilateral conflict rules. They see its advantage first of all in essentially *simplifying* the system, making it more transparent, while definitely leaving numerous traditional problems without legal relevancy. Classification (see §17), for instance, is a question conceptually impossible to raise in this system, for – the conflict norm and the rule of substantive law invoked by it always forming part strictly of the same legal system – the problems of interpretation and systematic arrangement of the legal category constituting the object of the fact governed by the choice-of-law rule, arise within this system of law alone.

The merits in the proposals of the unilateralists are worthy of note by all means, since they are able to ease considerably one of the most criticized problems of private international law based on multilateral conflict rules, namely its complication, its cumbersome armoury of conceptual-dogmatic devices (chiefly the institutions of its general part). This benefit, however, has a high price: disproportionate preference for the *lex fori*, the law of the proceeding court (forum), and, more importantly, the subsidiary role of special conflict rules.

In point of fact, special conflict rules are needed whenever there is a positive or a negative conflict between foreign systems of law in connection with their application to a given fact: several of the foreign legal systems involved require application of their own substantive-law rules. (Conceptually, the legal systems in positive conflict can only be foreign as the "demand" of the *lex fori* to be applied enjoys absolute priority in this system.) The unilateralists recommend application of the following special conflict rule to positive conflicts: where the laws of several foreign States command application, the law must be applied of the State which relies on the principles closest to the forum's (unilateral) choice-of-law rules for determining its (unilateral) choice-of-law rules, viz. we have here a case of using analogous domestic (unilateral) choice-of-law rules. In case of a negative conflict in the application of law the special conflict rule would provide for application of the substantive law of the forum as subsidiary law. All this is no less complicated since the conflict rules would be of two layers (planes): the unilateral choice-of-law rules would always require application of their own law, while in the absence of such a requirement an eventual conflict, positive or negative, between foreign laws would be resolved by special norms. So what is gained by simplification is largely lost "on the swings" of unilateralism.

(b) Some theories (Cavers, Currie, Leflar, von Mehren, Trautmann and others) are in favour of substituting *general clauses* for private international law based on multilateral conflict rules, arguing that by reliance on the system of stable, pre-established choice-of-law rules, which is rigid, blind, mechanical and devoid of values, private international law is incapable of giving adequate solutions and still less of contributing to the assertion of material justice. In addition, legal certainty, which is intended to be served by fixed choice-of-law rules, similarly fails to materialize, since the choice-of-law rules leading to solutions that, while perhaps predictable in themselves, are often frustrated by general institutions of private international law, such as the public policy clause (see §24), classification (see §17) or *renvoi* (see §19). It is therefore more appropriate to abandon *a priori* the inevitably inflexible choice-of-law rules and replace them with general clauses allowing free appraisal of individual cases, thus providing a guide to the applicable law.

According to the expectations common to these conceptions, the means of private international law should also be used to promote the achievement of *material justice*, a reason why the judge is furnished with no fixed choice-of-law rules but guidance in a more or less coherent system of general clauses indicating to him the path for finding the material norms likely to promote material justice.

(c) In contrast to the theoretical conceptions outlined above, a number of reform proposals aim to renew the private international law of conflicts, unable to face up to the economic and social challenges, by rejecting the system of *multilateral choice-of-law rules*, one of its most fundamental methodological devices. So these theories continue to stand more or less for the basic principles of the traditional private international law but wish to *improve* it in particular aspects.

(i) This corrective goal meant to preserve the foundations is clearly seen in the proposals which intend to make broader use of the public policy clause (see §24), the traditional *corrective tool* employed *a posteriori* by the private international law of conflicts, to enhance its function or to supplement it with another general clause, the so-called *escape clause*.

These conceptions, which are popular mainly in Switzerland (Bucher, Dietzi, Vischer), should serve to evade the governing law which proves to be inapplicable for any reason. (This endeavour is also conveyed by the use of new designations like *international Härteklausel, allgemeine oder besondere Ausweichklausel, Ausnahmevorbehalte, kollisionrechtliche Berichtungsnorm; clauses échappatoires, clauses d'échappement, clauses d'éxception, clauses correctives, clauses correctrices, clauses de correction; escape clauses, exemption clauses* etc.)

The arguments advanced for leaving aside the applicable law refer, besides violation of the basic principles of the *lex fori* as the traditional reason for the public policy clause, to acceptance of the parties' lawful expectations deserving protection, the unbearable burden for the parties concerned, closer links with another legal system, the need to avoid contradictory results, and the overriding interest of another State in enforcement. The Swiss Code of Private International Law of 1987 raises these scientifically elaborated proposals to the rank of positive law: in addition to the *ordre public* clause (Art. 17), an "escape clause" (Art. 165) enables the judge to dispense – exceptionally, if obvious reasons are present – with application of the law designated by the choice-of-law rule of conflicts law [cf. Kreuzer, *ZfRV,* 33 (1992), pp. 168–192].

(ii) The theory which proposes occasional consideration of certain foreign rules other than those belonging to the otherwise applicable system of law (the *lex causae*) has brought something completely new into the realm of the private international law of conflicts.

The first formulation of this conception is to the credit of Wengler, who advocated acceptance of foreign rules – chiefly of the foreign exchange law and the law of the external economy, which form part of the "cogent law of contracts" – if their "demand for their own territorial operation" extends to a particular case, even though, according to the applicable multilateral choice-of-law rule, the case is decided under a different system of law. In this way, in the application of private international law, consideration may be given not only to the forum's scale of values, and not only to the value selected by the foreign legal system chosen according to the conflict rules of the forum, but also to the *values postulated* by specific rules of an eventual additional law having a close, essential connection with the concrete fact. All this, of course, is permissible within reasonable limits which, again, may evidently be fixed only through the filter of values of the forum's world and, above all, by having regard to the close connection with the given system of law, while respecting the public policy of the forum.

The idea of considering and eventually applying foreign rules of *jus cogens* not forming part of the applicable law is an imposing perception of the economic, social and political challenges faced in this century by classical private international law and expressed in, among others, private international law assuming the character of public law, heavily charged with political and social elements. These changes have borne especially hard on international economic relations and, in general, private international relationships, owing not least to the coexistence between States with different socio-economic systems, their interdependence and their multifaceted relations – economic, commercial, touristic, etc. International relations in the nature of "pure private law" are not only framed within a hardly transparent web of provisions of foreign exchange law, labour law, etc. as well as of export-import bans, but their very existence, validity and possibility of coming to fruition are also basically determined by that web. For this very reason, consideration of these elements should not depend on the "connecting devilry" of conflicts law, which is unable, even under a most carefully devised system of choice-of-law rules to guarantee in each case the operation of the rules of all the legal systems concerned. Cases in point may be, for example, import bans by the law of the place of performance not regarded as the *lex contractus* (see §83) in a particular case or, conversely, export bans by the law of the obliged exporter not regarded as the *lex contractus*.

Wengler's "*special connection*" (*Sonderanknüpfung*) of rules, mostly in the nature of public law yet affecting private law relationships, which form no part of the legal system designated by the choice-of-law rules but have a significant and substantial effect on a particular fact, is capable of giving an ingenious and efficient response to one of the greatest challenges to private international law. No wonder, therefore, that this idea is gaining ground, though through sharp debates, in theory and is penetrating judicial practice and, lately, even legislation.

Of the statutory devices, examples may be furnished by Art. 7 (1) of the Rome Convention of 1980 of the European Community and by Art. 19 of the relevant Swiss statute, which seek to rely on all important criteria elaborated by theory for "special connection", providing for consideration of foreign rules which, though not forming part of the applicable law by being closely connected with the case to be decided, require exclusive application (i.e. are of an imperative nature).

(iii) In like manner, potential conflicts between values of legal systems connected with private international law facts and solutions thereof constitute one of the dominant motives of Ehrenzweig's forum theory ("*lex fori approach*", as he terms it), which emphasizes the *natural evidence of the scale of values of the forum* in three aspects, in three functions. The values of the *lex fori* are paramount to fixing the scope of operation of its own substantive law rules and, "in the absence of a demand for application", to designating the foreign rules in their place, this being a self-evident concomitant of the (*basic*) *function* of the *lex fori*, viz. its natural priority of application. The conception formed of the institutions in the general part of private international law is likewise based on values as postulated by the forum. Again, the *lex fori* fills the role of *ultima ratio* in the adjudication of private international law cases (see §25). Ehrenzweig otherwise continues favouring the traditional system of pre-established multilateral choice-of-law rules.

(d) We conclude this survey by a brief reference to the reform proposals aimed at eliminating, in a smaller or larger measure, the indirect method of traditional private international law, notably at replacing the conflict rules by application of the directly regulative *rules of substantive law*. The related theories have been mentioned in our summary of crisis phenomena in modern private international law (conflicts between international facts and rules geared to national problems) (see item 2 above). The substantive rules of private international law are of various *types,* including in general international (bilateral and multilateral) *agreements* regulating international facts directly, without reference to the law of conflicts, as well as those of the internal (State) rules which, applied only through reference by the conflict norm, were drafted in view of the international character of facts and control exclusively international facts. This latter type was often exemplified by the Czechoslovak Act of 1963 on International Trade, but such substantive rules of private international law are also contained in Law-Decree No. 8 of 1978 (still in force) on the Application of the Hungarian Civil Code to External Economic Relations (see §65).

The important sources of substantive private international law may be considered to include the rules of customary law which – formulated in international usages, decisions of judges or awards of arbitral tribunals, etc. – are applied as stipulated by the parties concerned, to the exclusion of conflicts law, mainly in order to meet the needs of international trade (see §68). During the past decades there has emerged an entire theoretical system called "*transnational commercial law*" to govern the principles of this method of regulation.

CHAPTER III

THE SOURCES OF PRIVATE INTERNATIONAL LAW

§12. THE TYPES OF SOURCES

The sources of private international law include *customary* and *statute* laws.

(A) In addition to written law, *customary law* has retained an extremely important role all over the world. More comprehensive works of codification did not appear except in the past hundred years (e.g. in Italy and Germany in the last century and then in Poland, in former Czechoslovakia, etc.), and the significance of customary law in the regulation of private international law facts is generally greater, even in the countries mentioned, than in other areas of the legal system. So far, no more than detailed draft regulations of private international law have been elaborated even in countries with notable traditions of codification (e.g. France), not to mention the world of common law, in which a decisive part is traditionally played by customary law. Consequently in most countries the *practice of courts* and other law enforcement agencies is the basic source of private international law.

International commercial usages (see §66) are also of great significance in the law of transactions (especially in the regulation of international sales), but they are not regarded as sources of law except when and where a particular international usage is, expressly or by implication, recognized or sanctioned by the State concerned.

(B) 1. A group of *written* private international law *sources* is found in the norms of domestic law, such as

– special enactment [e.g. in Austria, Czechoslovakia (whose law is now in force both in the Czech and Slovak Republics), Hungary Italy, Poland, Romania, Switzerland];

– comprehensive provisions of civil codes (e.g. the Portuguese *Código civil*) or enacting legislation (the German *EGBGB*); and/or

– several other statutes or decrees.

(The questions of private international law in the former Soviet Union were normatively covered by the Act called the Foundations of Soviet Civil Law

Legislation laying down uniform rules of civil law. It is not yet known exactly which of the successor States will draft its own code of private international law or will adopt the rules of the one-time Foundations. The Foundations will henceforth be referred to in this sense.)

(a) The sources of written domestic law (e.g. all those just mentioned) are constituted *mostly* by *conflict* norms using the indirect method of regulating facts of private international law, by remitting rules determining the applicable law.

(b) Exceptionally, however, there are also *direct* rules and even laws in the nature of a code (e.g. the Czechoslovak Act of 1963 on International Trade and the former GDR's *GIW vom* 5.2.1976, both of historical interest) that can be found among the domestic sources of private international law. Regulations of this type (including Law-Decree No. 8 of 1978 on the Application of the Hungarian Civil Code to External Economic Relations) contain special provisions for legal relationships with international elements.

2. Another group of written private international law sources is made up of *international agreements* which, in their origin, are sources of an *international character* and become part of domestic law through appropriate constitutional procedures (e.g. ratification and promulgation).

The international agreements containing conflict *norms* or substantive law rules form a special class (that of the so-called law-making treaties, *traités-lois*) and can be clearly separated from international agreements (political, military, etc.) that create no direct rights and obligations for natural and legal persons. Particularly in the wake of World War Two, international agreements have assumed a much *greater role* in regulating facts of private international law. Their provisions are applied with respect to some countries and to certain legal relationships more frequently than the so-called autonomous rules (laid down by one single State). Therefore, in the resolution of concrete cases the first thing the court (or another law enforcement agency) is to do is to ascertain whether a particular matter is governed by an international agreement.

The rapid growth of international agreements having the nature of private law gives rise to *specific problems*, too. It is not rare to find difficulty in merely having an overall view of international agreements (keeping up-to-date with modifications and additions) and determining *the text in force* covering a particular case, let alone agreements at cross-purposes or in direct conflict with one another. As often as not, the different meaning or interpretation of the terms adopted in the practice of States parties is an obstacle to a really uniform application of international agreements. (If, for instance, an international agreement attaches legal consequences to the time of making a loan contract, the meaning varies according to whether it is considered to belong in the category of a consensual or a real contract.) Given the specific problems they entail, international agreements in the nature of private law have become a field of law requiring independent scientific research (see Kropholler, 1975; Majoros and Volken in the List of Sources).

International agreements having the nature of private law can be *classified* by various criteria.

(a) Depending on the number of States parties, agreements are *bilateral* and *multilateral*.

Hungary has signed several *bilateral* agreements (*agreements on legal assistance*) laying down conflict rules for determination of the law applicable mainly to the status of persons as well as to family and inheritance matters. Its bilateral agreements on investment protection are likewise of importance. [The agreements on legal assistance and investment protection are listed under Section I. 2 (a) in the List of Sources.]

An important part in the elaboration of *multilateral* treaties on private international law is played in particular by the *Hague Conference on Private International Law*. Several such treaties have also been concluded under the auspices of the United Nations, the European Union and the Council of Europe (see §67).

A distinction between multilateral agreements is made by the *possibility of accession* to them. By this criterion, agreements are either

– *closed*, meaning that they are open only to specified States [e.g. those participating in their elaboration or belonging to a particular geographical, economic or political (regional) group of States]; or

– *open*, meaning that they are open to accession by all States.

Each class of agreement on private law may be illustrated by examples such as the *Rome Convention* signed by the member-states of the European Union on the determination of the law governing contract law relationships (a *closed* agreement; see §67), the *Code Bustamante* (an *open* agreement, though ratified to date only by States of South and Central America; see *Samtleben* in the List of Sources) and the *Vienna Convention* on the International Sale of Goods (an *open* agreement; see Chapter XXII).

(b) By the use of different methods, international agreements may formulate *direct* (substantive) or *indirect* (conflict) rules to govern cases of private international law. International law-making practice relies heavily on both methods: the said Hague Conference has produced scores of agreements on the law of conflicts since the Second World War, the aforementioned Vienna Convention lays down substantive rules, the agreements on legal assistance or the Code Bustamante establish conflict rules, and so on.

Further, the agreements on the law of conflicts employ partially different methods: some determine the applicable law (the way an autonomous, domestic conflict norm does), others designate the proceeding court or other authority (viz. determine jurisdiction) and at the same time ordain the application of the law of the State of the organ vested with jurisdiction (*lex fori in foro proprio*). The difference in regulation is rather one of method used in codification only.

(c) Moreover, international agreements differ by *scope of operation*. Most of them are applied *only in relations between States parties*, more specifically to facts of private international law connected only with the States concerned, e.g., to specified acts done in the territory of a contracting State (celebration of marriage, motor accident, etc.) or to legal relationships one of whose subjects is at least a national of any of the States parties. The application of such agreements as *special rules* to private international cases (and to them only!) takes precedence over other relevant rules of domestic law (conflict norms or substantive rules).

On the other hand, there are international agreements obliging States parties to change their own laws in a particular area and to incorporate into their internal laws the provisions of the relevant agreement which thus supersede or override the domestic norms. The *uniform* international *law* (*loi uniforme*) which is stated in such international agreements to be *binding* upon all States, may normally be applied only to *international* legal relationships (e.g. "international sales") in the area covered (but here with respect to non-parties, too), whereas in other cases the uniform law may also govern purely *domestic situations* (e.g. the Geneva Conventions of 1930 and 1931 on the Law of Bills of Exchange and Cheques; see §81).

Each international agreement determines its own scope of application. (If an international agreement allows the States parties to make reservations in this respect, the scope of application may also be limited by the incorporating rule of the State concerned.)

The sources of private international law may be *summarized* as follows:

(A) Norms of *customary law* and *commercial usages*

(B) *Statutory* (written) norms

1. *National* law
   - (a) *conflict* rules
   - (b) *substantive* rules
2. *International agreements*
   - (a) *bilateral*
     multilateral
     open
     closed (e.g. regional)
   - (b) *conflict* rules (indirect regulation)
     substantive rules (direct regulation)
   - (c) special rules
     uniform law (*loi uniforme*)

§13. THE SOURCES OF HUNGARIAN PRIVATE INTERNATIONAL LAW

1. Down to recent times, Hungarian private international law derived its sources largely from international customs and from *principles of customary law* moulded by the practice of courts (arbitral tribunals, etc.). This was characteristic chiefly of the international law of contracts but customs played a considerable role in other fields (e.g. the law of inheritance) as well. The same situation

persisted after the entry into force of the Hungarian Civil Code (Act IV of 1959): Law-Decree No. 11 of 1960, which brought the Code into force, expressly upheld the authoritative rulings of the Supreme Court (partly of the Curia prior to the Second World War) on matters of private international law (para. 3 of Art. 5).

Rules of private international law – mostly on matters of detail – were contained, in addition to customary law, in scattered sources of *written norms*.

Scattered rules on jurisdiction, and private international law provisions on the *lex personae*, the *lex loci et temporis contractus*, the capacity of foreigners to acquire immovable property, the legal status of foreign merchants, etc. can be found in various enactments from as early as the 14th century. (For a fuller discussion, see the works by Bónis and Zlinszky in the List of Sources.)

In the 19th century, with the quickening process of capitalist development in Hungary, there appeared a growing number of private international law rules in Hungarian legislation concerning foreigners' full equality of rights (1848, 1852), law on bills of exchange (1850, 1876), copyrights (1852, 1884), patent rights (1852, 1895) and trade-mark rights (1890); wills made abroad (1876) and probate proceedings (1894); foreigners' guardianship (1877) and marriage (1894), etc. Important jurisdictional and conflict norms can be found in legislation on civil procedure (1868) and the jurisdiction and competence of domestic and foreign courts (1896). The enforcement of foreign judgments was governed by a separate enactment (1881). This period witnessed a greater role assumed by international agreements as sources of Hungarian private international law, such as trade agreements with the United States of America (1829), Greece (1835, 1854, 1856), Russia (1860), France (1866), etc. and numerous agreements on legal assistance. The terms and conditions of trade and business were also controlled by international agreements which contained, moreover, jurisdictional and conflict rules (relating to the law of property and the law of inheritance).

This accidental and rather chaotic method of legislation on Hungarian private international law continued into the 20th century and even after the Second World War. Among comparatively more recent enactments, which include provisions on private international law (and in operation up to 1 July 1979), mention is deserved of, e.g., Act III of 1952 on Civil Procedure and Law-Decree No. 22 of 1952 on its Entry into Force, or Law-Decree No. 23 of 1952 on the Entry into Force and the Enforcement of the Family Law Act.

2. The uncertain and unsystematic state of the sources of private international law necessitated and placed again on the agenda a *comprehensive codification* of the law in this field.

Professor István Szászy's draft, which appeared in print in 1948, covered both the major general questions of private international law and the definitions of connecting factors, affording detailed justification for the bill, which was prepared with excellent scientific erudition and rested on impressive theoretical foundations. Since adoption of a code of private international law was not favoured by the domestic and the international situation at the time, the draft remained one of private initiative, with the idea of codification falling into oblivion for nearly two decades.

The need for a codification of private international law reappeared *in the mid-1960s*, a period by which the changed pattern of international and domestic conditions had created a more favourable atmosphere for the expansion of international economic and personal transactions, with quantitative growth accompanied by a qualitative differentiation in international contacts of a private law nature. This world phenomenon is of particular relevance to Hungary, which has a fairly open economy and consequently produces some 50% of its national income in foreign trade, while assuming a growing role in international tourism. These developments have considerably widened the scope of everyday situations calling for regulation by private international law.

All these circumstances combined to ripen the conditions for a comprehensive codification of Hungarian private international law. Foreign examples were also more numerous. Of the European countries, for instance, Czechoslovakia and Poland adopted their codes of private international law (in 1963 and 1965, respectively), which are still in force, even in the successor States.

Under the combined impact of these factors the work of codification was set in motion in 1966 under the guidance of the Institute of Political and Legal Sciences of the Hungarian Academy of Sciences, and the second draft was prepared by 1968. Thereafter, codification continued under the auspices of the Ministry of Justice, which produced a new draft in 1970. Owing mainly to still greater pressures on other legislative activities, however, a comprehensive regulation of private international law suffered a prolonged delay. It was not until 1978 that the fourth draft was prepared, which was adopted as a law in 1979 and was promulgated by *Law-Decree No. 13 of 1979*.

In the various sections of our book dealing with conflicts law we rely on this Law-Decree (hereinafter referred to as the Hungarian *Code*), which, embracing as it does the basic questions of private international law and the international law of civil procedure, is a product of legislation meeting the criteria of a code. It falls into the following chapters: I. General Rules, II. Persons, III. Law of Intellectual Property, IV. Property Law and Related Rights, V. Law of Obligations, VI. Law of Inheritance, VII. Family Law, VIII. Labour Law, IX. Jurisdiction, X. Rules of Procedural Law, XI. Recognition and Enforcement of Foreign Judgments. (The body of rules is followed by the usual Final Provisions.)

The Code is applied in the practice of courts, other authorities (notary public, guardianship authority, registry office, etc.) and arbitral tribunals on an ever broadening scale and with increasing frequency, especially to international cases involving family law, inheritance, damages caused by accidents, and even contracts within its remit. In this book we shall try to discuss cases of greater interest presenting theoretical problems in the various subject areas.

3. An important source of Hungarian private international law is invariably constituted by *international treaties* [see item 2 (a) in §12], including in part

multilateral agreements, e.g. the *Vienna Convention* on the International Sale of Goods: see Chapter XXII; conventions on the protection of copyright and industrial rights: see Chapters XXVII and XXVIII; conventions on the law of bills of exchange and cheques, etc.: see §81; and in part bilateral treaties (of which the agreements on legal assistance are of the greatest importance to our study).

Of course, the international treaties are not affected by the operation of the Code, which provides (in Art. 2) that "this Law-Decree shall not apply to matters governed by international treaty". [The Supreme Court ruled (Pf.IV.20. 841/1991; BH 1992/10. 631), *inter alia*, that "since the protection of copyright is also governed by international treaty, the Law-Decree on private international law is inapplicable by virtue of Art. 2 of the Code".]

TITLE 2

THE CONFLICT RULE AND ITS APPLICATION

CHAPTER IV

THE CHOICE-OF-LAW RULE

§14. CONCEPT AND TYPES OF THE CHOICE-OF-LAW RULE

1. As has been indicated earlier (item 7 in §6), Title 2 is devoted exclusively to the specific problems of legal science and policy concerning indirect regulation of private international law facts, with emphasis laid on questions relating to the *international conflict rule*.

The norms indirectly regulating facts of private international law belong to a special group of rules, that of conflict rules. On the broader plane, a conflict rule is understood to mean a *norm* regulating any conflict of law (hence its name!), to wit, *determining which of several relevant rules is actually to be applied.*

Given the nature of conflicts of law, one may speak of various types of conflict rules in the wider sense (see §7).

– Conflict cases may be international, when the choice is between the laws of several sovereign States; the norms resolving such conflicts are called *international* conflict rules. The focus of our discussion will be on the rules of this type.

– Conflicts may also arise between differing laws of non-sovereign parts of a sovereign State (member States, federal States, etc.). These are cases of *interterritorial* conflicts which are governed by interterritorial conflict rules. (This problem is of particular relevance in the United States of America, for instance, where the private laws of the various sister States often show wide differences.)

– In some legal systems (e.g. the Islamic laws of the Middle East) there still exist divergences between laws – especially in personal law, family law and the law of inheritance – applicable to different groups of people separated mainly by religion. Conflicts arising between such laws are governed by *interpersonal* conflict rules.

– Modification of an internal-law rule may lead to temporal conflicts of law if the facts of the case occurred wholly or in part during the operation of a repealed rule. Such problems are controlled by *intertemporal* conflict rules.

Hereafter by conflict rules we will mean international conflict norms and by the law of conflicts the domain of these norms.

2. Most conflict rules are designed to govern the choice of law between conflicting legal systems and to determine the law to be applied to a particular fact of private international law. These may as well be called choice-of-law rules since they establish a connection between the given fact and the legal system by which the former is to be decided *in merito*.

At the same time the law of conflicts, as a separate field of law also governed by rules of its own, contains some norms of a different nature, such as those providing either definitions or a general guide to the rules (for the choice of law) in relation to determining the applicable law (e.g. rules on renvoi or the public policy clause; see §§20 and 24). These rules of the law of conflicts may be considered to form, as it were, the general part of the choice-of-law rules which find formal expression in the fact that they are included in the early part of the comprehensive codes of private international law.

The rules for the choice of law do not all provide clearly and explicitly for the applicable law. It happens that the choice of law (determination of the applicable law) is governed by an implied provision of a norm of a different character, as is often the case with, e.g., jurisdiction and the applicable law being determined by one and the same rule. (For the link between jurisdiction and the applicable law, see §21.)

3. Most important to the typification of choice-of-law rules is their classification by *unilateral* and *multilateral* (*complete*) conflict norms.

A rule for the choice of law is deemed to be unilateral when it defines the scope of application of the domestic law with respect to foreign element cases only, namely it determines the situations in which a fact of private international law is to be governed by the domestic law. A classical example for the unilateral formulation of the choice-of-law rule is offered by the provision of Art. 3 (3) of the *Code Civil* quoted earlier: "French nationals shall, even if they are abroad, be subject to the French law governing the legal status and capacity of the person". This rule defines the scope of application of French laws governing personal status (which are applicable to French nationals in all cases, regardless of their place of residence, whether at home or abroad), but is unilateral for its failure to determine the law applicable to similar legal relationships of nationals other than French.

By contrast, a rule for the choice of law is called multilateral when it explicitly determines the law applicable to a particular fact of private international law irrespective of whether the process of selection leads to the consideration of *domestic* or *foreign* law. Thus, for instance, unjust enrichment and its legal consequences are, under the Hungarian Code (Art. 35), governed by the law of the State in which the enrichment took place. This rule is complete as regards the determination of the law applicable to the given fact or private international law (unjust enrichment) because it covers all situations and is not confined to fixing the scope of application of the Hungarian rules for unjust enrichment (§§361–364 of the Civil Code).

Differentiation between unilateral and multilateral (complete) rules for the choice of law is of relevance primarily at the legislative level. If permitted by the intention of the legislator, unilateral rules may also be made multilateral by legal practice. (This is evidenced by the example of German judicial practice, which has developed numerous unilateral choice-of-law rules of the *EGBGB* of 1896 into multilateral conflict rules. The new German law of 1986 has formulated multilateral choice-of-law rules.)

In a historical retrospect, the legislative method of formulating unilateral choice-of-law rules is akin to the proposition of the statute theory concerning the scope of applicability of a given rule as against the multilateral (complete) choice-of-law rule, based on Savigny's reasoning, concerning the law of which State is to control a fact of private international law. Indeed, in the dominant scientific view, multilateral (complete) choice-of-law rules can only be spoken of since Savigny, and facts of private international law were, during the many centuries of statute theory, governed by unilateral conflict rules. It is nevertheless to be noted that this sharp historical categorization is not fully borne out by recent research results which rather point to the use of both unilateral and multilateral choice-of-law rules in each period of the law of conflicts, with only a shift of emphasis or in proportion observed over the past hundred years towards the application of multilateral (complete) conflict rules.

Since Savigny, at any rate, it has been the more general scientific view that multilateral (complete) conflict rules are more suitable for fulfilling the function of the law of conflicts, whereas unilateral choice-of-law rules are confined to expressing the reservations of the national systems of law and to protecting the economic and socio-political interests of individual nations (e.g. in the typical field of foreign exchange control, where every State insists on upholding its own scale of values and hence enforcing its own rules of law).

Nevertheless there are, even in the 20th century, significant exponents of the scientific view (Niboyet, Pilenko, Quadri, etc.) arguing for the construction of the law of conflicts on a mutual system of unilateral choice-of-law rules [see item 3 (a) in §11B]. They maintain in the first place that no State must determine the scope of application of any but its own law (which in turn is to be done by each State) and that no State must fix the sphere of operation of the law of another State. In addition to the practical problems involved, the weakness of this view is in taking the question of State sovereignty to its extreme with respect to a set of problems in which it is absolutely necessary to give precedence to the most equitable possible adjudication of private international law cases (viz. disputes between private persons), while multilateral (complete) conflict norms are, in principle and ordinarily, more suitable for achieving this goal. This latter principle has been adopted by the Hungarian Code as well.

International legislative practice is tending to lean towards the dominant view that the overwhelming majority of choice-of-law rules are made up of multilateral (complete) norms; yet it is not rare to find unilateral conflict rules (cf. Conetti's study in the List of Sources) mainly in areas where every State deems it important to give effect to its political considerations and where, therefore, every system of law seeks to define its own scope of application. (Over the past decade, legislation in several States has regarded the questions of consumer protection or some aspects of adoption (see Conetti in the List of Sources) as constituting such a set of problems.) The range and structure of everyday relations that are of paramount legal-political significance, are reserved for regulation by domestic law according to its own scale of values and are subject to the control of its rules, are liable to change and are also largely dependent upon the degree of consolidation of international political, economic and other relations.

§15. THE STRUCTURE OF THE CHOICE-OF-LAW RULE. CONNECTING FACTORS

1. The indirect method of regulation by the law of conflicts necessarily results in the fact that the choice-of-law rule is never all-embracing in terms of wording or formal expression; it never decides a particular case on its merits but is confined to determining which of the legal systems connected with the given fact of private international law is to govern the adjudication of the merits of the case according to its substantive rules. In this sense the choice-of-law rule is a *legal norm* controlling selection of the legal system with the aid of the norms of other branches of law (civil law, family law, labour law).

The theory of legislation usually distinguishes between *three structural elements* of a legal norm: fact (hypothesis or premise), provision (disposition) and legal consequence (legal effect or sanction). The choice-of-law rule is a legal norm of special function and structure exhibiting some peculiarity in each of these elements.

(a) The very *facts* covered by the choice-of-law rules are peculiar in that they are always *formulated with the aid of substantive-law institutions, of basic systematic concepts*, their core being formed by categories like legal capacity, disposing capacity, extrinsic or intrinsic validity of marriage, contracts, etc. These concepts may as well be termed the *objects of choice-of-law.* Thus, for instance, *liability* for non-contractual damage (Art. 32) or the *substantive requirements of the validity* of marriage (Art. 37) are defined by the Hungarian Code as facts under the control of their relevant rules.

Of course, what we have behind the legal concepts as well as in the case of choice-of-law rules, are civil or social relations (damage to property, matrimonial relationships, etc.); the "primary matter" (as termed by Rabel) of the objects of choice-of-law rules are constituted by the corresponding everyday relations. While, however, substantive (positive) rules often have a direct bearing on a given relationship or fact (birth, death, attaining a certain age, etc.), the facts governed by choice-of-law rules are always and necessarily defined by the help of abstract legal concepts. The hypothesis of a conflict norm can never be directly wedded to everyday relations but it always "depends" on substantive rules, for preliminary appraisal and transmission. In the use of choice-of-law rules the problem to be solved does not emerge as a concrete fact of daily life as in the case of substantive rules; rather it appears as a question of law on a more abstract plane, with the typified question of law subsumed under the hypothesis of the choice-of-law rule. This peculiarity is of relevance mainly for the interpretation of the choice-of-law rule, namely classification or characterization (see Chapter V).

(b) The most peculiar element of the choice-of-law rule is the *provision* (disposition) subjecting a fact of private international law to the applicable system of law, national or foreign. As has been repeatedly stated, since the law of conflicts is the means of indirectly regulating facts of private international law, it finds expression in the remitting nature of the choice-of-law rule is confined to determining the applicable law, to designating the substantive rules for the adjudication of the merits of the controversy. It is the provision of the choice-of-law rule which gives a *normative character* to the selection of the applicable legal system, which makes the question covered by the conflict norm a concern of the law, thus establishing a connection between the facts of the case and the applicable legal system.

Under this approach to the *provision* (disposition) of the choice-of-law rule we rather emphasize its peremptory (imperative) aspect which, in the legal system of the forum, contains the *legislator's command* to apply the system of law (national or foreign) controlling the particular fact of private international law. At first sight this is doubtless the most emphatic element, especially when one has to explain the reason for the application of a foreign substantive law, or the way in which the fragment of a norm as formulated in the choice-of-law rule is accepted from a foreign law in order to achieve full effect: the normative command is certainly a part of domestic law, with the peremptory element residing in the conflicts law (choice-of-law rule) of the forum. (On the justifications for the application of foreign law, see §4, item 4 in §10 and item 2 in §11; on the special difficulties in the application of foreign law, see §23.)

In fact, however, the *rational* element in the provision of the choice-of-law rule is of no lesser importance as it constitutes the aspect of choice between systems of law having connections with the questions of law (ultimately the sets of facts) covered by the hypothesis. So the provision of a conflict norm is also expressive of the legislator's choice between alternative legal systems connected with a particular fact of private international law, of the result of appraisals concerning his decision. In this sense the provision of the choice-of-law rule is an expression of a value, as its imperative designation of the applicable legal system, results primarily from the legislator's appraisal of various factors leading to the selection of the legal system which is deemed desirable to control the given set of legal points.

(c) The choice-of-law rule never contains any *legal consequences.* This third element (legal effect or sanction) of the legal norm is always absent from the choice-of-law rule because it is determined by the relevant positive rules (in civil law, family law, etc.) of the legal system (national or foreign) invoked by the conflict rule.

2. (a) Unilateral choice-of-law rules (see item 3 in §14), in designating *in concreto* the law applicable to a particular case, define the scope of operation of the law of the State of the proceeding court (authority).

(b) Given their nature, multilateral (complete) conflict rules define *in a general way* the applicable law, by the use of connecting factors (localizers) which constitute an element of the provision (disposition) of the choice-of-law rule. Under the Hungarian Code, the law of the place where the property is situated is applicable to the right of ownership (Art. 21), the formal requirements of the validity of marriage are governed by the law of the place and time of celebration (Art. 37), etc.

3. (a) Accordingly a connecting factor (localizer) is a normative command expressed in the provision of the multilateral choice-of-law rule and *creating a connection between a fact*, condensed in a substantive-law concept, *and the applicable legal system.*

Thus, establishment of such a connection, leading to the choice of law, is a decisive criterion of indirect regulation concerning a fact of private international law. The connecting factor (localizer) is consequently a highly important element of the multilateral (complete) choice-of-law rule.

In the modern law of conflicts several connecting factors were developed on the principles of statute theory, while others were defined by Savigny and legal science evolving as it did under the influence of his theory in this century. The *major connecting factors* used by the various conflict norms, or the systems of law determined by reliance on them, are the following:

– nationality (domestic law), *lex patriae*;
– domicile, *lex domicilii*;
– seat of a legal person;
– the place where property is situated, *lex rei sitae*;
– the place where a transaction is effected, *lex rei loci actus*;
– the law chosen (stipulated), *lex pro voluntate*;
– the place where a wrong is committed, *lex loci delicti commissi*;
– the law of the proceeding court (authority), *lex fori*.

The various connecting factors will be given fuller treatment in the chapters dealing with cases of private international law.

(b) Some connecting factors at times fail to provide guidance for the judge in the discovery of the applicable law. Nationality, for instance, is a connecting factor which is inapplicable to stateless persons (having no nationality). In such cases *subsidiary connecting factors* are needed, which are often determined by the legislator himself. Under the Hungarian Code (Art. 11), for instance, the personal law of stateless persons is the law of the State of their domicile or, if they also have a domicile in Hungary, the Hungarian law. The same holds true for persons with multiple nationality.

If no subsidiary connecting factor is determined by the law, the judge has to apply the rules of the law *most closely connected* with the fact before him. This is also the case when in principle, because of uncertainty surrounding the use of a given connecting factor, several legal systems may be applicable. Thus, for instance, when it cannot be determined whether a person possesses Yugoslav or Italian nationality, the applicable law will be that of the country to which he is actually linked by closer contacts (domicile, habitual residence, etc.)

(c) Some connecting factors (nationality, domicile, residence, seat, location, etc.) are subject to change over time. It is therefore necessary that the point of time relevant to the choice of law should be defined in the choice-of-law rules. Under the Hungarian Code (Art. 36), for instance, inheritance relations are to be judged according to the law which was the personal law of the testator *at the time of his/her death.*

(d) Some of the connecting factors are themselves legal categories (e.g. nationality, domicile, place of performance), while others form *factual* categories (e.g. location). This distinction is, however, rather relative since even the factual categories as elements of the conflict rule may acquire a special legal meaning, a legal complexion, which, like legal categories, may result in uncertainty and be subject to interpretation.

4. The connecting factor is the core and substance of the conflict rule. Specification of the different connecting factors is therefore the touchstone of codifying private international law. It is not by chance, then, that since Savigny's time (see item 2 in §11) the *principles of selecting the connecting factors* have been a central concern of legal science.

(a) The *continental theory* sees the path to a solution primarily in the critical refinement of Savigny's theory by *Sitz* and in its adjustment to the facts of modern life, trying to define maxims of codification to meet this requirement.

In the main, continental *legislation* likewise follows this principle in an endeavour to provide connecting factors controlling the various types of legal relationships. The continental laws proceed from the assumption that the diversity of private international cases makes typification indispensable. While the validity of this conceptual approach can hardly be disputed, problems are, understandably, often encountered when it comes to legislative practice. Thus, the most recent laws of the Continent similarly show a strong tendency towards a formulation of connecting factors that is flexible enough to leave scope for judicial consideration. Examples can also be cited from the Hungarian Code: the so-called final clause (second sentence in §29) used to determine the law controlling contracts or the principle of equity (item 2 in §32) allowing for corrective connection in designating the law applicable to tortious liability.

(b) Science and judicial practice *in England* and especially *in North America* have taken a different path, applying more flexible principles in order to avoid the occasional rigidity, "divorced" from reality, "blindness" and unjust consequences of the connecting factors used in continental laws.

It is mainly in the determination of the law applicable to wrongful damage and to contracts that general rules in the United States are devised to leave a wider discretion for the judge to consider the specific requirements of individual cases ("the proper law of the tort", "the proper law of the contract", "the most real connection", "the most significant relationship", etc.). However, for the time being at least, this method has led to a notable degree of uncertainty, confusion and disorientation in judicial practice, while allowing more room for (probably well-intentioned) subjectivism.

5. The process of *choice of law* is part of the *administration of law*, meaning the application of the choice-of-law rule. Since, as has been noted, the choice-of-law rule is a *legal norm having a special structure, nature and function*, its application likewise poses partially separate questions, different from the problems (interpretation, analogy, etc.) that arise in the application of rules of law other than conflict rules (of positive law). The chapters that follow will discuss the most important problems as encountered in the application of choice-of-law rules.

A distinct question is raised by the very subjection of private international law cases to the relevant choice-of-law rules. This problem is called *classification* or characterization ("qualification" in French), and its substance is considered to be in the interpretation of the legal concept as constituting the object of choice of law (see Chapter V). Particular complications arise from the indirect regulation of private international facts, when the choice-of-law rules of the legal system, ordered to be applied by the conflict rules of the State of the court (forum) handling the case, refer back to the law of the forum or direct the case to the law of a third State (*renvoi*; see Chapter VI). Again, a separate problem is posed by the *application of the positive rules of foreign law* (see Chapter VII).

§16. FRAUD IN CONFLICT CASES

1. In the adjudication of private international law cases the choice of law is of decisive importance in selecting the applicable law and thereby, frequently, in finding the solution to the dispute on its merits. No wonder then that the parties (or either of them), accepting financial burdens and using a lawyer's services, often strive to have an influence upon the process of selecting or designating the applicable law.

When the parties (or either of them) create an artificial link with another legal system in order to evade the law which is rendered applicable to their legal relationship by the appropriate choice-of-law rule, we have the case of *fraud.* The *intention* of evading the applicable law is generally held to be a notional element of fraud, which often creates difficulties of proof. (To cite an *example*, it is not always easy to decide whether the parties celebrate their marriage at a foreign spa far from their common domicile in order to evade an impediment to marriage, to facilitate the conclusion of marriage, or merely to enjoy the pleasant environs of the location so chosen.)

On principle, fraud in the selection of law may lead to the application *either of the law of the forum or of a foreign legal system.* Its commonest form is that of the parties (or either of them) *artificially* changing the *connecting factor* by which the applicable law is determined. This is easy to achieve especially in the case of the so-called mobile connecting factors (place of residence, place of contracting, etc.), but deliberate change in domicile or even nationality is likewise a common recourse. (Well-to-do Italians, for instance, often resorted to a change in nationality so long as dissolution of marriage was inadmissible in Italy.) Artificial creation of legal conditions required for the determination of *jurisdiction* (see §21) and thereby evasion of the appropriate conflict rule is an additional method. For example, the forum authorized by law to take jurisdiction would decide the case according to the law of nationality, while the applicable law is the law of domicile under the conflict rule of the forum which the parties, by artificially creating the statutory conditions, manage to have for considering their case. The applicable law may further be fraudulently "determined" by manipulating the *object of choice of law* (the legal concept expressing the fact covered by the choice-of-law rule; see item 1 in §15).

By fraudulent selection of law, the parties (or either of them) seek to gain individual advantage: either to avoid the undesirable *consequences* of their legal relationship (e.g. the invalidity of a contract or a marriage) or to produce a *favourable legal effect* (e.g. dissolution of marriage) not incidental to their original legal status. Not infrequently, enterprises choose a foreign country (e.g. Liechtenstein) for their seat, or freighters (oil-tankers) fly a foreign (e.g. Liberian) flag in order to evade tax laws, etc. International family law, particularly the conclusion and dissolution of marriage, is a typical area of fraud in conflict cases.

2. The legal appraisal of and the sanctions for fraudulent conduct vary country by country. Some legal systems (e.g. the French) adopt a rigorous approach, others (e.g. the German judicial practice) take a broader view, and still others (the English, the American) show a tolerant attitude. The reaction of the law may also differ by classes of facts; fraud is sometimes deliberately tolerated because it allows evasion of a rule (mainly of foreign law) that is generally assumed to be inequitable.

If the factual element of the case resulting in the selection of a different law is merely a fictive one (e.g. the type of contract is misstated in the deed or the place of contracting is shown to be different from the real one), the legal consequences will be established in disregard of the feigned incidents, namely in accordance with the truly governing choice-of-law rule (provided, of course, that the fiction is disclosed!). If the wrongful selection is based on an actually accomplished artificial incident (e.g. the parties actually concluded the contract at the place shown in the deed, but did so in order to evade the applicable law), the most obvious sanction is *denial of legal effect to the result obtained by fraud* and application of the appropriate choice-of-law rule (in addition to fiscal, criminal and/or other consequences, if any).

The *intent* to evade the otherwise applicable law is regarded by the Hungarian Code (Art. 8) as a notional element of fraud in the selection of law, including both cases of foreign connection established either artificially or fraudulently as indicated above. On the other hand, the Hungarian Code imposes sanctions against fraud only in the event that it is likely to lead to the application of foreign law; where the Hungarian law would be applicable it must be applied. (It is hardly possible to provide a theoretical explanation for such partiality of the Code!) The foreign law "chosen" by fraud must be replaced by the rules of the otherwise applicable law.

CHAPTER V

CLASSIFICATION

§17. THE SUBSTANCE OF CLASSIFICATION PROBLEMS

1. The first and foremost question arising in the application of law is to decide which law is to govern a concrete case or, conversely, to which law is the case to be subjected. Essentially the same problem is faced in the indirect solution (by conflicts law) of private international law cases, namely in the application of the choice-of-law rule. *The selection of the appropriate choice-of-law rule (governing the particular fact) and its application to the legal relationship in question is called classification* (or characterization).

The classification problem lies essentially in *identifying the place in the system of conflicts law of the substantive-law issue involved in the facts of the case requiring decision* (prescription, claim to maintenance, validity of a will, etc.) *and in subjecting it to the appropriate choice-of-law rule*. The process involves the interpretation of the substantive-law category constituting the object of the choice-of-law rule (see item 1 in §15) and the definition of its scope of operation.

This question – e.g. whether the law applicable to testamentary capacity is to be determined by the choice-of-law rule relating to disposing capacity or to the law of inheritance – is often hard to decide even within the framework of a single legal system. The real problem of classification is nonetheless posed by the *need to consider several systems of law* in order to find the place of the related substantive-law concept in the law of conflicts.

The choice-of-law rule is part of a particular legal system, and bears mainly the imprint of the legal system in question, while creating a link with a foreign system of law and its concepts. Since the legal categories generally formulated in the fact controlled by the choice-of-law rule (the governing law of that fact being determined by the connecting factor) may have a different substance and meaning in the laws of the various countries, determination of the scope of application of the choice-of-law rule depends on the legal system by which the interpretation of the particular legal concept (used in the hypothesis of the choice-of-law rule) is accomplished.

This may be illustrated by the following example: Under the Hungarian Civil Code (Arts. 615 and 616) the jointure of the surviving spouse (*widow's portion*) is a claim to inheritance unknown to most European laws today. If a Hungarian national living permanently abroad brings an action for jointure before a foreign court, the nature of her claim – and hence the selection of the governing choice-of-law rule and often the outcome or the success of the action – will depend on whether the widow's action of jointure is classified by the court as being under the control of the law of inheritance (as under the Hungarian law) or as being in the nature of a right *in rem* (as under the *lex fori*). In the former case the action is governed by the choice-of-law rule for statutory succession (see Chapter XX) and hence, normally, by the substantive law of the decedent's nationality (perhaps domicile), whereas in the latter case the applicable law is indicated by the choice-of-law rule relating to rights *in rem* (see Chapter X) and accordingly by the substantive law of the place where the property (movable or immovable) at issue is situated. The pivotal question is therefore to decide *by which system of law* the substantive-law issue (widow's portion) is to be classified under the law of conflicts.

2. The classification problem posed by cases in judicial practice was first discovered at the end of the last century (by the German jurist Kahn in 1891 and, independently of him, by the French jurist Bartin in 1897, to whom the French term "qualification" is attributed). This has since become a much-analyzed and much-discussed problem of private international law which has not yet been settled.

(a) Judicial practice is mainly confronted with cases of classification when *a legal category is dealt with in different parts of the competing legal systems*. A common example is provided by the institution of prescription (see Edler and Will in the List of Sources), which is regarded as a matter of substantive law in the continental legal systems, but is still treated as one of procedural law in most component States of the United States of America (despite shifts observed in some sister States) (see Hay, *IPRax*, 1989). (In English law the Foreign Limitation Periods Act of 1984 has changed the classification of prescription to one under substantive law; see Carter, *The Law Quarterly Review,* 1985.)

A similar problem may arise from, e.g. the prohibition of joint testamentary disposition (Art. 664 of the Hungarian Civil Code), non-violation of which is considered to be a requisite of the intrinsic validity of a will (e.g. in Italy) or of extrinsic validity (e.g. in France).

In a similar manner, the systematic treatment of the status of the State in respect of estates is twofold in the different laws: in some legal systems (e.g. of Germany, Switzerland, Italy, Spain, Greece, Turkey) the State is statutory heir [as under Art. 599 (3) of the Hungarian Civil Code], whereas in others (e.g. of the common-law countries, most countries in Latin America, Austria, France, Belgium, Netherlands) the State has the right of escheat to unclaimed estates (reversion or appropriation exhibiting public-law characteristics). (See Bungert, *ZfRV*, No. 4 of 1991.)

(b) A problem of classification may also arise if a particular legal institution is entirely unknown to, or another of an essentially similar nature is not contained in, the law of the proceeding court *(forum)*. For example, the institution of *trust* at common law is unfamiliar to the continental legal systems, or important institutions like *bankruptcy, payment moratorium* or *prohibition of transfer* which have essential bearings on the performance of contracts, are unknown to certain systems of law, although related issues frequently emerge in international economic relations.

In group (a) of cases, covering different systematic approaches, the process of classification by the relevant system of law and by the law of the forum leads to opposite results (e.g. application to prescription of the choice-of-law rule of substantive or procedural law). In group (b) of cases, the *lex fori* may contain no appropriate choice-of-law rule because the given legal institution is unknown to its substantive law (as is trust to the continental legal system) and therefore has to rely specifically on another system of law. Such instances of classification may even serve to fill gaps in law, thus refining the law of the forum. (The problem of filling gaps in the law, the demand for legal development by the judge, is *per se* greater in the private law of conflicts than in other fields of law, since a number of questions is unanswered by regulation even in countries where private international law is codified.)

3. From the foregoing it becomes clear that, in our view, the root of the classification problem is to be sought in the *normative peculiarities of the choice-of-law rule* (see item 1 in §15).

We must proceed from the fact that the norms formulated in the choice-of-law rules come into full effect through the rules of the substantive law (domestic or foreign) invoked. This conceptually requires the hypotheses of choice-of-law rules (the substantive-law concepts contained in them) to be framed in such a way as to be duly receptive to the concepts of any legal system, or, put in another way, to leave room for the substantive-law rules of any legal system in the hypothesis of the appropriate choice-of-law rule. Such a requirement of principle can be satisfied, at least in a rough approximation, by formulating the hypotheses of choice-of-law rules in view of the substantive rules of both domestic and foreign law. However, this goal can hardly be achieved in full. Even works of codification relying on modern comparative law can at best drawn on but limited experience of foreign legislation (on conflicts law). In point of fact, in preparing a catalogue of choice-of-law rule hypotheses the legislator cannot have full regard except to the substantive rules of his own legal system.

The problems of classification stem from this inevitable "imperfection": legal practice may reveal differences in systematic arrangement between the substantive-law category contained in the hypothesis of the choice-of-law rule and the question of law arising in a concrete case to be decided [see item 2 (a) above]. The number of classification problems grows in proportion as the hypotheses of choice-of-law rules are formulated with adjustments for few other legal systems and with attention focused on the substantive rules and institutions of domestic law.

§18. ATTEMPT AT A SOLUTION

1. There are mainly two systems of law relevant to classification required for the application of the choice-of-law rule: the given legal category may be classified under the law of the State of the proceeding organ (*lex fori*) and, on principle, under the applicable (selected) law (*lex causae*). For instance, the prescription of a contractual money debt repayable to a Californian buyer may be classified by a Hungarian court as an institution bearing the character of substantive law under the Hungarian law (*lex fori*) but, in principle, the court may also take the view that the prescription is held to be a procedural matter under the Californian law (*lex causae*) as the law applicable to the litigated fact.

For a long time, legal science treated this problem as one of choice, carried to extremes, between the *lex fori* and the *lex causae*.

(a) The dominant view (including the concept of Kahn and Bartin) is still in favour of classification by the *lex fori*. Accordingly the forum may interpret the legal categories covered by its conflict norms only under the concepts and organizing principles of its own system of law and may select the appropriate choice-of-law rule of its own law of conflicts solely by using its own notions. This method is supported by the principle that it is for every State to decide the temporal and spatial limits of the application of foreign law by its fora. In case of doubt, therefore, a State should likewise answer this question by interpretation of its own system of law, all the more so since the question implies voluntary waiver of sovereignty.

In a similar manner, the legislative and judicial *practices* of most countries consistently follow the prevailing view of the science of private international law and seek to solve the classification problem under the domestic system of law.

In its practical application, however, the method of classification by the *lex fori* is *not flawless* in spite of its logical accuracy and of the attractiveness and weight of the theoretical arguments in its favour. It is particularly difficult to arrive at a decision in the case of legal institutions unknown to the law of the forum [see item 2 (b) in §17].

(b) Classification by the *lex causae* is hardly defensible on a purely logical basis, for it produces a *circulus vitiosus*: determination of the legal system relevant to classification requires the concrete (yet unqualified) issue of substantive law to be subjected to the appropriate choice-of-law rule of the forum, although that very rule is ascertained by a process of classification.

Yet this approach to classification cannot be discarded merely by formal arguments of logic, and it is always favoured by a definite minority of scholars (with the strongest arguments advanced by Martin Wolff). The exponents of this view assert that in the majority of cases the notional systems of contemporary private laws do not differ so much as to prevent the choice-of-law rules of the forum from providing an important guide to the applicable law. Classification as such may then be accomplished under the *lex causae*, thus ascertained. For instance, in the case of jointure as mentioned earlier, this method of classification would lead to the following result: the legal system applicable to property relations connected with death is to be determined by the choice-of-law rule governing the law of inheritance; if that law (the *lex causae*, in our example the Hungarian Civil Code) regards the widow's portion as an institution of the law of inheritance, it is appropriate to classify the related claim as pertaining to the law of inheritance and to subject it to the choice-of-law rule of the law of inheritance (to arrange it under its system).

Classification by the *lex causae* seems particularly obvious in the case of institutions unknown to the law of the forum. Here, too, its advocates argue, moreover, that this method allows for the legal categories to be harmoniously arranged in the given legal system by putting them into the context of the applicable foreign law; for instance, it is capable of distinguishing between movable and immovable property in accordance with the principles of the applicable law (rather than the *lex fori* which might treat them differently).

All in all, classification by the *lex causae* raises *many more problems* than classification by the *lex fori*, more often than not leading to inconclusive results. The sponsors of this approach try to eliminate its defects by several limitations, by supplementary and subsidiary solutions. As regards its *substance*, classification by the *lex causae* places the problem on a different plane, thus removing the otherwise unavoidable *circulus vitiosus* of logic; it implies that the core of the classification problem lies not in selecting the governing choice-of-law rule (*primary classification*), but in fitting the particular matter of law into the applicable legal system (substantive or procedural law, law of property or law of contracts, law of inheritance or law of matrimonial property, etc.) (*secondary classification*). This, to be sure, amounts to *evading the problem of primary classification*. When resort is had to the *lex causae*, such primary classification is corrected in the process of secondary classification.

2. Legal science has, from the outset, been aware of the difficulties inherent in the classification problem.

(a) The very title of Bartin's treatise is all that more resigned: "*De l'impossibilité d'arriver à une solution définitive des conflicts de lois*" (On the Impossibility of Arriving at a Definitive Solution of Conflicts of Law). The complications stem from the need to find some way of accommodating the ultimately different systems of notions as used in the law of the forum and the applicable foreign law. (As is aptly stated by Raape: "*Nichts ist schwerer, als Richter in zwei Welten zu sein*" – Nothing is more difficult than to be a judge in two worlds.)

(b) In recent decades the view has become increasingly dominant that a *general principle* (at least one giving a reassuring solution in each case) *cannot* be formulated to govern the classification problem. The notions of the various legal systems are bound to differ in substance (certain categories embracing diverse sets of questions even in one and the same system of law, e.g. the substance of usury is different under criminal and civil law). Differences can only be accommodated or balanced with an eye to the concrete circumstances of the case. Rigid and generalized employment of a single principle (be it the *lex fori* or the *lex causae*) cannot lead to success.

(c) On the other hand, *the problem of classification can be* greatly *reduced* by a functional appraisal and interpretation (of the purpose) of the dogmatically or systematically divergent categories of the various legal systems (a method which has happily been gaining ground over recent decades, chiefly as a result of intensive comparative inquiries). Under this approach (*functional classification*), differences appear merely superficial or outright fictitious. For instance, an institution of a legal system concerning matrimonial property, may be intended to provide material support for the surviving spouse in the same way as an institution of the law of inheritance does in another system of law; this means that the former may also be placed under the control of the choice-of-law rule relating to the law of inheritance.

Guided by this spirit, some scholars, mainly Rabel, seek to construct a more flexible and more appropriate approach to classification by a *comparative interpretation of the choice-of-law rules*, namely *by employing an autonomous method* rather than relying exclusively on the notions of a particular legal system. This attempt at a solution can be endorsed in respect of its point of departure, for the reason that often notional differences may be observed between the conflicts law (choice-of-law rules) and the substantive law of one and the same legal system.

Others, like Kegel, contend that these norms should be interpreted in the light of the purposes of the private law of conflicts, in view of the *interests intended to be served by the choice-of-law rules.* There are also views which argue for taking into account the *objectives of the* applicable *substantive law* (*teleological classification*).

(d) These theoretical approaches offer correct solutions designed to break down frequent rigidities and one-sidedness in dealing with the classification problem, but in aspects of detail they are not yet elaborate enough to win wider application in practice. *Legal practice may* therefore *be said to be still dominated by classification under the lex fori.*

In the case of legal institutions finding no counterparts in the law of the forum, however, the point of departure is represented by classification under the *lex causae*, namely in consideration of the function fulfilled by the given category in the foreign system of law. (Finally, in the case of *renvoi* (see Chapter VI), the categories (object of choice of law, interpretation of the connecting factor) applied in the foreign conflict rules are to be viewed as well in the context of the notional system of the particular foreign law.)

3. A special problem different from the classification of the internal conflict norms of the various States is presented by the classification of the choice-of-law rules laid down in *international agreements*. The content of the legal category covered by a choice-of-law rule is either indicated by the agreement itself or resort should be had to the principles governing the interpretation of international agreements (ascertainment of the intent of the contracting parties, etc.).

4. The Hungarian Code (Art. 3) contains specific provisions (almost without equal in international legislation) on the problem of classification.

(a) The adopted approach basically makes classification subject to the *lex fori*. Accordingly, where there is a dispute about the legal classification of facts or relationships involved in the case, its solution should be based on the interpretation of the rules and concepts of Hungarian law [para. (1) of Art. 3]. As can be seen, the Hungarian Code has adopted the approach which, despite its problematic and controversial nature, can be regarded as predominant in international theory and practice.

(b) On the other hand, the Code contains a separate provision for special cases in which an unknown legal institution or category is to be interpreted [see item 2 (b) in §17]. In dealing with such a problem the judge is required to correct the inadequacies of interpretation under Hungarian law by *paying heed to the foreign law familiar with the institution in question*. The Code therefore provides that if a legal institution is unknown to Hungarian law, or is known with a different content or by a different name, and cannot be defined by interpreting the rules of Hungarian law, the foreign law governing the legal institution must also be consulted for the purpose of classification [para. (2) of Art. 3].

5. After the above statements it seems desirable to sum up *our position* regarding classification, one of the most problematic institutions of the private international law of conflicts.

In the first place, we wish to point out that the two traditional basic forms of classification, notably classification by the *lex fori* and the *lex causae* as substantive-law methods of classification, seem to us to amount to a unilateral approach, for we see the substance of the problem in interpreting the hypothesis of the choice-of-law rule. Therefore we see no useful purpose served by accomplishing classification under a single substantive law, be it the *lex fori* or the *lex causae*. As has been indicated above, classification under the *lex fori* seeks to find a solution of the problem on the assumption that the hypothesis of a choice-of-law rule comprises all the domestic and foreign legal institutions (and only them!) which in the substantive law of the forum are covered by the legal concept used in the relevant choice-of-law rule. The *lex causae* method of classification is equally one-sided as it suggests the same (and, moreover, draws a conclusion hardly defensible on a logical basis) with respect to another substantive law. Such a one-sided and rigid approach is, in our view, unlikely to be consistent with the normative peculiarities of choice-of-law rules (see item 1 in §15). The characteristic traits of the structure of those rules and their openness also call for flexible receptivity to substantive laws in the process of thinking about classification. Consequently we have elaborated our proposition by reliance on several autonomous theories. We base ourselves primarily on Rabel's comparative classification and on Kegel's interest-oriented classification under private international law, conceding Rabel's postulate to emancipate the notional system of conflicts law, his argument for the openness of choice-of-law rule hypotheses and his comparative approach, while drawing on Kegel's proposition as regards mainly the functional and interest-oriented interpretation of norms.

For dealing with the two traditional groups of classification problems we propose the use of a basically similar method which, however, requires an approach with significant differences.

(a) *Unknown institutions.* The most obvious problem of classification consists of the fact that the system of choice-of-law rules does not embrace the type of legal issues involved in a particular case to be decided, because the legislator, in framing the hypotheses of choice-of-law rules, apparently did not keep in view the concrete legal institution in question [see item 2 (b) in §17].

We maintain that by appraising its actual purpose, function and role in the "parent system of law" a large number of the legal institutions, having no counterparts in the substantive law of the forum, can be subjected to one or other choice-of-law rule of the forum even if the *lex fori* as indicated by the conflict norm contains no specific choice-of-law rule covering the institution concerned. Once the function of the substantive-law institution has been ascertained, its subjection (subsumption) calls for an independent interpretation of the choice-of-law rule's receptivity as intended by the legislator in the hypothesis. It is this line of thought – the process of drawing the radius of the choice-of-law hypothesis – which, as we perceive it, amounts to *classification* as such in the case of unknown legal institutions, whereas ascertainment in the "parent system of law" of the actual function of the institution unknown to the substantive rules of the *lex fori* is a mere antecedent to classification. We believe that the Hungarian Code [para. (2) of Art. 3] provides an obvious yet useful guide to this latter process of "*prequalification*".

When classification has a negative result – when the legal institution in question cannot be subsumed under any choice-of-law rule of the *lex fori*, that is, the institution is unknown both to the substantive law of the forum, and to its law of conflicts – the case should be treated as a gap in conflicts law and be appraised accordingly. The law enforcement organs may attempt to fill such a gap by an extensive interpretation of a choice-of-law rule hypothesis or by analogy.

What has previously may be graphically illustrated by the example of *culpa in contrahendo* in German law. This institution is unknown to Hungarian civil law since the latter's breach-of-contract system is much more closed than that of the *BGB*, whereas conduct causing damage but not leading to the formation of any contract may be duly sanctioned as wrongful conduct (Art. 6). In the case of a claim to damages invoking *culpa in contrahendo* under private international law, the Hungarian forum would probably never have to refer to a gap in its own law of conflicts, even though the claim were based on an institution unfamiliar to its substantive law. Ascertainment of the concrete function of *culpa in contrahendo* by the aid of German substantive law (i.e. by way of "prequalification") serves as a solid basis, in the majority of cases, for finding the place of the claim in the law of conflicts, for subsuming it under the appropriate choice-of-law rule, namely for its classification. In some cases, *culpa in contrahendo* practically amounts to breach of contract (e.g. neglect of duty to provide information) and the case may therefore be subjected to the law of contracts (see §82). In other cases (in the absence of a contract) it is possible to establish a tortious claim and to apply the law of torts (see §84).

To sum up in brief, we have come to the following conclusions:

– The first step is to ascertain the real function or role of the institutions unknown to the substantive rules of the *lex fori* in the only possible way, by the aid of the "parent system of law" familiar with those institutions, notably by "prequalification" under the foreign substantive law.

– An attempt should be made to subject to the law of conflicts the given institution of a foreign substantive law, with its function thus ascertained, by interpretation of the choice-of-law rules of the forum, by clarification of the receptivity of the relevant choice-of-law rule hypotheses, namely by *classification* as such *under the lex fori indicated by the law of conflicts.*

– An institution unknown to the substantive law of the forum is often not unfamiliar to the conflicts law of the forum, but was considered and postulated in drafting the choice-of-law rules and is therefore capable of being subjected to or subsumed under the law of conflicts.

– Where a concrete institution of foreign law cannot be "received" into the conflicts law of the forum, the gap in conflicts law should be filled by using methods known to substantive law (extensive interpretation, analogy, etc.).

(b) *Differences in systematization.* As has been noted [see item 2 (a) in §17), classification problems are often posed by the fact that differences between the criterion of systematization used by the hypothesis of the choice-of-law rule and the notional system of the applicable foreign (exceptionally domestic) substantive law are discovered in legal practice.

(i) Classification problems are less frequent and their solution is simpler in the group of cases which shows differences in systematization between the substantive and conflicts law of the forum. The cause of this *discrepancy* lies in the fact that the hypotheses of choice-of-law rules and of substantive norms are chiefly framed on the abstract plane, even in one and the same legal system, and hence are usually of different types and are found to be relatively adequate. Thus, for instance, the institution of *culpa in contrahendo* (referred to earlier) has no direct counterpart in the choice-of-law rules of the German conflicts law. This special legal phenomenon should also be classified in German law, with related claims arranged by their substantive-law functions and perhaps subsumed under different choice-of-law rules.

Problems of classification arising from differences in systematization between the substantive and conflicts law of one and the same legal system are essentially *solved* in the same way as those encountered in the classification of legal institutions unknown to a foreign substantive law [see subitem (a) above], with a difference observed only in the process of "prequalification": if the problem arises within a single legal system, the function of the particular legal institution is naturally determined on the basis of the substantive law of the given legal system, while classification *per se* implies, even in the case of systematic differences within a single legal system, interpretation of the choice-of-law rules of the forum and subsumption under the conflicts law of the institution whose function has been ascertained by "prequalification".

In short, the process of "prequalification" takes place under the substantive rules of the lex fori and classification as such under the lex fori as indicated by the law of conflicts.

(ii) Classification problems involved in the second group of cases are more complicated as they arise from divergences in systematization between different systems of law and are, moreover, the commonest source of conflicts in classification. On the surface they appear in cases where the self-same institution (or rather one identical in essentials) is of a different systematic arrangement in the *lex fori* and in another law connected with the pertinent fact (in the potential *lex causae*) [for examples see item 2 (a) above].

In our view, the substance of these classification problems should be seen not so much in systematic differences between the substantive rules of the *lex fori* and another substantive law as rather in the uncertainty about the *receptivity of the choice-of-law rule of the forum* in this group of cases as well.

In the example of prescription presenting the most important problem in practice this question may be formulated thus: Can a norm of the choice-of-law rule governing prescription in the continental spirit be supplemented with substantive norms controlling prescription (e.g. in Californian law, to stick to our aforementioned case) despite the fact that in Californian law, in contrast to the continental approach, prescription is treated, for the purposes of systematic arrangement, as an institution of procedural rather than substantive law? Even a relatively superficial inquiry may disclose that the essential element of prescription, primarily its function, shows no such difference even in common law so as to question its appraisal under the choice-of-law rule governing the basic legal relationship, namely its classification by substantive law. (The situation is different with regard to classification of strictly procedural questions by the *lex fori.*) As general practice in private international law, classification of these questions under the *lex fori* is mainly justified by criteria of administration of justice, that is by the interests of judges, parties and their representatives. The parties to an action could hardly be expected to perform their procedural acts according to a foreign (more accurately, an oft-changing foreign) procedural law (rules of procedure, etc.). Seen from this angle, namely from that of conflicts law or *choice-of-law rules*, the essential aspects (effect, limitation period, date, suspension, interruption, etc.) of prescription, regarded as an institution of procedural law in several state laws of the United States of America, exhibit no such traits as call for connection of "genuine" procedural issues under the *lex fori*; on the contrary, they behave very like questions of substantive law from the viewpoint of connection under the law of conflicts. (Nothing but the mode and forms of pleading prescription in an action can be problems to be determined under the *lex fori*.) For all these reasons, it is deemed justified to classify prescription as an institution of substantive law even if the essential factual elements of a concrete case are connected with a system of law which systematizes prescription as a procedural category within its inner structure.

The position set out here is also supported by the change which has recently been witnessed in the common law with respect to the classification of prescription. Great Britain's Foreign Limitation Periods Act of 1984 has broken with traditional classification under the *lex fori* at common law and has definitely introduced classification of prescription by substantive laws (Carter, *The Law Quarterly Review*, 1985). Some member states of the United States of America have likewise effected such a change by legislation (Arkansas, Colorado, North Dakota, Oregon, Washington), and a similar change is taking place in judicial practice (Heavner v. Uniroyal, New Jersey 1973, etc.; Hay, *IPRax*, 1989).

In summary, we can state the following.

– Solution of classification problems arising from the diverse substantive-law structures of the various legal systems basically also requires interpretation of the choice-of-law rules, the ascertainment of the diameter of the choice-of-law rule hypotheses. This means that *classification* should essentially be accomplished *under the lex fori of conflicts* in this group of cases as well.

– Here, too, the process of classification may be preceded and assisted by "*prequalification*", i.e. by ascertainment of the function of a particular legal institution and its comparison under the substantive rules of the *lex fori* and the potential *lex causae*.

– In the *vast majority* of classification cases, ascertainment of the actual role of the legal institution in question and its comparison in the *lex fori* or the potential *lex causae* (process of prequalification) result in disclosing that the legal institution concerned performs, despite its different systematic arrangement, essentially the *same function* in both systems of law, thus raising no obstacle to its *similar classification*, and thus to its subsumption under the usual choice-of-law rule of the *lex fori*.

– In the mathematical remainder – a theoretically negligible part – of cases where "prequalification" discloses a different function behind the diverse systematic arrangements of a particular legal institution, classification should be left to judicial wisdom as a guide.

6. We shall single out two of the classification problems encountered in judicial practice concerning the application of the Hungarian Code.

– In some laws it is an unsettled question whether testamentary capacity is to be judged according to the general rules on disposing capacity or is governed by the special rules of testamentary law.

– Another problem is posed by the systematic arrangement of contracts of inheritance. We consider that the notarial decision delivering the movable estate of a German national living in Hungary was mistaken in classifying the contract of inheritance as a contract of maintenance rather than as a testamentary disposition (Baja, 2. Kjö. 1910/1981). (It is even more surprising that this classification served to arrive at the application of Hungarian law to the case at issue.)

CHAPTER VI

RENVOI

§19. THE SCOPE OF REFERENCE BY THE CHOICE-OF-LAW RULE: THE PROBLEM OF *RENVOI*

1. In principle, the choice-of-law rule refers to a *legal system as a whole*, directing the application of the rules either of the domestic law (*lex fori*) or of a particular *foreign* law. In case of reference to a foreign law, it may be of relevance to know whether the appropriate *conflict rules* of the given legal system should also be taken into account or only its positive rules (e.g. substantive civil law) are to be considered.

Where reference by a choice-of-law rule also extends to the conflict norms of the legal system invoked, directing that they should likewise be taken into account, sometimes there may arise *specific conflicts* between the relevant conflict rules themselves. It may occur that the appropriate conflict rule of the legal system invoked governs the case differently than the conflict rule of the remitting legal system: the conflicts law of the legal system invoked does not accept direction and ordains that the rules of the remitting (original) legal system or of a third legal system should be applied instead of its own rules. Thus, for instance, under the Hungarian law of conflicts (Art. 11 of the Code) the disposing capacity of a Danish citizen domiciled in Budapest or Vienna is to be governed by the law of nationality, namely Danish law, but the relevant conflict rule of Danish law thus invoked directs the application of the law of domicile, namely Hungarian or Austrian law. As can be seen, Danish law invoked refers back to the remitting Hungarian law or refers the case onto a third law, to the rules of Austrian law.

In the law of conflicts this case is known as *reference back* and *reference on*, or, by the general French term, *renvoi*. In the case of *renvoi* the problem is one of choosing between competing conflict rules and of deciding whether to follow direction from the domestic law of conflicts, ignoring reference back or on by the conflict rule of the legal system invoked, or to accept such reference from the latter as well.

The problem of *renvoi* was made known by a case dealt with in French judicial practice, namely *Forgo's case*, which was considered three times by the *Cour de Cassation* between 1875 and 1882. A Bavarian citizen, Franz X. Forgo had lived, since the age of five, and died in France where he left considerable movable property. Under the French law of conflicts his estate was to be governed by (then independent) Bavarian law (i.e. the decedent's law of nationality), but the Bavarian conflict rule referred to the *lex situs* (in some aspects to the law of the decedent's domicile), namely French law. In the end, the *Cour de Cassation* accepted reference back from the Bavarian law of conflicts and applied the rules of the French law of inheritance. (As regards the outcome of the case, it is hard to ignore the fact that the estate went to the French treasury, whereas the estate would have gone to Forgo's collateral relatives living in Bavaria if the case had been decided under the Bavarian law of inheritance.)

At any rate, with its adjudication of this case the French court presented legal science with a most difficult problem of the private law of conflicts, which cannot be said to be short of unanswered questions. No wonder, then, that Cheshire, the famous English scholar, has remarked: "Might Forgo never have been born!"

2. From the foregoing it emerges that, *in principle*, the *possibility* for the problem of *renvoi* to arise is created by cases where reference by the choice-of-law rule is understood in the broad sense also to extend to the conflict norms of the legal system invoked, for if reference is confined *a priori* to the positive rules of the legal system invoked, the possibility of *renvoi* is ruled out even in theory. It should be stressed that this concerns only the theoretical aspect of the problem.

For renvoi to emerge in a concrete case, it is necessary that the conflict rule invoked should contain a connecting factor different from that of the remitting (domestic) law and that connecting factor should also refer to a different legal system. Disposing capacity, for instance, is subjected to the law of nationality by most of the European laws of conflicts, including the Hungarian. Accordingly, these laws contain the same connecting factor as the Hungarian law for disposing capacity, meaning that the problem of *renvoi* arises in practice if the conflict rule of the legal system invoked differs from that of the remitting legal system, but its reference happens to lead to the same result. If, for instance, a Hungarian court is to consider the disposing capacity of a Danish national domiciled in Copenhagen, the law indicated by the remitting Hungarian law of conflicts (the law of nationality being applicable) and by that of the Danish conflict rule invoked (the law of domicile being applicable) is the same, namely Danish law in both cases. As can be seen, given the converging results of different references, the problem of *renvoi* (a theoretical possibility) does not actually arise in cases such as this.

What has been said (not least the instances given) further goes to show that the question of *renvoi* arises *mainly* in connection with determining the *personal law* (see §29), in respect of which one can observe the greatest differences between the laws of conflicts, some relying on nationality and others using residence (in Anglo-Saxon laws, domicile) as connecting factors. This does not mean, of course, that the problem of *renvoi* is irrelevant to other facts or other choice-of-law rules.

§20. THEORETICAL VIEWS AND PRACTICAL SOLUTIONS

1. The *science* of private international law was long dominated by the concept that *renvoi* should be inadmissible and that, therefore, reference by the conflict rule should be understood *a priori* to refer only to the positive rules (e.g. substantive civil law) of a foreign legal system.

Those *opposing* the admissibility of *renvoi* continue to advance *logical* arguments for the most part, saying that the function of conflict rules is to provide clear solutions for borderline cases of private international law which have essential contacts with several systems of law. This goal, however, can only be achieved if the conflict rules definitely indicate the positive rules of the relevant legal system applicable to a particular case rather than to refer to the law of conflicts of another State as well. In such a broad sense, reference to the conflict norms of the legal system invoked would basically run counter to the purpose of private international law rules, let alone the fact that mutual and consistent acceptance of the possibility of reference back would result in an endless kicking around of cases, a never-ending ping-pong match between the legal systems concerned, while reference on would also frequently give rise to the complicated problem of finding the system of law which eventually accepts the *renvoi*.

By using logical arguments it is indeed difficult to state the case for the *acceptance* of *renvoi*, since it may be said (and is actually voiced) that the role of the law of conflicts lies in, and is confined to, determining the applicable legal system as a whole, leaving the law invoked with the choice of directing the application of its own positive rules or those of another legal system (the remitting or a third one). The argument, that if the extent of reference by conflict rules is consistently limited to the positive rules of the legal system invoked then the eventual interterritorial (interlocal) and intertemporal norms of the particular law should also be ignored, carries more weight.

Undoubtedly penetrating to the heart of the problem are the views which, rising above purely logical considerations, seek to create a *greater harmony* in the adjudication of cases under the conflict rules of the *various States* by advocating acceptance, though limited, of *renvoi*. They assert that the international law of conflicts has the foremost aim of ensuring, so far as possible, uniform adjudication of private international law cases before the fora of the various States. So, if the law of conflicts of a State does not subject a given fact to the rules of its own substantive law, but refers it back to the remitting law or refers it on to a third law, it is more appropriate to accept *renvoi* than to force consideration of the rules which do not seek application, for this is the path to follow in achieving international uniformity or harmony of decisions. To take one of the above examples, if *renvoi* is excluded by both laws, the disposing capacity of a Danish national domiciled in Budapest is subject to Danish law (domicile) before a Danish court, but if the Hungarian forum accepts *renvoi* from the Danish law of conflicts, it is free to apply the Hungarian law, just as the Danish court would be, to the particular case. This position seeks to serve Savigny's ideal concerning the purpose of private international law "to arrive at the same predictable adjudication of private international law cases, irrespective of the State of the court handling the case". In addition, it is apt to ensure the necessary *flexibility* of decisions under the law of conflicts.

Still, the most important argument, declared or not, for the acceptance of *renvoi* is that *by admitting it the forum* may arrive at the application of its own law. In other words, the case can be channelled towards the legal system in whose rules, practice and literature the judge can best find his way around and where he is completely at home. Acceptance of *renvoi* is thus a useful instrument in the court's endeavour to apply its own law, an inevitable and understandable "homeward trend" (Nussbaum's now classical term: *Heimwärtsstreben*).

2. Repeated appraisals of these aspects have led the science of private international law gradually to abandon its rigid and categorical rejection of *renvoi*. The views which, within certain limits, endorse and *accept the renvoi* may now be said to be predominant.

However, authors differ on the *extent* to which *renvoi* can be accepted, though this aspect is the touchstone of the entire problem for all practical purposes: When to accept reference back? Where to cut the thread of the "logical game"? How far is reference on to be admitted?

The *principle to be followed* in answering these questions is rather clear: reference back or reference on by the foreign law of conflicts concerned is to be taken into account, when and where reliance on *renvoi* can be expected to result in the same decision which would be brought by the foreign forum in question. To use the oft-repeated *example*, this principle implies that the Hungarian judge will accept reference back from the Danish conflict rule because in that way he can arrive at the same decision as the Danish judge would, whose law does not accept the *renvoi*. In other words, the Hungarian judge by accepting the *renvoi*, and the Danish judge by excluding it, arrive at the same conclusion, namely the disposing capacity of a Danish national domiciled in Budapest is to be determined according to Hungarian law.

Again, this example goes to show that the said correct principle is far from easy to translate into practice, for if the Danish law were also in favour of accepting *renvoi*, the Hungarian judge would have to disregard it completely in order to reach the same decision as his Danish colleague. This conclusion is even of general validity in so far as practical postures on *renvoi* tend to create an international harmony between decisions under the law of conflicts only if the *renvoi* is accepted by one of the relevant legal systems, but is rejected by the other.

This idea is drawn upon by the "*foreign court doctrine*" (or "local court doctrine") prevailing in English judicial practice: under it the English judge will apply the substantive law which the forum of the legal system invoked by his own law of conflicts would deem applicable to the case. He is led on to this path by adopting the reserved position of the given foreign law (or court) on *renvoi*, to wit, by accepting *renvoi* it is rejected by the legal system invoked, and *vice versa*. It is easy to see, however, that this approach has no universal applicability either, for if it were applied by several countries in relation to one another, it would lead to an impasse, failing to offer any solution, as mutual and unlimited acceptance of *renvoi* would, but creating a situation in which polite individuals cede precedence to each other at the door, or people going in the same direction steer clear of each other in the street, only to run into each other over and over again. One law is to wait and another to move in order for the one biding its time to follow a different path, not to mention the fact that here we have but two countries challenged to take common ground about *renvoi*, with the need for each pair of countries to follow suit along parallel courses. This is a complicated, unworkable approach!

So one can hardly find a logical, unambiguously clear theory likely to give satisfactory answers to all questions and capable of practical application to the problem of *renvoi*. The *debate in legal literature* goes on, with a spate of suggestions which, having regard to the said principles and differing in approach to a greater or lesser extent, seek to define the range (class) of cases in which acceptance of *renvoi* would seem desirable.

Prevalent among them are those which admit *reference back and a single reference on*. On the other hand, there is the general view that *renvoi* should not be admitted in cases to be decided according to the law chosen by the parties under the international law of contracts (see §83), for what the parties intend to do is precisely to have the applicable positive law clearly determined and to avoid swinging between different laws of conflicts. [This position is also taken by Hungarian arbitration practice; see item 5 (c) below.] Moreover, there are significant proponents of the idea of ruling out the *renvoi* in the international law of contracts in general (i.e. even if there is no choice of law by the parties).

3. *Judicial practice in several countries* (e.g. Belgium, France, Sweden) cares little about sustained theoretical efforts and makes relatively short work of *admitting* reference back and, in some cases, even reference on.

In the case of reference back, legal practice seems to conceive of *renvoi* resulting from a foreign law of conflicts as a reference to the internal positive rules. There can be no logical objection to this approach, which leads to proper results even if the remitting foreign legal system does not accept *renvoi*, for reference back in such case may indeed be said to have been to the substantive law of the forum. For example, the estate of a Danish national formerly domiciled in Budapest is, under the Hungarian law of conflicts, governed by Danish law, but the Danish conflict rule refers back to the law of the last domicile, which is Hungarian law. Since the Danish law of conflicts regards reference by its own conflict rules as going to the positive law only, thus excluding *renvoi*, the Hungarian judge will correctly and logically decide the matter under the Hungarian law of inheritance. The Danish judge would do likewise, so the international harmonization of decisions is secured.

On the other hand, this approach is not devoid of logical flaws and does not help towards international harmony between decisions where the law invoked similarly admits reference back, taking a broad view of the reference by its own conflict rules, viz. considering it as extending to the law of conflicts as well. In such cases the forum's action is illogical, though *a fortiori* so, and breaks the logical *perpetuum mobile* of references between various legal systems when it comes to the application of internal law. Under the French law of conflicts, for instance, succession to immovable property is governed by the *lex rei sitae*, which in the hypothetical case is a foreign law even if the decedent is a French national. If, however, the foreign law invoked (e.g. the Hungarian choice-of-law rule) directs the application of the law of nationality (*lex patriae*), referring back to French law, the French judge will accept, and stop the game of, *renvoi* by applying the rules of the French law of inheritance. Conversely, the Hungarian forum would follow the same procedure, naturally arriving at a reverse result, viz. applying the Hungarian law of inheritance. There is no doubt that this practice in connection with *renvoi* is decisively influenced by considerations of sheer convenience on the part of the fora, by an inclination to apply their own law, for, as is also shown by the example, one cannot speak of harmony between decisions in such cases.

At the same time there are countries (e.g. Denmark, The Netherlands, Norway) whose legal practice still reject *renvoi*.

National legislation did not initially adopt any position on *renvoi*. The only exception was the German EGBGB of 1896 (Art. 27), which directed acceptance of reference back in specific cases. As theoretical debates brought some clarification of views, legislation became more specific on the problem of *renvoi*, at first tending to *reject* it (e.g. the Greek Civil Code, the Italian *Codice civile*), but now providing mainly for its (limited) *acceptance* (e.g. the laws of Poland, Portugal, Spain and Austria).

The greater inclination of more recent legislation to accept *renvoi* is clearly shown by the change in Italian positive law: the new Code of PIL in force from 1 September 1995 (*Legge*, 31 *maggio* 1995, n. 218) has made a decisive break with the apparently unshakeable rejectionist attitude of Italian law, accepting reference back (Art. 13) and making acceptance of reference on conditional solely on acceptance of *renvoi* by the law of the State invoked. (This condition is intended by the Italian legislator to avoid any logically insoluble contradiction resulting from eventual differences in approach between the Italian system of law and the legal system invoked by reference on.) Also, in making exceptions from its position of principle, the Italian law in force follows the recent international trend to rule out recognition of *renvoi*:

– in cases where the choice of law is made by the contracting parties;

– in respect of rules on the formal requirements of legal transactions;

– in respect of liability for non-contractual damages; and, naturally,

– in respect of matters controlled by international agreements (where even recognition of *renvoi* is subject to the particular agreement).

Finally, under the Italian law in force, if the rules governing the family status of children are chosen, *renvoi* may only be recognized if it is likely to strengthen the family status of the child concerned.

It is an empirical fact that mainly countries of the *lex patriae* have so far tended to accept *renvoi* while the States of the *lex domicilii* (see §29) have been more inclined to reject it. This has given rise to the idea that the conflicting basic postures necessary for easier achievement of international harmony between decisions could generally be secured by the legal systems of the *lex patriae* accepting, and by the conflicts laws of the *lex domicilii* rejecting, reference back.

The overwhelming majority of *international agreements* rule out the possibility of *renvoi*. Thus, for instance, all of the post-Second World War Hague Conventions explicitly provide for the application of the positive rules of the countries designated therein, excluding consideration of the law of conflicts and hence the *renvoi*.

4. According to the Hungarian Code (Art. 4), reference back is *accepted* by the Hungarian court: if the applicable foreign law of conflicts refers back to the Hungarian law, the latter's substantive rules must apply to the particular case.

On other hand, the Code *rules out* the acceptance of reference on: except for reference back, the conflict rules of the applicable foreign law are not to be taken into account but the rules of foreign law directly governing the matter must apply.

In the case of the introductory *example* this solution would mean the following:

– if the Danish national is domiciled in Budapest, his disposing capacity should be governed by the Hungarian civil law, with the acceptance of reference back of the Danish conflict rule (to the law of domicile);

– if the Danish national is domiciled in Vienna, his disposing capacity should be governed by the Danish law (of nationality), in disregard of reference on of the Danish conflict rule to the Austrian law (of domicile).

As the example indicates, the Hungarian Code's rule on *renvoi* is one of *compromise*: it does not always promote international harmonization of decisions under the law of conflicts but rather fosters the *"homeward trend"*, as it accepts reference back, but rejects eventual references on, which would indeed facilitate international harmony between decisions more than reference back does. As is known, *"Heimwärtsstreben"* is not a Hungarian-made device, the Hungarian law of conflicts is not the only one trying to "steal back" the security of its own law, considerations of convenience and the like, yet it could have been expected to adopt a more nuanced solution.

5. *Practice in the application of the Code* is most frequently confronted with the problem of *renvoi* when employing statutes of matrimonial property and of inheritance.

(a) For example, the property relations of a married couple who emigrated from Hungary in 1956, but are now of Swiss nationality and domiciled again in Budapest are made subject by the Code (Art. 39) to Swiss family law, the law of common nationality at the time of the action, whereas the Swiss private international law [para. 1 (a) of Art. 54], which is based on the principle of the law of common domicile of the spouses, ordains the application of Hungarian family law, the law of the common domicile of the spouses, the whole process resulting in reference back to Hungarian law.

(b) Even today, numerous laws of inheritance – e.g. the relevant rules of French private international law and of those of several states of the USA (e.g. the State of New York) – provide for different legal appraisals of movable and immovable properties. By contrast, the Hungarian Code (Art. 36) stands by the principle of unity of the property and subjects the entire estate (viz. the decedent's movable and immovable property alike) to the personal law of the deceased person at the time of death (i.e. to the law of nationality). Accordingly the Code makes immovable property situated in Hungary subject to the French law of inheritance or to that of New York if the decedent was a French national or a citizen of New York, but the conflict rules of the laws invoked refer back to the law of the *situs* of the property, viz. to the Hungarian law (for more detail, see §94).

In both groups of problems the rules of the Hungarian Code (Art. 4) lead to acceptance of reference back and to application of Hungarian law.

(c) As noted (in item 2 above), Hungarian arbitration practice does not recognize reference back in case where the choice of law is made by the parties (see §83). The Rules of Procedure of the Arbitration Tribunal of the Chamber of Commerce, which went into force on 1 September 1989, provide that "stipulation of a particular legal system shall be understood to refer directly to the substantive law rather than to the conflict rules of the given State". [It should be pointed out that in several countries *renvoi* is ruled out by the Code of PIL itself in case of choice of law and, only in case of doubt, by the Austrian Code [Art. 11 (1)] or, quite categorically by the FRG Code of 1986 [Art. 4 (2)]; cf. *IPRax*, 1989, p. 70.]

CHAPTER VII

THE APPLICATION OF FOREIGN LAW

§21. JURISDICTION AND THE APPLICABLE LAW

1. By jurisdiction is meant the power of courts and other State organs (notary public, guardianship authority, etc.), conferred on them by law, to adjudicate cases of private international law (i.e. ones connected with the jurisdiction of several States over the administration of justice). Thus jurisdiction may also be regarded as a sort of *"international (interstate) competence"*. The question of whether the courts (and other organs) of a State are invested with the necessary power to take jurisdiction over a particular case of private international law is governed in part by international agreements and, for the most part, by the relevant internal rules of the State concerned. (For a detailed treatment of the problems of jurisdiction, see Chapter XXXV.)

Jurisdiction is a special *procedural prerequisite* for the adjudication of private international cases (more specifically, it is the first such prerequisite, since power and competence, capacity to sue and to be sued, etc. are to be determined, as in purely domestic situations, after jurisdiction has been ascertained).

The procedural character of jurisdiction means that this category gives no orientation concerning the adjudication of private international law cases under the substantive law, namely the ascertainment of the applicable substantive law (civil law, family law, labour law, etc.). The rules on jurisdiction tell us whether the law enforcement agencies of a State may or may not take jurisdiction over, and thus adjudicate, a given fact of private international law. The Supreme Court ruled (Pf.III.20 No. 163 of 1993), *inter alia*, that "a Hungarian court may take jurisdiction over a litigated legal dispute by virtue of Art. 54 of Law-Decree No. 13 of 1979 in Private International Law". Then, once jurisdiction has been established, the question of applicable law is governed by the norms of the private law of conflicts. For instance, the existence of Hungarian jurisdiction does not categorically mean that a given fact is perforce subject to the rules of Hungarian substantive law (civil law, family law, labour law, etc.). This latter problem needs further consideration after the establishment of jurisdiction and should be solved under the appropriate conflict rules, that is to say, jurisdictional rules have no direct bearing on the determination of the applicable substantive law. However, the same can be stated in reverse: establishment or exclusion of jurisdiction is not influenced by the fact that the applicable law is domestic or foreign. It was in this sense that the Supreme Court ruled (Pf.III.21 No. 741 of 1994): "The need to apply a foreign law to a particular case does not by itself mean the non-existence of jurisdiction".

2. No clear distinction between jurisdictional rules and international conflict norms can be made in all countries and in all cases. It often happens, chiefly in English and US laws, that determination of jurisdiction implies applicability of the law of the forum as well (see item 2 in §14). In the laws of the USA, for instance, the rules on jurisdiction over divorce cases normally determine the applicable law, too; that is to say, they virtually contain conflict norms as well (such rules are usually called *hidden conflict rules*), as do the rules on jurisdiction over matters of e.g., adoption or children's maintenance. It should also be stressed that in general at common law the rules on jurisdiction play a basic role and are assigned a much greater significance than in the private international laws of a continental character.

3. In what has gone before, we have sought to make clear that existence of jurisdiction does not generally mean that private international law cases should also be decided on their merits under the substantive law of the State having jurisdiction. On the contrary, the problem concerning the existence of jurisdiction and the determination of the applicable substantive law necessarily involves logically two separate questions, and, indeed, what we have in a considerable part of cases are questions leading to different answers even in substantive terms.

Thus we have explained that:

– existence of jurisdiction and determination of the applicable substantive law are two different questions to be decided separately;

– determination of the applicable substantive law is reserved for conflict norms;

– "substantive law" in private international law is the counterpart of the "law of conflicts" (whereas in the case of rules on everyday relations controlled by a single legal system, it is more common to speak of "substantive law" as distinct from "procedural law").

4. There remains one more question to answer in this context: the *conflicts law of which State* is the proceeding court or other forum to apply (if it has jurisdiction)? This question can be answered clearly under the traditional and long-prevailing concept: the court (or other proceeding forum) applies the conflicts law of its own State and determines the applicable substantive law according to the conflict rules of its own legal system.

Nevertheless, this question needs to be examined in greater depth today.

(a) The traditional approach invariably prevails with respect to ordinary *courts* (notaries public, etc.), which are subordinated to the conflict rules of their own State, namely they determine the applicable substantive law by the aid of the conflict rules of their own legal system. [The only exception to this principle is acceptance of reference back and reference on (*renvoi*; see Chapter VI).]

(b) The prevalent view once dominating the practice of arbitral tribunals (both international and national) seems to have been relaxing its hold over the past decades. It has become questionable in both legal theory and practice whether the arbitral tribunal really has to apply the conflicts law of the State of its seat or the conflict rules of the *lex fori* are really to determine the substantive law applicable to a particular case. (For the latest work providing a summation of related aspects, see Sandrock in the List of Sources.)

The practical relevance of the problem is increased by the fact that a considerable part of private international cases are submitted to arbitral tribunals (rather than to ordinary courts), and its theoretical significance is not reduced by the fact that in a considerable part of such legal disputes the parties use their right to select the applicable law (see Chapter XXV), to determine the substantive law governing their contract, thus largely eliminating the need for conflict rules.

Some arbitral tribunals (including, for the time being, the Permanent Court of Arbitration attached to the Hungarian Chamber of Commerce) adhere to the old principle that where the parties failed to designate the applicable law, they determine the applicable substantive law by use of the conflict rules of their own seat. By contrast, other courts of arbitration (accepting the critical arguments against the traditional concept) reject the automatism in the application of the conflict rules of the *lex fori* and, considering all circumstances of the case before them, determine by themselves the applicable law of conflicts. This modern approach is reflected in, e.g., the European Convention on International Commercial Arbitration of 1961, which provides that if no law is chosen by the parties the court of arbitration is to apply the law indicated by the conflict rule it deems to be appropriate. The UNCITRAL Model Law on International Commercial Arbitration of 1985 recommends a similar rule under which, failing stipulation by the parties, the arbitration court is to apply the law determined by the international rules which in its judgement are to be applied. This same approach is manifested in the rules of procedure of the arbitration court attached to the Paris-based International Chamber of Commerce: where the parties failed to designate the applicable law the arbitrator is to apply the law following from the conflict norms which he deems to be applicable. Also, according to the rules of procedure of the arbitration court attached to the Chamber of Industry at Vienna, the applicable substantive law is to be determined by the arbitrators if the parties failed to choose their law.

As can be seen, during the past few years the new trend of theory has successfully made inroads into the practice of international and national arbitral tribunals: where the parties have failed to choose their law the arbitral tribunal does not automatically apply the conflict rules of its own seat, but, having regard to the real points of contact with the legal relationship underlying the case before it, determines the applicable law by reliance on the conflict rules chosen in its discretion. Here, too, discretion does not naturally mean arbitrary decision but is to be used within reasonable limits (fixed above all by the actual points of contact of the case with the given system of law: cf. Sandrock in the List of Sources).

§22. THE SIGNIFICANCE OF RECIPROCITY IN THE APPLICATION OF FOREIGN LAW

Reciprocity in international relations means the *mutual attitude* or conduct *of States vis-à-vis one another*. It may also be relevant in legal relationships between nationals and organizations of States, namely in those which have no direct connection with State sovereignty. It is of particular significance mainly in the field of special rules on foreign natural and legal persons (the *"law of foreigners";* see item 3 in §8) and in the *international law of civil procedure*.

By contrast, reciprocity generally has no role to play in the private international law of conflicts: *as a rule, application of foreign law cannot be made subject to reciprocity*. That course would reflect an approach that application of foreign law is a sort of gesture towards a particular State, a kind of "benefaction" or perhaps "favour" based on mutuality. Yet, as has been pointed out several times, application of foreign law is based exclusively on the requirement of arriving at correct adjudication of private international cases, namely on the recognition that the facts of life having contacts with several States and their legal systems should be adjudicated under the rules of the legal system most closely connected with them, having the most organic relationship to them. Postulation of reciprocity and its examination in each particular case would be incompatible with this fundamental criterion, let alone the fact that, very often, the reciprocity doctrine would even affect the nationals of the particular State who may have an elementary interest in the application of a foreign law, e.g. for the purpose of having the judgement (or other act) recognized abroad.

So, postulation of reciprocity is alien to the ideas sustaining private international law, and reliance on its application is quite exceptional in international legislative and judicial practice. One may and should therefore proceed generally from the fact that lack or violation of reciprocity cannot be a ground for non-application of foreign law; exceptional cases of this type may nevertheless occur, but only if reciprocity is specifically required by the law and if the party to a concrete case is able to prove the lack or violation of reciprocity.

In the absence of provisions to the contrary, application of foreign law is *not subject to reciprocity under Hungarian law*. This theoretical position is explicitly stated in Art. 6 of the Code. As a rule, reciprocity must be presumed, i.e. must be deemed to exist, until the contrary is proved, even if the law makes the application of foreign law dependent on reciprocity. Where, exceptionally, the law requires proof of reciprocity, the *Minister of Justice* gives a *declaration* as to the existence of reciprocity, such declaration to be *binding* upon the court or other authority.

§23. PROBLEMS IN THE APPLICATION OF FOREIGN LAW

Conflict rules direct the application variously of internal or of *foreign* substantive law.

The fact that the forum applies – naturally indirectly, pursuant to its own conflict rules – the law of another State, thus "obeying" the norms of a foreign sovereign, often presents a problem much too difficult for theory to overcome even today (see §4). Application of foreign law poses a still greater challenge to judicial practice.

1. (a) *Theory* has relied on different *fictions* for doing away with the problem, somewhat artificially exaggerated, as to why the forum applies the law of a foreign sovereign. Doctrine has followed upon doctrine during the past hundred years alone. (For the earlier history of theory, see item 4 in §10 and items 3–4 in Sect. A of §11.)

– There were some (first Dicey in England, Beale in the United States and Pillet in France) who held that what is involved is not actual application of the foreign law invoked but merely recognition and protection by the forum of substantive rights acquired under foreign law (theory of *"vested rights"*, or *"droits acquis"*).

– In Italian legal science there is the widely-held view recognised in several variants (sponsored by Santi Romano, Ago, Pacchioni, Quadri and others, but opposed by di Vignano, Cappelletti and others) that the forum, through its own conflict rules, practically adopts, receives, or incorporates the foreign norms in question, applying them as its own (theory of "*rinvio ricettizio*").

– Closely akin in result is the American theory (sponsored by Cook, Lorenzen and others) that what the forum does consists in reproducing, or copying the given rules of foreign law, thus applying in effect an identical domestic rather than a foreign norm ("*local law*" theory). (A finer distinction is made by the "data" theory of Ehrenzweig and Jayme, which treats as facts certain elements of foreign norms.)

(b) Behind these and similar theories of fiction there is a *real core* of import *with* numerous *practical and mainly procedural implications*. It is an unquestionable fact that application of foreign law cannot be equated with that of domestic law. Application of foreign norms, mostly unknown to the judge, raise a number of special problems having practical relevance. This explains why common law, for instance, still relies, at least for a point of departure, most heavily on the thesis that foreign rules should be treated as litigated facts.

Some major aspects concerning the application of foreign law should be given separate consideration.

2. The first and foremost question is whether the court applies the foreign law *ex officio or only optionally, in other words when requested to do so by one of the parties.*

(a) This same question concerning the law of the forum can be answered clearly in the affirmative from ancient times: the judge applies *ex officio* the norms of his own legal system. This axiomatic statement rests on the fact that the judge is familiar with his own system of law, knows its rules and is able to employ them: *iura novit curia* – says the ancient tenet, or at least presumption!

The situation is far from being that simple, and hence a position can by no means be formulated so clearly with respect to the rules of foreign law. *Logically* and merely in terms of *principles*, the conclusion would not be different on this point either: if the choice-of-law rules of the forum direct the application of a foreign law, the judge should, without more ado, abide by the particular conflict rule and apply the foreign law indicated.

It is not uncommon, however, for *practical difficulties* to impede full implementation of this well-recognized principle. The main problem is posed by the fact that, understandably, the judge cannot be as at home with and as certain of a foreign legal system as he is acquainted with his own: he was not trained for it, it is far from his everyday life, and often he finds it hard or even impossible to get access to the most basic aids (legislation, judicial practice, literature). It is no wonder, then, if the judge tries, whenever he can, not to use foreign law but to apply the norms of his own legal system ("*Heimwärtsstreben*", see, e.g., *renvoi*, item 1 in §20). Even if the reasons and grounds for such an endeavour are often debatable, one thing is certain: *the presumption of iura novit curia cannot be set up in respect of foreign law.* It would be as groundless to presume the judge's knowledge of foreign law as it is reasonable to expect his familiarity with the law of the forum.

Theory, especially in the continental legal systems, is *more* in favour of the *ex officio* application of foreign law, despite the difficulties we have indicated above.

(b) On the other hand, legislative and legal practice is *strongly divided* on the issue.

(i) The *common law* is traditionally a firm advocate of the *optional* application of foreign law: the judge must *not* employ, *ex officio*, a foreign law except at the express request of the parties to the case. Thus, from the point of view of proceeding *ex officio*, judicial practice treats foreign norms *on an equal footing with the facts of the litigation*.

England has sustained such practice to this day, the only change being that in the past half-century the appraisal and application of the foreign law invoked by the parties have come to fall within the competence of the judge rather than of the jury made up of laymen (cf. Kecskés, *Magyar Jog*, 1990, p. 775). For English judicial practice, a certain shift is also signalled by putting into force [1 April 1991: Contracts (Applicable Law) Act 1990] the Rome Convention (cf. §67), which provides [Art. 1(1)] for mandatory application, as part of

English law, of the law (foreign law, where appropriate) governing contracts within its scope of operation (Fentiman, *The Law Quarterly Review*, 1992, pp. 142–156).

The federal states of the USA do not follow a uniform practice in all matters, differences showing up chiefly with respect to the proof of foreign law. Legislation in most states has relaxed somewhat the more rigorous and more rigid common-law rules on evidence, particularly as regards state laws. (It must be borne in mind that state laws in the USA are viewed as foreign, even though, understandably, they are treated in many aspects differently from the norms of foreign sovereigns!) In the United States, too, the ancient maxim of common law continues to prevail with respect to the basic issue: foreign law is applied only at the request of one of the parties, never *ex officio* (cf. Kecskés, *Magyar Jog*, 1990, p. 886).

Some European countries (e.g. Spain, despite the strong criticism by Spanish learning) and several Latin American legal systems (e.g. Argentina and the Central American countries) insist on the optional application of foreign law as tenaciously as the common-law countries.

(ii) In recent decades, practice in some countries adopted and employed a certain intermediate solution: *the judge was not required to apply foreign law, but might choose to do so*, especially when requested by the parties. This position was maintained by, e.g., French judicial practice from 1959 (Cass. civ. 12.5.1959, J.C.P. 1960, II, 11733) until the latest practice of the *Cour de Cassation* (Cass. civ. 11.10.1988, J.C.P. 1989, II, 21327; 18.10.1988, J.C.P. 1989, II, 21259), which was followed from 1988 but has led to mandatory *ex officio* application of foreign law (cf. *RabelsZ* 55/1991, pp. 143–151).

(iii) Finally, there are legal system under which the judge is *obliged* to apply *ex officio* the foreign law as determined by the conflict norms of his law. This is the case in the judicial practice of several European States (e.g. Austria, Germany and, lately, Italy) and in some countries of Latin America (e.g. Brazil). Practice in other countries (e.g. the Scandinavian States) similarly tends towards this approach, though with some observed variations. [In its Resolution of 1989 (*IPRax*, 1989, p. 70) the *Institut de Droit International* took a position of principle in favour of *ex officio* application of foreign law.]

In these systems of law, the rules of civil procedure ordinarily follow (with certain variations in some countries) the *principle of hearing* and accordingly require the judge to apply *ex officio* the relevant foreign law by virtue of his office. Such is the case in Hungarian law, too. Both the Code of Civil Procedure of 1952 (Art. 200) and the Code of Private International Law (Art. 5) lay down the principle that the *court* or other authority must *proceed ex officio to ascertain* the content of a foreign law unfamiliar to it (Supreme Court, Pf.III. 20.998 of 1995).

Under the Code, the foreign law governing the case must nonetheless be disregarded at the common request of the parties (Art. 9) and the Hungarian law must be applied instead, whereas in choice-of-law situations the governing law shall be the law selected by the parties (Art. 24). This latter possibility was admitted by the Supreme Court (Pf.III.20 No. 895 of 1992) in ruling: "Since, however, the parties in the appellate procedure had by agreement requested the adjudication of their dispute under the Hungarian law (rather than the German law applicable by virtue of the Code), the Supreme Court applied that law in accordance with the choice of law by the parties" (see item 3 in §25).

3. *Proof* of foreign law presents another set of problems. The different legal systems maintain a basically similar position on the fundamental question: the principle of *iura novit curia* cannot operate in respect to foreign law, namely *the applicable foreign norms are subject to proof.*

(a) There are disparities of approach as to whether the onus of proof is on the party invoking the foreign law or essentially on the judge.

(i) In the legal systems favouring *optional* application of foreign law [see (i) and (ii) in item 2 (a) above], the burden of proving the necessary foreign law is clearly on the interested party unless the judge has official knowledge thereof. The interested party is usually in need of expert advice.

(ii) In the procedural laws following the *ex officio* principle [see (iii) in item 2 (b) above], it is *primarily for the judge* to secure access to the appropriate norms and to ascertain the content of the applicable foreign law. This position is adopted by the Hungarian law as well (formerly in Art. 200 of the Code of Civil Procedure and today in Art. 5 of the Code of Private International Law). The Supreme Court (Pf.III.20 No. 474 of 1992) reversed the decision of the court of first instance and ordered it to hold another hearing and to hand down a new decision, because it was "mistaken in respect to the substantive law applicable to the legal relationship of the parties and therefore its decision was so unfounded as to be unfit for a substantive revision". Again, in another case (Pf.III.20 No. 998 of 1995), the Supreme Court ruled that the new proceeding ordered must "extend to the ascertainment of the applicable substantive law and to the taking of any evidence that may become necessary as a result thereof".

It is a different matter that in the process of ascertaining the foreign law the judge may rely on the opinion of *experts* or of the *parties* (their lawyers) in addition to other means. As is provided in the Code, the court or other authority may, in ascertaining the content of the foreign law, invite expert opinion where necessary and may also take into account any evidence submitted by the party; information about the foreign law is furnished by the Minister of Justice upon inquiry by the court or other authority (Art. 5). Guidance by the Supreme Court is provided on this basis: in ascertaining the content of foreign law the court of first instance "may invite expert opinion, but may also accept any statement made or evidence presented by one of the parties and not challenged by the other party" (Pf.III.20 No. 998 of 1996).

This is only natural if one keeps in mind the difficulty faced by the judge in ascertaining the content of foreign law. Taking a position with respect to the law in force (statutory provisions, judicial practice), one may run into serious problems even in the case of the laws of States in geographical proximity, having legal systems grafted onto similar socio-economic structures, cultural and legal traditions, not to mention the alien legal world of remote countries. Therefore the courts often have to rely on the opinion of *experts* (from universities and institutes) familiar with the law in question.

No wonder that in view of the difficulties and expenses involved in the ascertainment of foreign law, a shift from the *ex officio* to the optional principle is advised time and again by literature on private international law (see Flessner and Sturm in the Bibliography). On the other hand, a definite stand against optional application is taken by the 1989 Resolution of the *Institut de Droit International* (Jayme, *IPRax*, No. 1 of 1990; Rigaux, *RabelsZ*, No. 1 of 1990), which (Sect. II/a) comes out for the equality of application of foreign law and the *lex fori*, regarding as mandatory the application of conflict rules and (if they lead to a foreign law) of foreign norms as well. (By contrast, on the proposal of common-law delegates, the Resolution included an important restriction to the effect that the *ex officio* principle in respect to the application of conflict rules and foreign law is to prevail to the extent "premitted by the general rules of procedural law".)

(b) The different legal systems exhibit a rather varied picture of *forms of evidence*.

In England and largely in the United States, the most widely used form is the hearing of *expert witnesses*.

In France, *written expert opinion* on the foreign law in question is the most common point of departure for evidence. Similarly, the German courts, which rely on traditions stretching back to medieval times, mainly request written expert opinion from universities (institutes) concerning *concrete matters of law*.

In several countries (Austria, Federal Republic of Germany, Sweden, etc.) the courts are assisted by *authorities*, above all the Ministry of Justice, in ascertaining the content of the foreign law in force.

In 1968 a European Convention was signed in London, under the auspices of the Council of Europe, on the mutual promotion of the exchange of legal information (mainly for the member-states of the Council). (In 1978 the Convention was modified in Strasbourg by an Additional Protocol.) In 1989, invited by the Ministerial Committee of the Council of Europe, Hungary deposited its instrument of accession to the Convention which also entered into force for Hungary as of 1990 [Decree No. 50/1990. (III.21.) of the Council of Ministers]. In the Agreement the State-parties mutually undertake to inform each other on their respective civil and commercial laws, rules of procedure and judiciaries. Requests for information must specify (in the official language of the State approached) the nature of the case and the relevant facts necessary for adjudication, enclose copies of the documents pertaining to the substance of the case and formulate the questions of law to be answered. In its reply the State requested must furnish information on the texts of the relevant statutory provisions and court decisions and enclose, as supplementary documents, quotations from legal literature and from draft laws with official reasoning thereto and excerpts from commentaries thereon. (Where appropriate, the judicial authority approached may also transmit the request to a private agency or a qualified lawyer for its/his preparation of the reply.) The reply must be given as soon as possible. The State-party requested may not decline a reply except when it is likely to interfere with the interests of the proceedings underlying the request or to prejudice, in its judgment, its sovereignty or security. The judicial authority making the request is not naturally bound by the information furnished in the reply.

Some legal systems offer examples of the use of services from both experts and authorities. Thus, as noted before, the Hungarian Code explicitly requires the courts and other authorities to rely on expert opinion. Accordingly the Supreme Court, for instance, stated (Pf.III.20 No. 474 of 1992) that "the Budapest City court, if unfamiliar with the Austrian law, must proceed *ex officio* to ascertain the foreign law, may invite expert opinion, but may also accept any statement made or evidence presented by one of the parties and not challenged by the other party". Further the Code provides (as does the Code of Civil Procedure, in Art. 200) that the Minister of Justice must give information on foreign law at the request of the court or other authority (Art. 5). In like manner, such information is provided in specific cases by the Minister of Justice in Poland, for instance. This does not, of course, mean that the courts cannot use other methods (e.g. expert opinion). In ascertaining the content of foreign law, the court is *not bound* by the information received from the Minister. A simpler way of proving the foreign law is available through *agreements on legal assistance* between States maintaining closer relations (and between them and some Western States).

(c) The fact that the judge cannot be expected to know the foreign law and that therefore he is (or may be) assisted by the interested party in ascertaining the content of the appropriate law *does not imply the burden of proof* in the proper sense of the word. The burden of proof *stricto sensu* (in respect to litigated facts) would entail losing the case (e.g. dismissal of the action brought by the plaintiff on a claim under the foreign law) if the party is unable to prove the foreign law invoked.

Nor does such burden of proof exist in the legal systems that require the party to the case to prove the foreign law [see (i) and (ii) in item 2 (b) above]. Although exceptionally it happened (e.g. in France, in some states of the United States, or seldom in West German practice) that an action was dismissed for failure to prove the foreign law, the general practice indicates that the judge applies subsidiary rules (see §25) instead of the foreign law in question in order to decide the litigation even in such cases.

In the legal systems that require the judge to apply *ex officio* the foreign law on a particular case [see (iii) in item 2 (b) above] it is notionally impossible to speak of the burden of proof for, as said, the judge may rely on assistance from the parties, in addition to using other means, in determining the foreign law, but failure to prove it may in one way result in the party losing his case. When confronted with such a problem, the judge must apply Hungarian law as subsidiary law (Art. 5 of the Code).

4. Finally, we should touch briefly upon some special questions concerning the application of foreign law.

(a) In theory, the forum may rely on such foreign legal institutions as are unknown to its own system of law. The important thing here is that the actual effects of the foreign law applied must not run counter to the fundamental principles, or the public policy, of the forum (see §24).

(b) The rules of foreign law should be applied, so far as possible, in the manner in which the courts of the State involved translate them into actual practice. This requirement holds above all for the *interpretation of foreign rules*, but also applies to other problems met with in the administration of law (lacuna, analogy, etc.).

(c) Under the practice of most countries, the courts of *appeal* treat the application of foreign law as a question of fact and do not review questions of foreign law. Hence there is generally no place for appeal on the ground that the lower court did not employ a foreign law or employed (interpreted, etc.) it erroneously.

Legal literature is increasingly critical of this practice for raising doubts about the wisdom of regulating facts of private international law by conflict law and failing to work towards the uniformity of judicial practice. Today the position of courts in many countries is also changing, allowing for the right of appeal on ever more questions related to the application of foreign law (the right of appeal is strongly supported by the *Institut de Droit International* in its Resolution of 1989: *IPRax*, 1989, p. 70).

The *right of appeal* is *generally* recognized by some legal systems. This concept is dominant in *Hungarian* law as well.

5. The specific problems involved in the application of foreign law are more susceptible to a solution if adjudication of private international law cases is properly *concentrated*, for concentration tends to ensure the necessary *specialization of judges* and thereby to increase the possibility for acquiring the required *knowledge and expertise*. In several countries, therefore, private international law cases are subject to separate rules on jurisdiction and competence.

§24. PUBLIC POLICY; IMPERATIVE RULES AND THE PUBLIC POLICY CLAUSE

1. At the "core" of every legal system is the objective to defend in a direct way the economic, political and moral foundations of the given system and, at the same time, to express the fundamental values of the particular social and legal order. This is usually done by formulating constitutional principles. This focal point of the legal system, which is the most sensitive from the economic, political, social and moral angles, is naturally projected to the branches of substan-

tive law that regulate the merits of private international law cases, namely to civil law, family law and labour law (private law), determining their basic principles and their scales of values. It stands to reason that private international law should also protect these principles, helping to assert them in the adjudication of private international law facts. In its specific language, private international law subsumes these inviolable principles under the category of *"public policy"* (*"ordre public"* in French).

The substance of public policy lines in its purpose to *defend and assert by all means* the institutions and principles within its ambit *vis-à-vis* the contrary effects of the applicable foreign civil (family, etc.) law. In the adjudication of private international law cases, this endeavour is expressed by the fact that the forum does not apply foreign norms offending its public policy or, more accurately, it disregards the foreign norms which, in their particular effect, would violate public policy. Thus, with a view to defending public policy, the law deviates, if need be, from the path indicated by its conflict rules, excluding application of the foreign law invoked by the conflict norms where it would be at variance with its own basic principles.

Public policy – like the value-judgement of law in general! – is a category subject to *change in content*, both in time and space, always in relation to the prevailing socio-economic system and politico-moral precepts. In the period of the Civil War in the United States, for instance, the rules which recognized slavery in the southern States and formed part of the basic principles of public policy in those States ran counter to the public policy of the northern States. Another example is that in contemporary Western States private property is defended by constitutional guarantees against expropriation without compensation, and, consequently, Western courts repeatedly declared that the post-Second World War East European laws on nationalization offended public policy.

Furthermore, these examples go to show clearly that the concept of public policy is strongly influenced, even if not always so manifestly and primordially, by the basic political posture of a given State and its prevailing system of law. At the same time, this throws light upon the perils of defending public policy: particularly in strained international situations, the law, under political pressures overt or covert, resorts to this means much too often, which results in unwarranted discrimination motivated by political impulses against foreign legal systems. In similar situations, defence of public policy is a most obvious pretext and a most appropriate channel for the growth of political intolerance in the international practice of the law of conflicts, which is meant to be guided precisely by, *inter alia*, the idea of tolerance between legal systems.

Legislation and practice in the field of private international law have developed *two methods* of defending public policy. Both are known to most legal systems, although some give preference to one over the other.

2. One of the methods relies on rules of a *peremptory* nature (civil law, family law, etc.) – which *require absolute application* even to cases of private in-

ternational law – for defending public policy against the contrary effects of foreign norms. (Here we focus on substantive rules in the narrow sense – namely norms of civil law, family law, etc. – governing facts of private international law, but recall that the rules of administrative or financial law, such as foreign exchange regulations or provisions on exports and imports, which often control highly important preliminary or partial questions, are normally of a peremptory nature in the adjudication of private international law cases.) This method may be called, if you like, the *positive* defence of public policy, positive in the sense that peremptory norms not only displace foreign norms likely to be contrary to public policy (this function is usually conceived of as negative defence of public policy), but also give an answer to the question at hand by regulating its substantive aspects. It follows that peremptory rules, though bearing the character of a principle, frequently of a general principle, all govern particular and specified sets of facts, even if normally not confined to a narrow sphere of life. We might as well say that peremptory rules are *not in the nature of a general clause*. Thus, for instance, the peremptory rule of Hungarian civil law (Art. 8 of the Civil Code) spelling out the general, equal and absolute character of legal capacity is a specific one, despite its doctrinal nature and significance, not least by reason of providing that any contract or unilateral declaration restricting legal capacity is null and void. This rule not only supersedes a foreign norm which is applicable to a case on the ground of its foreign element and which happens to recognize a legal transaction restrictive of legal capacity, but also provides positive guidance by spelling out the nullity of such transactions.

As can be seen, in the case of defending public policy by peremptory rules, the forum gives effect to the value-judgement of its own legal system by the absolute application of internal rules: the applicable foreign law must be superseded by the *peremptory* norms of the *lex fori*. [For the proposals to consider peremptory rules not forming part of the *lex fori* and the *lex causae*, see (ii) in item 3 (c), Sect. B of §11.]

This legal-technical approach can be traced back to the *Code Civil* (Art. 6): the French law was the first among modern laws to apply peremptory norms in defence of public policy (*lois d'ordre public international*). This method was then used by legal systems other than those codified on the pattern of the *Code Civil*.

The Hungarian law, too, employs the method of peremptory rules to defend public policy. A problem is caused only by the fact that the Hungarian theory of legislative sources lacks (as do laws and legal science in other countries) a clearly evolved concept concerning the criteria of a peremptory norm, namely the rules that should be deemed to require absolute application. According to the most acceptable position, those rules are peremptory which directly serve and defend the foundations, expressed mainly in the Constitution, of the economic and social system. In case of doubt, the purpose of the given rule should be taken as a guide. Fully to remove the uncertainty about the peremptory nature of rules is the common task for legal science and practice, for concreteness, the main asset of this dogmatic method, can only be attained in that way.

In some cases (e.g. Arts. 34 and 41 of the Code) the peremptory nature of certain substantive rules is clearly indicated by special norms of conflicts law, the so-called *special public policy rules* (cf. item 3 in §100).

3. Another tool used by the law of conflicts to defend public policy is the so-called *public policy clause*.

(a) This is a rule of law bearing the *character of a general clause* and directing non-application of a foreign norm, as indicated by conflict rules, where its application would violate the institutions and principles that lie at the heart of the legal system. Accordingly the public policy clause is a *safety-valve* of the law of conflicts, serving to defend the foundations of the legal system and achieving its goal by excluding, under a *negative* approach, the application of foreign norms likely to have undesirable effects.

It is essential to note that the public policy clause always prevents the *actual* application of a foreign norm (to a *given* fact of private international law), but does not imply a general appraisal of the particular foreign norm, which would add up to discrimination against the legal system involved.

When confronted with a different fact, the judge has to reconsider the need for defending public policy. There may also occur cases in which the public policy clause is not relied upon against the self-same foreign norm, as when, in particular, the forum deals with facts that have an occasional, accidental, or unimportant connection with its legal system [e.g. the legal dispute of foreign parties has no substantive link with the internal law and its consideration by an organ of the forum is a matter more of chance; see also subitem (d) below]. Consequently, a general, abstract evaluation of the foreign law is insufficient to substantiate the resort to the public policy clause; what is necessary is its appraisal in relation to a particular fact.

(b) The public policy clause being in the nature of a general clause implies great difficulties both for legislative *definition* and judicial *application to the substance* of the matter at hand. The clause is necessarily based on generally formulated categories, yet it should not be interpreted *in a too broad sense*. Finding the proper context is a *task for judicial practice*; it is only through constant refinement by legal practice that the criteria can be found by which to judge whether public policy is likely to be violated in a particular case. It is hardly possible to tell in general and abstract terms when and how far, for instance, the equality of spouses, a general principle of family law, is violated; to establish such violation requires appraisal of the foreign norm in relation to the instant case.

At the same time an adequate legislative *definition* also provides a satisfactory guide for the judge in defending public policy. It appears important to lay down the *following criteria* for the formulation of the public policy clause: a foreign norm is to be disregarded where its *actual* effect *obviously* offends *essential* principles of the legal system.

(c) Today every law of conflicts relies, to a greater or lesser extent, on the public policy clause to achieve non-application of foreign laws violating public policy. In the legal systems that also use *peremptory rules*, these norms *and the public policy clause* stand *in a relation of the specific to the general.*

The *Hungarian* Code, too, contains a public policy clause (Art. 7), providing that foreign law must be disregarded if its application is likely to violate the public policy of Hungary. This rule is to be interpreted by the aforementioned criteria. The requirement of appraisal free from discrimination is stressed by the Code in a separate provision to the effect that non-application of foreign law must not be based solely on the ground that the socio-economic system of the particular foreign country differs from that of Hungary.

(d) *Violation* of public policy is *obvious* in the case of certain foreign norms, such as those prescribing discriminative treatment on account of race, sex and nationality. Frequently, however, violation is relative, and defence of public policy is warranted precisely by the *close substantive relationship* of the given fact of private international law *to the legal system of the forum.* In order to avoid application of a foreign norm basically contrary to, for example, the security requirement of transactions, it is necessary for a fact of the contract at hand to take place in the domestic setting and, say, the Hungarian nationality of only one of the parties to the transaction is an insufficient ground. It would be equally ill-advised to regard exclusion of conjugal community property (a prevalent property regime in Hungarian family law but an optional one in several foreign family laws) as offending Hungarian public policy in the case of a spouse having Hungarian nationality and residing abroad.

Where a close substantive link with the forum exists, the fact of the case is connected in content with the legal system of the forum so much so as to justify application *ab initio* of the *lex fori* lest the "devil" of choice of law should lead to the application of foreign norms. (If this occurs all too often, something may be wrong with the given conflict rule as well!) So the notion of public policy is relative in this sense, too: the contact of the particular fact with the legal system of the forum may often be decisive.

In this context it must be emphasized again that reliance on the public policy clause is by all means an *exceptional* recourse and *must not result in discrimination* against any legal system. This tool of defence in the private law of conflicts is as necessary as it would be ill-advised and contrary to the fundamental objectives of private international law to resort to it too frequently. It is particularly dangerous immediately to suspect violation of the basic principles of the legal system wherever an unknown or simply a different solution is offered by the foreign law: defence of public policy must not serve as a pretext for escape from application of the foreign law, which is more difficult to handle; it must not be used as a justification for the ill-conceived "homeward trend".

From the fact that the public policy doctrine is subject to change with the passage of time as well, it clearly follows that the temporal aspect is to be taken as a guide in determining whether public policy is offended by a foreign norm.

§25. SUBSIDIARY LAW

1. In the foregoing discussion we have briefly stated that the law indicated by the conflict rule cannot be applied in several cases, particularly when

– the relevant foreign norms remain *unknown* to the forum after the available means of evidence have been exhausted (see item 3 in §23); or

– the applicable law gives no answer to the matter of law at hand; or

– the relevant rules offend the *public policy* of the forum (see §24); or

– the parties request non-application of the foreign law [see (iii) in item 2 (b) of §23]; or

– reciprocity subject to proof is non-existent (see §22); or

– there is a fraud in the choice of law (see §16).

In these cases the question arises as to which rules of law should govern the judge in deciding the fact before him.

The matter is clear when the forum applies peremptory rules to "fend off" a foreign norm offending public policy (see item 2 in §24): the appropriate peremptory rules of the forum give a positive answer to the issue, so there can be no gap in the law.

On the other hand, however, cases where *no foreign norm is known, no such norm applies or the application of one is excluded* by the public policy clause (see item 3 in §24) lead to a gap in the law. Filling that gap should be attempted first by the known methods (analogy, etc.), with an eye to the foreign legal system concerned. If the attempt fails, another system of law should be looked for, a subsidiary law is needed (see Schwung in the List of Sources). A similar situation obtains when the parties request non-application of the foreign law, no reciprocity exists or there is a fraud in the choice of law, with a not insignificant difference that in such cases the original governing law is inapplicable as a whole, so analogy cannot be employed and it is inevitable that reliance must be placed on a subsidiary law.

2. The practice of private international law in *most* States invokes the *lex fori* where the relevant foreign norms are inapplicable: the judge fills the gap in law by applying the rules of his own legal system. The use of the *lex fori* as a subsidiary law often leads to results satisfactory from all points of view, while in some cases simply no other solution can be found. This course is also warranted by the judge's greater knowledge of the internal law.

Yet, not infrequently, the supplementary use of the internal law is supported solely by the theory of "lesser resistance". The spirit of the "homeward trend" prevails along this path as well, even if the norms of the *lex fori* are totally unsuitable for consideration of the foreign element at hand.

Hence legal science generally recommends the supplementary use of the *lex fori in the last resort only*. Instead the judge should look for a subsidiary connecting factor to find another legal system which also has a sufficiently close link with the given case. If, for instance, decision by the law of nationality is impossible, application of the law of domicile should be attempted. The view is also held by many that the rules of the eliminated (inapplicable) law may be supplemented by the norms of a similar legal system (e.g. the norms of the Belgian law, which was codified on the pattern of the *Code Civil*, by the French rules) or the missing norms may be deduced from the *general principles of law* by employing the comparative method.

The chief flaw of these propositions, which are not unassailable on the theoretical plane either, is that for the most part they raise great difficulties in practical application. *Practice, therefore, sticks to the lex fori*. Cases in which the law of the forum is replaced by a law similar to the eliminated one or by rules deduced from general principles (e.g. in the judicial practice of (former) Yugoslavia or Germany) may be regarded as exceptional.

3. The *Hungarian* Code, too, looks primarily on the *lex fori* as a subsidiary law. Accordingly, Hungarian law is to apply if the content of the foreign law cannot be ascertained (Art. 5) and also if the foreign law is to be disregarded because of violating the public policy of Hungary (Art. 7).

Again, this is the case when the applicable foreign law is to be disregarded *at the common request of the parties* and Hungarian law must be applied instead (Art. 9). By contrast, in the law of contracts (where the parties generally have the right to choice of law), the parties may request application either of Hungarian law (Supreme Court, Pf.III.20 No. 895 of 1992) or of *another foreign law* different from that whose non-application was sought (Art. 9).

Also, in case of fraud, it is not necessarily the *lex fori* but the law which the parties sought to disregard, which will be applicable (Art. 8).

TITLE 3

PERSONS

CHAPTER VIII

HISTORICAL ANTECEDENTS AND REGULATION IN GENERAL

§26. PERSONS IN LAW – A HISTORICAL RETROSPECT

Since historical times, persons have been part of a process which has been gradually bringing them under the control of regulatory systems different from the norms (systems of social or legal regulation) that had previously governed their lives and relationships. This was brought about by the fact that, in part, people were moving from one place to another, thereby changing a given regulatory system, and, in part, political history was producing essential changes such as extension by an ethnic group or a State of its domination over another ethnic group or another State. The inevitable result was the emergence of the necessity for expressing somehow the changes that had occurred in the personal status of these people. The means of doing so were those of the particular era, namely customary law and the power of administrative measures. Of course, this was not yet a regulation considered by private international law as fulfilling that function in modern law, or by some other branch of law as known in modern times. In similar situations the personal status of immigrants or people who came under foreign domination was governed by customary law, statute or State administrative measures through direct commands, or, in current usage, directly regulating substantive legal norms which determined the treatment and status to be accorded to foreigners in individual cases. Although the differentiated system of modern regulation is a result of long historical development, the distinctive feature of the diverse legal systems, namely the evolution of separate rules for foreigners, a law different from that applicable to nationals, can be traced from the early period of history. The road travelled to our modern-day advanced legislation was naturally long. The main aspects of this process may be presented in the following outline.

1. The rise of the classical private international law, which provides a guide to conflicts and relationships between systems of law, including regulation of personal status, can be traced to the first part of the 19th century (Savigny, Story). That was the era of the creation of bourgeois society.

The status of persons *in pre-capitalist periods* showed the following main features.

(a) The status of persons revealed a dissimilar pattern even on the general plane, while that of non-foreigners was sharply differentiated by social standing. The law also expressed the traditional structure or feudal character of society in that respect. The picture was coloured even more by the processes under which the law of a State was extended to foreigners. It was only natural that in the situation then obtaining there could not emerge a kind of uniform legal regulation, particularly in "private international law" as we understand it today, concerning the status of foreigners, whereas the very designation "foreigner" is itself a backward projection of a present-day category. The seeds of such regulation had however been sown.

(b) A look at the substance of the status of foreigners reveals the following picture. The masses of people driven off during wars or the prisoners of war enjoyed in general no legal protection whatsoever. Usually they were even worse off than the slaves (or the future serfs). The occupied countries or territories were brought under the rule of the conqueror militarily, politically and economically. This meant two things in the domain of law, especially in the area of law under consideration. On the one hand, the internal law of the State or territory in question was tolerated with respect to the populations of occupied territories and, on the other, the conqueror's law was gradually increasing in influence. The best example of this is provided by the Roman conquests. In the territories under the rule of Rome there existed mainly two planes of legal regulation, with considerable interaction in places of lasting coexistence.

As for the legal status of foreigners within the State (e.g. in the Roman Empire), they were not granted the rights of Roman citizens (*civis romanus*); as aliens, they hardly enjoyed any legal protection or any positive legal remedy. In the so-called period of Augustan peace and also in longer periods without a war, there was a significant growth of personal transactions and international trade flows (appearance of foreign merchants and their transactions, settlement of such merchants and craftsmen). Under stabilized conditions this process raised such daily questions as to how to determine the legal capacity of those people, their capacity to do business, their rights to marry, their inheritance relations, etc. In the Roman law as much as in the laws of peoples creating States in Europe in the wake of the great migrations (including the early Germanic and Hungarian laws) there were traces, and even coherent systems, of regulation induced by the said circumstances and set in train by conscious efforts to govern the legal status of foreigners in a way consistent with the interests of the prevailing legal order, but largely discriminatory and going far to protect the interests of the given State.

(c) The above developments are well reflected in legal literature on the ancient world. The *Imperium Romanum* testifies to, e.g., a certain symbiosis of *ius civile* and local laws of different peoples in the various provinces. In addition, there were emerging certain sporadic elements of conflicts law, rather of an interprovincial private international law, precisely in respect of personal relations of individuals (see Hamza: the section entitled *The Question of Ancient Private International Law*). Despite similarities in the substantive laws of the Greek city-states there is evidence, equally sporadic, of a certain choice-of-law approach to personal status (notably in a legal dispute about inheritance as covered by Isocrates' writing entitled *"Aegineticus"*, virtually the text of a brilliant pleading, in which the author argues, as far back as 391 B.C., about which of the competing three legal systems – the laws of Aegina, Siphnos and Ceos – is to be applied; quoted in Vrellis's monograph on private international law published in Greek in 1988, p. 32).

The status of persons showed a rather varied picture in these periods of development. Differentiation by feudal or subject standing was but one of its aspects. Greater differences could be observed in the status of foreigners even in countries where this group of people was subject to separate regulations under substantive law. Consequently, the basic situation of private international law existed, to wit, large numbers of cases were controlled by different regulatory systems. However, a comprehensive system of private international norms, determining which law was to be applied in case of conflict between differing legal systems, was slow in developing.

(d) Significant developments could be observed in respect of the status of persons even before the emergence of capitalism. They were, in brief, the following: (i) the control of State laws, even if by internal social stratification, over a specific territory, or their extension to a territory as a whole (principle of territoriality); (ii) special regulation by substantive law of the legal relations of foreigners, and gradual practical realization by such regulation of the principle that foreigners should, for both economic and political reasons, be accorded equal treatment with nationals, at least in respect to economic transactions, and that the necessary legal capacity and legal frameworks should be recognized for them; (iii) assumption of an important role by canon law and Roman law on ensuring the uniformity of substantive regulation; (iv) evolution by legal science and practice of the first pivotal elements of private international law which were to constitute the doctrine of domicile with respect to persons, with a view to reconciling the still-existing disparities of legal systems and regulations (see §§9–10).

2. The full-scale development of the *capitalist social system* signified the emergence of the capitalist relations of production, the consolidation of uniform private property and the vast growth of commodity turnover. Property and commodity relations were shaping, as it were, on their own pattern the sets of economic and social relations in general and the domestic and international markets in particular. This meant equal treatment in respect of personal status and establishment of a uniform law applicable to all in the entire territory of the State with regard to legal capacity. Furthermore, these developments found expression in historically significant instruments on constitutional law, such as the American Declaration of Independence and the Declaration of the Rights of

Man, but mostly in the great civil codes of the 19th century, first of all in the *Code Civil* of France. As part of civil-law developments in the bourgeois nation States, the great codes regulated in detail the status of man as a subject at law (legal capacity, disposing capacity, personal rights), while the commercial codes and other laws laid down additional sets of rules for capacity to contract. There emerged detailed regulations, with a differentiated system of appropriate institutions, concerning the legal personality of commercial firms and various commercial companies (corporations). Subsequent periods saw the appearance of the category of cooperative as a subject at law as well as of the civil-law features of different State organs and public institutions as entities in civil law.

Large-scale commodity turnovers in the national and international arenas were accompanied by a fast-growing mobility of persons, physical as well as legal. An all-embracing regulation under substantive law of domestic origin to govern such international movement as comprehensively as domestic movement had not yet been evolved, or was only gradually being devised, by the national systems of law. A partial unification of international law was also a product of later times, mainly the 20th century. Therefore, in general, international operations of persons could not be controlled except by the internal substantive laws of the countries involved, which were basically designed to govern internal forms of operations. For this reason the intensive international movement of commodities, capital and persons always resulted in conflicts between the national legal systems concerned.

Nationality as a connecting factor is likewise a product of the capitalist era. The concept of nation was placed in the centre of the legal order by the French revolution, while nationality came to replace the former feudal (nobility-descent and ruler-subject) relationship and became instead the expression of one's allegiance to the nation. It was not accidental that the principle of nationality was first formulated in Art. 3 of the *Code Civil* and was to be adopted by private international law. The *Code Civil* provides that the personal status of Frenchmen must be governed by French law even if they stay or live abroad. In respect of other subjects at law, mainly corporations, the term "nationality" was applied to the category of legal persons, and so on.

The interests vested in the large-scale movements of commodities, capital and persons, physical as well as legal, led to the creation of more and more rules of internal substantive law to govern international aspects connected with persons. Through these rules the different States regulated certain basic questions precisely in order to facilitate the international mobility of persons, alongside solutions under the law of conflicts. The essence of such regulation was that foreigners gained legal capacity substantially identical to that of nationals. The principle of equal treatment with nationals became universal. The very last remnants of legal disability were eliminated, and the general principle that foreigners were entitled to equal treatment with nationals came to take hold. This in itself is not contradicted by the fact that from time to time some countries imposed and impose various restrictions on foreigners: acquisition of immovable property by foreigners may be made subject to special permission by government authorities; special authorization may be and is required for the establishment of foreign companies; the employment of foreign nationals may be and is governed by separate regulations different from those applicable to nationals; reciprocity is a general requirement for the equal treatment of nationals and foreigners and the absence of it entails limitations on the concrete implementation of this principle, etc.

§27. PERSONS IN MODERN LAW

1. The *advanced Western countries* have made significant progress in regulating the legal status of persons.

This is partly manifest in new forms presenting new needs. Thus, for instance, there came into being a broad scale of economic associations, from joint stock companies, through limited liability companies and other simpler forms of association or groupings forming economic communities, to corporate law institutions like holding companies, business concerns and various forms of inter-state joint ventures. Among natural persons, large-scale migration of labour, including temporary or permanent settlement of large masses of migrant workers and other professional groups in foreign countries, was a fresh phenomenon which not only accentuated the importance of regulation under the law of conflicts, but also called for appropriate legislation by the receiving (host) countries concerning the treatment of qualifications and diplomas, the adoption of labour laws and the provision of social services. In certain occupations the special capacity of persons to effect related transactions was not a self-understood and natural thing in the host countries, which adopted an attitude towards foreign labour in accordance with the rules of internal protectionism.

But labour as well as companies were needed, and this generated a growth of international mobility which in turn, expressing as it did the increasing interdependence of the national economies, called for a significant development of the legal material on persons through, among others, international agreements.

There was a significant increase in the body of domestic and international rules governing the recognition and establishment of foreign legal persons and their sphere of operation. The European Communities (see §39) issue guidelines for a progressive harmonization of the corporate laws of member-states with a view to facilitating the movement of companies in the context of integration. The long-standing draft statute, for instance, of the European Union providing for the creation of the legal institution of the "European company" (*Societas europea, "SE"*) is designed to facilitate the concentration of capital and the growth of big companies. This plan seeks to set up a corporate structure for large European enterprises which will bring the economy of the European Union into a better position to compete with the big corporations of the United

States and Japan. Paramount importance is attached, also in general, to the European Union having achieved a high level of generalization in respect of the free movement of persons through more than 300 legal instruments designed to institutionalize a single internal market.

Also significant are the norms relating to the State as a subject at law in economic transactions, as a founder of enterprises or as a shareholder, as a subject of large contracts under civil or commercial law, of the so-called State orders. Of a recent date in this field are the norms seeking to frame a system of relevant rules of law that are identical or harmonize in all member-states of the European Union or apply to the European Communities as subjects at law.

Along with these norms in the nature of substantive law, a notable change in respect to legal persons and persons in general is represented by the fact that in a large number of the advanced Western countries the law of conflicts has been codified or considerably developed by local judicial practice. This development is characterized by an endeavour of regulation and judicial law-making, which are largely expansive in scope, to govern nearly the entire domain of possible legal relationships between persons within the ambit of conflicts law (related matters are covered by 20 articles in the Swiss Code of PIL of 1987, 36 in the 1969 Restatement of the Conflict of Laws 2nd, an American compilation of related legal material, 12 in the French Draft of 1967, 19 in the FRG Code of PIL of 1986, 16 in the Austrian Code of PIL of 1978). Persons are also covered by or brought under international agreements, such as the Hague Convention on legal persons or the *Code Bustamante*, which is a comprehensive code of private international law, consisting of hundreds of sections and extensively regulating the legal status of persons.

2. As for the *countries of Central and Eastern Europe*, the forms of regulation governing international personal and economic transactions, particularly in respect of East–West relations, were already largely established, present partly in the pre-existing legal values of these countries, partly in the solutions prevalent in other countries. These countries gradually grew into highly industrialized ones and soon came to play a great role in international economic relations. They increased their share in commodity turnover as well as in financial and personal transactions, maintaining this upward trend at the enterprise level, too. Despite the inertial autarky of their systems, these countries, particularly Hungary, sought to uphold such fundamental institutions of modern private international law as national treatment (generally subject to reciprocity, of course) and to adapt or devise their private international institutions relating to natural and legal persons. They codified in private international law the rules on the legal and disposing capacity of persons and other personal rights (in the Czechoslovak Code of 1963, the Yugoslav Code of 1982, the Polish Code of 1965, the Hungarian Code of 1979), or they regulated these questions otherwise, normally covering them in bilateral agreements on legal assistance. In terms of both personnel and organization vested with rights to engage in external economic activities, they established a special foreign trade monopoly of

the State and its foreign trading companies, only to see it gradually dismantled and fade out during the switch to a market economy system coupled with a process of fully developing the range of subjects at law in this area (see §40). There emerged a body of internal substantive rules in relation to subjects at law formed through international economic association (see §46). In the field of foreign trade, the legal personality was also recognized of foreign economic units unknown to domestic laws, e.g. the Hungarian law (as is also stated in Law-Decree No. 8 of 1978 on the Application of the Civil Code to International Economic Relations). It may be stated in summary that this group of countries evolved a modern private international law and a system of substantive law rules governing persons, which followed the general trend of international development even if they used a number of devices that, geared to interstate cooperation during the previous period, have since disappeared from the stage (e.g. the CMEA rules for international economic organisations). As part of the transformations in Central and Eastern Europe and of its readjustment to the West, the law of persons is also characterized by solutions fashioned by the general line of development.

3. At this point we should add that the worst periods of relations between "real socialism" and the West were also marked by significant legal *confrontations* (both in the practical field and in legal literature) which had to do chiefly with how to treat nationalized enterprises and their foreign owners, or the relationship between the latter and the Hungarian State as well as between state enterprises and the State (see §37 and §§54–55).

4. In the context of the law of international economic relations consideration should be given to the general international organizations which have a highly important role to play in shaping the pattern of international relations (International Monetary Fund, GATT, UNCTAD, European Union, Council of Europe, etc.) and, given our interests on the world market and our legally regulated cooperation with them, form part of Hungary's external economic relations as well. Therefore they deserve serious attention in the context of persons (see §39).

§28. THE NATURE, SOURCES AND MAIN INSTITUTIONS OF REGULATION

1. As could be seen, as regards the *nature of regulation*, there evolved a diversity of forms with respect to the legal status of persons. One form of regulation is in the nature of private international law (on conflicts), determining which of the national laws among the relevant legal systems is applicable to a legal dispute where the legal status of persons contains a foreign element. Another form of regulation appears in the law of international economic relations, which mainly offers a complex regulation by substantive law and relies on norms directly controlling the personal status of the subjects at law in foreign element

cases, stating any modifications, additions, restrictions or differences that are applicable in respect of the foreign element in opposition to the internal substantive law governing nationals as subjects at law. It also determines which of the rules are of a peremptory nature, of mandatory application (and hence exclude conflicts of laws) and which of them are to apply only if a conflict norm directs the application of the national law, should it also contain such norms.

2. With regard to *sources*, they are basically of two groups, as is also indicated by the evidence of this book, namely those of domestic, or national and those of foreign, or international origin. In internal, or national legislation, the written law is predominant, of course, but judicial practice also has a notable role to play, particularly in the law of conflicts. In Hungary, too, customary law created by judicial practice was the dominant source until 1979. The sources of international origin – international agreements – are significant in the field of regulation by both substantive law and private international law (e.g. bilateral agreements on legal assistance, the said *Code Bustamante* and the Hague Convention on legal persons and on the solution of conflicts between domicile and nationality). The precepts of customary law evolved by judicial practice carry a considerable weight even among the international sources of law.

3. As regards the *main institutions* to be found in the said legislative sources and to be discussed hereafter, they comprise the legal status of (a) natural persons, (b) the State, and (c) legal persons, as well as that of (d) foreign natural and legal persons within the State (basically regulated by substantive law, its principles and special rules governing the establishment, operation and capacity to do business within the State of subjects at law possessing legal and disposing capacity and other personal rights).

CHAPTER IX

PEOPLE AS A SUBJECT AT LAW

§29. THE PERSONAL LAW

1. The personal law (*lex personae*) is not only an abstract concept created by legal science, not only a theoretical *notion*, but also a living phenomenon of legislation and practice. Article 10 (1) of the Hungarian Code provides: "The legal capacity, disposing capacity, personal status in general and personal rights of the individual shall be governed by his personal law". The personal law has an element of private international law and one of substantive law. In terms of substantive law, the personal law is nothing other than the totality of internal substantive norms relating to the person as a subject at law, namely to a person's legal and disposing capacity and their termination, and her/his personal rights. This is the substance of the personal law within the meaning of substantive law. Here also belong the substantive norms of international origin which are binding on the country by virtue of international agreements and as such take precedence over international law (Art. 2 of the Code). The element of private international law consists in private international law presupposing the existence of two real facts. One is that individuals, especially in their large-scale international movement at present, may change, for a long time or permanently, the country whose substantive law has determined the content of their personal law. The other fact which private international law must presuppose is that the personal law of individuals may be considered by the authority (court or other agency) of another country having a legal system different from their own. With these circumstances and facts presupposed, the personal law performs the function, in private international law, of determining the particular national system of substantive law by which its content is to be ascertained in respect of matters not covered by international agreement. The interrelation of the two elements of the described notion in private international law is called the personal law (or *personal status*), which governs the status of people as a subject at law.

2. As is also shown by the quoted provision of the Hungarian Code, the personal law *per se* is not a connecting factor. *In the institution of the personal law a connecting factor* is that which, from the legal relations that individuals as subjects at law have with the State, singles out the essential element for the formulation of the private international law rule under which the personal law of a given individual must be determined, in consideration of that element in case of a conflict between legal systems. That element is a legally expressed relationship of a person to a State and through it to its entire legal system. In Europe, since the French Revolution, this relationship has been not one of this or that kind, which people (citizens) have to the sovereign, but one of universally declared equality to the State, a relationship expressed by nationality. It was an essential principle of the idea of the nation State that the State extends its legal order to its citizens even if they reside or live abroad *(lex patriae)*. On the one hand, by so doing the State wanted to accord the protection of its law to its citizens residing or living abroad, but, on the other hand, it was a way of expressing the identity of the nation State, an indication of its intention to have its legal order extended to and asserted in this international setting as well. This important concept of nationality has become universal in continental Europe. The French *Code Civil*, in Art. 3, expressed it by providing: "French nationals shall, even if they are resident abroad, be subject to the French laws governing the capacity and status of persons". In the process of development of the Italian State this was spelled out in both principle and theory by Mancini, a great authority on private international law, in a political discourse entitled *Della Nazionalità come fondamento del diritto delle genti* (On nationality as the foundation of the law of nations), which he delivered at Turin in 1851. It should be noted that "nationality" in this context stood not for national minority but for national allegiance or citizenship.

The principle of nationality (*lex patriae*) became the determinant of the personal law in Germany, Spain, Austria, in continental Europe in general, and in other continents as well. The *lex patriae* was likewise adopted by the countries of Central and Eastern Europe and is reflected in their legislation, legal practice and literature in the field of private international law.

3. Nevertheless, the *lex patriae was unable to gain absolute application*, to the exclusion of all other principles, *even in the countries of continental Europe*. There emerged a great diversity of situations which, by their essential nature, required disregarding the *lex patriae* in some cases. Even the concise and annotated editions of the *Code Civil*, when dealing with Art. 3, cite numerous new statutes, and judicial decisions which, depending on the nature of the facts and types of relationships, departed in some way or another from the absolute applications of the nationality principle. This can also be observed in the legislation and practice of other States. Such departure is quite evident in the case of, e.g., stateless persons (having no nationality) or of persons of dual nationality. In such cases the principle of nationality in itself provides no guidance at all. One of the available solutions is to ascertain the substantive-law as-

pects of the personal law according to the law of domicile. Thus the *lex domicilii* as a connecting factor (generally called *domicilium*) has been carried over into the concept of the personal law based on nationality in the countries of continental Europe (Art. 2290 of the French Draft Code of PIL of 1967, Art. 9 of the Austrian Code of PIL of 1978, Art. 5 of the FRG Code of PIL of 1986, Arts. 33–35 of the Swiss Code of PIL of 1987).

4. The *principle of domicile* is the general connecting factor of the personal law first and foremost *in the common-law countries* but also in some others (e.g. Argentina). The domicile becomes an element of the connecting factor in ascertaining the personal law by reason of the fact that private international law emphasizes a person's relationship thereto, namely to that State in whose territory s/he resides, i.e. *was born, settles and acquires a permanent place of residence*. True, this too is a strong connection, which establishes a kind of relationship, quite close to nationality between the foreign State (host country) and the person choosing to reside in it with the intent of permanent or final settlement (taking up employment, acquiring property, contracting marriage, obtaining education, qualifications or diplomas, all of which link her/him to that country in terms of personal achievement and fortune). Even if this relationship is not as full as is implied by nationality in public law (right to vote, eligibility to public office, etc.), it is such form of relations and allegiance to the State and society concerned that operates as a decisive element of a rational and justified connecting factor along with or instead of nationality.

This concept became dominant in the common-law countries, England and the United States of America, where the general norms of private international law render the law of domicile applicable to the determination of the personal law. As is stated by Dicey with respect to English law (Rules 3–7), "the domicile of a person is the country in which he has his permanent home under the English law ... either by birth or by appropriate choice of the place of residence". According to the relevant articles (11 to 15) of the American Restatement 2d of 1969, "the domicile is the place, usually a person's home, to which private international law attaches paramount importance by reason of the person's relationship to that place, whereas the home is the place in which the individual resides and which is the centre of local social and civil life ... either by birth (domicile of origin) ... or by choice (domicile of choice)".

In addition to the above considerations, there was a special socio-political argument in favour of the domicile-centred approach in Anglo-Saxon law. In the former British Empire, but also in the latter-day Commonwealth, there was and is a great mobility of persons, with migration and British nationality extending to numerous dominions and States. On the one hand, application of the *lex patriae* would have been politically damaging to the countries involved, because it would have entailed disregard of their legal system in this respect as well, and, on the other hand, given the large-scale migration, the applicability of the law of the given constitutional units (countries, component States) would have resulted in the use of various laws at the same time throughout the territory of the Empire or the Commonwealth. Especially in the United States it became an established feature of the situation that a large part of the population had no American citizenship. While some inhabitants acquire American citizenship after a long period of residence, there is a continuing influx of new immigrants, so it is a standing rule that a certain segment of inhabitants has no American citizenship. Under such circumstances, application of the nationality principle by the American courts would give rise to numerous difficulties by causing the courts to be constantly faced with the problem of applying the laws of nearly all the countries of the world. Furthermore, it would create confusion because the personal status of people would show a permanent pattern of diversity due to the multiplicity of the immigrants' nationality. In that country, therefore, the principle of domicile is also an expression of and a substitute for "civic equality", while on the socio-political plane it forms part of what is called the American melting pot, to wit, the concept that the multitude of immigrants should be assimilated into the mass of Americans by the use of all available means.

Although the principle of domicile, which has thus become generally adopted in the common-law countries, was less forced to permit numerous exceptions and also to apply the *lex patriae* (for, among other things, an important norm of the *lex domicilii* permitted no one to have two domiciles at the same time), it was unable to win absolute applicability. On the one hand, the law of the forum is frequently applied and, on the other, someone can actually have several places of residence even if, in the legal sense, he cannot have several domiciles as one rules out another by virtue of legislation. So the concept of *place of residence, chosen with no intention of a permanent stay, as distinct from domicile and even that of sojourn* has likewise been carried over into private international law, particularly to the common law (see the pertinent chapters of Dicey's and Ehrenzweig's works in the List of Sources), but also to continental laws, the Hungarian included, as will be seen below.

5. Of course, the nationality-centred and the domicile-centred approach have caused serious difficulties during the 100 years' history of *attempts at the unification of private international law*. This was particularly evident in the process of codifying numerous conventions of the Hague Conference concerning the personal status of individuals (guardianship, obligation of maintenance, marriage, protection of minors, inheritance etc.). The bulwark of the European *lex patriae* approach as "canonized" by Mancini yielded relatively quickly to the Anglo-Saxon orientation towards *domicilium*, partly because the inner force of the *domicilium*'s rationality kept increasing, since it was due largely to the growth of migration, partly because unification of law without the participation of the common-law countries would have questioned the very pursuit of unification. It is an achievement that "habitual residence" (really permanent residence) as an institution of *domicilium* in the Hague definition appeared in the first Hague Convention of 1896 (on civil procedure), and since then "the work of The Hague shows a clear progression of thought from nationality towards

habitual residence" (see Droz-Dyer). Today, with a slight lead of "habitual residence", the compromise points to a constantly reproduced combination of the two concepts, as is indicated by the latest Hague Convention (1989) on the Law Applicable to Succession of Estates of Deceased Persons (Arts. 94–95) and, at the level of generality, by the Hague Convention of 1955 on the Settlement of Conflicts between the Law of Nationality and the Law of Domicile. In proportion as Hungary accedes to the Hague Conventions, the combination of these two approaches will also become part of Hungarian practice and legal thinking through this channel.

§30. LEGAL CAPACITY

1. Legal capacity is *one of the most general categories of law*, which means a legally expressed qualification of persons, primarily physical but also legal, and of the State to be subjects of civil-law relations. Thus, legal capacity is not only a part of people's moral condition but also a central element of their civil status in all civilized countries. According to advanced political and legal thinking, the generality, universality and equality of legal capacity are today congeneric to people to such an extent as to deny, and indeed one should deny, the "right" of positive law to restrict, let alone question, them. In more countries than one, legal capacity is not even covered by private international law (see, e.g., the stance of German law in the enactment putting into effect the *BGB*) on the assumption that conflict situations are practically impossible in respect of legal capacity; although formal conflicts may arise between legal systems, the laws of States should, in view of people's generic substance, be uniform in regard to legal capacity.

2. The fullness of a people's legal capacity is the *result of legal development*. Nevertheless, there are still retrograde laws drawing distinctions between one individual and another in respect of legal capacity. Therefore the United Nations' Declaration of Human Rights is not merely a solemn act of political relevance, but a necessary instrument giving legal expression to the said fullness as a product of historical development and combatting the still operative retrograde mental furniture of law. By virtue of that Declaration as an international instrument the fullness of people's legal capacity is to be considered as having the protection of the law in all member-states ("Everyone has the right to recognition everywhere as a person before the law"; Art. 6), including the ones whose private international law does not cover this question.

The need for the coverage of legal capacity by international law is also made obvious by the differences existing between the national systems of law concerning its commencement and termination as well as, in some aspects, its substance. A remitting rule is therefore needed to determine the national law to which these questions are subject in particular cases. This is why legal capacity is covered by the private international law of most countries, as is the case with the Polish Code of PIL of 1965 (Art. 9), the Czechoslovak Code of PIL of 1963 (Art. 3), the Austrian Code of PIL of 1978 (Art. 12), the FRG Code of PIL of 1986 (Art. 7), the Swiss Code of PIL of 1987 (Art. 34), etc. Given the significance of this problem, legal capacity is also regulated by Hungary's bilateral agreements on legal assistance.

3. The *international legislation* of Hungary *on private international law* will be dealt with in the following discussion. Legal capacity is *governed by the personal law* as set out below.

(a) The question of *whether a natural person is deemed to have legal capacity in any particular context is, according to the former law and the recent codification, to be governed by the domestic law of the person concerned (lex patriae).* This tenet of the former customary law was made written law by Art. 42 of the Law-Decree to bring into force the Family Act, providing that the existence and extent of disposing capacity must be governed by the domestic law of the person concerned, namely by the law of nationality. Since, however, disposing capacity presupposes legal capacity, the said legislative provision also naturally implied regulation of legal capacity in the sense mentioned above. The first provision of the Code in Chapter II on Persons (Arts. 10–11) ordains the application of the *personal law – law of nationality* under the Hungarian approach in general – to *legal capacity.*

Accordingly, the commencement, substance and termination of legal capacity are subject to the domestic law.

A reference to possible differences in the *substance* of legal capacity has been made in the preceding paragraphs. Equal treatment in this respect is a general postulate, also formulated by international law. This finds expression in, among other things, the fact that foreign nationals and stateless persons are, under Art. 15 of the Code, deemed to be on an equal footing with nationals in respect of legal capacity. This provision of the Code amounts to a virtual guarantee for the operation of Hungarian law in this field, albeit in defence of the fullness of a people's legal capacity. Nevertheless it follows from the same legislative source that the law may lay down contrary provisions overriding the applicable rules in the Chapter on Persons, which ordinarily render legal capacity subject to the law of nationality. If, however, the law of the State of the person contains provisions which, in respect of the substance of legal capacity, offend a general rule of international law or a fundamental principle of the Hungarian Constitution, such foreign norms are inapplicable to legal capacity in Hungary. Both the Constitution and the Civil Code of Hungary provide that legal capacity must be equal regardless of age, sex, nationality or religion. The pertinent rules (Art. 56 of the Constitution and Art. 8 of the Civil Code) are of mandatory or absolute application. Consequently, where the domestic law of a foreigner is otherwise applicable before a Hungarian forum and provides for discrimination between persons on racial or other grounds in respect of, e.g., a particular legal relationship and a legal dispute arising therefrom, the law of the foreign State involved must not be applied even if its application to the particular case is otherwise directed by Hungarian private international law. As against this, it is only a secondary question whether Hungarian law disallows non-application of these rules of internal law in view of their imperative nature or because the discriminative foreign law is violative of Hungarian public policy and disregarding it is required by the public policy clause (see §24). In point of fact, this may also be viewed from the angle that the said imperative rules, although disputed in jurisprudence, are a specific form and manifestation of the public policy clause.

As regards the *commencement* of legal capacity, systems of law may exhibit disparities having more far-reaching implications. Here, the connecting factor of Hungarian law may *even* assume a role of great practical relevance. As a rule, the systems of law recognize the legal capacity of persons not only in case of live births, but also from the moment of conception. Still, they differ in calculating that moment and in deciding a legal dispute about the personal law according to the personal law of a person yet unborn or to the nature of a vested right. In a case of inheritance, for instance, the latter concept means that the legal capacity of an unborn child is governed by the law generally applicable to inheritance relations, because the substance of the dispute consists of the fact as to whether a person has acquired inheritance rights, to wit, has become heir while a still foetus. This is of interest because under Hungarian law inheritance relations are to be governed by the law of the (last) nationality of the deceased person, not by the law of the heir's nationality. The problem may acquire practical relevance in deciding whether the legal relationship at hand is qualified as an inheritance relationship. As is provided by Art. 600 of the Hungarian Civil Code, a person who by operation of law cannot succeed to the estate at the time of its accrual must be eliminated from succession. On the other hand, under Art. 9 of the Civil Code, a person, if born alive, is vested with legal capacity from the date of conception. The same Article also states that the date of conception is the three hundredth day preceding birth, a period being the prenatal phase of legal capacity. Now, certain laws may define this period as being of a shorter duration. If, for example, in State A the legal relationship comes under the law of inheritance and the prenatal period of legal capacity is shorter than 300 days *vis-à-vis* State B, where the heir was born (and where the presumed date of conception is likewise 300 days preceding birth), the heir is considered to be eliminated from succession. Where the legal relationship is governed by the personal law, the legal capacity of the heir is subject to the law of State B, which counts a full 300 days in the prenatal period of legal capacity, so the person concerned is deemed to have legal capacity with retroactive effect and is entitled to acquire the inheritance. The regulation of this aspect is also ambiguous in the Hungarian Code of Private International Law. What we have is, in point of fact, a special instance of qualification (classification). Since, however, the core of this problem, which is not one of legal capacity alone, is constituted precisely by legal capacity, the correct and reasonable approach lies in the application of the personal law to this situation as well.

Nor is the concept of live birth unequivocal in international practice. Under Hungarian civil law, a person is legally capable even retroactively to the said point of time if she/he were born alive and lived for a period no matter how short. On the other hand, there are countries where viability is an added requirement (e.g. 24 hours of life is the criterion of live birth).

Legal capacity ceases upon death. In extreme cases the time of death may also give rise to a problem, for it is not sure that biological death and death in the legal sense clearly coincide in each and every legal system. Yet it may be said that this is seldom likely to acquire any particular relevance in private international law. On the other hand, legal capacity is terminated by *declaration of death*, which is given more extensive and diverse coverage by substantive law in the various legal systems. Regulation of this question by private international law is therefore equally important and will be given separate treatment below (§32).

(b) By contrast, practical importance attaches to those rules of private international law which *designate additional connecting factors (domicile, place of habitual residence)*, beside nationality as a connecting factor of the personal law, to govern legal capacity. Situations of daily life may cause the absolute allegiance of natural persons to a State to be complemented by such other facts which do not enable private international law to arrive at clear decisions by reliance on the law of nationality. Like situations are covered by Arts. 11–13 of the Hungarian Code.

(i) A group of these situations is connected with *dual nationality,* or with multiple nationalities possessed by one person. This may be attributed to the fact that according to the law of nationality of some States emigrating citizens do not ordinarily lose their nationality even if in the meantime they have acquired the nationality of another State. Our law provides that whenever such a situation obtains, legal capacity must be governed by the Hungarian law if the person concerned is also a Hungarian citizen. Where none of the several nationalities is Hungarian, the applicable law must be that of the State of *domicile*. As can be seen, the doctrine of domicile operates here as a subsidiary rule.

In another group of situations not clearly definable, namely those involving *stateless* persons, legal capacity is subject to the law of domicile. Hungarian law uses domicile as a connecting factor in this case as well. Of course, Hungarian law applies if in either of the two cases mentioned the person also has a residence in Hungary. This may be of relevance in cases where persons have more than one residence.

(ii) As mentioned earlier in connection with the law of domicile in the common-law countries (§29), the doctrine of domicile is not unequivocal even in those countries since their practice varies considerably with respect to this legal category. Considering the domicile (or residence) as a connecting factor was (and is) also used by the positive rules of Hungarian law, *clearly formulated provisions were needed to understand what was (is) meant by domicile and to deal with cases involving more than one residence*. As regards the latter aspect, a relatively flexible provision (Art. 11 of the Code) ordains the application of the law of the State with which the person concerned has the closest relationship. Accordingly it is by considering all the circumstances of the case that the court must determine to which State the particular legal relationship is most closely linked by its nature.

With regard to the legal concept of domicile or residence, international practice has evolved several criteria for its definition and delimitation. Thus, in the common-law countries, which have the broadest range of practice in this field, law distinguishes: a domicile existing by operation of law; a domicile to be established in consideration of all the circumstances of the case; a domicile presumed on the ground that in her/his place of residence the person obtained domicile for the purpose of permanent settlement; a domicile acquired by birth; and so on. The common element of these approaches is essentially choice of place with the intention of permanent residence. Another element is voluntary choice of residence (not through coercive measures by the State, deportation or expulsion, etc.). Generalizing the relevant legislative and practical experience, Hungarian private international law defines residence as the place where "a person resides permanently or with the intent to settle" [Art. 12 (1) of the Code]. Science and judicial practice have to rely on this general provision for devising partial solutions to meet situations, which, as was seen, might arise from continuing differentiation in the concept of domicile.

(iii) The last question about domicile relates to the need for coverage of the personal law of individuals having no residence as defined above. International practice offers no other solution than that adopted by Hungarian law (Art. 11 of the Code), namely that the personal law of such persons is to be determined by the law of their *place of habitual residence*. By habitual residence is understood that place where a person lives for a considerable length of time without the intention to settle. Following this line of logic, and considering the connections between such possible facts and legal aspects, Hungarian law covers the additional question of how to determine the personal law of individuals with more than one place of habitual residence. The answer is given by Art. 11 of the Code: the personal law of individuals having one of their places of habitual residence in Hungary is subject to Hungarian law, while that of persons having all their places of habitual residence abroad is governed, on the analogy of several foreign domiciles, by the law of the State with which they have the closest relationship.

(c) The regulation we have outlined boils down to the need for the personal law to be ascertainable through determination of either nationality or domicile or place of residence. Even if the personal law has been clearly established by this process, this may still not be the case where the personal law, in contradistinction to the one so established, was formerly governed by the law of another State. The question is whether *or not* the *earlier personal status* and the rights and obligations originating therein are *affected by the change in the personal law*. In other words, if the mentioned incidents change retroactively under the new personal law, can they do so, or not, *inpeius*, especially with respect to the person involved? According to the clear position of Hungarian law, the personal law resting on subsequent nationality, domicile or place of habitual residence has no such retroactive effect [Art. 11 (1) of the Code].

(d) The *legal status of refugees*, which presents an increasingly serious problem for Hungary, is of practical relevance to personal status. Refugees generally retain their original personal law (nationality, domicile) because their status is notionally temporary. As regards its political and legal substance, the situation of refugees is normally better in the host country than it would be in the country they have left. This may affect the content of the personal law, too. Since Hungarian law starts from the assumption that its standards with respect to the fullness of the personal law are higher than those of any such country, Art. 13 of the Code is prompted by favourable considerations to direct the application of Hungarian law to the legal status of refugees. However, this provision must not prejudice the aforesaid principle that the earlier personal status and the rights and obligations originating therein must remain unaffected.

4. Hungary associates itself, as well as by accession to *international conventions*, with the universal norms expressing the fullness of personality and legal capacity.

(a) The *Convention of 1951 relating to the Status of Refugees* considers and regulates the status of refugees in its many facets. It was a long time before Hungary acceded to it. During that time the ideology of the one-party State and its isolation in the world were actuated in this regard by the claim that by such a regulation of the refugee problem, Western circles with hostile intent gave anti-socialist protection to illegal emigrants from the socialist countries. That is now consigned to past history, while the treatment of refugee questions has acquired a dramatic relevance. Our accession followed soon after the transformations had got under way (Law-Decree No. 15 of 1989). Among the numerous provisions of the Convention we shall refer at this point only to those directly affecting legal capacity, such as application of the Convention without discrimination as to race, religion or country of origin (Art. 3), or acquisition of property, protection of intellectual property, right of association, etc. (Arts. 13 *et seq.*). The most important rule relating to *personal status* is contained in Art. 12 to the effect that the personal status of a refugee shall be governed by the law of the country of his domicile or, if he has no domicile, by the law of the country of his residence, and that the rights previously acquired by a refugee shall be respected by a Contracting State.

(b) Among the universal conventions relating to human rights and through them to man's legal capacity an important place is occupied by the Universal Declaration of Human Rights, which was adopted and proclaimed by the United Nations General Assembly on 10 December 1948. It is of outstanding importance primarily because it universally declares the aforementioned principle that "everyone has the right to recognition everywhere as a person before the law" (Art. 6). This has made legal capacity not only a universal human value, but also a universally binding maxim of law. Of course, the Declaration presupposes a wide range of human rights, thereby outlining, as it were, the substantive dimensions of legal capacity as well. These dimensions naturally comprise numerous elements of human personality and socio-political action, namely of disposing capacity and capacity to contract. Thus the Declaration states that "everyone has the rights to life and liberty" (Art. 3), that "all human beings are born free and equal in dignity and rights" (Art. 1), that no one must be held in slavery and thereby be restricted in his legal capacity (Art. 4), that all are entitled to equal protection of the law (Art. 7), that men's and women's right to marry must not be restricted by discrimination as to race and religion (Art. 16), that "everyone has the right to own property alone as well as in association with others" (Art. 17), to mention but a few major provisions of the Declaration.

Another important instrument of the United Nations is the *International Covenant on Civil and Political Rights*, with the *Optional Protocol* thereto, which were both adopted by the General Assembly on 16 December 1966 (and were promulgated in Hungary by Law-Decree No. 8 of 1976 and Law-Decree No. 24 of 1988, respectively). Like the Universal Declaration, these are comprehensive instruments on personal, civil and political rights, but also naturally express the fullness of human personality and legal capacity (see Arts. 2, 3, 6–9, 11, 17–18, etc. of the Covenant). The Covenant and the Protocol have the great merit of making a significant step towards giving effect to the rights declared in them, namely by the Covenant establishing a Human Rights Committee which may, on the basis of reports submitted by the States parties, study the legal practice thereof and take various measures in connection with it (e.g. transmit its comments to the State party concerned): may even receive communications from individuals subject to the jurisdiction of the States parties: to consider with the State party concerned such communications at the request of the Committee and to inform the Committee of its clarification of the matters involved and of the remedies taken (Arts. 28 *et seq*. of the Covenant and Arts. 1 *et seq*. of the Protocol).

(c) Legal capacity may also be affected by *bilateral agreements*. All of Hungary's agreements on legal assistance, for instance, provide that citizens and legal persons of either Contracting State are to enjoy, in the other Contracting State, legal protection of their person and property on an equal footing with the subjects at law of the other Contracting State (see, e.g., the Italian–Hungarian Agreement, promulgated by Law-Decree No. 11 of 1981, Art. 1; the Greek–Hungarian Agreement, promulgated by Law-Decree No. 21 of 1981, Art. 1; the Finnish–Hungarian Agreement, promulgated by Law-Decree No. 25 of 1982, Art. 1).

(d) In connection with international conventions, mention should be made of the relevant instruments of the Council of Europe. Our joining the Council entailed our accession to the *European Convention on Human Rights* (see §39), which was signed on 4 November 1950 and entered into force on 3 September 1953. The Convention has since been complemented by 8 Protocols. While it serves to protect human rights by a more detailed regulation than the United Nations instruments do, it has progressed beyond the legal structure devised by the United Nations especially by setting up the European Court of Human Rights, which affords judicial protection against violations of human rights (Arts. 19, 38 *et seq.*).

§31. DISPOSING CAPACITY

1. Most provisions of law on legal capacity are automatically applicable to disposing capacity. Being an element of personal status which in turn is *determined by the personal law as set forth above*, disposing capacity is likewise governed by the personal law. This is particularly true of the rules which, as we have discussed in connection with legal capacity, determine the personal law, i.e. the *lex patriae* or, in specific cases, the domicile and the place of habitual residence.

The applicability of the same connecting factor to both legal and disposing capacity is spelled out in part by Art. 42 of the aforementioned Law-Decree bringing into force the Family Act, which directs that the existence and extent of disposing capacity must be governed by the domestic law of the person concerned. A similar provision is contained in Art. 11 of the Hungarian Code of PIL: "The personal law of the individual shall be the law of the State of which he is a national". What we have said about the domicile and habitual residence as a subsidiary rule governing legal capacity, in addition to nationality, as the principal rule naturally applies to disposing capacity as well. Essentially similar provisions are contained in the continental laws which have adopted the *lex patriae* in respect to personal status. This is also generally reflected in the agreements on legal assistance which Hungary has signed with other countries. On the other hand, disposing capacity is governed by the domicile principle in the common-law countries. Both systems of law make the same exceptions in respect of legal and disposing capacity.

2. As already noted, the principle of man's full legal capacity is a matter of socio-political progress everywhere. It is therefore practically impossible to presume conflicts of laws with respect to the substance and extent of legal capacity. The situation is different with regard to *disposing capacity*, the regulation of which *in substantive law exhibits* fairly considerable differences usually arising from a background other than socio-political considerations or substance. Differences are due rather to the fact that the rules on disposing capacity are also part of the personal law, the civil law in general, which again is conditioned by varying patterns of historical development including aspects like timelags of codification in the legal development of countries, discrepan-

cies in legal practice, legal policies, and legal traditions in general. Therefore, since the substance and extent of disposing capacity differ notably by national laws, the regulation of disposing capacity in private international law has acquired great practical relevance.

Disposing capacity means a legally recognized and expressed capacity of the individual to acquire rights and to assume obligations by his own acts. Divergences between, and hence conflicts of, laws are likely to exist in any of those questions in which disposing capacity is fully covered by law. One such question concerns the existence or non-existence of disposing capacity, the age at which it commences and its aspects of limitation by reason of age or, irrespective thereof, due to restriction or lack of discerning capacity. Consequently, under Hungarian law, all of these questions are *governed by those rules of the differing and conflicting legal systems which make up the personal law of the individual concerned.* The personal law is also naturally applicable to the consequences of limitation or lack of disposing capacity and to the question of who is to be regarded as the legal representative of persons having limited or no disposing capacity.

3. Disposing capacity means general contractual or commitment capacity. However, some transactions are controlled by substantive-law rules different from the general rules on disposing capacity. *In specific cases, the discrepancies in the rules of substantive law reappear in the rules of private international law.* Those of more moment are the following.

(a) As distinct from general capacity to enter into transactions, *special commitment capacity* means, for instance, capacity to marry and to make wills. It implies, among other things, that the testator must have command of the language in which he is to make a will or he must be in the legally prescribed position to make a verbal will. Under private international law, the conflict rule governing a given legal institution (e.g. the law of inheritance) must also be taken into account in determining the special commitment capacity.

(b) Furthermore, disposing capacity may happen to be regulated differently by a new personal law (nationality or domicile) resulting from a *change* in the former. Thus, for instance, an individual has as yet no disposing capacity under the new personal law but he acquired it under the former. Under Hungarian private international law, majority already attained is not affected by such change in the personal law. Accordingly, a Hungarian court will hold to be of age a person who was to be deemed of full age under his earlier law, but would not yet be deemed to have reached majority under the new personal law otherwise applicable to the particular legal relationship.

(c) Disposing capacity is governed by two additional important rules of Hungarian law, both of which serve to strengthen the security of transactions and, as is shown by comparative studies, are in accord with international practice. One refers to transactions of non-Hungarian nationals who, under their personal law, have limited or no disposing capacity but enter into *transactions that are generally effected on a mass scale to meet the ordinary needs of daily life.*

These transactions – provided such persons are capable of action under Hungarian law – must be regarded as valid in Hungary [Art. 15 (2) of the Code]. Given the large volume of international personal transactions in our time, to ascertain whether a foreign buyer is somewhere subject to a law restricting his disposing capacity to a greater extent than Hungarian law does would be an unrealistic requirement, one impossible to meet in retail trade. Naturally, regulation by Hungarian private international law takes into account the domestic facts of life and the provisions of substantive law expressive of them.

The second rule relating to a common situation of a similar nature (in which an individual does not have unlimited disposing capacity under his personal law, but would be capable of action under Hungarian law) differs in one aspect, namely it refers not only to economic transactions effected in Hungary to meet the usual needs of everyday life, but all other economic transactions of such persons, *provided the legal consequences of their transactions of this kind occur in Hungary*. According to Art. 15 (3) of the Code, an individual having disposing capacity under Hungarian law must be considered capable of action in such a situation even if a non-Hungarian national has restricted or no disposing capacity under his personal law.

4. With the above statements projected on to the *practical plane*, reference may by made to the following instances or legal disputes which appear of interest from a variety of angles. A 17-year old British subject residing in Hungary sells his personal computer in Budapest to a Hungarian friend of his, who is also 17 years old, on condition that the buyer should pay the price, moderate in comparison with the market value, within two months. The buyer received the computer but failed to pay the purchase price within the agreed time-limit.

In an action brought before a court of Budapest the seller requests the court to order the buyer to pay the purchase price. Under Arts. 54–56 of the Code the court establishes the existence of the given facts (which is also proven by the delivery of the computer), and such everyday transactions are regarded by English law as valid in respect of minors as well. The application of English law follows from Arts. 25 and 30 of the Hungarian Code, which render the law of the seller's country applicable to contracts of sale. The buyer's legal representative pleaded the invalidity of the contract because the contracting parties are not of age, their legal dispute is subject to the Hungarian law, under which such a transaction could not be validly effected, so the original situation should be re-established.

Therefore, in the this instant case, the question is one of determining the law applicable to the settlement of the dispute. The procedure to follow is this. The material validity of the contract of sale is governed by the law of the seller's country or, more accurately, "the law of the state in which, at the time of contracting, the seller ... has his domicile or habitual residence ..." (Art. 25). Even if disposing capacity as a "preliminary question" is not separated from that of material validity (see §83), the said Article also directs the application of Hungarian law because the seller resides in Hungary. If the question is looked at from the angle of disposing capacity (capacity to contract), Hungarian law generally regards the law of nationality as applicable (Art. 11). However, the Code recognizes reference back (Art. 4): since in English law domicile is the connecting factor of personal status, which is Hungary in the instant case, the applicable law will, in this line of logic, again be that of Hungary by accepting reference back to it. In the case of a minor buyer, on the other hand, the application of Hungarian law follows from his Hungarian nationality (Art. 11). This same transaction is invalid under Hungarian substantive law, a fact which can be pleaded in favour of the minor buyer (Art. 21 of the Hungarian Civil Code). It is invalid because today in Hungary purchase of a personal computer cannot be regarded as "a contract of lesser importance for meeting usual needs of daily life" (Art. 14 of the Civil Code) which would be valid without the intervention of a legal representative. Furthermore, a contract may also be invalid for contravention of the law (Art. 200 of the Civil Code) of the seller since he is not considered as a native under the Foreign Exchange Act and hence the validity of the transaction in question is subject to permission by the foreign exchange authority [Art. 6, para. 1 (b), of the Foreign Exchange Act, promulgated by Law-Decree No. 1 of 1974]. For all that, the reasonable approach may be different today if purchases of personal computers are common transactions which can be deemed to be of lesser importance in view of the size or value of particular computers, but the system of rules of conflicts law as such is nonetheless unaffected by this circumstance.

§32. DECLARATION OF DEATH

1. People's legal capacity and disposing capacity cease upon death. In addition to natural death, however, the law knows a sort of civil death, viz. declaration of persons as dead or, sometimes, missing. As regards their *substance*, such declarations bear a similarity to death in having the same civil-law consequences, namely the termination of legal and disposing capacity, with their most important practical bearings consisting in eliciting effects under the law of inheritance and reviving the capacity of the surviving spouse to marry. The essential difference between someone being declared dead and being declared missing lies in that the declaration of death includes the presumption of death, whereas in the case of missing persons such presumption is not provided for by the law. In the latter case, however, this difference generally has no relevance for the subsequent phase of property relations because these behave as if such a person had died.

There are three major issues arising in private international law in connection with the declaration of death: they concern the applicable law, the jurisdiction, and the recognition of judicial judgments declaring a person legally dead.

2. As regards the *law governing* declaration of death, Hungarian private international law (Art. 16 of the Code) ordains that the applicable law must be the personal law of the missing person, with the content and criteria as discussed above in connection with legal capacity. If in a private international law dispute the Hungarian court, in support of an interest protected by internal law, declares a non-Hungarian national legally dead or missing, such a declaration of death is subject to Hungarian law by virtue of Art. 16 of the Code. In support of an interest protected by internal law, a Hungarian court may declare a non-national legally dead for various reasons: e.g. if a presumably dead foreign national had property or other unsettled legal relations in Hungary, or anywhere else, the relatives in Hungary would have an interest in settling, say, inheritance relations. An inheritance accruing to a Hungarian national upon death, natural or presumed, is seen as a legal interest which is accepted by the domestic court as constituting an interest of international law with respect to declaration of death. Since it may occur that in a particular situation a foreign national cannot yet be declared legally dead under his personal law, but a missing person may, under Hungarian law, be so declared by reason of the facts at hand, the Hungarian court proceeds accordingly and applies the Hungarian law. This is an exceptional procedure in Hungarian law, but in the practice of other countries the law of the forum (*lex fori*) is rather often the principal rule of private international law. Although most of our agreements on legal assistance provide that proceedings for declaration of death must be governed by the domestic law of the person concerned, some of them (e.g. the agreement between Romania and Hungary) direct the proceeding courts to apply the law of their own State to cases involving declaration of death.

3. At this juncture reference should also be made to the question of *jurisdiction* (and recognition of judgments) concerning declaration of death. In the specific situation discussed above with regard to the applicable law, it is hard to separate the governing law and jurisdiction even conceptually, and in reality the two are inseparable (on the one hand, the jurisdictional rules of Hungarian private international law stem from internal law and, on the other, they are included in the agreements on legal assistance between Hungary and other States).

Article 55 of the Code provides that Hungarian courts and other authorities have, as a rule, exclusive jurisdiction in proceedings involving the personal status of Hungarian nationals. So, considering that in the matter of declaration of death the Code makes no exception to the general rule, a Hungarian national cannot be declared legally dead except by a Hungarian court. Should she/he be declared dead abroad, the consequences of such declaration would be unrecognizable in Hungary (as it follows from Arts. 70 *et seq.* on the recognition of foreign judgments).

This is likely to give rise to problems in our practice, and the logic of such conclusion may be questioned even on the theoretical plane, since conversely this is not the case: suits on the personal status of foreigners are not among the matters excluded from the jurisdiction of Hungarian authorities (Arts. 56 *et seq.*). Accordingly, Hungarian authorities may generally take jurisdiction over cases involving the personal status of foreigners, declaration of death included. Moreover, the provision of Art. 16 of the Code that occasionally, on behalf of a domestic legal interest, a Hungarian court may also declare a foreign national legally dead cannot be seen as an exception to the general picture. That such judgments have indisputable effect chiefly in Hungary is another matter. It is not certain that such judgments would also be recognized by the State whose national was declared dead in Hungary: but that is highly likely since a similar legal solution is familiar to other legal systems, and the question again arises whether judgments of the courts of a given State are enforceable abroad in respect of foreign nationals as well. This duality of jurisdiction, at least formally competing, is also reflected in agreements on legal assistance with numerous countries; they generally provide for the jurisdiction of the local forum in proceedings for declaration of death, but further permit nationals of the other contracting party to be declared dead. The said dual and contradictory feature of the Code could likewise be eliminated by this two-way solution. It is to be asked, however, whether this "lapse", probably of codification, can now be corrected at least by "guidelines" of the Supreme Court, for it would amount to practice *contra legem*. By contrast, the Code has abandoned the rigour of our previous practice in matters of more moment: decrees of divorce granted abroad to Hungarian nationals are equally recognizable in Hungary (Art. 71).

4. Much less can be said on the *recognition of the validity of foreign judgments* passed in matters of declaration of death and on the *enforcement* of such judgment. Hungarian law does not refuse to recognize foreign judgments declaring foreign nationals legally dead [Art. 70 (1) of the Code]; what is more, as has been seen, Hungarian courts declare foreign nationals legally dead too. By contrast, in cases of Hungarian nationals, Hungarian law essentially knows no judgment other than Hungarian, inasmuch as the Code lays down the general rule that "the judgment of a foreign court or other authority on matters subject to the exclusive jurisdiction of a Hungarian court or other authority may be recognized only in cases specified herein" [Art. 70 (2)]. Since, as was indicated above, declarations of legal death of Hungarian nationals are generally within the exclusive jurisdiction of Hungary and the Code allows no exception to the rule just mentioned, foreign judgments are not recognizable within the meaning of Hungarian law (which is but a follow-through to the contradiction). The only permitted exception is the "loophole" left by the Code is in expressing that if an international treaty contains conflicting provisions, the rules thereof must apply (Art. 2). Indeed, there are cases in which agreements on legal assistance subject legal death declarations to conflicting provisions, which again vary by approach. Some of these state that a foreign legal death declaration of a Hungarian national is also recognizable in Hungary, provided that a similar decision of a Hungarian authority is recognized in the other State. Others provide for the recognition in Hungary of foreign judgments declaring foreign nationals legally

dead. According to still others, a judgment on the legal death declaration of a national of the other contracting party must have effect only in the judgment country, but the effect of the judgment must not be extended to the State whose national was declared dead.

§33. PERSONAL RIGHTS

1. The rights pertaining to individuals and, in numerous aspects, to legal persons are governed by a considerable body of differentiated rules in the various legal systems. Different factors of legal development, however, have caused *notable discrepancies* between national laws. Important changes in these rights have also occurred in the recent development of Hungarian civil law. To take but one example, claims for compensation as a remedy for damage to personal rights were available prior to the reform of civil law only if material loss had also resulted; no action lay for moral or consequential damage, but it is now permitted by the amended Civil Code. Furthermore, national laws show extremely great differences as to the range and amount of damages for non-economic loss.

It is these differences between national laws and the ensuing conflicts of laws with respect to personal rights that present a practical need for these rights to be regulated by private international law as well. The principal rule of Hungarian law is that *personal rights* are subject to the personal law, i.e. mainly to the law of nationality. This applies to such institutions as the individual's rights to his name, image, recorded voice, life, physical integrity, personal freedom, honour, secrets, the inviolability of privacy, or of the premises of a legal person, to all of the legal relationships which express and govern person's personality, as if protecting it externally, in its manifestations and identity.

With regard to the right to a name, a few words may be said on whether titles of nobility or other feudal ranks and names as incidents of the category of personal rights, which have been abolished in Hungary, can be protected if related claims are brought by foreigners before the Hungarian forum. The question is of little, if any, relevance today in the purely domestic setting, but a Hungarian court or other authority could hardly deny protection, for reasons of public policy, to such claims of foreigners based on foreign law.

3. A special duality, understandable in view of practical considerations, can be observed in the regulation that while the existence and extent of personal rights are governed by the personal law, "*claims arising from the infringement of personal rights shall be decided under the law of the place and time of the injury*" [Art. 10 (2) of the Code]. Moreover, the principle of the more favourable law comes into play here: "if the Hungarian law provides more favourable compensation for the person injured, the claim shall be adjudicated according to Hungarian law" (*ibid.*). Underlying this approach motivated by practical considerations is a phenomenon spilling over into the law of tortious liability and

the difficulty in having the legal consequences of wrongs separated in a generalized way from the values of the law applicable in the place where the tort was committed (see §§84–85).

While these rules are intended to protect any injured persons and to impose sanctions on any wrongdoers, the legislator directed that their practical application be chiefly by the Hungarian fora (courts). Seen from the angle of *judicial practice*, of concrete cases, the above provisions offer the Hungarian court the following main options for a solution: (a) A foreigner – a national of State A – brings an action in Hungary for violation of his reputation by a book published (also) in Hungary; its story is about him, told in a way revealing his identity, and gravely violates his personal rights (good reputation) by describing or alleging false facts, situations and characteristic traits. Within the meaning of the above rules, the Hungarian court will ascertain and establish the occurrence of the wrong, not under Art. 78 of the Hungarian Civil Code, but under the law of State A governing personal rights. As the next step, it will have to apply the relevant provisions of the Civil Code [Art. 84. and Art. 85 (2)] to the legal consequences of the wrong. (b) A Hungarian daily or periodical published abroad – in State A – violates the personal rights of a national of a foreign State – State B. The wrong itself is to be decided by the Hungarian court according to the law of State B, but the legal consequences thereof are governed by the law of State A. Since, by relying on the principle of the more favourable law, the court may also apply the sanctions of Hungarian law (the cited provisions of the Civil Code), it has to compare the law of State A with Hungarian law and if, in consideration of all the circumstances of the case, it finds the latter to be more favourable, it must decide accordingly. (c) A Hungarian national sues in Hungary an illustrated magazine of State A for carrying his image without his consent in the form of an advertising photo. The Hungarian court will judge the violation of personality by Hungarian law (Art. 79 of the Civil Code), but will rely on the law of the place where the tort was committed, i.e. of State A, for determining the legal consequences of the violation, while it will have to do so under Hungarian law if it finds that law more favourable to the person injured.

CHAPTER X

THE STATE IN PRIVATE INTERNATIONAL LAW

§34. THE CONDITION OF THE STATE AS A LEGAL SUBJECT AND ITS RELEVANCE IN PRIVATE INTERNATIONAL LAW

1. Private international law governs legal relationships presenting foreign elements and hence likely to give rise to conflicts between the legal systems involved. The norms of private international law resolve such conflicts of laws by indicating the international law of a State under which a particular case is to be decided. In respect of persons this means determination of the law governing their personal status and their condition as subjects at law, which, as was seen, comprise questions like legal and disposing capacity, their substance, commencement, change and termination, and protection of personal rights. *The condition of the State as a legal subject in general* is, in this sense, controlled not by private international law, but by internal law, namely constitutional law, and, in interstate relations, by international law. In this respect, the method of regulation by private international law, based on the assumption of conflicts between systems of law, is out of place. There can be no question of rendering the internal private law of a foreign State applicable to the legal capacity of the State, its existence and extent, by reference to a relevant remitting rule of private international law.

2. The condition of the State as a legal subject nevertheless implies that the State may be a *subject of civil-law relationships*. It is a clearly stated position, both in legislation and in legal literature, that the State may be a subject of any civil-law relationship except those of which, notionally, only a natural person can be a subject. The question of which *state organ* is *to represent the State in such relationships is decided by imperative rules of internal law*. In Hungarian law this organ is defined by the Civil Code (Art. 27) as being generally the Minister of Finance or the state organ which may be designated for that purpose. [With the coming into force of the Act on the Treasury Directorate for Legal Affairs and with it the repeal of the said Art. 27, the powers to represent the State has been vested in this new organization (the Directorate) within the meaning of Act XIV of 1991 amending the Civil Code]. The right of the State

to decide which of its organs may act on its behalf in civil-law relationships is, irrespective of the source of law governing it, an internal matter of constitutional law, an element of state sovereignty. The above-mentioned incidents of the condition of the State as a legal subject (both in general and in civil law) cannot be challenged under the law of a foreign State or under the terms of some foreign jurisdiction by invoking any norm of private international law. The relevant rules are consequently of absolute application, thus excluding *ab initio* the basic proposition of private international law, namely conflicts of laws and their resolution through conflict norms.

3. *However, one side of the civil-law transactions of the State comes under the rules of private international law, viz. the question of which forum has jurisdiction and what is the applicable law if a State is party to a legal relationship in civil law.* In fact, this is the question of immunity in private international law.

§35. ON THE IMMUNITY OF THE STATE IN GENERAL – THE STATE IN THE ECONOMY AND THE EVOLUTION OF FUNCTIONAL IMMUNITY

1. *Notionally* the immunity of the State means – most generally and traditionally – that the State cannot be subjected to the jurisdiction and substantive law of another State. The question emerges, however, whether the immunity of the State also extends to its civil- (commercial) law transactions and related disputes. No doubt, this is first of all a question of jurisdiction and, additionally, the applicable law in various types of transactions. While the existence of the State and its legal capacity as well as the organizational aspects thereof, namely the condition of the State as a subject at law, are notionally outside the scope of private international law, which also theoretically presupposes choice (of the law of another State), *jurisdiction and the law governing the civil-law transactions of the State (the facing of immunity in this context) turn into a problem of private international law.* The question is rightly posed on principle, and with no small practical relevance, that if the State is one of the parties to a civil-law transaction (is a member of or a shareholder in an economic association, or enters into a civil contract through a *sui generis* state organ), what should the reasonable answer of private international law be as to *jurisdiction* and the *applicable law.* According to the principle of absolute immunity, the answer of private international law should be that the State enjoys full immunity in all legal relations, including the domain of civil-law transactions. This was the generally accepted view in earlier periods but it is undergoing a change in our time. According to more recent concepts, *immunity is not enjoyed by the State when doing an act not of the nature of public law (iure imperii), but of civil or commercial law (iure gestionis), one ordinarily done by subjects of civil or commercial law. This is the doctrine of functional or relative immunity.* It is really

the appearance of this doctrine that made this problem a concern of private international law and opened up the theoretical possibility of choice as to the application of the law of a State other than the State concerned, in the form of the law governing a particular type of legal relation *(lex causae)*, and for the submission of disputes to a forum other than that of the State involved.

2. Speaking generally of state immunity, it should be stressed that the question of applicable substantive law has its rationale only on the assumption that the State, in a dispute involving its civil-law transactions, may be brought under a jurisdiction different from its own. If the latter is to be excluded by law and the State be brought before its own forum in all its civil-law disputes, the question of applicable substantive law would practically remain outside the scope of private international law. The forum of a State will adjudicate its own legal transactions under the law of another State only in cases and situations that rarely occur. *The key aspect of immunity is* therefore *principally jurisdictional.* Immunity becomes of relevance to the applicable law as well, if the law also recognizes the jurisdiction of a foreign forum over specified matters.

3. Finally, a general question of immunity concerns the *organs of the State* by whose acts the State may be regarded as the subject of a legal relationship, namely *whose acts are to be regarded as done directly by the State*. This question is fairly ambiguous unlike the widely held view, stated from different angles (see §37), according to which acts of state-owned enterprises do not imply the presence of the State in civil-law transactions, but are acts of the particular state-owned enterprise as a legal person distinct from the State. In general terms it may nevertheless be said that, admitting the functional immunity approach, an act is deemed to be one of the State when done by an organ of state power or administration, usually by central organs of state administration, in the exercise of *sui generis* public-law functions.

4. It should be stated that *historical and comparative surveys* point to the reign of absolute immunity at an early stage of legal development.

Absolute immunity is an outgrowth of sovereignty. When sovereigns acted only in constitutional functions deriving from their sovereignty, the principle that a sovereign had no power over another sovereign (*par in parem non habet imperium*) clearly asserted itself. In the 20th century, however, particularly in recent decades, this situation has basically altered. Pervasive state intervention in economic relations, including intensive participation by the State in legal relationships, under both public and civil law, is characteristic even of the modern capitalist States and, indeed, is their distinctive feature, while it notionally followed from the function filled by the former socialist States in the organization of the economy. *The State becomes a subject of wide-ranging international civil-law relationships as a corollary to the intensity of international* relations, including *economic relations*. The fact that, owing to intensive diplomatic, consular and other interstate relations, States hold property abroad to a much greater extent than previously (buy, erect and operate buildings and institutes, which entails the natural need for them to make contracts of sale, lease, services and labour), represents but one area of such involvement. Another domain of civil-law transactions is state participation in the establishment of enterprises, and in the execution of investment projects, where States not only have States as their counterparts, and the legal disputes of purely interstate enterprises are, by their nature, similarly subject to corporate law. Given the large volume of international personal transactions, the State is often involved in matters of inheritance, which are under the control of civil law. Furthermore, States make contracts of other types, such as various state orders (purchases, tenders) and other operative economic undertakings.

5. In the practice of capitalist States all these have combined in comparatively recent times to increase the number of private-law disputes to which States are parties. It became increasingly evident that the security of transactions and ultimately the interests of the State are adversely affected by situations in which the State is intensively involved in civil- and commercial-law transactions on the one hand and, on the other, seeks to avoid being subject as a sovereign to the kind of settlement which is commonly used in disputes arising out of such transactions. Under such circumstances there was no defence for the legal tenet referred to in a relevant English High Court decision and stating in part as follows: "No principle of international law ... has gone so far as to authorize a sovereign prince to assume the character of a trader, when it is for his benefit; and when he incurs an obligation to a private subject to throw off ... his disguise, and appear as a sovereign, claiming for his own time, all the attributes of his character ..." (Charkich Case, 1873). The said contradictory situation led one supreme court after another in the advanced Western countries *to adopt the doctrine of functional or relative immunity* in the 1950s and 1960s. This was done in the United States in 1952, in the Federal Republic of Germany in 1963 by a ruling of the Constitutional Court, and in France in 1969 by the Supreme Court (Court de Cassation). The Western countries went even further: since considerable variations could still be observed in the application of functional immunity by the various countries, the West European States signed in 1972 the European Convention on State Immunity, regional in scope, which extended the principle of functional immunity to, and made its application uniform in, all these countries through unification of international law. Moreover, functional immunity, which was increasingly relied upon in judicial practice, was also legislatively covered and confirmed by some States in more recent years (US Foreign Sovereign Immunities Act of 1976, UK State Immunity Act of 1978). Mention is further deserved by the fact that the Court of the European Communities, the European Court of Justice, as part of the legal mechanism of the West European economic integration, was granted jurisdiction, with elements of sovereignty, over several important matters connected with the process of economic integration on which no forum other than that of the State involved had previously had power to decide.

6. Substantial efforts for a general acceptance of functional immunity have also been made at the level of *multilateral conventions*.

(a) One alternative of related developments is represented by those draft conventions which would *generally* extend functional immunity *to the State* (to all *sui generis* state organs) if engaged in *iure gestionis* transactions. Such a draft convention is being discussed (though nevertheless not yet finalized) by the UN International Law Commission (on the state of the codification, see McCaffrey). After the Belgrade Conference of the International Law Association in 1980 (Hungary is also a member of ILA), when a resolution was passed to propose a draft convention on state immunity (Report of the Fifty-Ninth Conference, 1980, pp. 208 *et seq.*), a draft convention was codified at the 1982 ILA Conference in Montreal (ILA Montreal Draft Convention on State Immunity, declaring the doctrine of functional immunity in its long Article III).

(b) Hungary, too, acceded to the Vienna Convention on Diplomatic Relations of 1961 and to that on Consular Relations of 1963. The doctrine of functional immunity is present in these international treaties and in bilateral agreements related to the subject, but is *confined to diplomatic and consular missions*, as these instruments provide that exemption, i.e. immunity, shall be enjoyed in the known contexts by the staff members of diplomatic and consular missions but such extension will not apply when these missions and their staff members act or participate in civil- (commercial) law transactions.

7. It is in recent years that this problem has begun to attract more attention *in the literature of the Central and Eastern European countries*. The previous predominance of absolute immunity in literature is on the wane, chiefly under the impact of facts, emerging in legal development.

(a) In the course of codification of private international law *some countries introduced, though in different ways, the principle of functional immunity*, with definitions nearly as precise as found in the textbooks. This principle is formulated with respect to subjects within the ambit of the said Vienna Conventions in Art. 111 of Act No. 296 of 1964 on the Polish Code of Civil Procedure and, with a general reference to the State in Art. 47 of the 1963 former Czechoslovak Code of Private International Law: "... the jurisdiction of Czechoslovak courts shall extend to such occupations and commercial activities of persons otherwise enjoying exemption (including the state organs mentioned in para. 1) as are outside their official functions". The 1961 Act of the former Soviet Union on the Foundations of Soviet Legislation on Civil Procedure gave a unique response to the described process of development, choosing to apply functional immunity by way of reciprocity.

(b) The need also arose *in the system of relations, now a thing of history, between the former socialist countries*, particularly under the pressure of States undertaking ever more material (economic) commitments, for a legal regulation of state liability for those commitments. Although no general norms had been established (with no time left by the systemic change), the various concrete interstate economic organizations (*Interelektro, Interatomenergo, Intertextilmas*) practically came to admit functional immunity in their stipulations on dispute resolution. [See Mádl: *A külgazdaság és a nemzetközi beruházások joga* (The external economy and the law of international investment).]

8. Thus it may be stated in summary that functional immunity is an expression by private international law of the objective fact that under modern-day conditions the State directly and extensively participates in economic transactions. Therefore its admission within reasonable bounds is also a matter of streamlining the law, for the added purpose of furthering the economic role of the State.

§36. IMMUNITY AS REGULATED IN HUNGARIAN LAW

1. *Hungarian legislation* and legal thinking as its conceptual basis have been *developing in a creative kind of antagonism with respect to immunity.* The influence of the classical thesis of absolute immunity (in both literature and practice) has been strong. However, writers with innovative minds and responsive to new needs had argued for years that the modern relationship between the State and the economy in the matter of immunity was to be regarded as a negation of the old thesis and that the State's legal relations of a material (economic) nature and its legal disputes called for an institutional synthesis. Our previous references to comparative law have indicated where a synthesis is thought to be found in other countries and in international legislation. Though marked by no small contradictions of "progress with prudence", Hungarian legal development likewise is moving virtually in this same direction. The said creative antagonism also prevailed in the codification of immunity under the appropriate sections of the Hungarian Code of Private International Law (see Mádl: *Új szakaszban ...*, in the List of Sources). With the Code now in effect, that antagonism can be felt not in a wholly positive sense, as can be seen in the contradictory and complicated nature of regulation, which appears to have produced a multi-tier solution by progressive quests and which it is not even easy to understand without knowing the underlying basis. This does not imply the failure of the Code to represent progress over the previous situation. Yet the reader and anyone else seeking orientation in law, having grasped the actual substance of regulation, may well ask: "What does this mean?", or "Why was it not possible to have this expressed more clearly by means of a stricter drafting?". We can say by way of excuse that a law cannot spell out everything in one place, and that it is justifiable for more comprehensive statutes to be drafted within an appropriate inner structure, with principal rules and exceptions arranged in a general and a special part. At times this raises difficulties in recognizing the intention of the legislator, even in those cases complying with the legislator's intentions. Avoidance of these difficulties is only one instance of the possibility and necessity for both theoreticians and practising specialists to contribute by creative legal thinking to a modern and realistic implementation of the legislator's conception.

2. As noted earlier, the *Code* has made considerable progress *in the Hungarian positive law of immunity.* On the one hand, it has furnished a detailed regulation and written rules in comparison to the previous situation and, on the other, it has abandoned, albeit with some contradictions, the exclusivity of absolute immunity, thus opening the law to functional immunity in several aspects.

A clear-cut solution, free from contradictions either of logic or of drafting, would have been for the Code to prescribe the general application of the principle of relative or functional immunity (as did, e.g., the former Czechoslovak Code of Private International Law). Nonetheless, the progress made by Hungarian codification can be discerned in a more differentiated approach to both drafting and substantive solutions. The full answer of the Hungarian Code unfolds itself spatially in four steps (readings) which, however, do not, as will be seen, express logically closed sets of norms, a clearly stated position as to the acceptance of functional immunity. The Code's position has to be pieced together from its global approach.

(a) The first step determines the substantive law applicable to civil-law relationships of the State. According to Art. 17, *such relationships of the Hungarian State are, as a rule, governed by its own law* but *three important exceptions are allowed* for the application of foreign law, namely where (i) "the State has expressly consented to the application of foreign law"; or (ii) "the legal relationship concerns foreign real property owned or intended to be acquired by the State"; or (iii) "the legal relationship concerns participation in an economic enterprise involving foreign interests". True, this solution still leaves a whole range of civil-law relationships under the control of absolute immunity yet the said exceptions apply to frequent incidents of important transactions in respect of which it was reasonable to recognize the applicability of foreign substantive law. However, this procedure would acquire a real or full meaning only if the Code were also to have admitted functional immunity also with respect to jurisdiction over such cases, but it does not (at least in the first reading). What the Code did – if not in the first, then in the fourth reading – will be seen in the fourth step to be discussed below. At this juncture we can anticipate this much: it is not very practical to assume that if, e.g., in acquiring property for the purpose of establishing a foreign mission, we recognize the relevant substantive law of the particular foreign State but reserve the legal dispute for the Hungarian jurisdiction (as the legal relationships of a State are recognized as being subject to the jurisdiction of its own forum alone), it would imply that the Hungarian forum would apply foreign law to the legal dispute of a *sui generis* state organ of Hungary. A different interpretation is also possible: the application of a foreign substantive law requires foreign jurisdiction, to wit, functional immunity is to be recognized in the areas contemplated with respect to both the applicable law and jurisdiction. This seems to be supported, as will be seen, by the fourth step which may be construed as suggesting a general "heal-all" formula.

(b) Another element of the Hungarian concept of immunity, as conclusively formulated in the second step of the conditions, concerning *exclusive Hungarian jurisdiction,* appears in Art. 55 which provides that "Hungarian courts or other authorities shall have exclusive jurisdiction ... (d) in proceeding against the Hungarian State, a Hungarian state authority or administrative organ; (e) in proceedings against a Hungarian national acting as a diplomatic representative abroad or otherwise enjoying immunity from foreign jurisdiction, in cases where, *by virtue of an international agreement or of reciprocity*, no proceedings against such person may be instituted abroad". This is one more instance of a strict and clear formulation appearing, at first sight, to favour absolute immunity, albeit with very few exceptions allowed.

(c) The third step reveals this same approach, but conversely, in the case of *excluded jurisdiction*, where Art. 56 of the Code excludes from Hungarian jurisdiction legal disputes of foreign States. Yet on this point we are a little bolder: we proceed in the legal dispute of a foreign State if immunity has been waived by that State, and consider our forum as also having jurisdiction over counterclaims originating in the same case (Art. 57). Article 55 would not, on this ground, allow such course of action *vis-à-vis* the Hungarian State, although, following from its general legal capacity, such action might obviously be taken in any matter.

Accordingly, a generally valid solution is offered only by waiver of immunity. Thus, under a strict interpretation of the Code, functional immunity accorded by international treaty or reciprocity extends only to persons enjoying diplomatic immunity [Art. 56 (c)]. It is solely in their disputes that a State other than their own (i.e. the Hungarian State) is permitted to proceed, provided that the dispute arises out of a legal relationship connected with the exercise of some function under civil or commercial law, and not under diplomatic or public law. As is known, the Vienna Convention of 1961 on Diplomatic Relations and the Vienna Convention of 1963 on Consular Relations, which were ratified by Hungary (Law-Decree No. 22 of 1965 and Law-Decree No. 13 of 1987, respectively), are such international treaties of general application, and Arts. 55 and 56 of the Code referred to above adopted the corresponding provisions thereof.

But what is the case with the civil-law relationships of other organs of a foreign State? It would seem necessary at least for cases of functional immunity allowed by reciprocity and international treaty to be extended to these relationships as well, which it would perhaps be possible to do under a somewhat looser interpretation [see item 3 (c) (ii) below]. By not doing so, the Hungarian law would put itself in an unequal position. We can be as absolutist as we wish in the matter of exclusive Hungarian jurisdiction with respect to the Hungarian State, but this will hardly bring influence to bear upon anyone abroad, for the foreign fora will apply to Hungarian state organs their own rules on functional immunity, with effect mostly in their respective countries. It would thus be entirely asymmetrical and hence unreasonable for a Hungarian forum to treat foreign state organs with such absolutist reverence. This approach could be replaced by narrowing the scope of excluded jurisdiction, i.e. by expanding our possibilities of proceeding in respect to foreign state organs, notably by practising functional immunity, as indicated above, at least when justifiable on grounds of reciprocity. As a matter of fact, we should not rely on international treaty as a category for opening more channels since States might take that course of action in any matter, regardless of whether or not the code of private international law indicates such a possibility.

(d) It is all the more justified to adopt the said approach to our "excluded jurisdiction" since we take a disproportionately large view, again surprising and failing to endorse the foreign proposition, in the more sensitive area of recognition of foreign judgments against the Hungarian State. This is done in the fourth step, where functional immunity is admitted, yet not in favour but to the detriment of the Hungarian State. Article 72 of the Code states in general terms that a decision passed abroad against the Hungarian State is also to be recognized in case of *reciprocity*, in addition to waiver of immunity and to a similar provision of an international treaty, or more specifically, if in the particular case "the foreign court or other authority may also proceed by virtue of ... reciprocity". As here understood, reciprocity extends not only to civil- or commercial-law disputes of persons or agencies enjoying diplomatic immunity, but also to civil-law disputes of all state organs (by "dispute" is meant one in civil law although the term "civil law" or a similar limitative reference is not used in the Code). It stands to reason that in order for the forum of a foreign State to proceed on the basis of reciprocity in a civil-law dispute of the Hungarian State, it is necessary that the Hungarian court do likewise in a civil-law dispute of the foreign State concerned. Somebody has to start reciprocity. It would be meaningless to talk about reciprocity and exclude this possibility and assumption, and in both a notional and a practical context. The Code is therefore justified in laying down the pertinent provision which, if properly interpreted, can also be applied to this problem, namely that where a rule of law refers to reciprocity, the existence thereof must generally be presumed (Art. 6). By the presumption of reciprocity the Hungarian law has essentially taken the necessary step for eliminating the anomaly that application of reciprocity can in effect never be started by a State alone. Therefore, in order to furnish a take-off point for regulation, the Code spells out the fiction: there is reciprocity even if it has not been actually practised yet. So we recognize foreign judgments and, in the context of the foregoing statements, this notionally results, on our side of reciprocity, in our similarly passing judgments on foreign States so that they may also recognize our judgments (which they do nonetheless) and that we may also recognize theirs, even without the presumption of reciprocity. This is how, though intricately, the avenue is opened up to mutually admitted functional immunity, with the Code recommending, as it were, the practice of reciprocity regarding functional immunity (Art. 72).

Hence it follows, in our view, that with respect to civil and commercial law relationships, including those not specified in Art. 17 (i) Hungary may, with due allowance made for all the circumstances of the case, accept the action of a foreign forum in a legal dispute otherwise subject to exclusive Hungarian jurisdiction, and (ii) considering that this is based on reciprocity, a Hungarian court may also adjudicate on a civil-law dispute of a foreign State which would otherwise be subject to excluded jurisdiction. Thus, beside waiver of immunity and a relevant international treaty, reciprocity represents the third main and, in this case, general way as regards the acceptance of functional immunity, and it seems reasonable to have it judiciously applied in practice under the regulation by the Code and in keeping with Hungarian interests.

3. *Practice* will now be viewed from the angle of the above regulation.

(a) Numerous examples and legal proceedings, both old and new, could be cited, with bearings on Hungary, to illustrate how real issues are resolved. As the present volume is intended for a university textbook, too, it will perhaps be of interest to recall that in the wake of Wor!d War One a Hungarian university, then called Péter Pázmány (and now Lcránd Eötvös), brought an action, precisely as an entity distinct from the State, against the Czechoslovak State to recover its property that that had remained on Czechoslovak territory. True, the proceedings took place before the forum established by the Treaty of Trianon and then before the Permanent Court of International Justice at The Hague, but the action was brought by a person "in private law" against a State and not before the forum of that State, which represents two notable aspects of the functional immunity theory (the judgment is discussed by Váli). The literature (see Deák) records several judgments in which the former socialist countries were the passive objects of functional immunity, but even more of judgments that were passed against Western countries.

Pre-war Hungary received more protection from immunity judgments, often against the theoretical applicability of functional immunity. A Hungarian embassy building against which a writ of execution was issued was protected by the Czechoslovak Supreme Court against an arbitral award of 1928. In 1942 a court of New York dismissed the request of a private party for execution in satisfaction of his pecuniary claim to attach and surrender a picture owned by the Hungarian National Museum, by invoking the thesis that the Museum was a "government instrumentality" and as such was under the protection of immunity.

(b) Instead of citing further concrete examples on this subject, it will be more instructive to give a brief review of the *main types of legal relationships which also raise the questions of immunity and functional immunity in the practice of Hungarian organs.*

(i) To begin with practice concerning the aforesaid embassy context, Hungary operates abroad *sui generis* institutions acting on behalf of the State (embassies, consulates, etc.) and such institutions are also operated in Hungary. This gave and may give rise to the following types of legal disputes (with the involvement of the particular State): (1) property (purchase or lease of immovables, neighbour's rights, etc.); (2) contract of sale (car, energy, furnishings and equipment); (3) contract for service (repairs, maintenance, etc.); (4) insurance (cars, buildings); (5) contract of labour (local employees); (6) bank account contract; (7) non-contractual damages, all these being civil-law categories and potential grounds for legal dispute.

(ii) Given its role and its condition as a legal subject in general, the State participates in civil-law contracts or contracts of association and, conversely, Hungarian enterprises participate in contracts in which the State is (also) their contractual partner.

(iii) As heir general (of necessity), the State may enter into inheritance relationships and hence become a party to disputes under the law of inheritance.

(c) To confront all these and other possible examples, legal cases and relationships with the positive rules of law currently in force in Hungary and to solve them, as if by way of judgment, are no task for this volume to accomplish. Yet, *by way of indication of the possible ways and means of dealing with them*, let us present a few variants and "recommendations" by legal literature, taken to their logical conclusion.

(i) If a Hungarian *sui generis* state organ participates in an association established by international (interstate) treaty, it is practicable to stipulate by contract the mode of dispute settlement.

(ii) Where there is no such contractual stipulation, the applicable law will be that indicated by Art. 17 of the Hungarian Code in respect of legal persons (Art. 18). As regards jurisdiction, the Hungarian forum may proceed in cases where a foreign state organ, if involved in the dispute, has waived immunity (Art. 57). It may also proceed when paras. (a) and (b) of Art. 56 are viewed together, viz. are interpreted in such a way that the provision of para. (b) – under which proceedings may be instituted against a diplomatic agent by virtue of reciprocity or an international agreement – is extended to that of para. (a) – namely to a foreign State and also to its organs in general. By doing so we can say that the Hungarian forum may also proceed in the dispute of a foreign State, and not only one of a diplomatic agent, if, apart from waiver of immunity, the dispute is subject to reciprocity and an international agreement. And considering that reciprocity must be presumed (Art. 6), the proceedings can be deemed to be in accordance with the law. On the other hand, the said "joint interpretation" can be justified by the grammatical collation of the two provisions [the said paras. (a) and (b) contemplated] and by the fact that the Code itself relies on such collation. Article 72 covers recognition of foreign judgments against Hungarian diplomatic agents and others state organs; the three prerequisites of recognition (waiver, international agreement and reciprocity) apply to both categories, so it does not appear unwarranted to suppose that the said result of collation is actually inherent in the Code.

(iii) The same can be said to apply, *mutatis mutandis*, to a legal dispute involving immovable property purchased by a diplomatic mission of the State in, say, Italy or to other possible civil-law contracts of that mission. This situation is more clear-cut and requires no such interpretation as is outlined above, because functional immunity accorded to foreign missions, including those of Hungary, by virtue of an international agreement or of reciprocity is spelled out in the Code (Art. 56), and its provision is also confirmed by the above-mentioned Vienna Conventions from the position of public international law.

(iv) The question of whether a Hungarian enterprise is likely or unlikely to have success, in respect of jurisdiction and substantive law, before the forum of foreign State A, in the case of a contract to which State A is also a party, will be governed by the immunity concept of State A. With regard to the EU countries and the USA the success can be taken for granted in view of what was stated above (§36). True, cases of state involvement in those countries are most rare but not excluded, e.g. in the event of winning a state order (tender). State participation in the developing countries is more frequent; if some form of waiver of immunity cannot be stipulated by contract (it is advisable to do so, e.g. by stipulation of arbitration), there remains the immunity rule of the forum to which the Hungarian party submits its dispute.

(v) As regards now enforcement the following can be said.

– International agreements generally rely on the principle of voluntary (i.e. mandatorily voluntary) enforcement, as it follows from, e.g., the European Convention on Immunity referred to above.

– In the absence of international convention the relevant rules of the particular forum apply. These rules generally cover cases of waiver and reciprocity, as does the Hungarian Code (Art. 72). However, the practice of Western countries goes even further as, under the internal immunity rules, enforcement is effected even in cases not covered by international agreement or reciprocity. The only major obstacle here is the inadmissibility of levy on such property (embassy building, account, etc.) of a foreign State as are destined to support the *sui generis* state function of that State. This principle of law was upheld by, e.g., the judgment passed in 1977 by the Constitutional Court of the Federal Republic of Germany, often cited in international literature and comparing well with a monographic study, concerning the request of a lessor for a writ of execution. In its judgment (*Urteil des BVerfGE vom 13.12.1977 im Filippinen-Fall*) the Court dismissed the lessor's request for a levy of execution on the Embassy of the Republic of the Philippines, to be fixed on its account held at the *Deutsche Bank AG*. It did so despite the fact that the competent German courts had passed a final judgment on the basic issue, and had ruled that the rent claimed by the lessor from the Embassy had been judged without regard to its immunity, on the basis of functional immunity. However, the Constitutional Court held that execution was a different matter. In vain did the complainant plead that the substance of the principal suit was constituted by the nature of the transaction rather than its purpose and function, which had not changed, and that, by its nature, a bank account was also a civil-law institution that could be used to effect any payment. The Court in fact set out the principle of law applicable to this case in the following ruling: while in respect of a claim under substantive law, functional immunity is to be accepted in civil-law transactions in view of the nature (rather than the purpose or function) of a transaction, in respect of execution it is precisely the purpose or function of the asset in question that will mark the confines of functional immunity. The purpose or function of an embassy account consists first of all in ensuring the operation of a *sui generis* state organ, and consequently that is where the realm of absolute immunity begins.

§37. THE STATE AND ITS ENTERPRISE

1. *The relationship between state enterprises and the State comes into the open in connection with the very problem of immunity.* On the one hand, the presence of state-owned (publicly-owned) enterprises in the modern national economies is a common phenomenon, and state enterprises can be expected – despite the process of privatization (see §§59–60) – to retain a significant role for a long time to come in the countries of Central and Eastern Europe. On the other hand, a state enterprise is also deemed to be a State under the laws of some countries, e.g. the USA, even though it is deprived of the cloak of the absolute immunity of sovereign States. As is stated in the American Foreign Sovereign Immunities Act cited earlier, the notion of "foreign State" comprises any agency or instrumentality, which is a separate legal entity either in the form of a corporation or in another form, but the majority share or other proprietary position in it is held by the State or an organ thereof (this "State" nevertheless enjoys no immunity in respect of its commercial-law transactions). By contrast, it is a matter of public record that in Hungary, for instance, state enterprises possessing separate legal personality generally did not and do not require the protection of immunity. However, as will be seen below, their identification with the State nonetheless carries implications in private international law.

If we are to treat distinct things separately, as we indeed should because they are covered by different notions, we should be aware that the problems of immunity cannot really emerge except in *iure gestionis* transactions of *sui generis* state organs. But, as is asked by many, where are the confines of a *sui generis* State? Life does not always fit into the pure abstractions of law. The reason for state enterprises being qualified as a State by the aforesaid American legislation lay in the different immunity concept of other countries. However, once an enterprise relatively distinct from the State and owned by the State with a minimal majority share had been deemed by legislation to be a State, this same Immunities Act naturally had to spell out, under the doctrine of functional immunity also espoused by American law (and, indeed, having unfolded itself first in the American practice), that not even a State so broadly conceived is entitled to immunity if its operation is manifested in *iure gestionis* acts. Well, this is precisely the approach that is embodied in the American Immunities Act.

This is partly an extensive concept of the State, partly a definitely limitative concept of immunity, which extends the protection of immunity only to explicitly *sui generis* state acts of a public-law nature and is also manifested in different court decisions on legal disputes between East and West. These decisions first declare a particular state economic organization existing as a legal entity in the given country to be a State, and then spell out that such an organization is not entitled to the protection of immunity in the concrete legal dispute because its acts are deemed by their nature to be *iure gestionis* by their nature [see Mádl: *A külgazdaság és a nemzetközi beruházások joga* (The external economy and the law of international investment)].

However, the relationship between the State and its enterprise also emerges *in areas other than immunity*. It came to present a significant problem precisely in the previous context, namely with regard to this aspect: where are the confines of the State, for if a state enterprise is involved in an economic transaction, which is an incident of a usually mass phenomenon, can it still not be identified with the State in certain matters of property or contract? How are the acts of both related to each other, are they related at all, or is a particular state enterprise to be regarded as completely distinct from the State as owner when it is moving about in the domain of contractual relations while attending to its business and gets involved in routine disputes as well? Is it that enterprise alone which is before the forum or the owner is also to look behind it, especially when a dispute between it and its partner has erupted over an act of the State?

This set of problems should be discussed for various reasons. One reason is the obvious relevance of the aforesaid questions. The other is that, under the well-known economic concept, state enterprises played a dominant role and will for long retain a significant one in many countries of Central and Eastern Europe, while a large public sector also operates in the advanced market economy countries. The third lies in the fact that the described questions are governed by articulated concepts and jural postulates according to which the separate autonomy of state enterprises, conforming to market requirements, is accepted in the Western countries as well. Also to be discussed here are the main elements and the evolving pattern of this trend, while it should be stressed, in consideration of what has been said in connection with immunity, that the designation "state enterprises" refers in our exposition generally to state-owned enterprises, be they economic units operating either in the form of enterprise in corporate law or of a *sui generis* state enterprise in a particular case.

2. Similarly, the relationship between the enterprise and State is a subject of thorough scientific analysis *in international literature on comparative law*. Therefore we will not go into details here. Analyses in comparative literature extend, within the framework of this relationship, to the determinant conceptual proposition that a state enterprise is an economic and legal entity relatively distinct from the State. Still, an additional problem to be addressed here, state enterprises were in the past often identified with the State in the arena of interna-

tional economic relations and conversely, because, among other things, state enterprises are designated with the term "state" and (mainly) because they are owned by the State and as such act as enterprises of the State in the said arena. Repeated attempts have been made to sue the State itself for liabilities of particular enterprises, or to recover debts (collect assets) of the State as such. There are examples of cases of the converse, too, namely of similar actions taken against state enterprises to satisfy economic claims against the State. Again, it was occasionally challenged that, in the case of state enterprises, general economic management by the State was not sufficiently separated from the exercise of owner's rights. Partners were not therefore content with state enterprises pleading such general acts of the State (e.g. an enterprise was unable to perform the contract because it was also subject to an export ban in the nature of act of God, or *vis major*). It is claimed that the State and its enterprise are one and the same thing in this matter as well, and that neither can perform such a schizophrenic act except at its own risk. Thus the core of the problem is that the separate identity of state enterprises was denied in such situations because a state enterprise was in fact the *alter ego* on the State. The thesis which can be propounded on the basis of international literature and of judicial practice concerned with East-West relations is the opposite of these contentions, namely the conclusion, drawn from comparative studies indicated above, that a state enterprise is *an independent economic and legal entity relatively distinct from the State*, just as a limited liability company is from its shareholders.

3. The said thesis prevails in this vein not only in the public sector of the developed market economy countries, operating under corporate law, but *held and still holds also in respect to the countries of Central and Eastern Europe*, as is evidenced by legislation and legal literature alike.

(a) Internal (national) legislation and practice are unambiguous. It is trite to say that limitation of legal entities' liability to their own property is a general principle of modern corporate and company law. The state enterprise as a legal person, as a legal and economic entity, occupies an outstanding place in the regulation of legal persons and in the related sources of law. Under the Hungarian Civil Code (Art. 31) and Act VI of 1977 on State Enterprises (Arts. 22 and 27), a state enterprise is a legal person, enjoys autonomy, within the framework of laws and regulations, in managing the assets entrusted to it, and is liable for its obligations with the assets entrusted to and administered by it.

In some countries the identity and autonomy of state enterprises have been strengthened in the course of reforms and particularly in the process of transformations. In general, the State has retreated or is retreating to positions of general strategy, legislation and direction. Parallel to this went the process, in Hungary at any rate, of state enterprises receiving practically full autonomy in the domain of transactions and operative economic activities. Among other things, legislation went so far as to restrict sharply state intervention in the economic dynamics of enterprises, by subjecting the withdrawal of the assets of enterprises or instructions to carry out specific activities, to statutory requirements like procedure for privatization or exceptional situations (e.g. war or emergency).

From the general principles described above and from the corresponding legal regulations, it follows that a state enterprise may be sued and that final court orders or arbitral awards are enforceable against it to the extent of its assets.

(b) In line with the above concepts, it is clearly emphasized in *legal literature* that recognition of state enterprises as legal persons and their treatment as entities relatively distinct from the State in accordance with the important substantial element of the former are actually a key aspect of the normal workings of the economy and an indispensable precondition for cooperation on the market.

4. In the light of *international legislation and practice* it is an equally well-known fact that state enterprises in the Central and Eastern European countries were and are capable of being sued for their liabilities in the field of their international relations. They are also liable to levy of execution on their assets under a final judgment. This follows from, *inter alia,* the fact that these countries are parties to the European Convention on International Commercial Arbitration done at Geneva in 1961 and to the New York Convention of 1958 on the Recognition and Enforcement of Foreign Arbitral Awards. These are all indications of the capacity of state enterprises to sue and be sued in the said countries as well as of the enforceability of judgments against them in the international sphere. Consequently a state enterprise cannot plead its condition as such nor state immunity in order to be exempted from compliance with its obligations. Furthermore, the external partner to the contract has neither chance nor any need to sue the State or another state-owned enterprise for the liabilities of a particular state enterprise. Finally, as regards recognition and enforcement of foreign judgments against state enterprises, related procedures are clearly available not only under the said international conventions but, by virtue of international law, also under bilateral interstate agreements and on the basis of reciprocity (for a fuller treatment of immunity, see §§35–36; on the recognition and enforcement of arbitral awards and foreign judgments in general, see §§117–121).

5. The preceding item referred briefly to legal practice in general. Next we shall deal with *major cases and legal developments*, often discussed in international literature and at other fora, in which judicial practice can be said to have established the thesis that a state enterprise cannot be regarded, and the reasons why, as the *alter ego* of the State. This thesis is, in accordance with the above statement, naturally valid even if a state-owned enterprise is operated as one in corporate law.

(a) "In the beginning" there was, has existed for a long time and *gained general acceptance* a recognized principle of private international law, namely that the status of legal persons is, regardless of their owner, to be governed by the law of nationality, or the law applicable to them (as a general rule, the law of the place of registration or of the seat). The motives of this concept, shared by the private international law of both Eastern and Western countries, are well known (see §§42–43). If this approach is applied without differentiation and discrimination, it should also naturally be applied to state-owned enterprises, with the obvious conclusion that if state enterprises come into being and operate as independent legal entities, they are liable for their obligations with their assets to the extent regulated by the law of nationality. This is normally the internal law of the State in which the particular state enterprise has its seat. And within the meaning of that law, as was seen, state enterprises are no *alter egoes* of the State and hence may not be sued for liabilities of the State as owner, and *vice versa*.

(b) Yet this state of affairs was followed by *differentiation,* with support from the evolution of enterprise (company) structures and from changes in the international forms of enterprise (company) behaviour. States grew sensitive to the application of their own tax laws, rules on competition and consumer protection, and laws of bankruptcy. Such sensitivity and its consequences resided essentially in States insisting on application of their own laws, controlling the given sphere and matters, to foreign enterprises as well, and even in cases where the nationality principle indicated a law different from that otherwise applicable to foreign enterprises. More and more ground was gained by the practice under which the law of proceeding fora refused to recognize the protecting shield or umbrella of the law indicated by the law of the foreign nationality of the particular foreign enterprises against the relevant rules of internal law. So the process set in of splitting the integument of corporate law in order to enable the fora to reach the real owners and "principals" (e.g. the parent companies), and furthermore, to treat foreign enterprises as non-foreigners in the given areas. This approach soon achieved a "status of its own". The phenomenon of disregarding traditional corporate law (*Durchgriff*) developed as it were into a powerful natural concept; as such, it soon reached by intensive efforts the state enterprises of foreign countries, namely their legal personality, as well. By partially disregarding the legal status of enterprises governed by the traditionally applicable law of nationality, legal literature moved towards challenging, under the said special internal-law approach, the view that state enterprises were relatively independent of the State. In so doing legal writing was motivated, moreover, by the home trend (*Heimwärtsstreben*), which is apt to conceive of external phenomena in keeping with the internal scale of values on the general plane, too. In this case it led legal thinking to view the relationship between the State and the enterprise according to the State's own scale of values concerning the enterprises rather than to the foreign law, alien to it, as indicated by the law of nationality. This was the essence of the aforementioned *disregard theory* or *Durchgriffstheorie* as referred to in English and German literature on the subject. Both designations are good expressions of the substance of this theory, namely the fact that, by reliance on it, the fora do without the law otherwise applicable to the particular legal person, as if reaching beyond it and thus deciding its disputes under another statute.

The core and substance of the problem – as to whether a state enterprise is sued for an act of nationalization by the State or a state act of economic policy (e.g. export licences) is involved in a particular case – is that the State and its enterprise appear as the same identity under this concept. The state enterprise is but the *alter ego of the State.* Even if state enterprises are distinct from the State, they embody the property of the State, their economic activities are those of the State. In case of unlawful expropriation, it should be necessary and possible to take action against state enterprises on account of this act of the State. In the other context it is claimed that the State, proceeding as an authority (issuing export or import licences), certainly will not act against the interests of its own enterprises. The State will always tend to consider the interests of its enterprises in deciding on licences, namely granting a licence if it is of commercial advantage to its enterprise and denying or withdrawing it if compliance by a state enterprise with its contractual obligations is disadvantageous to the enterprise. In other words, there is a kind of conspiracy at work between the State and its enterprise. In it, the state enterprise pretends to have relative autonomy while it is actually a forward-based entity, an undercover agent of the State, which performs state functions in international economic processes according to the criteria of the State's economic policy. Of course, this reasoning leads to the logical conclusion that the enterprise should bear full responsibility for its breach of contract, despite the fact that performance was prevented by a State-imposed ban on exports or imports, a circumstance which is seen as an act of God, i.e. a saving grace, everywhere. Here, however, one cannot speak of *vis major*, because for it to be an extenuating circumstance it should have been caused by the State as distinct from the enterprise, as a public-law entity outside the latter's sphere. It is only in this case that one can speak of an act of the State that is beyond the scope of identity and control of the particular state enterprise. However, such is not the case in this state enterprise–State relationship, so the reasoning goes, because the enterprise and the State either have the same identity or are intertwined so closely that as phenomena they pass into each other and hence the same should be said of their obligations. Here an act of the State could be seen as *vis major* only if in this enterprise–State relationship the State were unable to put itself now in this, now in that position, yet it does so: the enterprise of the State enters into a contract and then both "withdraw" from the contractual obligation, one invoking the conduct of the other.

(c) No matter how appealing and consistent this line of reasoning may appear, *this concept is no longer in the main supported by the more recent judicial practice.*

In the *Czarnikov v. Rolimpex Case* (1979) the Polish foreign trade company *Rolimpex* was unable to fulfill its contractual obligation to deliver to its British buyer the quantity of sugar fixed by contract. Performance by the Polish company was prevented by a general ban imposed by the Polish Government on sugar exports because the country was short of that product. In the ensuing legal dispute *Rolimpex* pleaded *vis major*, which had been caused by the wholesale government measure and which exempted it from liability for breach of contract; this function of *vis major* is usually accepted by international commercial practice. Czarnikov responded by saying he would accept the plea of *vis major* and the resultant exemption from liability, for the added reason that a *vis major* clause of like nature was contained in the contract itself. All very well, perhaps, but his partner, *Rolimpex*, was a state trading company, and the State and its enterprise are so close so as to preclude the decisive prerequisite of *vis major*, namely that an enterprise invoking *vis major* must be definitely distinct from the State, but it was not, rather the two were essentially congeneric. The case was even submitted to the House of Lords; it upheld the judgment of the appellate court (and the award originally proceeding from an arbitral tribunal), and granted the plea of *vis major* raised by *Rolimpex*. After thorough argumentation and intensive exchanges of views between the parties before the judicial fora, all the three courts formulated the following theses: *Rolimpex* as a state enterprise was an entity distinct from the State, so it could not be made liable for the State-imposed export ban, which by its nature of *vis major*, led to its breach of contract; the Polish foreign trade company was not the *alter ego* of the Polish State; it was also impossible for the proceedings to establish any collaboration or connivance between *Rolimpex* and the Polish Government in the matter of the export ban, which had been an act of state intervention beyond the control of the seller and which substantiated *Rolimpex*'s rightful plea of *vis major* [for this and similar British judgments, see Mádl: *A külgazdaság és a nemzetközi beruházások joga* (The external economy and the law of international investment)].

In the *First National City Bank v. Banco para el Comercio Exterior de Cuba Case* (1983), the Supreme Court of the United States held that state economic institutions distinct from governments, established as legal units acting independently thereof (such as the Bank of Cuba operating as a state enterprise involved in the case), should indeed be treated as such in general. The legal entity integument of such economic and legal units could be split, and the legal identity of them as such challenged, only in exceptional situations in which, for instance, a grave abuse had been incurred by the State in the particular state institution, such abuse manifestly resulting in an unlawful situation. Pronouncing this general thesis, the Supreme Court found, and accordingly reversed the decision of the Court of Appeal, that in that concrete situation the State of Cuba had misused its proprietary power at the Bank in order to exempt the Bank from its liability under international law. According to the facts of this case, the Cuban party sued the American bank, and the American First National City Bank presented a counterclaim for damages against the Bank of Cuba on the ground that Cuba had previously nationalized its economic interests without compensation. Soon after the presentation of the counterclaim, the Government of Cuba dissolved the foreign trade bank of Cuba in question, thereby terminating it as an economic unit (against which the counterclaim had been presented) and transferring its assets to other state enterprises of Cuba. In its judgment the Supreme Court of the United States held that the said act of the State, namely the termination of the legal personality of the other litigant and the distribution of its assets among other economic units, had been accomplished through the fact of an abuse and manifest wrong, as it ruled out the possibility for the counterclaim (for the text of the judgment, see *International Legal Materials*, Vol. 22, 1983, pp. 840 *et seq.*). For all its logical arguments, the judgment is ultimately contradictory, because even though the manifest wrong was true, the principal should have been sought in the State rather than in a non-existent enterprise (the question of what can be done against the State is a different matter; see Chapter XVI). Its contradictory nature and its inconsistency leap to the eye when one considers the judgment passed by this same court (the American Supreme Court) in another case, *Leteiler v. Republic of Chile* (1984), in which the Supreme Court ruled that the otherwise final judgment handed down against the State of Chile as such was not enforceable against the property of the Chilean airline company. According to the facts of the case, one of the problems lay in nationalization: the property of the claimant American company had been nationalized in Chile at the time. The American plaintiff obtained a final judgment on compensation for that property. In order to secure the enforcement of the judgment, it instituted proceedings under the *alter ego* theory to levy execution on the property of the Chilean airline company. However, the American Supreme Court decided to sustain the structural doctrine, under which legal entities distinct from the State could not be deemed identical with the State. It stated furthermore that in that dispute, it had found no such elements of "abuse" between the parties as it had established in the above BANCEC case (see 748 F.2d 790, 2 Cir. 1984). It appears therefore that the *alter ego* theory has become less prevalent in the practice of recent years. This is not contradicted by the fact that at times one can meet with judgments which seek, even if disputably, to translate this theory into practice (see Mádl: op. cit.).

All this leads to the obvious conclusion that state enterprises are to be regarded as legal entities distinct from the State. They cannot be held liable for acts of their respective governments. The situation is different where such acts are done directly in respect of a particular enterprise and result in a manifest wrong in international relations between enterprises. Such is the case when specific acts of a State are artificially committed with the aim of unlawfully creating a favourable situation for the enterprise in question, thereby facilitating its exemption without sufficient cause from the performance of its contractual obligations. Concepts and doctrines contrary to these theses would, if widely prevalent in practice, lead to erosion and disruption of international contractual relations while, indeed, what is needed in this domain is precisely the opposite, notably fruitful cooperation and its security in law.

CHAPTER XI

THE STATE AS ARCHITECT OF INTERNATIONAL ECONOMIC RELATIONS

§38. ON THE ROLE OF THE STATE IN GENERAL

1. In the legal rules expressing international economic relations, the State does not, of course, appear as a subject of private international law or of civil-law relationships in the first instance. Its decisive and paramount role consists in creating, by its activity in the domestic and international spheres, those organizational and administrative conditions and those legal prerequisites – within the ambit of public international law and other branches of law – which enable Hungary to participate to the greatest extent possible in the international division of labour. In dealing, as we did above, with the State as a subject at law we must also discuss the role of the State as such in the law of international economic relations, all the more so since what the State does in this domain is ultimately to shape an optimal pattern of transactions by natural subjects and economic entities in the international field for the benefit of the national economy, including citizens and enterprises. What is involved here is virtually *state management of the external economy in a broad sense*, as is also required under conditions of a modern market economy.

The role of the State in the external economy *can best be depicted in the context of* the following *four topics* to be addressed at this juncture, viz. the main elements signalling and embodying the external economic role of the State in historical perspective and in present-day Hungary (§38); the set of international conditions of the external economic mechanism (§39); its domestic organizational structure (§40); and management of the external economy (§41).

Recent years have witnessed particularly dramatic and historic changes on the stage of the external economic mechanism, and the play still goes on. Changes of historical significance have occurred in comparison to the prolonged period during which the State practised, quasi *totum et totaliter*, control of microeconomic processes, both in the economy in general and in the external economy, on the principles of a centrally-planned economy and foreign trade monopoly in a large part of Europe. This new panorama presents a sharp contrast to the long-drawn proscription of private property, the market, and commodity and money relations: on 12 April 1990 all States participating in the Conference on Security and Cooperation in Europe (CSCE), including Hungary and the rest of the Central and Eastern European countries, among them the former Soviet Union, reaffirmed their faith, at the follow-up conference in Bonn, in free elections, a pluralist system of political parties and a state ruled by law, a market economy, respect for private property, a liberalized external economy and organic international economic cooperation, and a market-governed system of prices. Even if the road to travel to the actual achievement of these goals is long and even if the countries of Central and Eastern Europe register different rates of development, there is no denying that – and this is well illustrated by the CSCE statement cited above and the experience of the past years – the core and substance of the trend is clearly visible despite all the retarding factors, many of which combine to act as an obstruction to progress along the path indicated.

2. In order for the present day to be seen more clearly it is worthwhile to cast a brief glance at the past, at *the kind of role the State has played in the course of history* with respect to international economic relations. Here we have in mind not the military operations motivated by interests of the State's existence or the wars of conquest generated by economic interests. Unfortunately, the greater the distance we look back, the more discernible it is how harshly determinant that role of the State was in the system of international relations between peoples, rulers and countries. While that role practically continues into our time, it is only now that the nearly century-old faith and aspiration (Peace Conference of the Hague, conventions on economic cooperation, League of Nations, United Nations and its specialized agencies, GATT, WTO, International Monetary Fund, World Bank, CSCE/OSCE, European Union, EFTA, Central European Initiative, cooperation agreements between countries of Central and Eastern Europe and the Western world, etc.) are gaining momentum. This has the effect that global, regional and bilateral systems of international institutions can and should serve to eliminate military confrontations mainly of economic origin, to coordinate the economic strategies of nations, and to maintain a reasonable and balanced pattern of international economic cooperation.

(a) So, if we inquire into the role of the State in peaceful and legally regulated international economic relations, its notable elements can be found as far back as the times of the ancients with regard to our own historical past in Europe. It is well known that ancient Greece owed its standing (disregarding for now the wars it waged for the aforesaid reasons) not only to its culture, but also to its internal socio-economic and political forces, its alliances, or its international political, military and economic strategies seeking and allowing alliances, its internal and international trade and its merchant shipping. Of course, the State played a decisive role in that trend of development, while the external economic and politico-military aspects of the *raison d'état* were strongly intertwined. In times of peace a great role was reserved for legal settlements (formation of alliances), for regulation of foreign trade by internal law as is evidenced by the *Lex Rhodia* and the *ius gentium*. This sphere of state life was similarly covered in detail by Plato in "The Laws" (Part XII of Book V; Part XII of Book VIII).

In Rome the role of the State in shaping international economic relations, *mutatis mutandis*, was likewise significant, its model being similar to that of its Greek predecessors. While adopting precisely many things from the Greeks in this area, Rome advanced much further in several respects. In its relations with aliens (foreign merchants) and other powers, Rome developed differentiated regulations within the frameworks of the *ius praetorium* (law of aliens) and the *ius gentium*. The historic role of Roman law in shaping international economic relations is well reflected in, among others, its having become the law of contemporary world trade, known as the *lex mercatoria*, from the time of the prospering city-states in Northern Italy. Through the reception of Roman law the Holy Roman Empire offered that law to govern international transactions at the time.

(b) Again, *in the States that emerged during the great migrations*, we see the international relations of the State and the "civil" world in a closely entwined symbiosis. In Hungary, too, the king and the royal court (with the royal estates and crown revenues in the background) invited to the country not only monks and artists, but also craftsmen, contractors, architects and jurists, as was done by St. Stephen or later by King Matthias in particular (*Secula Hungariae*, Budapest, 1985, Vol. 1438–1526). As is known, the laws of St. Stephen and St. Ladislas contained separate provisions on foreign merchants. Thus the royal courts were at once subjects and regulators of international transactions. By granting the right of holding fairs and other privileges, they strengthened their role in the country's international economic transactions in some cities and even enlarged it in regions far from the centre. The royal treasuries assumed a significant role and raised sizable revenues by pursuing fiscal and customs policies on various international trade routes (of salt, cattle on foot, etc.).

(c) With the emergence of *nation-states*, the civil society and the State appeared to pull apart, the State gradually putting on the nightwatchman's gown in respect of the economy, guarding the "order" and the country's military and foreign policy interests. It was at that time that Adam Smith said that public law was the science of practising politics and exercising state power and authority (*Inquiry into the Nature and Sources of the Wealth of Nations*, Edition Cannan, 1937, p. 397). A quite different and separate world was that which, almost at the same time, Savigny characterized as one in which civil (commercial) law was the science of the subjects of economic transactions, of private autonomy, of economic freedom (*System des heutigen römischen Rechts*, Berlin, 1840, Bd. I, p. 55). Indeed, the private sphere, i.e. the capitalist economy, started and expanded its large-scale movement governed by its own laws (freedom) on both the domestic and the international plane and, engineered by the means of production, soon came to force its way unrestrained into the postindustrial era.

Then this situation, subject as it was to its own rules, came to be accompanied by harmful consequences, presenting the well-known scenario of poverty, sharp class antagonisms and social strains, social revolutions, colonial oppression and liberation struggles (uprisings and wars) of colonies, ruthless national and regional hostilities, economic crises, wars and world wars. The reaction is likewise of public record: Utopian and Marxist socialists, social democracy, the Church's social conscience manifested in the papal social encyclical letters (*Rerum novarum*) on the plane of political-ethical thinking; social legislation as early as Bismarck's day on the plane of government practice; later the philosophy of state intervention of a more general nature in the form of economic law, which was first thought to be a mere transitory phenomenon, a symptom of a disease; the *New Deal* philosophy, the economic policy concept of Keynes and Müller–Armack, which came to be generally known as a necessary new part of the modern market economy in national and international economic contexts; the shocks and lessons of the world wars, which were truly drastic demonstrations of the lack of the State's balancing, organizing and influencing role; the magnitude of the instrumentalities which became necessary and were used by the State for the technological and economic strategies of postindustrialism; the effect of the promised social and economic programmes of the Soviet and subsequent revolutions in anthropomorphizing the West, to mention but the major elements and causes of what occurred or materialized under the impact of all these events and developments. The manifested consequences are known to be these: active internal involvement of the State (considerable proprietary participation and above all comprehensive coordination of interests; balancing, financing, economy-developing and intensive regulatory role); a large system of institutions of international economic relations established in active international cooperation between States, this being, for decades now, the fabric and guarantee, visibly more than a mere promise, of economic cooperation on a global scale, of the effectiveness of market economy mechanisms as modulated by the State(s), of the development of productive forces, of a more organic readjustment of the world economy and its different regions, of a more balanced development of national economies and the world economy, and thereby of the material, cultural and, what is perhaps no vain hope, moral progress of the human race. This modern concept and practice of the symbiosis of the market economy and State involvement, viz. a social market economy, continues to prevail in the developed part of the world and is also postulated by the pertinent literature (see Schlecht, Buxbaum–Mádl (eds.), Hahn-Gramlich, Mestmäcker, Pescatore).

Among the absolute dictatorships, the crisis "real" socialism came to a head; its abortive attempt (see the third Hungarian edition of this book, pp. 165 *et seq.*) was followed by a complete systemic change, which Hungary, too, experienced in a revolution accomplished through law, in order for the different countries to catch up, in both their domestic and international economic systems, with the advanced countries, with the development of the world economy and the European economy.

3. The question now is one of the role which the State *in Hungary* today is to play or should play, in consequence of the processes outlined above and in pursuit of the described goals, in the shaping of international economic relations. *Paradoxically, this role probably is or will be larger than hitherto* (at least in certain respects), although it would stand to reason to say that it is or will be definitely smaller in somehow reaching the stage where the countries with a developed market economy find themselves in this field. Still, as regards the concrete aspects and the details, we should, in referring to the following phases (§§39–41), seek the cause and substance of this paradoxical situation under a more general approach.

(a) In the first place we underline the *need for a complete overhaul of the country's external economic strategy.* In terms of its substance and goal, this overall rapid and consistent opening to the world economy called and calls for accomplishing integration into and catching up with Europe. In wider contexts this meant and means three things: (1) the need to bring the country's relations to a qualitatively new level with the developed market economy countries, with the "West", with the determinant international organizations (European Union, OECD, Council of Europe, etc.) and to strengthen our cooperation with the developing world; (2) the need to rearrange or "rewrite" the "Eastern" world, to frame new regulatory systems of cooperation in place of the disintegrated CMEA; (3) the need to reshape our relations and cooperation with our close neighbours in the interest of openness, actual integration of enterprises and optimal development of national economies and the region, the scheme of cooperation between the Adria–Danube countries (Pentagonale, then Hexagonale and now Central European Initiative) as well as between the Visegrád States forming part of this process as an added contribution to a more intensive and faster integration of the countries concerned into the larger European unity. All this required a high degree of intensity without parallel of interstate and other international negotiations and efforts to conclude agreements in terms of both quantity and quality or substance.

(b) It was and is likewise necessary to rewrite the internal legal order of the external economic mechanism in order to establish the domestic framework and regulatory system of cooperation based on a market economy, although much had been done in this field during the previous period. We are facing a special challenge of social engineering. What should be done is for a largely artificial (not self-regulatory, not organically developed) system to be carried over, again "artificially" (by programmes of human or government action like privatization, foreign investments) to a market-oriented (external) economic system, which is presumed to be organic. Of course, a revolution waged and stabilized by legal means cannot tackle this task except by a large new wave of legal regulations.

(c) Then we still have the public sector as against the actual market economy of the future operating with real owners, and we probably will continue to have some of it (which it certainly seems right to maintain to a reasonable extent), in which the State is also owner and which calls for special regulation and conditions of operation and management in the sphere of the external economy as well.

Once all that we have described as a state task of "rewriting" has been accomplished, once the "work is up and running" (even if not so perfectly done as to allow the creators to rest) and once the market economy functions better to meet society's material and cultural needs at a higher standard and in a more balanced way, the role of the State can settle at a lower level of intensity which remains necessary but is already sufficient for a relatively good work to run with ordinary efficiency. *Hic et nunc*, however, we must address what the State did and does at the stage of intensive action in pursuit of this goal. We will discuss these points next (§§39–41).

§39. THE SET OF INTERNATIONAL CONDITIONS OF THE EXTERNAL ECONOMY

1. A vast terrain of implementing the aforesaid external economic strategy is that of creating an appropriate set of international conditions. By the "set of international conditions" is to be understood the totality of international instruments (conventions, agreements, organizations, forms of interstate cooperation) enabling the country's economy to participate to its utmost in the processes of the international division of labour, in which the country's general and economic policy objectives, national as well as international, can largely be achieved. To create such a set of international conditions for the external economy is *a sui generis state function, a right and a duty of the State*, which follows from the State's sovereignty and from the role it performs in modern times, constituting a substantial element thereof.

Today this means the following:

(a) an awareness of the fact, and an ability to turn it into intensive action by economic diplomacy, that Hungary, given its historical and geographical determinism, has always been strongly oriented towards foreign trade (the external economy) and is especially so today (with over 50% of national income earned in external economic processes); its economic prosperity can thus only be achieved through a successful working of the external economy. In its new historical situation – under conditions of economic crisis, the systemic change and the necessary external market reorientation – the country is heavily dependent on those political and economic resources which can be mobilized by a new international strategy and which the advanced countries use to support the historical transformations taking place in this part of Europe;

(b) an awareness that the set of international conditions of the external economy, or the whole complex of various regulators and institutions, is largely at hand, being a product of human and historical development. Our task is to join these systems, to play an active role in them and to make the most of the available benefits;

(c) in addition, an awareness that a new situation of global-historical significance has emerged in Central and Eastern Europe, one that has made it necessary for international economic policy doctrines and strategies to be redesigned in both East and West. This in turn is coupled with a considerable transformation of the large regulatory systems and the establishment of new ones. Hungary has played a pioneering role and still has much to do in this enterprise.

All that we have stated above concerning the external economic role of the State and the related set of international conditions is, in its concrete aspects, embodied in the instrumentalities discussed below: multilateral, regional, bilateral agreements and institutions, and those supporting the transformations in Eastern Europe, including Hungary.

2. The *multilateral (universal, or global) regulatory systems* are naturally of various types as regards both their objects and subjects and legal peculiarities. They appear in the following three groups (a, b, c).

(a) The first institutions to be addressed are those *in the nature of organization*; their members are States, the subjects of their statutes (conventions relating to them) are mostly the States parties and, only indirectly, economic actors of States. Another feature of them is that, after all, they govern state behaviour concerning the movement and legal relationships of the subjects of transactions but, in numerous respects, they pass into regulations of enterprise behaviour (e.g. GATT rules on dumping or World Bank rules on project credits).

(aa) Certainly the most important of the global institutions are the General Agreement on Tariffs and Trade (GATT) and the World Trade Organization (WTO).

(i) Historically, until the establishment of WTO, GATT had also been more an institution than an organization. The International Trade Organization (ITO) was not established as originally planned; in 1947 "only" GATT was signed, and it became a comprehensive international agreement, yet one of a dual character. On the one hand, GATT grew into a comprehensive system of rules governing the external economic policy behaviour of the Contracting Parties, into an agreement operating as a source of international law. On the other hand, it was more than a simple international code as it also had an important machinery and procedure for its operation and built-in development (meetings of the Contracting Parties, country or working groups, bilateral *ad hoc* deliberations, roundtable talks, ministerial conferences, Secretary-General, Secretariat, etc.). Over time, however, this had proved insufficient for the implementation of the GATT principles, and the need was increasingly felt for devising a more efficient implementation mechanism. GATT reform was also urged by other important considerations, e.g. the fact that international transactions involving services and intellectual property were outside the scope of GATT, or the necessity and practicability of ensuring that these spheres, as highly important sectors of the world economy, would likewise be covered by the rule of law in international economic relations.

The reform of GATT was formulated at its Uruguay Round (1986–1994). The new agreements were signed in Marrakesh in Morocco by over 100 countries, Hungary included (15 April 1994), and by other GATT countries at a later date. Among the numerous agreements highly important to the order of world trade, the major ones include (1) the Agreement on the establishment and operation of the World Trade Organization (WTO); (2) the agreements streamlining GATT on trade in goods (1947), namely GATT (1994); and (3) various other agreements supporting and complementing the former (e.g. new or renewed agreements relating to and regulating agriculture, technical trade barriers, trade-related investment measures, dumping, subsidies, origin, quantitative restrictions, the protective clause); (4) the General Agreement on Trade in Services (GATS); (5) the Agreement on Trade-Related Aspects of Intellectual Property Rights, Including Trade in Counterfeit Goods (TRIPs); (6) the Understanding on Rules and Procedure Governing the Settlement of Disputes; (7) the Agreement on the Trade Policy Review Mechanism; (8) Plurilateral Trade Agreements.

(ii) The *organic structure* of WTO as a legal entity now includes really new and promising elements designed to promote effective implementation of the principles and provisions of the Agreement and reasonable dispute resolutions. The main institutions of WTO are the Ministerial Conference held as a rule every two years with the participation of all member-states, the General Council, various committees (on trade, development, balance of payments, budget) and councils (on commodities, services, intellectual property) as well as the Dispute Settlement Body.

(iii) The *role* of GATT and WTO is manifest in the above aspects, too. GATT (1947) was also a trade agreement and as such a global one which, in representation of over 100 member-states, has sought, ever since it was concluded, a reasonable liberalization of world trade conditions as existing from time to time. Despite all its crises and problems it has coped with to date (see Bán, Mádl, Náray), GATT has long attracted the attention of policymakers in Hungary with a view to accession, as was expressed in contemporary Hungarian statements of position on economic policy and economics as well as in legal literature, as a way of improving the efficiency of the Hungarian economy in foreign markets. The accession took place in 1973 and was promulgated by Decree No. 23/1973. (IX. 9.) of the Council of Ministers. Under the new conditions of the world economy, when the countries of Central and Eastern Europe participate in the world economic processes with economic policy endeavours attuned to the developed world, the renewed system of GATT agreements, completed with WTO, is equally of outstanding importance to Hungary.

The great significance of the system of GATT and WTO agreements for us naturally lies in the value of institutions and principles. The most important of these include the granting of most-favoured nation treatment on a multilateral basis (see §45), more favourable customs tariffs in foreign markets, national treatment in taxation, limitation (elimination) of different state protectionist measures and coordinated regulations (contingents, subsidies, dumping, integration preferences, settlement of the relationship between support for the developing countries (General System of Preferences, GSP) and the most-favoured nation clause, regulated procedure for dispute settlement, protection of intellectual property, etc. All this has resulted in much better conditions for external economic contracts and undertakings, favouring more harmonious international relations (for more detail on the new developments concerning GATT and WTO, see Cocuzza–Forabosco, Ipsen–Haltern, Náray).

(ab) What in the field of international trade is represented by GATT and WTO is, with some simplification, embodied in the International Monetary Fund (IMF) and, directly connected with it, the International Bank for Reconstruction and Development (IBRD), also called the World Bank (WB), in the domain of international payments, the money markets and credit transactions. These so-called Bretton-Woods institutions were established, in cooperation with, among others, Professor Keynes, basically by the United States and the United Kingdom (and 42 countries allied with them) during World War Two, at Bretton Woods, New Hampshire in July 1944, to create, for the new postwar world, the legally institutionalized frameworks of and arrangements for international payments and turnover of capital (see Loewenfeld: *The International Monetary System*). Hungary joined these institutions in 1982 (Law-Decrees No. 1 (6) and No. 15 of 1982). In 1985 we joined the International Finance Corporation (IFC) and the International Development Association (IDA), two subsidiary institutions of the World Bank. Thus Hungary became a party to this large system of financial institutions numbering as many as 182 member-states at the time [Mrs. Lőrinc: *Pénzügyi világszervezetek* (World Financial Organizations)].

Our accession, already at that time, was seen to be motivated by the following major benefits: (1) taking an effective and a more active part in growing economic relations without the State, as well as joining the international financial organizations that determine the international money markets and credit transactions which was in general a difficult task to accomplish because trade flows are hard to separate from financial conditions; (2) Hungary needs favourable credit terms, and its accession ensured and ensures considerable easy-term credits for implementing concrete investment programmes (projects) and maintaining the balance of payments; (3) our enterprises are granted the right of direct competitive bidding for participating in investment projects financed from World Bank credits.

Our membership in and active cooperation with the IMF and WB are more timely today than ever. On the one hand, the loans of the IMF and those catalyzed by it are indispensable for preserving the country's liquidity position, which is no simple priority objective of economic policy after that of easing the heavy debt servicing burdens existing as a real factor endowment. On the other hand, economic restructuring and technological development, which also serve to improve the country's liquidity position, are in need of IMF support and World Bank project credits (see item 5 below).

As regards the difference in functions and emphasis between the IMF and WB, the Articles of Agreement for the IMF deal with the equilibrium of national currencies and of their relationship *inter se*, exchange policies, convertibility, balance-of-payments equilibrium, availability of Fund resources for these purposes (standby credits within the frameworks of general economic policy programmes between the IMF and particular countries, credits required for keeping balance of payments in equilibrium), coordination of economic policies, and the administrative structure of the IMF as an organization (Corden; Gold; Mrs. Lőrinc: *Pénzügyi világszervezetek*; GATT Articles 1 and especially V on "Operations and Transactions of the Fund"), whereas the Articles of Agreement for the WB cover, in addition to organizational aspects, the Bank's sources of capital stock (paid-in capital subscriptions by member-States in proportion to national income, the great "contributors" including, as in the case of IMF, the most developed advanced countries, primarily the USA), various kinds of credit to beneficiaries (countries producing national income below a certain level, i.e. mostly developing countries, including in this respect the countries of Central and Eastern Europe), and the mechanism of credit operations (see Broches: The World Bank; Mrs. Lőrinc: *op.cit.;* IBRD Articles of Agreement). The IFC "breaks down" the World Bank's role to small and medium-sized (mainly private) enterprises (Camacho: The IFC).

The significance of the *Bretton Woods* institutions is indicated by the magnitude of credit granted to Hungary through these channels and under schemes costing in the order of several billions of dollars and co-financed by the World Bank (see Mádl: *A külgazdaság...*, pp. 46–49).

(ac) Within the framework of the *United Nations Conference on Trade and Development* (UNCTAD) Hungary has participated in working out and implementing instruments that are of relevance to its external economic policy, too, such as the Convention concerning the Transit Trade of Landlocked Countries, the General System of Preferences applied within GATT (see §46), the Code on Transfer of Technology drafted with special attention to the interests of developing countries, and so on. Within these frameworks, Hungary is concurrently seeking to assist the economic growth of developing countries and to build solid economic positions for itself and its enterprises in those regions.

(ad) Hungary is working constructively and cooperatively with the *United Nations Industrial Development Organization* (UNIDO) in supporting the implementation of programmes and undertaking other activities for the benefit of developing countries, essentially in keeping with the objectives pursued within UNCTAD. In addition to concrete development programmes, UNIDO plays a significant role in elaborating general conditions for various industrial development projects. Stipulating general conditions of contract, these have been of considerable practical assistance to related undertakings and transactions, with respect to, among others, the contractual practice of Hungarian enterprises as well (such conditions apply, e.g., to delivery of machinery and equipment, design and construction of establishments, technical supervision). Similarly, numerous UNIDO initiatives have reached a promising stage in creating the legal conditions for technology transfer.

(ae) Our country is naturally taking an active part in the work of the *United Nations Commission for International Trade Law* (UNCITRAL), not only because this institution of the United Nations has been set up at Hungary's initiative in earnest recognition of its achievements and legal science, but also because it derives a stimulating experience from the success of that initiative. Development (and unification) of international trade law results in essentially better conditions for increasing the effectiveness of our extensive trade orientation. Great significance is attached to the very fact and process of the unification of law, but of particular importance is a type of unification that serves to develop the substance of international trade law by rewriting the international conventions, so far based mainly or wholly on the interest model of the highly industrialized countries, in such a way as to assert the interest models of developing countries as well. Among the many initiatives (bank guarantees, letters of credit, arbitration procedure, various contracts), the Vienna Convention on the International Sale of Goods of 1980 has already proved to be a great success and has every chance of becoming a uniform law of general application as a result of accessions by a large number of countries (see §67).

(af) Hungary is equally active in the *Institut International de l'Unification de Droit Privé* (UNIDROIT), which was established by an international treaty in 1926 and is based in Rome. Within its framework Hungary contributes to developing the law of various international commercial transactions and institutions (international sale, commission, carriage and conveyance of goods, insurance, leasing, etc.). We played an especially effective role in the elaboration of the leasing and factoring conventions (which were signed at the diplomatic conference of Ottawa in 1988 and were ratified by Hungary in 1995) and in the elaborations and publication of the Principles of International Commercial Contracts in 1994 [on their publication in Hungary (Budapest, 1996), see Burián and, in general, Bonell].

(ag) Our membership in the *Hague Conference on Private Law* through the Austro-Hungarian Monarchy has an interesting history. Initially *ad hoc* in nature, this Conference came into being in 1893 and has since grown into a permanent institution. Its Statute as an international convention entered into force in 1955. Our cooperation with it, dead-and-alive for a long time after 1945 and intensified during the 1980s, is motivated by the interests manifested in the programmes for the unification and development of law within the sphere of activity of the Conference (the subject areas in the work of codification include the law of conflicts of international sale, jurisdiction, legal persons, succession, recognition of foreign judgments and arbitral awards, etc.; cf. §§67, 69, 94, 112–115). In connection with our accession to the European Union it is worthwhile to take into account that in this domain the Hague Conference has so far elaborated 32 conventions, many of which have entered into force, and that the number of accessions by countries of the European Union (EU) is on the increase, meaning that the legal infrastructure of Europe will before long be constituted by these conventions in the subject-matter under discussion. Whereas the West European countries have acceded to between 15 and 24 conventions, Hungary has acceded only to 4, so it is timely to speed up our strategy of accession in this field as well (see Mádl: *Ius Commune Europae*).

(ah) Hungary acceded to the *World Intellectual Property Organization* (WIPO) in 1970 (Law-Decree No. 18 of 1970). The relevance of the WIPO to our country lies in the importance of the unions for the protection of copyright and industrial property (see §§87 to 93), specifically in the possibility for our effective participation in this sphere of international cooperation and economic action concerning the protection and utilization of the values of copyright and industrial property. There are significant interests involved if one keeps in view that in the Convention establishing the WIPO, "intellectual property" embraces the whole spectrum of rights pertaining to scientific discoveries, inventions, industrial designs, trademarks, trade names, protection against unfair competition, literary and artistic and scientific works, sound recordings and broadcasting, in brief, all rights deriving from intellectual activities in literature, the arts, sciences and industry.

The purpose of the Organization is to promote the international protection of intellectual property throughout the world in the interest of creative activities in the domain indicated above and thereby to enhance such pursuits and the commercialization of their results for the benefit of society. WIPO plays a significant part in ensuring that legislation on intellectual property increasingly serves the special interests of developing countries that are of paramount importance in this field. Also, its purpose is to administer the unions for the protection of copyright and industrial property and to ensure their cooperation in administration without prejudice to the competence of the different unions (for more detail see Title 7 and Boytha).

(ai) Investments by foreigners in Hungary and Hungarian investments abroad play a significant and growing role in Hungary's external economic strategy (see §§46–47). Hence the importance of our country's participation in the work of the *Multilateral Investment Guarantee Agency* (MIGA; Law-Decree No. 7 of 1989) and of the *International Centre for Settlement of Investment Disputes* (ICSID; Law-Decree No. 27 of 1987) (for a full discussion see Chapter XVII).

(b) A special place among the multi-regulatory systems is occupied by the so-called *commodity conventions*. These are of a special nature on the basis of the following main grounds. First, they aim to ensure an internationally coordinated and regulated mechanism and balance of the production of and trade in specified raw materials. Second, by their legal nature, they are at once conventions regulative of behaviour and organizational phenomena as well as institutions operating organizational mechanisms. Further, they are specific for the considerations mentioned below. It is evident that the regulation of production, trade and the market is contrary to the philosophy of economic competition (opposition to cartels, namely the anti-trust law); moreover effective anti-trust law even found its way from America to Europe in the wake of World War Two in the economic policies of the advanced capitalist countries as well as in theory, e.g. in that of Keynes. However there arose a need for the prices of certain basic commodities and raw materials to be fixed in the interest of ensuring the equilibrium of the world market. Stability and equilibrium were necessary for the added reason of fostering the economic development of the newly-liberated colonies by stabilizing and guaranteeing income from raw materials. Such international efforts for the sake of developing countries came to be intensified particularly under the hallmark of UNCTAD. It was believed that world-wide organization of the production of certain basic commodities, of trade in them and of related information as well as stabilization thereof through relevant conventions, could contribute to the progress of developing countries and ultimately promote the interests of the advanced capitalist countries as chief consumers. UNCTAD endeavours in that direction initially encountered a great deal of difficulties. At the UNCTAD Conference of 1976, which formulated and adopted an integrated raw materials programme, the countries of both West and East showed a more active and more positive economic policy attitude. That raw materials programme offered a reformulated synthesis of coordinated international action in the field of economic policy (containing elements like agreements on stock-building and their coordination, determination of prices, coordination of supply and demand, market information, additional sources of finance), while envisaging the elaboration, by appropriate application of the elements of the aforesaid synthesis, of agreements covering 18 commodities ranging from bananas through bauxite, sugar, coffee, tin, copper and many others to steel. The preparation and operation of the various commodity agreements proceeded by slow degrees.

Given the international relationship of market and other forces, the last few decades have seen the conclusion of several conventions one after another, such as the International Sugar Conventions. Under these latter were set up the International Sugar Council and its Executive Committee, which consist of eight exporting and importing countries each. The new Sugar Convention created better conditions for Hungarian sugar exports, better than those which the country would otherwise have enjoyed on the international market. In 1969 we acceded to the International Tin Convention, notably the Third Convention, to which Czechoslovakia and Poland were also parties and which had become of importance for Hungary too, while we continued to cooperate within the frameworks of the Fourth Tin Convention concluded in 1971 and the Fifth Convention signed in 1976.

The different countries participate in the aforementioned 18 commodity conventions with varying degrees of intensity depending on the mechanism of, and the measure of interest in, each particular convention. As an important development in recent years, Hungary has acceded to the International Meat Convention, which contains the specific elements of most commodity conventions such as the quota system, price policy, warehousing, mutual information, other conditions, and regulation by the International Meat Council. It ratified this convention by Decree No. 35/1980. (IX. 1.) of the Council of Ministers. The same can be said, *mutatis mutandis,* of the International Dairy Convention also signed at Geneva in 1979; our accession to it was ratified by Decree No. 36/1980. (IX. 3.) of the Council of Ministers. Again, Hungary has adhered to the International Wheat Convention and its implementing organization, the International Wheat Council based in London. All these three commodity conventions operate on a looser philosophy of economic policy, contain no provisions regulative of the economy, but exert their effects by circulating market information and affording possibilities of consultation at the appropriate Council meetings on questions of distribution and production and circulation of appropriate information; they play a significant role in the international market of the particular products. A country greatly interested in wheat exports, Hungary's participation in the Wheat Convention offers the added benefit of getting into direct contact with partners on the world market of this product, holding out to it a promise of the commodity conventions (see Wo: International Commodity Trade; Ernst and *HVG* No. 8 and No. 51–52 of 1986). The significance of commodity conventions for world trade is indicated by the fact that the aforementioned multilateral trade (commodity) conventions such as the Convention on Trade in Aircraft, the International Milk Convention and the International Beef Convention (these apply only to those WTO countries which explicitly accede to them) have been incorporated into the system of WTO Conventions [see Ipsen–Haltern–Náray: *GATT uruguayi forduló* (Uruguay Round of GATT)].

An international cartel at state level, OPEC as the commodity convention of oil-exporting countries represents an entirely different world and interest mechanism in many aspects, but it is nonetheless an identical economic policy and legal instrument in respect of its essential elements, and its importance exceeds by far that of the other conventions. Whereas in most commodity conventions consumers and producers, i.e. exporters and importers, generally figure together and accordingly have proportional representation (naturally with notable divergences observed in them as well), OPEC is a powerful international interstate cartel exclusively of oil-producing countries. The reason that it deserves mention here in the East–West and North–South contexts lies in its very significance and its exercising a great influence on the energy market of both the advanced capitalist and other countries and even on the development and the international price structure of a range of oil-related industries.

Apart from the unilaterally dominating-dictating commodity conventions, the international ones are, in sum, useful components of the world economy for these reasons:

(ba) they contribute considerably to the production of the particular commodities and the stability of their respective markets;

(bb) thereby and owing to a reasonable price mechanism, they are preferred as a tool for greatly promoting the economic interests of developing countries;

(bc) numerous countries are both producers and importers of the raw materials in question, and thus their cooperation on the basis of commodity conventions results in a balanced system of relations among them;

(bd) given their *value as models* (their existence and operation), the international commodity conventions play an extremely important role in the international regulatory system of the external economy: on the one hand, they serve to strengthen the belief in the possibility of considerably reducing, within the framework of intergovernmental economic cooperation, the contradictions and difficulties emerging in international economic processes and, on the other, the concrete effective international commodity conventions actually fulfil this function, in addition to belief, with respect to the particular commodities. Notwithstanding the philosophy of GATT and the rational requirements of liberalizing world trade, one should keep in mind the State's role of this nature in shaping the pattern of international economic relations.

(c) The next large group of multilateral regulatory systems is constituted by the *conventions regulating enterprise trade relations (mostly contracts).* The uniform rules of this type, addressed to enterprises and governing their behaviour, as well as the practical application thereof (unification of law, uniform law) represent the modern *lex mercatoria strictu sensu* (modern law merchant), the law of world trade, to the extent that the particular conventions are shared in large measure by different countries. The view is gaining strength that considers the body of public-law rules on international economic relations (GATT, IMF, EU, WB, etc.; indeed all that is discussed in this paragraph; see Mádl: *Ius Commune Europae*) as now forming part of the *lex mercatoria*. Still, it is mostly the terrain of trade law, as strictly understood, in the unification of law that has become the classical realm of the *lex mercatoria*.

The related multilateral *conventions* have grown broader in scope and include, among others, the following major international trade agreements and other forms of international economic activity: international sale; carriage of goods by air, sea, rail and road; various forms of payment like bills of exchange and cheques; leasing as an important new form of international transaction; different fields of intellectual property such as copyright, patent rights, trademarks, the entire domain of industrial property; settlement of international commercial disputes, international arbitration, enforcement of foreign arbitral awards and other court decisions. These conventions are discussed in the relevant chapters and section of this book. We have mentioned them here in order to emphasize their importance, to give a full picture of them and to indicate that

Hungary has generally acceded to them, thus having a hand in fashioning the *ius commune* of world trade although much more remains to be done in this area. The related tasks will be addressed below in connection with the appropriate institutions.

3. Although much has been achieved, most of the tasks to be accomplished are in the field of Hungary's highly important *regional* relations. The outstanding importance of these relations is explained by obvious and well-known reasons: historical and geopolitical endowments; centuries-old traditions of political, cultural and economic relations, at times fraught with "problems"; the decisive role of Europe with regard to economic aspects, including both the absolute volume of economic transactions and the current historical process of political and economic transformations. All these factors appear in the large European regulatory systems: Conference (now Organisation) on Security and Cooperation in Europe (CSCE/OSCE), Council of Europe (CE), European Union (EU), European Free Trade Area (EFTA), European Bank for Reconstruction and Development (EBRD), Central European Initiative as a new mechanism of basically bilateral cooperation replacing CMEA, Central European Free Trade Agreement (CEFTA) successor to the "Visegrád Three", which now includes Slovenia, Czech Republic and Slovak Republic (instead of Czechoslovakia), Poland, Romania and Hungary. Our active and constructive (reconstructive) participation in them is therefore of paramount importance since the stakes, for the sake of revolutionary transformations in Eastern and Central Europe, are precisely in joining the said regulatory systems, in a fuller European integration, in building the "common European house".

(a) Moving from the lower to the higher degree of economic orientation, we should in the first place touch briefly on CSCE/OSCE. In addition to the chapters of the Helsinki Final Act (1 August 1975) on security policy and culture, a significant place is occupied by the chapter on the economy, the so-called third basket. Its relevance was (and still is) seen in its historical weight, its declarative force, and the commitment of the participating States to establish economic cooperation, along with peace and security, in Europe. Although the direct norm-potency of the Final Act is not of the same degree as that of other international conventions of a "more technical" nature, the Final Act carried a great weight especially at the time of its signature, namely in expressing a great historical compromise between the spheres of interests and groups of States involved. As such, it came to generate a number of regulatory systems of East–West economic cooperation more operative in nature as well as cooperative efforts and international codification projects during the subsequent period.

As a result of the historical turn, the formerly opposing and hostile spheres of interest have developed from the position of antagonistic confrontation towards a kind of harmony between political, social and economic philosophies. This, however, does not eliminate the need for CSCE in the historical perspective and with regard to the future of Europe. Through the harmonization of substance, the change rather results in removing the previous drawbacks and facilitating more effective progress. The signs of this are clearly visible in the arms reduction talks, in the question of Germany's unification, in the remodelling of relationships between the countries of Eastern and Central Europe, in the questions concerning the extinction of the Warsaw Pact Organization and the enlargement of NATO, all of which are important conditions for building a new structure of economic cooperation in Europe. The signs are also clearly visible in economic readjustments. Under item 1 above, we have referred to the declaration made at the 1990 Follow-Up Conference to CSCE and expressing the adherence of *all* Europe to such basic tenets of economic philosophy as a market economy, private property and organic economic cooperation. Recent years have given an especially dynamic impulse to the role of CSCE, as is convincingly expressed mainly in the Charter of Paris for a New Europe (*Charte de Paris pour une nouvelle Europe*) signed by the Heads of State or Government of the participating countries at Paris on 21 November 1990. This is indeed a harbinger and a promise of a new Europe in the form of such a solemn yet highly substantial legal instrument. The Charter addresses numerous fundamental issues of the external economy beside political and security questions. In effect, it embodies a European constitution of responsible, mutually advantageous international economic cooperation, economic freedoms and a social market economy, with special emphasis laid on human dimensions (State under the rule of law, including, human rights and moral fullness). In a peculiar and certainly regrettable way, CSCE was unable to make "European peace" in the matter of European security, in the Yugoslav war, in which, as is known, it fell to NATO and the United Nations to rise to the occasion, true, with a significant contribution by Europe.

(b) The Statute of the *Council of Europe* (5 May 1949) and, among its numerous conventions, primarily the Convention on the Protection of Human Rights and Fundamental Freedoms (4 November 1950) and the Additional Protocols express in clear terms the value criteria of cooperation in political, economic, social, cultural and scientific matters (Art. 1 of the Statute), notably respect for human rights and fundamental freedoms (including economic freedom), a state under the rule of law, a pluralist parliamentary democracy, and a market economy operating in accordance with economic freedoms (Statute, Preamble, Arts. 1 to 3; Convention, Preamble, Art. 1; Art 1 of Additional Protocol No. 1 of 1952). These are regarded by the CE as part and parcel of the universal political, legal and cultural heritage of Europe, and it was on the basis of respect for them that the CE decided to institutionalize cooperation in the aforementioned fields, with a view to maintenance and development of peace, human society and civilization (Statute, Preamble).

All this is expressed, perhaps most unequivocally, in the Preamble to the cited Convention, which states, *inter alia*, that the Governments of the CE, guided by the spirit of the Universal Declaration of Human Rights (United Nations, 1948), proceed on the assumption that one of the CE's aims is to achieve a larger measure of understanding and unity among Members and that a means of attaining this aim is that of protecting and developing human rights and fundamental freedoms; reaffirm their profound faith in these fundamental rights as they form the basis of justice and peace in the world and their maintenance rests, on the one hand, on a true and genuine democratic political order and, on the other, on a shared and upheld concept of human rights as European Governments imbued with the same spirit, sharing a common heritage of European intellectual values and political traditions, and having a shared interest in respect for freedom and the rule of law, they resolved to take the first steps in CE towards collective assurance of the rights proclaimed in the Universal Declaration.

From the foregoing it becomes clear why the Governments of the Eastern and Central European countries had previously been unable (and why, out of a kind of schizophrenia and hypocritical false superiority, had refused) to join the Council of Europe. As outlined above, the situation has radically changed since the historical change. After its Parliament's decision on accession adopted on 30 October 1990 [Decision No. 76/1990. (XI. 2.) of the National Assembly], Hungary was the first among the countries of Central and Eastern Europe to be admitted to membership in the Council of Europe on 6 November 1990. It is in this context that we must touch briefly on the reasons for our accession and on the organizational-operational specifics of the CE.

(ba) *Accession* is a decisive element of our catching up with Europe, stabilizing our belonging to Europe, institutionalizing the Hungarian political and legal system in the European framework, and ensuring its further development on the CE scale of values.

The EU scale of political values is that of the CE. The principal objective of Hungary's new (international) economic policy strategy is to join the European integration process, to become a member of the European Union. Our accession to the CE was a move of paramount importance in this context as well.

Although in terms of its concrete activity the CE is a basically political rather than an economic organization, its objectives are, as indicated in its legal instruments referred to above, also economic on a wide spectrum through better economic cooperation to a fuller European unity.

The activities of the CE include economic and social cooperation programmes in addition to economic goals and extend to education, culture, sports, environmental protection, local administration and, naturally and particularly, general legal and human rights fields. To participate in these forms of activity (to adjust our internal systems to CE standards and criteria, to be a party to various conventions on economic matters, to make use of mutual benefits, etc.) is likewise deemed to be an objective demand of our development.

(bb) Viewed from the angle of *organization and operation*, an outstanding role is naturally played by the central organs of the CE. Article 10 of the Statute contains these provisions: "The organs of the Council of Europe are: (1) the Committee of Ministers; (2) the Consultative Assembly. Both these organs shall be served by the Secretariat of the Council of Europe". "The Secretariat shall consist of a Secretary-General, a Deputy Secretary-General and such other staff as may be required" (Art. 36). The Committee of Ministers acts on behalf of the CE (external representation, conclusion of conventions, determination of programmes and tasks, internal rules, rules of procedure, etc.) and consists of the Ministers for Foreign Affairs of the member-States; in case of the Minister for Foreign Affairs being unable to perform his duties, another member of the Government concerned may sit on the Committee of Ministers; each representative on the Committee is entitled to one vote (Arts. 13 to 18 of the Statute). The Consultative Assembly is the deliberative organ and presents its conclusions, in the form of recommendations, to the Committee of Ministers; the member-States have different numbers of representatives in the Consultative Assembly (e.g. Austria 6, San Marino 2, Portugal 7, Italy, France, Germany and the United Kingdom 18 each); the representatives are delegated by the Parliaments of the member-States (Arts. 22 *et seq.* of the Statute).

Both the Committee of Ministers and the Consultative Assembly may set up committees in the different fields of the CE activity. There are a good number of such committees (steering committees), which submit their proposals to the establishing organ. Among other things, legal instruments, especially conventions on human rights, are prepared in the Committee on Legal Affairs and Human Rights.

Among the non-central, but highly important organs of the CE, special mention should be made of the European Committee on Human Rights and the European Court of Human Rights established by the aforesaid Human Rights Convention; the members are elected by the Committee of Ministers and the Consultative Assembly from among the candidates of member-States (Arts. 19 *et seq.* and Arts. 38 *et seq.* of the Statute).

(c) Seen from the aspect of the international conditions for the external economy, it is hardly questionable that our system of relations with the European Union (EU) and its full development – into membership status – is a high priority of economic policy.

[It may be remarked parenthetically about the name of this organization that while people knew what the earlier, frequently used denominations "Common Market" and "European Economic Community" stood for, these designations were not really accurate when used to refer to the Community as a whole. The official designation which came into general use later is "European Communities" (EC) – "*Europäische Gemeinschaften*" (EG), "*Communautés Européennes*" (CE) – covering the European Coal and Steel Community (the so-called Montanunion) established at Paris in 1951 and organizationally integrated in a separate treaty, as well as the European Economic Community (EEC) established by the Treaty of Rome of 25 March 1957 and the European Atomic Energy Community established by a separate treaty at the same place and time. In its narrow sense the EEC Treaty is usually called the "Treaty of Rome", while the latter is officially referred to as the "Euratom Treaty". In Hungary the European Atomic Energy Community is also referred to as the European Atom

Community (the latter being the official and legally accurate designation), the official German text refers to the Euratom Treaty as *Europäische Atomgemeinschaft*, although the English literature uses mainly the designation "European Atomic Energy Community". The Single European Act adopted at Luxembourg (17 February 1986) and at The Hague (28 February 1986) and covering the three communities, or the three founding documents as well as the conventions and instruments supplementary thereto, specifically provides (in Art. 1) that the European Communities are based on these instruments. The "European Union" was established by the Treaty of Maastricht at a new stage of integration, its Art. 1 stating that by this Treaty the Contracting Parties establish the European Union among themselves.]

(ca) The general political, geopolitical and historical considerations in favour of our integration into and accession to the European Union have been stated earlier, by way of prelude, among the principal motives of our joining the Council of Europe. Now we should specify the underlying (external) economic reasons and interests in more concrete terms.

Along the most comprehensive line, we refer to the economic weight of the EU in general and from the angle of Hungary's external economy in particular. With their more than 300 million inhabitants, the 15 countries of the Union constitute the largest market in the world. They account for one quarter of world production and for one third of foreign trade. They rank first or among the first in areas like steel production, motor-car construction, outlays on technological development, international movement of investment capacity (working capital), regional development programmes, number of large corporations, number and ratio of small and medium-sized enterprises, and large state or inter-enterprise projects (e.g. Airbus, cooperation in European aircraft manufacture). Given the interest of its economy and the resolve of its economic policy, the European Union stands ready to support Hungary in its efforts at catching up and integration. As for this country, its decisively European identity was established and is substantiated by its system of political, cultural and economic relations and cooperation dominating its entire history as well as by geopolitical considerations, with a quantitatively large part of its foreign trade turnover, and a particularly important part in terms of its structure, handled in this continent. From the EU and its member-States come most of the investment projects and other economic action programmes [credit, assistance; see item 3 (d) below]; the same can be said of technology and management skills; EU has acted as the major "pulling power" for the Hungarian systems of transport, traffic and telecommunications. Understandably, the flow of cultural and scientific values continues to be particularly intense in this region and promises to give further impulses in both directions; owing to centuries-old interactions, the European structure, concepts and institutions of the legal regulation of the economy have been traditionally compatible with Hungarian legal thinking (see Mádl: On the Way to the EU; *Ius Commune Europae; Quo Vadis* Europe?).

All these aspects combine to create most important conditions, and to act as a powerful catalyst, for the described strategy, namely for catching up with the centre by relying heavily on these frameworks and possibilities and by increasing national development efforts, as the country did with no small success after St. Stephen, King Matthias, the Age of Reform of the 1840s or the 1867 Compromise [see Mádl: *Az Európai Közösségek és Magyarország* (The European Communities and Hungary); Palánkai].

(cb) Before focusing below on the European Union we should refer briefly to the *objectives, principles and institutions* of this integrative community and the relevant treaties mentioned earlier. By institutions we mean here legal institutions, systems of political and economic policy concepts rather than organizations.

(i) Like the other instruments, the Treaty of Rome, in its Preamble and Art. 2, deals with *objectives* on the most general plane, those of the greatest importance being the solidarity and union of the European peoples, socio-economic progress, higher living standards, economic growth, development of productive forces, cooperation with other countries of Europe and world peace and freedom – by freedom the EU also means economic freedom, a market economy freedom, a market economy conforming with the values of CE [see item 3 (b) above] –, and establishment of a common market, integration of economic policies and creation of an economic community in pursuance of these goals.

(ii) The *principles and institutions* indicate the EU's true mission and substance specific to it, and their significance is conveyed by their simple designations.

Under the heading "The Foundations of the Community", the famous four freedoms figure in the first place in the Treaty of Rome and the supplementary treaties (Single European Act, Treaty of Maastricht): (1) customs union, free movement of goods (Arts. 9 *et seq.*), a separate section covering agriculture and agricultural policy (Arts. 38 *et seq.*); (2) services (Arts. 59 *et seq.*); (3) free movement of workers (Arts. 48 *et seq.*) and (4) capital (Arts. 67 *et seq.*). These are followed by the remainder of the principles and institutions as policies of the Community (numbering continued): (5) agricultural policy under the Articles referred to; (6) transport policy (Arts. 74 *et seq.*); (7) competition policy (rules on cartels, monopolies, dumping and subsidies; Arts. 85 *et seq.*); (8) economic policy (Art. 103); (9) financial and currency policies, monetary union (Arts. 102 *et seq.*); (10) trade policy (Arts. 110 *et seq.*); (11) social policy (Arts. 117 *et seq.*); (12) research and technological development policies (Arts. 130f *et seq.*); (13) policy on environmental protection (Art. 130r); (14) cooperation in foreign policy (Art. 30 of the Single European Act). While determining the basic elements of the common strategy of member-States and thus of the Community with respect to these policies, the constituent instruments have made it a right and a duty of the Community organs to translate them into practical terms through their own acts directly operative in member-States and through harmonization of the relevant laws and regulations of member-States; (15) what is really involved here is a "policy" which may also be called independent and which is termed by the Treaty of Rome as harmonization and approximation of laws (Arts. 99 to 110); (16) it is a new phenomenon that the Maastricht summit meeting of EU decided to make the Union still more comprehensive and to strengthen European political, economic and social cohesion through an economic and monetary union [Art. B of the EU Treaty; see item 3 (c) and (ce) in §38].

(cc) Although the various EU treaties have evolved both the static foundations and dynamic elements of the integration process, the core and substance of the EU and its instruments lie in a gradual realization of purposes through constitutional acts of its *organs*. which are called upon to create a Europe as conceived of in the principles, foundations and policies mentioned above.

(i) The *European Parliament*, elected by direct ballot since 1979, consists of directly elected members (numbering 628 since the latest accessions). Its powers of cooperation have been strengthened along with its consultative and control functions. Before adopting decisions the Council and the Commission are required to obtain the Parliament's views, position and occasionally consent (e.g. to the admission of new members) concerning their most important acts. While formerly they had to "consult" the Parliament, the new procedure requires them to "cooperate" and at times even to "decide jointly" (co-decision) with the European Parliament (Arts. 137 *et seq.*; Art. 189b; Art. 6 of the Single European Act). The Parliament is entitled to decide on the EU budget and may even make a motion of no-confidence against Commission members (Art. 144). In general, it decides by an absolute majority of the votes cast (Art. 141).

(ii) The *Council* or, as generally named, the Council of Ministers is the EU's real power and legislative organ and the representative body of member-States. It has 15 members, 1 from each member-State. Its role as the EU's highest power, legislative and decision-making organ has developed in the Hegelian dynamics of thesis–antithesis–synthesis. Of course, the concept of majority decision-making as formulated in the Treaty of Rome for the post-transition period has cut deep into the member-States' national sovereignty with regard to economic policy and therefore has more than once provoked strong resistance by the forces of disintegration. Since the Single European Act was signed, the synthesis has appeared to be gaining strength, owing to the rising trend of integration, the reassertion of the "creed of a united Europe". Along with cooperation with the Parliament as previously indicated with the requirement for proposals to be made by the Commission and, occasionally, for the Council to adopt unanimous decisions, the general majority principle has come to be constitutionally established (Arts. 145 *et seq.*, Arts. 6 to 12 of the Single European Act). Where the Treaty of Rome requires a qualified majority, the votes of member-States must be weighted as prescribed (10 each for the United Kingdom, France, Italy and Germany, 8 for Spain, 5 each for Belgium, Greece, the Netherlands and Portugal, 4 each for Austria and Sweden, 3 each for Denmark, Finland and Ireland, 2 for Luxembourg). Qualified majority consists of 62 votes, for which the Treaty of Rome requires votes jointly cast by 10 member-States (Art. 114). So the four larger member-States cannot dominate the rest even in cases of simple majority.

(iii) The Commission is the executive organ of EU. It is a *sui generis* institution rather than one representative of Governments. Its function is to achieve goals and to implement strategies. To this end, the Commission has to make thousands (if not hundreds of thousands or millions) of initiatives (preparing and submitting proposals to the Council and the Parliament), to implement measures and decisions (Art. 155). The Commission is the motor of EU. Its constitutional function is to act as the motivating force of implementing the European creed in the manner set out by the founders in the constituent instruments. The Commission has 20 members, quasi ministers, headed by the President, all of whom must act with high professional competence and with full authenticity of their independence. While not a representative organ, the Commission may not have more than two members who are nationals of the same member-State. It adopts decisions by a simple majority of votes. Subordinate to its members are the various Directorates-General (DG) and other administrative bodies (for more detail see the Convention of 8 April 1965 establishing the joint Council and Commission of the European Communities).

(iv) The *Court* (with 15 judges and 8 advocates general) is an important institution of the operation and development of the European Community, or, on a more general plane, of its operation and development in the spirit of a State under the rule of law in Europe. Its significant functions and competence include interpreting the constituent instruments, ensuring constitutionality in respect of acts of the EU organs, deciding legal disputes between member-States and EU as well as between legal entities of member-States and the European Community, to mention but the most important matters (Arts. 164 *et seq.*).

(v) The *Economic and Social Committee* consists of a total of 222 representatives of trade unions and other representational organizations. Its function is to ensure proper representation of this sphere in the operation of the EU. It must be consulted on matters within its competence (Arts. 193 to 197).

(vi) The *Court of Auditors* (of 15 members) is the financial control organ of EU and its institutions.

(vii) The *European Investment Bank* (EIB) assists a balanced economic development of the EU by, *inter alia*, non-profit banking transactions (credits, guarantees) in the case of projects aimed at developing poorer regions, modernizing industrial structures, creating job opportunities, effecting investments that can only be undertaken in cooperation between several member-States (Arts. 129–130). From 1977 EIB extended credits to Yugoslavia, the Mediterranean countries (Algeria, Morocco, Tunisia, Egypt, Lebanon, Cyprus, Israel, etc.), and EU's associate States of Africa, the Caribbean and the Pacific (ACP) under the Lomé Convention. A new phenomenon in EIB's history is the opening of credit lines from 1989 on with the consent of the Commission, to Hungary, Poland and the other newly democratic countries of Central and Eastern

Europe for purposes of project finance. The total amount of such credits exceeded ECU 3 billion between 1990 and 1996 (see European Investment Bank – Financing in Central and Eastern European Countries, EIB Report of January 1995; Act III of 1996 promulgating the Framework Agreement on Financial Cooperation between the Republic of Hungary and the European Investment Bank).

(viii) The *European Council* is a new institution of EU, one that, in recognition of actual practice, was confirmed by Art. 2 of the Single European Act and, after its repeal, by Art. D of the EU Treaty (of Maastricht). It is not to be mistaken for the Council of Europe (*Conseil Européen – Conseil de l'Europe; Europäischer Rat – Europa Rat*). It is nothing more than the regular (summit) meeting between the Heads of State or Government of the member-States and the President of the Commission to discuss highly important internal or international questions of the EU (e.g. the summit meetings at Copenhagen in 1993 and at Madrid in 1995 on EU's institutional reform and enlargement). Article D cited above reads as follows: "The European Council shall provide the Union with the necessary impetus for its development and shall define the general political guidelines thereof „. The participants are assisted in their work by the Ministers for Foreign Affairs and a member of the Commission.

(ix) Political cooperation is served by the conference of Ministers for Foreign Affairs, meeting at least four times a year, under the scheme of *European Political Cooperation* established by the Single European Act and assisted by the *Political Committee* consisting of political directors of the Ministries for Foreign Affairs (Art. 30 of the Single European Act).

(x) Although the EU's *professional administrative staff* is not a separate legal entity, it is worth noting on account of its importance, that the number of such employees now exceeds 15,000 and is close to 20,000. This "force" is a highly trained and well-paid "eurocracy" equipped with a modern technical infrastructure and supporting with a relatively high degree of efficiency the work of the above organs, the implementation of EU strategies and the performance of other tasks.

(cd) The *law of Europe* and the *legal acts* of the EU are a remarkably significant and exciting phenomenon of legal development, both universal and European, already representing a large domain of professional activities, literature on law, research and educational programmes, which we cannot but briefly mention here. The underlying substance is in social and economic development, a new quality and magnitude of political, economic and human relations, Eurocentripetal value-orientation of political and general thought. Removal of and progress beyond restrictions and controversies hindering development, have called for a new legal and organizational mechanism appropriate to act in this direction. There are many who have recognized the new, transcribing it into the law, and continue to do so by reliance on a wide-ranging armoury of differentiated tools and institutions. This process started with the Treaties of Paris and Rome and continued with the devising of instruments supplementary thereto, a long series of international treaties and other institutions, numerous fruits of unification and harmonization of law, an elaborate practice of law enforcement by the EU, interactive cooperation between European legal structures and national systems of law. The process goes on...

The dazzling variety of this phenomenon – the painstaking efforts at setting priorities, crises and euphoria, strains and contradictions witnessed in the law of Europe and the national legislation, yet with the main stream always capable of resolving related concerns – can only be seen in its true depth in the voluminous literature, books, hundreds of journals and, of course, the practical functioning of the relevant institutions (of the many possible sources see, e.g. Ipsen, Kecskés, Király, Martonyi, Pescatore, Mádl; Weatherill–Beaumont: European Perspectives – Thirty Years of Community Law, edited by the EU Commission). Here and now, however, a brief reference should be limited to legal acts like (1) international conventions on integration (e.g. constituent and supplementary instruments of the EU, the European Patent Convention, the Rome Convention on the PIL of Contracts); (2) regulations, (3) directives, (4) decisions, (5) recommendations, and (6) opinions issued or formulated within the competence of the Council and the Commission in accordance with the provisions of the Treaty of Rome (Art. 189); (7) statements of position (resolutions and proposals) by the other EU organs (Arts. 141 and 198); (8) judgments and (9) preliminary ruling (*Vorabentscheidung*) as the most important legal acts of the Court; the latter may be requested by national courts when proceedings before them require interpretation of a source of the EU law (Art. 177).

As regards the *relationship* of legal acts *to national laws,* the priority of the former is unambiguously clear in the case of international conventions. The core and substance in respect of Court decisions lies in direct enforceability and execution (Art. 176). The regulations of the Council and the Commission are directly applicable and are binding on all member-States, while the substance of their directives is binding on the member-State(s) to which they are addressed, but the legal form of expressing the substance falls within national competence. The decisions of the Commission are binding on the member-States to which they are addressed, but the recommendations and opinions are not (Art. 189).

(ce) For all the problems encountered, the past decade has witnessed *notable progress in the EU integration process*.

(i) The *Single European Act* (SEA) amended and supplemented the constituent instruments of the EU. Its provisions aim to strengthen the process of integration and the EU unity and to increase the efficiency of EU institutions. The main aspects thereof have been addressed, and the amendments to the relevant articles cited, in our discussion of the EU's principles, institutions, organs, and legal acts.

The preparatory document for SEA was the *White Book*, or the programme for a single internal market and its schedule of implementation. Its elaboration was decided upon by the Brussels European Council Meeting of 29–30 March 1985. Elaborated by the Commission, the White Book formulated that programme in 222 paragraphs with three parts, annexed thereto mapping out the detailed timetable, and stressed that the programme was designed to implement the objectives and principles set forth in the constituent instruments of the EU (paras. 1 *et seq.*). Envisaging over 300 legal acts (conventions, regulations, directives, decisions and recommendations), the White Book found it possible and necessary to deregulate, i.e. dismantle, the legal obstacles to a single market and to create a harmonized or uniform legal order replacing the nationally non-integrated domestic systems, naturally through the actions of EU organs, paradoxically by the aid of a multitude of norms. Each partial timetable scheduled the legal acts for the periods 1985–1986 and 1987–1992 [on this and on details of implementation, see Király: *Az EU belső piac szabályozása* (Regulation of the EU Internal Market)].

(ii) Another important milestone in the realization of the EU creed is constituted by the conclusion of the *EU Treaty* in 1992. The *Maastricht Council Meeting* of 9–10 December 1991 [see item 3 (c), (cc), (viii) in §39] made another great stride in the process of European integration by the *EU Treaty* of 7 February 1992 formulating the principles, devising the institutions and determining the schedule of establishing a political, economic and monetary union as a move towards a fuller development of the EU. The new agreements, the significant amendments to the Treaty of Rome, and the protocols governing the operation of the new institutions represent progress of historic import (source: *Conseil Européen, Maastricht, les 9 et 10 Décembre 1991, Conclusions de la Présidence*, Doc. SI/91/910.). Articles A and B of the EU Treaty state in this respect that by signing the present Treaty the Contracting Parties establish a European Union among themselves; this Treaty marks a new stage in the process of creating a closer union of European peoples in which decisions will be brought as close as possible to citizens; the Union is built on the European Communities, supplemented by policies and forms of cooperation as envisaged by the present Treaty; the aim of the Union is to promote economic and social progress, particularly by establishing a space without internal borders, strengthening economic and social cohesion, creating an economic and monetary union and, finally, a single currency.

Also expressed is the need for cooperation in the fields of common foreign and security policies and the administration of justice as well as in the introduction of citizenship of the Union. Beside economic policies, great emphasis is laid on advancing the policy of environmental protection, research and development policies, general political cooperation, and a uniform European social policy.

However, the most decisive new element should be deemed to be constituted by the full development of the *European Economic and Monetary Union*, a single European system of monetary policy, payments and finances, which is being introduced as planned in this last decade of our century. The high stakes are doubtless in the creation of a single currency (euro) and the establishment of a European Central Bank (ECB), the preparations for which are facilitated by several new institutions, namely the Monetary Commission, the European System of Central Banks (ESCB) and the European Monetary Institute (EMI).

It is appropriate to single out for attention two of the Maastricht resolutions: the one stating that European integration *is to enter irreversibly its third stage of development* along the lines described above; again, in addition to the many aforementioned agreements and planned institutions and measures, this is spelled out, as if by way of summation, in a separate instrument called the Protocol on the transition to the third stage of Economic and Monetary Union, the first paragraph of which contains the highly important declaration to the effect that the Community is to enter irreversibly the third stage of development. The third paragraph of the Protocol provides that this new stage, with the institutions supporting it, must start operating not later than 1 January 1999.

(iii) The dynamic advance of the European integration process also concerns the *EU's institutional reform and enlargement.* The *declaration concerning the enlargement of EC and the admission of new members* was already adopted at Maastricht. This is not a normative agreement but "only" a general policy statement by the Twelve to the effect that any European State whose system of government is based on the principles of democracy may apply for admission to membership in the Union (Doc. SN. 271/1/91). However, the need for further progress (internal institutional reform and enlargement) and a political declaration thereof has since been reaffirmed by the summit meetings of the European Council (Corfu, Essen, Copenhagen and Madrid) on the general plane. The many challenges (global competition, environmental protection, security, unemployment, integration of the market now embracing 15 countries, more efficient operation of EU institutions, need for a more effective international identity and involvement, revolutionary transformation in the Central and Eastern European countries, accession of their new democracies to the EU) have evoked at the EU summit meetings the main strategic elements of the responses to them. The responses include EU efforts to grow closer to its citizens through better legitimation and to enhance the development of its integration, increase its international weight and effectiveness, and face the need for enlargement through institutional reform. As is stated in the final declaration by the Presidency of the 1995 Madrid summit, enlargement is a political necessity and a historical opportunity for Europe, it will guarantee the Continent's stability and security and thereby offer both the applicant States and the current members of the Union new perspectives for economic growth and general welfare (see Mádl: *Quo vadis* Europe?, pp. 424 *et seq.* and State and Economy in Transformation, Sections 53–58).

(cf) The cited final declaration leads us on to the system of relations between EU and Hungary, in which three phases can be distinguished in the historical perspective.

(i) In the aftermath of negative attitudes, indecision and hesitant steps during the previous decades, when the former socialist countries did not even want to hear of recognizing the European Communities despite their heavy dependence on trade with them, the relationship between the European Communities and the Central and Eastern European countries arrived at *a new stage in 1988–1990*, with the latter recognizing the former and with the status of relations thoroughly rewritten in a short time. Indeed, a new chapter was opened in the law of international economic relations as well [see Balázs; Dienes–Oehm: *Az Európai Közösségek* (The European Communities); Martonyi: *Az EGK hatásköre a nemzetközi kapcsolatok terén* (The Competence of EEC in the Field of International Relations); Mádl: *Az EGK és Magyarország* (EEC and Hungary); Mádl: *State Economy in Transformation.* "Rewriting International Conditions"]. Significant events of this process were the East–West Conferences of 1987 and 1990 organized by Geneva University's Institute for the Law of Europe on the "political and legal frameworks of commercial and economic relations between the EC and the Eastern countries" (see Maresceau).

Following upon the earlier technical and sectoral treaties, the first decisive breakthrough was represented, beside recognition and the establishment of diplomatic relations, by the *Agreement* between Hungary and the EEC *concerning Trade and Commercial and Economic Cooperation*, signed at Brussels on 26 September 1988 (published in *Magyar Közlöny*, No. 4 of 1989).

The Agreement consists of three important parts (chapters), the first governing the application of such fundamental principles as the most-favoured-nation treatment conforming to GATT, non-discrimination, mutual benefits, liberalization, and mainly the gradual lifting of quantitative restrictions by the EEC, which were formerly highly prejudicial to Hungarian interests.

The chapter on economic cooperation opened a relatively wide panorama of programmes for intensive cooperation by specifying the economic sectors covered, defining the forms of cooperation and envisaging scientific cooperation.

These programmes are also facilitated by a Mixed Commission set up by Chapter III to encourage the implementation of the Agreement and the development of cooperation.

(ii) The great historical turn around in Hungary was effectively brought about in 1989–1990 by well-known pioneering political efforts. In the wake of the Agreement signed in 1988, it resulted in EEC adopting a new policy towards Hungary.

Under the Agreement of 1988 the gradual lifting of quantitative restrictions by 1995 was "set aside", with most of the quantitative restrictions on exports suspended without further delay (Council Decree No. 3691/1989 of 4 December 1989, Official Journal No. L 362, 12.12.1989), while the system of special facilities, or the General System of Preferences (GSP; see §45), under which Hungarian commodities placed on EC markets are subject to more favourable customs tariffs than those of the advanced countries, was extended to Hungary (Council Decree No. 3896/1989 of 18 December 1989, Official Journal No. L 383, 30.12.1989).

In addition to the abovementioned and other forms of support for transformation and reconstruction (see item 5 below), the *Association Agreement* was the next decisive step forward. Called the Europe Agreement concerning the establishment of association between the European Communities and its member-States on the one hand and Hungary on the other, it was initialled on 22 November 1991 and then signed on 16 December by the EC Commission and the Government of the Republic of Hungary and, while operative *ad interim* (until its ratification), it was promulgated in Hungary by Act I of 1994 after its ratification by EC and its member-States (Art. 238 of the Treaty of Rome, Art. 118 of the Agreement).

The Association Agreement imports many things. As a prelude to the complete *opera*, it expresses in the Preamble a promise of full accession, albeit without the EC's legal commitment, but also declaring its aim to help create the conditions for Hungary's full membership status. However, more important is the fact that, in terms of its basic thrust, the Agreement refers to goals and cooperation rather close to membership status and involving aspects of membership, thus naturally going much further than the Agreement of 1988. In respect of the four main freedoms – free movement of goods, capital, services and workers – the Agreement does not imply a fully-fledged status (for it presupposes the required level of development). However the said freedoms do serve as a framework, with the different headings and chapters envisaging our legal approximation in terms thereof, by gradually removing customs tariffs and lifting quantitative restrictions with regard to industrial free trade and according special treatment to certain "heavy" branches like textile and steel exports as well as to agriculture as regulated in a separate chapter, thus opening growing possibilities for integration in nearly all fields of economic life. Mention is deserved by the major fields (titles of the Agreement): political dialogue; general principles; free movement of goods (subject to transitory regulation as indicated above, with full freedom to be achieved by stages); movement of workers, services and capital; approximation of laws and regulations related to integration (customs, company law, industrial property, consumer protection, taxes, etc.); cooperation in all important fields of economic life (industry, investments, scientific and technological development, education, agriculture, energy, environmental protection, transport, telecommunications, postal service, insurance, banking, regional development, social policy, development of small and medium-sized enterprises, information and audiovisual media, tourism, statistics, collaboration of economists); cultural cooperation; financial cooperation; EC aids. Particular emphasis should be given here to Chapter III on the approximation of laws for the added reason that it also "looks to" full membership, with the Contracting Parties recognizing that a basic precondition for Hungary's economic integration into the Community lies in approximating the country's present and future laws and regulations to those of the Community, and with Hungary ensuring that its future laws and regulations will be as compatible as possible with those of the Community (Art. 67). What we have is, indeed, an association agreement exerting a more intensive attraction than ever. The heading "Institutions" dealing with the organizational set-up similarly marks a new feature compared to the earlier EC–Hungary Agreement inasmuch as there appear in it organs named the Association Council and the Association Committee, which are called upon to monitor the status of implementation of the Association Agreement and to deal with any matter which the Parties may deem to have relevance for the development of cooperation.

After this review, it is perhaps worth noting that the Preamble to the Agreement refers to all the political theses and values as well as those of social and economic philosophy (basic principles of the CE, EC, CSCE, the Charter of Paris) which govern the establishment and operation of organizations of European integration. Hungary's association means its definite and natural acceptance thereof and its sharing the common heritage of Europe.

(iii) The third stage involves the *process of accession* lasting until adoption of a favourable decision on accession or full membership.

Full membership is covered by Art. 237 of the Treaty of Rome, its essential elements being the right of every European country to apply for admission, the application to be submitted to the Council, which is to decide by an unanimous vote after hearing the Commission and after the Parliament giving its consent with an absolute majority. The provisions on the necessary adaptation and the conditions for admission are laid down in a treaty between the EC member-States and the applicant State, the treaty to be subject to ratification by all States parties in accordance with their respective constitutional procedures.

The Hungarian decision on external economic policy was defined in the submission of the application for full membership as early as 1994 (*application for accession to EU*). It is outlined in the application that by national efforts to implement the strategy for accession Hungary will meet the requirements of full membership on the basis of its historical, cultural, political and geopolitical peculiarities, its process of social, political, cultural and economic transformation, a pluralist democracy established and gathering force, building a state under the rule of law and a social market economy, and sharing the common European heritage.

The EU summit meetings referred to earlier (Copenhagen 1993, Corfu 1994, Essen 1994, Madrid 1995) gave expression to the rationality and historical topicality of enlargement, as is expressed in the cited declaration of the Madrid summit. In that declaration it is stated, furthermore, that the negotiations on accession can be started six months after the conclusion of the Intergovernmental Conference, that is, at the beginning of 1998. The decision will depend on the degree of compliance by the applicant States with the conditions determined by the Copenhagen summit, namely (1) stability and appropriate functioning of democratic institutions (pluralist democracy, law-governed State, human rights, minority protection); (2) a working market economy; (3) competitive position of the economy in the internal market of the Union; (4) ability to assume all the obligations emanating from membership, including the established system of rules (*acquis communautaire*) as well as the objectives of the political, economic and monetary union; (5) the Union's ability to admit the new members by keeping to the schedule of integration with the aid of its institutional reform (Together in Europe, EC Newsletter for Central and Eastern Europe, 18 December 1995, No. 80, pp. 2 *et seq.*; Balázs–Maresceau: *Magyarország felkészülése* (Hungary's Preparation); Mádl: *Quo vadis* Europe?; *idem*: EU Integration Process – Enlargement and Institutional Reforms).

The necessity for development under these conditions and for a corresponding economic policy strategy – together with several other demands such as operation of a balanced social structure and a cultural and moral order – naturally follows primarily from Hungary's own internal exigencies of development (or additionally from them). Yet, or precisely for this reason, particular importance is attached to intensifying general and economic policy efforts at all levels in order for us to contribute with shared responsibility to the economic, cultural and moral advancement of Europe. For this to be achieved it is also necessary that the large national systems of legal regulation affecting the integration process in particular should be adjusted, to the limit of possibilities, to the currently prevalent EU system of economic and legal regulation and that the endeavours of individuals, society and the political sphere should also be in keeping with this process (see Andorka; Balázs–Maresceau; Mádl: On the way to the EU; Mádl: On the Legal Regulation; *idem: Ius Commune Europae; idem:* EU Integration Process).

(d) In similar manner, it is for the same stated reasons that relations and cooperation with the *European Free Trade Association* (EFTA) could not start to develop until comparatively recently.

EFTA came into being in 1960. The Convention establishing it entered into force on 3 May 1960. Its members were Austria, the United Kingdom, Denmark, Finland, Portugal and Sweden, all of which have since become EU countries. Its present members are Iceland, Liechtenstein, Norway and Switzerland. EFTA formed part of the European integration process which was intended to turn the hostile Europe of the world war into a new Europe, a Europe of cooperation and unity freed from the trade barriers raised by the world economic crisis. Ever since the EU established its own community, more closed but of great attractive force, EFTA, hesitantly seeking both cooperation and compensation for non-adherence, has itself also become a significant institution of integration, albeit with a lesser degree of efficiency, for Hungary (Resch).

EFTA has adopted, just as the EC has, the CE scale of fundamental philosophical and political values [see subitems (b) and (c) above]. The Preamble to and Art. 2 of the EFTA Convention contain the same general objectives as are set out in the Preamble to the Treaty of Rome (improvement of living standards, expansion of production, intensification of cooperation, peace, financial stability, harmonious increase in world trade, etc.).

(da) The EFTA Convention formulates the following concrete *economic policy principles and institutions*; (i) gradual abolition of customs duties (in full measure by 1966) on industrial products (Arts. 3 *et seq.*), with no customs duty internally, and every member-state applying its own tariff system externally;

the Association envisaged no free trade system in respect of agricultural products (Arts. 21 *et seq.*); (ii) the "50% rule", under which preferential tariffs apply only to products that are of at least 50% EFTA origin (Art. 4); (iii) gradual lifting of quantitative restrictions (Arts. 10–11); limitation and gradual abolition of subsidies (Art. 13); suppression of forms of behaviour restrictive of competition and of dumping (Arts. 15 and 17); cooperation in economic development programmes (in coping with balance-of-payments problems, developing poorer regions) in the fields of agriculture and fisheries (Arts. 22 to 30).

(db) The EFTA *organs* are (i) the Council; (ii) such organs, committees and other forms of organization, established by and subordinate to the Council, as the Council may deem necessary for fulfilling its function (Art. 32); (iii) consultative and supervisory committees to resolve disputes between members (Art. 31); (iv) the Secretariat (based in Geneva) set up by the Council and headed by the Secretary-General; and the representations in Geneva (Art. 34; Rieber).

(dc) *Closer cooperation with* the Central and Eastern European countries, including *Hungary,* is developing progressively.

The breakthrough has occurred. On 14 June 1990 the greater EFTA (before Austria, Finland and Sweden had become EU members) and the Governments of the Central and Eastern European countries adopted a *Joint Declaration* calling for closer cooperation in the fields of the economy, tourism, transportation, environmental protection, scientific and technological development; proclaiming assistance in economic restructuring and creating a market economy. This latter goal was realized in 1993, when the EFTA member-States and Hungary signed a free trade agreement (promulgated in Hungary by Act LXXXIII of 1993).

(e) The *European Economic Area* (EEA) is a new vision (Reisch) of EU and EFTA, which took on a more concrete form first at the joint ministerial meeting of these two institutions of integration in December 1989. Today's political visions are also known to become tomorrow's realities. After the full development of EU's single internal market EEA became a functioning institution: the EU member-States and the then member-States of the EFTA (Austria, Finland, Iceland, Liechtenstein, Norway, Sweden and Switzerland) signed the Convention on the European Economic Area at Oporto on 2 May 1992. The EEA now forms part of the European reality and has even acquired a notable volume of literature (see Laursen, Rhein, Weatherill–Beaumont, pp. 7–8), although its weight has diminished with the admission of Austria, Finland and Sweden to membership in EU. The main purpose of the EEA is to promote economic cooperation among EU and EFTA member-States and the full establishment of an integrated single market in the whole region under identical terms and rules of competition (Art. 1 of the EEA Convention).

Also, the EEA is destined to be integrative in the sense that it should not dig a trench around the EU and EFTA, but should facilitate, directly or indirectly, the full integration into Europe of the Central European countries, including

Hungary. In this sense it is an intermediary phenomenon, an active catalyst for bringing about a more mature, more fully developed system by contributing its share to the efforts in that direction. Nor can matters be envisioned otherwise, if only for the reason that Hungary, for instance, is maintaining intensive and strengthening relations, as indicated above, with both the EU and EFTA. From this it obviously follows that the new common organization thereof cannot but have a positive effect on EU–Hungarian and EFTA–Hungarian relations, all the more so since the EEA, EU–Hungarian and EFTA–Hungarian cooperation equally serves to strengthen the same integration processes.

(f) The Danube–Adria scheme of cooperation originally embraced five countries [*Pentagonale*: Austria, Czechoslovakia (Czech Republic and Slovakia after the separation), former Yugoslavia, Hungary and Italy] and extended to include Poland (*Hexagonale*) at the summit meeting of the Five at Dubrovnik on 27 July 1991. Since 1992 it has been operating as the *Central European Initiative* (CEI) with the participation of Croatia, Slovenia, and Bosnia and Herzegovina from this region under the impact of the Southern Slav developments, and is an added element of the international conditions for the external economy of Hungary. This scheme was launched as part of the great transformations in Central and Eastern Europe by the countries concerned (with Czechoslovakia joining them later) at the Budapest conference of Deputy Prime Ministers and Ministers for Foreign Affairs in November 1989. After numerous previous intergovernmental conferences the first summit of the Prime Ministers of the parties to the Pentagonal Scheme of Regional Cooperation took place in Venice on 1 August 1990. It adopted the Political Document of the Pentagonale, together with concrete proposals and a three-year programme of work containing projects of cooperation, which in the meantime have naturally widened in scope.

CEI is not an organization and has no statute, but, in the given historical and geopolitical situation, it acts as a forum which has evolved from intensive political, economic and cultural cooperative operations between the States mentioned above. However, as it can be stated in the light of its work and declarations, it is a forum where the participants not only hold meetings, but also make concrete political, economic and other initiatives in pursuance of specific goals and formulate programmes of action envisaging cooperation in concrete development efforts in fields like the transport infrastructure, environmental protection, cooperative operations between small and medium-sized enterprises, migration research, cultural and scientific cooperation, and telecommunications. By ensuring greater efficiency of implementation, CEI can be a significant motive force of national development and of integration.

(g) The *United Nations Economic Commission for Europe* (ECE) is one of the regional institutions. Hungary participates in its activity which is of importance for us. This forum operates to create better economic policy conditions for European economic relations. In the legal aspect we contribute to ECE's work of codification, which is of relevance to the contractual practice of Hungarian foreign trade, namely to the elaboration of a variety of general conditions intended to facilitate the development of international trade law (see §68) and to the drafting of conventions (see §117).

(h) France proposed (in President Mitterrand's speech in the European Parliament on 25 October 1989) the establishment of the *Banque Européenne pour la Reconstruction et le Développement* (EBRD), which led to its constituent instrument being initialled at Paris on 29 May 1990. The Bank is an important regional (European) institution, although its founders and providers of finance include advanced non-European countries to the tune of nearly 25% of its capital (with 8.5% of shares held by Japan and 10% by the USA, which are the largest individual contributors of capital).

The Bank's importance to Hungary is evident as its function is to assist with the economic transformation of the Central and Eastern European countries by acting as an institution which seeks to ensure proper utilization of the advanced countries' capacity and readiness to provide finance. On the Government's proposal the Parliament decided on Hungary's accession in November 1990 [Decision No. 78/1990. (XI.17.)], and the Agreement establishing the Bank was promulgated by Act LV of 1991.

The order of magnitude is noteworthy: the new Bank started operating with a capital stock of ECU 10 billion, amounting to more than US $10 billion, contributed by the founders, which include 40 countries: all the European States except Albania, the USA, Canada, Mexico, Japan, Australia, New Zealand, South Korea, Israel, Egypt and Morocco, as well as the EC Commission and the European Investment Bank. The Bank's majority shares, totalling 51%, are held by the EU member-States, but the largest individual package of shares (10%) is held by the USA. A total of 13.5% of capital is contributed by the Central and Eastern European countries, with the former Soviet Union having a share of 6%. Hungary contributes 0.79% of the capital stock, amounting to ECU 79 million, of which 30% – one half in cash and one half in promissory notes – had to be paid during the following five years, so that Hungary's share imposed no additional great burden on the state budget. On the other hand, the probable benefits were sizable. The Bank was established to assist the Central and Eastern European countries in economic restructuring, speeding up privatization and launching new projects.

Thus, according to its planned strategy, the Bank extends *60%* of its loans *to private undertakings* and 40% for the purpose of facilitating the development of publicly-owned enterprises and the implementation of certain infrastructural programmes. Since the capital is contributed by the founders in the above shares, but credit may only be granted to the Central and Eastern European countries, the amount of credits will always exceed by far the contributions paid by the latter. As no preliminary quotas were fixed for the different countries, the Bank decides on each individual matter submitted to it.

(i) Like EBRD, the *Organization for Economic Cooperation and Development* (OECD) is a European regional international organization having extra-

European members as well (e.g. Japan and Australia). Its constituent instrument was signed at Paris on 14 December 1960. The founders included the USA and Canada, because OECD came into being as the successor in title to the Organization for European Economic Cooperation (OEEC), which had been established originally in 1948 to facilitate the Marshall Aid operations and the post-war economic consolidation. Today it is an organization for interstate cooperation between the industrialized countries with a developed market economy. Its main purpose is to coordinate the economic, trade and development policies of member-States. While it has no administrative powers to sanction its objectives, its decisions based on consensus have considerable authority and actual weight. Membership means that the given country justifiably forms part of the family of countries with a developed market economy as well as of their mechanisms for economic cooperation, with the inherent possibilities thereof open to them.

Within the framework of the Memorandum on Cooperation with the Visegrád countries, adopted in 1991 following the systemic changes, the OECD facilitated the processes of transformation with a view to creation of market economies. On the basis of the experience of international relations and of favourable decision by the OECD Council, Hungary submitted its application for accession in 1993 (Várkonyi, p. 200). It was an important development that after Czech Republic (1995), Poland and Hungary were also admitted to membership in the OECD in 1996.

(j) An important place among the regional sets of international conditions was occupied in the past by the *Council for Mutual Economic Assistance* (CMEA), which was established as an organ of economic cooperation among the former socialist countries in 1949 and, when in a state of collapse, it went out of existence in 1991. Its role is now history, but its considerable negative effect is still felt (for an analysis, see the third Hungarian edition of this book, pp. 229 *et seq.*). At the Council's (closing) session at Budapest on 28 June 1991 the member-States decided to abolish CMEA without a successor in title and signed the relevant instruments, which provided for the settlement of the Organization's assets and other matters, and, to that end, they set up a Liquidation Commission. In Hungary, the Charter of CMEA and the instruments of accession to it were abrogated by Act XXXV of 1991 "in view of CMEA's extinction".

(k) Finally, among the regional systems of cooperation, mention should be made of the latest one, that of the *Three* (now Five) *of Visegrád* (Czechoslovakia – later Czech Republic and Slovakia –, Poland, Hungary and Slovenia which subsequently joined). Given their geopolitical situation, their historical links, the similar degree and intensity of their political democracy based on a state under the rule of law, of the development of their market economy and of their European commitment, the three founding countries saw and see a better possibility for future development in a new special form of cooperation, in pursuance of the fundamental goal of full integration into the political, economic, legal and security systems of Europe. Closer cooperation between the Three (Five) is directed towards this end rather than some sort of separation. This regional scheme of cooperation is aimed at building a system of relations between regions, with particular emphasis on that part of Europe which was previously excluded from the process of European integration, at establishing a network of relations that will link the centre of Europe with the Baltic region and the countries in the east.

It was at the Cracow summit (15 October 1991), following those at Bratislava and Visegrád, that the Visegrád Three formulated most clearly their philosophy and strategy of economic policy and economic cooperation. In addition to discussing and coordinating ways of improving cooperation in the process of political, security and European integration, this forum has, in its *sui generis* strategy for cooperation, outlined the main elements of an agreement establishing a certain kind of free trade zone. With the break up of Czechoslovakia, the *Central European Free Trade Agreement* (generally abbreviated as CEFTA on the analogy of EFTA) was signed by four countries (Czech Republic, Hungary, Poland and Slovakia) at Warsaw on 21 December 1992.

According to the provisions of Chapter I, the States parties to the Agreement decided to complete the development of their markets into a free trade region by 1 January 2001, with customs duties on industrial products to be phased out symmetrically and with other protectionist measures to be abolished by that date.

In Chapter II the set of rules on trade in agricultural products similarly follows the symmetry ensuring a global balance of benefits, but this global symmetry seeks to give effect to the criteria of global balance in keeping with the national specifics of the agricultural market.

Chapter III on general provisions contains institutions and elements of cooperation like rules on origin, non-discrimination, payments in convertible currency, anti-trust and anti-dumping rules, anti-dumping measures based on GATT rules, rules on the functioning of mixed commissions, etc.) (see Mádl: CEFTA).

4. The *bilateral conventions and agreements* make up a significant part of the set of international conditions and are of vital importance to international economic cooperation, owing to the large number of these regulatory systems as well as their considerable operative efficiency and normative potential on the practical plane. As is known, bilateral international agreements generally contain less esoteric commitments and declarations and much more concrete operative rights and obligations, which commitments are easier to fulfil.

Generally speaking, the *panorama thereof opens up broad perspectives*, embracing important agreements regulative of details, such as agreements on friendship, general trade agreements, agreements on industrial cooperation, agreements on customs and taxation (including agreements for the avoidance of double taxation) which have assumed profound importance recently, payments and credit agreements, consular conventions covering problems of economic cooperation, and agreements on legal assistance. This enumeration does not indicate by any means the full weight and range of bilateral agreements, running to volumes even for individual States, as they are one of the major instruments of active state participation in the international division of labour (for more detail, see item 3 in §63).

5. A considerable set of international conditions for the operation of the Hungarian (external) economy and for the process of profound transformation (especially in the initial period) was and still is constituted by the *foreign assistance and credit programmes* under which the EEC, the OECD countries, IMF, WB, the European Investment Bank, EBRD, the 24 and several other countries which have supported economic restructuring and the development of a market economy and Hungary. This support has been forthcoming with a view to facilitating the operation of the world economy and their own economies on the one hand and the process of transformation and the better operation of the economy in Hungary on the other, the declared purpose being to help enhance the values as proclaimed at the most general level in the philosophy of the Council of Europe [see item 3 (b) in §39], and cherished by the Western countries, as well as in the Central and Eastern European countries, Hungary among them. In addition to the implementation of related policies, at issue is the stabilization of the economy which, given our economic difficulties and indebtedness, would hardly be possible without the said credits and assistance programmes.

These programmes, while in a state of flux in terms of both scope and form of assistance owing to the obtaining circumstances (the transformations which have taken place in the countries of Central and Eastern Europe), comprise the following *main components*: IMF and WB credits [item 2 (a) in §39]; untied credits, project credits for investment purposes, credit guarantees and *stand-by* credits from governments and the EU (for export credits and projected credits); grants-in-aid for training programmes, business venture funds, foundation of joint ventures, regional projects of environmental protection, professional and technical development plans for public administration and democratic institutions, etc., and the establishment of EBRD [item 2 (h) in §39) handling capital flow from the advanced to the Central and Eastern European countries. The importance of the assistance and credit programmes may be indicated by the following brief statements.

The volume of grants-in-aid ranges from a few million to 100 million dollars (e.g. the EC PHARE and USA SEED programmes are of the latter order of magnitude).

The implementation of the EU programme covering a period of several years is supported by a "framework agreement" (3 September 1990, published in *Magyar Közlöny*, No. 54 of 1991) laying down the rules and procedures for organizing the different financing and development projects in cooperation between the EU Commission and the Hungarian Government.

Of course, the credits which, in view of our debt burden, provide external finance for the economy are in the order of billions of dollars.

It will certainly not be amiss to give a few practical examples in the world of science. First, we refer to the EC TEMPUS Programme, which made it possible, *inter alia*, for several hundred students to attend universities of the EU countries in cooperation between the EU and Hungarian universities and with the financial assistance of the EU. Second, we had an easy-term WB loan facilitated to develop human resources required for economic development and restructuring. Opened to Hungary in 1991, amounting to 150 million dollars and combined with a similar amount of Hungarian support, it served to finance for years such important projects as streamlining higher education, professional training and retraining, establishment and development of the informational infrastructure, and support for young research workers to study abroad. Third, the said American Support for East European Democracy (SEED) is destined for the implementation of various educational and information projects for Hungarian institutes and specialists; further the Hungarian–American Enterprise Fund was likewise established within its framework [see item 2 (d) in §60].

§40. THE INTERNAL ORGANIZATIONAL STRUCTURE OF THE EXTERNAL ECONOMY

1. The main objectives and principles concerning the external economy, covered in greater depth by item 3 in §38 above, mean, *inter alia*, the following in respect to the organizational system: organizational rights and duties of the State which serve to have the Hungarian economy as efficiently as possible involved in and integrated into world economic processes in general and the European economy in particular; and further economic freedom and a set of rules on association, investment and transactions on the basis of which enterprises and natural persons enjoy the largest possible measure of autonomy in extending their business ventures to other countries, increasing their foreign trade activities and attracting foreign entrepreneurs to Hungary. *Generally speaking*, they constitute *an organizational structure at state, social and entrepreneurial levels* which serves to facilitate the attainment of these goals and the implementation of the principles of action.

In its main aspects, all this has called for two things.

First, dismantling the state monopoly in foreign trade. As will be seen below, the organizational pattern of the external economy clearly indicates that the foreign trade monopoly has disappeared from present-day reality (on its substance and erosion, see Chapter XI in the second Hungarian edition of this book). Its "abrogation" with general effect by positive law was provided for in Art. 54 of Act XXII of 1990 on Deregulation.

Second, in a constructive aspect, institutionalizing state involvement by creation of appropriate organs and powers that are natural elements of an efficient external economy in modern democracies and market economies. It means not so much new organs and institutions as rather intelligent cooperation between the classical bourgeois state organization and economic actors. Of course, there are also new organs and institutions, but modernity appears more in new and more efficient functions like building our relations with the EU, participating in the establishment and operation of large international organizations, concluding and applying comprehensive conventions, to mention but a few such roles, "small" and new. There was and still is a need to improve the domestic infrastructure and to enrich the experience of related activities in this domain, representing as it does the realm of action described in the preceding (39) and the present (40) paragraph. Of course, the static order of things (the organization and its terms of reference) is of equally great import and is just as inseparable from success as the combined role of hardware and software is. Today, given the economic transformation of Hungary, the involvement of the State – both hardware and software – is still very important for paving the way for its own withdrawal at a time when a strong economy will have been created in the external economic context (see item 3 in §38).

As regards now the *concrete actors of the external economic system*, they are the corresponding institutions of the state organization (item 2), the different social organizations (item 3), and the subjects of actual economic and business actions (item 4). The following picture may be presented of them.

2. *Viewed as well from the angle of the organizational pattern of the external economy, the institutions of the state organization* are identical with themselves, namely they include the Parliament, the President of the Republic, the Government with its ministries, other central administrative organs with their general competence as defined by the Constitution and other laws in accordance with the principles of a state under the rule of law and the division of powers. The focus here is on the role which these organs play in relation to the external economy. Next we will cast a brief glance at this role, with its intensity and with the manifold activities of the various organs discussed in the chapters of this book dealing with concrete institutions and questions of regulation.

(a) The *Parliament* ratifies international treaties of paramount importance to the external economic relations of the Republic of Hungary; determines by laws and regulations the government structure, including the organs directing the organization of the external economy (ministries and other organs); adopts the laws governing the operation of the external economy in accordance with the social and economic system of the country; further approves the state budget bearing on the external economy; approves the government programme, including the main elements and directions of the Government's external economic strategy. These powers, fundamental to the external economy, are determined by the Constitution (Art. 19).

(b) The *President of the Republic* has or can have an indirect role to play in the field of the external economy by, *inter alia*, sanctioning laws relative to the external economy; appointing, on the Prime Minister's proposal, ministers, ambassadors and envoys, as well as secretaries of state and the President and Vice-Presidents of the Hungarian National Bank; and concluding international treaties concerning the external economy (Arts. 30/A and 33 of the Constitution). He has general authority to represent the Republic of Hungary [para. 1 (a) of Art. 30/A], but conclusion of treaties the subject-matter of which falls within the competence of the legislature is subject to the prior consent of Parliament [*idem*, subpara. (b)]. Presidential functions are unlikely to be frequently exercised on related matters of lesser importance.

(c) At the level of executive power, the broadest functions in respect of the external economy are naturally performed by the *Government*. The main instances thereof are determined by Arts. 33 and 35 of the Constitution.

(ca) The Government formulates its programme, submits it to Parliament and implements it, once it is approved. A comprehensive external economic programme naturally forms part of the government programme.

(cb) Following from the programme and on the general plane, a decisive role is played by the Government in preparing and giving effect to laws, agreements and other measures concerning the external economy in respect of which Parliament is vested with constitutive powers [see subitem (b) above].

(cc) The Government directs and coordinates the work of ministries and other organs directly subordinate to them (e.g. State Privatization and Property Managing Company Enterprise, Inc., National Committee for Technical Development). By elaborating and approving their statutes (see, e.g. Government Decrees Nos. 39 to 51/1990 in *Magyar Közlöny*, No. 91 of 1990), defining the functions and responsibilities of ministers, making proposals for the appointment of ministers or appointing other senior executive officers and ensuring their constitutional activities, it directly determines or brings decisive influence to bear on the country's external economic strategy. Also, in a state of danger, the Government may, on the mandate of Parliament, issue decrees and adopt measures conflicting with certain laws (Art. 35 (3) of the Constitution). The strong position of the Government is similarly expressed by its right to annul or alter, with the exception of laws and regulations, any decisions or measures of subordinate organs that are contrary to the law (*idem*, para. 4).

(cd) Acting within its competence to issue decrees [Art. 35 (2) of the Constitution], the Government ensures and facilitates by detailed regulations the efficient operation of the external economy e.g. by ending the foreign trade monopoly or the old product-mix monopoly of foreign trade companies [Government Decree No. 112/1990. (XII.23.) on exports and imports of goods, services and intangible assets] or regulating trade in internationally controlled high technology [Government Decree No. 111/1990. (XII. 23.)].

(ce) In the exercise of its functions the Government may also conclude , on its own behalf, international agreements on any matter that does not fall within the competence of Parliament or the President of the Republic [see subitems (a) and (b) above]. These are mostly of an administrative nature (executive agreements, *Verwaltungsabkommen*) by which the Government seeks to shape the international conditions of governance. They naturally include treaties and agreements relating to the external economy [e.g. Hexagonale (CEI) agreements: see item 3 (f) in §39] or agreements on investment promotion and protection (see Chapter XVII).

(d) The *ministries and other authorities or institutions with nationwide competence* (Hungarian National Bank, National Committee for Technical Development, etc.) likewise have important functions to perform in respect of the external economy. In accordance with Art. 37 of the Constitution and their own statutes [see subitem (cc) above] they direct the governmental and economic policy institutions attached to them, prepare and enforce the relevant Government decisions, and the ministers issue decrees within their respective spheres of competence. All of these may, and a large part of them do, affect external economic processes. The same holds for the following major areas of activity as defined in the statutes of ministries: maintenance, on behalf of the Government, of direct contact and cooperation with international economic organizations (GATT, WPO, OECD, IMF, IBRD, EU, CE, EBRD, etc.: see items 2 and 3 in §39); conclusion, on authorization, of international agreements concerning governmental activity; promotion of investment of foreign working capital in general and in privatization in particular; coordination of assistance programmes; on authorization, representation of the Government in international organizations; collaboration in determining the main directions of external economic policy; credit policy, drawing international credits; shaping international conditions for tourism, transport and energy; international financial cooperation; and international scientific and technical cooperation. These amount to but a few important areas where the different ministries and institutions with nationwide competence have significant functions and responsibilities to perform in respect to the external economy. In the government cycle of 1990 to 1994 an outstanding role was played by the Ministry of International Economic Relations (see the third Hungarian edition of this book, pp. 238–239). Since this Ministry and the Ministry of Industry and Trade were merged, with the lines of activity recast, in 1994, a decisive governmental role in the external economy has been assigned to the Ministry of Industry and Trade and the Ministry for Foreign Affairs.

(e) The administrative *direction of foreign trade* requires a special device to be employed abroad in matters involving Hungarian subjects at law active in other countries, and other Hungarian interests. The related tasks abroad are attended to by the commercial sections of the diplomatic missions of the Republic of Hungary or by other foreign trade state organs authorized thereto (Art. 24 of the Foreign Trade Act). In the performance of their duties these organs exercise such functions as are delegated by the minister competent in matters of international economic relations, representing Hungarian foreign trade interests, assisting in the establishment of contacts with authorities and enterprises in the receiving countries and with international organizations based in those countries, and directing and controlling, within their respective areas of activity, the foreign and related transactions of Hungarian economic organizations.

3. A significant role in the organizational system of the external economy is played, in addition to the *sui generis* state organs, by a variety of *social organs* functioning in the economic sphere, such as the National Alliance of Manufacturers, the National Alliance of Entrepreneurs, the National Organization of Craftsmen, the Hungarian Farmers' Association and economic chambers as regulated by Act XVI of 1994, including the Hungarian Chamber of Commerce and Industry (HCCI), the successor in title to the Hungarian Chamber of Commerce (Art. 78 of the Act).

As is known, these organizations are voluntary professional organizations of enterprises, economic associations, institutes and institutions, firms and natural persons operating within the particular areas.

Among them, with a greater pedigree, and playing a manifold role according to the new principles and dimensions of the cited Act, particular are in the economic chambers and HCCI [see Chapter IV of the Act on the tasks of economic chambers, Chapter VII, and the transitional rules of Art. 78; for a full discussion of the economic chambers, see Révész–Szakál: *Fejezetek a gazdasági kamarákról* (Chapters on the Economic Chambers)]. With a view to ensuring the success of economic activities and the efficient operation of the economy, the work of economic chambers extends, *inter alia*, to safeguarding interests, development of cooperation, information, training, maintenance of contact with national and foreign institutions, and various areas of efficient cooperation in formulating economic policy, shaping the economic environment and its legal regulation. Their varying involvement in economic relations and processes is likewise significant.

Pars pro toto, as it were, HCCI maintains wide-ranging international relations, carries out intense international activity, represents the interests of its members in similar international organizations, collaborates in exploring and procuring new markets and finding new business partners, and organizes abroad Hungarian business days, exhibitions and displays to popularize the Hungarian economy.

The chambers make proposals and express views to promote the development of a legal regime governing economic organizations. With a view to international commercial dispute settlement, HCCI provides facilities for a standing court of arbitration functioning under its auspices, elects and removes its arbitrators, and establishes its rules of procedure.

In order to facilitate the legal and technical handling of foreign trade, HCCI publishes in foreign languages the principal Hungarian laws and regulations on foreign trade and prepares compilations of the Hungarian versions of the major international agreements.

In its informational activity the Chamber keeps its members posted on the long-term and current economic development goals and tasks, on foreign and domestic market outlets, and on the fundamental laws and regulations affecting the possibilities open to members. Moreover, it issues publications in Hungarian and foreign languages on topical issues of international economic relations.

4. In the organizational structure and the actual practice of the external economy, the decisive role is played by *enterprises as subjects of external economic and foreign trade transactions.*

In point of fact, the question no longer concerns a part of the external economic organization, at least not in the sense it conveyed prior to the systemic change, when foreign trade rights were conferred on a specified range of subjects (organizations) and a real state organ was established under the concept of foreign trade monopoly. As was expressed in Art. 3, since repealed, of Act III of 1974 on Foreign Trade, "the State...shall devise the *organizational set-up* of foreign trade on the basis of the foreign trade monopoly". In practical transactions this meant at first a few dozen state foreign trade companies, with all the rest, for the most part, numerous state enterprises, having to handle trade in their products through these 25 to 30 channels. This rigid monopoly concept was considerably relaxed during the last two decades of the previous regime.

In this field too, the decisive step was taken, or the qualitative change effected, by the new world order on the basis of the freedom of economic undertaking, a market economy and owners' equal rights. This was provided for in Government Decree No. 112/1990. (XII.23.) on exports and "imports" of goods, services and intangible assets. With the relevant earlier decrees repealed (by Art. 15), the said Government Decree laid down the thesis, prevailing and applied in every free market economy, that *everyone is free to establish a business enterprise* in the external economy, just as in the internal one. This might appear to be a broad formulation, but it is essentially the reality even in the language of the law, the relevant section of the Government Decree reading: "The right to export or to import goods in accordance with the provisions of this Decree shall be conferred on (a) legal persons, (b) economic associations possessing no legal personality, (c) specialized groups, (d) individual entrepreneurs" (Art. 2). Thus the range of subjects is complete. The restrictions still remaining "in accordance with the provisions of this Decree" [see item 2 (b), (bb), (viii) in §41] do not affect the qualitatively new system to any significant degree.

The range of subjects of foreign trade activity *strictu sensu* was completed by the above measures. Under the broader concept of the external economy, the other sphere of activities in which the subjects were entitled to engage includes joint investments with foreigners, investments abroad and investments by foreigners in Hungary. The freedom of business undertaking without discrimination was provided for in respect of each by Act VI of 1988 on Economic Associations, Act XXIV of 1988 on Investments by Foreigners in Hungary and Act III of 1974 on Foreign Trade (Arts. 46 and 47).

§41. MANAGING THE EXTERNAL ECONOMY

1. Generally speaking, the following introductory remarks may be made about the *management of the external economy by the State or the Government.*

State management of the external economy forms part of the country's or government's economic policy concept and of government action to give effect thereto. Together they serve to realize the goals and to implement the principles that could be predicated above in this respect (item 3 in §38).

While respecting and maintaining the forces and laws of the market, and even playing in order to guarantee efficiency and security in this respect, the role of state or government direction, exercised with an intensity varying according to the specific conditions of the particular country, both in general and in the external economy, is a commonly represented and asserted concept in the developed market economies (see item 2 in §38). We would therefore be unwarranted to say that such role of the State played for whatever reason stems from the concept of some sort of state monopoly in foreign trade. The new text of the Constitution justifiably states in these contexts that Hungary's economy is a market economy (Art. 9) and that the Parliament and the Government determine, on the basis of *national sovereignty*, the organization and direction of governmental activity, including the Government's external economic programme (Art. 19). Our prevailing conditions certainly call for "above-average" state involvement to help develop and direct the ongoing transformation to the extent practicable (see item 3 in §38). It is equally certain that in transcribing this into practical action and into law it is not easy to define the optimum, with the intensity of effort likely to exceed the necessary measure. Therefore, keeping in mind the needs and lessons of practice, one should constantly rethink state action in order to ensure that the main thrust comes into play. It is a commonly known thesis of social theory that, unfortunately, the multivariable socio-economic processes and the effects of state and political actions on them cannot be indicated or determined with scientific exactness except until the time of their occurrence, to the present day, or *ex post facto* with regard to the future. "Scientific" foresight by scientific thinking, by refined economic policy and legal "empathy" is not possible except by some creative sort of anticipation and with regard to the very near future and the probable major developments. On the border of today and the morrow, conscious efforts to shape the pattern of multivariable conditions are for politics to undertake, even with respect to state management of the external economy. In order not to overplay its practicable role, politics should be executed under the strong control of a pluralist democracy and the opinion of the professional world.

2. The management of the external economy is a *complex phenomenon* and is administered accordingly. Its conditions lie in the laws and demands of the market economy and the international division of labour, which are concurrently the goals of management, namely it should seek to be moulding optimal patterns thereof by exercising influence on them. Consequently, management is

adequate to the system if it influences the market, international and domestic transactions, basically by way of overall macro-regulation. The Hungarian system of managing the external economy is devised to operate under this concept, which has external economy-oriented aspects, both general and particular.

(a) Speaking of the set of international conditions and the system of internal organization, the *general aspects* naturally can and should be said to imply no genuine forms of management, but macro-level conditions for the operation of the external economy and its management. It should be seen, however, that, paradoxically, it is really in them that the management of the (external) economy by, and the economic management philosophy of, the State of a modern social market economy is best expressed; namely in the fact that the State creates the conditions for a market-like operation of the actors of the market, then withdraws and only intervenes with more concrete instruments of management where and to the extent so required by the reasonable operation of the market and international economic processes. So an ingredient of external economic management is constituted by all that which is stated in §39 on the set of international conditions and in §40 on the internal organizational system of the external economy and on the rights and functions of the corresponding organs. It is easy to realize without any particular argument advanced that serious incidents of external economic management are furnished by the agreements and conventions regulating our relationship to the EU, EFTA, GATT, WTO, CEI, CEFTA, IMF, IBRD, EBRD, foreign assistance and credit programmes. Similarly, hardly any evidence is needed to prove the determinant role of the related laws and regulations in channelling and influencing external economic processes, that is to say, of state management. The said enactments stem from the rights conferred on the different levels of the internal organizational system of the external economy. Consider, for example, the legislation of foreign investments in Hungary, privatization, concessions and economic associations, or the Government Decree "vesting foreign trade rights in everyone", and many more laws and regulations mentioned in the above-cited and other sections of this book.

It is only in appearance that this approach of "management is everything – everything is management" seeks to be all-embracing. In fact, quite the opposite is true, especially if by management we mean the usual content and bearings, basically the fact that the State uses direct means of management and often resorts to "manual guidance". It is precisely this intensive direct management by the State that is losing ground and becoming superfluous, because attainment of the external economic objectives having social relevance is actuated by the general framework conditions and macro-regulations themselves, playing as they do a decisive role in this process.

(b) The means more fully and concretely oriented towards the external economy, or the *strictu sensu management of the external economy*, generally follow from the functions of the State outlined in our preliminary remarks (§38). Here we should add that the possible models of economic management, both presently and in the future, cannot do without pursuing an active external economy-oriented development policy and using the incentive tools generally accepted in the market economies, in the interest of ensuring successful adaptation to the world economy and the integration process.

(ba) One level of directly external economy-oriented development policy and instruments is represented by general economic policy as well as by the *elaboration and implementation of external economic strategies* appropriate to it. This follows from the described functions of the Government, the ministries competent in external economic relations, other ministries and central organs [item 2 (c), (d), (e) in §40]. To give an example, obligations were imposed on government organs by programmes like those on "state involvement required for an external economy-oriented economic policy" (1990) and on "external economic strategy and plan of action for external economic programmes covering the years 1991–1994" (1991). The "property policy guidelines" determining the privatization process and particularly important at the beginning thereof as well as the government programmes concerning proprietary and privatization strategies, deserve special attention for their essential bearings on the external economy. According to their target-oriented contents, these programmes and strategies formulate and envisage individual measures, long-term objectives, preparation of legislative proposals and parliamentary decisions, issuance of government decrees and adoption of government decisions. They prescribe mandatory action by the Government and the government organs concerned. By providing orientation, they naturally serve a useful purpose in informing the interested public, particularly the actors of the market, but, as a rule, impose no direct obligations on them. Such obligations derive only from normative or individual measures adopted on their basis. As will be seen below [subitem (bb)], the concrete and operative instrumentalities of external economic management appear in the complex whole of the said programmes and strategies.

(bb) At this juncture reference can be made only to the major *instruments of shaping and directing an active* external economy-oriented *development policy*. One should be aware that, as software in the hardware structure (meaning the set of international conditions for the external economy and its internal organic structure and related competencies), they are in a state of flux, being suitable and effective when responding to the objective demands of the prevailing conditions and concrete economic policy goals, following them without questioning the structural stability of the system and the main thrust of the process.

(i) One of these instruments – the following enumeration implying no order of importance – is support for investment of foreign working capital, primarily by economic and legal policy regulators like tax benefits and transfer of profit in convertible currency regardless of the currency in which income is produced (see §46). Or further, the Investment Promotion Fund which, under Government Decree No. 41/1991. (III.8.), "is a separate state fund destined to encourage foreign investments in Hungary, principally for production purposes, in keeping with our national economic priorities and to improve conditions for the operation of economic associations with foreign participation" (Art. 1), but it may be supplemented by voluntary contributions from national and foreign entities and private persons (Art. 2). The Budget for 1991 allotted an initial amount of 1.5 billion forints to the Fund (Act CIV of 1990 on the Budget for 1991, Annex I, Sect. 4 of Chapter X). It is a not insignificant fact that in the case of foreign investments of particular importance to the national economy (General Motors, General Electric, Suzuki) guarantee agreements providing some support were also signed between the investors and the Government. In the long term, these arrangements as well as the tax benefits certainly deserve some critical attention from the perspective of competition, equality of opportunity and the *régime national* (equal treatment) and have already received such consideration (for gradual reduction of tax allowance, see §46).

(ii) A considerable role is reserved for various export subsidies which are, however, subject to GATT rules. A case in point was the Trade Development Fund, which was formed by Government Decree No. 46/1991. (III.26.) and for which the Budget for 1991 and 1992 earmarked 5 and 4 billion forints, respectively. The purpose of the Fund was to facilitate the introduction of exportable goods, services and intangible assets in foreign markets. A significant role was and is also assigned to other funds in support of external economic strategies (see, e.g., the role of the Economic Development Fund and its resources to the tune of several billions of forints, Act CIV of 1994 on the Central Budget for 1995, XIX. IKM, Title 24). Outstanding importance is attached to the activities of Eximbank and of Export Credit Insurance, Co. in support of the external economic strategy; as state-owned banking institutions, they support the subjects of external economic transactions with easy-term credit and insurance (Act XLII of 1994 on Hungarian Export-Import, Co. and Hungarian Export Credit Insurance, Co.). Mention is deserved on this score by e.g., Government Decree No. 105/1995. (IX.8.) on the Interest Equalization System Related to Export Credit.

(iii) Agricultural export subsidies, naturally conforming to GATT, are employed as an important tool of external economic policy. Act VI of 1993 on Agricultural Regulations and Their Functions and Government Decree No. 177/1995. (XII.29.) on budget subsidies in 1996 for certain objectives of the agricultural sector lay down detailed rules relative to exports and other tools of intervention in the market.

(iv) The credit guarantees provided by the Government serve to facilitate, among other things, sales of surplus grain in the former CMEA countries, as there was, or could be, generated a greater demand for credit or deferred payment. On the other hand, the credit bank demands repayment guarantees from Hungarian exporters. Such guarantee is afforded by the State which ultimately runs the risk. Credit guarantee must conform to GATT rules.

(v) A significant indirect role in the external economy is certainly played by provision of support for individual economic organizations [for 1996, see Government Decree No. 55/1996. (IV.12.) on such support].

(vi) The foreign exchange authority (generally the National Bank) carries out significant activities affecting the external economy in the fields of foreign exchange control, credit transactions and external economic operations, issuing foreign exchange permits, authorizing taking up and providing of credit, making available foreign currency for the operation of the economy in accordance with the Act on the Central Bank (Act XCV of 1995 on Foreign Exchange; Act LX of 1991 on the Hungarian National Bank; Glatz, pp. 265 *et seq.*).

(vii) Exchange rate and interest policies naturally have a strong influence on the external economy. For instance, devaluation of the forint obviously serves to make exports more profitable and to check imports. Under the Act on the Central Bank, formulation of customs and exchange rate policies vests in the Government and the National Bank.

(viii) The Act on the Prevention of Money Laundering and the responsibilities defined therein have an important defensive role to play in reliably shaping the pattern of external economic conditions (Act XXIV of 1994 on the Prevention of Money Laundering).

(ix) Economic freedom is the general rule in respect to the system of licensing exports and imports (everyone is entitled to engage in foreign trade, see item 4 in §40), while most imports (about 90% of products) are liberalized (the products affected may be imported without a license in foreign currency purchasable for forint). This philosophy and practice are adopted by Government Decree No. 112/1990. (XII.23.) on the exports and imports of goods, services and intangible assets.

The main restrictions upheld are the following: (1) some kind of foreign trade right is still necessary for trade in certain products (e.g. in the case of firms undertaking to have in stock a fixed quantity of energy carriers; see Annex II to the above Decree); (2) a licence is required for the exportation or importation of certain goods as enumerated in Annex I; this applies to the remaining 10% of the other 90 percentage share indicated above; (3) licensing or restriction may be "tightened" when so required by the country's needs or international obligations (Art. 4); (4) the latter motivated the adoption of Government Decree No. 61/1990. (X.1.), amended by Government Decree No. 66/1992. (IV.10.), on licensing trade in certain internationally controlled products and technologies (those on the COCOM list).

It is thereof essential that, in respect to exports and imports outside the scope of specific provisions of law, licensing by the foreign trade organ or the foreign exchange authority – the previous dual licensing or other administrative procedure – has been abolished (by Art. 67 of the Foreign Exchange Act), there remaining but one thing, notably the requirement to apply the general rules of foreign exchange control to foreign trade activity as well (see Art. 1 of the Foreign Exchange Act; Glatz, p. 274).

(x) Other means are likewise known to be used with varying intensity for the regulation of imports and the protection of the internal market. In some way, all States try to hinder or regulate dumping-like inflows of foreign consumer goods, which may be a natural attendant upon the freedom of trade. This function is fulfilled in Hungary by, e.g., Government Decree No. 69/1994. (IV.4.) on anti-dumping and value-equalizing (countervailing) customs (Kovács, p. 12).

(xi) In the process of privatization the State performs a series of strongly external economy-oriented acts through the state institutions of privatization in order to exert a decisive influence on, *inter alia*, investments of foreign working capital (see §§59–60).

(xii) Authorization of the establishment of commercial representations of foreign enterprises and banks as well as of banks and banking partnerships is regarded as a state instrument directly affecting external economic relations and processes (see §46).

(xiii) Regulation by customs law is an important component of external economic policy (Act C of 1995 on Customs Law, Customs Procedure and Customs Administration). Customs duties perform several functions. A most important one is to produce budget revenues. Another is to promote human and animal health protection and plant sanitation. A third one is to exert an appropriate effect on the prices of imported goods, thereby influencing the inflow of products. A further and more specific function is to help implement the principles of equality and mutual benefit, while contributing to observance of the GATT rules [see item 2 (a), (bb) in §39].

(xiv) In connection with taxation, we have already referred to benefits accorded to foreign investors [subitem (i) above]. In respect of the external economy mention should also be made of bilateral agreements for the avoidance of double taxation, which Hungary has concluded with all its major trading partners (see List of Sources).

(xv) The Hungarian regulation of economic competition in close conformity with the EU law of competition, as is provided for by Art. 62 of the Europe Agreement, is likewise of relevance to the external economy and prevails over any restriction of competition in Hungary (see Vigh, pp. 238 *et seq.*, and Art. 1 of the new Act LVII of 1996).

(xvi) The requirement for all or any economic actors to make a specified contract or to show a specified form of behaviour with a view to compliance with the country's international obligations is seen as a drastic tool of management. It was codified only as *ultima ratio regis* even by Act III of 1974 on Foreign Trade (Art. 20). The related Law-Decree of 1984, in instructing economic organizations to carry out a specified economic activity, provided – in the way of prescribing incentives for enterprises as a general rule – that an enterprise suffering material loss caused by a compulsory contract must be entitled to compensation for such loss (Art. 4).

Under the present-day conditions of a market economy and the autonomy of the economic sphere, administrative instructions are a phenomenon especially alien to the existing system. There is no denying the fact, however, that the cited provision of the Foreign Trade Act currently in force could be given effect if the orderly process of transactions (domestic supply, market protection, fulfillment of international obligations) were impossible to ensure otherwise. Seen in a wider context, it should be said that direct state intervention – prescription of compulsory behaviour and action – is not actually an unknown phenomenon, even though a rare one, in modern law. Such action is, for example, compulsory transformation of anti-competitive cartel contracts and mergers under the law of competition, which may be ordered by the Cartel Office or the Office of Economic Competition, or compulsory raising of prices under the anti-dumping procedure, which may be decreed by the anti-dumping authority [see, e.g., Government Decree No. 69/1994. (V.4.) regulating anti-dumping and price equalization customs (in the Preamble and Arts. 10, 25 *et seq.*) in the spirit of statutory authorization by Art. 20 of the Foreign Trade Act].

CHAPTER XII

LEGAL PERSONS

§42. LEGAL PERSONS IN INTERNATIONAL ECONOMIC RELATIONS AND LAW

1. The concentration of national wealth, as required by the development of the means of production, was started and given full rein fundamentally through economic associations during the nineteenth century. People in the United States prefer to term that process as one in which the *shareholding system* and *corporate democracy* emerged and took shape. The commercial companies and economic associations (joint stock companies and other forms of association) as legal persons became the basic cells of the *modern market economy*. Partly through the process of expansive development, partly competition between them, such associations assumed ever greater proportions and started a large-scale international movement in the last century. The trend of internationalization of economic processes (production, development and trade), which grew particularly strong during the 20th century, caused enterprises to stretch beyond the boundaries of their home State on a massive scale, operating producing and administrative units, branches and affiliated companies simultaneously in several countries. Through partnership and purchase of other firms, these enterprises continued to enlarge their empire until they came to control formally and legally independent enterprises in the forms of holding company. Multinational corporations came into being. (It will be noted by way of illustration of the magnitude that the 1,000 largest American corporations have on average 48 affiliated firms; Mobil Oil has 625 in 62 countries, BP a total of 1,000, Unilever 800 (Loewenfeld: Obligations of International Companies, p. 248). Numerous multinational corporations [BP, GM (Opel), Audi, Suzuki, Shell, etc.] have affiliated firms in Hungary, too, involving the Hungarian economy in this process.)

The need was created by legal development to bring the described processes under *legal regulation* through the positive-law institutions of corporate law as well as the norms of the law of competition (cartels and monopolies) and the law of international economic relations.

Legal persons came to acquire growing importance in the newly democratic countries of Central and Eastern Europe. These countries share the view that a significant area of economic cooperation is represented by a two-way movement of enterprises, namely establishment of enterprises abroad and operation of foreign enterprises within the country. In the new situation this strategy, in particular, for investment of foreign working capital has become a highly important objective of economic policy. In Hungary nearly 20,000 foreign investment projects have so far been implemented, largely within the framework of company law, whereas in 1993 there operated abroad 1,250 enterprises with Hungarian participation, mostly as a result of rapid development in the years following the systemic change [see Mádl: *Állam és gazdaság* (State and Economy), §44; the value of foreign investments reached the 13 billion dollar mark by the end of 1995, while this figure was 7 billion in Poland, 6 billion in Czech Republic, and 0.5 to 1 billion in the rest of the smaller newly democratic countries, see Diczházi].

2. In the latter field of legal regulation this basically involves a *double set of rules* to govern, on the one hand, the status of legal persons (personal law, nationality) and to give them, on the other, full coverage under substantive law in view of their international movement. Again, in its main aspects, the latter body of rules appears on two planes. On one plane we find the norms, both of national and of international origin, which constitute a separate regulation of a complementary nature in respect to and with allowance for the distinctive features of enterprises founded and operated within the framework of international cooperation. On the other plane are those rules of internal substantive law by which the State regulates the domestic status of legal persons – foreign companies or joint ventures – operating in their territories. At this point we will discuss the legal status of legal persons under private international law, while the internal law aspects will be treated in the section on the status of foreigners (Chapter XIII).

§43. LEGAL PERSONS IN PRIVATE INTERNATIONAL LAW; THE PERSONAL LAW AND NATIONALITY OF LEGAL PERSONS; THE CONTROL THEORY

1. The concept of personal law governing the legal status of natural persons was carried over – by legal practice and learning – to the legal status, or personal status of legal persons as early as the last century. In accordance with this concept, all legal relationships expressing the condition of legal persons are to be *considered under the personal law* in any private international dispute involving the legal status of legal persons; this includes their establishment, legal capacity, merger, separation, liquidation, personal rights, and inner organizational and operational patterns. In respect of natural persons the personal law gave rise to no special problem, for the physical presence of individuals in the

territory of a country is a single and concrete phenomenon: an individual cannot be present in more than one country at the same time and therefore, given some contact with a particular State (nationality or domicile), the connecting factor of the personal law can clearly be determined. The situation is different with respect to legal persons, which are not natural persons, currently functioning in various countries and possessing a definite organizational and legal identity. Regulation by private international law varies from one country to another according to the element of identity by which the personal law of legal persons is determined.

2. Among the *existing connecting factors* used to determine the personal law the seat theory *(siège social)* is dominant in Europe, whereas the incorporation theory prevails in the common-law countries, and primarily in the United States. According to the seat theory, the personal law of a legal person is the law of the State in which the legal person has its place of business, and according to the incorporation theory, the applicable law is that of the incorporating State. Article 154 of the 1987 Swiss Code of PIL lays down the following general rule guided by the incorporation theory: "*Gesellschaften unterstehen dem Recht des Staates, nach dessen Vorschriften sie organisiert sind*" (Commercial companies shall be subject to the law of the State under whose rules they have been organized). As against this, cases are rather frequent in which the law of the seat *per se* is not unambiguous, for in the corporations in question the seat may refer to the place of administration as distinct from the seat designated in the articles of incorporation or of association and from the State of actual business, or *vice versa*. On the other hand, there may be countries (and accordingly commercial companies or associations) where (or in respect of such companies) incorporation is not compulsory and therefore the place of establishment or some seat may be used as the decisive connecting factor.

A combination of the two systems may be considered to have been accomplished by the Hague Convention of 1956 on the status of legal persons in private international law. However, this Convention only deals with the recognition of legal personality. Under it, the States parties recognize legal personality for all the units of an economic association which qualify as legal persons under the law either of the State of establishment (incorporation) or of the place of business. It would certainly be practicable for Hungary to accede to this Convention for, on the basis of Hungarian law, no objection of principle can be raised to the said regulation. First, the relevant provisions do not affect the regulation by the Hungarian law of conflicts (see item 3 below), which defines the law applicable to legal persons and to questions of their organization and operation. The Hague Convention is confined to stating that a unit recognized as a legal person by a State party is also to be recognized as such in the other States parties in transactions governed by commercial law. Second, such a normative statement is contained in similar wording in Hungarian law: under Art. 2 of Law-Decree No. 8 of 1978 on the application of the Civil Code in international economic relations, "the State shall, in the domain of international economic relations, recognize the legal persons established in accordance with foreign law". Third, Hungary exhibits a rather varied normative "attitude" in its regulation of legal persons by private international law: while the general rule is oriented to incorporation (albeit with exceptions allowed), several of our international agreements chose to use the seat of the legal persons as the connecting factor (see, e.g., Art. 23 of the Yugoslav–Hungarian Agreement on Legal Assistance promulgated by Law-Decree No. 1 of 1969).

3. Now, if we are to ascertain the *position of Hungarian law*, the following analysis may be instrumental.

(a) First, we have to look for sources of law to the *interstate treaties* of Hungary – agreements on legal assistance, trade agreements and consular conventions –, in which we find two main localizers and their variations. Of course, with respect to a given country, the connecting factor must be deemed to be that which is formulated in the corresponding agreement on legal assistance, trade agreement or consular convention. These sources of law, however, do not offer a uniform regulation on which to rely for ascertaining the position of international law. Prior to the Code of PIL, Hungary had no internal legislation in this area, nor was its judicial practice well settled in the conflict field.

(b) For the correct position to be taken it is probably impossible to ignore the *concept*, not only held by *legal science*, which deems it difficult to define the personal law of legal persons in a uniform statute, especially and exclusively on nationality, or allegiance to a nation or State, patterned on citizenship as applied to natural persons. In the case of natural persons, nationality is the expression of a political relationship between citizens and a nation or State, but in the case of legal persons we have economic or business relations, regulation of assets, and the necessary organizational structures with property law implications. This means in concrete terms that if a State is the host of a company established (incorporated) in another State, the host country will act according to its own law in a number of questions – initiate bankruptcy proceedings, draw up requirements to bar action *ultra vires*, regulate the legal standing of employees in company law, prescribe requirements of publicity and apply the rules on merger and competition – even if it recognizes the existence and the legal capacity of a legal person under the law of the incorporating State.

Therefore reality sheds light on legal persons having basically *two statuses*. One is the so-called *genetic status*, the sum of rules governing the establishment, existence and legal capacity of legal persons as well as the internal relations of their members. The other is the so-called *activity status*, the sum of corporate norms expressing the actions, short of contractual transactions (!), of legal persons under corporate law. Whereas the reasonable localizer of the personal law is incorporation in respect to the former, it is the actual place of business in respect to the latter, for it stands to reason that only the law of the State of incorporation (foundation or establishment) can be a test of whether an economic unit established conforms to the requirements prescribed by that State for the formation of legal persons. It is no less obvious, however, that States do not permit questions of the second category (bankruptcy, liquidation, *ultra vires*, requirements of publicity, aspects of the law of competition), falling under the activity *statutum,* to be governed by laws other than their own. Hence it logically and necessarily follows that the personal law in this respect must be determined according to the law of the State of the actual place of business. This is also unambiguously clear from, e.g., the Hungarian law of joint ventures covered by Act XXIV of 1988 on investments by foreigners in Hungary.

(c) The *regulation by Hungary's internal law* is in harmony with the described panorama of the theory and practice relating to the personal law of legal persons, as is reflected in Art. 18 of the Code of PIL, which provides: "The legal capacity, economic status and personal rights of a legal person as well as the *inter se* relationships of its members shall be governed by its personal law. The personal law of a legal person shall be the law of the State in whose territory the legal person was incorporated". It is clearly seen that the personal law – the law of the place of incorporation – relates exactly to the generic statute, namely to legal capacity, economic character, personal rights and relations among members. The regulation does not cover the aforementioned activity statutum as part of the personal statutum of economic organizations and other legal persons. This allows Hungarian judicial practice to take into account the law of the actual place of business in control of the latter aspect.

The Code is more specific about the personal law only if incorporation *per se* is not unambiguous either because the legal person is incorporated under the laws of several States or the law of the seat named in the statutes of the legal person does not require incorporation; in this case the personal law of the legal person is the law of the seat named in the statutes (para. 3 of Art. 18). If, however, a legal person has no seat named in the statutes, or has several seats, and is not incorporated under the law of any of the respective States, its personal law is the law of the State in whose territory the legal person has its central administration (para. 4 of Art. 18).

The consistent use of the incorporation principle is reflected in the rule of the Hungarian Code under which the personal law of a separately incorporated branch or subsidiary of a legal person is the law of the State in whose territory the branch or subsidiary is incorporated (para. 5 of Art. 18).

(d) Company-law practice may embrace, numerous, almost all, questions relating to the law of legal persons. This could be exemplified by a whole series of legal cases encountered in real life.

A dispute concerning the management rights of a foreign partner to a joint venture founded in Hungary (say, a limited liability company incorporated here) is to be settled under Hungarian law, as is provided for by Art. 18 of the Code. Having regard for the contract of association, this means the laws and regulations relative to economic associations with foreign participation on the one hand and the relevant provisions of the Act on Business Associations (Companies Act) (see §48) on the other. In view of the foregoing and by virtue of the activity *statutum*, the applicable law will be the Hungarian law with respect to the liquidation of the limited liability company as well.

A limited partnership of Hungarian nationality (Arts. 94 *et seq.* of the Act on Business Associations) implements a project abroad under a contract for work, labour and materials and its contracting partner raises a related claim which the contractor is unable to satisfy because of insolvency. The foreign partner brings an action before a Hungarian court against a member of the partnership, pleading that under Art. 26 of the Hungarian Code the dispute concerning the partnership is governed by the law of the place of the undertaking, namely the law of his country, and maintaining that his claim is lawful and that in the case of such a partnership the member sued bears unlimited liability.

The Hungarian law offers the following practical answer. True, the existence of the claim is to be established by the Hungarian court, too, under the particular foreign law because, according to Art. 26 of the Code, "contracts of *locatio conductio operis* (designing, installation, work for hire, etc.) shall be subject to the law of the State in whose territory the activities of the undertaking shall be performed or the results shall be accomplished under the terms of the contract". However the question of whether the claim against the limited partnership can be enforced against a member of it (senior or silent partner under both the old and the present law of business associations) is to be governed by the Hungarian law. This is the course to follow because the question concerns the legal personality of an association incorporated in Hungary and, as incidents thereof, the relationship of members to the partnership and the extent of their liability for the partnership's obligations. It is in this sense that Art. 18 of the Code can be properly applied to the concrete case. Beyond this point, the solution depends on whether the member sued of the partnership or a senior or a silent partner. If he is a senior partner, he bears unlimited liability (Art. 94 of the Business Associations Act), and if he is a silent partner, he may not be sued as a general rule, although if he has not yet contributed his share of capital, he is deemed liable for the amount of his share, albeit only to that shown in the register of firms (Companies Register) (Art. 99). However, a silent partner also bears unlimited liability if his name figures in the partnership's trade name (Art. 100).

4. As has been seen, the personal law of legal persons is subject to the nationality principle, according to which the personal statute of a legal person is governed by its connection with the given State and is, in this respect, independent of its proprietors (e.g. shareholders) and of their nationality, that is, their personal law. The *control theory*, now manifested in several mutations, has a different implication (takes a different approach) in terms of both motivation and legal substance.

(a) In its original form the control theory, which may be called *wartime or, paradoxically, classical control theory*, appeared in the post-World War One period and became dominant particularly during World War Two. Its essence lay, already at the time of its appearance, in the claim for a legal person to be judged not only by its own nationality, but also by that of its proprietors under the special circumstances obtaining. A practical instance of its application was that, for instance, German companies with American nationality (incorporated in the United States), which would have been regarded as American companies according to the prevailing connecting factor of the American private international law, were deemed not to be American companies by reason of having German proprietors. Although these companies, operating in the United States, were legal persons relatively detached from their owners, in economic life they held their own assets (legal owners) and handled their operative dealings through their own organs, their policy decisions were taken by their real owners (beneficial owners), who in turn were nationals of a State at war with the United States. Thus the control theory meant that even a legal person, which had its seat within the State where its business operations were carried out, was regarded as foreign if it was under the real control and management of such foreign nationals who, with the state of war prevailing, could be supposed to act against the interests of the country of the actual seat.

The *practical application of the wartime control theory* was manifest in the fact that during World War Two the United States set up the so-called Alien Property Custodian Authority in 1942 to exercise state control over foreign property in the said context. Indeed, that Authority brought under strict financial and other economic control the USA-based companies and related entities of Germany and Japan, which were then at war with the United States, including the property assets owned by nationals of these countries (the original idea was to seize such foreign property).

Nor did Hungary escape the effect of the wartime control theory. For the country, this theory did not remain a concept to be contemplated from outside, one only of concern to other countries, but adversely affected Hungarian interests as well. It was applied to Hungary in the Peace Treaty of Paris. Article 29 of Act XVIII of 1947 ratifying the Peace Treaty authorized the Allied and Associated Powers to seize, retain, or liquidate all property assets and rights – including industrial and company rights and interests – owned or held within their territories by Hungary or its nationals at the date of entry into force of the Peace Treaty. The Allied and Associated Powers effected liquidation and sale according to their own laws and were entitled to apply the proceeds to all their claims and those of their nationals against Hungary or its nationals. Under the same Article of the Peace Treaty, the Hungarian Government was obligated to indemnify the Hungarian claimants expropriated. Obviously, the relevant procedure was governed, irrespective of the American nationality of the affected companies, by the nationality of Hungarian claimants behind those companies, namely by the control theory.

(b) In conditions of peace, under the present-day pattern of international political and economic relations, however, the control theory cannot generally be employed in this respect. Nevertheless, it should be noted that *treatment as foreign of foreign-owned domestic enterprises and consequently the existence of special regulation are not unknown in current law and recognized economic practice.* Such mutation of the control theory is a rather frequent phenomenon in cases where the activities of foreign companies or of enterprises operated with foreign participation happen to be subject to some conditions (complementary rules of company law) even though, by their incorporation or seat, they are deemed to be domestic enterprises in private international law. Provisions of this type are those which, e.g., prohibit the operation of foreign companies or of economic associations involving foreign participation in certain sectors of the economy, or those regulating the formation and registration process, or others on the possible share the foreign partner may acquire, etc. Experience in this field shows that countries have different practices and that the relevant economic and legal considerations are in a state of flux. At any rate, the case at hand involves something other than application of the control theory, and a brief reference to it has been warranted by motives of similarity and distinction only. Here in fact we have regulations of foreign investments, generally permissive and incentive, the tendency being towards gradual extension to them of rights equal to those of entities entirely in national ownership (national treatment and even benefits, e.g., tax allowances). Therefore this may be called a *positive control theory*, albeit such entities are also brought under regulations occasionally restrictive of them with consideration for the national economic interests of the countries concerned (see Chapter XIII).

(c) The *control theory of concern law* relative to multinational corporations may be considered to be a third mutation. As is indicated by the figures furnished above (items 1 and 2 in §42), the companies extending their operations to several countries (operating in various forms, generally as joint stock companies governed by corporate law) have come to play a rather large role in international economic relations. It is characteristic of them that the so-called parent company or controlling company operates affiliated firms abroad with controlling property shares or under controlling contractual arrangements; such controlled firms are legally independent, operated under the local law as domestic enterprises in the country of seat and subject to the general principle of private international law that their liability should be limited to their own assets under the domestic law.

However, the numerous grave enterprise–economic catastrophes of the past decades have thrown more light on the fact that a particular affiliated form is, on the one hand, unable to meet its material liability (for compensation), and, on the other, is not really independent in asserting its will, that its decisions and business activity depend heavily on the controlling parent company of the multinational empire, and hence it should share the latter's liability. A case in point is American Standard Oil, which was made liable for the vast environmental pollution caused by the catastrophe of a tanker of its small affiliated firm in Liberia (when the *Amoco Cadiz* sank, 1.5 million tons of oil poured into the sea off the French coast). In general, too, the adequate and equitable legal solution cannot be other than this: it is necessary tc exceed the scope of the private international law regulation of the affiliated form causing the damage, to lift the corporate veil (as is cast in the language of corporate law), to ascertain the owner, or the entity on control, of the firm, and to establish its liability under the applicable law. Based on an analysis and summation of international practice, this principle was declared in the Resolution adopted by the *Institut de Droit International* at its Lisbon Session of 1995 on the codification of the Obligations of Multilateral Enterprises and Their Member Companies (*Annuaire de l'Institut de Droit International*, vol. 66-II, 1996, pp. 463–473). For that matter, this concept is in keeping with the approach of the Hungarian Act on Business Associations and the genetic statutum as mentioned earlier.

CHAPTER XIII

THE LEGAL STATUS OF FOREIGNERS

§44. ON THE LEGAL STATUS OF FOREIGNERS IN GENERAL, NATIONAL TREATMENT AND RECIPROCITY, THE LEGAL STATUS OF FOREIGN NATURAL PERSONS IN HUNGARY

1. The status of persons in private international law means, as was seen, the internal substantive law of a State governing their personal status in cases where a set of facts leads to a conflict between legal systems. The international movement of persons, however, raises several other questions in real-life situations. Of greater importance and practical relevance to the movement of persons are, in point of fact, those rules of *substantive law* (partly of internal, partly of international origin, such as the rules of civil law, administrative law and others) *which make that movement possible at all, a movement which then creates conflict problems with respect to personal status*. More specifically, these are (a) rules expressing elements of police control and administrative procedure affecting the movements and transaction of persons (e.g. norms relating to entry visas, residence permits, employment, industrial and commercial activities); (b) rules governing the recognition of foreign companies and the domestic conditions for their operation, or regulating specific company rights in the various fields of the law of international economic relations; and (c) legally expressed general principles normally governing transactions of foreigners under internal civil and commercial law.

The sum of these rules is generally also known as *Fremdenrecht* in literature in non-German languages (called the law of aliens after the Latin *ius peregrini*). [For its designation in Hungarian practice, see Glatz–Martin–Nagy: *Az idegenjog és a konzuli jog* (The Law of Aliens and the Consular Law).] *Fremdenrecht* is the body of rules determining the special status (*Sonderstellung*) of foreigners, granting them rights different from or identical to those of nationals. As can be seen, these rules are not conflict norms but rules of substantive law (*Sachnormen*), and are destined to regulate the legal status of foreign persons, natural and legal, supplementing and occasionally modifying the norms relating to foreigners precisely in view of their condition as such.

2. The *Fremdenrecht* governing the legal status of foreigners has, in point of fact, both *a narrower and a broader sense*.

In the narrower sense, it encompasses the norms (mostly of an administrative nature) which regulate the legal status of foreigners differently from that of nationals.

In the broader sense, it is a body of all the rules devised to govern the status of foreigners in every respect, some of them regulating a status different from that of nationals, some of them recognizing their equality with nationals, including those which, by the nature of things, are necessary for the activity of foreigners as such within the State (rules relative to employment, permission to reside).

The interrelated nature of *Fremdenrecht* and private international law and the differences between them may be illustrated by the following examples: whether a legal person has legal capacity, if disputed, is a matter of private international law, but if with respect to the same legal person the question is whether its activity within the State is subject to special restrictive or other rules, the governing provisions of law are not norms of private international law, but rather rules of substantive law applicable to the status of foreigners and belonging to the broader notion of *Fremdenrecht*. Whether a foreign national has disposing capacity or not is to be established before a Hungarian forum under the rules of private international law, with regard had for the law of the given foreign State but the conditions for his residing or taking up employment in Hungary are determined by Hungarian administrative norms (in the nature of *Fremdenrecht*).

3. As mentioned above, the legal regulations on the status of foreigners include legally expressed general principles which *govern in a general way the contractual capacity of foreigners under international civil and commercial law.* One of these principles is that of *national (equal) treatment* known as *régime national* in legal literature, both French and non-French.

(a) *The principle of national treatment expresses, in the given context, the equal status of foreigners with nationals.* This means that foreign nationals in Hungary are subject to the same rules as nationals, namely that, in principle, the participation of foreigners in the social relations covered by legislation entails no difference in the application of Hungarian law. The content of this principle is conveyed by its denomination, which is to say that under the principle of national treatment a foreign national enjoys equal status with nationals of Hungary, not with nationals of his own country under the internal substantive law of the latter. Should that not be the case, the principle of national treatment would entail serious discrimination against nationals of Hungary, or perhaps *vice versa*.

It should be stressed that national treatment does not presuppose the stay of a foreign national in Hungary. His capacity to acquire property, e.g. an inheritance, exists in Hungarian law in the same manner and with the same substantive-law content as in the case of Hungarian nationals, irrespective of whether the foreign heir happens to reside in Hungary or lives abroad. In its classical sense the principle of national treatment applies to legal capacity as broadly understood, thus comprising legal capacity, contractual capacity, or capacity to have personal and property rights, to inherit, etc.

(b) This point brings us to the *position of Hungarian law*. Article 56 of the Constitution as amended provides that "everyone in the Republic of Hungary shall have legal capacity". This provision is restated in Art. 8 of the Civil Code. Under Art. 70/A of the Constitution, "the Republic of Hungary shall guarantee for everyone in its territory all human and civil rights without distinction of any kind, such as race, colour, sex, language, religion, political or other opinion, national or social origin, property, birth or other status". Any discrimination against persons is ruled out by law. Pursuant to the Constitution, Hungary undertakes to promote the achievement of equality of rights as well, through measures aimed at eliminating inequality of opportunity (para. 3 of Art. 70/A).

In dealing with the legal capacity of persons in a previous section (§30), we have referred to the rules of international origin which, also adopted in Hungary, give universal expression to legal capacity. The equal treatment of foreigners follows from this very position, although the relevant rules do not spell out the capacity of foreigners to enter into economic transactions, to make contracts in Hungary, to inherit, etc. This does not mean, however, that Hungary fails to give effect to the principle of national treatment in this respect. Before the entry into force of the Code, Hungarian private international law was essentially based on customary law. Its force in customary law was emphasized by Art. 5 of the Act to bring into operation the Civil Code by upholding the old tenets in this domain. Thus, Decision No. 203 of 1888 of the Curia, which expressly stated that, subject to reciprocity, foreigners who had the capacity to contract could also acquire property, could be considered to have remained in effect. This norm was accordingly deemed to express the stand of Hungarian law for nearly a century. Furthermore, this principle was embodied in several international treaties of more moment, such as the Hungarian Peace Treaty of Paris ratified by Act XVIII of 1947. In Art. 26 of Part 6, this Treaty provided that, any restrictive legislation notwithstanding, "the legal capacity, disposing capacity, personal and property rights as well as the obligations of foreign nationals and stateless persons shall, unless otherwise provided by law, be governed by the same law as is applicable to Hungarian nationals".

4. Evidently, national treatment presupposes *reciprocity*, which enables Hungarian nationals to be accorded equal treatment in foreign countries in relation to which reciprocity prevails. The old aforesaid tenet of Hungarian customary law expressly presupposes reciprocity as a prerequisite for the enjoyment of national treatment, as is the case with many codified laws as well. As regards the substance of the problem, reciprocity is a natural requirement. It should be stressed, however, that the legal capacity of natural persons is a generally absolute element of legal status – naturally in Hungarian law, too (see §30). Article 15 of the Code does not make national treatment subject to reciprocity outside the scope of legal capacity either, but contains the phrase "unless otherwise provided by law", which leaves scope for Hungarian authori-

ties to resort, on statutory authorization, to retaliation with a view to eliminating discrimination to which Hungarian nationals may be subject in foreign countries. The first prerequisite of retaliation, however, is that discrimination by a foreign State against Hungarian nationals must be proved either by the interested party or by an act of the competent government authority, whereas it is a generally held view that discrimination gives cause for recourse to retaliation by the courts and other authorities of the affected State. If a Hungarian authority has doubts as to the existence of reciprocity in some aspect, it has to apply to the Minister of Justice for a declaration thereon, which is binding on the court or other authority (Art. 6 of the Code).

It should be observed, however, that under the Code, the existence of reciprocity must be presumed as a general rule, so Hungarian courts are not required to look for evidence *ex officio* as to the existence of reciprocity. According to Art. 6, "unless otherwise provided by law, the application of foreign law shall not depend on reciprocity; if a rule of law makes the application of foreign law subject to reciprocity, the existence of reciprocity shall be presumed until the contrary is proved". With reasonable and appropriate interpretation, the presumption of reciprocity may also be applied, *mutatis mutandis*, as regards the proper treatment of, or national treatment accorded to, Hungarian nationals in foreign countries. Such approach and application of the Hungarian Code are supported by the fact that national (equal) treatment is similarly confirmed by numerous international treaties, including agreements on legal assistance. For instance, Art. 1 of the Yugoslav–Hungarian Agreement on Legal Assistance (Law-Decree No. 1 of 1969) provides that citizens of either Contracting Party are to enjoy in the territory of the other Party, in respect of their personal and property rights, the same legal protection as citizens of the other Party and that this provision is to apply to legal persons as well (paras. 1 and 3). Under the German–Hungarian Treaty of 1992 on European Partnership (Act LXXIX of 1995), both Contracting Parties are to create the most favourable conditions for the economic activities of natural and legal persons of the other Party (Art. 11).

5. It is to be noted in conclusion that *national treatment does not mean* that a foreigner has an equal standing with a national in all related aspects of substantive law. However it does mean that, as a rule, he is controlled by the same rules of law as the national, whereas a foreigner is, or may be, subject to other statutory provisions than those which are intended precisely to accord him national treatment. This may be illustrated by the following examples and legal devices in some of the more typical areas.

If the heir is a foreigner, he needs permission to export (transfer) the inheritance from Hungary. This does not mean, however, that he is incapable of inheritance; he is on an equal footing with his Hungarian counterparts, who are similarly required to obtain permission for the export of inheritance or of any property. The grant of such permission to Hungarians as well as to foreigners is not without limits, however, or there would be no need for the related rules.

The rules on foreigners' settlement and employment in Hungary cannot even conceptually apply to nationals, yet they may treat foreigners differently to nationals: e.g. the right ("capacity") of a foreigner to take up employment may be limited to a definite period of time, as will be discussed in more detail below. The differences are, however, of a technical nature and are due to the fact that the regulative process of national treatment bears, *a fortiori,* upon foreigners only, that national treatment cannot be extended to them except by such regulation, and that the grant of national treatment may necessitate interposition of transitional phases. A strange contradiction resides precisely in this duality: the rules of law which apply only to foreigners, and hence are formally "discriminative", actually seek to delimit the possibility of substantive discrimination and to achieve national treatment. Regulations of this nature affect foreigners' acquisition of property, stay and employment in Hungary, which are to be discussed below.

6. *Acquisition of immovable property by foreigners* is a special field of the related set of problems. Under Art. 9 of Act XCV of 1995 on Foreign Exchange, Art. 88 of Act LV of 1994 on Arable Land and Art. 1 of Government Decree No. 171/1991. (XII. 27.), a foreign legal or private person must have permission from the Ministry of Finance or the Central Corporation of Banking Companies to acquire immovables in Hungary by either purchase or exchange or gift under the conditions specified by the Government Decree. One such condition is that acquisition of property must not prejudice Hungarian State, local government, economic, touristic, cultural, public welfare and other social interests. Under Arts. 7 and 8 of the said Arable Land Act, ownership in arable land and nature conservation areas may not, as a rule, be acquired by foreigners, except for arable land in connection with the termination of joint ownership. Thus the right to acquire immovables is basically limited to building plots, housing property, and other immovables outside the former category. No permit to acquire property is required for Hungarian nationals living abroad, for persons with an identity card entitling them to permanent residence in Hungary, for persons recognized as refugees under Art. 1 of Law-Decree No. 19 of 1989 on the status of such persons and under Art. 3 of the Government Decree referred to above, and for legal persons with foreign interests established (incorporated) in Hungary under Art. 19 of Act XXIV of 1988 on foreign investments (for additional regulations, see Glatz–Martin–Nagy, Chapter 6). It should be seen that the limited scope of the requirement of permission does not amount to discrimination against foreigners in the first place, but is a limitation dictated by and adjusted to the distinctive feature of the given thing, immovable property (arable land in particular). Similar restrictions are also recognized in other countries.

Under Art. 11 (2) of the Foreign Exchange Act, a permit of the foreign exchange authority is required for an alien, in respect of his *movables* in Hungary, to make a contract of sale, commission or use with a Hungarian national or another alien, with the exception of contracts in the domain of international economic activities. Furthermore, Art. 9 of the Act requires a permit of the foreign exchange authority for aliens and Hungarian national to transfer to each other foreign currency, national currency or material values (i.e. movables) inside and outside the country, except for international economic activities with respect to material value (Art. 67) and other privileged cases like travel exchange without settlement in money, if natural persons pay each other's expenses of stay abroad (para. 2 of Art. 9).

7. The administrative norms relative to the *stay in Hungary* of foreign natural persons today represent a large body of legal material [see Glatz–Martin–Nagy: *Idegenjog, I. fejezet* (Law of Aliens, Chapter I)]. In general, they are not of a restrictive nature, although they express a status of foreigners different from that of nationals, namely they relate to foreigners who are subject in every country to certain administrative norms governing their stay and employment within the country. Nevertheless, they do not generally tend to restrict the rights of foreign persons. On the contrary, foreigners who had never previously any connection with Hungary are, as a general tendency, given an ever wider coverage by Hungarian law. In effect, these norms are an indication that a foreigner passes from his "non-existence" under Hungarian law into an active legal existence for Hungary, assuming a positive role here. This function is actually fulfilled by the provisions that determine the conditions under which foreigners may cross the Hungarian border and stay in the country.

At the same time, it should be stated that, despite the said currently prevailing general tendency, the present-day large waves of international migration have concurrently intensified the defensive legal mechanisms of States. This is shown by Hungarian legislation and practice as reflected in institutions like expulsion, aliens' control custody, deportation, etc., which are regulated by Act LXXXVI of 1993 on Aliens' Entry, Stay in Hungary and Immigration (Arts. 31 *et seq.*).

As regards the said general tendency, the first thing to mention in connection with the regulation of foreigners' settlement in Hungary is that Act XXIV of 1989 on Emigration and Immigration considers these two matters to be a fundamental human right in conformity with the International Covenant on Civil and Political Rights, which was promulgated in Hungary by Law-Decree No. 8 of 1976. This approach is likewise bolstered by Act LXXXVI of 1993 mentioned above and which also has a bearing upon immigration.

Here we are concerned only with the rules on *immigration*. The main provisions of the Act (Arts. 17 *et seq.*) are the following. *Permission* for immigration of foreigners too is required by the new regulation. As a general rule, an immigration permit may be granted to a foreigner who has been lawfully living in Hungary without interruption for at least 3 years and has no grounds for disqualification (e.g. has no assured livelihood). A dispensation as to the period of 3 years may be granted by reason of family reunion and renaturalization.

The procedure for immigration is initiated by the foreigner submitting his application. Under the general rule, the application is to be submitted to the

Hungarian foreign representation, having jurisdiction by reason of the applicant's place of permanent or habitual residence. If though the applicant is staying in Hungary on a valid permit (see below), he may also file the application with the central police office having the relevant jurisdiction according to his future domicile. The rule that the application must be considered within 120 days is in the nature of a safeguard. The impediments to immigration are regulated by the Act in conformity with the cited International Covenant. As for their effect, the impediments are either of an imperative nature or are subject to consideration. Appeal against rejection of applications is admissible.

Entry into Hungary is subject to an entry or a transit visa. Under Arts. 8 *et seq.* of Act LXXXVI of 1993 and Arts. 7 and 8 of Government Decree No. 64/1994 on its enforcement, a transit visa is good for a stay of 48 hours in Hungary, while the validity of an entry visa is stated therein, but is usually not longer than 90 days. No Hungarian entry visa is required for nationals of a State with which Hungary has signed an agreement on visa-free travel; such nationals may enter and stay in Hungary, for a period as defined by the agreement, in possession of a travel document issued by their own authority. It should be noted that Hungary has recently signed non-visa travel agreements with a great number of advanced Western countries. It is further to be emphasized that while the provisions of law on entry into and stay in Hungary are of general applicability, arrangements vary in relation to countries with which Hungary has agreed otherwise, different rules apply to the entry of diplomats (Arts. 2 and 4 of the Act).

A *residence permit* is required for foreigners intending to remain in Hungary for a longer period (Arts. 14 *et seq.* of the Act). Residence permits for a period stated therein – temporary residence permits shorter than one year and permanent residence permits longer than one year – are issued and prolonged by the police offices in the relevant territorial jurisdiction. Under a general provision of the Act, to be issued with a permit of stay in Hungary, foreigners must have sufficient means to pay subsistence expenses (Art. 5 of the Act).

8. *Employment of foreigners in Hungary* is regulated by Act IV of 1991 on Employment Promotion and Provision for the Unemployed (Art. 7) and, under its authority, by Decree No. 7/1991. (X. 17.) of the Minister of Labour. The substance of these regulations is that a foreigner may take up employment in Hungary if the labour centre, which has the relevant jurisdiction by way of the place of employment, issues an employment permit on the employer's application. As a rule, such permits may be granted if no Hungarian labour with appropriate qualifications is available in a particular district. Permits are normally issued for not more than one year, but may be prolonged. Under the provisions of the Decree, employers may apply for, and may be granted, group permits (within aggregate ceilings). The range of persons exempt from an employment permit (persons covered by interstate agreements, persons delegated to diplomatic missions, refugees and immigrants in possession of an identity card entitling them to permanent residence, leading officials of economic associations

with foreign participation, persons invited under programmes of scientific, educational, artistic and cultural institutions) is determined by Art. 7 of the Act and Art. 5 of the Decree referred to above. Applications are to be submitted by the domestic employers, who receive the permits from the competent labour centre (Art. 6 of the Decree).

§45. THE MOST-FAVOURED-NATION CLAUSE AND THE SYSTEM OF SPECIAL PREFERENCES

In addition to national treatment as a general principle, the *most-favoured-nation clause*, seeking to accord equal treatment to foreigners (foreigners *vis-à-vis* foreigners), is of outstanding importance to international personal and economic transactions, especially to international economic relations. Its scope of application is conceptually smaller in comparison to that of the principle of national treatment, partly because it is not a general maxim of internal substantive law, but is only applied to relationships specified by interstate treaties, and partly because it is applied not universally, but "only" in commercial and economic transactions. Its significance in this domain is great by itself, but its importance also results from the fact that it has become an essential component of international economic policies, even on the general plane of international politics.

1. The *concept* of most-favoured-nation status can be said to have the following meaning: if natural and legal persons of a foreign State *enjoy, under a pertinent international treaty, most-favoured-nation treatment in the State concerned, this latter State grants them, on this ground, all the rights and facilities accorded to natural and legal persons of the State which enjoys the most favourable situation in relation to that State.* Under an appropriate bilateral or multilateral international treaty, the domestic status of the nationals and companies of the foreign State in question is determined by legislation on two planes. On the one hand, these nationals and companies are naturally entitled to specific facilities (concerning tariffs, taxes, etc.) as specified by treaty in respect of economic relations between the two States concerned. On the other hand, however, they are entitled to such other facilities, partly known, partly not yet known, which one State has already accorded to nationals and companies of other States, including those which it will, at any future point of time, grant to nationals and companies of any State. This, too, shows clearly that what we have here is actually the principle of equality of foreign companies and natural persons as between themselves.

2. What lies behind this formal equality of rights, behind this principle expressing the possibility of action under equal economic conditions, is the working of *fundamental economic interests*. Mutual granting of the most-favoured-nation treatment is a condition for the development of international trade and general economic relations. While Hungary, for instance, did not en-

joy most-favoured-nation status on the American market (until the promulgation of the American–Hungarian Trade Agreement of 1978), its products were subject to higher customs tariffs, or American internal law placed other restrictions on Hungarian goods and commercial transactions. With those conditions prevailing, amid sharpened international economic competition, it was, of course, particularly difficult to develop Hungarian–American trade relations and to strengthen the positions of Hungarian companies on the American market. Therefore, practically speaking, the unequal situation compelled Hungarian companies to sell all their products at much higher customs tariff rates than their competitors from other States which enjoyed most-favoured-nation status in the United States. Obviously, non-application of the most-favoured-nation clause serves to shield or protect the domestic market against some importers on the one hand and to restrain the growth of international economic relations on the other, while causing specific disadvantages to the State which is denied this status.

3. As regards Hungarian law, most-favoured-nation treatment is seen as a central element of the law of international economic relations. This is reflected in the *bilateral trade agreements* between Hungary and several other countries, and this principle can be found in, e.g., the Tanzanian–Hungarian Trade Agreement (Art. 1), which was promulgated by Law-Decree No. 15 of 1967, and in other agreements of a more recent date, such as the Finnish–Hungarian Trade Agreement (Art. 6) promulgated by Law-Decree No. 5 of 1975, the Japanese–Hungarian Trade and Navigation Agreement (Art. 1) ratified by Law-Decree No. 10 of 1977, and the US–Hungarian Trade Agreement (para. 1 of Art. I; paras. 2 and 11c of Art. III; para. 3 of Art. V) promulgated by Law-Decree No. 12 of 1978, the Hungarian–EEC Agreement of 1988 on Trade and Commercial and Economic Cooperation, the Association Agreement with the European Communities and their member-states concluded in 1991 after the systemic change [see item 3 (c), (cf), (iii) in §39], and several other bilateral agreements like the German–Hungarian Treaty on Friendly Cooperation and European Partnership (Art. 11) signed in 1992 and promulgated by Act LXXIX of 1995.

4. Apart from the previous, mostly strong political considerations and motives which have caused and still cause some countries to grant this status reluctantly and with reservations, the most-favoured-nation clause is a general expression of the objective needs of international economic relations, notably of the possibility for nationals and companies of foreign States to carry out economic activities in the countries concerned, and generally in all countries, on an equal footing and with the same advantages. Differentiation between and discrimination against countries naturally hinder the normal development of international economic processes and generate conflicting interests between companies on the markets, thus leading to clashes of interests between States, ultimately in interstate and hence international politics. Application of this principle is therefore an inner and general demand of international economic

relations between States, being reflected in several multilateral instruments of international law.

(a) It is not accidental that the most-favoured-nation clause carries considerable weight in such important *international instruments of general applicability* as the Charter of Economic Rights and Duties of States (Art. 26) adopted by the United Nations in 1974 and the Final Act of the Helsinki Conference on Security and Cooperation in Europe (sections on economic relations, commercial exchanges, and general introductory provisions). These significant legal instruments show how the most-favoured-nation clause is both an economic and a political phenomenon.

(b) This is indicated as well by the *General Agreement on Tariffs and Trade* (GATT), one of the most universal international agreements on trade, which was ratified by Hungary in 1973 and its accession was enacted by Decree No. 23/1973 of the Council of Ministers. GATT and its latest developments – the Uruguay Round and the establishment of WTO – have already been addressed in this work, along general lines [item 2 (a), (aa) in §39]. What should be emphasized here is that the most-favoured-nation clause has, from the outset, been the central institution of GATT, which has grown into a general principle of world trade through the medium of this highly important multilateral agreement. It is of great significance even if GATT itself "envisages" exceptions, or, given the various difficulties besetting the world economy, it is not always properly applied where required by GATT. The central role of the most-favoured-nation clause is indicated by the provision of GATT Art. I to the effect that, in respect of all rules on imports and exports (tariffs, charges, payments, etc.), any advantage, facility, privilege or immunity which any Contracting Party accords to any product imported from or exported to the territory of all other Contracting Parties. Hungary's accession to GATT entailed the extension to it of the generally highly favourable terms and conditions associated with these mutual rights and obligations, together with the need for its tariff system to be adjusted to the GATT standards attained by that time. Indeed, right after the accession, the Council of Ministers modified, by Decree No. 24 of 1973, Hungarian trade tariffs, which have since been adjusted several times. Our accession was not without problems, however.

We will single out for attention the following *problems* of the many that accompany the most-favoured-nation clause of GATT.

(ba) For a long time, GATT *could not by itself eliminate* all discrimination. The question involved was not only that, owing to the supersaturation of its internal market, the Common Market generally placed restrictions on the imports of meat and other agricultural products from non-Common Market countries. It also involved the fact that, in effect, such restrictions were coupled with discrimination in so far as the consignments for exports from Hungary as a "state-trading" socialist country were fixed at a much lower level than was the case with other countries not members of the Common Market. Of course, the situation is different today. The aforementioned agreements between Hungary and the EEC on trade and commercial and economic cooperation as well as on association were signed in 1988 and 1991, respectively. In them, the Contracting Parties reaffirmed their commitment to the *exchange of most-favoured-nation treatment* in accordance with the Protocol for the Accession of Hungary to GATT.

(bb) Especially a few years ago, the *relationship between GATT, or the most-favoured-nation clause and economic integration* was the subject of debate. An essential element of economic integration consists of coordination or unification by the member-states of specific aspects of their economic policies in an endeavour to create a uniform legal status for their nationals and companies in specific areas and to establish a legal framework for identical facilities in respect of economic transactions. Thus this process will gradually place nationals and companies of the member-states on an equal footing in relations between member-states, a situation which will enable them to enjoy such economic, economic-policy, financial and legal advantages as the community of an economic integration will progressively evolve through intra-integration cooperation. A highly important manifestation of this trend is, e.g., complete elimination of internal tariffs (between member-states) in the European Economic Community and establishment of uniform tariffs for external application. Staying with this example, numerous countries signed such bilateral agreements with EEC which provided for the most-favoured-nation treatment. Thus the need was raised for all those advantages which the member-states accorded to one another in the Common Market to be extended to third countries for reasons of legal arrangements and requirements, legal logic, and, of course, economic interests. Indeed, there were signs of such efforts by the most advanced countries *vis-à-vis* the Common Market. This was reflected in the activity of GATT, too. The problem which evoked considerable debate was resolved by GATT adopting the principle that economic integrations having reached a certain level, e.g. the level of a customs union (and the Common Market qualifies as such), cannot be compelled to extend, under the most-favoured-nation clause (GATT Article XXIV), membership treatment to nationals and companies of third countries. If this were allowed to occur it would practically bring the integration to an end inasmuch as it would require States seeking to build an economic integrationist structure to form such an organisation with all States with which they have signed an agreement on the application of the most-favoured-nation clause.

This relationship of economic integration to GATT reflects the weight of the most-favoured-nation clause. For the preferential system of an economic integration to be left intact, however, GATT is clearly guided by the principle that the application of preferential systems thus maintained must not result in discrimination among the member-states of GATT and must not impede the development of economic relations among them. For the moment, facts show that international economic relations have strengthened, and that the preferential systems of integration have by themselves raised no obstacle to the implementation of the GATT principles.

(bc) Another significant problem concerns the *relationship between GATT, or the most-favoured-nation clause and the developing countries*. The essential point here is that the developing countries need preferences *vis-à-vis* the advanced countries to further their development and the general improvement of international economic relations (the establishment of a new international economic order). If nothing but the principle of equal opportunities continues to prevail, the rich will become richer and the poor poorer. The first result achieved by the concerted efforts of developing countries in this question was the complementing of the GATT Convention in 1964. In Article XXXVI of Chapter IV on "Trade and Development" the substance of the new results was expressed in these terms: the advanced Contracting Parties expect no reciprocity in respect of the commitments they have undertaken during the trade talks to reduce or to eliminate customs tariffs or other restrictions in their trading with the less-developed Contracting Parties (para. 8). So there is no question of granting facilities which is for the Contracting Parties to decide. The only question is that once facilities are granted, which is naturally desirable under the said GATT Article, the advanced States are not to demand reciprocity.

In addition, the United Nations Conference on Trade and Development (UNCTAD) has long been urging the advanced countries to grant preferences to the developing countries, while not extending them to the advanced countries, on the understanding that such preferences do not come under the most-favoured-nation clause. This led to the adoption of the General System of Preferences (GSP) in 1970, its essence consisting of the advanced countries determining non-reciprocal preferences varying from one country to another and refraining from applying them among themselves as part of the most-favoured-nation treatment. Since no uniform international agreement was concluded on this matter, States follow the GSP principle in the form of "non-mandatory commitment" and give it a substance varying by country. With respect to Hungary it may be mentioned that the Hungarian Trade Tariffs Act, referred to above, similarly grants preferential tariffs to developing countries. Under the impact of the political changes, Austria extended to Hungary the preferential tariff treatment with effect from 1 July 1988, and then, on 1 January 1990, Hungary was accorded the same treatment under specified arrangements by the European Community (which, in consequence of the Association Agreement, chose to grant more favourable preferences as a matter of course) and the United States. This treatment has been extended to Hungary by Canada, Japan and New Zealand as well.

There is no special need to underline the significance of these developments for the competitive capacity of the Hungarian economy. All this is in keeping with the general endeavour also expressed in the United Nations Charter of Economic Rights and Duties of States, namely to give increasingly more substance to GSP. As is provided by Art. 26 of the Charter, international trade should be conducted without prejudice to generalized non-reciprocal preferences in favour of developing countries, on the bases of mutual advantage and the most-favoured-nation clause.

§46. FOREIGN COMPANIES IN HUNGARY – FOREIGN INVESTMENTS IN HUNGARY, TRADE REPRESENTATIONS, FOREIGN BANKS

1. The *general economic policy conceptions* about joint ventures and foreign investments have been formulated in various ways and with shifting emphases.

(a) On the side of *capital exports* they embrace interests in the utilization of surplus capital; exploitation of comparative advantages (qualified yet cheap labour, rich sources of raw material and energy, reduction of transport costs by supplying markets through locally-based enterprises); proximity to markets and hence to market demands and challenges; increasing the stability of investing companies and the efficiency of their business strategies by establishing a wide network of undertakings; support for the restructuring of entire national economies where these historical processes are under way, as in, e.g., Poland, Hungary, Czech Republic and the rest of newly democratic countries.

(b) On the side of *capital imports* they express interests involved in encouraging investments for the purpose of establishing or lagging industries; utilization of modern technologies, streamlining the industry with a view to competitive production; development of skills in business and market organization; procuring new markets by improving the balance of trade and payments as well as by increasing the competitive capacity of foreign trade and receipts in convertible currency; streamlining the economy in general and obtaining support for programmes of restructuring and switching to a market economy model.

(c) Of course, it is a commonly held view that *international dependence* rooted in technological processes, production and trade cries out for *international cooperation*, for a division of labour embodied in foreign companies and joint ventures and in the movement of investment capital.

(d) Then there is the realization, commonplace but expressing an indisputable truth, that close economic cooperation (with joint ventures and foreign capital investments creating especially strong mutual interests) contributes greatly to *reducing political tensions and the chances of armed confrontation.*

2. Foreign investment capacity and foreign capital in general *appear within the State in the following institutions as broadly understood*:

(a) *loans and bonds:* these are not *sui generis* forms of investment but serve to channel capital (i.e. investment capacity, financial resources available for investment in goods) from one country to another;

(b) *leasing:* this is, by its nature, a special tool of investment strategy widely employed even in the Central and Eastern European as well as in the developing countries, not to speak of the countries with a developed market economy.

While international leasing is not covered by any special legislation in the countries of Central and Eastern Europe, internal commercial laws and the modern *lex mercatoria* have achieved a great deal towards having this legal institution established. With Hungarian participation, UNIDROIT has drafted the International Financial Convention, which was adopted by the International Diplomatic Conference in Ottawa on 28 May 1988 and has since come into force. Hungary, too, has acceded to it (after the relevant Government Decree of 1992 and Parliament's Decision of 2 May 1995 the instruments of accession were deposited by the Republic of Hungary with the Canadian Government on 7 May 1996);

(c) *contractual joint undertakings:* channelling considerable investment capacity from one country to another. They include joint or coordinated research projects, development and market regulatory systems, joint production based on specialization and on repurchase agreements, agreements on designing factories and putting them into operation, turn-key systems, franchise, etc. In pursuance of these goals, countries make extensive use of the appropriate institutions of civil and commercial law. We will now confine ourselves to emphasizing that the freedom of contract is the most fundamental institution or general principle of the complex cooperation contracts and will not speak of the types and forms of cooperation contracts, nor of the voluminous literature and the theoretical considerations relating to framework agreements, model agreements and general terms and conditions. Then we have the various types of associations, some categories of syndicates, consortia, etc. The European Economic Interest Grouping (EEIG) (*groupement d'intérêt économique*) appears to be gaining acceptance both in the law of the European Communities and in national laws (for the variety of forms, see Mádl: Forms of Joint Ventures; Bobkin, J.A. *et al.*: International Joint Ventures).

3. The range of *foreign investments in the narrow sense* practically embraces the diverse forms of associations and the administrative provisions which seek to regulate the inflow and outflow of investment capital in one way or another. Under Act XXIV of 1988 ("Investment Code"), the forms of foreign investments in Hungary include economic associations with foreign participation, economic associations founded by foreigners, and acquisition by foreigners of shares in economic associations [para. (b) of Art. 2]. However foreign participation in investment funds should also be deemed to belong to this category, as Act LXIII of 1991 on Investment Funds provides that investment shares in investment funds may also be acquired by foreigners (Art. 51).

(a) As a general rule, the forms of associations are those classical (national) forms which are known throughout the world. For foreign investors, these represent the background structure in corporate law with respect to both foreign-owned subsidiary companies, as well as partnerships and joint ventures established by Hungarian and foreign partners.

Some investment codes list all types and forms of economic units, associations and entities other than associations, which the particular national legal system recognizes, regulates and recommends for economic units established by foreigners or joint ventures. Under Hungarian law, associations with foreign participation may be established in the manner and form regulated by Act VI of 1988 on Economic Associations ("Associations Act"). These associations are subject to the rules of the Associations Act. In countries where such codes of association or generally recognized modern forms of associations do not (yet) exist or are not sufficiently developed, establishment of special forms of joint ventures/associations is attempted by the investment codes themselves. Of course, the latter regulations are of necessity rather general, often not detailed enough to give orientation or a clear coverage. With some simplification, the forms of joint ventures thus "invented" may be said to follow the models of joint stock companies and limited liability companies.

(b) Foreign investments are likewise encouraged by a wide range of *inter-governmental agreements* including, *inter alia*, general trade agreements, agreements and conventions on investment protection, agreements for the avoidance of double taxation, etc. (see the List of Sources: 2. Major International Treaties), providing, as it were, a background to the theatre of international investments.

(c) Moreover, there exists a rather large number of investments (and regulations governing them) with *direct state participation*, so that States, individually or jointly with others, act as investors as well (see §48). This holds for, among others, the member-states of the European Union (see the joint public-law enterprises established under the Euratom Treaty, European Investment Bank, *Eurochemic*, larger airline companies, Airbus, etc.).

(d) We have had to make at least a brief reference to the above-mentioned categories in order to give a more or less full picture of them, but naturally we cannot focus much attention on them. This also holds true for two more areas which we shall touch on presently.

(da) One area is represented by large-scale investment projects to which *one Party is a government* and the other a private person. This was an arrangement mainly in the philosophy and practice of the former socialist countries, an inter-system scheme of East and West, such as the Soviet-Fiat Agreement establishing a large motor-car factory in the former Soviet Union.

(db) The other area is that of *concession* agreements under which Governments grant licences to foreign companies, operating and intending to effect investments in their territories, for purposes of prospecting for and exploiting gas, oil or coal deposits.

Concessions in Hungary are regulated by Act XVI of 1991. This regulation allows the State or a local government to transfer temporarily, by onerous contract, the right to pursue activities specified by law, thus securing for the concessionaire a partial monopoly on the market. A concession seeks to carry out activities or to operate specific assets (e.g. railways, electricity works), or is linked to exclusive state activities, aimed at public supplies of strategic importance (e.g. prospecting for and exploitation of mines). Here, too, within the meaning of the Act, belong activities that yield very high extra profits (e.g. operation of casinos).

The conclusion of concession contracts is subject to compulsory tendering, and the State or a government may sign a contract only with the winning bidder, who in turn must found with his own participation an economic association, within the country. Such association is entitled to engage exclusively in the activity specified by the contract and to conduct such other operations as are organically related to it.

4. *The history of legal regulations relative to joint ventures* or foreign *investments* is in itself the subject of extensive analyses. By way of reference to the pertinent literature (see Buxbaum, Mádl), we will confine ourselves to making a few observations.

(a) As is known, the *developed market economy countries* have no special legislation on joint ventures or foreign investments under corporate law, simply because this domain is governed by a system of corporate laws, one of highly-developed national corporate laws, which is in some cases supplemented by international instruments of harmonization as applied in, e.g., the European Communities (see Martonyi, Király). Thus, foreign investments in the host countries are controlled by internal corporate law on the basis of the principle of national treatment. This legal basis (national treatment, *régime national*) prevails as well with respect to special rules, which are either incentive or restrictive, occasionally analytical and monitoring norms, and mostly administrative. Thus, for instance, the Swedish law on acquisition of property by foreigners establishes thresholds (10, 20, 40 and 50%) on investments in the various categories, which may not be exceeded except with permission. In countries with a developed law of competition, a critical-level market position or behaviour of international joint ventures may be seen as restrictive of competition and activate application of the antitrust law. For considerations of defence, some countries have adopted special restrictive or prohibitive rules to control business dealings with specific countries, which naturally brings profound influence to bear on the flow of working capital between the countries concerned. For instance, the so-called COCOM bans and restrictions may, and were able to, wield a heavy influence on the affected transactions (see Dobkin, J.A. *et al.*: International Joint Ventures, "Antitrust Laws", "National Security Restrictions", Chapters 9–10).

In some advanced countries, special legislation and government measures encourage the foundation of joint ventures in developing countries. Schemes of insurance (see §58) like OPIC (USA) and HERMES (FRG) similarly give encouragement and provide highly important incentives to investment projects in other countries, where the "political risk" is (or is deemed to be) much greater than in the stable market economies.

(b) The existence of investment codes *in the developing countries of the Third World* is a general phenomenon. Without going into detail, we would point out that from the end of the 1940s to the end of the 1980s more than 70 countries framed special legislation controlling foreign investments (Buxbaum). Some laws are rather liberal, granting not only national treatment, but also strongly articulated facilities, while others reflect a rather harsh and restrictive approach and even one appearing to be oriented somewhat against "aliens".

(c) According to the economic and legal philosophies of the former "socialist" countries, the presence of capitalist ownership in foreign private capital (see shareholding) was regarded as alien to the system, as contrary to the socialist order, and, as such, was prohibited. These countries were opened to foreign investments by a series of transformations, the first reform measures followed by really revolutionary developments in comparatively recent years. Legislation on joint ventures appeared in them in the late 1960s and during the 1970s (first in Hungary and, within a narrower scope, in Romania). The initially reluctant, restrictive, controlling special law-making concept, adding up to a kind of *ius praetorium vis-à-vis* joint enterprises and foreign capital in general, came to be replaced by measures of gradual liberalization and, under the hallmark of the systemic change, by a permissive-incentive attitude, by national treatment under the classical corporate law.

This is known to mean that all forms of foreign investment came to gain acceptance in the whole spectrum of acquisitions 100% in foreign ownership, traditional mixed enterprises in which foreign and domestic founders join in establishing and operating new economic associations.

7. The *main elements of regulations* on foreign investments in the form of association (independent units, acquisition of shares in existing units, and joint ventures) will be reviewed below [subitems (a) to (1)] (for general comparative characteristics of other than Hungarian legislation, see Buxbaum–Dobkin–Mádl: Forms of Joint Ventures).

(a) *By the object* of undertakings, some codes expressly prescribe or at least recommend the industries where foreign investment is seen to be desirable. In certain cases the codes happen definitely to prohibit specific categories of investment in a few areas. Other legal systems require joint ventures to promote introduction of modern technologies and skills in business organization, to facilitate supplies to the domestic market, to contribute to the growth of exports, to improve the balance of payments, etc.

Of course, in countries where such requirements are formulated, the competent authorities also consider, in the licensing process, the activities of future joint ventures by these criteria. The system of norms conceived under the third "Philosophy" (Hungary) contains no restriction or prohibition by the object of undertakings. Obviously enough, the activities of joint ventures, just as those of the other economic actors, must not be contrary to law, must not offend public morals, etc. This, however, should not be declared in the investment codes for it follows directly from the principle of national treatment, whereas investment in the preferred industries is stimulated in addition by Hungarian law granting extensive *tax benefits* rather than governing it by compulsory provisions.

(b) The host countries determine different *ranges of potential foreign and domestic investors*. Formerly most of them allowed foreign legal persons to be partners to domestic economic organizations. In the course of later development this range of investors was widened to include economic associations possessing no legal personality and even private persons, as is further reflected in the Hungarian investment code.

With respect to domestic business partners, Act XXIV of 1988 spells out clearly that "in associations with foreign participation the State, legal persons, economic associations possessing no legal personality, and natural persons may equally participate either as domestic founders or members thereof in accordance with the provisions of the Associations Act".

(c) *State influence* or control is of varying intensity at the time of foundation or liquidation: it may be strong or marginal as dictated by the economic philosophy of the particular State.

In the once state-dominated "socialist" systems, central administration ultimately sought to exercise the prerogative of deciding on the economic rationality or efficiency of each and every new undertaking. As in other cases, lack of confidence in the independent role of the market resulted in predominant state intervention. It was thus rather common that in addition to the registration of firms existing in every country, the permission of the Government (practically a minister or a government committee) was required, as a quasi prerequisite for registration, for the establishment of foreign interests. The licensing procedure was unduly long and complicated in general, with no possibility of judicial review. At any rate, it allowed scope for controlling or demanding fulfillment of the specific economic policy expectations, declared or disguised, placed on joint ventures.

With the switch to a market economy, *simple registration,* inscription in the registry of firms (Companies Register), became the general rule. In fact, the Companies Register became the general rule. All the court of registration has to do is to examine the legality of the foundation or acquisition of shares in the associations, and it may not deny registration except in case of violation of law. The Hungarian investment code requires no permission of the foreign exchange authority for the foundation of an association with foreign participation or for participation in an association (para. 2 of Art. 9), so the fact of foreign participation does not by itself entail any special licensing procedure. This regulation by the Act is a definite step towards the granting of national treatment and essentially simplifies the foundation of associations. Of course, if the law makes the activity of a Hungarian economic association subject to administrative permission, the permission should also be obtained for an economic association with foreign participation (Art. 34). As regards the liquidation of joint ventures, there is no special state intervention as in the past, but the appropriate rules of the law of association or of bankruptcy are applicable.

Pursuant to the special rules relative to the introduction and circulation of securities, including shares, the circulation in other countries of securities involving domestic investments is subject to the provisions of law on authorization.

The Securities Act requires the permission of the Banking and Capital Market Supervisory Body for circulating abroad *securities involving corporate property and investment* (Art. 66 of Act CXI of 1995). Concerning the circulation and sale of securities abroad, the Foreign Exchange Act requires the permission of the foreign exchange authority in the case of open-end collective investment securities or if a Hungarian national intends to circulate in Hungary shares in foreign currency or other securities embodying shares held in an undertaking (Art. 35).

(d) As against the earlier restrictions concerned about the erosion of "socialist" ownership, Hungary has put no ceiling, under the new conditions, on the *ratio of foreign participation* in joint ventures, which may be as high as 100% both in partnerships and in newly-founded independent economic associations, with no permission required. Hungarian legislation grants tax benefits as an incentive to secure the desirable minimum ratio of foreign participation.

As regards the *assets contributed*, the following will be noted.

(e) *Money contribution* is subject to no special regulations other than the rules applicable to transfer. Under Art. 12, as amended, of the Hungarian investment code, a foreigner may pay his money contribution in convertible currency or, under the foreign exchange regulations, in forint convertible into convertible currency; this latter possibility is not extended to the monetary contribution by associations set up in the (tax-) free zone.

With respect to *contributions other than money*, the Hungarian law provides that "as a non-monetary contribution, account may only be taken of realizable assets as well as of intellectual property rights or rights which an economic association may subsequently transfer without the consent (permission) of a third person. A foreigner may offer, as a non-monetary contribution, compensation vouchers other than those which are, by virtue of law, due to him as a beneficiary of compensation" [Art. 12 (2) of Act XXIV of 1988 as amended by Art. 48 (2) of Act LXV of 1991]. It is to be noted that the *means of production* which the foreign member of an association makes available as non-monetary contribution may be imported *free of customs duty* (Art. 18). Such means of production are understood to include primarily machinery and equipment, installations, vehicles, building components that are "directly necessary" for manufacturing goods, supplying services or carrying out activities (Art. 18).

A special problem is posed by *valuation* in cases where, in the process of privatization, foreign investment involves partnership in an operating state enterprise, or *acquisition of minority or majority shares or full ownership* therein (see §§59–60).

(f) The mode of *decision-making* is governed by the principles of the classical corporate law in the countries where the legal regulation of foreign investments is based on corporate law. Such is the case in Hungarian law.

(g) *Indigenization* is today a notably weaker trend. National preferences are established by only a few legal systems, requiring, e.g., that the chairman of the board of management be a national or restricting the employment of foreign staff (managers and subordinates).

The more liberal investment laws (of Poland, Hungary) have lifted all previous restrictions: "Foreigners may also be senior executives and managers of an association, members of its board of supervision, and its employees" (Art. 27 of Act XXIV of 1988), meaning that even an association with foreign participation is free to decide on its employment policy. In addition to the regulation by corporate law, account shall be taken, in the employment of foreigners, of the rules of internal law governing the stay of foreigners, social insurance, and certain questions of labour law.

(h) *Taxes* play an outstanding role both in the economic policies of capital-importing countries and in their strategies for foreign investment. The host countries wish to encourage foreign investments by according tax preferences, formerly "more generous" and today tapering off gradually. This trend naturally cannot reach the point of greatly prejudicing national treatment, the competitive ability of domestic economic subjects and investors. This is why the tendency is strengthening for a reduction in preferences. Fiscal policies combined with this system of preferences show the following picture.

Tax rates in the countries according preferences are generally lower than those applicable to domestically-owned undertakings. The usual rates are fixed at 20% to 40% of annual profits realized by enterprises operating with foreign participation.

Reinvestment of profits generally enjoys sizeable benefits and is occasionally encouraged even by full exemption from taxation. Foreign investments are supported by take-off preferences in the first years of operation. Finally, the third group of benefits is related to certain *priorities of the national economy*, i.e. to investments in *priority industries*.

At the beginning, *Hungarian law* was also guided by this philosophy, but, with the evolution of market economy conditions, the interests attached to taxation and to the equality of competitive conditions, have led to a gradual reduction in special tax benefits. In time the benefits already granted were made "closed-end" by legislation providing that they might be enjoyed only until at the latest 2003. Of course, associations with foreign participation are entitled to all the benefits due to other domestic economic associations (see Art. 14 of Act XXIV of 1988 and, on the extremely flexible rules of taxation, Glatz–Martin–Nagy: Chapter 5/III).

It is obvious that the position of foreign investments is likewise strongly influenced by agreements for the *avoidance of double taxation*. Clearly enough, foreign investors are, in theory, liable to taxation both in the country of investment and in the country of their nationality, the country to which profits are transferred. This double burden would certainly act as a retarding factor. In order to avoid it and to promote the international flow of capital, the capital-receiving countries, including Hungary, concluded numerous agreements for the avoidance of double taxation in recent decades (see Agreements for the Avoidance of Double Taxation in the List of Sources).

(i) The *transparency of profits* due to foreign investors is a vital precondition for more pronounced capital flows. This means first of all the free transferability of the foreigner's share in the association's profits and of the amount due to him from the foreign property share in case of the association's liquidation or of the alienation, in full or in part, of that share (Art. 32 of Act XXIV of 1988).

Equally important is the transferability of the income earned from a joint venture by the foreign members of the staff (senior executives, managers, members of the board of supervision, employees) (in Hungary the ratio of such transferable income after taxation is up to 50% under Art. 33 of Act XXIV of 1988). Since difficulties raised in this field would bring joint ventures into an impossible situation, the investment codes generally seek to provide some sort of guarantee, but regulations differ, especially in respect to the transferability of profits.

Under Hungarian law, the transfer of profits in convertible currency is guaranteed *regardless of the currency* in which the profits of joint ventures are realized. Accordingly, gains may accrue either in Hungarian forint or in non-convertible currency, and the amount due to a foreigner is freely transferable in the currency of investment.

(j) The *alienability of* foreign investors' *property share* is an important element of investment regulations. In case of inalienability, investors would be reluctant to invest, would feel themselves "soil-bound", as it were, so the flexibility of the market of securities, capital and immovables is an essential prerequisite for participation in the international flow of capital.

In previous years, in particular, the investment codes made the sale of foreigners' property shares subject to various conditions. Other corporate laws now simply recognize the owners' agreement, and its implementation, concerning alienation as contained in the memorandum and articles of association. Hungary belongs to the latter group of countries.

(k) National treatment is the general rule with regard to the *general economic and legal environment* (terms and conditions of contract, access to credit, economic planning, foreign trade, administration of justice, supply of raw materials and energy, price regulation). Already in the preamble, the Hungarian code emphatically refers to enjoyment of *national treatment*, which is restated in the particular rules. Thus, in respect to price formation, regulation of competition, liquidation procedure, etc., economic associations with foreign participation are subject to the same rules as those controlling the rest of domestic economic organizations (Arts. 20 to 25 of Act XXIV of 1988).

In effect, the Hungarian law accords national treatment to enterprises with foreign participation with respect to *acquisition of real property* as well, since an association needs no separate permit to acquire ownership or other rights in immovables necessary for its economic activity as defined in the memorandum and articles of association (Art. 19).

(l) The guarantees provided for foreign investors must perforce be discussed, as will be done in Chapter XVII in connection with the protection of foreign property.

6. In the domain of foreign investments a special role is played by economic associations established in customs-/tax-free zones, referred to hereafter as *"free-zone associations"*. This institution was called into being by economic policy interests and considerations involved in increasing foreign investments, as it affords *preferences* able and destined to exercise a considerable attraction for investors. The substance of the relevant regulation consists of a high degree of flexibility and of independence from domestic regulations. The free-zone association found its way into our law in 1982 (Joint Decree No. 62 of 1982 of the Minister of Finance and the Minister of Foreign Trade, which was refined by Act XXIV of 1988, Arts. 37 to 43) in the following main provisions.

Establishment of a free-zone association is subject to a decision of the Ministry of Finance to the effect that the real estate on which the association is planned to be established has been declared to be a customs-free area, or zone.

A customs-free zone is a site separated under specified conditions from the surrounding area of the country and qualifying as non-national territory for the purposes of *customs and foreign exchange regulations* and, with certain exceptions (see below), of *foreign trade regulations*. Consequently, a free-zone association qualifies as alien from the point of view of the said regulations.

As a general rule, a free-zone association is required to effect its transactions *in convertible currency*, may draw credit from both domestic foreign sources and from abroad, and is free to dispose of its assets deposited in convertible currency inside and outside the country.

The most obvious concomitant of the free-zone status is that the association may import goods duty free, but its deliveries from the compound to the domestic market are liable to customs duty. In addition, although it is regarded as alien for the purposes of foreign trade regulations as well, the free-zone association is under the control of the foreign trade-related provisions of the international treaties by which the Republic of Hungary is bound as well as of certain rules relating to exports and imports.

The benefits recognized for free-zone associations may be extended by the Minister of Finance to *non-free-zone associations* operating with full or partial foreign participation unless the particular association is engaged in an activity involving movement of goods across state boundaries. This type of association is regarded as alien in accordance with the foregoing statement and represents, in point of fact, a special mutation of free-zone associations, a kind of off-shore company. A most important instance of such undertakings is the International Investment Bank for Central Europe, Co. Ltd. in Budapest. A normative variant of associations not operating in a customs-free zone has been introduced recently by Act IC of 1993 (Art. 14/A) amending Act LXXXVI of 1991 (see Glatz–Martin–Nagy: Chapter 5/IV).

7. Under the recent pattern of international economic relations the said developments in enterprise movement, which are gaining momentum in Hungary, are also manifest in the appearance of many associations operating with foreign participation. A further element consists in leaving a broad scope for the *trade representation of foreign companies within the State*, namely the organizational presence of foreign firms in a specified area of activity. Their operation is governed by Decree No. 3/1989. (II.26.) of the Minister of Commerce on the trade representation of foreigners as well as their information and service offices.

(a) The function of trade representations is to join in transmitting, preparing and concluding contracts of foreign trade, or to make such contracts between the represented foreign company and the respective Hungarian enterprises. Furthermore, their activity may include maintaining a consignment depository of the represented foreign company, shopping and post-sale services related to goods supplied and services provided by foreign companies as well as marketing and promotion concerning the products and services of the represented company (Art. 7).

(b) The same Decree authorizes foreigners to set up information or service offices in Hungary in order to inform Hungarian partners of their products and services, control quality, give expert advice, service machinery and equipment, and carry on marketing and promotion activities (Art. 8). However, a foreigner may not, in his capacity as such, engage in foreign trade, namely transmit and conclude contracts, etc.

(c) At the statutory level, the commercial activities of foreigners in Hungary (including trade representation) had been governed by Art. 25 of Act III of 1974, but para. 3 of that Article covering the licensing procedure was repealed in the meantime by Act XXII of 1990 on *Deregulation*. This is in keeping with the much more liberal provisions of the already mentioned Decree No. 3/1989. (II.26.) of the Minister of Commerce.

(d) The permanent trade representation of foreigners in the territory of the Republic of Hungary may be assigned to a *Hungarian economic organization* [Art. 685, para. (c) of the Civil Code] or to a direct trade representation the foreigner establishes with a seat in Hungary. The former case is governed by Decree No. 1/1987. (XII.29.) of the Minister of Commerce establishing the procedures for pursuing foreign trade activities.

(e) A *direct trade representation* may be established by a foreigner who has a firm in accordance with his domestic law and has it entered into the registry, kept by the Ministry of Industry and Commerce, of foreign firms maintaining a representation in Hungary. Registration is made on notification by the foreign party, and it may not be denied except for the reasons specified by the Decree, notably –

(ea) the activity of the foreign firm offends against the public order;

(eb) the activity of the foreign firm is contrary to the generally accepted customs in international commercial practice;

(ec) the activity of the foreign firm prejudices or jeopardizes Hungary's obligations under international treaties or its compliance therewith;

(ed) the country of the notifier's place of business restricts or prevents the settlement or operation of Hungarian firms for similar purposes (para. 2 of Art. 5). The same procedure applies to the registration of information and service offices, with the exception that consent may not be denied except in the cases mentioned in subitems (ea) and (ec) in accordance with para. 6 of Art. 8.

(f) It may be stated in general that, parallel to the changing regulations on economic associations with foreign participation, the "consessionary" regime based on authorization in each individual case was replaced by a general permissive regulation (the so-called "general legal regime") with respect to the foreign trade representations of foreigners as well.

8. The role of *foreign banks* in Hungary is an important element of international economic cooperation and of the development of the Hungarian economy, particularly the Hungarian banking system. This is manifested in bank-like operation based on property shares and in bank representation.

(a) Under Arts. 15 and 69 of Act LXIX of 1991 (Banking Act), bank-like operation with *foreign property share* – foundation of a banking institution wholly or in part in foreign ownership, a foreigner's share in a banking institution incorporated in Hungary (if the total shares of foreigners exceed 10% of the bank's subscribed capital) – was subject to the Government's consent in principle on the proposal of the Banking Supervision Board and in concurrence with the President of the Hungarian National Bank [see, e.g., Government Decision No. 1036/1992. (VII.10.) on consent in principle to the foundation of "Crédit Lyonnais Bank in Hungary, Co. Ltd." in partial foreign ownership]. Further in connection with the conditions for our membership in OECD, the restrictive provisions of the said Act were repealed by Art. 3 of Act XII of 1996 amending the former, and the new Banking Act (Act CXII of 1996 on Credit Institutions and Financial Undertakings) naturally follows the principle of national treatment. The proprietary role of foreigners may not be subject to discriminative provisions of law. With these regulations adopted, Hungarian legislation has already satisfied EEC Council's Guidelines No. 73/193/EEC of June of 1973 concerning the abrogation of statutory provisions restrictive of the freedom to settle and to provide services in connection with the activities of banks and other credit institutions (see the new Act's No. 6 Annex "EU Guidelines Considered", para. 1).

(b) *Establishment of a bank representation* is required by Art. 34 of the new Act on the Banking and Capital Markets Supervisory Body to be notified only to that Body.

§47. HUNGARIAN ENTERPRISES ABROAD – ENTERPRISE INTERESTS AND TRADE REPRESENTATIONS

The modern economy and modern international economic cooperation call for a dynamic role to be played abroad by investments, or enterprises in general. Foreign investments have become an increasingly significant factor of the world economy as regards both their volume and economic importance. Given its existing situation, Hungary is involved, especially as a host country, in such movement of capital, in the expansion of the transnational group of corporations, and, as was seen in the preceding paragraph, in the efforts to promote foreign investments in its territory by the aid of law as well. However, the other side of the story is also the fundamental need for Hungarian investors to increase their direct presence abroad through practical implementation of intensive investment programmes.

1. Hungarian enterprises started to appear abroad in conjunction with the economic reform processes in the late 1960s. That was an indispensable and necessary move because the large-scale internationalization of development and production processes and, in that context, of trade relations had entailed the necessity for the international movement of investment capacities. Unilateral participation as host country in that process would have been tantamount to renouncing *a priori* an intensive involvement of Hungarian enterprises.

There are several concrete forms of direct presence abroad, such as *foundation of enterprises abroad, acquisition of enterprise interests and establishment of joint ventures*. Such direct activities abroad were slow to increase over the last few decades, but were quick to gain momentum after the systemic change (see item 2 in §42).

Another important form of direct presence is the *trade representation* of enterprises in other countries, which effectively contributes to implementation of the strategies abroad of enterprises in Hungary. Trade representations are publicly known to carry out a wide range of activities. For instance, they cooperate in transactions like preparation, conclusion and execution of contracts for large-scale cooperation, which ultimately result in international investment projects as well. Furthermore, their functions include cooperation in establishing subsidiary companies abroad and launching (investment) projects involving other proprietary positions in corporate law.

2. As regards the *foundation of enterprises and partnerships abroad* (subsidiary companies, joint ventures and other investment projects in the form of association), they are governed by *three levels of legal regulation*.

(a) First, we have the *bilateral trade agreements* or, functioning along with or instead of them, the *general intergovernmental agreements on cooperation*. These instruments of international law create a legal framework for Hungarian enterprises effecting investments, in any of the forms described above, in the country of the other Contracting Party. We refer by way of example to the US–Hungarian Trade Agreement of 1978, which enumerates in Art. 3 the facilities enjoyed by firms of either Contracting Party for their operation in the territory of the other Contracting Party (establishment and operation of agencies and trade representations, prompt procedure of authorization, etc.). The EC–Hungarian Agreement on Trade and Economic Cooperation of 1988 and the Association Agreement of 1991 (see §39) are still more specific. Article 11 of the former specifically refers to creation of a favourable environment for investments and joint ventures, *inter alia*, by making arrangements under which Hungary and the member-states of the Community will make greater use of agreements to encourage and protect investments and, in particular, to allow transfer of profits and repatriation of invested capital on the basis of non-discrimination and reciprocity. Concerning the establishment and operation of Hungarian enterprises in the European Union, the Association Agreement provides that from the entry into force of the Agreement the member-states will grant to the establishment of Hungarian enterprises and nationals a treatment not less favourable than that accorded to their own enterprises and nationals, and will grant to the activities of Hungarian enterprises and nationals established in their respective territories a treatment not less favourable than that accorded to their own enterprises and nationals (para. 3 of Art. 44).

(b) The most important element of *internal regulations* consists in stating that economic organizations may effect investments abroad and in determining the conditions for such activity. Article 13 of the Foreign Trade Act (Act III of 1974), which has been repealed in several aspects, is still in force with respect to the *foundation of enterprises and partnerships abroad.* It provides that, with a view to establishing their foreign market organization, the economic subjects "vested with foreign trade rights" may, within the framework of the law, post delegates abroad, employ foreign natural or legal persons as trade representatives, set up representations, branches or offices abroad, found enterprises or acquire interests in enterprises abroad (for more detail, see §§40–41). As indicated earlier (see item 2 in §42), the range of such economic subjects has considerably broadened during more recent times. It should be kept in view however that, despite the trend to liberalization, legal regulation remained restrictive in so far as it covered only the economic organizations vested with foreign trade rights and prescribed a double licensing procedure, with permits to be obtained from the Minister of Finance and the Minister of Foreign Trade (for a fuller and a critical presentation of regulations, see Kolben, pp. 412–413).

International investment activities guided by a modern market-economy approach have called for a larger freedom of movement, to which the new regulatory system has contributed the following assertive elements. On the one hand, with the complete abolition of the foreign trade monopoly, the "right to engage in foreign trade" has become, as it were, a subjective right, naturally subject to the applicable general rules of commercial law (see §§40–41). Today thousands of entities carry on foreign trade, and investment projects are likewise in the order of thousands. On the other hand, under Arts. 31–33 of Act XCV of 1995 on Foreign Exchange, inhabitants may, subject to notification to the foreign exchange authority, found enterprises or partnerships, increase capital shares, establish or enlarge affiliated firms abroad without permission, which is required in exceptional cases only [e.g. because the amount of investment does not exceed 10% of the capital of a foreign undertaking; the law of the country concerned does not allow transfer of profits or repatriation of capital; the host country is not a member of OECD or has no investment protection agreement with Hungary, proceedings in bankruptcy or liquidation are conducted against the domestic economic association (regarded as such under the Foreign Exchange Act)]. In accordance with Art. 35 (2) of the Foreign Exchange Act, circulation by aliens of shares within the State, representing as it does a special form of investment abroad, is subject to the permission of the foreign exchange authority. A similar provision is contained in Art. 61 of Act CXI of 1996 on Securities.

It is a special rule of *banking law* that under Act CXII of 1996 on Credit Institutions and Financial Undertakings the permission of the Banking and Capital Markets Supervisory Body is required for establishing abroad a branch office or a subsidiary company of a credit bank (loan office, financial or other undertaking) or for the acquisition by a credit bank of the controlling shares in an undertaking regarded as alien under the Foreign Exchange Act (Art. 14).

The purpose and object of investment may equally be served by *immovable property*. As a general rule, Art. 38 of the Foreign Exchange Act requires the permission of the foreign exchange authority for acquisition of foreign real property, but this restriction does not apply to tenancy of premises for foreign representations and for *ad hoc* building and fitting work done by a natural person under a foreign trade contract.

(c) The third layer of the legal regulation of foreign investments is represented by the investment, administrative and corporate laws of the particular countries. It is only natural that Hungarian enterprises carry out their investment activities in accordance with the rules of foreign corporate law, make use of the possibilities and enjoy the advantages afforded by the said foreign laws, and comply with the obligations imposed by these systems of legal regulation on associations in general and on foreign investors in particular.

3. The statements made on the regulatory system of investments abroad apply, *mutatis mutandis,* to the *foreign trade representations* of Hungarian enterprises. These representations function within the frameworks of bilateral trade agreements or general agreements on cooperation, enjoying the rights and facilities granted therein, whereas they are under the control of the Hungarian regulations described above, in application thereof as appropriate to them. Under the special provisions of the Act on Credit Institutions and Financial Undertakings, establishment of a foreign representation of a banking institution is subject to the permission of the Supervisory Body (Arts. 14 and 34 of Act CXII of 1996). Thirdly, Hungarian trade representations function abroad in accordance with the relevant rules in force in the host countries.

§48. INTERSTATE ECONOMIC UNDERTAKINGS

The internationalization of productive processes and the growing complexity of international cooperation not only lead to the appearance abroad of private capital, enterprises, associations and extensive empires of international companies, or transnational corporations, but also bring in their wake the *establishment, directly by States* and groups of States, of comprehensive, capital-intensive *interstate (supranational) public enterprises* to operate economic undertakings embracing several countries. Although similar undertakings had been established prior to World War Two, this process acquired real impetus in the post-war period. Literature uses different terms to designate these interstate enterprises. In the English-speaking and French-speaking countries, for instance, the designations are multinational public enterprises and international bodies corporate, or *établissements publics internationaux* (international public establishments). These terms are meant to indicate that such interstate undertakings are established to perform certain economic functions generally in the public interest, ones that demand large volumes of long-term capital investment and need an enterprise organization for their operation.

1. In the advanced countries of Western Europe there emerged interstate enterprises as early as the 1940s. Thus, for instance, Britain is one of the Contracting Parties in the foundation of *British Commonwealth Airlines Limited*, which, though incorporated in Australia, is operating largely under the control of the British Government, legally in the form of a limited liability company, within the framework of a relatively brief agreement and functions according to the corporate-law rules of common law.

The *Scandinavian Airways System* (SAS) came into being as a consortium of three national airline companies (Sweden, Norway and Denmark). As regards its legal form, it functions as an unlimited partnership obligating the partners to mutual cooperation and entailing their own liability. Accordingly, the States concerned are indirectly involved in the consortium. Moreover, even the Agreement of 1951 on cooperation in civil navigation between the three countries provides nothing but an indirect state framework for the operation of SAS.

The *Basel-Mulhouse Airport* is a state enterprise established by a convention between France and Switzerland which, with its detailed regulation and annexes, creates a quasi separate *ius singulare* to govern the joint undertaking.

The *European Company for the Chemical Processing of Irradiated Fuels (Eurochemic)* was established in 1957 by a convention between 12 West European countries for the purposes of research into, as well as industrial production and utilization of, atomic energy. Its legal and organizational structure qualifies it as a joint stock company, which was incorporated in Belgium. On the part of the different member-states, only a few state organizations are shareholders in *Eurochemic*, the rest being private institutions (enterprises). It therefore seems logical to refer here to the joint enterprise established by the Euratom Treaty which, on the one hand, operates under the control of the Common Market authorities in accordance with the Treaty rules and, on the other, is governed, within the meaning of the corporate-law mechanism, by its domestic law as it may be in force from time to time.

The *Company for the Sale of Coal from Lorraine and the Saar (Saarlor)* came into being in 1956 by virtue of the bilateral treaty under which France and West Germany had settled the post-World War Two status of the Saar region. The legal form of *Saarlor* is similarly a joint stock company, its purpose and function being to supervise coal-mining in the Saar and Lorraine coal fields and of the sale and distribution of coal in keeping with the economic policy concepts approved by the two Governments.

Jochenstein Kraftwerk A.G. was established by and interstate agreement of 1951 between Austria, FRG and the State of Bavaria for the construction of a power-generating plant and the installation of navigational equipment by harnessing the water of the Danube. Participating as members in the joint enterprise, founded in the form of joint stock company, are the appropriate electric utilities of the States parties. The joint stock company is operated in accordance with German corporate law, but is subject to the restrictions stated in the treaty of the founding States (limitation on transactions in shares, requirement of the consent of the founding States to a modification of the Statutes, etc.).

International Mosel GmbH (Société Moselle) was founded in 1956 under an interstate treaty signed by France, FRG and Luxembourg. Its economic function is to make the Mosel navigable by canalization, having regard to the demand for electricity and to the needs of agriculture, fishery, hydrology and tourism. This river control in the form of interstate enterprise was motivated by the fact that a 280 km section of the Mosel is in France, one of 36 km is between Germany and Luxembourg, and an additional section of 200 km is in Germany, constituting a significant waterway, which had previously been unsuitable for navigation. Under German law the enterprise is a limited liability company which was incorporated in Trier.

Of both legal and economic relevance is the international economic undertaking called the *Mont Blanc Tunnel*, in which France and Italy are partners under the relevant Convention of 1953. Its purpose was to construct and operate a tunnel under Mont Blanc. To that end, the two Governments founded two enterprises by contract or, it is better to say, organized and authorized their establishment with concessions specified in the contract. Such concessions were to the effect, *inter alia*, that the two enterprises were to be granted the exclusive right to construct and operate the corresponding sections of the tunnel, the exclusive rights of operation to be enjoyed for 70 years. Both enterprises took the form of a joint stock company, but were subject to conditions of operation and management minutely specified by the contract so as to allow both States the opportunity for appropriate control and eventual intervention. The future situation of the large-scale project in property law was also settled by the contract stipulating that upon expiry of the concession the tunnel and all its installations must become the undivided property of the French and Italian States.

Each country must have a share of 50% in the responsibilities of operation and administration as well as in material gains and eventual losses.

The *European Company for the Financing of Railway Equipment (Eurofima)* was founded by 16 countries of Western Europe under an interstate treaty. It is a multinational state company established to modernize and standardize railways and wagon parks in Western Europe and to devise and operate a uniform system of financing for that purpose. Like *Eurochemic*, *Eurofima* is a joint stock company, and its legal structure, differing greatly from that of traditional joint stock companies, is regulated in detail by the memorandum and articles of association as *ius speciale*. The law of the seat (Switzerland) is allotted but a secondary role in dispute settlement.

It is also worth mentioning the inclusion of European member-states (France and The Netherlands) in the *Latin American Forest Research and Training Institute*, which was established as a joint undertaking of some Latin American States and the European States just mentioned under an interstate treaty concluded within the framework and at the recommendation of FAO. The purpose of the Institute is to research with a view to conserving, exploiting and developing forest resources in Latin America. Its legal form is an international institute possessing independent legal personality. The founding States take part in the Institute's work and management and bear its costs, but the necessary immovables (site, buildings, etc.) were made available and are owned by Venezuela, the country of its seat.

Again, there is a form of international enterprise that is entirely the product of the European Economic Community. It is the joint enterprise regulated by the Euratom Treaty, and the issue has also been raised of using it outside the domain of the atomic energy industry. As to its form and type, it is a company under traditional commercial law, but "subjected" to a Community system of control, with private enterprises participating in it as founding owners in addition to EEC and its member-states.

2. Furthermore, within the framework of economic cooperation among the *former CMEA-countries*, there existed joint economic organizations such as *Intermetal, Intransmas, Agromas, Haldex,* the still more important *International Bank for Economic Cooperation* and the later *International Investment Bank* of later date, and *Intertextilmas, Interatomenergo,* etc. CMEA was unable, despite efforts in that direction, to consolidate the various legal rules on them (see §48 in the second Hungarian edition of this book) into a uniform treaty law; the operation of each of these organizations was governed by its own deed of foundation. With the demise of the CMEA, all that remained to be done was to establish the fact of their extinction and to settle outstanding legal issues.

3. As regards *Hungary*, a significant role was assigned to other types of interstate economic undertakings. At this juncture we will give a brief description of two of them.

(a) One is the *Győr-Sopron-Ebenfurth Railway* (its Hungarian acronym being *GYSEV*), which had originally been established as an inland joint stock company to construct and operate a railway line for fast transport of Hungarian agricultural exports (chiefly from *Kisalföld*) to the region of Vienna. However, the western section of the line was annexed to Austrian territory after World War One. At the same time, the Peace Treaties guaranteed the joint operation of the railway, which was also recognized by the Austrian Government in 1923. *GYSEV* has since been operated as a united line in the form of joint stock company, which has its seat in Hungary and an operating unit in Austria, as well as maintaining a corporate representation and an operational management in that country. Its operation is under the control of its articles approved by the Hungarian and Austrian Ministers of Transport on 16 November 1973.

(b) The other undertaking (deserving mention here for the similarities of its legal regulation) came into being between Hungary and Czechoslovakia. The Governments of the two States signed an interstate treaty on the construction and operation of the *Bős-Nagymaros Dam* on the Danube. The Treaty was promulgated in Hungary by Law-Decree No. 17 of 1978. It did not set up a joint organization for the implementation of the project, but envisaged a programme for joint investment and exploitation. It designated governmental commissioners to take charge of directing and controlling implementation, to set up joint permanent and *ad hoc* bodies and to determine their terms of reference. On grounds of environmental hazards, which had not been sized up in advance and which, with the growing body of knowledge about environmental protection, came to be deemed more and more alarming, Hungary stopped its participation in the construction in 1989. It proposed stoppage of construction and rehabilitation of the region, transforming it into a kind of national park, but the proposal was opposed by the Government of Czechoslovakia (Slovakia after the separation) and, with the unilateral diversion of the Danube, Slovakia put into operation the Slovakian section of the Dam on its own territory. Thereupon the Hungarian Government denounced the interstate treaty but the Slovak party refused to accept the denunciation. The parties therefore decided to refer the legal dispute thus arising to the International Court of Justice in The Hague.

TITLE 4

PROPERTY

CHAPTER XIV

THE ROLE OF PROPERTY IN INTERNATIONAL TRANSACTIONS AND GENERAL QUESTIONS OF ITS REGULATION

§49. THE ROLE OF PROPERTY IN THE PAST AND AT PRESENT

1. *In earlier times* the role of private international law in property-law relations was not determined by the different countries rejecting private property in varying degrees or placing on it various restrictions to any considerable extent, for the property regime was grounded, both in principle and in practice, on the uniformity of property in the form of private property. Existing differences in approach were due rather to legal traditions which resulted in differing national legislation on property-law relations with respect to the protection of property and possession, to the range of aspects considered to fall within the field of property law (which was deemed to include, e.g., the law of bankruptcy in some countries and to exclude it in others; there was some controversy about the property-law approach to intellectual property, and so on), and to the varying measures of protection slowly recognized for foreign property, or to the diverse treatment of the category of "public property". National legal rules concerning property-law relations thus showed differences in these and similar aspects, and the differences in substantive law naturally warranted as well the role played by private international law at that stage of historical development.

2. However, the property-law approach which – in the current international situation, with its diverse legal structures as expressed in legislative developments too – confines the international aspects of property law to the domain of conflicts law is neither understandable nor defensible *today*, and for various reasons. First, the public sector has assumed a greater role (partly through nationalizations, partly through state investments, foundation of state, public and interstate enterprises) even in the countries with a developed market economy. Second, the developing countries have likewise assigned, in varying degrees, a significant role, e.g. through nationalization, to economic units not in private ownership. Third, nationalization, state investments, cooperativization, etc. in the Central and Eastern European and other countries have operated to split up the former property regime, and although in Europe most of these phenomena

have already receded into legal history, they continue to bear appreciable property-law aspects (in the ongoing process of privatizing state property). Both internally and externally (in inter-country contexts), all these developments have combined to give rise to legions of substantive-law problems and legal disputes pointing beyond the conflict area (various problems of nationalization and compensation, relationship between state enterprises and the State in matters of liability, requirements for state-owned economic units to be in a neutral position with respect to competition, etc.). Consequently, it was not long before this even caused writers on private international law to take a definite interest with related questions, awakening to the fact that thinking on private international law could not afford to avoid the issues related to the existence of different property regimes and the legal problems arising in relationships between them. Nor was it possible to do so on the plea that *the issues involved were mostly of concern to internal substantive law and international law* and that, no doubt, *only some of them had bearings on private international law.*

3. Given the underlying set of factors governing the current development of international economic relations, *the law of property has witnessed the appearance of new important phenomena* whose regulation obviously cannot be confined to the law of conflicts. The first such phenomenon is the growth of *foreign investments*, a form of operation characteristic of modern international economic relations, and the rather general recognition of the interests involved in them. We are living in the age of an upsurge in international investments, as is manifested in internal legislation, and in the systems of legal regulation concerning the protection of and support for domestic and international investments (property). Thus it is for these reasons, too, that property has acquired great relevance to our subject

4. Parallel to the growing role of the State in organizing the economy, the highly-industrialized countries have also placed greater emphasis on interstate economic organizations, *joint investment projects and joint ventures*, i.e. on state property that is common in one way or another. Such operations bear on several concrete aspects of the relationship between state property and private property. In the European Union, for instance, countries are seeking at the Community level to find a harmonized solution to this phenomenon in its property-law aspects as well (e.g. the proprietary status, in respect of fissionable materials, of joint state enterprises or of enterprises half-owned by States and half-owned by private persons within the framework of Euratom). From the 1960s onwards, joint international investments and economic organizations were assumed a growing role in the former socialist countries as well (oil pipelines, *Intransmas, Intermetal, Interatomenergo*, etc.). The continuing operation or termination of these undertakings raise a series of issues in property law.

As can be seen, our era has in respect of property law, set in train a large-scale movement which, on the one hand, has extended far beyond the conflict area and, on the other, has caused every participant to take interest in it somehow or other.

5. *The fundamental character of property naturally finds expression in the private international law of property too*, which has historically adopted the *lex situs* as the general localizer in conflict cases involving property. Since in earlier periods, particularly under feudalism, land and other immovables constituted the main object of property, application of this principle virtually ensured the hold of the domestic economy and legal policy over the wealth of a country. Property, primarily immovable property, is bound to the territory of a State much more than a person is. Given the small scale international mobility of property, Savigny could still express this by saying that control over property is gained by the person who, so to say, goes where the property is found and thereby shares the law of the country where the property is situate, together with the system of regulation under the law of property. By contrast to previous practice, the *lex situs* was, mainly under Savigny's concepts, extended to movables. The connecting factor thus generalized – the place where property is situate – is the same for things as the personal law is for individuals, as is expressed by Savigny in Volume VIII of his work: *System des heutigen Römischen Rechts*, §366. The personal status of an individual is determined by his personal relationship to a particular State (yet, with Savigny, by his domicile, although the nationality principle was gaining ground during his time), whereas in respect of things this role is fulfilled by a fixed location, objectively existing.

6. To the extent, however, that the movement of persons and commodities was growing under modern conditions, the *lex situs* came to be surrounded with more and more exceptions. New phenomena emerged which in many respects defeated the earlier assumption that things are and remain fundamentally at some objectively defined place. A distinct category of these phenomena is represented by the increasing role which securities embodying enterprise or corporate property play in the law of property and mainly in the large volume of related international transactions. Another category is constituted by goods involved in international shipping, whose inherent feature is a change of place, even movement across several countries. Commercial vessels and aircraft as well as their cargoes are assets representing a form of property which, in the process of commercial exploitation, keeps moving not only across state boundaries but, often on or above the high seas, outside national territories. These new phenomena were and are also given a different legislative coverage in the substantive law of countries, so private international law has a major role to play in related conflict cases. As against the *lex situs*, the law of the place of destination in respect of goods in transit and the law of the flag (place of registration) with respect to commercial vessels and aircraft became the connecting factors generally used in most cases.

§50. THE FEATURES OF LEGAL REGULATION

1. For the reasons set forth above, international transactions involving property have created a host of international property-law relations. Here is the place to give their treatment a reasonable systematic framework. Grasping the most essential aspects of these legal relationships is decisive to this approach as well. They include the following: (a) The status of property in private international law, namely the domestic system of law by which a given case is to be governed, may need to be determined in some of the international property-law relations. Viewed from the angle of the manner and form of legal regulation, this is the most general category which becomes of relevance whenever there is no uniform international or mandatory internal rule to govern a particular legal relationship. (b) The next main aspect concerns the diversity of property regimes and the related problem of nationalizations. (c) Protection of property invested abroad is a special and increasingly important area of international property-law relations. (d) A significant new aspect is presented by privatization and its international bearings in the law of property. Hereafter we will be discussing these principal issues (Chapters XV to XVIII).

2. The *specific features of regulation* flow from the diversity of property-law relations and their objective peculiarities that we have described. The conflict approach in regulation by private international law is used wherever and whenever the legislator does not subject a legal relationship involving property to a peremptory rule of international law (e.g. within the conceptual framework of state property) or to a rule of substantive law originating in international legal rules.

CHAPTER XV

PROPERTY IN HUNGARIAN PRIVATE INTERNATIONAL LAW

§51. THE *LEX SITUS* AS THE PRINCIPAL RULE

1. The *lex situs* (or *lex rei sitae*) is a generally accepted basic principle of private international law in the field of property-law relations, but is subject to the exceptions to be discussed below. In the modern civil-law systems this principle became part of European law as an essential substantive element of the medieval statute theory. Its conceptual substance is clear: if a legal relationship involves property (rights *in rem*) in the broader sense, the matter at hand should be adjudicated under the law of the State in whose territory the object of property or of the property-law relationship is situate. Here is a foreign example to illustrate the universality of the aforesaid principal rule: Art. 99 of the Swiss Code of PIL of 1987 lays down the general rule that "*Dingliche Rechte... unterstehen dem Recht am Ort der Gelegenen Sache*" (rights *in rem* ... shall be subject to the law of the place where the thing is situate).

This stand has been expressly adopted by Hungarian private international law as well. Article 21 of the Code states: "Unless otherwise provided by this Law-Decree, property rights and other rights *in rem* as well as mortgage and possession shall be governed by the law of the place where the property is situate. The controlling law of the place where the property is situate shall be the law of the State where the property is located at the time of the occurrence of the legally relevant fact". (The principle of the *lex rei sitae* was applied by the Hungarian Code in, e.g., the litigation of a Greek plaintiff against a Hungarian defendant concerning the surrender of movables: *Legf. B. Pf.*VI.21 600/1993.)

This clear regulation includes what has not been discussed so far but is, as if by the nature of things, reasonable, namely that the *situs* should always be understood to comprise a temporal factor relating, of course, to movables, for these are apt to be found in the territory of different states. Thus inclusion of a temporal element renders this rule unambiguous in the determination of the applicable law. Such a temporal element is the point of time at which the fact producing the legal effect in question has occurred. This makes the *situs* clearly definable even in case of a change in the location of the movable.

2. The above general rule is so unambiguous that adherence to it is definitely evidenced by *judicial practice*, which often follows it without reference to the applicability of Hungarian law on the ground that the particular thing is found in Hungary. The termination of joint ownership in Hungary was the object of Judgment No. 4.P.20210/1982 of the District Court of Kaposvár, which involved a foreign element by reason of the fact that the defendant was resident in England. Similarly, the foreign element in Judgment No. 4.P.21806/1981 of the District Court of Szeged, concerning the establishment of joint ownership in Hungary, was represented by a German defendant. Within the meaning of the Hungarian Code, the incidents of joint ownership were clearly governed by the rules of Hungarian Civil Code relating to joint ownership.

§52. EXCEPTIONS

We have noted earlier that in the field of property-law relations there have appeared such new phenomena which make exclusive recourse to the *lex situs* objectively impossible or at least unreasonable. This applies, on the one hand, to movables which for some reason (e.g. shipping or, in the case of personal effects, travel abroad) pass through several countries in the shipping process. True, they are at any one time on the territory of a particular country, yet this is but incidental. Hence the emergence of a rule different from that of the *situs* and permitting an exception thereto in governing similar situations. On the other hand, some property-law relations and disputes may happen to require parallel determination of the law applicable to a variety of assets situate in the territories of several States. Such is the case with universal succession of title (devolution of business assets as a whole). It would be unreasonable to bring under separate statutes all of the things situated in various countries, when the underlying cause thereof is connected with a particular person. This is why private international law has allowed an exception to the principal rule, namely it has rendered the personal law of the predecessor in title generally applicable to this group of cases as well. The crux of the matter is, therefore, that, within the scope of exceptions, the law of the *situs* is not employed despite the fact that the case otherwise involves real things that in principle are at one and the same place at the same time and it is property-law relationships that are connected with them.

1. One of the broadest categories of exceptions in Hungarian law relates to *commercial ships*, the so-called registered vessels, and *civil aircraft*, whose property law or statute is governed in Hungary, too, by the generally accepted principle of the *law of the flag* (*lex bandi*, or *loi du pavillon*). The *lex bandi* is the law of the State whose flag or other insignia the vehicle is using. This means the country in whose territory the vehicle was registered. Like cars, ves-

sels and aircraft are officially registered (even more so than cars). Registration takes place only if they comply with the appropriate traffic safety rules. According to the Code, "the creation, existence and termination of property rights relating to registered vessels or aircraft shall be controlled by the law of the State under whose flag or other insignia the vehicle is operating" (Art. 23).

2. Another important category is represented by *goods in transit (res in transitu)*, which are generally controlled by an exception to the principal rule both in the law of other countries and in Hungarian law. This category has acquired great significance in view of the present-day intensity of international economic relations. As is known, a large part of raw materials, semi-finished products and consumer-ready goods as well as producing equipment comes to the stores through shipping, which accounts for a considerable volume of import and export transactions. In this process goods pass through a whole range of countries. Movables in transit may be, and often are, the object of change in property rights (e.g. change in ownership or conclusion of a contract of lien). The legal effect of such acts will occur, on the strength of contract or by operation of law, irrespective of whether the goods are momentarily on the high sea, at a port or on the railways of a country. So the question arises, to which phase of the entire process should the given property-law relationship be linked? Both practice and literature are divided on this score, with some countries employing the law of the owner's domicile or the domestic law and others preferring the law of the country of consignment.

(a) Hungarian law renders the *law of the State of destination applicable as a general rule*. The Code provides that "property rights relating to goods under transportation shall be controlled by the law of the State of destination" (para. 2 of Art. 23).

(a) This is in itself a reasonable solution, which, however, needs interpreting in certain cases in the field of, e.g., protection of possession or property rights. A lorry of a Hungarian enterprise and its cargo, which is to be transported to Baghdad, are attacked along the journey in country A. The driver averts the attack by using his own force. The resultant dispute is brought before a Hungarian forum. The problem concerns the measure of such self-help (self-defence), which bears on the justification for or the groundlessness of the claim for compensation. The legal problem consists in this: is the Hungarian lorry, too, an article of merchandise in transit, or only its cargo? In the former case, the question of reliance on self-help should be controlled by Iraqi law, which is certainly an unreasonable solution, one that need not be explained here. However, the cargo is in all certainty an article in transit. Yet this fact does not create any closer connection between the problem and Iraqi law. The reasonable solution can obviously be afforded by the law of the place of assault where – in which context of moral and legal values – the situation producing the said legal effect occurred. Viewed from the angle of the conflict rule of property law, this law is the *lex situs*, the place where the lorry was divided, namely the principal rule outlined above (see §51). This solution can be supported by linking the attack to the lorry, which in turn is, as against its cargo, no *res in transitu*, but a vehicle transport, which is not governed by the cited provision of Art. 23. It is therefore the principal rule – the *lex situs* – that comes into play. This solution is warranted, furthermore, by the fact that, in cases like this, justifiable self-defence as a means of protecting possession is blended with liability for damage as another legal means coming into play here. Self-help can also be appraised in the law of damages (see Art. 343 of the Hungarian Civil Code). On the other hand, the Code makes legal disputes involving compensation for damage subject to the law of the place of the tortious act (Art. 32).

(b) In addition to this general rule, however, Hungarian law distinguishes between goods in transit in general and the *legal effect of certain emergency measures* as regards their appraisal *under the law of property*. If, for instance, an article in transit must be sold, stored or pledged for some compelling reason, the legal effects of such actions are ordained to be determined by the legal system of the State *in whose territory the thing is found at the time the emergency measure is taken*. For the most part, the motive behind this rule is that legal acts such as these, which are largely unpredictable, are rather difficult to appraise at a place other than the scene of action and that some of the said acts are done under the local law. Cases of this class are governed by the law of the *situs*: "... the property-law effects of forced sale, storage or mortgage of such property shall be subject to the controlling law of the place where the property is situate" [Art. 23 (2) of the Code].

In principle, of course, it could indeed be a debatable point as to whether this double statute should be applied merely to property-law relationships. If we add that the contracts by which movables are sold and then transported are governed by different laws we must see that one and the same legal relationship, namely the sale of goods and their delivery to a particular customer, *can be subject to various (in our case, four) systems of law*. This in itself may seem to be artificial and to amount to legalistic surplusage. While such criticism is not entirely without justification, we must perceive the rationale for the application of various laws in such extreme situations. One of the reasons lies in the general principle of private international law that the parties may choose the law to govern their contractual relations. Selection of law is part of their entire concept of business and, ultimately, of the entire economic process which is unable to function without the control of an appropriate law. If the parties ship their goods to a place some 1,000 kilometres away, it is equally natural that the goods reach their destination by passing through the area of jurisdiction of several legal systems. Along the way the goods become the object of contracts for carriage and forwarding which, again, are subject to a regulative system of domestic and international law different from the body of rules governing contracts of sale. And if the merchandise is forcibly sold owing to a train accident or to some other unexpected event, the case obviously cannot be adjudicated under, say, the law chosen by the parties to govern the sales contract itself. Emergency measures may be taken, say, in England, where they are subject to the rules of internal substantive law, and those taking the measure act under that law without regard to the provisions of say, Swiss law chosen by the parties to govern the contract of sale. Of course, judicial practice may and does endeavour to consider identical economic relationships in their entirety despite their extreme fragmentation and to keep this complexity in mind, so far as possible, in looking for an optimal private international law approach to their solution under substantive law.

Again, *in certain practical aspects*, it is reasonable that a small bus left in England and resting at a public place for a long time should be forcibly sold by the British authorities and that the new owner's original title to the property thus acquired should be recognized under English law. This further follows from Art. 23, para. (2) and even para. (5) of the Hungarian Code. In similar situations, the claim to property of the original Hungarian owner subsequently legitimizing his title may similarly be adjudicated upon by a Hungarian court only under the English law.

An Iranian lorry in Budapest had to be towed away for reasons including traffic safety. The enterprise owning the lorry failed to take any measure (it was not even to be located because of the acts of war and its manager left the country). The reasonable solution as to what the Hungarian organs can do in such cases (responsible custody, sale, etc.) obviously cannot be offered except by Hungarian law, as it follows from the cited provision of the Code.

(c) A special sub-variant of goods in transit is *passengers' luggage*, which differs from other goods in international trade. Its main feature consists of the fact that it "travels" together with the owner or holder and has the only function of meeting his personal needs. Therefore a property-law relationship involving such things obviously cannot be separated from the individual since his personal law, by its very unambiguity, precludes the classification of goods in transit being extended to this category of goods, which would thus be regarded as likewise being incidentally now in this, now in that country. As application of the law of the *situs* would be rather casual, this group of cases calls for a clearly-defined connecting factor. A safe guide in this field is offered by the personal law of the individual with respect to luggage as it is by the place of destination in respect to merchandise. The Hungarian Code is guided by this consideration in providing that "property rights relating to the personal effects of a passenger shall be subject to his personal law" [para. (3) of Art. 23].

3. We have pointed out before why it is unreasonable to render the law of the *situs* applicable to assets situated in different countries, which all become, simultaneously, the object of property-law effects in consequence of *universal succession*, namely change in the person of the subject at law. Hungarian private international law has also adopted the rule which is objectively warranted by the situation described: "If enterprise (business) assets devolve as a whole upon the successor in title, the property-law changes shall, with the exception of such changes concerning immovable property, be under the control of the *personal law of the predecessor in title*" [para. (4) of Art. 23]. A Hungarian

enterprise enters into a lease and uses in Hungary the equipment of enterprise B of country A. During the term of lease the Hungarian enterprise (lessee) is informed by enterprise C of country E that enterprise B went out of existence as a result of merger with enterprise C, which will thenceforth be entitled to the rent. The Hungarian enterprise is uncertain as to the lawful process of the merger as well as about the settlement of the situation of the leased equipment. Motivated by that uncertainty, it fulfills its obligation to pay the rent by deposit in court in accordance with the Hungarian Civil Code (Art. 287), although the law stipulated to govern legal disputes is the law of country D, a solution also recognized as lawful by the Code of PIL (Art. 24). All well and good but the stipulation is contained in the contract made with enterprise B. Finally, enterprise C brings an action before a Hungarian forum to clarify its entitlement to the rent. The Hungarian forum has to adjudge universal succession, not under the law of the place where the equipment on lease is found, i.e. not under Hungarian law, but under the law of country A as the successor in title to enterprise C (i.e. enterprise B).

As could be seen, *immovables* represent an exception to the rule just discussed. Immovables are controlled by the *lex situs*. This has to do with the generally recognized and legally expressed fact that immovable property is firmly fixed to a place, forms the basis of national wealth in every country and, moreover, creates the primary condition of existence for populations everywhere. Hence, in respect of transactions involving immovables or, as in our case, to property-law effects, no exception is allowed to the law of the *situs*, or to the State exercising sovereignty over the particular territory.

4. Property-law effect, namely a change in owner or title, likewise occurs when title in property passes from one owner to another *under a court order or a writ of execution*. Since in such a case the property-law effect results from an order of an authority of a particular State, and the corresponding powers of that authority are conferred by the domestic law of the State involved, the legal effects produced (the entire property-law relationship) cannot even conceptually be removed from the powers of the State in question. Accordingly, unless public policy intervenes, such cases may reasonably be governed only by the law of the State which has caused the said inevitable legal effects to occur. This is why the Code provides that "if rights of ownership in a thing are transferred by a court order or by way of execution, acquisition of rights shall be governed by the law of the State whose court issues the order or whose authority proceeds in the matter of execution" [para. (5) of Art. 23]. One should not, however, overlook an essential element of this provision, namely that the given property statute (the law of the proceeding State) applies to acquisition of rights only, that is to title and the result of the act of acquisition. All other legal effects of such property, as for instance any legal dispute of earlier or later origin in connection with it, are naturally governed by the *lex situs*.

Enterprise A in Austria is subjected by a court order to bankruptcy proceedings. In Hungary, too, it has property, *inter alia*, through leasing and in representative consignment stores. Hungarian and Romanian creditors/buyers (B and C) also aspire to acquire that property. If in the course of execution a dispute arises with respect to a question of acquisition by B and C which was not covered by the Austrian court order, the Hungarian forum will, by applying Art. 23 (5) of the Code, decide in accordance with the Austrian law.

5. Property-law problems may also arise in respect of *securities* embodying things, including goods in transit (e.g. consignment note, bill of lading) or ownership rights (e.g. bonds expressing the proprietary position of a company, or shares as securities). Since, however, the status of securities under the law of property has a close connection with the law of contracts and considering that securities are treated by the Code of PIL in its section on the law of contracts, we too will discuss securities in the chapter dealing with the law of obligations. It should nevertheless be anticipated here that the property-law status of securities must, in a given case, be decided under Hungarian law despite the fact that securities are not specifically covered by the Code in its chapter on the law of property. The significance of property-law aspects is otherwise indicated by the fact that the status of securities in the private international law of numerous countries, generally of the common-law countries, is discussed in the chapter on the law of property (Dicey and Cheshire). Nevertheless, the complex nature of the regulation of securities by private international law is emphasized even in the countries following this system, it being stated that picture and treatment respectively of the whole presuppose consideration of the aspects of corporate law and contract law, along with the property-law bearings, and formulation of appropriate private international law rules.

§53. SCOPE OF APPLICATION OF THE CONNECTING FACTORS GOVERNING PROPERTY

1. In the preceding two sections we have presented an overall view of the connecting factors that control property-law relationships with foreign elements. The problem now is to ascertain the scope of the private international regime of property, thus determined. The property statute obviously extends not only to rights of ownership in the narrow sense, but, along with the general rules on ownership *stricto sensu*, to the rights of use and to possession, as is also reflected in the approach of the Hungarian Civil Code in Part III on the Law of Property. What we have here is, in point of fact, *right-in-rem relations in general*, a term we have made occasional use of before. Therefore the pertinent chapters of the codes of private international law in the European countries are headed "Rights *in Rem*" and deal, for the most part, with legal relationships involving rights *in rem*. This arrangement is followed by the Hungarian Code too. Accordingly, a mortgage arising from operation of the law is also naturally governed by the general rules of the law of things. Still, the Hungarian Code

deals with mortgage among contracts as well, subjecting contracts of mortgage to the control of contract law.

2. Related to this is the fact that *the internal civil-law codifications of some countries no longer use the term "right in rem"* and the corresponding systematic arrangement. Accordingly, the pertinent part is headed "Law of property" instead of "Rights *in Rem*", and mortgage, a classical institution of the law of things, is discussed in the chapter on the law of contracts, although this does not bear upon the right-*in-rem* effects of mortgage. The category of right *in rem* is not used by the Civil Code either in terms of structure or on the general plane, nor is it accepted and employed by the common law, in which the continental concept of right-*in-rem* relations is discussed within the ambit of property-law relations. This aspect is worth noting because, owing to the world dimensions of contemporary transactions, systemization by rights *in rem* has both benefits and detriments in comparative private international law. This systematic approach should always be inserted into a larger frame of reference, into the appropriate systematic categories of the legal systems adopting the property-law approach, and thus it should always be determined whether in a concrete case an apparently right-*in-rem* relationship is not really one, but is in the nature of, say, contract law (see, e.g., contract of mortgage) or of contract law and corporate law (see, e.g., securities), or whether possession is an independent institution of law or is part of the law of property or of things; a mortgage is also in the nature of a right *in rem*, although it is covered by the Hungarian Civil Code in the law of contracts. Finally, an argument for making property law – rather than the abstraction of rights *in rem* – a comprehensive category determining the structure of this chapter lies in the need for our discussion of property law to be extended to its substantive- and economic-law aspects and even to its political bearings (see Chapters XVI to XVIII). In this context the abstraction of rights *in rem* is no longer serviceable. In dealing with the protection of foreign property and the property-law problems of joint ventures in connection with nationalizations and foreign investments under the different property regimes, this category is not only out of use but would be quite unreasonable; insistence on it would mean trying to have social reality fitted at any cost into the Procrustean bed of old categories that were justified in the context of their time, but now appear antiquated.

3. As regards now the scope of application of the *connecting factors of property law*, we should say that the *law of property (relationships involving rights in rem in older language)* is generally under the control of the law indicated by the connecting factors discussed above. Accordingly, the *lex situs* and the laws shown by the said connecting factors to govern property-law relationships are in principle applicable, subject to the exceptions previously referred to (e.g. a mortgage based on a contract), to all legal relations that involve things and are of an absolute structure and of a negative content.

According to the Hungarian Code of Private International Law, "... property rights and other rights *in rem* as well as mortgage and possession shall be governed by the law of the place where the property is situate" (Art. 21). True, this provision does not amplify our point but its reference to "property rights and other rights *in rem* as well as mortgage and possession" suggests that the law determined by the said connecting factors is applicable to the following main aspects: (a) classification of the objects of property (movable–immovable, negotiable–non-negotiable, etc.); (b) types of property rights or rights *in rem* (right of ownership, right of use, possessory right, mortgage); (c) modes of acquisition; (d) substance and extent of rights *in rem* and their protection. Briefly and mainly in the context of Hungarian law, the law determined by the connecting factors is understood to apply to all matters covered by the Civil Code in Part III on the Law of Property, including mortgage save as based on contract. This latter aspect, except where subject to contrary stipulation by the parties, is treated by the Hungarian Code of PIL in connection with the law of contracts so as to avoid, *inter alia*, fragmentation resulting from the right-*in-rem* approach.

4. This completes our review of the main provisions of the Hungarian private international law of property (or of things). One important rule, that on *limitation*, remains to be mentioned. Under Art. 22 of the Code, limitation is ordinarily governed by the law of the *situs*. In the case of immovables this is a clear and unambiguous rule both in principle and in practice. Immovables change neither place nor statute of limitation. Owners may be in different countries, but the Hungarian law governs acquisition of Hungarian immovable property through expiry of the limitation period even with respect to foreign owners, just as cases in which the limitation period may not be running and entry of change in ownership in the land register. This is amply evidenced by court judgments (see, e.g., Judgment No. 2.P.20.999/1982 of the District Court of Kaposvár).

In the case of movables, however, the *situs* is subject to change during the limitation period, for things may pass to another country where the limitation period is shorter than in the country where it commenced. This by itself may be generative of conflict cases covered by Art. 22 of the Code, which states that limitation is controlled by the law of the State in whose territory the thing was situated at the expiration of the limitation period, that is to say, where the thing was to be found at the time of the occurrence of the fact giving rise to the legal relationship at hand. Plaintiff C had left a valuable painting with defendant A in country B. After five years, A settled down in Hungary again, bringing the painting with him, of which he remained in possession for an additional seven years. At that point of time plaintiff C sued A for return of the painting because, although he had not claimed it back before and had not disturbed the defendant's possession of it, the limitation period had not yet expired under the law of country B. The Hungarian forum, applying Art. 22 of the Code of PIL and referring to Art. 121 of the Civil Code, will consider the limitation period to have expired, because the limitation period in Hungary is 10 years and the painting was in Hungary on the expiry of that period. Article 22 of the Code furthermore provides that "a change in the place where the property is situate shall not by itself interrupt the limitation period", although the national laws of property usually contain no provisions against which this rule should be enforced. In general, no rule of internal substantive law ordains interruption of the limitation period by a change in the *situs* of the thing, yet this clear regulation is provided by Hungarian law to meet any possible case.

CHAPTER XVI

SOME QUESTIONS CONCERNING THE DIFFERENT PROPERTY REGIMES

§54. AN OVERALL VIEW OF LEGAL PROBLEMS IN THE DIFFERENT PROPERTY REGIMES

1. In the light of the current political, social and economic development in Central and Eastern Europe, particularly in the context of Hungary, this chapter could be regarded largely as an inquiry into legal history, partly because we are well past the time of the nationalizations of 40 years ago, with questions now of state divestiture or privatization at the forefront of minds and partly because today the property regimes of this region and the Western world are faced with questions of approximation rather than differences on the agenda of history.

Certain aspects of the related set of questions should be discussed, despite their apparently wide coverage in private international law and the law of international economic relations, because there do exist different systems of property. The property regime of the former socialist countries is progressing towards the private property regime of the market economy countries, but will certainly reveal notable differences for a long time to come. It is a matter of record that there exists a public sector even in the advanced countries of Western Europe. The questions mentioned in the heading should be treated for the added reason that problems of the past are commingled with those of the present. The earlier nationalization of foreign property continues to give rise to problems. In like manner, the law of foreign investments started developing with a blending of foreign private capital and domestic state-owned property, which still makes its effects felt in numerous countries, with bearings on Hungarian law as well. Privatization, though, as a process pointing to the future is interlocked with the present, with the law of international investments, since privatization and foreign investments are mutually complementary processes. It is possible to list the reasons which support the importance of dealing with the related set of problems together.

2. If we are to be more specific about the questions arising in this context, *the following may be singled out for attention*:

(a) mutual recognition of the legal system in countries with different social and property systems and of the existence of different structures (see item 1 in §55);

(b) disposal by States of national wealth and problems of nationalization (see item 2 in §55);

(c) property of foreigners and their legal status with respect to acquisition of property (see Chapter XIII);

(d) protection of foreign investments and property within the ambit of present-day international economic relations (see Chapter XVII);

(e) the new property regime: privatization and its international aspects (see Chapter XVIII).

§55. RECOGNITION OF THE DIFFERENT PROPERTY REGIMES AND A SURVEY OF LEGAL ATTITUDES TO NATIONALIZATION

1. In the recognized practice of coexistence and cooperation of varying intensity on the stage of history there are (or partly were) three types of countries whose political, economic and social peculiarities, property regimes and related philosophies are, under a general approach, similar or identical in their basic features: countries with a developed market economy, developing countries, and countries whose property regime shared or still maintain (e.g. Cuba, China) a model of Soviet origin. This generalization apart, one should of course be aware that numerous differences exist within each group of States, with a considerable degree of convergence observed even between the large groups, and that first of all, every country should ultimately be viewed within its own identity. However, when private international law and the law of international economic relations came to be confronted with inter-system questions of property law, the problems to be addressed under the most general approach consisted in the appraisal of property regimes in the said groups of countries. And, in the given context and under this general approach, the legal maxims *expressing mutual recognition of the different legal systems (inclusive of property regimes)* gained acceptance in the long process of mutual adjustments fraught as it was with numerous controversies of common knowledge and determined by shared interests of a global nature. The principle, or rather the *raison d'être*, of private international law that property regimes are equal has become generally accepted (see §9). This principle is expressed in the vast number of bilateral agreements between States, in accessions to international conventions, in the Charter of the United Nations. In the specifically European context, it finds expression particularly in the Final Act of the Helsinki Conference and, amplified with respect to the property regime, in the Charter of Economic Rights and Duties of States adopted by the United Nations in 1974; it explicitly spells out the sovereignty of States over national wealth, including the sovereign right of nationalization, while declaring compensation to be desirable and referring it to

national competence [Art. 2, 3281 (XXIX) Charter of Economic Rights and Duties of States, adopted 12 December 1974]. Obviously, on the most general plane, the concrete questions of law that emerged and still emerge in the inter-system context of property should likewise be viewed against this background.

2. *Nationalization is a specific issue* compared with the recognition of property regimes. In this respect, distinction should be made between nationalizations (occasionally resorted to) in countries with a developed market economy, the former socialist countries, and developing countries as regards both their purpose and conditions. In the first group of countries the function of nationalization is to maintain the whole economic system based on private property, to improve its operation and to save occasionally loss-making but necessary industries by using state resources for their rehabilitation, which is often followed by privatization, while the conditions always include compensation under appropriate procedures. Such nationalizations usually give rise to no antagonistic problems in international relations. Problems arose chiefly in the wake of nationalizations in the former socialist countries, where the economic system as a whole was transformed on the Soviet model, with the entire national wealth except businesses and personal property nationalized without compensation, although compensation was envisaged in the relevant legislation.

This was a source of the following problems within an international context.

(a) The affected foreign countries gradually acknowledged the fact that they were unable to call into question the *domestic effect* of legislation on nationalization (the internal property regime). The acceptance of that effect is also manifested in the practice of Western countries (see Makarov, pp. 94–96; Dicey, p. 668).

(b) Non-recognition of the *extraterritorial effect* of nationalization laws was one of the possible paths, long trodden, of manifesting understandable opposition and taking action at Western fora. The owners of nationalized companies, who were living abroad, claimed for themselves those assets and accounts receivable of their companies that were to be found abroad, claiming them as their own, because they considered expropriation without compensation to run counter to the legal maxims of western countries and to international law. Later (particularly from the mid-1960s onwards) there has been a gradual change in attitude, the problems involved "have run their course", partly because the legal actions followed with varying results (mostly with success), partly because the principle of peaceful coexistence and the slowly evolving practice of cooperation between the different systems were gaining momentum at the macro level. Today everything is different as a result of the historical turns and transformations. A further contributory factor to the aforesaid change was the relative acceptance, from the 1960s, of the so-called Act of State Doctrine, which was actually passed in the United States. Under it, the courts of foreign States are not to question the extraterritorial effects of *sui generis* acts of other States, such as nationalization. The Supreme Court of the United States based its ruling on that Act in the famous *Sabbatino* case, which was to take different turns

(*Banco Nacional de Cuba v. Sabbatino*, 376 U.S. 398, 1964). Claims of injured foreigners for compensation from state companies of nationalizing States for acts of such States damaging them were similarly rejected, even if not always consistently (see §37 on the State and its enterprise). While there continued to be occasional lawsuits with varying degrees of success on the plea of violation international law, such views did not gain general acceptance. It is worth mentioning, for example, that when after the nationalization of the copper mines in Chile the nationalized American companies sued for seizure of copper shipments, under way to foreign ports, of the new state-owned Chilean companies, the *Hamburger Landesgericht* rejected an American claim, first attaching and then relieving attachment of a copper shipment at the port of Hamburg, on the ground that the claim (that nationalization was unlawful) was impossible to honour on the basis of the generally accepted principles of modern international law (for the court judgment of 1973, see Loewenfeld, Vol. II).

(c) Another trend of related actions was represented by efforts of the States of affected owners which mainly resulted in the conclusion of claims *settlement agreements*. These bilateral intergovernmental agreements covered a series of matters in order to improve relations between the parties. During the negotiations the Western parties sought compensation for the nationalized companies. The nationalizing State admitted that, during and after World War Two, nationals of the other party had suffered material loss for various reasons (e.g. owing to nationalization) and offered lump-sum compensation in settlement of such claims. It was for the Western Contracting Parties to decide how, by which process of legitimization and to what extent, individual claimants were to be compensated. Hungary, too, signed such agreements with several countries, among them the United States in 1973.

(d) The period beginning with the 1970s opened *new perspectives* and presented different problems associated with demands for foreign working capital and investments in most socialist countries of the time and everywhere in the years since (see Chapter XIII). Related operations were combined with legal guarantees for the protection of foreign investments (property) and with general application of the relevant internal and international norms in these countries as well (see Chapter XVII).

(e) As part of the revolutionary transformations in the countries of central and Eastern Europe, there has emerged a *completely new situation* with these countries revising nationalizations originally effected without compensation and offering some measure of compensation to the former owners in the process of privatization (see Chapter XVIII). This contributes towards the general application of the thesis of the Charter referred to above that nationalization is a matter within the internal sovereignty of States, it cannot be questioned by foreign States, but compensation is to be paid to the former owners under a procedure appropriate to a State governed by the rule of law.

CHAPTER XVII

PROTECTION OF FOREIGN INVESTMENTS AND PROPERTY IN CONTEMPORARY INTERNATIONAL ECONOMIC RELATIONS

§56. ON THE PROTECTION OF PROPERTY AND INVESTMENTS IN GENERAL

1. Generally speaking, the following brief statements may be made at this point *on the protection of* foreign property or, more precisely, *foreigners' property*.

(a) One aspect of the matter concerns the *assets that may be owned by foreigners in Hungary*. By the nature of things, this aspect might appear to bear only (or mainly) upon the bounds or scope of immovable property. We have advanced, however, far beyond that point, for a host of movables are also owned by foreigners in Hungary (foreign nationals have ownership, or have the permanent use, of vehicles, machinery and equipment, enterprises and other institutions), let alone the growing bulk of shares in enterprises established through foreign investments. Nevertheless, as regards the question of what may be owned by foreigners, we would refer the reader to Chapter XIII on the Status of Foreigners.

(b) The second aspect concerns *foreigners' disposal of their property in Hungary*, the special rules, if any, relative to the use, utilization or disposal of property. By way of an answer we refer again to the aforementioned chapter, but regard should also be had to foreign investments, estates, the law of matrimonial property, foreign exchange law, intellectual property, and the relevant conflict rules governing property (see the corresponding parts of Chapters XIII, XV, XVII–XIX).

(c) The third aspect, constituting the essential point in this Chapter, concerns the *protection of foreign property*. As for a general reference to the protection of foreign property and possessions, we are again in an easy position, for the answer is the principles of national treatment (*régime national*), as has been broadly outlined in the cited sections of this book (particularly §45 on national treatment in Chapter XIII). The situation is different with regard to the protection of foreign investments, which need a fuller treatment here in view of their specific features.

2. The protection of international investments is as important as the role and appropriate legal regulation of foreign investments in international economic

relations, in general, and in the economic development of Hungary, in particular.

(a) *Investment protection is an especially important area of legal regulation.* The explanation is obvious. An investor seeks security and intends to implement his investment strategy, thought to be economically rational, within legally guaranteed frameworks. He tries, and is able, to size up the commercial risks to the planned project, against which he seeks and finds protection (by an appropriate statute and decision-making mechanism, assessment of the market and the sources of supply). Yet there exist types of risks that are beyond the limits of any, however careful, precautions, planning, and economic activities. Such risks include war, uprisings, radical economic and social transformations, uncertain political and economic situations, state bankruptcies, restrictive state intervention or nationalization in the host country. They are called "non-commercial or political risks", which may eventually cause grave damage to the investor or the invested property of the foreign partner. Understandably, investors look for protection against such risks as well, for protective arrangements encouraging the movement of working capital toward regions that are likely to hold such dangers in store (mostly capital-importing, "stimulating" developing countries that are poorly supplied with capital), and they do invest if there is protection, but do not invest if there is little or none. The risk to which investments in the Central and Eastern European countries were exposed represented a special type of risk. After the lapse of long decades and in the light of their experience, the Western countries formed an image, a historically-justified social consciousness, of the former socialist countries in Central and Eastern Europe. This image portrayed opposition to private capital as a notional attribute of those countries so much so that their systems had become what they were, economic systems called socialist, precisely through the expropriation of private capital. They eliminated even the notion of capital from their economic armoury and philosophical system and then these very same countries invited foreign investors or, *horribile dictu*, foreign capital, which they themselves came to call capital, promising profit, and even effect investments abroad.

So what kind of guarantees were there? The answer of the law was the affording of legal guarantees designed to balance the said contradictions under special legal mechanisms for investment protection. Such requirement in the relations *inter se* of countries with a developed market economy was not naturally raised because their domestic legislation, oriented to investment and tailored to the needs of capital movements, accorded equal treatment to all, nationals and foreigners alike, usually with few elements in the nature of *ius peregrini*. The so-called "investment codes" and "investment protection agreements" originated in the developing countries after World War Two and then found their way into the socialist countries as well. In the West, they were motivated by interests attaching to security and, in the capital-importing countries, by a strange duality of restrictions (particularly in the earlier years) and preferences.

(b) This is how the regulation of protection turned into a "philosophy" of contradictions in a field of force marked by opportunities of action and charged with diverse energies. *The theses and antitheses cried out for some sort of synthesis.*

Of course, everyone knows, and Western investors are also generally aware, that the world has undergone a profound change. The world economy has become civilized. In the North–South context, colonialism has been replaced by the stabilizing multiformity of the Third World, with a notable development and world-economic significance of some of its countries, which have grown into active protagonists of the political and legal transformation of the world economic order. With the historical finality of the Cold War in East–West relations, the future now belongs to economic and political cooperation, first articulated at the most general level in the Final Act of the Helsinki Conference on Security and Cooperation in Europe. This has been the objective trend of development despite all its periodic setbacks. Ascendancy has been gained (especially in Europe) by the values of historical and cultural traditions binding countries together and shaping attitudes of mind. The role of international regulatory systems (GATT, IMF, IBRD, EU, etc.) in integrating the world economy is on the increase. At the turn of the 1980s and the early 1990s, peaceful or armed revolutions gathered speed in the former socialist countries of Eastern and Central Europe, where commodity and money relations, the market and capital have been re-established in their own right and a market economy holds out ever greater promises, with its elements being translated into reality, while the forces advocating a return to Europe have gained the upper hand. The year 1989 created the conditions for full-scale development along this line, with a pluralist democracy, a State under the rule of law and elements of a social market economy, which are now in the process of achieving their full potential, serving as the foremost guarantees thereof.

Everyone is aware that, with the new conditions prevailing, working capital can be expected to launch larger-scale undertakings. The relevant figures for Hungary are particularly promising (see §42). It is equally common knowledge that precisely the aforesaid countries, and even a large number of developing countries, are in dire need of intensive cooperation with the advanced countries, including foreign working capital – as one of the major guarantees –, in striving for economic prosperity (economic survival in some countries).

This was and is generally known to all. Yet it was precisely this knowledge that, with said developments in the background and as a reflection thereof, generated efforts to introduce investment protection which, legally institutionalized, i.e. regulated by positive law, is capable of working as a tangible reality and as a system of guarantees to be applied in concrete cases.

§57. INTERNATIONAL REGULATORY SYSTEMS FOR THE PROTECTION OF FOREIGN INVESTMENTS

1. As regards the international regulatory systems governing the legal mechanisms for investment protection, it was not a simple matter to devise them, but *gradual efforts were needed to attain their present stage.* One of the reasons lay in the fact that behind the said general common interests and realizations (namely that international movement of investment capacities is in the interest of every country to some measure), there were hidden notable conflicts of interest at the level of the specific. This is to say that on one side were the advanced Western countries exporting capital, which had an objective interest in securing as absolute a protection as possible for their companies (including multinational corporations). Hence it is understandable that the capital-exporting countries were the first to insist on investment protection, including guarantees by the poorer recipient countries for the security of investment, and to obligate the latter countries, by virtue of international law, to appear before the court if they interfered with or eventually nationalized invested property and/or to bear the burden of insurance or other guarantees, paying appropriate compensation for any loss of capital. On the other side were the poorer capital-importing countries, which saw their interest in developing their economies with the fewest possible commitments, with the lowest possible degree of mortgage to working capital. Understandably, they stressed time and again that it would impair their (economic) sovereignty to tie their hands in advance with some sort of ban on nationalization or transformation, to let every small investor summon them to court in every legal dispute connected with new investments.

These contradictions caused numerous international initiatives to fail; it was mainly draft international conventions, dictated by the stronger parties and one-sidedly capital-oriented, that fell through (see Király–Mádl: *"Multilaterális félsikerek..."* ("Multilateral Half-Successes...", §4). Then from the 1960s and the 1970s, the situation underwent a gradual change as it came to be generally recognized that, as mentioned earlier, the international flow of investment capacities and a more balanced development of the world economy generated by it, more allowances needed to be made for consideration of the poorer and thereby a better functioning international market, were in the interests of all parties. This led to the protective arrangements for investments which may be said to be modern and lawful at both multilateral and bilateral levels as well as at the level of domestic law. In this section we will be discussing the multilateral, regional and bilateral levels (items 2 to 4 below).

2. The *multilateral* half-successes referred to above were followed by successes, notably the Washington Convention and MIGA.

(a) In 1965 the International Bank for Reconstruction and Development (World Bank) elaborated the *Washington Convention* on the Settlement of Investment Disputes between States and Nationals of Other States. With its few rigid legal limitations, liberal flexibility and non-imposition of substantive-law bans on nationalizations, the Convention was guided by the Bretton Woods spirit and could *a priori* expect more success than its abortive predecessors. It guarantees a minimum level of investment protection in procedural law. A Convention which merely offers conciliation of disputes, organizing it at request, it has become over time a common denominator between States often having conflicting interests. The Convention, with the Statute of the Dispute Settlement Centre, was ratified by 126 States (mainly advanced countries, but also a great number of developing countries) up to 30 June 1996 (see International Centre for Settlement of Investment Disputes 1996, Annual Report, p. 6). Hungary acceded in 1987 (Law-Decree No. 27 of 1987). Thus the Washington Convention became a living law, an instrument of importance for Hungary as well. This, too, warrants a full treatment of it here. Therefore, and considering the numerous aspects of the topic, it is worthy of note that Hungary's several bilateral agreements on investment protection, which will be discussed in item 5 of §57, have explicitly incorporated the Washington Convention by rendering its rules generally applicable to disputes. Through such bilateral agreements the Convention will become a legal instrument of mandatory application (by Hungary, too), while otherwise it functions through voluntary submission to its provisions. With regard to this matter, the Convention is open to signature by the member-states of the World Bank and, under specified conditions, by any other State party to the Statute of the International Court of Justice (Art. 67).

(aa) The substance of the Washington Convention and its International Centre for Settlement of Investment Disputes consists in having *created, by voluntary submission, an international jurisdiction (conciliation and arbitration), with a well-regulated procedure, in this field.* This will be extensively discussed in the Chapter on arbitration [item 4 (a) in §117]. At this juncture, too, mention is deserved of *a few borderline disputes about jurisdiction* which, though relating to jurisdiction in concrete cases, ultimately concern the material protection of the interests of investing parties and, in this context, the scope of action of the Convention and the Centre as protective shields.

(i) Of course, voluntary submission served and serves to express a high degree of party autonomy as well. In case of agreed submission, party autonomy is essentially limited by one provision only, notably the rule that once the parties have subjected themselves to the Court's jurisdiction, such *agreement may not be withdrawn unilaterally by either party* (para. 1 of Art. 25). It was the interpretation precisely of this rule that became a key issue in numerous cases, such as the *Alcoa Minerals of Jamaica v. Government of Jamaica case* (Yearbook of Commercial Arbitration, Vol. IV, 1979, pp. 206–209). In 1968 the said firm with an American interest (Alcoa Minerals) entered into a long-term contract with Jamaica for bauxite and aluminum production. In the basic contract the Contracting Parties subjected themselves to the arbitration procedure as regulated by the Washington Convention in case of any dispute. However, after the lapse of a few years, immediately before the adoption of the Bauxite Act radically changing the economic environment, the Government of Jamaica modified its original declaration of accession and communicated a reservation to the International Centre for Settlement of Investment Disputes to the effect that it had withdrawn investment disputes connected with the extraction and processing of mineral deposits from the jurisdiction of the Centre. Under Art. 25 (4) of the Convention, States are, in theory, entitled to act in such a way. In the concrete case, when the foreign company applied to the arbitration court of the Convention, invoking the irrevocable consent to jurisdiction as stated in the contract and pleading the almost ten times higher rate of tax, Jamaica questioned the competence of this forum by invoking its reservation made subsequent to its accession.

Like a drop in the ocean, this dispute is well illustrative of the contradictions generated by the economic activity of the State, its interest in capital imports on the one hand and in the defence of its own sovereignty on the other. As for the investor, he is likewise interested in the deal regarding capital imports (capital exports as seen from his side), in investment in the recipient country but, for him, a special risk factor is constituted by the phenomenon that although he might have surrounded the agreement with private-law guarantees (e.g. irrevocability of the jurisdiction clause), his commercial partner is at the same time a sovereign power, which may, in a given case, use the means of public law (modification of the legal system, notification of reservation concerning the Washington Convention) to abandon its obligations felt by it to be burdensome.

Finally, keeping in view the principle of *pacta sunt servanda* as well as the integrity and operational capacity of the Washington Convention, the arbitration court rejected the objection of the Jamaican Government and consequently declared the State's subsequent notification of reservation to be invalid with respect to the earlier agreement of the parties. In other words, as the court understood it, the irrevocability of consent to jurisdiction enjoys precedence over the possibility of making reservations. And, albeit the dogmatic purity of the decision is at least debatable, we must agree with the court in that a different decision "would have largely, if not wholly, deprived the Convention of all its practical value".

(ii) Following the dilemmas of practice, we should deal at some length with a further element of the Convention's rule on jurisdiction, notably with the definition of the term "legal entity of the other Contracting State". The question arises because State recipients of investment generally expect foreign investors to carry out their activities through "domestic" undertakings, namely ones established under the law of the host country. That form of operation often affords advantages to working capital of foreign origin as well. No doubt that, in a technical legal sense, such undertakings qualify as nationals, but, at the same time, invested foreign capital would also claim protection by the means of international investment protection, including the procedure established by the Convention. If the interest of foreign capital are not honoured, a notable area of foreign investments remains outside the protective arrangement of the Convention. If they are honoured, such investments acquire, as it were, a *dual nationality*, and will be generally regarded as national. So the point is whether the *personal law of a legal entity* is determined exclusively by its attachment to a particular State or is, in certain cases, also governed by the nationality of the owners (e.g. shareholders). On the negative side, this question was formulated in the 20th century, as far back as World War Two, in the control theory concerning strict control and restriction of investments in the United States (see §43). In our case, however, the old theory is fortunately filled with a positive substance, and the economic role of foreign owners is accentuated rather for the sake of a wider range of guarantees.

By way of option, the Washington Convention regulates this matter by framing the so-called "foreign clause exception", by virtue of which the application of the Convention extends to any legal entity that, although possessing the nationality of the Contracting State involved in a legal dispute, is to be treated, under an agreement of the parties, as a national of another Contracting State for the purposes of the Convention [para. 2 (b) of Art. 25]. Since the Convention merely allows this solution, and leaves the actual decision on agreement between the parties, it remains for the court of arbitration to ascertain the intent or eventual agreement of the litigants in legal disputes, all the more so since the Convention is silent on the formal requisites of the aforementioned declarations. Under the existing practice (see, e.g., *Holiday Inns v. Morocco*, Yearbook of Commercial Arbitration, Vol. X, 1985, p. 77), which does not constitute a *stare decisis* system and is therefore in the nature of orientation for the future, the parties' simple, informal agreement is sufficient determining jurisdiction over domestic firms established with the participation of foreign capital. At the same time, such agreement must be explicit as a general rule, and implied agreement may not be accepted save in exceptional cases.

(ab) The Washington Convention does not define the *concept of investment*, owing obviously to its rich and complex semantic content. The very Preamble adds but a single adjective to the noun in referring to the role played by international private investments in economic development. However, the said expression – if an introductory provision has any normative force at all – does *not exclude from the scope of application of the Convention anything except the direct economic activities of sovereigns* qualifying as aliens (in respect of the host country) in accordance with the rules on jurisdiction (Art. 25). Emphasizing this obvious thesis becomes of relevance *in relation to state enterprises*, namely in answering the question whether the jurisdiction of the International Centre for Settlement of Investment Disputes extends, with other conditions prevailing, to companies of another State. The answer can only be in the affirmative in this case, for Art. 25 of the Convention refers in general to "legal entities" in determining the Centre's jurisdiction, and state enterprises are also usually vested with this required attribute of independent legal personality. And in the context of international economic relations as a whole, the separate entity of State and enterprise, their independent legal personality, has also been established during the last few decades by numerous court judgments of the West parallel to the retreat of the alter ego doctrine asserting the opposite (see §37).

(ac) Although the Washington Convention originally regulated matters of procedural law, its scope of application relating to subject-matter extends to international investments, so the legal relationships emerging within the ambit of the legal systems of several States call for the Convention to face up to the task of determining the *applicable law* as well, which is a question basic to the law of conflicts. Indeed, this question is covered by Art. 42, under which para. (1) the court is to decide the dispute under the law which the parties have agreed upon. Failing such agreement, the court is to apply the law of the litigant Contracting State (including the conflict rules of private international law) and the applicable rules of international law. Paragraph (3) the provisions of para. (1) do not derogate from the right of the court to decide the dispute *ex aequo et bono*, provided the parties have agreed thereto. Thus, this Article recognizes *three main options* as constituting the legal basis for a decision: the law chosen by the parties (whose autonomy is also not subject to any restriction in this respect); the equity rules of *ex aequo et bono*; and, save as otherwise provided, the law of the Contracting (host) State involved in the dispute. In the latter case, however, the national system of law is to include the *conflict rules of the host country*. Consequently *renvoi*, or recourse to another system of law, is deemed to be admitted by the applicable law. So, at least in theory, an investment dispute will not be decided under the national legal system of the host country in this case either.

The picture will be even more tinted if we recall the last sentence in Art. 42 (1) expressing that the basis for deciding legal disputes is provided by the law of the Contracting *State together with the "rules of international law as may be applicable"*. This *"international law clause"* poses several problems of interpretation in practice. Thus, for instance, the enigmatic provision fails to define the concept and position of international law even with respect to investment disputes. Therefore the legislative instruments of international law and its usages that are rather difficult to reconstruct are to be appraised by States in the light of their own, rather different systems of law.

Projecting the norms of their legal systems (based on private property) concerning expropriation to the international domain, the Western countries demand, in addition to non-discrimination or national treatment, *fair and equitable treatment* (see Martonyi), which includes *prompt, adequate and effective compensation*. On the other hand, the developing countries, coping as they do with various economic and political constraints, are reluctant to recognize the absolute precedence of this principle (formerly the socialist countries were equally and militantly so, but the situation has changed; see item 4 in §57) and prefer invoking the more permissive rules of the UN Charter of 1974, which leave the question of compensation to the standpoint of domestic legal systems (see §55). As can be seen, the brief reference to international law acts to reintroduce, willingly or unwillingly, all the dilemmas of international investment protection into the Articles of the Washington Convention, which otherwise seek neutrality and consensus.

This is all the more so since Art. 42 of the Convention fails to determine, moreover, the relationship between the controlling national law and the applicable international norms. Is it that the "international law clause" seeks nothing other than to *supplement* the law of the Contracting State, filling its lacunae, or attempts to set some minimum *standard of protection* in the realm of national legal systems, extremely divergent and variable as they are? Can international law, which is in itself of a contradictory nature, serve as a kind of etalon, as a stabilizating factor in the field of investment protection? In several cases the arbitration courts set up under the Convention have answered this question in the affirmative. Thus, for instance, the arbitrators acting in the *AGIP v. Government of the People's Republic of the Congo* case found that although the Constitution of the disputant State allows nationalization without any special restrictions, the reference in the Convention (and one in the contract of the parties) to international law is sufficient for the establishment of the *irregular nature of a nationalization* effected (Yearbook of Commercial Arbitration, Vol. VIII, 1983, pp. 133–143), that is to say that the Government is to pay reasonable compensation to the entrepreneur damaged. It is known that, while the former socialist countries shared, especially earlier on, the said reluctance of developing countries to pay compensation as claimed in due process, under a rejectionist interpretation of international law (see §55), the more recent international legal instruments of these same countries now postulate due process and compensation of corresponding value as a norm to be followed (see *infra* item 4 on bilateral agreements on investment protection).

(b) *The Multilateral Investment Guarantee Agency* (MIGA), which was established by an international convention signed at Seoul in 1985, lent new colour and brought a new actor to the stage of investment protection. Protection against political and other risks to foreign investments by means of insurance law and practice (insurance contracts, purchase of insurance policies, payment of premiums) is no novelty, as will be discussed at some length in §58. Still, what is new is the creation of such international institution to strengthen insurance as a protective institution. A new feature is its establishment within the framework of the World Bank and its function, as one of such a large, worldwide institution, to keep in view the interests of developing (recipient) countries. Another new feature is its purpose to intensify capital movement toward countries poorly supplied with capital, both through investment and by many other means. Finally, what is essentially new in it, compared with the multilateral system of investment protection discussed above and with the bilateral ones to be discussed below, is its encouragement of investors, not by promising compensation *a posteriori* and through a legal mechanism for keeping that promise, but by handing them in advance a letter of guarantee directly convertible into money to settle any claims for eventual damage (to pay damages); this is like attaching to it an asset of invested property and saying, go and invest, and if the money is eventually lost, here is as much to make up for it. Needless to say that under a well-covered mechanism the "norm potential" of the insurance contract, i.e. its guarantee-creating force, is much greater than that of the investment protection promise of an international convention, however elaborate.

Based on the related sources, the *history of MIGA's emergence* can be told as follows. The idea of facilitating and improving the worldwide movement of investment capacities, chiefly toward the developing countries, by an international institution of insurance had also been raised under the auspices of the World Bank, in addition to numerous other fora, as early as the beginning of the 1960s. After abortive initiatives the World Bank was more resolute in stating its case for it in the early 1980s. With a great input of energy and consultations with different fora, the Bank's Board of Governors prepared, by September 1985, the draft Convention establishing MIGA in a long series of sessions. At its annual ordinary session held at Seoul on 11 October 1985 the Board of Governors approved the draft and invited the member-states and the Government of Switzerland to sign the Convention so as to open the process of ratification. Article 61 of the Convention set the following conditions for its entry into force: 5 ratifications in Category I as established by the Convention (advanced countries), 15 ratifications in Category II (all other member-states of the World Bank), with the added requirement for ratifications to cover one-third (Art. 5) of MIGA's capital stock of one (exactly 1.082) billion dollars. The process of signature and ratification was much quicker than usual, indicating the great interest shown by States in MIGA. By the end of 1987 the Convention had been signed by 50 developing and 12 advanced countries, of which 20 (exactly 5 advanced and 15 developing) countries had also ratified the Convention by that date, but those ratifications had not yet covered one-third (about 360 million dollars) of the capital stock. In the first months of 1988, however, ratifications by the USA (with a quota of 205.19 million dollars) and Great Britain (with a quota of 48.6 million dollars) took place, and additional developing countries acceded to the Convention. In brief, the MIGA Convention took effect. Hungary's accession followed soon after (Law-Decree No. 7 of 1989).

(ba) MIGA intends to attain its general *purpose*, as indicated above, *under a double strategic approach*:

(i) on the one hand, by *favourable schemes of insurance* against non-commercial risks to foreign investments, with the following main elements.

The scope of possible *non-commercial risks* is clearly definable: (1) obstacles to currency transfer raised by state measures; (2) nationalization and similar measures; (3) "repudiation risk", if the host country authorities refusing to provide legal protection for the investor, who is thereby prevented from obtaining a court decision regarding his lawful claim; (4) war, armed conflict, revolt of the civilian population; (5) the Board of Governors may, at the request of the host country and the investor, extend insurance coverage to other risks (Art. 11).

Article 12 of the Convention determines numerous requirements concerning the *nature of investments*. The major ones include capital transfer in monetary form or in kind; short- and long-term credits secured by the investor for the investment project operating with his participation; other direct forms of investment as may be determined by the Board of Governors; the need for investments to be reasonable, to promote the economic development of the host country in a way deemed by MIGA to be appropriate, and to be in keeping with the host country's economic priorities, law and other conditions for investment, including equitable treatment as desirable for foreign investments and legal protection of investments.

Investors entitled to MIGA insurance may be privately or publicly owned legal entities incorporated in a member-state other than the host country, if they operate on a commercial basis, and natural persons of member-states who are not nationals of the host country. However, exceptions may be made in favour of nationals of the host country and of legal entities incorporated there, if the property to be invested is secured from a State other than the host country.

MIGA insurance is available only to *investments in* member-states of Category II (usually *developing countries* under this scheme) and only if the member host country has consented to the planned MIGA insurance against a particular risk (Art. 15).

The *terms and conditions of insurance contracts* are governed by MIGA's general conditions of insurance (Rules and Regulations). Concrete contracts are to be approved by the President of MIGA on the part of the Board of Governors (Art. 16).

The member States recognize MIGA's *right of subrogation* (substitution), which means that once MIGA has indemnified an investor under the insurance contract, it will take his place with respect to all claims for compensation due to him under the law of the host country (Art. 18);

(ii) on the other hand, by *general investment promotion* (in the wording of Art. 23), which may mean many things in actual activities, such as collection and circulation of information describing investment opportunities, conditions and modalities; efforts to limit factors restricting or hindering investment; co-operation with national and international institutions facilitating or supporting investment, particularly with those of the World Bank functioning in this field, such as the International Finance Corporation (of which Hungary is also a member); organization of investment missions (conferences, advisory programmes), professional and technical assistance – at the request of member-states – in the formulation of national investment strategies; support for the establishment of domestic and bilateral systems regulating investment protection, etc.

(bb) For its *resources* MIGA relies chiefly on its capital stock, receipts (insurance premiums) and reinsurance schemes (Arts. 19–20), not to mention now the aforesaid general activities in support of investment, the resources of which vary by the nature of programmes and which call for mobilization of MIGA's personnel capacity. The insurance cover undertaken could not initially exceed 150% of the subscribed capital stock plus reserves (receipts and reinsurance background), but the Council may by decision allow this magnitude to rise to five times the previous items at a later date (Art. 22). If we take the whole capital stock plus the said supplementary assets to amount to, say, 2 billion dollars, the total value of current investment insurance policies may come to 10 billion dollars. However, MIGA expects the capital stock and the supplementary assets to rise considerably over time. Even 10 billion dollars may allow for the insurance of 1,000 (!) investment projects costing 10 million dollars each. MIGA supplements its own financial sources outlined above with resources mobilized through the Sponsorship Trust Fund, in which the sponsoring States make available, or undertake to provide, finance for insurance cover, and MIGA relies on such funding for underwriting commitments to investors supported by sponsoring States (Art. 24, Appendix I). With advantage taken of this possibility, MIGA's insurance capacity will certainly increase and may even surpass several fold the figures given above.

(bc) As for its *status*, MIGA is legally and financially (materially) independent of the World Bank (Arts. 4–9, 25–29 and 30–37), although it has links with it. Such linkage is to be seen, e.g. in the foundation process and in the fact that the President of the World Bank is the President of MIGA's Board of Governors (Art. 32). In accordance with its constitutional order as defined in the cited articles, MIGA is an independent economic entity functioning under a separate organizational mechanism (Council, Board of Governors, office of administration), discharging the responsibilities and functions determined by the Convention. MIGA is based in Washington (Art. 36).

Membership in MIGA is open to the member-states of the World Bank and to Switzerland, if they accede to the Convention by ratifying it in accordance with their domestic laws (Art. 61).

The Council, vested with general competence in questions of strategy, consists of governors nominated by the member-states, each member-state having one governor representative in it, and it elects its Chairman from among its own members (Arts. 30–31).

The Board of Governors is the MIGA organ responsible for general operations, has at least 12 members and is chaired by the President of the World Bank (Art. 32, Schedule B).

MIGA's President is appointed by the Board of Governors on the proposal of the Board's Chairman. His functions are to carry out operative activities and to exercise employer's rights (Art. 33).

The substance of the detailed regulations on the decision-making mechanism ensures that major shareholders – advanced countries of Category I – may not obtain majority over the rest by their majority share. Therefore, for instance, the decisions of both the Council and the Board are to be adopted by special majority in the first three years or by an even greater majority in specified cases (Arts. 39–42).

(bd) *MIGA's capital stock consists of member-States' subscribed shares and the corresponding funds made available.* The quotas of member-states are fixed by Schedule A and are divided into special drawing rights totalling 1 billion dollars. At a later date the Council may raise the capital stock by special majority. The 1 billion drawing rights total 100,000 shares of equal face value (Art. 5). Schedule A establishes the size of capital (shares) to be subscribed by each of the 21 advanced countries' members of the World Bank and an additional 128 member-states of the World Bank, the rates amounting to 59.473% of the total for advanced countries and the remaining percentage (of 40.527) to be divided among the other member-states; for instance, the percentage share is 20.519 (205.19 million rights) for the United States, 0.775 (7.75 million rights) for Austria, and 0.564 (5.64 million rights) for Hungary. Those member-states of the World Bank acceding to MIGA after 30 October 1987 may subscribe to less shares than are indicated for them in Schedule A, but not less than 50 shares (Art. 6), meaning 50×10,000, or 500,000 rights in capital share, i.e. "input". The counter-value of subscribed shares falls due after accession, 10% in cash within 90 days, an additional 10% in non-negotiable securities (e.g. bills of exchange), and 80% is to be secured under a commitment to pay MIGA's concrete obligations for indemnification (with MIGA "calling in" payments at rates equal to each share). Developing countries may effect payments in their own currencies to the tune of 25% of their payments in cash, otherwise all payments are to be made in convertible currency, and the material liability of member-states is limited to the payment of subscribed shares (Arts. 7–8).

3. Remaining with Europe, it may be stated that no investment protection agreement in the above sense has been concluded on the *regional* level, partly because that role is fulfilled by the Washington Convention and MIGA in respect of Europe as well, and partly because the system of protection in this continent can be considered as complete with the bilateral agreements and the domestic protective arrangements. Nevertheless, in order to get a full picture, it is necessary to point to certain specific features with regard to the EU and Europe.

(a) The *European Union* (EU) bears on investment protection chiefly on three planes.

(aa) Article 222 of the Treaty of Rome provides that "this Treaty shall in no way prejudice the rules in member-states governing the system of property ownership", thereby referring the protection of property and, with it, investment to the internal national competence of member-states. On the other hand, since the EU member-states function in a market economy system based on private property, on which basis the EU originally came into being, and this Article of the Treaty postulates and protects that system of property ownership.

(ab) An important principle of the Treaty of Rome is freedom of establishment capital, and its progressive development (Arts. 52 *et seq.*). *Therefore the law of EU means investment protection in the positive aspect* as it spells out the need to facilitate and give free rein to the movement of investment to the extent possible within the region. This is assisted by considerable legislative activity at the EU level. Consider, for example, the EU Convention on Establishment, promoting the free movement of enterprises, and the efforts at the harmonization of company law.

(ac) Western literature on the subject is rather unequivocal in stating that, in a philosophical and socio-political sense, the EU is built on a social system, or postulates one, in which *economic freedom as a fundamental principle of human rights is under the protection of the law.* This is why references are made to the Universal Declaration of Human Rights (United Nations, 1948), which provides (in Art. 17) that "everyone has the right to own property..." and "no one shall be arbitrarily deprived of his property".

(b) However, in addition to the Declaration of 1948, EU's philosophy really rests on the *Council of Europe*'s First Protocol of 1952 to the European Convention on the Protection of Human Rights and Fundamental Freedoms, of 1950 which is also regarded as relevant to this question. The Protocol spells out that everyone has the right to (her/his) property, of which s/he must not be deprived except in the public interest in accordance with the general principles of law and international law. With Hungary's accession to and membership of the Council, this norm applies to us, as well by virtue of the cited international instrument. Our more recent bilateral agreements (see item 4 in §57) and the latest provisions of our domestic law (see §58) are likewise adjusted to this thesis.

(c) The Concluding Document adopted on 12 April 1990 by the *CSCE* (see §39) follow-up conference held at Bonn in March and April 1990 to discuss economic questions is extremely noteworthy from the point of view of regional legal values, and not only by reason of its theses concerning property, but chiefly because what emerges from it is *a kind of united economic policy creed for the whole of a future Europe*. In the light of the drifting historical developments and experiences, even as perceived back in 1990, one was able to observe quite a new perspective in the fact that the commonly-accepted Closing Document was also signed by the Soviet Union and all Eastern and Central European States. From closing documents, or conferences adopting them, there is usually a long way to go to implementation, to appropriate transformations of the social, economic, political and legal systems of nations. However this one conveys an unexampled message moulding the shape of the future in so far as it involved the signatory States all reaffirming their faith in free elections, a multi-party system, a State under the rule of law, a market economy, *private property*, development of international investments, enterprise cooperation and free convertibility of currencies, and stating that they regard these principles as the basis for the establishment of an all-European economic order.

4. Hungary's bilateral agreements on investment protection form part of this and are indicative of its domestic transformation, a change in its international economic policy strategy, its Europeanism, and a modern legal order concerning foreign investments. With constant promptings by theory, such agreements were signed with numerous partner countries (France, FRG, Great Britain,

Netherlands, Austria, Sweden and others) in the second part of the 1980s (see the List of Sources and, for a theoretical-historical background, Mádl: *Beruházások Magyarországon* (Investments in Hungary); *idem: A külgazdaság* (The External Economy), p. 179; Király–Mádl, §§6–7). The new political, social and economic order of this country naturally shares the investment policy values of the said agreements, and a further series of agreements has been concluded (with Canada, Australia, Greece, Uruguay, Thailand) in recent years (see the List of Sources).

Since they were born of an advancing international process, the investment protection agreements generally employ the so-called *Hull standards* of guarantee (see Martonyi). In effect, these standards imply *fair and equitable treatment* as well as *prompt, adequate and effective compensation* in the case of expropriation.

Considering that the agreements show a basic similarity in their "hard core", it is possible to analyze these international legislative instruments (see the List of Sources) in their totality and to sum up the main elements common to them.

(a) Each bilateral agreement on investment protection tries to give a refined *definition of investment* comprising a broad area. Thus, for instance, in the *British–Hungarian Agreement* (1988) and the *Canadian–Hungarian Agreement* (1995) the term "investment" means *any investment asset connected with economic activity*. Serving as a guide, the non-exhaustive enumerations include movable and immovable property, mortgage, lien, pledge, share, bond and debenture, any other form of enterprise interest, any account receivable involving money or other asset or any service based on contract and having a monetary value, as well as intellectual property, good will or even a business concession based on law or contract (Art. 1).

As is also indicated by this definition, the *scope of application* of these bilateral agreements *in relation to subject-matter* embraces all complex phenomena of the investment process, including the contractual (corporate) and property-law aspects of undertakings. Some of the agreements state that their provisions apply to investments effected after 31 December 1972. The temporal limitation suggests the paramount importance attached by the agreements to the promotion of all joint ventures with foreign participation, the foundation of which was made possible in Hungary definitely from 1 January 1973.

(b) A similarly serious task to be accomplished is to determine the *scope of application of the law in relation to persons*, namely to outline the group of investors. The complexity of the question is due to the dissimilar institutional structure of the legal systems of Contracting States (albeit such dissimilarity is less marked from the adoption of the Hungarian Associations and Investment Acts). Thus, for instance, in the Swedish–Hungarian Agreement it was sufficient to refer to nationals and legal persons (para. 2 of Art. 1), but in the British–Hungarian Agreement it was practicable to replace the term "legal person" by "companies, firms and associations of persons" in respect of the United Kingdom (para. 3 of Art. 1). In like manner, the FRG–Hungarian Agreement extends its scope of application generally to commercial and other companies in respect of legal persons, while nationality is combined with domicile in respect of natural persons (Germans and Hungarians domiciled within its territorial scope) (para. 3 of Art. 1). However, the differences resulting from the interaction of the divergent corporate laws and conflict norms do not affect the common purpose of agreements to draw under their protective shield possibly all categories of potential entrepreneurs. It is particularly important to emphasize this fact with regard to Hungary in the awareness that other countries have, for their part, limited the range of investors to economic organizations and foreign-trading companies (see Dienes–Oehm).

(c) The first stage of support for investments is naturally associated with support for *foundation.* Accordingly, every bilateral agreement contains an article declaring an *intention to encourage the setting up of undertakings.* As is worded in the FRG–Hungarian Agreement, each Contracting Party will, to the extent possible, promote investments in its territory by investors of the other Contracting Party and will authorize such investments in accordance with its laws and regulations. Both Parties will accord just and equitable treatment to all investments (Art. 2). The effectiveness of such support *depends on the interpretation of authorization,* a key notion of this Article. As is known, during the past decade Hungary has established a normative system that is quite remarkable even by international standards; the relevant laws, as amended in early 1991, require no licence for the foundation of investment-related enterprises (see §46).

(d) As regards now the assurance of the normal operation of undertakings and of owners' rights, the Contracting States seek to undertake multiple *general commitments* to afford appropriate guarantees.

(da) *Non-discrimination* figures in all bilateral agreements on investment protection which Hungary has promulgated to date. Consequently, neither Contracting Party will accord to investments in its territory, by investors of the other Contracting Party, less favourable treatment than that extended to investments effected by investors of a third State (Art. 4 of the Swedish–Hungarian Agreement). In other words, this clause can be taken to mean *most-favoured-nation treatment,* for non-discrimination can only be ensured by application of this principle. This means that investors of the Contracting States are mutually entitled to all the preferences granted to investors of a third State, in the particular State party to the Agreement.

(db) Furthermore, a common core of the agreements is constituted by a readiness to accord *national treatment,* which serves to give effect to the *neutrality of state regulation* not only in relations of foreign investors *inter se,* but also in the wider contexts of relations between foreign and domestic entrepreneurs, ensuring a greater degree of transparency of economic regulators and the development of competition as determined by economic rationality.

(dc) The *emergence of economic integration* appears to act as a limitation on the implementation of the principles of most-favoured-nation and of national treatment, because the advantages otherwise granted to undertakings by investment protection agreements do not comprise those granted by one of the Contracting Parties to investors of a third State in connection with its participation in a free-trade zone, customs union, common market or any other regional economic organization. An inverse arrangement might disrupt the economic unity of integration, which try to achieve the maximum amount of economic cooperation among their members, bearing the related burdens as well.

(dd) Of course, these corrective rules do not prejudice the basic purpose of bilateral agreements concluded by Hungary to create favourable conditions for the entrepreneurial activities of foreign investors. In addition to the foregoing, this is guaranteed by state commitments to accord *just and equitable treatment* to investments. One might say that justness and equity are uncertain notions, as their meanings and application are likely to change with the current of historical and social processes. Still, it is indisputable that these categories seek, by their very nature, universality, for they are impossible to interpret under a single national system of law. Therefore, by accepting the guiding principles of justness and equity, the Contracting States have concurrently subjected their conduct, at least in respect of investments, to the international standards prevailing in the larger legal community of nations. And they have often proved to be an efficient check on the unsteady, occasionally authoritative investment policies of States, however contradictory and uncertain these standards may be, as was also evidenced by the application of the Washington Convention [see item 2 (a) in §57].

(e) Along with the previous philosophical categories, *free transfer* is a vitally important, though less comprehensive requirement, since there is usually a direct relationship between the lifting of financial restrictions and a growing propensity to invest. In order to increase the latter, all investment protection agreements of Hungary guarantee free transfer of income, including returns on capital, profits, interest, dividends, royalties and other fees in appropriate convertible currency and without delay. Free transfer is similarly guaranteed in respect of loan repayments, proceeds from conveyances or full or partial liquidation of investment undertakings, and earnings of foreign nationals (or such proportion thereof as may be established by law).

(f) However, the investment protection agreements under discussion not only enumerate the mutual benefits granted to investors of the Contracting States, but, in accordance with the related international practice, also impose limitations on acts of State, *subjecting nationalization to strict conditions*. Accordingly, every bilateral agreement provides that nationalization, expropriation or any measure entailing similar consequences (limitation of ownership) must be *in the public interest*, under appropriate *legal procedures, free from discrimination* and for *full compensation*, this is to include the market value prior to the limitation of ownership and interest calculated up to the period of its payment. The amount of compensation thus calculated may be transferred without delay.

(g) As can be perceived, the normative formulation of the Hull standard requires sovereign powers to observe in no small measure the basic principles of classical civil (private) law (prohibition of causing damage and obligation to pay compensation). Nevertheless, the question may arise as to the *assurance that the "fine words" of investment protection agreements will be kept.*

So far as Hungary is concerned, the following arguments could be listed in brief for the assured implementation of agreements.

(ga) All bilateral agreements have framed a *system of fora* to which recourse may be had in case of violation of treaty obligations. The essential elements thereof will be discussed at a later stage [see item 4 (b) in §117].

There is one more aspect to be addressed here in addition to those we will consider presently. The question of which persons can be regarded as *foreigners,* that was also covered in discussing the Washington Convention [item 2 (a) in §57], arises again in connection with the *procedural rights* of investors.

Notably, the direct legal link by reason of which an investor may initiate an arbitral procedure against a contested measure of the host country is associated with this capacity only. The Agreements with Sweden and Great Britain explicitly contain the foreign control clause, recognizing the capacity to sue and be sued also for enterprises established under the rules of the host country but held mostly in foreign ownership. In particular, the Swedish–Hungarian Agreement spells out that a legal person, which was founded in accordance with the legislation of one of the Contracting Parties, where the majority of shares is held by investors of the other Contracting Party prior to the emergence of the dispute, is to be treated as an investor of the other Contracting Party within the meaning of Art. 25, para. 2 (b), of the Washington Convention (para. 3 of Art. 11). In case of legal disputes within the scope of application of the other bilateral agreements, subsequent recognition of investors as foreigners is permissible under Art. 25, para. 2 (b), of the Washington Convention, analyzed earlier in the corresponding section, which functions as the underlying law.

(gb) Another guarantee for keeping the said "fine words" is afforded by the *environment of domestic law* (see §§48 and 58), which is not only basically amicable but welcoming in its own avowed self-interest and to which the institutional system of international commitments protection can be harmoniously adjusted.

(gc) The *most decisive guarantee*, however, is provided by a peculiar circumstance, namely the objective fact that a *conditio sine qua non* for recovery from the economic crisis and for the structural adjustment demanded by it assures the operation of foreign working capital, as is suggested by its very name.

§58. GUARANTEES UNDER DOMESTIC LAW

Without seeking to be exhaustive and to cover all details, we can state in the light of practice that national laws offer three important sets of tools for the protection of investments (foreign property), viz. through constitutional postulation of forms of property and their general legal protection, specific protective institutions of investment, and investment insurance.

1. The internal legal sphere of *general protective tools* is, in effect, the *national property regime itself*. Under a general conceptual-theoretical approach, this is a question of whether the domestic system of property ownership carries in it some sort of immune reaction to investments embodying foreign property or one of *how foreign investments are assimilated under the general law of property*. As is known, this was originally one of the strongest implications in the reservations of the then socialist countries concerning the question of how the so-called socialist (state and cooperative) property, dominant under the hallmark of superiority and exclusivity, was to coexist with private property [Király–Mádl: §8; Mádl: *A külgazdaság* (The External Economy), §§39 *et seq.*].The property regime has since changed, and private property as a value category has been re-established in its own right.

Concerning this generality of the domestic legal atmosphere, we refer to the new Constitution, which provides that "Hungary's economy shall be a market economy ... according equal protection to public and private property on an equal footing" (Art. 9) and spells out the thesis, most important in this respect, that "property shall not be expropriated save in exceptional cases in the public interest and in the manner defined by law, and expropriation shall be subject to full, unconditional and immediate compensation" (Art. 13).

2. *The domestic investments legislation has devised a special form of investment protection.*

(a) The legal protection of foreign investors has in general been raised to the level of the Constitution, whereas the investment codes (laws on joint ventures) of the different countries lay special emphasis on the protection of foreigners' property rights and of foreign investments. This provides a statutory guarantee for the concrete process of investment and for the post-investment period alike.

Article 1 of the Hungarian Investment Code (Act XXIV of 1988) declares the full protection and security of foreign investments in Hungary and provides furthermore that any loss to a foreign investor resulting from future measures of nationalization or expropriation affecting his property is to be compensated for without delay at the actual value of the property. Within the meaning of the Act, the amount of such compensation is to be paid to the person entitled thereto in the currency in which the investment was effected. This provision has thus introduced the State's direct liability, based on law, for any damage caused by measures of the Government or its organs.

(b) In addition to the general guarantees afforded by internal law, national legislation has developed more concrete forms of guarantee. Thus, for instance, Hungarian law allows, or virtually recommends, as it were, resort to *bank guarantees*. At the request of the foreign partner, a bank guarantee may be provided in respect of any damage to the foreign investor's property which results from any government measure, either restrictive or damaging. Investment protection with bank involvement includes assumption by a bank of a guarantee, under the usual business conditions, for the obligations of an association arising from membership relations *vis-à-vis* a foreign member. Obviously associated with bank involvement, but functioning "only" as a legal guarantee, is the provision which entitles a bank to transfer abroad, on withdrawal of a foreign member, his property share, to the extent of the amount paid to the bank, in the currency of the investment; which permits tax-free transfer abroad of the foreigner's net property share in case of liquidation (see Act XXIV of 1988 on Investments of Foreigners in Hungary, Arts. 32 and 36).

3. Even though the law offers a perfect system of protection by operating all the aforesaid protective mechanisms, it is the means of protection against investment risks under commercial (civil) law, namely "ordinary" insurance of investment with an insurance company, that have proved to be the most efficient in practice. This is why, among other reasons, MIGA [item 2 (b) in §57] has come into being at the international level, with its armoury employed in Hungary and elsewhere, and has fine prospects before it.

(a) Albeit an everyday occurrence today, this phenomenon *first appeared in the advanced Western countries.* To illustrate more clearly the substance and role of insurance in external economic strategies, it is worthwhile to take a closer look at the system of insurance as it evolved in this field in the USA, a country handling a particularly large volume of capital exports. The post-World War Two period saw the emergence of various large-scale programmes aimed at increasing the activity of capital abroad. The most important of them was naturally Marshall Aid, destined for the reconstruction of Western Europe and the activation of its economic growth. Subsequently, though, the American state economic strategy supported a more general expansion of working capital in institutionalized form as well. Achievement of the goal of expansive economic policy by the aid of State capital was facilitated through the American Export-Import Bank (Ex-Im Bank), whereas the expansive strategy of private capital was promoted by Overseas Private Investment Company (OPIC), a large institution of insurance established by the use of state resources. Seemingly contrary to its name, this is not a private insurance company, but a state institution insuring foreign investments of private capital; OPIC offered favourable conditions of insurance for investments abroad as a way of contributing to the implementation of America's international strategy on the world market. Under its contracts of insurance OPIC undertook to pay compensation in cases of non-commercial (political) damage caused by events like war, civil war, other similar political developments, expropriation, nationalization, and state measures which, in the place of investment, prevented repatriation of income or, in case of liquidation, of remaining assets. Today these are well-known categories of insurance which have grown up and taken shape in the practice of OPIC, with billions of dollars paid under its schemes to, e.g., *General Motors, ITT, Chase Manhattan, Chile Copper* and other American companies on grounds that they had suffered damage "due to political risks" in Vietnam, Bangladesh, Zaire (now the Democratic Republic of Congo), Argentina, Chile and elsewhere (see Loewenfeld, Vogel).

It is necessary of record that, in Hungary's new situation, extension of the protective shield of OPIC insurance to American investors here has become of great relevance to American investment projects benefiting the country.

Soon afterwards there were put into operation similar institutions and schemes *in the rest of the advanced Western countries*, such as *COFACE* in France and *HERMES* in FRG (see Mádl: Political Risks). It is characteristic of these insurance mechanisms to operate in a mutual legal relationship with bilateral agreements on investment protection, since it is stipulated that a contract of insurance under favourable terms is open, by way of protection, to a foreign investment project. This is in keeping with the international or domestic economic policy objectives of the capital-exporting and capital-importing countries concerned or it is implemented in a country with which the capital-exporting country has signed a bilateral investment agreement under which both parties recognize the subrogation clause (Loewenfeld, pp. 424 *et seq.*). The latter obviously serve a dual purpose: to rule out double compensation to the damaged party and to increase as far as possible the role of host countries in devising actual guarantee arrangements or meeting their obligations to pay compensation. True, the essential point in the domestic mechanisms for investment insurance is that, ultimately, a future loss to the expansive external economy of the capital-exporting country is also borne by its economy (which is, through the said link-up, a kind of logistical background insurance for an efficient external economic strategy). Yet by virtue of the *subrogation clause* in the bilateral agreements, a part of the invoice is put on the table of the host countries. Seen from this angle, similar roles are also allotted to the parties under the MIGA mechanism as well. Yet this is the viable path, as we have tried to make clear [item 2 (b) in §57]. For foreign investors, the substance of insurance is this: with state or private insurance in their own country in the background, they had enjoyed a large measure of security in Hungary even before its accession to MIGA. Now, though, coupled with a series of other guarantees, insurance may also continue to offer them increased protection in future, all the more so since this legal institution is similarly well tuned to bilateral agreements.

(b) In recent years, as is well known, the *system of investment insurance* has become greatly differentiated *in Hungary* as well. Within the framework of insurance contracts generally regulated by the Civil Code, export credit insurance has likewise come into use and the figure grown in practice. Along with economic risks (Conditions G) and risks materializing in exchange-rate deviations (Conditions A), it extends to political risks (Conditions P). Under the practice of insurance against political risks, Hungarian enterprises may enter into a contract of insurance with the insurance company to cover risks to invested capital as well (P–III). In general, the inner or notional content of political risks is in line with the notional elements as applied in international practice [and as was seen in the case of, e.g., MIGA discussed in item 2 (b) in §57: war, revolt of the civilian population, nationalization, etc.], while concrete cases are covered by Conditions P completed with a specific supplementary content. Thus, for instance, it is a natural specific of contracts that insurance premiums vary by country, and risk factors, periods of coverage and clients' shares are variable, etc. [for insurance practice in Hungary, see Knapp: 8.2, *Politikai kockázatok biztosítása* (Insurance against Political Risks); Mádl: Political Risks]. It is thus trite to say that one should insure well, just as to invest well. These two desiderata plus investment protection go together, constituting a general framework and complementing one another.

CHAPTER XVIII

A NEW PROPERTY REGIME: PRIVATIZATION AND ITS INTERNATIONAL ASPECTS

§59. THE NEW PROPERTY REGIME AND PRIVATIZATION

1. In recent years Hungary has experienced a peaceful revolution resulting in a profound transformation of social, political and economic relations, a process still under way. The core and substance of transformations is this: the institutional system of a pluralist political democracy has evolved and is functioning; a social market economy and a corresponding new property regime are in the making; a new kind of the country's integration into the systems of political, economic and cultural relations prevailing in Europe and the world has been set in train and is growing intensively. Society and the different political forces have reached a high degree of consensus on these objectives and the acceptance of related values.

Here is the place to address the market economy and the new system of property ownership. This *historic programme finds legal expression* above all in the Constitution, which provides that "Hungary's economy shall be a market economy ... according equal protection to public and private property on an equal footing", spells out the freedom of enterprise in stating that "the Republic of Hungary shall recognize and support the right of enterprise and the freedom of economic competition", and expresses that "the Republic of Hungary shall ensure the freedom to property" (Art. 9). All these rights have been translated into reality by numerous legislative enactments. Obviously enough, it has been one of the historical tasks gradually to dismantle the so-called socialist property regime, scaling down the nearly 90% predominance of state property, and to give free rein to private enterprise. This is the essence and mission of privatization in the legal context.

The greatest role in transforming the property regime was reserved for legislation on privatization along with several other enactments (relating to, e.g., economic associations, private businesses, local-government property, cooperatives, settlement of the situation of certain immovables formerly owned by the churches). There were four stages of legislative activity: (1) Based on the Acts on Business Associations and State Enterprises, Act XIII of 1989 on the Transformation of Economic Organizations and Economic Associations (as amended by Act XVIII of 1990 and Act LXXII of 1990) opened the way to a voluntary (spontaneous) privatization of enterprises, to their transformation and formation of partnerships. (2) Act VII of 1990 on the State Property Agency as well as on the management and utilization of property within its purview, as amended by Act LIII of 1990 and Act LXXVII of 1990; Act VIII of 1990 on the Protection of State Property Entrusted to Enterprises, as amended by Act LXXI of 1990; Act LXXIV of 1990 (Preliminary Privatization Act) on the Privatization of Enterprises Providing Services in Retail Trade, Public Catering and the Consumer Sector; and the Provisional Property Policy Directives approved by Parliament which were adopted for the purpose of strengthening proprietary (state) control. (3) In 1992 the abovementioned laws except the Preliminary Privatization Act were superseded by new enactments: Act LIII of 1992 on the Management and Utilization of Property Retained in Permanent State Ownership; Act LIV of 1992 on the Sale, Utilization and Protection of Property in Temporary State Ownership; Act LV of 1992 amending the legislative enactments on state business property; and Act XLIV of 1992 on the Programme for Worker's Share Ownership (PWSO). (4) Act XXXIX of 1995 on the Sale of State Owned Business Property.

By these consecutive enactments the legislature carried a stage further the concepts, principles and institutions of privatization (scope of state property to be privatized, generality of sale to private owners, exceptional nature and framework of property management, sale and utilization on a market basis, competitive bidding, incentive benefits, proprietary role of the State, organic structure of privatization, etc.). Drawing on existing experience and responding to new demands, the latter-day enactments injected significant new elements into the process (PWSO, scope of property remaining in permanent state ownership and its management, general extension of the right to form associations, revamping of the state organs of privatization (State Property Agency, State Property Management Corporation, State Privatization and Property Management Corporation) and a better definition of their rights and duties, introduction of new privatization techniques, clearer definition of the scope of property to be retained in permanent state ownership, etc.). It was an important task to improve the inner coherence of the legal system (e.g. incorporation in the Privatization Act of the rules on transformation with bearings on privatization, inclusion in the Associations Act of the general rules on transformation).

There were two more enactments of great importance which contributed to the laying down of the legal basis for the new property regime: Act XXV of 1991 on partial compensation for damage unjustly caused to citizens' property, with a view to settlement of property relations [First Compensation Act for short; on its enforcement see Government Decree No. 104/1991. (VIII.3.) as amended] and Act XXIV of 1992 on partial compensation, with a view to settlement of property relations, for damage unjustly caused to citizens' property by the application of laws and regulations adopted in the period from 1 May 1939 to 8 June 1949 [enforced by Government Decree No. 92/1992. (VI.10.)].

Three functions of these enactments need emphasizing. First, settlement and stabilization of property relations under the hallmark of the said constitutional scale of values. In order for the abovementioned privatization acts to help establish a new system of property ownership through positive mechanisms, it was necessary to create security for both national and foreign entrepreneurs and would-be owners, a certainty that no one would question the right of ownership in the immovables acquired and put into operation, viz. to rule out by law the possibility of reprivatization. Second, within the national framework of general sharing in taxation and the limits of the country's available resources, compensation to owners deprived of their property. Failure to compensate them would amount to a legal and historical schizophrenia hard to combat and likely to generate social conflicts, for it is impossible to speak of a new constitutional order protecting property on the one hand and to say, on the other, that it applies only to the present and the future, but not to the property of millions of people living here and dispossessed yesterday. Third, the mechanism of compensation – use of a security (bond) issued for purchase of state property destined for privatization. This became a source and a strength of privatization, for the rise of a new layer of entrepreneurs or a middle class, whereas acquisition of arable land by compensation bonds issued in settlement of claims of agricultural origin served to contribute towards development in the direction of a modern farming system. A notable social element of the compensation mechanism consists of entitling the holders of compensation vouchers to by state-owned dwellings or to convert the vouchers into life-annuity (Act XXXI of 1992 on Redemption of Compensation Vouchers for Life-Annuity).

2. Lying deep beneath the briefly described regulation by positive law of the new property regime and privatization are naturally fundamental *theoretical considerations relevant to the philosophy of history as well as to economic and social philosophy*.

Mankind has accumulated a wealth of experience borne out by history that, translated into practical terms of a man-centered social theory – one seeking for man's economic, cultural and moral development and hence socially balanced –, is bound to travel a toilsome road, long and stricken with contradictions. History similarly testifies to man's experience that "real" socialism did not prove to be a viable option in this respect: on the contrary, it hurled a large part of the world into a grave material and moral crisis, let alone the burdens of political dictatorship. Moreover, man has historical evidence that, of all social and economic systems known to date, the best able to operate a balanced social structure, to increase economic efficiency, to harmonize patterns of distribution and to ensure a pluralist democracy is a system based on private property and a social market economy.

3. The *more immediate* principal *goals* of privatization can be deemed to be the following.

(a) A balanced social structure functioning without any greater stresses and strains and allowing for an organic inner development and, through it, a pluralist democracy which call for a strong and responsible and well-structured layer of owners; for a strong and equally well-structured middle class capable of economic activity by reliance on its skills and own capital and thereby having an existential autonomy; for a broad segment of intellectuals rewarded for its capital of knowledge and skills and with an appropriate material position; for a large number of individual small entrepreneurs in industry, commerce and services and especially in agriculture; and for this structure to allow room for a sound inner mobility. All these factors have combined to make it a purpose of privatization to ensure that privatization of state property will not lead to the sway of huge private wealth, but will *contribute to shaping a sound structural pattern of society as outlined above*. Therefore the preponderance and prevalence of forms of privatization, e.g., in ready cash, that are open only to high net individuals worth high purchasing capacity are a source of concern.

(b) It is an important goal to increase the efficiency and competitive ability of economic subjects (enterprises, associations, firms, individual economic undertakings) and to *modernize* the economy with a view to meeting domestic needs and the demands of the international market.

(c) Attainment of these goals requires real motivation, proprietary responsibility, a proprietary attitude to economic activities, a new property regime based mostly on *private property*, but operating with considerable state and public and, under the hallmark of the freedom of cooperation, cooperative property. The new property regime should assign a significant role to local government property.

(d) *Competitiveness on an international scale and involvement of foreign capital* are outstanding goals for two reasons. First, Hungary produces a very high ratio of national income in international economic processes, a real factor endowment that cannot do without competitive ability. Second, privatization attracts foreign capital and know-how, no less indispensable for economic development. Effective presence of working capital in the national economy is a general and apparently important element of a modern international division of labour. The percentage ratios are variable, but are usually around 25 to 30% in the advanced countries, and there are also glaringly lower and higher figures [for Hungary, the ratio in 1995 was a *warning signal* (!) with a 40% share of foreign property in the Hungarian property structure; this figure was 5% for the Czech Republic and 3% for Poland.

(e) Another major goal is the *restructuring of the economy*, or the structural adjustment of enterprises, meaning, *inter alia*, increasing the number and weight of small- and medium-sized enterprises, dismantling the monopolies, decentralization, shaping a modern structural pattern of enterprises, creating adequate job opportunities, full-scale privatization of retail trade and services.

(f) An equally important goal is *free supply of funding to the social insurance scheme* which is likely to improve the standard of social insurance services and to increase their economic security, while indirectly meeting the needs of a broad segment of proprietors.

(g) Moreover, *receipts from privatization* – in addition to covering the costs of reorganization, job creation, repairing earlier environmental damage, etc. – may be used for reducing the state debt and may serve to promote attainment of goals set by Parliament.

4. Privatization means strengthening and reinforcing *the following spheres and proprietary positions*: domestic private undertakings, the so-called private sector, which has already registered a dynamic growth and produces a notable ratio of national income; foreign investors; joint ventures; investment projects largely with the participation of domestic private entrepreneurs, now numbering many thousands and representing billions of dollars in aggregate; and the gradual development of the farming system, particularly under the probable impact of the Compensation Act. In comparison to state property, the property of local governments, churches and other institutions as well as its operation with proprietary motivation fall in line with privatization. Finally, privatization means transfer to private ownership of productive state property, or state enterprises, which is privatization in the narrow sense, so called in everyday language, by public opinion and literature alike.

Thus, the *targeted range of owners* in the privatization process includes Hungarian private persons; economic and other associations of Hungarian private persons: Hungarian private persons as enterprise employees participating in property-sharing programmes; Hungarian private persons indirectly involved through various institutions (local governments, social insurance company, insurance companies, other investors and owners); foreign natural and legal persons.

5. The *main elements of the privatization mechanism* – in accordance with the enactments on privatization referred to in item 1 above – are as follows.

(a) On the side of organization and competence, mention should be made first of the *State Privatization and Property Management Corporation* (Hungarian acronym: *ÁPV Rt.*) established by Act XXXIX of 1995 (Arts. 9 to 26). Its functions and duties are to organize and accomplish privatization, through assessment of state property as a general rule (Art. 1) and to operate, usually under appropriate contracts, the property management mechanism for property in permanent state ownership (Arts. 7 *et seq.*). Thereby the said Act consolidated these functions formerly performed by the State Property Agency and the State Property Management Corporation, which operated under the earlier laws, into one organization (*ÁPV Rt.*)

ÁPV Rt. is a one-man joint stock company in state ownership; its shares are non-negotiable; the shareholder's rights are exercised by the minister in charge of privatization and the Government; its foundation and operation are, but for the contrary provisions of the Act establishing it, subject to the rules of Act VI of 1988 on Economic Associations; it may be terminated by Parliament (Art. 9).

The 11 members and the Chairman of its Board of Directors are appointed and relieved of office by the Government (Art. 12). Its activity is controlled by the State Audit Office, and the Government renders to Parliament annual accounts of *ÁPV Rt.*'s work and the process of privatization (Art. 25).

It is important to note that, in accordance with law, the conceptions about the privatization of associations significant for the operation of the national economy are adopted by the Government and that the classification of associations as ones operating with the participation of property in permanent state ownership is to be determined by an Act of Parliament (Art. 8).

(b) Under Act XXXIX of 1995, sales *in the process of privatization* are, in accordance with the previous practice, subject (as a general rule) to competitive bidding directly through the institutions of the capital market, investment funds or associations, or, under a simplified procedure of privatization, through senior officers of associations (Art. 27). Sales are supported by privatization techniques offering facilities (payment by instalments, leasing, buy-outs by managers and workers, start-up credit, PWSO; see Arts. 46 to 60). The contractual systems of property management operate, in accordance with the earlier laws and practice, under contracts of commission, contracts for work, labour and materials, naturally with the aim of promoting and enlarging state property and subject to appropriate guarantees (Arts. 62 *et seq.*).

§60. INTERNATIONAL–EXTERNAL ECONOMIC ASPECTS OF PRIVATIZATION

1. Generally speaking about the international and external economic aspects of privatization, we should state the following.

(a) European integration, *integration* into the system of political, social and legal relations of the advanced countries, and extension to us of economic, financial and other assistance that can be expected from that world (security, science and technology, credit, working capital, and financial assistance) naturally presupposed and presuppose establishment of a new property regime, creation of private property and the freedom of enterprise and economic activity: in short, the release of man's creative potential. Our accession to the international and European institutions of integration, so important to us, and continued co-operation with them make this necessary in a legal technical sense as well. One of the conceptual-political pillars of the Council of Europe is constituted by the institutions of a free market economy and private property along with a pluralist democracy, a state governed by the rule of law and human rights [see item 3 (b) in §39]. The Declaration of Bonn adopted within the CSCE framework and the Paris Charter of Europe spell out the commitment of member-states to a market economy and private property [see item 3 (a) in §39]. And, what is of particular importance to us from political, cultural, scientific, human and economic points of view, the European Union and its legal instruments. Even the Preamble to the EU–Hungarian Agreement on Association ("Europe Agreement") clearly proclaims the freedom of market economy and private property, making it an unambiguous condition for accession, as has been repeatedly stated at the EU summits dealing with enlargement [see item 3 (c), (cf) in §39].

(b) Foreign capital, technology, management skills, and an increase in market outlets are indispensable for recovery from the economic crisis caused by the previous regime, for building a new economic structure, and for promoting gradual economic growth. Private capital is "willing" to contribute to the attainment of these objectives, really for rational business considerations, in countries where private enterprise and property are protected by stable property relations.

The other side of the matter is that establishment of partnerships, associations and purchase of enterprises by foreign private capital should also be guaranteed by the privatization acts in a legal technical sense.

(c) In respect of compensation, a special sphere of privatization, it is an essential point that *compensation is also due to those foreign nationals* who, at the time they were deprived of their property, were Hungarian nationals or lost their property by reason of deprivation of Hungarian nationality (Art. 2 of the First Compensation Act). Equally entitled to compensation are those non-nationals who were habitually resident in Hungary up to 31 December 1990 (Art. 2). This latter provision pays regard to Bulgarians, Poles, etc. who had been living in Hungary for decades and suffered the same injury as Hungarians, but retained their foreign nationality. The First Compensation Act is applicable to loss of property after 8 June 1949, but it provides that claims for compensation must also be settled by law in respect of those materially damaged on racial and political grounds as well as in consequence of the post-war resettlement of Germans (Art. 1). This will affect a very large number of former Hungarian nationals now living abroad and having a foreign nationality as well as interstate relations or agreements (e.g. through possible bearings of agreements on exchange of populations, i.e. agreements on compensation of displaced persons or victims of racial persecution). The Second Compensation Act of 1992 settles matters of compensation with retroactive effect to 1 May 1939.

2. Also, privatization appears in several, more concrete international–external economic aspects covered by specific legal regulations.

(a) The related large areas of regulation are represented by *foreigners' investments in Hungary* (see §46) and *protection of foreign investments* (see Chapter XVII).

(b) Hungarian economic policy thinking sets a limit of 25 to 30% to *total foreign shares*, possible and desirable, obtained in foreign investments and through privatization of Hungarian enterprises. Expressly or impliedly, this conforms to the international average share of foreign investments and international capital transactions. Going far beyond this limit may adversely affect the interests of the national economy and the general social peace [similar concerns have been voiced about the privatization of the energy supply system and the high foreign participation; see item 3 (b) above]. With regard to state enterprises, the current law sets limits only with respect to about 200 enterprises that will remain fully or partially in permanent state ownership (Art. 7), providing that "in case of bids of equal value, preference shall be given to those of domestic investors" (Art. 27).

(c) A large role in the privatization process is played by *consulting firms, including foreign ones.* Through the medium of hundreds of internationally known investment banks and consulting firms, it is possible, *inter alia*, for Hungarian offers to evoke a global interest on the international capital markets and investment capacity and to find their way to them. It is probably to their credit, too, that the composition of foreign capital invested in Hungary can be said to be of global origin (with the presence of South Korea, Japan, India, Australia and others in addition to the traditional European countries and the USA).

(d) A significant role in strengthening and widening the process of privatization, naturally including green-field investments, is played, along with Hungarian and foreign consultants, by *various so-called Hungary funds and banking partnerships initiated and financed from abroad.*

Vested with the function of investment counselling and supplied with financial resources, these are established by foreign governments and natural persons interested in Hungary's development and the success of privatization. Such is, for example, the Hungarian–American Enterprises Fund, which was established by the American Government in the form of a commercial association, with 60 million dollars of capital, under the SEED Program (see item 5 in §39) and which has already initiated, organized and participated in numerous investment projects as part of the privatization or of joint ventures (Hungarian–American Enterprises Fund, First Annual Report, April 17 – September 30, 1990). Another one is First Hungary Fund Ltd., which came into being, with headquarters in the Channel Islands, as a private undertaking with the participation of, among others, the Hungarian National Bank and IFC [see item 2 (a), (ab), in §39] and with a capital stock of $80 million subscribed on the international capital market. For its part, it founded "First Hungarian Investment Counselling Joint Stock Company", functioning under Hungarian law, to provide professional guidance for investment undertakings in Hungary. In it, the Hungarian National Bank holds a share of 50% besides foreign shareholders.

(e) The *compensation bond* is part of the compensation arrangement, for which a great role was reserved in privatization. It is a "freely negotiable bearer-bond with a face value equal to the amount of compensation and embodying a claim against the State" and serves for acquisition of property in the process of privatizing state property (Arts. 5 and 7 of the Compensation Act). Within the framework of his own compensation, a foreigner as acquirer may also obtain and sell it (Art. 7). Such foreigners are subject to no foreign exchange restrictions with respect either to acquisition of property or to export and import of compensation bonds [Sect. 13 of Government Decree No. 104/1991. (VIII. 3.)].

TITLE 5

CONTRACTS

CHAPTER XIX

MAJOR GENERAL QUESTIONS OF CONTRACTS

§61. CONTRACTS OR THE LAW OF OBLIGATIONS – AS DISCUSSED UNDER THIS TITLE

1. Contracts are the truly large terrain of international personal and economic transactions. It is contracts which internationally link subjects of law and economies attached to and gravitating towards national boundaries; which legally express and organize the worldwide movement of persons and material values; which gradually bring our contracted world within reach of all; which, in the economic context, provide legal protection and assistance for the unity of various regional markets and of the world market; and which formulate daily programmes for the international division of labour. Of course, a great role in this is also played by the other institutions of law we have discussed earlier (persons, property, etc.), but the category of contract is of the greatest mobility, facilitating the international movement of States as well as individuals and enterprises, while the latter preserve, and do intend to preserve, their attachment to the State of their nationality in most of its aspects.

Well, this large and general view of contracts naturally *exceeds the scope of the traditional law of obligations governing contracts*. The realm of contracts is also illustrative of the fact that life, especially in this sphere, does not tolerate categories that have emerged under different sets of conditions and naturally have their rationale in their particular contexts. In the simplest terms, the law of obligations is that part of civil law which encompasses civil law contracts, non-contractual liability and, as a sort of appendix, unjust enrichment. Many writers on private international law have construed the law of obligations as being wider in scope and have integrated into it their discussion on international agreements and conventions embodying substantive law, the utilization of intellectual property (as is also treated in the Hungarian Code) and many other aspects which constitute much more than the classical law of contracts, or at least for which their classification is in dispute. Substantive-law regulation as embodied in the unification of international law has led some countries to look on private international law as pertaining, on this account as well, to the domain of public international law. The Italian private international law explicitly bears the hallmark of this approach. If now, in keeping with what we have stated in the Introduction, we add to this the aspect of those new dimensions ("the revolt of facts") that in the sphere of international economic relations the contracts of enterprises as regulated under domestic and international law cannot be seen and understood as having any sense except in combination with the contracts of States expressing their international economic function; if we in addition include also the interstate treaties directly determining the civil-law conditions and the conditions and mechanism of international economic processes; taking these circumstances into consideration, we move very far from the traditional framework of the law of obligations. This is nothing other than the *unity of the contract rules of private international law and the part of the law of international economic relations dealing with contracts*, as was generally referred to in the introductory chapter. This is a "mule" approach. A mule is known to combine to great advantage the qualities of its two progenitors. Likewise the said solution is eager to claim something for its own. In it there appears a unity of the regulation of contracts by the law of conflicts, the substantive-law rules of domestic and international law governing the different types of contracts, and the body of rules of international treaties by which States regulate their own conduct in order to help the contracts of economic subjects to be optimally concluded and to function under appropriate conditions.

2. Next we will discuss the following questions in this complexity: contracts in domestic law and international agreements, with particular emphasis on the unification of law as well as on the role of interstate treaties and the civil-law mechanism of contracts (Chapters XIX); system of contracts governing international cooperation between economic subjects, a survey of contract types in foreign trade: sale, contracting, carriage and forwarding, complex contracts for large projects, international payments transactions (Chapter XX to XXIV), and finally the private international law of contracts as the underlying law governing the large substantive-law mechanism of contracts (Chapter XXV).

§62. CONTRACTS IN DOMESTIC LAW – A HISTORICAL AND COMPARATIVE SURVEY

1. Here we naturally understand contracts to mean contracts with foreign elements and a regulation thereof purported to aid personal transactions and international economic relations.

In historical retrospect, the first more general reaction of law to "international contracts" (i.e. contracts presenting foreign elements) consisted in the application of internal substantive law. It was not until the beginning of the second worldwide revival of Roman law, the *period of the glossators*, that *the trend slowly evolved towards recognition of conflicts and formulation of the lo-*

calizers of private international law governing the applicable law and then a modern and differentiated definition thereof in recent times.

Large-scale international economic mobility in the modern era, together with the system of remitting conflict rules, made it increasingly evident that *international contracts of sale and other transactions also called for a special regulation of numerous aspects under internal substantive law*. This presents the following picture.

2. Under the impact of modern commodity trade, every country with a developed market economy evolved a differentiated system of contracts under domestic civil and commercial law (rise of commercial codes along with civil codes on the Continent, long-time unity of law in the common law countries, by emergence of the actual duality of civil and commercial law, particularly adoption by all common-law sister states of the USA of the Uniform Commercial Code in recent decades). Yet one more step was needed to "indicate" whether contracts with international elements were, if subjected to internal substantive law, to be governed by these same norms or additionally by other rules, at least subsidiarily. Well, this question was and is answered, of course, by the law of all advanced countries, albeit not in a uniform way.

The rules in this field form two main groups. The *first group* of rules appears on the plane of contracts governed by civil and commercial law, indicating where the otherwise advanced and integral contractual mechanism of domestic commercial law needs to be supplemented by specifics relating to the external economy. This could, in theory, take the form of applying separate rules to all aspects of the contracts used in foreign trade transactions, even though the result would be a duplication of numerous rules because domestic contracts would, in several aspects, evidently be governed by the same rules applicable to external contracts. In other words, just as the commercial law is in many respects a duplication, a sort of mutation, of civil law, it would amount to a secondary mutation here – but this time with respect to the law of foreign trade contracts. The law of Western countries was not and is not developing along this path, but legal development was and is complementary to domestic commercial and contract law where this is so required by external economic aspects. Thus, for instance, separate laws were framed and noted cases were adjudicated which served to provide some guidance on how to deal with contractual agreements (cartels) impeding economic competition and involving foreign partners, as well as with export insurance, insurance of international lines of merchant vessels, international shipping contracts, and the type of foreign trade contracts under which seller grants the buyer an exclusive right of sale on a particular product in a particular country. Consequently, in the advanced Western countries, the law of foreign trade contracts is nothing more than the regulation of domestic economic transactions plus the sum of subsidiary norms originating in, and bearing the character of the external economy.

The *other group* of rules relates to the formulation and implementation of the State's external economic policy (control, management) in the province of foreign trade contracts, embracing procedures for authorizing contracts, regulations of contingents, subsidies to encourage, or special taxes and other charges to discourage, contracts and, in part, foreign exchange regulations. All these categories exist and function in the laws of the market economy countries with varying degrees of intensity and in veritable symbiosis with the law of contracts pertaining to the former group. They represent so much weight that at larger universities of the USA, for instance, they constitute a special branch of learning (A.F. Lowenfeld's *Trade Control for Political Ends* takes nearly 1000 pages to sum up the pertinent legal material, devoting only 100 pages to East–West trade).

3. *Hungarian law*, too, has adopted the second solution as outlined above. Law-Decree No. 8 of 1978 on the Application of the Civil Code to External Economic Relations reflects the concept that whenever the governing law is that of Hungary, the pertinent rules of the Civil Code are to be applied, subject, however, to the exceptions prescribed by this Law-Decree. Nevertheless, the exceptions are not great in number. Disregarding contracts for trade representation and customer services, which are extensively covered by the Law-Decree, the exceptions relating to contracts are stated in only 14 articles. Accordingly, the general rules of the Civil Code apply to foreign trade contracts when these are controlled by domestic law. With respect to contracts, the relevant institutions of the Hungarian law of obligations (its general rules and legal material governing the different types of contracts) are to be regarded as constituting the law of foreign trade contracts, with the exceptions which the said Law-Decree ordains to apply under the principle of *lex specialis derogat legi generali* (for more detail, see §65).

Once the Civil Code has been recodified with a full orientation to a market economy, this arrangement is certain to be changed as well, for the provisions of the said Law-Decree were largely necessary for Hungary to offer, in international application, a regulation conforming to international (market economy) standards in place of the other provisions that were still tailored in part to the needs of a planned economy.

And as regards the State's external economic policy and economic management in the domain of contracts, there is no need to emphasize in particular that aspects thereof are also covered by the relevant laws and regulations. The questions regulated in this respect are those discussed earlier in connection with the management of the external economy (§41).

§63. CONTRACTS IN INTERNATIONAL AGREEMENTS: REGULATION OF INTERNATIONAL ECONOMIC COOPERATION BETWEEN ENTERPRISES AND STATES

1. Regulations by domestic laws, no matter how advanced and differentiated, break up the unity of international or world economic processes by compelling

economic actors to fashion economic policies and to mould individual contracts on the assumption that several domestic laws are in control. This naturally injects complexities and difficulties into international transactions. A remedy to this situation is sought by the endeavour of States, particularly in recent decades, to frame a uniform law through international treaties (international legislation, agreements, conventions) to govern specific classes of economic legal relationships.

Like the domestic sources of law, the international ones can be divided into two groups as they *appear on two planes*. On one plane are the agreements or conventions which unify the international contracts of economic subjects. On the other plane we can see the interstate treaties which regulate and coordinate the economic policy conduct of States in order to shape an optimal pattern of the international movement of enterprises (of their contractual relationships).

2. A *uniform legal regulation of enterprise contracts* ranks high in the general economic policy conceptions of the Hungarian State. Just as Hungary has joined, at the state level, all important international economic organizations (see §39), it has participated in the work of codification under way within the frameworks of those organizations and has acceded to most of the major international conventions and other instruments. These instruments of international legislation seeking to establish a uniform law will be discussed in the corresponding sections under this Title (§§64 *et seq.*). At this juncture we will list but the major ones: Vienna Convention (1980) on the International Sale of Goods; *Incoterms* (1953/1980, and lately 1990); standard contracts of ECE and UNIDO; conventions on the carriage of goods by rail (CIM); Brussels Convention (1924) on the Carriage of Goods by Sea; conventions on the carriage of goods by road (CMR, TIR); Warsaw Convention (1929) on the Carriage of Goods by Air; Geneva Conventions on Bills of Exchange (1930) and Cheques (1931); collection of uniform usages compiled by the International Chamber of Commerce concerning letters of credit and encashment (1963); Conventions on Leasing and Factoring (1988); UNIDROIT Principles of International Commercial Contracts (1994).

3. Viewed from the angle of legislative sources, the unification of international law in the field of contracts generally takes the form of an international treaty pertaining to public international law. Nevertheless, the object and content of such treaties relate to this or that type of contractual relationship in the nature of civil law, *but some treaties regulate the conduct of and relationships between States*.

Besides the rules merely of a civil-law nature, as noted earlier, the norms directly formulating the State's external economic policy with regard to contracts are growing in importance. These norms operate together with civil-law regulations, presenting a combined view of contracts in domestic law. Such perception of contracts also appears in international legislation. The State provides a significant international regulation not only of contractual relationships of a civil-law nature between subjects at law, but further concludes a series of international treaties on questions which, while directly bearing upon the relationships and conduct of States as such, are covered with a view to improving the operation of the civil-law plane. This is why we could, and had to speak of a symbiotic coexistence of these two planes in the introductory chapter.

(a) Among the *multilateral conventions*, special mention should be made of the conventions adopted by GATT, WTO, IMF and the World Bank (§39) as well as of the United Nations Charter of Economic Rights and Duties of States (§55) and the Final Act of the Helsinki Conference (§46).

Mindful of their significance, but directing the reader to literature for details (Csanádi, Ernst), we should refer to the so-called *international commodity conventions* (see §39).

(b) The *bilateral agreements* relating to Hungary are rather broad in scope and present a varied picture. At this point we should address the major and most frequent types thereof, while anticipating the following remarks. The types of contracts as outlined here do not always appear in "pure" form, but often converge (e.g. interstate relations where not so intensive and comprehensive, an all-embracing treaty covers nearly all aspects of the subject-matter to be discussed presently. In other cases a particular matter is covered by the whole spectrum of treaties because this is required by the scope and differentiated nature of interstate economic relations). This classification may nevertheless be regarded as warranted by the multitude of such treaties and the peculiarities of the subject-matter covered by them.

(ba) Treaties regulating the comprehensive legal frameworks of trade relations usually take the form of *trade agreements that lay down principles recognized in the field of international cooperation*. Trade agreements lay down principles recognized in international commercial practice, namely those which, as if to provide the static elements of cooperation, States wish to apply in their economic relations (most-favoured-nation treatment, its scope and exceptions to its application, national treatment, preferences – e.g. customs duty concessions – stipulation of reciprocity, endeavours to maintain the balance of trade, exchange of information, non-discrimination, principles of market protection, support for the operation of trade representations, agreement to submit disputes to arbitration, currency of commercial payments, use of world market prices prevailing at any one time, see, e.g., American–Hungarian Trade Agreement as a comprehensive treaty, promulgated by Law-Decree No. 12 of 1978). In some (few) cases, trade agreements are completed with commodity lists enumerating the products which the parties find it desirable to sell or buy in the first place or intend to restrict trade in (quantitative restrictions). In such cases it is the general practice to set up mixed commissions to promote implementation of the agreements and to review the commodity lists periodically. Some trade agreements are combined with elements of *economic cooperation*, as was the case with, e.g., the Agreement on Trade and Economic Cooperation of 1988 and the Agreement on Association of 1991 signed by the European Communities and Hungary (see Chapter XI). They contain, beside the elements of classical trade agreements, aspects of agreements on scientific, industrial, economic and commercial cooperation, and set up mixed commissions as well.

(bb) *Agreements on scientific-technical cooperation* are of great importance, mainly in relations with developing countries. The principal areas covered by them include exchange of advisers and experts, study tours and scholarships, training of academics and practitioners, exchange of scientific and technical data, information, equipment and documentation, establishment of research centres and their equipment with physical facilities, organization of exhibitions and fairs, etc. Some agreements even outline the sectoral centres of scientific cooperation. The agreements on scientific-technical cooperation merely provide a legal framework for programmes of works and protocols which specify all details embraced by the will and programme of the parties concerning the achievement of the goals set forth in the particular agreements.

(bc) *Payments agreements* regulate the modalities of settling liabilities with regard to the parties' enterprises or other organs, nowadays almost without exception in convertible currency.

(bd) *Intergovernmental credit agreements* determine, along general lines, the utilization of government credits secured by States for each other, designate the central state banks responsible for related operations, and fix due dates, conditions of repayment and rates of interest.

(be) *Intergovernmental agreements on cooperation* lead States (governments) on to the dynamics of economic cooperation, quite close to the microsphere. They are of two types by nature.

One type is represented by *general agreements on cooperation* in which States define the general economic and legal frameworks of longer-term intensive cooperation, mark out the desirable areas of enterprise cooperation (industry, agriculture, transfer of technology, etc.), occasionally set up mixed commissions to develop cooperation further, and determine timely concrete aspects of cooperation.

Fortunately the other type – *special agreements on cooperation* (let us call them *treaties of cooperation* by way of distinction) – is relatively rare in Hungary's practice (consider the lessons of the agreements concerning the Tengiz–Yamburg project and the Bős–Nagymaros Dam on the Danube). One of their features lies in the circumstances that they relate to the implementation of a specified, mostly large and complex project. Another feature is that they define the main elements of the undertaking by concrete means of civil-law (commercial) commitments. The third feature consists in a direct linkage with inter-enterprise commitments transcribing the entire cooperative project into foreign trade (civil-law) contracts.

(bf) A special group of bilateral intergovernmental agreements was constituted by the five-year *bilateral goods exchange and prompt payment (clearing) agreements* with the CMEA member-states and the annual *protocols* for the implementation thereof. This has receded into legal history, however [for an in-depth analysis, see Mádl: *A külgazdaság* (The External Economy), §50; Nagy].

(bg) Brief mention should also be made of the essentially *self-restricting contingent agreements* as a type which were formerly concluded by, e.g., Hungary with the EEC concerning steel, textile, goat and mutton. Although the contingents (quantitative restrictions) run counter to the spirit of GATT, such voluntary restraints imposed on the other party were established with respect to the large GATT States (USA, Japan, UK) as well, throwing the cloak of voluntary restraint agreement (VRA) over one of the problems faced by GATT.

(bh) The large number of our bilateral agreements for the *avoidance of double taxation* in recent years is of growing relevance to international economic relations (such agreements were signed with, e.g., Austria, Denmark, FRG, Italy, Japan, Norway, Sweden, Switzerland, Great Britain, USA; see the List of Sources). These agreements represent the interests of economic subjects and nationals of both signatory States and have contributed considerably to removing the obstacles to international commercial and personal transactions and thereby to developing contractual transactions.

(bi) With regard to investments, the same can be said, *mutatis mutandis*, of the bilateral *agreements on investment protection* (see Chapter XVII).

CHAPTER XX

A SUMMARY VIEW OF THE MAJOR TYPES OF FOREIGN TRADE CONTRACTS

§64. THE FOREIGN TRADE CONTRACT AND ITS MAJOR TYPES

In view of their significance for the national economy, Hungary's *foreign trade contracts* are among the most significant among those contracts which belong to the domain of private international law. Decree No. 7/1974. (X. 17.) of the Minister of Foreign Trade enforcing on the Execution of the Foreign Trade Act (Act III of 1974) defines a foreign trade contract as any contract made by a national with a foreigner in the field of economic activity under the control of the Act. Accordingly the concept of "foreign trade contract has" *subjective* and *objective* criteria.

1. From the angle of the *contracting parties*, one of the subjects of a foreign trade contract is always a *national* and the other a *foreigner*. A national or a foreigner is a natural or legal person considered as such *under the foreign exchange regulations*. A *national* is deemed by these regulations to be:

– any natural person who is in possession of a valid identity card (or, in the case of persons under 14 years of age, an identity paper) issued by the competent Hungarian authority or is required by law to possess one (on crossing the border this condition of the holder of a Hungarian passport is to be presumed);

– any undertaking or organization whose seat is in Hungary;

– the owner or the senior officer of an undertaking or organization having its seat in Hungary, any member of its board of supervision and any of its employees in their capacity as such (even though they otherwise qualify as aliens) in respect of their transactions and other legal acts performed on behalf of the undertaking or organization if they establish a right or an obligation for the undertaking or organization;

– the place of business in Hungary of a foreign undertaking or organization, except for its place of business established in Hungary for the purpose of fulfilling a foreign trade contract;

– any foreign representation abroad, and a national's representative in respect of his transactions and other legal acts performed in that capacity (even though he otherwise qualifies as an alien).

A *foreigner* is deemed by the foreign exchange regulations to be

– any natural person who has no valid identity card issued by the competent Hungarian authority or is not required by law to possess one;

– any undertaking or organization (regardless of its legal form) if it has its seat abroad;

– the place of business or any branch abroad of a national's undertaking or organization, except for its place of business established abroad for the purpose of fulfilling a foreign trade contract;

– any foreign diplomatic or consular mission in Hungary, any trade or other representation in Hungary of a foreigner, and a foreigner's representative in respect of his transactions and other legal acts performed in that capacity (even though he otherwise qualifies as a national);

– any free-zone association, any association authorized by the Government in the interest of the national economy and controlled by Art. 85 of the Foreign Exchange Act, and any association meeting the special requirements of the Act on Corporate Tax.

2. The *objective criteria* of foreign trade contracts are expressly stated in the Decree [Sect. 4 (1) and Sect. 7] and the Execution of the Foreign Trade Act, meaning that a contract made by a national with a foreigner is deemed to be a foreign trade contract only if it relates to any one of the objects enumerated in the Decree.

A large group of foreign trade contracts has the object or economic function of transmitting commodities (rights involving a material value) or services through the channels of foreign trade. Contracts of *sale*, contracts of *locatio conductio operis* (assembly and other contractor's contracts), *licence*, contracts for *specialization*, and contracts for the *establishment of foreign enterprises* (acquisition, transfer, operation, etc. of such foreign interests) are the *most important* instances (see Chapter XXIII). Very often these contracts are coupled with *subsidiary* ones like contracts of representation or agency, agreements on market organization, contracts for promotion and advertising, contracts of carriage and of forwarding, contracts of storage, insurance contracts, etc., with the basic transactions including in each case various payment agreements (modalities of payment) (see Chapter XXIV). All these subsidiary contracts are in addition naturally deemed to be foreign trade contracts.

3. As for the form of foreign trade contracts, the law [Decree No. 7/1974. (X.17) of the Minister of Foreign Trade, Sect. 6] requires them to be *in writing*. Agreements through exchange of correspondence, telegrammes and telegraphic (telex) communications are to be regarded as contracts in writing as well. Where permitted by business usage, or where the nature of the commodity or some other special factor makes conclusion of a contract so urgent as to leave no time for exchange of telegrammes or telegraphic communications, a contract

may be made via telephone, but the agreement thus reached must be put into writing without delay: failure to put a contract into writing however does not affect its validity. This latter possibility is construed rather broadly by the most recent judicial practice. In one of its judgments (Gf.VI 32 706/1992, BH 1994/4, 208) the Supreme Court went so far as to state that the laws and regulations on foreign trade transactions prescribe no compulsory written form as a condition of validity, except formalizing them in writing. This evidently served for an authentic documentation of such transactions and to facilitate evidence. Accordingly, the very fact that the defendant is unable to produce a written declaration of acceptance concerning a contractual offer communicated in writing has no other effect than that of the defendant bearing the consequences, under the rules of the *onus probandi*, of the incertitude of his contention as against the other data presented. Moreover, this led the Supreme Court to draw the generalized conclusion that "failure to put a foreign trade contract into writing does not affect the validity of the contract". On the other hand, it is not reassuring that another Division of the Supreme Court appears to make validity subject to written form (Legf.B. Pf. VI.22 892–1993, BH 1996/11, 594).

§65. SPECIAL RULES OF HUNGARIAN CIVIL LAW ON FOREIGN TRADE CONTRACTS

1. If an international treaty, the agreement of the parties, or the applicable (conflict) rule of private international law places a foreign trade contract under the control of Hungarian civil law, the application of the *Civil Code* is subject to certain *exceptions* as determined by Law-Decree No. 8 of 1978 on the Application of the Civil Code to External Economic Relations. The most important special rules (Sections 4 to 18 of the Law-Decree) will be summed up below.

2. In respect to the *conclusion* and *validity* of contracts, they are the following:

– in the field of external economic relations the obligation to make a contract may not be prescribed by law even in exceptional cases;

– in the field of foreign trade contracts departure from the dispositive rules of the Civil Code may be based not only on agreement between the parties [Art. 200, para. (1) of the Civil Code], but also on international agreement or regulations;

– a preliminary contract, an agreement to agree (Art. 208 of the Civil Code) must contain the essential conditions of the contract to be concluded. If one of the parties refuses to conclude the envisaged contract, the court (or arbitral tribunal) may, at the request of the other party, order conclusion of the contract if the parties agreed thereto in the "preliminary contract". The "preliminary contract" contains the essential elements of the contract to which the parties agreed in their agreement to agree. But the conclusion may be denied by the interested party if he is able to prove that – owing to a circumstance which occurred after the conclusion of the "preliminary contract" – he is incapable of fulfilling the proposed contract or if, in view of that circumstance cancellation or termination of the contract were in place. In such a case the contract may not be enforced by the court (or arbitral tribunal) either;

– in the field of external economic relations a contract may not be impugned on the ground of a conspicuously great difference in value between performance and counterperformance [Art. 201, para. (2) of the Civil Code];

– the guarantees offered by the Civil Code (Art. 20) against misuse of the general conditions of contract are not applicable in the field of external economic relations.

3. With respect to the *fulfillment* of contracts, emphasis should be laid on the special rule under which, in case of a money debt being repaid before the due date or before the beginning of the due date, interest or compensation may be stipulated for the period between actual payment and expiry.

4. *Breach* of contract is subject to the following main exceptions:

– claims for damages in excess of the agreed penalty [Art. 246, para. (2) of the Civil Code) may not be enforced;

– in case of warranty (Art. 248 of the Civil Code) the obligor may be relieved of liability for damages upon proof of non-culpability;

– in external economic relations guarantee rights may be enforced, as against the time-limit fixed by Art. 308, paras. (1) and (2) of the Civil Code, within a six-month limitation period and, in cases where the limitation period is not running, within one year of the date of performance, the expiry of this period extinguishing all rights;

– the parties may restrict or exclude liability for breach of contract (Art. 314 of the Civil Code);

– by way of compensation the defaulting party is liable to pay for the damage [Art. 355, para. (4) of the Civil Code] which he caused directly by his conduct and which at the time of making the contract he could foresee as a possible consequence of a breach of contract;

– as an exception to the general rule contained in Art. 318 of the Civil Code, damages in external economic relations are amenable to reduction by the court (arbitral tribunal);

– the limitation period [Art. 327, para. (1) of the Civil Code] in respect of foreign trade contracts is not interrupted by written notice to satisfy a claim.

5. In connection with the reasons for the special provisions briefly described, it should be noted that in external economic transactions it appears advisable not to apply, so far as possible, those rules which are considerably different from or are unknown to the relevant provisions of most foreign laws. Such non-application would thereby save foreign partners from sudden or unpleasant surprises in case of applying the Hungarian law, as well as avoiding the equally undesirable situation that application of the Hungarian law grants foreign partners such advantages (e.g. exclusion or restriction of liability under Art. 314 of the Civil Code) which foreign laws generally do not confer on them.

CHAPTER XXI

INTERNATIONAL HARMONIZATION OF THE SUBSTANTIVE LAWS OF CONTRACT

§66. STANDARD CONTRACTS. INTERNATIONAL COMMERCIAL USAGES; *INCOTERMS* 1990

The Babel-like disparities of national laws perhaps raise most of the difficulties in international commercial transactions. It is therefore understandable that since ancient times merchants have been striving for an international uniformity of *standards* and *usages*.

1. *Standard contracts* (blankets, general conditions of contract, etc.) are also frequently used in the international field, especially in the *sale* of goods. The extensive use of standard contracts in international commercial transactions is motivated by the same factors as in the domestic field, such as the massive and recurrent flow of identical or similar products under identical or largely similar contractual terms.

As regards their origin, standard contracts are either contractual terms (blankets) formulated by large enterprises or general conditions elaborated at international fora. The latter are accepted by enterprises, employing them, perhaps with some modifications, in their business dealings. Products of such "private codification" are, for example, the UNIDO terms of contract (see §39) and the general conditions established under the auspices of the United Nations Economic Commission for Europe (e.g. General Conditions of Sale for the Import and Export of Durable Consumer Goods and Other Engineering Stock, Article No. 730 or General Conditions for Supply and Erection of Plant and Machinery for Import and Export No. 574A).

The sociological and legal problems concerning standard contracts used in the international arena are identical or largely similar to those of standard contracts in the domestic field: standard contracts of international sale likewise leave room for an economically stronger partner (perhaps even enjoying a monopolistic position) to take an *unfair* advantage of its economic superiority. Therefore, among the legal issues of interest here, the greatest importance is attached to legal protection against misuse of such contracts.

Related problems have grown more numerous during the past decades, and recent legislation has devised measures in the law of international sale to provide protection against such misuse. Thus, for instance, the law of the Federal Republic of Germany on the general conditions of business (the *AGB-Gesetz* of 9. 12. 1976, which entered into force in 1977 and is naturally concerned chiefly with the domestic aspects of the problem) contains special provisions for the use of standard contracts in international transactions and extends the protection of the law, under specified conditions, even to international transactions controlled by a foreign law (Art. 12). It was by refining these provisions that the FRG's new Code of PIL (1986) devised general guarantees of conflicts law in respect of consumer contracts (Art. 29).

2. Commercial practice, primarily with respect to sales transactions has evolved a special form of standardizing the conditions of contract. During the practice of many decades, the established terms of contract used recurrently over time on a mass scale came to be formulated and generalized in commercial transactions, became *usages* (usances) which, being commonly known, even lent themselves to abbreviation and were reduced to a few words or marked with a few letters.

Usages are short forms of expressing the substantive elements of a given type of sales contract which are of legal relevance: defrayment of freight charges and other expenses, transfer of ownership, transfer of risk, the main rights and obligations of the parties in general.

Commercial usages are of special significance in international transactions and have long been employed in *international trade,* rapidly operating and laying great emphasis on a clear regulation of the legal relationships involved.

While of great utility, commercial usages have often led to problems rooted in the fact that their essential contents, though commonly known in general, accepted and clearly interpreted, are not infrequently vague on matters of detail and some of their definitions lend themselves to interpretations varying from country to country. It is thus understandable that the different commercial associations have long sought, first at national and then at international level, to achieve full clarification of the international usages in order to ensure uniform interpretation of their contents.

Most important to the unification of commercial usages are *Incoterms* (International Commercial Terms), a collection of usages compiled by the International Chamber of Commerce (ICC) based in Paris.

In addition, the ICC has made various collections (first in 1923 and for the last time in 1953) of Trade Terms used in some countries, mostly at major ports, and published them under that title. (The compilation of 1953, for instance, contains the usages of 18 countries, which differ even on essential aspects, in connection with 10 contractual clauses.)

3. *Incoterms*, which had taken on special importance in international trade, were first published in 1936 and updated in 1953 by the ICC, which later (in 1967, 1976 and 1980) added new usages to the nine included in *Incoterms* of

1953. In 1990, drawing upon practical experience, ICC published *Incoterms* 1990, a revised version of *Incoterms*, which became operative on 1 July 1990. Periodic revisions (as that of 1990) are called for by the development of commercial techniques. For instance, in 1936 (when *Incoterms* were first published), carriage of goods was marked by the predominance of maritime and river navigation and that fact was also expressed by usages. In the course of more than half a century which has since passed, notable ground was gained by other means of carriage (by rail, road, air) which came to be reflected in the usages as well. Again, the revision of 1990 was required primarily by the use of new means of transport (particularly containers), the widening use of combined means of transport, and the spread of exchange of electronic data in international trade.

Incoterms of 1990 changed the earlier structural arrangements as well, with usages in parallel enumerating the obligations of seller and buyer and thereby increasing the ease of review. Compared to the version of 1980, the usages themselves did not change except that *Incoterms* of 1990 do not contain FOB Airport and FOR (FOT), but include the new DDU clause. The compilation of 1990 contains *13 leading terms* at present.

As has been mentioned above, *Incoterms* are an official compilation of the most important usages in international trade. Their application has been repeatedly and strongly recommended by the ICC. Indeed, these terms are actually used with increasing frequency. (For the unabridged Hungarian edition of the 1990 text of *Incoterms*, see the List of Sources.)

Of course, *Incoterms* are not of a normative character, and their validity, like that of any other condition of contract, depends on the contractual agreement of the parties. The contracting parties may even depart, if they so choose, from a particular term and employ in their contract a different set of rules. Any reference in the contract to a given term should also indicate whether the term is to be understood in accordance with the text of *Incoterms* (e.g. "CIF *Incoterms* 1990"). This is warranted by the fact that precisely the most frequent and most important usages have different meanings in other compilations (e.g. the Trade Terms cited above).

Ordinarily *Incoterms* provide guidance on the following essential aspects:

– obligation of seller to make delivery and obligation of buyer to effect payment;

– obtaining export and import licences (and complying with other administrative formalities);

– conclusion of the contract of carriage and the insurance contract;

– place of making and taking delivery;

– geographical point of the transfer of risk;

– division of costs between seller and buyer;

– mutual obligation to give notice of making and taking delivery;

– obligation to hand over the document of making delivery and the freight bill (or an equivalent electronic communication);

– seller's obligation to check on quality (packing) and buyer's obligation to control quality.

Some usages may include additional obligations. It should be stressed that *Incoterms* do not cover questions concerning transfer of title.

The legal arrangements furnished under these terms for the above questions are called *freight terms*. From the legal point of view, primary importance is attached to *defrayment of costs* and to *transfer of risk*. The said usages are formulated in English and abbreviated in capital letters.

Of *Incoterms* 1990, 6 are applicable in maritime and river navigation (FAS, FOB, CFR, CIF, DES, DEQ) and the additional 7 terms (EXW, FCA, CPT, CIP, DAF, DDU, DDP) may be employed in all (including combined) forms of transport.

(a) *EXW*: seller places the goods at buyer's disposal at the site of his own establishment, plant, etc.; buyer bears all costs of transport and (once delivery has been made) all risks, and obtains all licences. (Risks also pass to buyer in cases where he fails to indicate in due course the place of taking delivery and seller sets apart the object of the contract.)

(b) The so-called *F-clauses* (FCA, FAS, FOB) present the common feature that performance is effected by delivery to carrier. (In this sense, forwarder is also deemed to be carrier.) Risks pass from seller to buyer at this point of time. In the case of these clauses, freight charges are to be borne by buyer.

Where FAS is stipulated, buyer is to obtain all licences, but in the case of FCA and FOB this obligation is divided: seller is to obtain export licences and to make other administrative arrangements, while buyer is to obtain import licences and to comply with other formalities (customs clearance, etc.), with the related expenses incurred to be defrayed by seller and buyer accordingly.

Under the FCA clause, goods are effectively delivered into the custody of carrier on the premises or at the place named in the contract (e.g. a railway terminal), whereas in the case of FAS seller is to deliver the goods "alongside the vessel" named and, under the FOB clause, "on board the vessel" named. These points indicate the line of division between freight charges to be borne by the contracting parties and also the place of transfer of risks (which, in the case of FOB, is the point where the goods pass the ship's rail at the port of shipment).

(c) The feature common to the *C-clauses* (CFR, CIF, CPT, CIP) is in seller defraying freight charges and buyer bearing the risks from the time of delivery into the custody of carrier. In addition, seller is to obtain export documents and buyer is to comply with import formalities (as in the case of FCA and FOB).

Where CIF and CIP are stipulated, insurance of goods during carriage is also the obligation of seller.

(d) The *D-clauses* (DAF, DES, DEQ, DDU, DDP) all imply seller's obligation to bear all costs and risks until arrival of goods at the point of destination named in the contract. (Thus, since seller must deliver the goods to buyer at his own cost and risk, the D-clauses are also called "arrival" terms.)

In the case of DEQ and DDP, seller is to comply with both export and import formalities, whereas in the case of DAF, DES and DDU the related obligations are divided: seller is to comply with export formalities and buyer with import formalities. Compliance with administrative (e.g. customs) formalities in an intermediate (third) country is seller's obligation in the case of all D-clauses.

As can be seen, the EXW-clause is the least burdensome, while DEQ and DDP are the most burdensome for seller. The situation mentioned in respect of EXW may occur in the case of other *Incoterms* (i.e. the F-, G- and D-clauses) as well: by setting apart the goods seller may transfer risks to buyer if the latter failed to name the time and place of taking delivery.

§67. EFFORTS AT THE UNIFICATION OF THE INTERNATIONAL LAW OF CONTRACT

In the 20th century the harmonization of the national laws of contract has likewise been facilitated by intensified efforts at the unification of law (cf. Reinhart, in: Encyclopedia of Public International Law, 8, pp. 463 *et seq.* For the problematical aspects and financial implications of the unification of law, see Behrens, Kötz, *RabelsZ* and Puttfarken in the List of Sources). Special mention is deserved mainly of three "workshops for unification of law": the Hague Conference on Private International Law, the UNIDROIT Institute based in Rome, and UNCITRAL, a United Nations organ based in Vienna. The first is chiefly concerned with the unification of conflicts laws, while the latter two are engaged in the harmonization of the substantive laws of contract.

1. The *unification of the law of conflicts* has the advantage that any forum dealing with a particular matter will apply the same law of conflicts. Therefore, determination of the substantive law governing the adjudication of a concrete case will not depend on the proceeding forum (or its conflict rules), because the same (unified) localizer will lead any forum to the same system of law in the particular case.

(a) The conventions elaborated by the *Hague Conference on Private International Law* and adopted by a growing number of States are directed primarily at the unification of conflict rules.

Among the pertinent efforts we underline the significance of the 1955 Convention relating to the Law applicable to the international sale of goods, which embodies a uniform law (*loi uniforme*) incorporated in the laws of the nine State parties, meaning that the State parties apply the uniform law not only in relations *inter se,* but also in determining the law applicable to contracts of sale involving (non-contracting) States which are not a party to the Convention. In 1985 the Hague Conference drafted a new Convention on the law applicable to the international sale of goods, which is intended to replace the Convention of 1955. The updating of that Convention was required mainly by its harmonization with the Vienna Convention on International Sale (see Chapter XXII). The

Diplomatic Conference was attended by numerous countries, including Hungary, but the Convention is not yet in effect for lack of the prescribed number of ratifications.

Further, the Hague Conference on Private International Law registered notable results in other areas of unifying the *international law of civil procedure*, making treaty arrangements for recognition and enforcement of foreign legal acts, and promoting mutual *assistance in private law*. The post-World War Two period has seen the adoption of more than 30 conventions under the auspices of the Hague Conference; Hungary is also a party to some of them. (For an enumeration of the Hague Conventions in force with respect to Hungary, see the List of Sources.)

(b) In the field of the unification of conflicts law – with the increasing importance of *EU* and the prospective growth in the number of its member-states – the *Rome Convention* of 19 June 1980, concluded by the one-time Common Market countries, is becoming of greater relevance to ascertaining the governing law of contractual relationships under the law of obligations. This Convention is a closed international treaty open to accession by the EU member-states only. It entered into force on 1 April 1991 and is in effect at present (1998) for these member-states: Belgium, Denmark, France, FRG, Greece, Ireland, Italy, Luxembourg, Netherlands, Sweden, United Kingdom. Moreover, in several member-states, it replaced the national conflict rules governing contracts (in forms of incorporation differing in their coverage of details), thereby determining the applicable conflicts law with general effect in the said countries (i.e. in respect of private-law contracts affecting non-member-states as well) (see Plender's book in the List of Sources).

2. More ambitious goals are pursued by the efforts at the harmonization of laws directed towards the *unification of substantive law* and by the resultant international conventions.

(a) Special mention is deserved, in view of its more comprehensive nature, by the work of codification going on within the framework of UNIDROIT in order to formulate Principles for International Commercial Contracts, or uniform *model rules* controlling the general problems of commercial contracts. The draft is intended to harmonize the contract rules of both the continental and the common-law legal system in the fields of formation and interpretation of contracts as well as of substantive validity, performance and breach of contract (see Tallon's study in the List of Sources).

(b) Among other efforts at the international unification of the rules on *types of contracts* (cf. Chapter XXIII), mention should be made of the following conventions elaborated under the auspices of UNIDROIT:

– Brussels Convention (1970) on *Contracts of Travel*, which entered into force for some countries as early as 1976;

– Geneva Convention (17 February 1983) on *Agency* in the International Sale of Goods, which is not yet in force (cf. Bonell: Am. Comp. L., 1984, pp. 717 *et seq.*);

– Ottawa Conventions (1988) on *Leasing* and *Factoring*, which have not yet entered into force.

3. The conventions aimed at unifying the *substantive law of international sales* affect the central transactions of international trade and therefore need separate treatment.

(a) The first to be discussed are those of a *regional* nature.

(aa) Among the initiatives for a regional unification of the law of sales, reference should be made, if only for its historical precedence, to the solution found by the *Nordic States* (the Scandinavian countries and Finland), which, though not framing a uniform law to govern the contract of sale in the form of an international convention, formulated their relevant rules of internal (national) law in essentially identical texts as far back as the beginning of the 20th century, thereby practically ruling out (just as they did in their convention of a later date) the possibility of conflicts between national laws in this important area. The Nordic States have upheld their regional uniformity of law even after the adoption of the universal Vienna Convention on International Sale (see Chapter XXII) in the field of regulating international contracts of sale. (They ensured this position by expressing a reservation under Art. 94 of the Vienna Convention. We anticipate at this point that the Nordic States, by making a reservation under Art. 92 of the Vienna Convention, excluded the application of Part II of that Convention concerning the conclusion of contracts of sale both in relations *inter se* and with general effect.)

(ab) Today, among the regional efforts, the agreement of the one-time CMEA member-states on the General Conditions of Delivery (*GCD*) is virtually reduced to a relic of legal history. Both CMEA and GCD are now consigned to the past: the GCD adopted in 1958 (modified on comprehensive lines in 1968 and partially in 1975 and 1979, and again on comprehensive lines in 1988; published in Hungary in the Annex to Law-Decree No. 5 of 1989) lost effect on 1 January 1991. However, in a certain narrow field, GCD may still be applied in the following main respects (see Ujlaki: *Friss Hírek,* 7/93);

– the GCD of 1968/1975 are of mandatory application in their wording of 1979 to legal disputes arising out of foreign trade contracts made before 1 July 1989 unless the contracting parties agreed on the application of the GCD of 1968–1988;

– the GCD of 1968/1988 (with the exception of Chapter XI on payment procedures) are of optional application (e.g. in case of an express agreement between the contracting parties) to contracts of delivery made after 1 January 1991.

(b) Among efforts at a *universal* unification of the *substantive law* of sales, mention should be made of the *Hague Conventions*, albeit, for lack of acceptance by a sufficient number of States, they have never been of too much practical relevance and, following the entry into force of the Vienna Convention on International Sale (see Chapter XXII) and owing to its wide acceptance, even this limited practical role is on the wane. Yet their conceptual and theoretical influence is outstanding even in the process of their becoming a relic of legal history. For this reason, their basic features are worthy of brief treatment.

In 1964 at The Hague two conventions were adopted on international sale, viz.

– the Convention relating to a Uniform Law on the International Sale of Goods (abbreviated ULIS in English), and

– the Convention relating to a Uniform Law on the Formation of Contracts for the International Sale of Goods (abbreviated ULF in English).

These Conventions have been signed but not ratified by Hungary.

The Hague Conventions were adopted after decades of preparatory work on the basis of four drafts (1935, 1939, 1956, 1963). The rules formulated therein do not constitute a body of norms pieced together from different groups of laws governing sale. Of course, the codifiers drew upon the dogmatic approaches of the major legal systems but, on the whole, they framed an independent uniform law, even incorporating compromises.

The Hague Conventions were prepared *for universal acceptance*, so their scopes of application were defined accordingly. They take the *broad view* of international sale and are also intended for application on a rather broad scale: the court of a State party must apply the rules of the Hague Conventions to international sale covered by them even if neither contracting party is a national of, or has his domicile or seat in, one of the signatory States, nor is such State the place of contracting or performance.

The Hague Conventions evoked highly critical comments for their claim to so wide a scope of application, but their strong thrust towards *simplification* received a more favourable response.

These Conventions effectively and deliberately *ruled out* the possibility of the use of *conflict norms*, thereby accepting, of course, the challenge of certain problems. This means that the court of a signatory State must apply the rules of the Hague Conventions to international sale as defined by them, and must use the conflict norms of its own State only to ascertain the governing law of a sales transaction that is not qualified as international sale, but contains a foreign element.

The Hague Conventions, especially the one relating to a uniform law on the International Sale of Goods, go far to ensure the autonomy of contracting parties by extensive reliance on *permissiveness* and *informality*, and leave no broad scope for subsequent court intervention in the contractual relationship of the parties.

Given the complexity of the problems involved, the Hague Conventions have so far been ratified by only nine, mainly West-European countries, most of them expressing reservations concerning important aspects and allowing room for excluding the application of the Conventions by subjects of sales contracts.

For all these reasons, the Hague Conventions were not nearly sufficient in themselves to solve the problem of unifying the law of international sale. This prompted years-long serious efforts at unification by applying the lessons of experience within the framework of UNCITRAL (United Nations Commission on International Trade Law). That international work of codification was completed by the adoption at Vienna in April 1980 of a new convention, the United Nations Convention on Contracts for the International Sale of Goods (henceforth called the Vienna Convention).

The Vienna Convention (see Chapter XXII) is expected to replace the Hague Conventions in all their aspects, since membership in it is subject to denunciation of the Hague Conventions [paras. (3) to (6) of Art. 99]. [The States that have "switched" from the Hague Conventions to the Vienna Convention (in chronological order: Italy, FRG, Netherlands) have fulfilled this obligation for denunciation by ensuring that the Hague Conventions cease to have effect on the day preceding the entry into force of the Vienna Convention.] Today the Vienna Convention is the most significant legal system governing international sale and is certain to gain wider acceptance.

CHAPTER XXII

THE VIENNA CONVENTION ON THE INTERNATIONAL SALE OF GOODS

§68. CONCLUSION AND PURPOSE OF THE CONVENTION

The 1980 Vienna Convention on the International Sale of Goods, concluded under the auspices of the United Nations (abbreviated *CISG* in English and henceforth called the *Convention* in this Chapter), is intended to give a uniform regulation of problems concerning the law of international sales and hopes for acceptance by as many States as possible. The circumstance (first of all, the international political conditions) under which it was adopted were undoubtedly more favourable than they had been in the case of the Hague Conventions on International Sale. This is evidenced by the very fact that nearly one half of the United Nations member-states were represented at the Vienna Diplomatic Conference and that numerous States immediately signed the Convention.

The ten ratifications (accessions) required for the entry into force of the Convention were nevertheless a relatively long time in coming: as of 1 January 1988 the Convention came into force in respect of 11 States. In 1996, as a result of additional accessions (and owing to the separation of several States and to the clarification of problems concerning State succession), there were 46 States parties to the Convention.

Considering the outstanding practical significance of the Convention, we will list the States parties (indicating in parentheses the date of entry into force for each State): Argentina (1 January 1988), Australia (1 April 1989), Austria (1 January 1989), Bosnia and Herzegovina (6 March 1992; formerly as part of Yugoslavia: 1 January 1988), Bulgaria (1 August 1991), Belarus (1 November 1990), Canada (1 May 1992; Federal State of Yukon: 1 January 1993), Croatia (according to reliable information: 1991; formerly as part of Yugoslavia: 1 January 1988), Cuba (1 December 1995), Chile (1 March 1991), People's Republic of China (1 January 1988), Czech Republic (1 January 1993; formerly as part of Czechoslovakia: 1 April 1991), Denmark (1 March 1990; the Convention is not in force for the Faroe Islands and Greenland), Ecuador (1 February

1993), Egypt (1 January 1988), Estonia (1 October 1994; formerly as part of the Soviet Union: from 1 September 1991 on its attaining independence), Finland (1 January 1989), France (1 January 1988), Georgia (1 September 1995), Germany, Federal Republic of (1 January 1991), Guinea (1 February 1992), Hungary (1 January 1988), Iraq (1 April 1991), Italy (1 January 1988), Lesotho (1 January 1988), Lithuania (1 February 1996), Mexico (1 January 1989), Moldova, Republic of (1 November 1995), Netherlands (1 January 1992), New Zealand (1 October 1995; the Convention is not in force for some smaller islands), Norway (1 August 1989), Poland (1 June 1996), Romania (1 June 1992), Russia (1 September 1991; formerly taking the place of the Soviet Union: 24 December 1991), Singapore (1 March 1996), Slovakia, Republic of (1 January 1993; formerly as part of Czechoslovakia: 1 April 1991), Slovenia (25 June 1991; formerly as part of Yugoslavia: 1 January 1988), Spain (1 August 1991), Sweden (1 January 1989), Switzerland (1 March 1991), Syria (1 January 1988), Uganda (1 Mach 1993), Ukraine (1 February 1991), USA (1 January 1988), Yugoslavia (1 January 1988), and Zambia (1 January 1988).

For the former German Democratic Republic, the Convention was in force between 1 March 1990 and 2 October 1990. (Its operation in the territory of the former GDR between 3 October and 31 December 1990 was a disputed contingency, but we believe the view excluding that possibility is the correct one; cf. Magnus, *ZEuP* in the List of Sources. For problems of operation associated with the succession of States, see also Karollus in the List of Sources.)

The Convention (unlike the Hague Conventions on International Sale; see Chapter XXI) has consolidated the provisions concerning the formation and substantive incidents of contracts of sale (rights and obligations of the parties, passing, of risk), breach of contract and its consequences. At the same time, any acceding State may declare, by way of *reservation* (Art. 92), that it will not be bound by Part II of the Convention on the formation of contract or by Part III on the substantive incidents of sale. The overwhelming majority of the States parties have acceded to the Convention as a whole, while the *Nordic States* (Denmark, Finland, Norway and Sweden) declared that they would not consider themselves bound by Part II on the *formation of contract*.

§69. SCOPE OF APPLICATION OF THE CONVENTION

First we will examine the personal and territorial scope of application (item 1 below) and then extend our inquiry to the possibility for the parties to a contract of sale to exclude the application thereto of the Convention either totally or partially (item 2), to the scope of application relating to objects (item 3) and to aspects which the Convention deliberately omitted to cover (items 4 and 5).

1. In respect of the *personal and territorial* scope of application (Art. 1), it is fundamental that the places of business of the parties to a contract of sale should be *in different States*. This phrase merely imparts to a contract of sale an

international character for the purposes of application. (Thus, for instance, questions concerning the different or identical nationality of the parties, the place of contracting and performance, etc. are of no motion.) Since the international character of sale (and hence the application of the Convention) depends on this single circumstance, the Convention demands, in the interest of meeting the requirement of legal certainty, the fact that the places of business are in different States should appear from the contract or from any dealings between, or from information disclosed by, the parties. If a party has more than one place of business (Art. 10), the place of business is that which has the closest relationship to the contract or its performance. If, however, a party does not have a place of business, reference is to be made to his habitual residence. From all this it follows that the Convention may, in principle, be applied even between parties of the same nationality and, in the absence of another foreign element, if the places of business of the subjects of a contract of sale are within different States.

The provisions of the Convention apply in either of two ways to a contract of sale between parties having their places of business in different States:

(a) *autonomously*, i.e. without the agency of conflicts law, if both parties have their respective places of business in States that are Contracting States [States parties to the Convention; para. 1 (a) of Art. 1]. It was on this basis that the Convention was applied by, e.g., the Arbitration Tribunal of the Hungarian Chamber of Commerce and Industry to a legal dispute arising from a contract of sale between a Romanian seller and a Hungarian buyer (Vb./92092). Unfortunately, the Hungarian courts still often forget to apply treaty law (the Convention included). Thus, for instance, the Supreme Court ordered, by reliance on conflict rules, the application of the internal substantive law of the seller's country (notably the rules of the Austrian *ABGB*) to an international sales contract conducted between an Austrian and a Hungarian party (Pf.III.20. 998/1995), disregarding the fact that from 1 January 1989 the Convention had been autonomously applicable to sale between parties having their respective places of business within Austria and Hungary.

The condition of the parties as traders (just as the commercial or private law nature of sales transactions) is irrelevant to the application of the Convention in respect to persons;

(b) *by reliance on conflict rules*, if the places of business of the contracting parties (or the place of business of one of the parties) are not in the territory of a State party, but the conflict rule (*lex obligationis*) of the proceeding forum (which may even happen not to be in a State party) ordains the application of the law of a State party [para. 1 (b) of Art. 1]. Such is the case when the legal system invoked by an objective connecting factor or by choice of law is the law of a State party in which international sales are thus governed by the Convention (rather than by the law of sale under the general civil or commercial law).

(ba) In German judicial practice, for instance, the Convention was regularly applied under *objective* conflict rules to international sales contracts in which the State of the foreign seller was a State party (e.g. in relations between Italy and Germany) at a time (between 1988 and 1991) when the Convention was not yet in force in respect of Germany (cf. Reinhart, *IPRax* 1990, pp. 289 *et seq.*; Magnus, *ZEuP,* in the List of Sources). In several cases (e.g. VB/92205) the Arbitration Tribunal of the Hungarian Chamber of Commerce and Industry acted likewise, applying the Convention as the governing Hungarian law under Art. 25 (a) of the Code [by relying on the *"designating norm"* contained in Art. 1, para. 1 (b), of the Convention] to a contract between a German buyer and a Hungarian seller at the conclusion of which the Convention was already in force in Hungary, but not in the FRG.

Another interesting example of the Convention and conflict rules "working together" is provided by a judgment of the Metropolitan Court of Budapest (12.G.41.471/1991) [see item 2 (b) in §71].

(bb) According to the prevailing view, the Convention also applies in cases where the law of a State party is chosen, for the selected law is, as a rule, the governing law of international sales. A German high court (OLG Düsseldorf 8.1.1993; cf. Magnus, *ZEuP,* in the List of Sources) decided in this sense a legal dispute in which a Turkish seller and a German buyer agreed, by subsequent choice of law during the proceedings, on the application of German law. Thus, in case the law of a State party is chosen, the Convention applies except when the parties, in selecting their law, clearly express their intention to place their contract under the control of a particular national law (e.g. civil code or commercial law), in such a way to exclude the application of the Convention (Art. 6).

(A qualitatively new situation arises in cases where the Convention is chosen to govern their contract of international sale by parties to whose contract the Convention would not apply either autonomously or by virtue of a conflict rule, viz. by parties

– who have their places of business (or one of whom has his place of business) not in a State party and hence the autonomous application of the Convention is out of the question, and

– to whose contract the Convention would not be applicable either by the aid of an objective connecting factor or through choice of law.

The view dominant in legal literature recognizes such applicability of the Convention, but only as the chosen substantive law, meaning that the *jus cogens* rules of the law otherwise applicable to a particular contract cannot be avoided by recourse to the Convention as the selected system of law.)

(bc) Reliance on conflict rules serves markedly to *widen* the scope of the application of the Convention because the Convention may, in principle, apply even if neither State in which the parties have their places of business nor the State of the proceeding forum are parties to the Convention; it is sufficient if the State of the legal system applicable under the law of conflicts is a State party. Nevertheless, the typical case in which the Convention is applied by virtue of conflicts law is that in which one of the contracting parties has his place of business in a State party and the law of the State of that party (seller) will be the applicable law. Ordinarily the application of the Convention is more acceptable even for a contracting party having his place of business in a State other than a State party than a foreign law would be, if only for the reason that the Convention is more readily accessible and easier with which to become acquainted with than the national systems of law are. Another reason for applying the Convention by reliance on conflicts law lies in the fact that the rules of the Convention are explicitly tailored to international sales.

All these considerations notwithstanding, most of the States participating in the Vienna Diplomatic Conference deemed it necessary to block the way of conflicts law leading to the application of the Convention. This majority will be embodied in Art. 95 permitting any State party to declare, by way of *reservation*, that it will not accept the applicability of the Convention pursuant to the law of conflicts. Reservations to that effect have so far been made by five States (Czech Republic, China, Singapore, Slovakia, USA). (Canada had originally expressed a partial reservation, in respect of British Columbia, but withdrew it with effect from 1 February 1993.) Exclusion by reservation of the application of the Convention pursuant to conflicts law often makes it difficult in practice to establish the applicability of the Convention (see Vékás, *IPRax,* in the List of Sources). [It is in the interest of avoiding some of these difficulties that, for instance, the German Act incorporating the Convention (5 August 1989) spells out that if the Convention happens to apply as part of the law of a State having made a reservation, the conflicts-law way of applying the Convention will not be followed by German courts either, although Germany did not make a reservation to that effect under Art. 95 (cf. Schlechtriem, in: v. Caemmerer–Schlechtriem, in the List of Sources; Art. 2. VertragsG Rn.1.).]

2. The possibility of establishing the Convention's territorial and personal scope of application does not always mean the requirement of actual application as the Convention *may be excluded* by the contracting parties even in case of its applicability.

(a) The Convention is guided by the principle of party autonomy and therefore declares the *permissive* nature of its provisions [allowing derogation from them if the parties agree thereto] (Art. 6). This means that the parties

– may by agreement exclude application entirely ("opting-out"), or,

– may by agreement derogate from *certain provisions*. Derogation (subject to the relevant *jus cogens* rules) may, in a given case, form part of the general conditions of contract as well. [Pursuant to the reservation expressed by Hungary under Art. 96, the rules prescribing written form (Art. 12; cf. §70) are in the nature of *jus cogens* permitting no derogation by Hungarian contracting parties.]

(b) The Convention may be excluded in its entirety first of all by a common and *express declaration* of the parties to that effect.

In general, this is also the case when the parties, exercising their right to choose a law, designate a national law to be applied. However, a special problem arises when the Convention is part of the selected law as well. The question is one of whether the choice of law means implied exclusion of the Convention (and selection of the internal substantive law invoked) or the Convention is still to apply as part of the chosen law. According to the view generally held especially in German legal literature, choice of law usually cannot be conceived of as an exclusion of the Convention, because in such cases the rules of the chosen legal system applicable to international sale are constituted by the provisions of the Convention. Under that approach, the Convention can ordinarily be regarded as excluded by choice of law only if the parties expressly refer to a specific national rule of the legal system they wish to apply (e.g. to the relevant provisions of its civil code), whereas selection of the law of a State party, which is subject to no particular restriction, ordinarily leads to the application of the Convention (cf. Schlechtriem, 1996, in the List of Sources). Weighty arguments are also advanced by exponents of the opposite view: it is contrary to the purpose of the right to choose a law as recognized by the Convention, if within the framework of the selected law the transaction of the parties still comes under the control of the Convention (cf. Kramer, *Juristische Blätter*, in the List of Sources). It should therefore be stressed that a convincing position can only be taken by interpreting each concrete stipulation of the contract (e.g. stipulation of choice of law). (On legal disputes decided by the Arbitration Tribunal of the Hungarian Chamber of Commerce and Industry, see Harmathy: *Friss Hírek*, 4/91; cf. Vékás: *Magyar jog*, 5/1987.)

(c) The view prevailing in legal literature also deems it possible for the application of the Convention to be excluded *by implication*, subject to the only requirement for the common will of the parties to be safely ascertainable in that case as well. Similarly, according to the dominant view of literature (see Schlechtriem, 1996, in the List of Sources), stipulation by the parties of a national arbitration court or application by them of a general condition of contract linked to a national law, etc. cannot be regarded as exclusion of the Convention without further consideration. This statement may further be deemed to hold also for other cases of implied exclusion (e.g. stipulation of exclusive jurisdiction).

(d) The existing practice concerning the Convention shows that the parties make little use of their right recognized by Art. 6. Cases are frequent in which the Convention is excluded particularly by firms with considerable practice in foreign trade (cf. Best–Winsconsin in the List of Sources). [This is evidenced by, e.g., the vast majority of cases involving international sale and adjudicated by the ICC Court of Arbitration (Paris) (with an exception provided by Award No. 7153/1992, Clunet 1992, p. 1005; cf. Magnus, *ZEuP,* in the List of Sources).] In like manner, German enterprises frequently exclude the application of the Convention, mainly in an endeavour to avoid complications around Art. 25, which leaves wide scope for interpretation by the courts in connection with a "fundamental breach" (see §74; cf. Vida, *Jogtudományi Közlöny*, 1993).

3. As regards scope of application relating to *objects*, the Convention applies to the international sale of *goods* (in our view, to chattels).

Foreign judicial practice has so far considered machinery, motor vehicles, food, shoes, textiles, steel, etc. to be goods (and hence to be under the control of the Convention) (cf. Schlechtriem, 1996, p. 19). The Metropolitan Court (3.G.50.289/1991) regarded aircraft engines as goods (Decision upheld by Supreme Court Ruling, *Legf. Bír.* Gf. I.31 349/1992). The Arbitration Tribunal of the Hungarian Chamber of Commerce and Industry (Vb./92205; Vb./1993.XII.20.: Vida, *IPRax* 1995, p. 52) correctly held that the Convention was not applicable to transfer of business shares in a limited liability company.

Under Art. 2, the Convention *does not apply* to consumer sales, chiefly in order to leave scope for the application of increasingly frequent special devices for consumer protection provided for in national legislation. Moreover, the Convention does not apply to sales by auction and on execution, to sales of stocks, shares, investment securities or money, to sales of ships, vessels, aircraft and electricity. These exceptions are warranted by the peculiarities of handling sales transactions or of the objects of sale.

The scope of application relating to objects is extended by the provision (Art. 3) under which contracts for the supply of goods to be manufactured (i.e. practically transactions combining elements of undertaking and sales contracts) are likewise treated as contracts of sale (thus, for instance, in Decisions OLG Frankfurt 17.9.1991, NJW 1992, 633; ICC Paris 7153/1992, Clunet, 1992, p. 1005; cf. Magnus, *ZEuP,* in the List of Sources) unless the party who orders the goods undertakes to supply a substantial part of the materials necessary for such manufacture or production. (The Convention is also generally inapplicable to contracts of sale mixed with undertakings in which the preponderant part of the obligation of the party who furnishes the goods consists in the supply of labour or other services.)

Legal literature is in favour of applying the Convention to international *barter deals* (barter agreements), referring by way of argument to the special difficulties in finding the applicable law by reliance on conflicts law (difficulties that are increasingly encountered in the case of barter) as well as to contracts of barter having features akin to sales. In our view, legal arguments in favour of such extensive application can be adduced, without cause for concern, mainly if the rules of the Convention are chosen by the parties. Failing express choice of substantive law, however, we think that the conditions for analogous application are rather difficult to meet (cf. Lurger, *ZfRV* 6/1991, pp. 415–431).

4. The Convention does not cover the whole set of legal problems concerning contracts of international sale. Its rules extend basically to the *formation of contract and* to the *rights and obligations of the parties*. Foreign judicial practice has so far tended for the most part towards an extensive interpretation. Thus, for instance, a German judgment (LG Hamburg 26.9.1990, *IPRax* 1991, 400) deemed the Convention also to be applicable to an agreement on postponed payment of the purchase price. True, another German judgment (AG

Frankfurt 31.1.1991, *IPRax* 1991, 345) stated that set-off was not, as we similarly hold it not to be, a point of law under the control of the Convention.

(a) On the other hand, the Convention is admittedly *not concerned* with problems relating to the *invalidity of contract* and the *transfer of title* (Art. 4), which consequently remain to be judged under the substantive law rules indicated by the law of conflicts. (All we can do on this point is refer to the fact that several partial matters concerning the invalidity of contract can also be deemed to amount to breach of contract, e.g. a problem of warranty ensuing from invalidity on grounds of error, and as such they can be judged by the rules of the Convention.) Similarly, the validity of business usages employed in contracts of sale are to be judged under the substantive law rules selected by the aid of conflicts law.

(b) The Convention explicitly excludes its own application to seller's liability for death or personal injury caused by the goods to any person. This opens the way to application of the *product liability* rules of the governing national law (or a pertinent international convention), at least to liability for damage to life, physical integrity and health. In other words, the Convention applies only to liability for damage caused to things by a defective product (Art. 5).

5. In view of its importance, we make special mention of the fact that the problems of *prescription* similarly remain outside the scope of the Convention. Therefore, just as other unregulated matters, these problems are subject to the substantive law rules of the applicable national law indicated by the *lex fori* of conflicts law.

It is to be noted, however, that mindful of the significance of related problems, UNCITRAL has framed an international convention on the period of prescription applicable to international sales, notably the New York Convention of 1974, which in 1980 was brought into line (by a Protocol signed at Vienna) with the Vienna Convention. The New York Convention as amended by the *Vienna Protocol* entered into force on 1 August 1988, and it was promulgated and incorporated into the Hungarian law with effect from that date by Law-Decree No. 1 of 1989.

Parties to the New York Convention on prescription, with its modified text of 1980, are the following States (from 1 August 1988 unless a different date is indicated in parentheses): Argentina, Czech Republic (1 January 1993; formerly as part of Czechoslovakia to the original text: 1 August 1988 and to the modified text except for Art. 3 (1), instead of which the original Art. 3 invariably applies: 10 October 1990), Egypt, Guinea (1 August 1991), Hungary, Mexico, Romania (1 November 1992), Republic of Slovakia (1 January 1993; formerly as part of Czechoslovakia to the original New York text: 1 August 1988 and to the modified text except for Art. 3 (1), instead of which the original Art. 3 invariably applies: 10 October 1990), Uganda (1 November 1992), Ukraine (13 September 1993), USA (except for Art. 3 (1), instead of which the original Art. 3 invariably applies: 1 December 1994), Zambia.

Also parties to the New York Convention on prescription (but only to its original text of 1974) are (from 1 August 1988 unless a different date is indicated in parentheses) Bosnia and Herzegovina (6 March 1992; formerly as part of Yugoslavia: 1 August 1988), Dominican Republic, Ghana, Norway (but, by expressing a reservation under Art. 34, it excluded the application of the New York Convention on prescription, just as that of the Vienna Convention, to transactions in which the contracting parties have their places of business in Denmark, Finland, Iceland and Sweden), Yugoslavia.

The New York Convention as amended by the Protocol was, just as the Vienna Convention, in effect for the one-time GDR between 1 March and 2 October 1990, but its continued applicability in the former GDR after the unification of the two German States (3 October 1990) is an issue in dispute. We hold that the view excluding that possibility is the correct one (cf. Magnus, *ZEuP,* in the List of Sources).

(a) According to its original text, the New York Convention applies only to contracts of international sale in which both parties have their respective places of business in different *State parties* (Art. 3). Moreover, in keeping with the principles governing the application for the Vienna Convention, the amendment of 1980 opens the way to the application of the New York Convention by reliance on *conflict rules* as well: the New York Convention as amended applies to contracting parties having their respective places of business in different States even if the States of the contracting parties are not State parties (or the State of one of the contracting parties is not a State party), but the rules of private international law (designated by objective connection or by choice of law) lead to the application of the law of a State party to the New York Convention as amended. This recourse to private international law widens the scope of application of the New York Convention. The possibility of application by reliance on private international law may be excluded by any State expressing a *reservation* to that effect. To date, as was indicated in the above enumeration of States, such reservations have been made by the USA and Czechoslovakia (with the validity of the reservation also accepted by its successor States).

The contracting parties *may exclude* the application of the New York Convention, but the declaration of exclusion must be "express", which is to say that implied exclusion is not recognized by the Convention (Art. 3).

(b) The New York Convention establishes a single *four-year* period of prescription in the nature of *jus cogens* in respect of all claims (purchase price, faulty performance, etc.) which arise from a contract of sale and for the enforcement of which the Vienna Convention itself establishes no separate time-limit (Art. 8). However, this relatively long period of prescription is also applicable to enforcement of warranty rights emanating from faulty performance (naturally subject to observance of the separate time-limit fixed by Art. 39 for giving notice to the seller).

The period of prescription starts running from the due date of claim (from the time of breach of contract in case of claims arising from the breach: Arts. 9–10).

§70. GENERAL RULES

1. The Convention itself seeks to give rules for *interpreting* its provisions and filling emerging *gaps* (Art. 7).

(a) It is commonly known that the greatest danger to the uniform law created by international convention is posed by eventually differing in interpretation by practices of courts in the State parties. In the absence of a single high court, the Convention itself cannot provide for national courts a guide to maintaining the uniformity of law except by laying down maxims of interpretation. Such maxims usually focus on emphasizing the international character of the rules and formulating the requirement of maintaining the unity of the law.

These same principles are relied upon by the Convention to govern *interpretation*: in the interpretation of its provisions, regard is to be had to the international character thereof and to the need to promote uniformity in their application. These criteria serve primarily to restrain national courts (arbitral tribunals) in their involuntary return to their own domestic law in the application of the Convention, for it is unfortunate to revert to categories of national law even in cases where the notions used by the Convention and a national law show conspicuous similarities. The domestic law is not tailored to the requirements of international sale; such sales transaction should be governed by the Convention as interpreted by its own standards, on the basis of documents preliminary to its adoption, in its own purity rather than in a way permeated with the notion of national laws. Where necessary, reliance may be placed mainly on international usages and collections of usages (e.g. *Incoterms*; see §66) for solving problems of interpretation.

Uniform interpretation can be greatly facilitated in practice by collections of decisions also including judgments of foreign fora. Foreign judgments may be of effective help in interpreting the rules of the Convention without serving directly as precedents: it is indispensable to be familiar with them but it is not mandatory to follow their solutions. Legal literature (foreign legal literature in given cases) may likewise play as significant role as foreign judgments do in forming a correct and uniform interpretation of the rules of the Convention. Observance of good faith is a leading maxim of the entire Convention, so reliance on it as a principle of interpretation follows from the very spirit of the Convention.

If we are to appreciate realistically the need to maintain a uniform interpretation of the Convention and to preserve the uniformity of law regarding the Convention, we should be aware that such a practice is bound to take many years to crystallize.

(b) Nor is filling gaps in the practical application of the Convention a less difficult problem to tackle. (It is not accidental that the question of gaps was the subject of heated debates in the course of framing the Convention.)

The Convention does not seek to invoke a national law by immediate reliance on conflict rules for filling possible *gaps,* nor does it carry matters to extremes (as did the Hague Conventions on International Sale) in allowing gaps to be filled solely and exclusively by applying the general maxims of law that constitute the basis of the uniform law. According to the solution adopted by the Convention, which appears to be a sound middle course, gaps are to be filled primarily in conformity with the general principles on which the Convention is based but, in the absence of such principles, recourse should be had to the law of conflicts and the missing rules of the Convention should be substituted for by the applicable national system of law as indicated by the relevant conflict norms. So the judge should do all he can to fill the gap in the Convention with its own principles, thereby preserving the integrity of the Convention, but if the general principles of law on which the Convention is based do not give sufficient guidance, the lacuna is to be filled by the aid of the rules of the given national system of law as indicated by the law of conflicts.

A decisive preliminary question concerns what should be regarded as a gap within the sphere of the Convention. In certain cases in which the Convention spells out its own position this question is relatively easy to answer. If, for instance, transfer of ownership is not regulated by the Convention, as was pointed out earlier, the related matters cannot even be regarded as a gap falling within the scope of the Convention: they should therefore be appraised *a priori* by reliance on the applicable national system of law determined by the law of conflicts. (Accordingly, such gaps are automatically apparent ones and are not to be filled in by relevant principles of the Convention.) Real gaps are those emerging in respect of matters settled, but not "explicitly covered", by the Convention. Obviously, real problems are presented by borderline cases, by gaps emerging in the borderland between apparent and real gaps. In seeking solutions for such borderline cases one should proceed, in our view, from the fact that, of the several means of legal dogmatics governing one and the same problem (e.g. right to impugn on grounds of error and warranty claim), application of a single one in the Convention places the problem at hand under the control of the Convention, viz. the gap thus arising is to be treated as a real one. (For this set of problems, see Bonell in the List of Sources.)

In filling real gaps conceived in the above sense, use of the following methods is advisable in the order given:

– interpretation (extensive where necessary),
– analogy,
– general principles on which the Convention is based,
– rules of the national law applicable by virtue of conflict rules.

Thus, although within rather wide limits, the Convention keeps under control the means for gap-filling. For instance, a gap may not be filled by using the comparative method (say, by a comparative application of the corresponding provisions of the laws of States parties). (A similar proposal, rather ill-defined despite its demanding nature, had also been made in connection with the Hague Sales Conventions, but the method suggested was not practically employed.) The autonomous methods available for gap-filling (e.g. those based on the provisions and principles of the Convention) take absolute precedence over reliance on conflicts law: subsidiary recourse to the provisions applicable by virtue of conflict rules should necessarily be preceded by the use of autonomous methods. For that matter, the gap-filling role of the national law invoked by the law of conflicts may not go so far as to allow the judge to transfer to the contract of the parties any legal institution not regulated by the Convention (e.g. penalty established by law) from the legal system determined by the rules of private international law. (For a fuller treatment of gap-filling, see Barry, Magnus; Vékás: *Magyar Jog,* XXXIV, in the List of Sources.)

2. The general rule of the Convention on the *interpretation of legal declarations (statements) and other conduct concerning contracts* can be considered to have furnished a successful solution (Art. 8). This provision applies to the interpretation of basic declarations (offer, acceptance) establishing a contract as well as of declarations cancelling or revoking and rejecting an offer. Moreover, the principles formulated in Art. 8 are to be applied to the interpretation of declarations made in the course of performing the contract as well as of those modifying or terminating the contract and indicating the consequences to be drawn from a breach of contract.

[An equal appraisal and treatment of legal declarations and other conducts runs through the Vienna Convention: other conduct has equal effect to express declarations; assent to an offer may also be indicated by performing an act (para. 1 of Art. 18); only the avoidance of a contract is subject to an express declaration (Art. 26).]

A question preliminary to the interpretation of legal declarations (statements) concerns the *language used in a particular declaration.* Certain principles of the Hague Sales Conventions have already crystallized in practice concerning the language in which the validity of a declaration cannot be called into question. The fundamental requirement is that the addressee should be able to understand the declaration. Some orientation in this respect is provided by the fact that, within the framework of an existing legal relationship, the presumption is in favour of the validity of declarations made primarily in the language used previously. A similar principle is that a declaration proposing a new business deal (particularly one not addressed to a trader) can be considered valid without a dispute and without any restriction only if made in the language customarily used in the addressee's place of habitual residence (if another language is used, the risk of failure to understand a declaration is to be borne by the party making the declaration). It may be stated in general that in the case of a written declaration the addressee can be expected to use the services of a translator (particularly if the addressee is a trader), whereas in the case of an oral declaration (not made by a formal notice) the addressee's ability readily to understand the declaration is a requirement of its validity. In case of dispute, one may start from the fact that a substantive declaration in reply suggests understanding of the basic declaration and that the understanding of subsequent declarations made in the language of the basic contract should be presumed. By contrast, the presumption is in favour of the failure to understand a declaration (and hence of its invalidity), if the declaration was made in a language of communication other than that expressly agreed upon by the parties (or made in one entirely uncommon even as a commercial language in the addressee's country).

With regard to the *principles of interpretation* themselves, the Convention does not run into the error of insisting unilaterally on the principle of declaration, but deliberately seeks to avoid a rigidly exclusive application thereof. In the case of interpretation one should proceed from the assumption that the will of the party making the declaration is decisive if it was known, or could not remain unknown, to the other contracting party. In case of dispute the party making the declaration should prove that the other party was really aware of his (the first party's) intention regarding the deal. Acquaintance with the will of the party making the declaration may be supported primarily by negotiations and the documents relating to them, prior dealings (if any) between the parties, commercial usages, and the conduct of the parties after the conclusion of the contract. In other aspects, the criterion for the possibility of understanding the will of the party making the declaration is provided by the standard or faculty of understanding of a person showing reasonable conduct. Further the Convention relies on the criterion of reasonable conduct in cases in which it was impossible to ascertain the will of the party making the declaration. In such cases the statement (other conduct) should be interpreted in the way a person being in a situation similar to that of the addressee and showing reasonable conduct could have understood it in similar circumstances. (The circumstances to be taken into account should include the distinctive features of the given line of business, the country in question, the employed method of making deals, etc.)

Many writers on the subject refer to the Convention's principles of interpretation [discussed in item 3 (1)] as ones helping to interpret transactions. Although the Vienna Convention rejected this approach, we would hardly be correct in stating that in difficult situations, one should not rely on the Convention's principles of interpretation, primarily on its requirement to observe good faith, for the interpretation of legal declarations as well.

It follows from the fundamental principle guiding the interpretation of transactions that a secret reservation of that party (as his will remains unknown to the addressee) is to be disregarded.

3. The (international and national) *commercial usages* stipulated by the parties become incidents of the content of the contract (para. 1 of Art. 9). Commercial usages may also impliedly be made substantive elements of a contract. It follows from the permissive rules of the Convention (Art. 6) that the commercial usages stipulated by the parties (just as the business practices estab-

lished between themselves with regard to documents, invoicing, enforcement of claims, complaints, etc.) take precedence over the application of the Convention, while in cases where commercial usages and direct business practices of the parties differ preference should be given to the Convention.

International commercial usages impliedly stipulated by the parties similarly become substantive elements of a contract (para. 2 of Art. 9). (We stress that only international usages are involved here!) Such usages are instrumental mainly in reasonably facilitating the performance (handling) of the contract. This naturally holds only for usages that fall within the Convention's scope of application relating to objects, provided that a particular usage is also known to (and regularly employed by) the subjects of transaction in a given line of commercial business and that it is or should be known to the subjects of a particular contract as well. (Such usages undoubtedly include *Incoterms* as well as similar commercial usages of smaller branches of business that are widely known and regularly employed in the international sphere.) If commercial usages expressly or implicitly stipulated are in conflict, the former become a part of the contract. It is questionable, however, whether commercial usages implicitly not stipulated take precedence over the permissive rules of the Convention. Failing a clearly established rule, we believe that one may accept the view which, prevailing in the commentaries published to date, argues for giving precedence to commercial usages even over the permissive rules of the Convention.

It may be stated in summary that the Convention recognizes the effect of commercial usages and practices in accordance with their significance in commercial practice, namely

– the parties are bound by any usages to which they have agreed and by any practices which they have established between themselves;

– the parties are considered, unless otherwise agreed, to have impliedly made applicable to their contract a usage of which they knew or ought to have known and which in international trade is widely known to, and regularly employed by, parties to contracts of the type involved in the particular trade concerned. (For this set of problems, see Takáts: *Friss Hírek*, 12/90; Székely: *Friss Hírek*, 1/93; and for the relationship between some Incoterms and the Convention, see Faragó: *Friss Hírek*, 3/93.)

§71. FORMATION AND MODIFICATION OF CONTRACT

1. Under the Convention, as under the Hungarian civil law, a contract is formed by acceptance of the offer (*concurrent declarations of will* by the parties).

(a) A proposal for concluding a contract constitutes an *offer* if

– it is addressed to a specific person, viz. the legal declaration is *addressed* to someone (a proposal other than one addressed to a specific person is to be considered merely as an invitation to treat, not as an offer, unless the contrary is clearly indicated; Art. 14), and

– it is sufficiently definite and indicates the intention of the offeror to be bound in case of acceptance. *For an offer to be sufficiently definite,* it is absolutely necessary to specify clearly the goods and to determine the quantity and the price, if not expressly at least implicitly.

The Supreme Court (Gf.I.31 349/1992) considered that the declaration of an American seller concurrently (alternatively) proposing, without fixing the exact purchase price, the sale of different aircraft engines was not sufficiently definite (and hence was not an offer).

The Convention affords an exceptional possibility in connection with the price: where a contract has been validly concluded but does not expressly or impliedly fix or make provision for determining the price, the parties are considered, in the absence of any indication to the contrary, to have impliedly made reference to the price generally charged, at the time of the conclusion of the contract, for such goods sold under comparable circumstances in the trade concerned (Art. 55).

An offer becomes *effective* when it reaches the offeree. An offer, made but not yet effective (even if it is originally irrevocable), may be withdrawn if the withdrawal reaches the offeree before or at the same time as the offer. (An offer cannot be revoked if it indicates that it is irrevocable, or else it was reasonable for the offeree to rely on the offer as being irrevocable and the offeree has acted in reliance on the offer.) Until a contract is concluded an offer may be revoked if the revocation reaches the offeree before he has dispatched the acceptance. Otherwise the offer is terminated when a rejection reaches the offeror (Arts. 15–17).

(b) An *acceptance* may take the form of a declaration addressed to the offeror or of an indicative attitude (dispatch of the goods or payment of the price). Silence (or inactivity), however, does not in itself amount to acceptance. A court of New York held the opening of a credit by seller to derogate from silence and to be an acceptance of a new offer [Filanto S.p.A. v. Chilewich International Corp., 789 Federal Supplement (F. Suppl.) 1229 (S.D.N.Y. 1992), quoted by Magnus, *ZEuP,* in the List of Sources].

An acceptance of an offer becomes *effective* at the moment the indication of assent reaches the offeror. An acceptance is late (and hence not effective) if the indication of assent does not reach the offeror within the time he has fixed or, if no time is fixed, within a reasonable time (due account being taken of the content of the transaction and the means of communication employed by the offeror). An oral offer is terminated at once unless the circumstances indicated otherwise. A contract results at the moment the assent is indicated by performing an act (such as one relating to the dispatch of the goods or payment of the price) (Arts. 18 and 23).

(c) A reply to an offer which differs therefrom (contains additions, limitations or other modifications) constitutes a *counter-offer* except when the reply differing from the offer in the said aspects does not materially alter the terms of the offer, unless the offerer objects to the discrepancy without undue delay. In such a case the content of the contract is determined jointly by the terms of the offer and the modifications in the acceptance. Additional or different terms in a reply to an offer, relating to the price, payment, quality and quantity of the goods, place and time of delivery, extent of liability or the settlement of disputes are of necessity considered to constitute a counter-offer (Art. 19). A court of New York held that the buyer's stipulation of jurisdiction different from that indicated in the offer, was a declaration of acceptance materially altering the terms of the offer and hence a counter-offer [Filanto S.p.A. v. Chilewich International Corp., 789 Federal Supplement (F. Suppl.) 1229 (S.D.N.Y. 1992), quoted by Magnus, *ZEuP,* in the List of Sources].

(d) The Convention (Art. 20) specifies the manner of computing the *periods of time* fixed for contractual declarations. If an acceptance reaches the offeror with delay, but from the circumstances of the letter of acceptance (or other written communication) it can be stated that, in case of normal transmission, the acceptance would have reached the offeror in due time, the late acceptance is considered effective unless the offeror gives notice without delay to the offeree that he no longer considers his offer to be effective. [The Convention generally allows reliance on legal declarations which, through error in transmission, reach the addressee with delay or do not reach him at all; (Art. 27).] Otherwise a contract results from a late acceptance only if the offeror himself accepts it and, without delay, informs the other party to that effect (Art. 21). An acceptance, too, may be withdrawn if the withdrawal reaches the offeror before or at least at the same time as the acceptance would have become effective (Art. 22).

Any legal declaration or declaration of intention concerning the conclusion of a contract can be considered to have "reached" the addressee when it is made orally to him or delivered by any other means to him personally (Art. 24). (For problems concerning the conclusion of contracts, see Mirk, *Friss Hírek*, 12/91.)

A declaration of avoidance of the contract is only effective if made by notice to the other party (Art. 26).

The parties may by agreement modify or terminate a contract.

2. The Convention formulates the general principle of *"informality"* (Art. 11), i.e., in order to be valid, contracts of sale need not be in writing and are not subject to any other formal requirement. Legal declarations need not be evidenced by writing, and any means of evidence (witnesses, etc.) may be adduced.

(a) The principle of informality applies to *all legal declarations.* A contract of sale may be validly concluded, modified and terminated by the mere agreement of the parties. The possibility of informal modification and termination is specifically expressed in Art. 29 of the Convention, and in principle even in cases where the contract itself was made in writing. Modification and termination need to be in written form only if so required by a contract in writing (Art. 29). The principle of informality naturally applies even if the national law applicable under the law of conflicts subjects contracts of sale to some formal requirement, because the Convention takes precedence over the application of national law.

For all this, by relying on the permissive nature of the Convention (Art. 6), the parties may by agreement validly prescribe formal requirements (e.g. written form) for any of their contractual declarations. Under Art. 13 of the Convention, "*writing*" includes *telegrammes* and *telexes*. According to the prevalent view in legal literature, this provision applies, *per analogiam*, to *faxes* as well (Schlechtriem, 1996, p. 42, in the List of Sources).

(b) Since there are countries whose internal law requires international (sales) contracts to be concluded in writing as an essential of validity, the Convention (Art. 96) *allows expression of a reservation*: the State concerned may declare that the provisions of the Convention spelling out the principle of informality (Arts. 11 and 29) will be inapplicable if the place of business of either party is in a State requiring a written form. This compromise reservation was accepted by most of the States participating in the Vienna Diplomatic Conference, although modern commercial law is moving much rather in the direction of informality. This tendency is eloquently evidenced by the fact that very few States have made such a reservation (Argentina and, practically, the People's Republic of China, and, among the States which acceded later, Belarus, Chile, Estonia, Lithuania, Russia and Ukraine). (Characteristically, not even the onetime GDR availed itself of this possibility, not to mention Bulgaria, Czechoslovakia, or its successor States, and Romania, all of which acceded later.)

Hungary, too, made such a reservation (Sect. 3 of Law-Decree No. 20 of 1987) rather hastily (and unfortunately even at the time). This is all the more objectionable since in Hungarian substantive law, the written form in the realm of contracts was an exceptional phenomenon already at the time of the ratification of the Convention, and cases of such exception are still rarer today. In the light of recent judicial practice, the rule requiring foreign trade contracts to be in writing (Sect. 6 of Decree No. 7/1974.(X.17.) of the Minister of Foreign Trade) is especially in need of reappraisal as regards both its interpretation and the penalties for its violation. As we have indicated in our discussion on the peculiarities of foreign trade contracts (see §64), the Supreme Court has recently been inclined to appraise failure to put a contract into writing as a difficulty of proving the formation of the contract rather than as a cause of its invalidity (Gf. VI. 32 706/1992, BH 1994/4. 208).

Consequently it appears to be absolutely warranted for the Republic of Hungary to withdraw the reservation made under Art. 96. Withdrawal is permitted by Art. 97 (4).

(c) Furthermore, the *consequence* of reservation is a disputed issue in both theory and practice. (It would be appropriate for Hungary to withdraw its reservation made under Art. 96 for the sole reason of avoiding problems of this nature.)

(ca) The view can be regarded as logical (Reinhart, Art. 12. Rn. 3, in the List of Sources) which argues that in case of a reservation the *formal requirements* of the State making a reservation should, as norms replacing the rules of the Convention, be heeded by all fora regardless of whether or not the State of the proceeding forum has made a reservation, because this is the motive and purpose of the reservation itself, and indeed, this solution is likewise confirmed by the *jus cogens* provisions of the Convention (Art. 12) and the requirement of international harmony in the adjudication of related cases.

(cb) At the same time, prominent writers on the subject are of the view that while the expression of a reservation results in excluding the Convention's principle of informality (Arts. 11 and 29), that principle is not automatically replaced by the formal requirements of the law of the State making such a reservation, but the formal requirements of the *governing law as determined by conflict rules* will come into play (Schlechtriem, 1996, p. 41, in the List of Sources). So, if the law indicated by conflict rules requires no written form (and the State of that law expressed no reservation under Art. 96 for this very reason), the principle of informality will nevertheless apply by virtue of conflicts law. Accordingly, under this approach, the written form is a requisite of the validity of a contractual declaration only if the conflicts law of the forum ordains application of the substantive law rules of the State having made a reservation. [According to a strongly disputable view (Schlechtriem, 1996, p. 42, in the List of Sources), the rule of Art. 13 interpreting the written form ("writing" includes telegramme and telex) would prevail even in such cases.]

This interpretation of law is logically incontestable, and (just as the first view mentioned above) it also satisfies the requirement of international harmony in the adjudication of cases, for the occurrence of the consequences of reservation (i.e. the requirement of written form) does not depend, in this case either, on a legal dispute arising in a State having made a reservation or in a State having made no reservation under Art. 96; the forum of every State interposes its own conflict rules, and the form of contractual declaration will be determined by the applicable substantive law indicated by those conflict rules: if the governing law is that of the State having made a reservation, the formal requirements of that State will apply, but if the applicable law is that of a State having made no reservation, the Convention's principle of informality will prevail. (For related problems, see Vékás, in: *Das Einheitliche Wiener Kaufrecht*, in the List of Sources.) There is no doubt however that if this second view is accepted, the intention of the State having made a reservation under Art. 96 (and of the rule in Art. 12) cannot be asserted consistently, viz. the reservation (in accordance with the one-sided declaration) will only operate unilaterally.

Hungarian judicial practice appears to confirm this second view. In one of its judgments the Metropolitan Court (12.G.41.471/1991; cf. Székely: *Friss Hírek*, 3/92; Vida: *IPRax* 4/93) held that the reservation in question exists only as part of the Hungarian law, but forms no part of the (German) law otherwise applicable to the particular contract and that therefore the oral contractual declaration had also been validly made. The same position was taken by the Supreme Court's judgment (Pf.VI.22 892/1993) which, on the strength of Hungary's reservation, "opted out" of the Convention with respect to the form of an international sales transaction between an Austrian seller and a Hungarian buyer and applied the (Austrian) seller's law. On the other hand, these court decisions are strongly disputable on account of applying the national law (the German *BGB* and the Austrian *ABGB*) as the law of seller's country instead of the Convention, although the States concerned (Germany and Austria), being States parties, render the Convention (with no reservation made under Art. 96) rather than *BGB* and *ABGB* applicable to international sales. (The cited judgment "fled" the Convention to the rules of private international law perhaps because they were "bothered" by the lack of the unity of law between the two countries in respect of the problems of formality, precisely on account of the unilateral reservation: Hungary is a party to the Convention with a reservation made under Art. 96, while Germany and Austria are parties without a reservation. This situation is natural, however, because the reservation breaks the unity of law between State parties.)

§72. OBLIGATIONS OF SELLER

The main obligations of the seller (Art. 30) are

- delivery of goods;
- transfer of ownership in the goods; and, where necessary,
- handing over of any documents relating to the goods.

1. The seller must deliver *goods* which are of the quantity, quality and description required by the contract and which are contained or packaged in the manner required by the contract. Except where the parties have agreed otherwise, the goods do not conform with the contract unless they are fit for the purposes for which goods of the same description would ordinarily be used, and fit for any particular purpose made known to the seller at the time of the conclusion of the contract. In case of sale by samples, the goods must possess the qualities which the seller has held out to the buyer as a sample (or model). The seller is not liable for any lack of conformity of the goods if, at the time of the conclusion of the contract, the buyer knew or could not have been unaware of such lack of conformity (Art. 35).

Delivery of goods depends on the place of performance (Art. 31). If the seller, in accordance with the contract, is bound to arrange for carriage of the goods, he must make such contracts as are necessary for carriage of the goods to the place of destination. If the seller hands the goods over to a carrier, he must hand over to the buyer the documents identifying the goods or the consignment specifying the goods (Art. 32).

Very often, the contracting parties agree in *Incoterms* concerning the sale of goods, and naturally may modify and complement those terms.

The Convention contains specific provisions regarding the date of performance as well (Art. 33). If the seller has delivered goods before the date for delivery, he may, up to that date, deliver any missing part, make up any deficiency, or deliver goods in replacement of the same, provided that the exercise of this right does not cause the buyer unreasonable inconvenience or unreasonable expense. However, the buyer retains any right to claim damages (Art. 37).

2. The seller is liable for any *lack of conformity* which exists at the time when the risk passes to the buyer, even though the lack of conformity becomes apparent only after that time. The seller is also liable for any lack of conformity which occurs after the time the risk passed to the buyer, but is due to a breach of any of the seller's obligations, including a breach of any guarantee (Art. 36). In order for the buyer to enforce his rights concerning any defect in the quality of the goods, the Convention requires him to examine the goods (Art. 38) and to give notice thereof to the seller (Art. 39). Nevertheless, the seller may not invoke the buyer's omission in connection with the examination of the goods or with his notice thereof if the lack of conformity relates to facts of which he knew or could not have been unaware and which he did not disclose to the buyer (Art. 40). Moreover, the Convention requires the seller to undertake a warranty of title (Arts. 41 to 43).

3. In the case of international sales, it is rather often a fundamental obligation of the seller to hand over to the buyer the documents relating to the goods. In such cases the seller's performance conforms to the contract if he also furnishes the documents accompanying the goods (Art. 34).

§73. OBLIGATIONS OF BUYER

The main obligations of the buyer (Art. 53) are
- to pay the price, and
- to take delivery of the goods.

1. The buyer's obligation to *pay the price* includes taking such steps and complying with such formalities as are required under the contract or any laws and regulations so as to enable payment to be made. Failure to take the preparatory steps for the payment of the price is by itself a breach of contract by the buyer (Art. 54).

Unless otherwise stipulated, the price must be paid at the seller's place of business or, if the payment is to be made against the handing over of the goods or of documents, at the place where the handing over takes place. If there is a change in the seller's place of business subsequent to the conclusion of the contract, the seller must bear any increase in the expenses incidental to payment (Art. 57).

Failing stipulation to the contrary, the buyer must pay the price when the seller puts the goods (or the documents embodying the right to dispose of them) at the buyer's disposal. In this case the buyer's obligation to pay the price and the seller's obligation to hand over goods (or the documents) presuppose mutuality and concurrency. Otherwise the buyer is not bound to pay the price until he has had an opportunity to examine the goods except when the contract affords the buyer no such opportunity (Art. 58). For the buyer to pay the price there is no need for notice by the seller (Art. 59).

The *currency* in which the price is to be paid is for the parties to determine. The Convention grants the parties full liberty in this respect. That the parties must comply with the foreign exchange regulations regarding the contract is a different matter. If the parties did not determine the currency of payment in the contract (including of course any subsequent modifications thereof or any additions thereto by agreement), guidance may be provided by previous business practice between the parties or, failing such practice, by commercial usages. (Today it is exceptional for bilateral interstate trade agreements to fix the currency in which the purchase price is to be paid in relations between subjects at law of the States concerned.) Once all of the above avenues have been exhausted, the prevalent view is that the price is to be paid in the currency of seller's State even in cases where the contract as a whole happens to be governed by a law other than that of the seller's country (see Magnus, Székely, in the List of Sources). (The majority of the participants in the Vienna Conference rejected the view that, failing a separate stipulation to that effect, the seller should be entitled, quasi *facultas alternativa*, to claim the price, or the buyer should be entitled to effect payment, in a currency other than the official means of payment in the seller's country.)

Legal literature deems it possible for any loss of value of the currency in which the price is payable to be compensated for by a claim for any damages for breach of contract to be established in accordance with the foreseeability rule of the Convention (Art. 74) (Magnus, *RabelsZ,* in the List of Sources).

2. As regards the buyer's *obligation to take delivery,* he must do all the acts which could reasonably be expected of him in order to enable the seller to make delivery in accordance with the contract (Art. 60). The parties may specify by contract the mode of taking delivery (often by relying on *Incoterms*).

3. Although it is not a main obligation, the buyer often undertakes in the contract to specify the characteristics of the goods (*specification*). If he fails to meet this obligation (within an additional reasonable time), the right of specification devolves upon the seller (Art. 65).

§74. RIGHTS OF SELLER AND BUYER IN CASE OF BREACH OF CONTRACT

1. *Fundamental breach of contract* is a category central to the Convention's law on breach of contract. A breach of contract is fundamental if it results in such detriment to the other party as substantially to deprive him of what he is entitled to expect under the contract, unless the party in breach did not foresee and a reasonable person of the same kind in the same circumstances would not have foreseen such a result (Art. 25).

(a) The definition by the Convention of fundamental breach of contract can be traced back to a similar category of the Scandinavian law of contract adopted early in this century. (English legal practice also relies on this category, which however is given a different substance.)

Again, according to the most notable commentary in German, a fundamental breach of contract can be established by *three criteria*:

– breach of contract;

– causing of detriment;

– foreseeability of consequences (see Caemmerer–Schlechtriem, Art. 25. Rn. 7–11, in the List of Sources).

The essential point is that a breach of contract being fundamental depends on the legal consequence occurring and on the rightful expectations under the contract, with "rightful expectations" as a subjective criterion complemented by the objective criterion of "detriment". It is for the courts to define (by relying in part on practice concerning the Hague Uniform Law of Sale) the conceptual limits of fundamental breach.

The *commentaries* published to date appear to make it clear that non-adherence to a fixed time-limit may be regarded as fundamental (even if no detriment resulted to the obligee), but, in case of non-adherence to a time-limit not fixed, the obligee must, in order for a fundamental breach to be established, furnish separate evidence of a substantial detriment to his expectations under the contract (even though no damage was suffered). Thus, for instance seller's default in the delivery of seasonable goods may substantiate a fundamental breach (Vida, *Jogtudományi Közlöny*, 1993, in the List of Sources). Similarly, the case in which the seller delivers goods different from those specified in the contract (*aliud* delivery) can certainly be deemed to be one of a fundamental breach, whereas faulty performance ordinarily requires proof of a specific detriment to the obligee's expectations. According to the view prevailing in literature, the burden of proving is borne by the obligee in respect of the detriment and by the party in breach in respect of foreseeability. Violation of a subsidiary contract securing the buyer's exclusive rights to trademark protection amounts to a fundamental breach of a contract of sale (OLG Frankfurt 17.9.1991, NJW 1992, 633, *IPRax,* 1991, 950; cf. Vida, *Jogtudományi Közlöny*, 1993, in the List of Sources). Similarly, the violation of the "exclusive clause" of a contract of sale ensuring exclusivity for the buyer was held by a German court to be an essential breach of contract (LG Frankfurt 16.9.1991, RIW 1991, 952) (even though the court did not recognize the right to avoid the contract in that particular case; cf. Magnus, *ZEuP,* in the List of Sources).

(b) A breach of contract being fundamental is of relevance to *penalties for breach of contract*, chiefly because the legal consequences of breach (primarily the right to avoidance) (para. 1 of Art. 49, para. 2 of Art. 51, para. 1 of Art. 64, para. 1 of Art. 72, paras. 1 and 2 of Art. 73) may be enforced without fixing an additional period of time. On the other hand, the seller or the buyer must fix an additional period of time of reasonable length for performance by the other party of his obligations, in order that legal consequences of a breach of contract other than fundamental may be enforceable (Arts. 47 and 63).

The right of the parties to qualify, by agreement, any breach of contract as being fundamental and thereby to impose more severe penalties follows from the *permissive* provisions of the Convention.

2. In case of the *seller's breach of contract* the Convention ensures for the buyer

– warranty rights (Arts. 46 to 52) and

– a right to damages (Arts. 74 to 77).

It follows from the *permissiveness* of the rules on penalties for a breach of contract by the seller (Arts. 46 to 52) that the parties may by agreement depart from those penalties in favour or to the detriment of either party.

(a) The buyer is not deprived of any right he may have to *claim damages* by exercising his right to other remedies: in addition to warranty rights, he has a right to claim damages (Art. 45). The buyer's claim to damages for breach of contract will be discussed in more detail in connection with the rules common to breaches of contract (§76).

(b) The existing judicial practice (just as in the case of the Hague Uniform Law of Sale) has been chiefly concerned with claims arising from *faulty performance.*

As regards the details of a *claim to warranty*, the following can be stated.

(ba) In case of a breach by the seller, the buyer may require first of all *contractual performance* by the seller unless the buyer has resorted to a remedy which is inconsistent with this requirement. The buyer may require the seller to remedy the lack of conformity *by repair* in the first place.

(bb) The buyer may require delivery of *substitute goods* only if the lack of conformity constitutes a fundamental breach of contract, provided that he has given the seller notice thereof within the prescribed period of time. If the goods do not conform with the contract, the buyer may require the seller to repair the goods in case of any breach of contract (not only of a fundamental breach) unless this claim is unreasonable having regard to all the circumstances (Art. 46).

(bc) The seller may, at his own expense, remedy his breach *after the date of delivery*, if he can do so without causing the buyer unreasonable inconvenience. The remedy does not affect the buyer's right to claim damages (Arts. 74 *et seq.*) and to avoid the contract (Art. 48).

(bd) As has been noted above (item 1), the buyer may, without further procedure, avoid the contract of sale only of the seller's failure to perform in accordance with the contract amounts to a fundamental breach. In other cases of breach the buyer's *avoidance* of the contract is subject to additional conditions, notably

– in case of non-delivery, if the seller does not deliver the goods within the additional period of time fixed by the buyer or declares that he will not deliver within the period so fixed;

– in case of late delivery, only if the buyer declares the contract avoided within a reasonable time after he has become aware that delivery has been made;

– in case of any breach other than late delivery, if the buyer declares the contract avoided within a reasonable time after he knew or ought to have known of the breach, or after the expiry of any additional period of time of reasonable length fixed by the buyer, or after the expiry of any additional period of time indicated by the seller (Art. 49). Avoidance of the contract releases the buyer from his obligations under it, and if the buyer has performed the contract either wholly or partially, he may claim restitution from the seller (Art. 81).

In case of the buyer's avoidance of the contract, he must account to the seller for all benefits which he has derived from the goods (Art. 84). The buyer loses the right to declare the contract avoided (or to require the seller to deliver substitute goods) if it is impossible for him to make restitution of the goods substantially in the condition in which he received them except when such impossibility is not due to his act or omission (Art. 82). [Loss of the right to avoid the contract does not affect other remedies for breach of contract (Art. 83)].

(be) In case of the seller's breach of contract, the buyer may – apart from claiming delivery (repair or substitute goods) and avoiding the contract – *reduce the price* if the goods do not conform with the contract. The reduction in price must be in the same proportion as the value that the goods actually delivered had at the time of the delivery bears to the value that conforming goods would have had (at that time) (Art. 50).

(c) The buyer must give notice to the seller of any defect in the quality of the goods, specifying the nature of defect, "*within a reasonable time*" after he has discovered it or ought to have discovered it. Upon the expiry of this period, the buyer does not lose his right to claim damages (not including reduction in the price and loss of profit) if he has a "reasonable excuse" for his failure to give the required notice (Art. 44). The buyer loses his right to rely on a lack of conformity of the goods if he does not give the seller notice thereof (at the latest) within a period of two years from the date on which the goods were actually handed over to the buyer, unless this time-limit is inconsistent with a contractual period of guarantee (Art. 39).

Foreign judicial practice has so far insisted on strict (in some cases, too strict) adherence to time-limits fixed for the enforcement of the buyer's warranty claims (Magnus, *ZEuP,* in the List of Sources). The court held to be belated a notice with two weeks' delay in the case of defective shoes (LG Stuttgart 31.8.1989, *IPRax,* 1990, 316) and one with seven day's delay in the case of decayed cucumbers (OLG Düsseldorf 8.1.1993, *IPRax,* 1993). This rigour may have been overshadowed by the Hague Uniform Law of Sale, although one should be aware that the Uniform Law prescribes "immediate" notice, whereas the Vienna Convention expects the buyer to give notice within a "reasonable time".

The buyer's notice to the seller must *specify* the lack of conformity (a simple reference to such lack is not sufficient). For instance, a mere reference to "bad processing of goods" in a claim arising from a lack of conformity was held by the court to be insufficient (LG München I.3.7.1989, *IPRax,* 1990, 316; cf. Magnus, *ZEuP,* in the List of Sources).

(d) The abovementioned provisions should be applied, *mutatis mutandis*, to *partial breach of contract* except that the buyer may avoid the contract in its entirety only if the failure to make delivery completely or in conformity with the contract amounts to a fundamental breach of the contract (Art. 51).

(c) If the seller delivers the goods *before the date fixed* or delivers a quantity of goods greater than that provided for in the contract, the buyer may refuse to take delivery or to take delivery of the excess quantity, respectively (Art. 52). If the buyer accepts the goods delivered before the date for delivery, he retains any right to claim damages resulting therefrom against the seller under the rules on damages (Art. 37). (The question of whether or not the buyer's declaration of retaining his right to claim damages is a condition for the enforcement of his claim to damages is the subject of debates in literature for the time being.) If the buyer accepts the excess quantity (or a part thereof), he must pay the corresponding contractual price.

3. In case of the *buyer's breach of contract*, the seller's rights include requiring the buyer

(a) to *take delivery* of the goods in the first place, and

(b) to *pay the price*.

The seller may fix an additional period of time of reasonable length for performance by the buyer of his obligations. Unless the seller has received notice from the buyer that he will not perform within the period so fixed, the seller may not, during that period, resort to any other remedy. [However, the seller is not deprived of any right he may have to claim damages (Arts. 62–63).]

As noted earlier (item 1), the seller, just as the buyer, may not avoid the contract without further consideration except in case of a *fundamental breach*. The seller, too, may exercise the right to avoid the contract only after the expiry of the additional period of time fixed for performance by the buyer (or if the buyer refuses to perform within that period). If the buyer has paid the price, the seller loses the right to declare the contract avoided unless he does so

– in respect of late performance by the buyer, before the seller has become aware the performance has been rendered; or

– in respect of any other breach, within a reasonable time (after the seller knew or ought to have known of the breach, or after the expiry of any additional period of time fixed by the buyer (Art. 64). What has been stated in connection with the buyer's right to avoid the contract (item 1) holds for the substance and consequences of avoidance (Art. 81). The obligation of the seller to refund the price to the buyer with accrued interest derives from the nature of avoidance (Art. 84).

In addition to the right to require performance and the right to avoid the contract, the seller has the right to *claim damages* for the buyer's breach of contract. The legal conditions for exercising this right will be discussed in detail in connection with the rules common to breaches of contract (§76).

§75. PASSING OF RISK

(a) In regulating the passing of risk, the Convention brings into focus the *seller's right to claim payment of the purchase price*. This means the need for this right of the seller to be appraised under the rules on the passing of risk in case of loss of, or damage to or destruction of, the goods. The Convention starts from the basic principle that loss of the goods or damage thereto or destruction thereof after the risk has passed to the buyer, does not discharge him from his obligation to pay the price unless the loss or damage is due to an act or omission of the seller (Art. 66). The majority view in literature is that the seller's act or omission should not necessarily amount to a breach of contract for him to lose his claim to the price.

On the other hand, however, the Convention explicitly provides that if *the seller has committed a fundamental breach of contract*, the rules on the passing of risk do not impair the remedies available to the buyer on account of the breach (Art. 70).

(b) The *place and time* at which the risk passes to the buyer *depend on the mode of delivery*.

– If the goods are delivered through a *carrier*, the risk passes to the buyer at the place and time at which the goods are handed over to the first carrier for transmission to the buyer in accordance with the contract; provided that the goods are clearly identified in the contract (whether by markings on the goods, by shipping documents, by notice given to the buyer or otherwise).

– The risk in respect of *goods sold in transit* passes to the buyer from the time of the conclusion of the contract unless the circumstances indicate otherwise.

– In case of *other* modes of delivery, the risk passes to the buyer when he takes over the goods or, if he does not do so in due time, from the time when the goods are placed at his disposal. The risk does not pass to the buyer, even in these cases, until the goods are clearly identified to the contract (Arts. 67 to 69).

§76. RULES COMMON TO BREACHES OF CONTRACT

1. *Anticipatory breach* (Arts. 71–72) is covered by the Convention among the common rules, under which any party may suspend the performance of his obligations if, after the conclusion of the contract, it becomes apparent that the

other party will not perform a substantial part of his obligations. Anticipatory breach may result from a serious deficiency in the obligor's ability to perform or his creditworthiness, or from his conduct in preparing to perform or from performing the contract.

In the exercise of the rights deriving from anticipatory breach, the seller may prevent the handing over of the goods already dispatched to the buyer, even though the buyer holds a document which entitles him to obtain them. A party suspending performance on account of an anticipatory breach must immediately give notice of the suspension to the other party and must continue with performance if the other party provides adequate assurance of his performance. The contract may, even in case of an anticipatory breach, be declared avoided only if prior to the date for performance of the contract, it is clear that the other party will commit a fundamental breach of contract. Moreover, since in the last analysis such cases involve only a possibility of breach preliminary to a fundamental breach, the Convention requires the party intending to avoid the contract to give reasonable notice to the other party in order to permit him to provide adequate assurance of his performance.

2. The right to avoid a contract of sale for *delivery of goods by instalments* may, even in case of a fundamental breach, generally be exercised only in respect of the instalment affected by the breach of the contract. This right may be exercised in respect of the contract if delivery may be made by instalments but, by reason of their interdependence, those deliveries could not be used for the purpose contemplated in the contract (i.e. delivery by instalments is ultimately indivisible in law). In other cases, the obligee may abrogate the entire contract (the abrogation resulting in the *ex nunc* termination of the contract), only if the obligor's non-compliance with his obligations concerning any instalment gives the other party good grounds to conclude that a fundamental breach of contract will occur with respect to future instalments (Art. 73).

3. Under the Convention, *claims for damages* include full compensation of damages consisting of the actual damage and loss of profit.

(a) The general principle is that the *sum of damages* may not exceed the loss which the party in breach *foresaw or ought to have foreseen* at the time of the conclusion of the contract, in the light of the facts and matters of which he knew or ought to have known, as a possible consequence of the breach of contract (Art. 74). These limits on foreseeability were defined by English law with the aim of setting down a framework for a proportional sharing of risk by seller and buyer.

(aa) The obligee may claim as damages the *interest in excess* of the legally-fixed rate, if he incurred a credit at a higher interest rate in order to reduce the consequences of the breach of contract (LG Hamburg 26.9.1990, *IPRax,* 1991, 400; LG Aachen 3.4.1990, RIW 1991, 491; LG Frankfurt 16.9.1991, RIW 1991, 952; cf. Magnus, in the List of Sources).

(ab) The *additional expenses* intended to be claimed as damages must have been caused by, and be proportional to, the breach of contract (LG Frankfurt, 169, 1991, RIW 1991, 952; cf. Magnus, *ZEuP,* in the List of Sources).

(ac) In cases where the buyer, following avoidance or abrogation of the contract, satisfies his contractual needs, in a reasonable manner and within a reasonable time, by purchasing substitute goods (making a purchase to cover), he may also claim the difference between the original contractual price and the *purchase price* for the substitute goods. The seller may have this same claim against the buyer if, following the latter's avoidance or abrogation of the contract, he can resell the goods to a third person at a price lower than the original price.

(b) For *calculating the sum of damages*, the market (current) price of the goods is the starting point of comparison, the current price being the price prevailing at the place where delivery of the goods should have been made. If there is no current price at that place, the price at such other place as serves as a reasonable substitute should be fixed making due allowance for differences in the cost of transporting the goods and in the expenses (Art. 76).

(c) The Convention prescribes for both parties a general *obligation to mitigate the loss* (Art. 77). The parties must take such measures as are reasonable in the circumstances to mitigate the loss (actual damage and loss of profit). Failure to take such measures entails a reduction in the damages in the amount by which the loss should have been mitigated.

(d) The Convention (unlike the Hungarian civil law) provides for *exemptions from liability* for damages that are based on *objective* circumstances and are *unrelated to culpability* (Arts. 79–80). This means in concrete terms that in order to be released from liability for damages, the party in breach must prove that the breach was due to an impediment beyond his control and that he could not reasonably be expected to have taken the impediment into account at the time of the conclusion of the contract or to have avoided or overcome it or its consequences.

The party who fails to perform must give notice to the other party of the impediment and its effect on the performance of the contract. Failure to give such notice may increase the liability of the party in breach to pay damages (chiefly the sum of damages rising in proportion to the loss).

The Convention formulates a principle also known to Hungarian civil law in providing that a party may not rely on a failure of the other party to perform, to the extent that such failure was caused by the former's act or omission (Art. 80).

(e) In cases where an obligation is fulfilled *with the involvement of a third person* (*a sub-contractor*), the obligor in breach must prove the existence of an objective impediment in respect of himself as well as of the third person in order to be released from the consequences of breach regarding damages.

4. Among the problems common to breaches of contract, reference should be made to the fact that the Convention prescribes the obligation to pay interest in

case of late performance involving payment of the price and any other obligation in terms of money. Just as in Hungarian civil law, *interest* is the price of money unduly used, and as such it burdens the party in default regardless of liability for breach of contract or of exemption therefrom: consequently it does not reduce the sum of damages claimed, if any.

(a) The Convention (Art. 74 and para. 1 of Art. 84) does not determine the rate of interest on late payment of money. The prevalent view *in literature* (see Sándor, *op. cit.*; p. 294, in the List of Sources; Magnus, *RabelsZ* and *ZEuP,* in the List of Sources) is that the law otherwise applicable to the contract (*lex obligationis*) should be relied upon for determining the rate of interest on default. (For a discussion of this problem, see also Dósa, *Friss Hírek*, 5/91, and Székely in the List of Sources.) In Hungarian private international law this is all the more unambiguous since, under Art. 30 of the Code, the governing law of contracts extends to all elements of the contractual relationship.

After temporary hesitations (see Magnus, *ZEuP,* in the List of Sources), *foreign judicial practice* follows the prevalent view in literature and determines the rate of interest under the *lex obligationis* (LG Hamburg 26.9.1990, *IPRax* 1991, 400; OLG Frankfurt 13.6.1991, NJW 1991, 3102; ICC Paris 7153/1992, Clunet 1992, 1005).

(b) This position is likewise followed by *Hungarian judicial practice* [*Fővárosi Bíróság* (Metropolitan Court), 12.G.41.471/1991]. Of course, where the *lex obligationis* is the Hungarian law, Hungarian rates of interest may only be applied to claims to be satisfied in Hungarian currency (*forint*). The Supreme Court has repeatedly held and clearly expressed (e.g. Pf.III.20 701/1990; Pf.VI.22 046/1993; Pf.VI.22 189/1993; Pfv.IV.23 083/1994, BH 1995/6, 342) that if a money debt is to be paid in foreign currency, the *rate of interest on default as fixed by the Civil Code* may not be applied as it relates *exclusively to claims in forint*. Under consistent judicial practice, the rate of interest established by the international money market for the particular currency should be taken as a basis for fixing the rate of interest on default payable in foreign currency. [Where necessary, the Supreme Court ordains such rates of interest to be determined with the assistance of the Hungarian National Bank (Pfv. 23 083/1994, BH 1995/6, 342); in its cited judgments of 1993, for instance, the Supreme Court fixed at 6% the rate of interest payable on a sum awarded in US dollars.]

Finally, special mention is deserved of the fact that the *special rates of interest* fixed by the Civil Code [para. (c) of Art. 685] for "economic organizations" *do not apply to legal relationships established by foreign firms* with Hungarian economic organizations (*Legf. Bír.* Pf.VI.22 046/1993; Pf.VI.22 189/1993).

5. Among its rules common to breaches of contract, the Convention covers the seller's obligation for *responsible custody* whenever he is in possession of the goods or otherwise able to control their disposition without being entitled or obliged thereto. He is entitled to retain such goods until he has been reimbursed his reasonable expenses by the buyer (Art. 85).

CHAPTER XXIII

OTHER MAJOR TYPES OF CONTRACTS

§77. CONTRACTS IN THE NATURE OF *LOCATIO CONDUCTIO OPERIS* (CONTRACTOR'S CONTRACT)

In international economic relation – just as in the domestic field, – the greatest role is played, in addition to sales contracts, by transactions in the nature of *locatio conductio operis*. The object of such transactions is the *result of a process of work*, but the legal relationship often extends to the performance of work as well.

Given their economic significance, contracts of this type are also witnesses to the efforts aimed at the *unification of law* and constitute topical examples of *standard contracts*.

A large part of the *general conditions of contract* elaborated by the United Nations Economic Commission for Europe and published in two series (1953 and 1964) is in the nature of undertaking and applies to transactions presenting elements of undertaking (e.g. "export of equipment and machinery", "import and export of equipment and machinery").

Due to the absence of uniform substantive law rules, contracts of *locatio conductio operis* are also under the control of conflicts law. Within the meaning of the Hungarian PIL Code, the law chosen by the parties is applicable in the first place (Art. 24) and, failing a *choice of law*, the applicable law is the law of the State in whose territory the activity of the undertaking is to be performed or the results are to be achieved under the terms of the contract (para. 2 of Art. 26), to wit, the applicable law is that of the *place of performance* where no law has been chosen.

Contracts in the nature of *locatio conductio operis* used in international economic relations are of a great variety; the diverse forms often differ in essential matters and constitute, or are in the process of becoming, independent nominate sub-types, such as contracts for *assembly* or *servicing*.

Among international contracts of *locatio conductio operis* we find contracts for *delivery* and *installation* of *equipment* to be of outstanding importance to the national economy. Their object is formed by completely-equipped installation (factory, workshop, hospital, etc.) or complex machinery or equipment (bridge, ship, etc.). Contractual agreements may relate, in addition to supply of machinery in the narrow sense, to design of an establishment, trial operation, bringing a plant into operation, etc. The basic deal, which is often *complex* and not purely in the nature of an undertaking, is coupled with other services (building, after-sales service, transfer of the manufacturing process, on-the-job training (induction), etc.). The contractor may also undertake on-site installation (with his own workforce or with labour and materials provided by the buyer), but he commonly undertakes nothing more than overseeing assembly or providing professional advice.

Large equipment is often delivered under contract with a *general contractor*, who harmonizes his own activity with services provided by several subcontractors, but who is alone liable to the buyer for bringing about the result he has undertaken to produce. Among the numerous *special legal problems* involved in contracts of *locatio conductio operis* for the delivery of large equipment, attention should be drawn in particular to the existence of legal grounds for partial performance, to questions concerning the complex nature of performance, and to warranty.

§78. CARRIAGE OF GOODS, FORWARDING

Among the contracts used in international economic relations a significant place is occupied by the contract of carriage, especially *carriage of goods*, which, in terms of economic function, constitutes a subsidiary transaction of paramount importance ordinarily serving to perform contracts of other types, chiefly the underlying transactions (sale, *locatio conductio operis*).

By the nature of the vehicle used, carriage of goods in international transactions has different forms: carriage by train, lorry, air and water (sea and river). All these forms of carriage are *typically international in character*.

It is thus understandable that by the time of the late 19th century *international conventions* were concluded which provided direct frameworks of rules for this field of business (e.g. the Berne Convention of 1892 on the Carriage of Goods by Rail). Next we will discuss the major questions concerning international contracts of carriage, placing emphasis on the sets of rules applicable to the various forms of carriage.

1. The legal questions concerning international carriage of goods by rail are governed today by the *Berne Convention* of 1980 on the International Carriage of Goods by Rail (abbreviated COTIF in French), which was promulgated in Hungary by Law-Decree No. 2 of 1986.

Appendix A to the Berne Convention is constituted by the convention on the *Carriage of Persons and Luggage* (CIV) and Appendix B by the Convention on the *Carriage of Goods* (CIM), both laying down the respective sets of international rules. (Of course, these Conventions were also promulgated by Law-Decree No. 2 of 1986.)

The International Convention on the Carriage of Goods by Rail (CIM) is applicable to all European countries, except the former Soviet Union, as well as to several non-European States of the Mediterranean region. Its applicability is conditional on the dispatched goods passing through at least two States and on the transport route figuring in the official list of CIM railways. The railways are under obligation to provide such service except in cases where they are unable to perform carriage for reasons beyond their control, or the station of dispatch has no technical facilities for loading, or the acceptance of freight is impeded by extraordinary circumstances. The central rule of CIM is contained in Art. 35, which provides for the joint and several liability of the railways cooperating in carriage.

2. In recent decades increasing use has been made of *carriage by lorry (camion)* in international transactions as well. Therefore, in 1956 a convention was signed at Geneva on the rules of international carriage of goods by road (CMR). Hungary is a party to the Convention (promulgated by Law-Decree No. 3 of 1971). Concerning a carrier's liability, CMR contains rules essentially similar to those of CIM. (For a monographic treatment of CMR, see Clarke's book in the List of Sources.)

CMR is supplemented by the so-called TIR Agreement (*Transport International Routier*; promulgated in Hungary by Law-Decree No. 16 of 1978), in which the State parties grant passage-free customs control for vehicles bearing standardized signs and marked with a specified customs-house seal.

3. The international rules on *carriage by air* are laid down in the *Warsaw Convention* of 1929 (as amended at The Hague in 1955). Hungary is a party to this instrument (which was promulgated by Act XXVIII of 1936 and by Law-Decree No. 19 of 1964, respectively). The rules of the Warsaw Convention are applied to any contract of carriage by air under which the points of departure and destination are in two different State parties to the Convention, or the two places are in the territory of one and the same State, but the aircraft makes a scheduled landing *en route* in the territory of another State. A rather large role in the law of carriage by air is played by the *conditions of carriage (standards)* of air carriers. Unlike the generally accepted principle applied in other forms of carriage, the liability of an air carrier is not an objective one, but *is based on culpability*: the carrier is relieved of liability upon proving that it and its crew took all the necessary measures to avert damage or to do so was an impossibility. Moreover, the amount of damages is ordinarily fixed.

4. *Carriage by sea* is historically one of the most regulated fields of transport in international trade. Of course, legal regulation is still in the nature of *customary law* in many respects; it was shaped mainly in the practice of maritime courts (particularly in the English Admiralty Court from the late eighteenth century onwards). Charter party and bill of lading (practically a contract of carriage) are two basic institutions of the complex law of maritime transport.

Under a *charter party* the owner of a vessel temporarily assigns, wholly or in part, his vessel to a charterer, either retaining operation of the ship (providing crew) or placing it at the disposal of the charterer. A charter party has various sub-types. The conditions of this contract are governed by *usages* existing from the early part of the last century, and the resultant clauses have over time come into general use as models or standard contracts relied upon in relation to ports or sometimes to ports of a specific maritime region (e.g. the Baltic Sea), or reserved for specific cargoes.

The most important document of a *contract of carriage by sea* is the *bill of lading*, a documentary evidence of contract, an acknowledgement of receipt of goods, and a security embodying the right to dispose of goods.

The major rules relating to the obligations and the liability of sea-carriers were shaped by customary law. Some of them were laid down and adopted by many countries in an international agreement, the *Brussels Convention* of 1924 (more commonly known as the Hague Rules; and in their more recent formulation, the Hague–Visby Rules), which was promulgated in Hungary by Act VI of 1931. The Convention governs the major questions of liability for damage under a contract of carriage certified by a bill of lading. As a rule, the carrier's liability is very limited, generally to fixed amounts, and the grounds for release from liability are specified by the Convention.

In view of its numerous flaws the Brussels Convention has long been the focus of criticism, addressed largely to its rules according unilateral advantages to carriers and shifting onto the sender a large part of the still considerable risks of maritime transport.

In 1971, UNCITRAL set up, at the initiative of UNCTAD, an enlarged working group to review international regulations concerning the bills of lading. The result was the elaboration of a *convention* (at Hamburg in 1978) on the carriage of goods by sea (Hungary is among the signatory States). The *Hamburg Convention* is to replace the Brussels Convention (see Kreskay and Martonyi, in the List of Sources), but the 20 instruments of ratification (or accession) required for its entry into force have not yet been deposited.

5. Naturally, among the international rules on *carriage by river*, the conventions on carriage of goods on the Danube are of special relevance to Hungary. The freedom of navigation on the Danube was proclaimed by the countries of the Danubian basin in a convention signed at Belgrade in 1948. The *Belgrade Convention* was promulgated in Hungary by Act XIII of 1949.

In 1955 the Danubian shipping companies of Bulgaria, Czechoslovakia, Hungary, Romania and the Soviet Union laid down the principles of commercial shipping on the Danube in a separate agreement (DAF). In 1966 the Agreement was acceded to by two Yugoslav, one German and one Austrian shipping companies. Under present-day conditions the rules relating to commercial shipping on the Danube may be regarded as outdated, and their reformulation is absolutely warranted particularly by the operation of the Danube-Main Canal. (The legal regulation of the forms of international carriage is extensively treated in a study by Vattay, in: Martonyi–Vattay: *Kézikönyv* (Handbook), Chapter IX, in the List of Sources.)

6. Conveyance of goods, preparations for carriage, establishment of the relevant legal relationship itself is an often complicated activity which, especially in the international field, requires special expertise and knowledge of related procedures to ensure the smooth conduct of business. This area of activity, differentiated by the division of labour, was given a separate legal regulation adjusted to the needs of *forwarding* as an independent type of contract. The forwarder as a commission agent *concludes the necessary contracts* for the conveyance of goods on his own behalf for the consignor with third parties (carriers, other forwarders, warehouse) and may also attend to *collateral tasks* (issue of bills of lading) and perform other preparatory acts (storing and handling of goods). In the field of international forwarding great importance is attached to usages (especially to the *Business Conditions of Forwarding* published by the International Organization of Forwarders' Federations). Based on international models, the "Hungarian General Conditions of Forwarding" were also published by the Hungarian Forwarders' Association.

In international forwarding transactions (as in all contracts under the control of the law of obligations), the Hungarian Code allows the parties to choose the law applicable to their legal relationship (Art. 24). If no law has been chosen, the law applicable to a contract of forwarding is the law of the State in which, at the time of contracting, the forwarding agent has his seat or business headquarters [para. (i) of Art. 25]. This regulation, by a somewhat rigid and schematic application of the principle of "law of the obligor of characteristic performance", (usually) leads to the unilateral application of the law of the State of the foreign forwarder (cf. Vattay's study, in: Martonyi–Vattay: *Kézikönyv* (Handbook), Chapter VIII, in the List of Sources).

CHAPTER XXIV

INTERNATIONAL PAYMENT TRANSACTIONS

§79. INTERNATIONAL MONEY DEBTS, PAYMENT TRANSACTIONS

1. International money debt, an obligation to pay, undertaken in basic transactions (sale, *locatio conductio operis*, etc.) is a constant incident of international economic relations.

Generally speaking a money debt is a special form of services; all the more *peculiar* is an international money debt, where charge (determination of the amount of debt) and discharge (settlement of debt) are often effected in different currencies, while the value of the particular currencies (exchange rates) are subject to change during the intervening period, etc. The peculiar nature of international money debt raises numerous legal problems, some of which are governed by the Civil Code (Art. 231). Most of these problems, however, are controlled by *foreign exchange regulations*, which are of mandatory application (*imperative norms*). The rules of foreign exchange law *determine the procedure for enforcement of foreign claims and the use of foreign means of payment.* A detailed discussion of them goes beyond the scope of our topic.

International payments are made (the monetary countervalue of contracts under private international law is paid) *by the agency of banks*: the obligor contracts with a bank for the payment of his debt. Such contracts – *banking transactions* for the settlement of money debt – are normally *in the nature of agency*: the bank effects payment from the money and on the order of a client.

Another large group of banking transactions is formed, also in international economic relations, by various *loan and credit contracts*.

A growing role in international trade is played by a third type of banking transactions, the contract of *bank guarantee* providing an assurance of performance. Under it, the bank undertakes, on payment of an appropriate consideration, to pay a fixed amount to the beneficiary (transferee) within the set time-limit under specified conditions such as, in particular, the occurrence or non-occurrence of some event or presentation of documents.

The most important *payment transactions* (major forms in which international money debts are settled) are:

– transfer;
– order to collect;
– letter of credit.

2. In case of *transfer*, the transferor orders the bank to transfer from his account a specified sum of money to the credit of the person named by him (transferee). The remitter (principal) is always the obligor of a money debt.

In the civil-law sense, the transfer is a remittance which becomes payment upon acceptance (usually tacit) by transferee. Transfer is direct if the accounts of both transferor and transferee are held at the same bank, and is indirect if they are held at different banks (the two being interconnected by the banks). In international practice indirect transfer is the typical mode of payment: the bank ordered to pay by the transferor notifies such order to the bank in the transferee's country, which in turn will effect payment. In case of transfer to another country, the transferor pays or transfers to the account of the particular bank the equivalent in national currency of the amount payable in foreign currency [or, if the transferor's account happens to be held at the same bank (the one ordered to pay), authorizes the bank to charge his account with the equivalent sum of money].

In international banking practice, an order to transfer may only be withdrawn up until the transferee's notification of the transfer, because upon notification it is only the transferee who in law disposes of the amount transferred. (Today the technical facilities are rather limited for withdrawing orders to transfer, since the banks effect transfers through the electronic media of telecommunications.)

3. In the case of an *order to collect (collection)*, the obligee of the basic transaction, or the money debt (creditor), orders the bank to collect his claim from the obligor's bank account. The bank ordered to collect normally collects through the obligor's bank.

Order to collect is a frequent mode of collecting the monetary value of international economic contracts (chiefly international sale). Considering that, when this method is employed, the remittee has usually performed his part of the deal (e.g. has delivered the goods sold) and that the bank, for lack of sufficient cover, is not in a position to compel the debtor (e.g. the buyer of the basic transaction) to pay, an order to collect may not work with assured success. This danger is averted by *collection with a lien*, whereby the bank delivers the object of contract to the other party only after payment has been made (e.g. the buyer may not like possession of the goods ordered before payment of the purchase price).

An order to collect (even collection with a lien) gives no guarantee for payment to the obligee of a money debt, for the obligor himself is in a position to decide on effecting payment, the bank ordered to collect will transfer no amount without his consent (Thus, for instance, the bank will not be able to collect if, in case of collection with a lien, the obligor fails to take out the documents sent by the obligee and entitling him to dispose of the goods.) This is why order to collect as a form of payment is used in practice mainly by partners who have been in business contact for a longer time and therefore show confidence in each other.

With a view to settling the problems of collection, the International Chamber of Commerce based in Paris adopted and published a uniform regulation (operative in its current text from 1979) called Uniform Rules for Collections. This regulation is not a rule of law, but a compilation of provisions in the nature of usages, which the banks concerned must (by a declaration made either individually or through their central banks) recognize as binding on themselves. The International Chamber of Commerce publishes periodic lists of the countries whose banks have submitted themselves to the regulation. (Such declarations have been made by the banks of most countries, including Hungary.) Using special printed forms, the banks notify their clients to the effect that the collecting procedure has been placed under the control of the Uniform Rules.

4. In the case of a *letter of credit* the bank undertakes, on the remitter's behalf, to open credit to a third person named by him with the amount of his debt and to pay such amount on maturity (e.g. against surrender of the document verifying the performance of the contract). A letter of credit (as any payment transaction) is always based on another (basic) transaction, normally a contract of sale. By a letter of credit the remittee (typically the seller) receives from the bank an assurance in advance that his claim (the purchase price) will be paid, while the remitter's (buyer's) interests are also assured by an arrangement under which the bank will not pay until counter-performance has been effected (the goods have been delivered) on documentary evidence.

A letter of credit is frequently used in international trade because this mode of payment gives an assurance (without any separate guarantee) to both parties (typically to seller and buyer); the letter of credit is capable of ensuring concurrently that the seller will receive the purchase price and of safeguarding the buyer's interest in that the seller will not receive the purchase price unless he has performed the contract. The seller can be sure that the bank (obligated to him under the legal relationship created by the letter of credit) will honour his claim even if the buyer should be unwilling or unable to pay, while the buyer can be sure that the bank will not pay the purchase price to the seller until his performance of the contract.

A letter of credit embodies a legal relationship between three parties: a contract of *agency* between the obligor of a money debt (principal) and the bank; and a contract of *payment* between the bank and the obligee of the money debt. Under the contract of agency the bank is obliged to open a credit, to check on the documents verifying the performance of the underlying deal (sale) in accordance with the contract, and to pay out the money debt. The bank's declaration to the remittee of having opened a credit for him (such declaration being based on the contract of agency) is the direct source of the latter's right to claim payment and determines the conditions for its existence. As regards its legal conditions, the letter of credit is independent of the basic deal and, unlike, surety, for instance, is not incidental to it. Practice has evolved and employs a great many forms (sub-types) of the letter of credit.

International banking practice has devised several *usages* in connection with the letter of credit. The most important of them were complied in the form of rules by the International Chamber of Commerce, which published them as Uniform Customs and Practice for Documentary Credits, valid in their current text from 1984. These rules (like the Uniform Rules for Collections) are not rules of law and are applied on the basis of declarations made by banks of the different countries (either individually or through the central banks) to the effect that they recognize those rules as binding on themselves. (According to the list published by the International Chamber of Commerce, the banks of nearly all countries of the world, including Hungary, have submitted themselves to these rules.) It is stated in the rules themselves that their applicability to a particular legal relationship must be indicated in any letter of credit.

For that matter, the said rules are to be applied to all letters of credit honoured by the banks concerned, including "stand-by" letters of credit (used mainly in the USA).

§80. GUARANTEES FOR INTERNATIONAL PAYMENTS

In numerous cases, international payments are in need of legal means that are specifically in the nature of a guarantee, ones that, at least in their basic features, are known and employed even in domestic payment transactions and assume special aspects when used in international commercial transactions. Bank credit (surety) and bank guarantee are the most frequently used legal means of securing payment by the debtor.

1. *Bank credit* is, in essence, suretyship (Arts. 272 to 276 of the Civil Code) undertaken by a bank. Accordingly its basic feature is in being an incidental liability, namely in the surety's obligation being adjusted to that of the principal obligor. The practical consequence of this fact consists primarily in the fact that the bank standing surety may make not only its own possible exceptions to the obligee (either under suretyship or on the basis of another legal relationship), but also those of the principal obligor.

2. *Bank guarantee* means a bank's assumption of an obligation that, under specified conditions – particularly upon the occurrence or non-occurrence of some event or upon presentation of certain documents – it will, within the set time-limit, effect payment to the beneficiary up to the amount stipulated. (This is the definition of bank guarantee also given by Art. 249 of the Civil Code.)

The legal relationship of bank guarantee is similar to that of bank credit in there being a basic legal relationship (typically sale) behind both, but it differs essentially from the latter in that the bank may not make the exceptions to the beneficiary of the bank guarantee that the obligor of the basic relationship (typically seller) may take to the obligee of the basic relationship (typically buyer). (Of course, the bank may take its own possible exceptions to the beneficiary of the bank guarantee.) In this sense the bank guarantee is independent of the basic deal.

The bank's obligation is determined by the terms of the contract of guarantee, which fixes the limit of the sum secured by the guarantee, sets the time-limit of validity, defines the mode of making use of the guarantee and the conditions for presenting the relevant document, etc.

The "*tender guarantee*" serving to assure the seriousness of bids made in a tender (essentially substituting for a cash guarantee), the guarantee securing repayment of advance money, the guarantee securing payment of the purchase price, and the guarantee securing contractual performance are typically used in international commercial practice.

3. Bank credit and bank guarantee may only be differentiated by analyzing the contract of the pertinent document in each case. (The more denomination of the document may be misleading if only for the reason that the two legal notions are not clearly distinguished in every language or the terminologies used in the different languages may cover different contents. Thus, for instance, the German "*Garantie*" refers, usually but not always, to bank guarantee, while the English "guarantee" tends to mean suretyship in general.)

A security is deemed to be an obvious bank guarantee if the bank declares in the document itself that it will effect the payment undertaken in the document, without examining the basic legal relationship between the parties. Similarly, the bank's declaration to effect payment without taking any exceptions which its own clients, the parties to the basic transaction or any third party are entitled to make suggests the existence of a bank guarantee. On the other hand, a security containing an obligation for the bank in case of a breach of a concrete contract, without the bank waiving its right to examine the basic deal or to make exceptions, suggests the existence of a bank credit.

§81. BILLS OF EXCHANGE AND CHEQUES

Securities embodying pecuniary claims, particularly the bill of exchange and the cheques, are of paramount importance in payment transactions forming part of international economic relations. The international use of securities is facilitated by their strict forms rooted in centuries-old traditions and by the ease with which such transactions are conducted.

1. The international significance of securities explains the conclusion of comprehensive international conventions relating to uniform rules on both bills of exchange and cheques. The uniform substantive rules of the law of bills of exchange are contained in the Geneva Convention of 1930, which was acceded to by Hungary in 1964 [and was promulgated by Law-Decree No. 1 of 1965 and Decree No. 1/1965. (I.24.) of the Minister of Justice on its execution]. Nearly

50 States are party thereto. The substantive rules of the law of cheques were unified by the Geneva Convention of 1931, which was also ratified by Hungary in 1964 [and was promulgated by Law-Decree No. 2 of 1965 and Decree No. 2/1965. (I.24.) of the Minister of Justice on its execution].

In terms of legislative source, the international conventions concerning substantive-law rules on bills of exchange and cheques are characterized by the fact that they do not apply only to securities issued in international transaction. Since they constitute a uniform international law (*loi uniform*; see item 2 (c) in Section B of §12), their rules are also applicable to bills of exchange and cheques used in purely domestic transactions. (A deplorable "flaw" of the uniform law in this field consists of the fact that the common-law countries have not acceded to the Geneva Conventions on Bills of Exchange and Cheques).

2. The unification of substantive-law rules relating to bills of exchange and cheques has ruled out, in this field, the possibility for conflicts of laws between the States party to the Geneva Conventions, but the possibility of conflict situations has remained in relation to States not party to these Conventions establishing uniform substantive rules. With a view to reducing such possibilities, there were adopted, concurrently with the above uniform laws, conventions for the *unification of conflict norms relating to bills of exchange and cheques*. Hungary is a party also to these *conventions on conflicts of laws* (which were promulgated by the legislative acts mentioned above). The international treaties in question have, for the most part, codified the known conflict rules; e.g. the form of bills of exchange and cheques is governed by the law of the place where the declarations at law are signed (*lex loci actus*).

3. In respect of States not party either to the Conventions on the substantive law of bills of exchange and cheques (item 1 above) or to the conventions on conflict norms relating to bills of exchange and cheques (item 2), the applicable law is determined by Art. 28 (1) of the *Code*: "The existence and extent of an obligation deriving from securities shall be subject to the law applicable at the *place of performance*". It was by virtue of this provision that the Supreme Court (Pf.III.21 093/1994) applied the Austrian Bills of Exchange Act, for instance, in an action involving a claim based on a bill of exchange and to be settled at the branch of a bank in Austria of an Austrian obligee of a bill of exchange.

CHAPTER XXV

CONTRACTS IN PRIVATE INTERNATIONAL LAW

§82. HISTORICAL ANTECEDENTS, EXISTING SOLUTIONS AND THE HUNGARIAN REGULATION

The preceding paragraphs (61 to 81) presented the mechanism of contracts that function in international economic relations, in international trade, and the working of that mechanism in substantive law. The pertinent substantive law is one generally unified by international conventions and fundamentally controlling the civil (commercial) law content of contracts, but also covering contracts appearing in public-law form. The law of conflicts recedes into the background in cases where the relevant rules of substantive law govern. Yet the unification of substantive law is far from complete, full-scale unification being a goal not even pursued in respect either of the possible catalogue of contracts or of accessions to the pertinent conventions. By way of a background solution, however, there was a need for the law of conflicts even in relationships where full coverage was seen, as it were, to be a conceptual objective.

The private international law of contracts is consequently an important element of contract law. The present chapter is devoted to expressing this fact.

1. In the *historical processes leading to the birth of private international law* (see §§10–11), the credit for the delimitation and determination of the governing law of contracts through differentiation between personal statutes goes back again to legal learning fostered by the glossators and commentators.

Relying on considerable antecedents, Bartolus (1314–1357) was the first to devise a more comprehensive theoretical system, *inter alia*, of the private international law of contracts. In his great *Commentary* he naturally devotes a large chapter to contracts and to methods of solving conflict problems. He distinguishes between formal requirements (form) and substantive (subjective) rights, the former being controlled by the *lex loci contractus* and the latter needing subdivision. Later, e.g. with Balus (1319–1400), predominance was won by the theory of *lex loci contractus*. In his writing *Conclusiones de statuties et consuetudinibus*, generally considered a masterpiece on private international law, and commenting on the decree *"Cunctos populos"* in the *Codex*

Justinianus (C. 1.1.1), Dumoulin came to the conclusion that the various elements of a contract, in the different phases of its existence, can be deemed to be firmly established in law if they are inferred mostly from the substance of the contract. It may thus be stated that most of the major connecting factors had also been defined (and reinforced by the French, Dutch and German schools of thought in the 17th and 18th centuries) in respect of contracts before modern times which saw the appearance of codifications and the development of modern legal learning in the sphere of private international law.

2. The theory of private international law in the bourgeois period, which in Europe exercised the greatest influence on contracts as well, was worked out by Savigny in §§367–74 and 381–82 of his book *System des heutigen römischen Rechts* in Volume VIII on Private International Law. The main elements of his theory are these: (a) a distinction should be drawn between jurisdiction in respect of contracts and the applicable law; (b) the main connecting factor of jurisdiction is contractual agreement emanating from the autonomy of the parties or, failing such agreement, from the rules determining the applicable law (p. 246); (c) the applicable law, just as jurisdiction (*Gerichtsbarkeit*) over contractual relations, is determined in the first place by the choice of the parties (giving preference, according to Savigny, to the place of performance either expressly or by implication); "special jurisdiction over obligations rests, just like the real seat of them, on free choice by the parties, which appears tacitly implied rather than expressed in the contract" (p. 206); (d) in the absence of choice of law, the seat of contractual relations and hence the governing law are to be determined in the following sequence: (i) the place of performance, if clearly evident; (ii) if the obligation arises from the debtor's lasting business, the applicable law is that of the permanent seat of business; (iii) if the obligation arises from an individual act of the debtor, the applicable law is that of the place of such act; (iv) the debtor's residence, failing any of the above conditions; the debtor's residence may be a subsidiary connecting factor because, with this possibility open to them, the parties are more inclined to consider this rather than another place to be the place of performance; (v) the formalities of the transaction are subject, as a general rule, to the *locus regit actum*, i.e. the law of the place of the legal act (contracting).

By reference to our analysis of legal history in §§10–11 of this volume, it remains to be added that the parties' right to choice of law in the domain of contracts had been fully established as an institution chiefly by Mancini and his Italian school of thought and came to be generally accepted under his and his followers' influence. Although Mancini's work appeared later (1851) than Savigny's (1849) and the contractual will of the parties also became a decisive factor in Savigny's theory, Savigny held that will could prevail in a more indirect way (e.g. through the place of performance or the appearance of some other contractual factor). It was the Mancinian school that turned the right to the stipulation of law, this category of party autonomy which was to be allowed to operate by itself, into a general institution of private international law.

3. This doctrine has continued to develop *in our century*. Changes have occurred mainly in the following aspects.

(a) The *connecting factors* have come to form a *more differentiated* system, with the emergent need for the law-maker to formulate specific localizers for the different types of contracts. So, as can be seen, each of the pre-existing connecting factors, no matter how differentiated a picture they showed, bore on contracts in general with none to govern, say, contracts of sale, shipping or licence, though evidence of incipient progress in this direction could be discerned in Savigny's system of thought described above. An inquiry into the codes of the 20th century or other sources of private international law, reveals a notable spread of in-depth regulations governing the different types of contracts. In modern laws, individual contracts like sale, agency, commission, *locatio conductio operis*, carriage, publishing, licence, purchase by sale on a stock exchange and by auction, liability on securities, purchase of real property, contracts concerning vessels and aircraft, etc. are governed by specifically formulated principles, even though they often remain subject to the same connecting factors as before.

Of course, the freedom of choice of law everywhere ranks first and is followed by differentiation. Numerous types of contracts are made subject, *a priori*, to private-law rules by the PIL Codes of Poland (1965, Arts. 27–28), Czechoslovakia (1963, Art. 10), Yugoslavia (1982, Art. 20, which specifies 20 types of contracts) and Switzerland (1987, Arts. 97 *et seq.*).

(b) In addition to Savigny's conceptual approach, namely that the contract should be linked to the seat of contractual relations, there appeared other concepts and considerations, such as the principles of the closest link, or the most significant relationship, and of typical performance, according to which the legislator subjected a contract to the legal system with which it was most closely connected in terms of economic, social and legal function, with whose territory the most typical element of contractual performance had the closest contact. In most countries and in most types of contracts this has led to preference being given to the law of the debtor (over Savigny's place of performance, which cannot always be considered to be sufficiently characteristic: in case of purchase, for instance, the typical element is the seller's performance according to appropriate quality and other standards, whereby the economic and social function of the entire contract is fulfilled).

Failing choice of law, the French draft of 1967 (Art. 2313) renders a contract subject to the law with which it has the closest link in respect of its economic function and especially its performance (*Par son économie, et notamment par le lieu principal de son exécution*). In most cases this is obviously the obligor's law, for it is but one formulation of several aspects regarding the law of the place of typical performance. Article 25 of the Greek Act of 1940/1946 favours the most convenient law having regard to all the circumstances of the particular case. It is nevertheless characteristic of these sources of law not to go into further detail, leaving scope for amplification by practice.

(c) Differentiated solutions are offered by the Austrian Code of PIL of 1978 (Arts. 35–45), the Swiss Code of 1987 (Arts. 112–122) and the German Code of 1986 (Arts. 27–30), each of which deserved considerable credit for its modern regulation, as well as by the Rome Convention of 1980 concluded by the European Communities on the private international law of contracts (Arts. 3–7) and the Hague Convention of 1986 on the conflict rules governing international sale (Arts. 7–11), but their differentiation is of a different nature. In general, the point is that recent international practice has shown *more and more signs of there being no advantage in subjecting contracts exclusively to one or another connecting factor, traditional or a priori, extensively regulating a particular type of contract*. Seen in a historical perspective this is a new sort of integration following upon differentiation. A regulation going too deep into detail ties the judge's hands too tightly, barring him from arriving at a decision more consonant with the peculiarities of the case at hand and with the values of substantive law as determined by the legislator.

Therefore, in countries with great practice in this field, efforts have recently been made to formulate flexible rules governing the status of contracts under private international law or to allow scope for judicial practice to seek ways and means to brush aside inappropriate or much too rigid conflict norms. In dealing with individual contracts, larger textbooks start in each case from the existing conflict norms of a country, either written or established by courts in earlier cases, and go on to give detailed treatment of the different solutions sought and chosen by practice either through the intermediary use of *renvoi* or qualification as general institutions of private international law or through the application of a private international subnorm different from the general rule.

This tendency – namely a flexible regulation under an integrated and *a posteriori* approach – has become rather general in recent times. This is exemplified by the aforementioned Convention of the European Communities on the unification of the conflict norms of the law of contracts, which contains comprehensive and flexible rules rather than attempting to enumerate and to regulate every possible type of contract and to prescribe application of a special irreplaceable rule to each type of contract. In a few paragraphs its Art. 4 lays down general rules formulated in the following trichotomy: (i) in the absence of a chosen law a particular transaction is governed by the law of the place to which it has the closest relationship; (ii) that law in turn is presumed to be primarily the law of the party rendering the characteristic performance; (iii) the law of the place of characteristic performance may be avoided if, in consideration of all the circumstances present, the contract can be stated to have a closer connection with the law of another State. That is all there is to it. Everything else depends on concrete facts and on judicial discretion. Judicial practice will, of course, typify cases in general, without offering prefixed solutions for any particular matter. An essentially similar approach has been codified in the German and Swiss PIL Codes (Arts. 28 and 117, respectively).

On the other hand as regards differentiation under the new approach, or the general rules indicated above, the applicable law is chosen by the parties or, failing choice of law, by the judge, but certain types of contract are nonetheless excluded from the control of the applicable law so determined, from the scope application of the *lex obligationis* thus established. Such contracts include those (e.g. consumers' contracts, labour contracts) in respect of which it is appropriate for some special measures of protection for one of the parties (generally the weaker party) to take precedence over the otherwise applicable law (Arts. 28–30 of the German Code, Arts. 117 *et seq.* of the Swiss Code, Arts. 4 *et seq.* of the EC Convention). More specifically, we have here an extremely important phenomenon of modern times, notably one postulating that the value orientation of substantive law, some minimum of material justice should, to a reasonable extent, prevail even among the conflict norms, which, by their nature embody no value. In terms of legal technique, this secondary, separate or subsequent connection takes place through disregard (*Durchgriff*) of the given statute of contracts, which ensures that such matters are governed by typified special rules instead of by the principal rules of general application [for a detailed treatment, see §11; Mádl: *Érték vagy jogbiztonság* (Value or Legal Certainty)].

4. There are various reasons to justify a separate discussion of the Hague Convention of 1986 mentioned earlier and called upon to codify a uniform private international law of international sale. On the one hand, Hungary is a member of the Hague Conference, which framed the Convention, and has participated in the work of codification. On the other hand, one should be mindful that the Convention will come into play and thus become of relevance to Hungary as well whenever it affects cases with Hungarian bearings at foreign fora. Moreover, Hungary can be expected to ratify the Convention, as it would indeed be advisable for it to do, thereby forming part of the legal infrastructure of Europe [see Mádl: *Ius Commune Europaea. Hágai Egyezmények* (*Ius Commune Europaea.* Hague Conventions)]. The major rules of the Convention are these: (1) free choice of law (Art. 7); failing choice of law, the following connecting factors come into play: (2) the seller's law (para. 1 of Art. 8); (3) the buyer's law, if the negotiations and the conclusion of the contract took place in the buyer's country; if, under the contract, the seller is to perform in the buyer's country; or if the contract was made under the buyer's terms or upon invitation to tender (para. 2 of Art. 8); (4) exceptionally, if in consideration of all the circumstances the contract is linked most closely to another law, that law is to control (para. 3); (5) purchase by auction is controlled by the law of the place of auction (Art. 9); (6) the law of sale, apart from the usual exceptions (capacity of action, bearings on third persons, etc.), extends to the contractual relationship as a whole (Art. 12), but quality reception is governed by the *lex loci* unless the contract contains a different stipulation on the examination of goods (Art. 13); (7) while not recognizing the *renvoi,* the Convention explicitly ordains observance of the peremptory rules and the public policy clause (Arts. 15,

17–18); (8) in order to ensure uniform application, it is desirable for courts to interpret the Convention in view of its international character (Art. 16). As can be seen, discounting the group of cases under item (4), the Convention is not in conflict with Hungarian law, to be discussed presently, in regard to sales. This is an added argument in favour of Hungary's accession. As regards the said group of cases, the Convention follows the general modern approach in distancing itself from a totally *a priori* regulation that would admit no exception.

5. This leads us on to the *attitude of Hungarian law to the aforesaid modern developments in the field of contracts*. A substantive answer will be given in §83, but it may be indicated at this juncture that in some aspects it was a pity that the Hungarian law did not take a bolder step towards a higher degree of flexibility, a more value-oriented solution by substantive law.

A very through Hungarian study written on the maritime contract (highly important, for Hungary is a busy shipper!) has found that the law of the carrier is usually a disadvantage to Hungarian parties (see Martonyi's book in the List of Sources). Still, our previous drafts of private international law prescribed the application of that law, and so does the current Code [para. (i) of Art. 25]. And no improvement in our situation can be expected from this rule, because in the long run we are more likely to have our goods carried than to increase our carrying business even though the Hungarian sea-going vessels were to enlarge the volume of goods shipped.

Under these circumstances, it would serve us better to apply the Hungarian law (once it had developed an internal regulation) or a law determined by another element of contract (e.g. the law of the place of contracting). Here are three examples in illustration. (1) In the first example (similar cases are cited in known textbooks like Dicey's and Morris' with English orientation toward carriers' interests) a Hungarian enterprise makes a contract of carriage in the United States with a British firm for the shipment of its goods to England. The contract contains a stipulation of the carrier that excludes his liability for damage caused through the captain's or the crew's negligence. This stipulation is held valid under English law (England has been a big power in maritime transport for centuries, so it is not accidental that its law of carriage and related conflict rules render the legal relationship subject to the carrier's law). Therefore, if such cases before a Hungarian court were subject to the law as determined by our Code, the Hungarian enterprise would lose its action under the English law. A more flexible regulation, with this same contract made in the United States and with possible dispute governed by the law of the place of contracting, would eliminate the disadvantage of that stipulation, because it is invalid under American law, and the action would stand a chance of favourable adjudication. (2) The second example is from judicial practice previous to the adoption of the present Code. A Hungarian plaintiff sued a defendant carrying company of Yugoslavia because the goods had been short-shipped. Then, following a protest by the Supreme Court on legal grounds involving full disregard of the foreign element, one party wanted to apply the law of this country and the other the law of that country in order to achieve a favourable result in substantive law during the new proceedings. The court had several options to consider and, failing choice of law by the parties, found it most reasonable, having regard to all the circumstances of the legal relationship, to apply the law of the place of contracting (Budapest City Court 56 Pf. 29 406/1964). Today, failing choice of law and contrary provisions of the international convention, the court is clearly bound to apply the law of the Yugoslav carrier. (3) In the third example a contract of purchase on commission is made in Hungary between a Hungarian and a foreign party, the purchase is to take place abroad but performed in Hungary, involving *del credere* liability. The applicable law (under the Hungarian Code) will be that of the commission merchant, who has no such liability under his own law, but does have under Hungarian law.

These examples go to show that the strict commands of the Hungarian Code are not always an advantage, nor are they certain to be the simplest when the contract or transaction is viewed in its entirety rather than solely from the angle of Hungarian interests. Surpassing the previous drafts, the current Code covers the law of contracts only in a few instead of many articles, offering modern and workable solutions even in its present form. It nevertheless enumerates nominate contracts and, this is where it does not yet follow the aforementioned tendency, ordains the application of a predetermined law to each of them (law of carrier, law of seller, etc.).

Yet the rationale of that tendency has, as can be seen, appeared on each side. How far this is true is shown by the Czechoslovak PIL Code which gives a clear expression of the said tendency. Though the Czechoslovak Code did not remain on the level of general regulation, as is the case with the aforesaid EC Convention, it laid down the principal rule ("where the parties failed to select the applicable law, their contractual relations shall be governed by the law whose application is apt for a reasonable settlement of the given relationship": para. 1 of Art. 10) and then directed the application of this or that law to specified contracts as enumerated therein, stating, however, that the specified contract rule would apply "as a rule". In the light of what we have said before, this seems to be a modern regulation: on the one hand, it injected no rigidity into practice and, on the other, provided a sufficient guide for ensuring legal certainty, for the law determined by the conflict norms relating to the different contracts could only be avoided if it were inapt for a reasonable settlement of particular case. The Hungarian Code does not use the phrase "as a rule", but its lesser flexibility is compensated for by the values of greater predictability and legal certainty.

§83. HUNGARIAN REGULATION ON THE GOVERNING LAW OF CONTRACTS *(LEX CONTRACTUS)*

1. The *freedom of party autonomy* (choice of law) is expressed in Art. 24 of the Code (the first article in the chapter on the law of obligations) in these terms:

"The law chosen by the parties at the time of contracting or later shall be applied to their contracts". This right of the contracting parties to choose the applicable law is similarly recognized by several bilateral agreements of Hungary on legal assistance [e.g. item 1 (a) in Section B of §12]. [The Hungarian law expressly chosen by the contracting parties was applied by the Supreme Court, for instance, under Art. 38 (1) of the Hungarian–Czechoslovak Agreement on Legal Assistance (Pf. VI. 22 046/1993).]

The above basic provision of the Code calls for some comments, the most important of which are the following.

(a) The parties, who in Hungarian law enjoy full liberty in choosing their law, may *stipulate a law having no bearing on the concrete transaction.* In contractual practice it is rather common to stipulate, *inter alia*, the Swiss law (in most cases even Swiss jurisdiction), partly because the Swiss law of obligations is highly developed, partly because it is widely known to be such, Switzerland being a neutral State and having gained considerable practice in commercial arbitration, and also partly because, occasionally, each party stipulates that law by way of concession, being unable to designate his own law.

Unlike the Polish Code (Art. 25), Hungarian law does not require the stipulated law to have at least some connection with the contractual relationship. The full freedom of party autonomy is guaranteed in all modern laws practically without exception.

(b) Certain objections or restrictive approaches to the full freedom of party autonomy are nevertheless on record. The objections voiced related to, among others, the *legal nature* of the right to choose a law. Some held that this right could only be granted with regard to *dispositive rules*, but not against the *jus cogens* rules (this is but a substantive-law theory of domestic law claiming that the parties are free to shape their contract under their domestic substantive law, and when they opt for a foreign law they use their freedom by defining *brevitatis causa* the substance of their contract). According to the conflicts-law theory of party autonomy, the parties may choose their law, not by virtue of the dispositive rules of civil law, but under the general provision of private international law, and thus their autonomy prevails over the *jus cogens* norms as well. The sponsors of this theory used this argument against the former theory, contending that the stipulation of law was thus made in a vacuum and was at best a phenomenon of the law of nature. This dispute, somewhat legalistic, can be answered by saying that the Code explicitly states party autonomy to be a fundamental institution of private international law, from which it follows further that this right is not in a vacuum, nor is it a phenomenon of the law of nature, but it is a permitted and functioning institution because it is provided for in the law of the country of the forum. This is a command of the country of the forum, just as the provision which, in the absence of stipulation of law, determines the "otherwise" applicable law, again sometimes likely to be other than the law of the country of the forum. The current Hungarian Code adheres to the conflicts-law theory of party autonomy.

(c) The Hungarian law does not provide for *implied* stipulation of a chosen law, nor does it forbid its acceptance. In the laws of several other countries, which have adopted a similar solution, implied stipulation of law is an allowed or accepted practice, if it clearly follows from all the circumstances of the case. In the wording of, e.g., the Czechoslovak Code: "if in consideration of the circumstances there is no doubt as to the intent manifested" (Art. 9); a similar formulation is found in Art. 35 of the Austrian Code: "contractual relations shall be under the control of the law chosen by the parties expressly or by implication". Consequently, along with the concrete regulation by the Code, it is for theory and practice to take a stand on this question. The high degree of autonomy and permissiveness characterizing Hungarian civil law and (this part of) private international law suggests the acceptance of implied stipulation of a chosen law. Frequent references in a contract of A and B and in other related documents, particularly as regards legal dispute, to the commercial or civil law of country C can be regarded as implied choice of law, and it is reasonable for the court to apply the law of country C.

(d) As to the *time* of selecting the law, the Hungarian law is clear in stating, in accordance with international practice, that the parties are free to choose the applicable law at any time prior to the adjudication of the case (Legf.B. Pf.III.20 998/1995). [For example, the Supreme Court applied the Hungarian law chosen by the parties *during the proceedings* (Pf.VI.22 046/1993) and even *in the appellate procedure* (Pf.III.20 895/1992).]

(e) Problems may be caused by *change in the law chosen*: have the parties selected a given legal systems in its organic, hence changing, whole or with its content prevailing at the time of selection? In line with international practice, the Hungarian regulation should also be construed as meaning that stipulation of law applies to the law of the particular country as a changing whole, unless the parties have expressly agreed otherwise.

(f) Finally, attention should be drawn to what *remains outside the scope of the autonomy of the parties* in spite of their generally recognized liberty in choosing their law.

It should be stated as a general rule, and this follows from the quoted text of the Code, that the stipulation of law applies to "contractual transactions", meaning that it does not extend to non-contractual disputes (for its applicability to inheritance relations and labour contracts, see the chapters on the law of inheritance and on labour law).

Even the laws admitting any extreme interpretation of *reference on and reference back,* that stipulation of law does not mean acceptance of the conflict rules of the selected law. Where there is stipulation of law, therefore, it is always the internal substantive-law rules of the given legal system that are applicable.

The *legal and disposing capacities* of the parties are likewise subject to the domestic law of the parties, not to the law stipulated by them [see "preliminary question" in item 4 (c) below].

Under the law of numerous countries, the *formal validity of transactions* is governed by the law of the place of contracting (*locus regit actum*). However, this exception to the applicable law chosen by the parties is irrelevant to Hungarian private international law, because the Code (para. 1 of Art. 30) renders the rules of the governing law (namely the single *lex obligationis*) applicable to the formal requirements of validity as well (see item 4 below).

In the absence of an express agreement, the selected law does not apply to *certain aspects of acceptance of delivery* (obligation to inspect, mode of inspection, objections raised) which are also brought by Hungarian law under the control of the law of the place of destination or of the State where delivery is taken (para. 2 of Art. 30).

(g) The *Hungarian practice* of selecting a law likewise points clearly to full party autonomy (as conceived of under the conflicts-law theory).

In most contractual disputes arising between private parties (or involving one private party) the "otherwise applicable law" is ascertained and determined by the forum (PKKB. 4.P.86 327/1978; PKKB. 4.P.89 579/1982). However, the possible foreseeable advantages of selecting a law may be worth considering in case of a larger amount in dispute, because the parties usually do not choose a law, although they are free to do so. It tends to be a general practice of the enterprises to agree on the applicable law in their foreign trade contracts. Cases are also frequent in which the parties stipulate a law on the emergence of a dispute if they failed to do so in the contract. One of the cases adjudicated by the Arbitration Tribunal of the Hungarian Chamber of Commerce (Vb. 83.069), for instance, shows a differentiated practice in the stipulation of law. The Hungarian defendant and the Kuwaiti plaintiff made a contract for exclusive representation. In the dispute (complex of disputes) which arose from that legal relationship there appeared several variants of chosen law: (a) the contract of representation stipulated the jurisdiction of the Arbitration Court of the International Chamber of Commerce (Paris) and the French substantive law to govern any dispute concerning the contract; (b) in a separate contract the parties submitted themselves to the Arbitration Tribunal of the Hungarian Chamber of Commerce in the dispute about the formation of the contract at the time the dispute arose; (c) the defendant presented a counterclaim arising from another contract of sale made with the plaintiff concerning a commodity "represented" in the previous contract. In the counterclaim the parties stipulated different arbitral tribunals (if the seller sues, the seat of the arbitration court is the capital city of the buyer's country, and *vice versa*), but they were free to go to the ordinary court of the defendant's country as well. The substantive law was the law of the seller's country in each case; (d) the defendant submitted the counterclaim to the Arbitration Tribunal of the Hungarian Chamber of Commerce, which was to apply the Hungarian substantive law because it followed from the arrangement under (b) and was also provided for in the Statutes of that Tribunal (see §117).

2. Having discussed the stipulation of law as a way of determining the law applicable to contractual relations with international elements, we will now turn to cases in which the parties do not use their right to choose their law. It is here that the "*otherwise applicable law*" comes into play.

(a) *International practice knows of diverse solutions* according to the element of the legal relationship which is used as the connecting factor for the determination of applicable law.

(aa) One aspect of diversity concerns the emergence and use of various connecting factors in both legislative and judicial practice, such as the law of the place of performance *(lex loci executionis)*, the law of the place of contracting *(lex loci contractus)*, the law of the place of payment *(lex loci solutionis)*, the law of the State of seller *(lex loci venditoris)*, the common *lex personae*, stipulation of arbitration, the law of the forum, etc. This is sufficient to show that, owing to the extreme diversity and complexity of contractual relations, no solution of one kind or another suited to the nature of concrete transactions can be rigidly prescribed in advance. The reality is that, failing a clear command of the law, the court will employ the law best suited to the character of the case at hand and will, *quasi ex post facto*, determine the "*a priori*" conflict rule. It is a matter of record how great a role is played by the influence of the forum, or the inclination of the courts to secure, with a sort of endogenetic ease, the values of their own substantive law and to disguise that propensity in some principle of the law of conflicts. When dealing with general doctrines we have referred to the homeward trend (*Heimwärtsstreben*) or the phenomenon of staying at home (*zu Hause bleiben*) in private international law. Well, this holds true especially in respect to the *lex obligationis*.

(ab) Another aspect of diversity consists in the fact that, according to some conceptions (synthetic, deductive method), contractual relations in general and concrete cases in particular are to be placed under the control of *a single legal system, a single statute*, while, according to other views (analytical, inductive method), it is held advisable to render the different contract types and even concrete legal relationships, by reason of their nature, subject to *connecting factors varying by type of contract or by the inner specifics* of legal relationships, the result being that a particular legal relationship may be governed by several statutes of private international law.

All this is true if, in the absence of choice of law, we see the different variants of the *lex obligationis* in a somewhat abstract form, on the general plane. If, however, we examine a particular system of law more closely, we find that it does not follow this or that method or solution in general, but is flexibly adjusted, in conformity with the legislator's intentions, to the specifics or real-life characteristics of the different legal relationships.

(b) In determining the connecting factors, the Hungarian law bases itself on the general need to have a legal relationship determined by the law within whose jurisdiction its economically, socially and legally most characteristic element is realized (characteristic performance, *spezifische Leistung* theory, which is generally associated with Schnitzer, although it was formerly known by another designation: e.g. Savigny's doctrine of seat of the legal relationship is not very different either).

From this point of view the Hungarian Code (Art. 25) has determined the connecting factors for the most important contract types.

The applicable law of contracts shall be the law of the States in which, at the time of contracting, –

a) the seller, with respect to *contracts of sale*;

b) the lessor, with respect to *contracts of lease and tenancy*;

c) the licensee, with respect to *contracts for the exploitation of rights under copyright protection* (this connecting factor was correctly employed by the Supreme Court in its Ruling Pf.IV.22.284/1994);

d) the licensor, with respect to *contracts for the exploitation of industrial property rights and other rights representing material value*;

e) the bailee, with respect to *contracts of deposit (storage)*;

f) the agent, with respect to *contracts of agency*;

g) the commission agent (consignee), with respect to *contracts of commission*;

h) the representative (agent), with respect to *contracts of commercial representation*;

i) the carrier or the forwarding agent, with respect to *contracts of carriage or forwarding*;

j) the banking institute rendering service, with respect to *contracts for banking and credit transactions*;

k) the insurer, with respect to *insurance contracts*;

l) the lender, with respect to *contracts for the use of money and contracts for the use of goods*;

m) the donor, with respect to *contracts of gift* – has his domicile or habitual residence, or seat or business headquarters.

As can be seen, the seat (place of business, habitual residence) of the above-mentioned contracting parties is considered by Hungarian law as constituting the element which gives best expression of the distinctive feature of a particular contract in view of the performance or activity stipulated therein.

[The Supreme Court (Pf.III.20.895/1992) corrected the obvious error of the court of first instance: the typical performance under the contract of sale was the commodity rather than the purchase price. A similar decision was handed down in its Ruling Pf.III.20.998/1995.]

We have mentioned earlier (cf. item 5 in §82) that the Hungarian regulation, though modern and flexible, may have laid down rules that, owing to partial rigidity, are disadvantageous to us in respect of certain contract types (e.g. carriage).

In its subsequent provisions, for the very reason of directing the application of the law of the State where the most characteristic element of the contract is realized, the Code departs from the foregoing rules, namely from the law of the seat of the party rendering the most characteristic performance. (1) Obviously, a contract of *locatio conductio operis*, for instance, is really capable of fulfilling its function at the place where, under its stipulation, the activity is to be carried out or the result is to be brought about, so the governing law is the law of the particular place (para. 2 of Art. 26). (2) The *lex rei sitae* is the dominant governing law of contracts concerning *immovables* in all laws of the world, and the *lex bandi* is applied to contracts concerning registered *vessels and aircraft* (para. 1 of Art. 26). (3) Contracts concerning *purchase on a stock exchange and by auction* are also generally governed by the law of the particular place (para. 1 of Art. 27). (4) Contracts for *maintenance* and for *life annuity* are subject to the law of the State where maintenance is to be provided or life annuity paid (para. 3 of Art. 26). (5) Contracts of *association* are governed by the law of the State in which the association carries out its activity or, in the case of establishing a legal person, by the personal law of the legal person (para. 2 of Art. 27). (6) Obligations based on *securities* are determined by the law of the place of performance (para. 1 of Art. 28); legal relationships connected with bonds issued *under public loans* (assumption, transfer, etc. of obligations) are subject to the personal law of the bond issuer (para. 2 of Art. 28); if a security confers a *right to dispose of goods*, the property-law effects are governed by the law of property (para. 3 of Art. 28); if a negotiable instrument embodies a *right to membership* in a legal entity, the governing law is the personal law of the legal entity in question (para. 4 of Art. 28).

(c) If the above rules are viewed from the angle of *practice*, the real substance of the Code provision will be illustrated by a few typical examples or legal cases rather than by a full-length commentary in a separate book.

In connection with a *contract of publishing*, Hungarian author A has a legal dispute with a publisher of country B because the parties failed to clearly determine the amount of the honorarium and the conditions under which it was due to the author. The author relies on Hungarian law, under which a contract of publishing is an onerous one, and is entitled to an honorarium equal at least to the lowest amount due under Hungarian law. Since, however, such contracts are governed by the law of the licensee's State under Art. 25 (c) of the Code, the dispute is to be judged under the law and practice of country B.

The Hungarian law is applicable, on two grounds, to *recovery of a gift* from a foreign defendant in accordance with the judgment (passed by the District Court of Szekszárd, 9.P.20 018/1980) in a case in which the Hungarian plaintiffs demanded the return of Hungarian real property donated to a foreign owner: Art. 25 (m) of the Code renders contracts of gift subject to the law of the donor's State, while Art. 26 (1) prescribes the general application of the *lex situs* to contracts concerning movables.

In connection with the settlement of accounts concerning a very costly construction project abroad, the Hungarian defendant entrusted an expert in country A with the technical-financial review of the accounts and came into conflict with him. The expert brought an action before the Central District

Court of Budapest for the payment of his fee. The Court correctly qualified the contract as one of *locatio conductio operis*, which, under Art. 26 (1) of the Code (and earlier under customary law as well), is controlled by the law of country A, because the plaintiff (contractor) carried out his activity in that country (PKKB 4.P.86 327/1978). Also, on the ground of a similar contract, this same Court judged the expenses of the claimant German car repairer under the German law (BGB), because the Hungarian defendant had had his car repaired in the FRG and subsequently contested, by invoking various reasons, the amount of the bill, the date of delivery (repair) and the demand to pay for the damage caused by an unknown person. Before passing the judgment, the Court sought information from the Ministry of Justice about the German law in accordance with Art. 5 of the Code.

3. The third step in the Hungarian concept of regulation, following upon the stipulation of law as the first step and the law otherwise applicable to types of contracts as the second step, consists in offering an answer when the question involved cannot be solved in the first two steps, namely *non-typical or too complex contractual relations* cannot be brought clearly under any of the above "otherwise applicable law" rules.

(a) Such cases are covered by two subsidiary rules of the Code which require careful consideration by the judge.

(aa) According to the first of these subsidiary rules, "if the applicable law cannot be determined within the framework of Arts. 24–28, contracts shall be governed by the law of the domicile, habitual residence or seat (place of business) of the obligor of the most characteristic performance" (Art. 29).

[The Supreme Court (Pf.III.20 895/1992) correctly pointed to the obvious error of the court of first instance: the subsidiary rule in Art. 29 of the Code cannot be applied to typical and nominate contracts enumerated in the Code, but the concrete type of contract in question is to be governed by the pertinent connecting factor under Art. 25.]

(ab) If the first rule does not help either, then the second subsidiary rule applies; it is quite certain to lead to the applicable law as it provides that "the law most closely connected with the essential elements of the particular legal relationship shall apply in cases where the applicable law cannot be determined in the aforesaid either" (second sentence in Art. 29). As has been seen, the most significant relationship principle is in many countries virtually competing with, and even overriding, the principle of characteristic performance. We might as well say that the most significant relationship rule is in effect oriented to the same substance as the principle of characteristic performance, only that it can be safely relied upon even in cases involving several characteristic performances or complex relationships, because it deduces, from the totality thereof, the closest of all links with the particular legal system concerned. The Hungarian law has included this solution in its repertory to meet contingencies in which the clearer aspects of characteristic performance (which it has built upon so far) are not perceivable and there is no other recourse than to look for such connection.

(b) Of *practical* interest are costly and complex contracts like contracts for installation (or cooperation) which include purchase of patents and know-how, delivery of machinery, construction, company credit, carriage, lease of machinery, assembly, viz. several types of contracts. It is obviously impossible to determine the law controlling such type of contract by the many types of contracts functioning in it and hence to apply six or seven laws. In reality such contracts do not dispense with a "jurisdiction and applicable law" clause, i.e. stipulation of law. This is evidently the correct practice to follow. Should the need still arise to ascertain the applicable law, it is for the court to find the most reasonable law according to the "closest link" principle. Let us take a case in which the foreign party, concurrently with the transfer of his patent for exploitation in Hungary, undertakes to deliver and assemble a line of machinery, and to operate it for a specified period of time, one that is indeed capable of turning out the object of the patent with the properties indicated in the patent and in a *per diem* quantity. In a legal dispute the element of licence attracts the law of the foreign party's country under Art. 25 (d) of the Code, while the element of undertaking is controlled by Hungarian law in accordance with Art. 26 (2), since in such a situation both the orientation to Hungary of the contractual interests and the place of the activity aimed at performance, viz. the place of performance of both elements as well as the personal law of one of the contracting parties and other circumstances link the entire legal relationship most closely to Hungary, we can state, in the wording of the Code, that "the essential elements of the contractual relationship ... are most closely connected" with Hungary (Art. 29).

4. Now, in the fourth step, we must gain an answer to the question as to the content of the governing laws indicated above. Here the *content of applicable law* should be understood to mean the elements of a contractual relationship *to be placed under the control of the legal system determined by the said methods*; in other words, it should be ascertained whether all or only some aspects of a contract or a contractual relationship are to be adjudicated under the given system of law. A contractual relationship similarly presupposes the legal and disposing capacity of the parties, but the material and formal incidents of validity and jurisdictions may be controlled by different rules, and a contract is often accompanied by some agreement (mortgage, surety) securing it, involving set-off, assignment, and assumption of debt. In brief, a contractual relationship may, even in the case of a concrete transaction, be all-inclusive, comprising questions and doctrines that pertain to the general part of the law of obligations.

(a) In the law of numerous countries, specific questions of detail pertaining to the law of obligations, regulated by separate rules of private international law, are brought within the scope of separate statutes. Thus, for instance, the validity and the legal effect of a transaction under substantive law may be subjected to the law of the place of performance, but its formalities are controlled by the law of the place where the contract was made, and a contract of mortgage is placed under the control of yet another law. It is rather common that qualitative acceptance of delivery is made subject to the law of the place of destination or to the law of the State of acceptance.

It may be said in general that whereas occasionally, having regard to all the circumstances of the case, there may be a reason for subjecting some partial question of a contractual relationship to a separate (analytical) examination in order to reach the applicable law, it may be unwarranted to have a daily transaction, *in a concrete case*, split by legal means and to become entangled in contradictions between legal systems, a course leading up a blind alley so characteristic of legalistic alienation. This resort is justified only when it is not an overcomplicated form of legal regulation, but is dictated by the natural need to find a reasonable settlement for the given relationship.

(b) The *Hungarian regulation* has adopted the approach of seeking to *determine a contractual relationship so far as possible under a single statute*. It follows that Hungarian law conceives of the *lex obligationis* in a broad sense and with flexibility. Article 30 of the Code provides that, as a general rule, the *lex obligationis*, or "the governing law of contracts shall apply to all elements of the contractual relationship". This general rule is then broken down into details, with some exceptions allowed.

(ba) Accordingly, *the law of contracts extends to*: (i) the conclusion and formation of contract (Legf.B. Pf.III.20 998/1995); (ii) substantive and formal validity; (iii) legal effects; (iv) agreements securing the contract (mortgage, surety, etc.); (v) set-off claims arising from the contract; (vi) statute of limitation is also subject to the law applicable to claims; (vii) unilateral declarations, ordinarily subject to the rules on contracts.

(bb) The Code lists the following *exceptions*: (i) in the absence of contrary agreement, qualitative acceptance (obligation to inspect, mode of inspection, objections raised, etc.) are subject to the law of the State of acceptance; (ii) if there is agreement between the parties, the law agreed upon (other than the law governing the basic transaction) is applicable to independent contracts like mortgage, surety, etc.; (iii) the upholding of contracts is determined by the rule that a contract which for a formal defect is invalid under the *lex obligationis,* should be deemed valid if it is valid according to the law of the proceeding court or of the State in whose territory it was made or the purported legal effect is to occur (para. 3 of Art. 30).

(c) The so-called *preliminary question (Vorfrage)* has emerged in the practice of establishing the substance of applicable law. Given its weight, general nature and concept in literature, it may virtually be counted today among the general institutions of private international law. We will consider it briefly at this juncture because it arises most frequently, though not exclusively, in the domain of contracts.

Practical examples will highlight the following aspect. (1) A given case involves a claim for penalty arising from a contract of sale between a claimant

Hungarian foreign trade company and its foreign partner and the prescription of that claim (Arbitration Tribunal of the Hungarian Chamber of Commerce, VB/83050). The applicable law is clear: the parties stipulated Hungarian law. Owing to the peculiarities of the inner structure of the defendant company, the question was raised that the real defendant was not that company, but a "unit" thereof, a foreign trade organ with a partially different name. So, before prescription was to be judged under the rules of Hungarian law, the preliminary question had arisen as to who was the party on the other side, what was the name of the firm, what was the personality status between them. However, these questions of corporate law are governed, under the Code too, by the law of the place of incorporation, notably the particular foreign law (Art. 18). (2) A Hungarian national sells a video cassette to an Italian minor in observance of the foreign exchange regulations. There arises a dispute between the parties. The seller is a Hungarian, so the contract of sale is subject to Hungarian law under Art. 25 (a) of the Code, but a preliminary question arises in the meantime as to whether the contract was invalid because of the boy's minority, and this aspect is to be controlled by the personal law (Arts. 10–11 of the Code), namely by Italian law. (3) The next example shows that a preliminary question may emerge not only in respect of contracts. A Hungarian forum is to decide on the inheritance (juncture) of a Greek widow, a refugee. Since the testator was a Greek national, the question was to be judged by his personal law, the Greek law, under Art. 36 of the Code. However, the validity of the decedent's and the widow's marriage turned out to be questionable. The underlying case cannot be adjudicated without first deciding this question. So here we have the validity of marriage as a preliminary question, which in turn is governed by the common personal law at the time of marriage (Art. 37 of the Code).

Consequently the institution of preliminary question means that adjudication of the principal legal relationship necessitates that of another one as well, which is itself a significant and independent relationship. By reason of its identity and significance, the latter cannot be judged, at least sensibly and reasonably, by the conflict norm governing the principal legal relationship: it must be judged though because it logically precedes the "principal" question. As a general rule, the preliminary question can and must be judged, for the sake of inner harmony (*innere Entscheidungsharmonie*), by the conflicts law of the forum. Nor can the possibility be ruled out, however, for the judge to ascertain and accept the conflict rule of the law invoked (this is the so-called external harmony of decision, or *äussere Entscheidungsharmonie*). While the said institution of preliminary question clearly follows from the relative independence and comparable weight of the institutions covered by the Code, it should be judged by the criteria of the inner or external harmony of decision and in consideration of all the circumstances of the case.

Thus, regarding the scope of contracts law as discussed under this item, it is warranted to recognize the legitimacy of the preliminary question (e.g. legal and disposing capacity) in this respect as well, even though, in the wording of the Code, "the governing law of contracts extends to *all elements of the legal relationship*, particularly to ... the material and formal validity (of the contract)" (Art. 30). In fact, legal and disposing capacity is not a contractual relationship, a reason why its material and formal validity should be seen in relation to the incidents of validity other than those of legal and disposing capacity.

(d) A few words should be said about the fact that in the contractual autonomy of the parties or, failing choice of law, in the otherwise applicable law, notably in the conflicts-law statute of contracts (*lex obligationis*), there has appeared a peculiar partial statute, a set of rules on *"special protection requirement" (besonderes Schutzbedürfnis),* which is a new phenomenon in private international law. It forms part of the new Austrian Code (Art. 41) and is also explicitly manifest in some other codifications regulating private international law in greater depth, such as the Swiss Code of 200 articles (Arts. 120–121) and the ECE Convention on private international law (Arts. 5–6).

What is it all about? The point is that these sources of law subject contracts to the selected law or the law to which a particular contract can be linked according to the principle of typical performance or of the closest connection. Then these general rules are not followed up by a separate conflict rule for each type of contract. We have at hand the law determined by the given general rules to govern a particular contract, say the law of seller's country or of the place of contracting in case of a contract of sale or the law of creditor's country in case of a contract of credit, which will be the governing law of contract, the *lex obligationis*, in general. In recent years, particularly under the impact of consumer protection efforts, several countries have established different rules (partly of a public-law nature) for consumer protection and others devised to "protect the weaker party". [For example, these rules govern general conditions (protect buyers *vis-à-vis* sellers or banks in case of payment by instalments); prescribe the obligation of sellers to observe measures protective of buyers (indication of toxic substances, deadlines for the consumption of canned food, etc.) and confer related warranty rights on consumers; include specified social and other compulsory norms protecting workers in their country or places of work. Well, whichever the governing law of contract under the general rules of conflicts law, including the law chosen, it may not prevail over these protective norms, which will be controlled by the consequently favourable law of consumers in need of protection (e.g. the law of domicile).] This is how a partial *lex obligationis* comes about to govern the compulsory protective structure alongside the general *lex obligationis* of contracts. This is the core and substance of the above sources of law, of the said concept in general. As these norms interfere, *quasi a posteriori*, with the otherwise operative conflicts-law statutes of contracts, ordaining subsequent connections, they are also called rules of intervention or, as referred to above [see item 3 (c) in §82 on foreign legislative sources], "interfering norms" (*Eingriffsnormen*).

The question now is one of how this can be manifested in Hungarian legal practice, considering in particular that contracts are not even under the control of the general rules outlined above. As a matter of fact, the general rules may also lead the court, in consideration of the special interests of protection, to place the entire contract under the control of the law governing the protective structure. However, this is hardly possible because, under the Code, each type of contract is subject to a separate conflict norm. In case of purchase, for instance, the entire transaction with all its elements is mandatorily governed by the law of the seller's country, as there are no special rules in the Code (except where the parties agree on such rules, but in that case there is no problem, and that is not our concern here anyway). It is for practice to seek an answer to the problem and to take another step forward. In so doing practice may be guided by the following considerations. (1) These protective norms are in the nature of administrative law and as such are not under the control of the "all elements of the contractual relationship" rule (determining the scope of the governing law of contract) as laid down in Art. 30 of the Code. (2) Given their nature just described, they constitute a nominate group of virtually peremptory rules (see §24) which have the inherent attribute of "seeking" absolute application generally in all systems of law, this attribute being usually recognized even in aspects to which the norms of conflicts law contain no reference at all. The need and justification for absolute application are established in view of the nature of the given norm. (3) In the case of protective norms that appear largely in the sphere of the law of obligations (e.g. sale with instalment payment, general conditions of partial deals, norms of control), a similar position can be taken by an analogous interpretation of the above rules. Under international practice, such a development of customary law can be regarded as reasonable. For that matter, a guide to splitting the *lex obligationis* is also provided by the Hungarian Code, which, in Art. 33, lifts the law of the place of the tortious conduct out of the conflicts-law statute of liability and renders it mandatorily applicable to violations of traffic or other safety regulations, notwithstanding the fact that in a given case the otherwise applicable law would, under Art. 32 (2), be that of the State in which the damage occurred.

TITLE 6

LIABILITY FOR NON-CONTRACTUAL DAMAGE. UNJUST ENRICHMENT

CHAPTER XXVI

LIABILITY FOR NON-CONTRACTUAL DAMAGE. UNJUST ENRICHMENT

§84. DELICTUAL LIABILITY (TORTS) IN PRIVATE INTERNATIONAL LAW

For a long time the law of the place of wrongdoing (*lex loci delicti commissi*) in the domain of liability and claims for damage had the strength and certainty of a dogma in the law of nearly all States. It is only natural that this theoretical stand was also taken by Hungarian private international law. In the various systems of law there was greater or lesser controversy about what exactly was to be as regarded the place of wrongdoing – the place where the wrong was done or where the result occurred or both – but in the last analysis the guiding principle was always the *lex loci delicti commissi* of either place and this was a different matter. The essence was the wrongfulness of delictual conduct, which naturally entailed the application of the law of the place where the wrong was committed, because whether an act is socially and legally culpable and imputable can reasonably be determined under the law of the place where it was done.

In Volume II of his *Private International Law* Rabel wrote: "In the law of damages the *lex loci delicti commissi* is still the universally adopted principle, as was pointed out by the canonists and later by the statutists", and on this score he went on to state that "the advantages of the *lex loci* proved to be so strong as to lead this principle to almost universal acceptance".

2. As against this, *recent decades have seen a considerable change* in legal thought. This change occurred in the essential aspect of the law of damages, namely the attention of the law shifted from the tortfeasor to the injured party, the focus of the problem was moved from the wrongful act and personal responsibility to compensation for damage. While the tortfeasor and personal responsibility were predominant and the law looked for instruments for optimal repression and prevention, the answer of private international law was obviously in the law of the place of wrongdoing; it was this law the parameters of which made it optimally possible to appraise the wrongful act and liability and to "mete out" the sanction. Indisputably, this aspect of the law of torts still re-

flected vestiges, and was a guise, of the delictual approach. As was also stressed by Rabel, the principle of the *lex loci delicti commissi* probably emanated from the criminal law spirit of the law of liability, which in turn contradicted the spirit of private international law.

The shift of emphasis to the injured party and to optimal compensation, however, entailed the need for taking into account the fact that, on statistical evidence, damage is necessarily caused on a mass scale and not infrequently for reasons impossible to detect, whereas society has made provision to secure quick compensation by reliance on insurance and on the financial capacity of the tortfeasors. In this situation the law cannot build exclusively on the fortuity and eventuality of the *lex loci*. To simplify the analysis, the insurance company is in a position to calculate the annual volume of damage claims to be made *a fortiori* on the basis of numerous contingencies, it does not care if a car accident occurred one kilometre beyond the State boundary where the injured party may sue for smaller or larger amounts of damages rather than at a place one kilometre less from that point; it is thinking in terms of large volumes of accidents and compensation claims respectively, it is established for this general indemnification function, based of course on the premiums collected. The injured party is not in a position to make preliminary calculations; his knowledge is limited to whether he will be better or worse off on the strength of eventuality and of the *lex loci*.

Well, it was this situation that in the advanced countries in the field of the private international law of liability led to what Ehrenzweig, in Volume I of his *Comparative Private International Law*, calls a revolution, or dethroning of the *lex loci delicti commissi*. The result was the realization that in the sphere of sanctions in the law of torts based on compensation (as against reprobatory or admonitory sanctions), it was no longer possible to think and judge exclusively in terms of a single and absolute *lex loci delicti commissi*. This process, motivated by the said theoretical considerations and the government interest as interpreted by the *lex fori*, began with the "discovery" in 1963 by American judicial practice (in *Babcock v. Jackson*, 12. N.Y. 2nd 473, 191 N.E. 2nd 279, 1963) of a better law than the *lex loci delicti* for the injured party. The legal formula is to consider all aspects of the case and to render the legal relationship involving liability for damages subject to the substantive law offering the most reasonable solution. This law can be the *lex loci delicti* itself, or the law of the common residence of the parties, that of the country where the insurance policy is valid, etc. The essential point is that the *lex loci delicti commissi* is no longer of exclusive applicability. Motivated by court practice involving corresponding typical cases, this new approach is also expressed in the American "Restatement ... Second" (Arts. 145 *et seq.*). The exclusively operating *lex loci delicti* came to give way to the said modern tendency in several other countries as well. Perhaps the EC draft convention on the law of obligations may be an example (though remaining a draft only as regards torts, it still reflects the direction of thinking): while retaining the old principle of *lex loci delicti* as the general rule (para. 1 of Art. 10), the so-called subsidiary connecting factors (*subsidiäre Anknüpfung*) as regulated in paras. 2 and 3 show the breath of new times. The common core of these rather flexible rules is that they acknowledge situations in which there is no characteristic connection between the injured party's position and the place of wrongdoing or the occurrence of damage, but the injured party's position shows a stronger connection with another legal system, in which case that law is ordained to apply (para. 2). Where there are several connecting factors the draft leaves the judge with discretionary powers to decide, and this is really the point, i.e., which element of the case is of greater weight.

Recently this concept was also formulated in the Austrian PIL Code of 1978. Beside the *lex loci delicti* as the general rule, Art. 48 provides that if the law of another State has a closer connection with the delictual relationship, the law of that State must be regarded as the applicable law.

The concept of differentiated regulation is even more definitely expressed in the Swiss Code (Arts. 129–137), and still on the point of weight, the said shift of emphasis is growing in importance with the spread of this approach to other specific areas like unfair competition and product liability, whereby the revolution in the law of delictual liability tends to spill over, as is known to be increasingly the case, into the sphere of contractual liability. Whereas the draft of the European Community and the Austrian Code seek to allow scope for differentiated judicial practice by laying down flexible, general clauses, the Swiss Code expresses this trend at the legislative level. The main elements of progress in this direction include choice of the law of the forum; failing choice of law, the law of common domicile; failing that, the *lex loci delicti commissi*; the law of the place where the damage occurred (if the injured party had had to foresee the place of occurrence); the governing law of the legal relationship (if the wrongdoing encroaches upon the legal relationship existing between the tortfeasor and the injured party); applicability of the Hague Convention of 1971 to claims arising from road accidents (see item 3 below); in case of product liability, the law of the tort-feasor's domicile or the law of the place where the product was procured, as the parties may choose; in respect of claims arising from unfair competition, the law of the country where the effect occurred; in case of damage by emission, the law of the place where the damaging effect occurred or the law of the place where the establishment emitting pollutants is situate; in case of torts violating personal rights (through the press, the radio, television, etc.), the law of the domicile of the injured person or the tort-feasor, as the injured person may choose, or the law of the place where the result occurred, if the tortfeasor had had to foresee the place of occurrence.

By its inner stretch and formally through the channels of comparative legal thinking, the said development of substantive law and conflicts law, which was gathering momentum generally after World War Two, has broken the original predominance of the *lex loci delicti commissi* in the PIL codes of other countries as well. The Polish Code came to render the law of the same nationality or domicile rather than the place of wrongdoing applicable in case of the same nationality or domicile (Art. 31). The Czechoslovak Code adopted the solution which, in addition to the law of the place where the damage occurred, allowed the alternative use of the law in whose jurisdiction (country) "the circumstances founding the claim for damages have arisen" (Art. 15). The same solution is offered by the Yugoslav Code (Art. 28). Thus the *lex loci delicti commissi* has lost its absolute applicability in these laws as well, albeit not in spectacular judicial decisions or disputes in literature and not in such an extreme form that, as momentous claims for damages occasionally illustrate, the courts do as they please in order to reach the "better law", which would be of dubious value even if the courts are presumed to be acting with the best of intentions, because legal certainty and predictability are certainly important values of law enforcement.

3. Again, the said course of development is reflected in the two *Hague Conventions* on the governing law of road accidents (1971) and on the governing law of product liability (1973). Both Conventions are in force. Although Hungary has not acceded to them, they are important sources of law for this country as well, and for more reasons than one. First, our country is likely to accede to them in the near future. Indeed, it is appropriate to give serious consideration to the earliest possible accession for these Conventions represent modern codifications, Hungary is a member of the Hague Conference, it is practicable for it to share Europe's legal infrastructure in this field, too, and accession is certain to enhance the modernization of its domestic law. Second, these Conventions may affect the legal relationships of Hungarian parties in cases with Hungarian bearings before the fora of neighbouring countries. Article 11 of the Hague Convention of 1971 on the governing law of road accidents states that the forum of the acceding country is to act according to the Convention even if the country of the applicable law is not a party thereto. A similar provision is contained in Art. 11 of the other Convention.

As regards now the main connecting factors covered by the two Conventions, and with references made to the Convention of 1971 on the governing law of road accidents, the general rule is the traditional *lex loci delicti* (the law of the place where the accident occurred: Art. 3), but the controlling law is of the State where the vehicle is registered if it is not the place of the accident (Art. 4). In case of several countries of registration, the law in control is that of the State where the motor vehicle is habitually stationed or is to be found (Art. 6). Whichever the governing law, in establishing liability regard must be had to the traffic safety rules prevailing at the place of the accident (Art. 7). The injured person may, under the applicable law, enforce his claim directly against the insurer (Art. 9). The law applicable under the Convention may not be disregarded except on a plea of prejudice to public policy (Art. 10).

The Convention of 1973 on product (producer's) liability first provides that the concept of "product" is to embrace both natural and industrial products, whereas damage is to include damage both to persons and to things as well as economic loss (Art. 2). The applicable law is that of the place of wrongdoing if it is identical to the injured person's business headquarters or with the place where the product is procured (Art. 4). However, the injured person's domicile takes precedence if it is identical to the wrongdoer's business headquarters or with the place where the product is procured (Art. 5). Where neither of the two rules provides guidance, the law of the tortfeasor's business headquarters is to be regarded as the applicable law except when the injured person bases his claim on the law of the place of wrongdoing (Art. 6). The law of the place of wrongdoing and that of the injured person's domicile are inapplicable if the tortfeasor proves that he could not foresee the availability of his products at those places (Art. 7). In addition to the law applicable under Arts. 4–6, regard is to be had to the safety rules of the country in which the product in question was put on the market (Art. 9). The law applicable under the Convention may not be disregarded except when it is explicitly contrary to public policy (Art. 10).

§85. THE HUNGARIAN REGULATION

1. The Hungarian regulation may be considered to offer a modern but moderate solution: *while following the described trend of development instead of the rigidity and exclusivity of the lex loci delicti commissi, it seeks legal certainty* by determining the alternative forms of solution in the Code itself. Room is left, of course, for judicial consideration but the law defines its scope, thus giving a more predictable answer to those looking for the applicable law.

The concept of liability in the Hungarian Code of Private International Law has the additional advantage, by comparison with the more condensed laws of numerous countries, that, going to the theoretical limit of practical need, it minutely specifies forms and conditions (though not all the ones which are covered in this way by several of the aforementioned foreign laws or conventions) which the law is sure to encounter in this field. To refer to but one provision, "whether the tortious conduct consisted in violation of traffic or other safety regulations shall be determined according to the law of the place of the tortious conduct" (para. 1 of Art. 33). In a concrete matter this provision makes the principle of the *lex loci delicti commissi* indisputable for, obviously, one must not frustrate its purpose by going to the other extreme and saying that this doctrine has lost its relevance in all cases. It may well be that a relationship and a dispute involving a claim for damages resulting from an accident between two Hungarian nationals in Vienna are adjudicated upon by the court under Hungarian law because their respective personal laws, insurance policies, etc. are also Hungarian, but the question of who (the Hungarian injured party or the tortfeasor) violated which signal at the particular intersection in Vienna can only be decided according to the local traffic regulations, i.e. the Austrian law.

2. As concerns now the *inner structure of the Hungarian regulation*, it appears on three planes: (a) general rules, of which one is the *lex loci delicti commissi*; (b) supplementary interpretational rules serving as points of guidance in important partial aspects of the modern conception; (c) the so-called minimum statutory requirements of liability as prescribed by Hungarian law.

(a) The *general rules* contained in the first three paragraphs of Art. 32 of the Code offer three options concerning the governing law of liability for damages: (i) the law applicable at the place and time of the wrongful act or omission (this is the classical *lex loci delicti commissi*); (ii) the law of the State where the damage occurred, if that is more favourable to the injured party (on this point the judge has considerable power of discretion as he can "look for" the concrete place of occurrence and can consider the extent to which the law of that place is more favourable than the law of the place where the wrong was done); (iii) the law of domicile, if shared by the injured party and the tortfeasor.

(b) This triple option is *complemented* by the Code with three additional provisions for specific aspects within the defined scope of flexibility: (i) "if, under the law of the place of the tortious act or omission, liability is subject to fault, the existence of culpability may be determined either by the personal law of the tortfeasor or by the law of the place of tort" (para. 4 of Art. 32); (ii) the absolute applicability of the *lex loci* to violation of traffic regulations was noted above; (iii) wrongful acts committed on registered vessels or aircraft are controlled by the *lex bandi* (para. 2 of Art. 33). This latter rule is naturally employed only if the court uses the wrongful act or omission as the main connecting factor, for if the law of the place where the damage occurred or the shared domicile were applied, the applicability of the *lex bandi* on the said ground would be notionally ruled out.

(c) The liability rules of domestic substantive laws differ in degree of rigour and of protection for the injured party, or in the use of criteria for considering conduct to be wrongful or lawful and in the application of sanctions. For a long time the Hungarian law of the former regime did not acknowledge intangible (moral) damage (*dommage moral*) and did not award material compensation for such damage, while this institution of the law of torts had been (and still is) known in other countries, again in varying degrees. Although the tendency of general legal development is toward a harmonization of the substance of the law of torts, there still exist considerable differences: individual countries may stop short of providing for an optimum measure of some sort of compensation either because of limited availability of material resources or of fears of losing the preventive force of regulation by introducing, say, a system of full and direct compensation (through insurance). For the said reasons the following view, for instance, is warranted on the one side, but is disputed on the other: once the Hungarian law has acknowledged intangible damage as a legal consequence or institution, compensation for such damage may not, by reference to the measure of compensation established by Hungarian legal practice, be of a lesser extent than that established by practice under the otherwise applicable foreign law, viz. be made equal to the extent reached by Hungarian practice. If damage is suffered in the injured person's country, compensation should also keep up with the levels of restitution and compensation attained by that country. The list of reasons could be extended, but the essential point is that country's regulative system of liability is reflective of definite values safeguarded by legal policy and that the legislator is disinclined to allow application by his forum of a profoundly different system of liability for damages. This postulate is formulated in the so-called *minimum statutory requirements of liability*. These are the concrete peremptory norms of domestic law which seek to prevail over the otherwise applicable foreign law. The fact is that, failing them, the law of the forum would be able to meet the said requirements only by resort to the public policy rule. Evidently, however, the legal institutions involved are not of the kind to be fought with the "heavy artillery" of the public policy clause. True, they are disputable and are actually disputed precisely for this reason.

The said minimum requirements are set forth in Art. 34 of the Code with respect partly to torts, partly to sanctions, the relevant provisions reading: "A Hungarian court shall not establish liability for conduct not considered unlawful under Hungarian law" (para. 1). "A Hungarian court shall not, on the ground of liability for damage, establish legal consequences unknown to Hungarian law" (para. 2).

3. If the Hungarian regulation is viewed from the angle of *practice*, Hungarian as well as foreign, and regard is also had to considerations of comparative law, the following statements may be made.

(a) The *general rules*, including the *lex loci delicti commissi*, are followed by Hungarian judicial practice (both old and new) *without problems*, often without the use of *renvoi*: the Austrian law was applied against a Hungarian tortfeasor in the case of a road accident which had occurred in Austria and in which the injured party was a Czechoslovak national (PKKB.4.P.87150/1978); the Hungarian law was applied in claim for a damage case resulting from a traffic accident which had occurred in Hungary and in which the injured party was a German and the tortfeasor a Hungarian national (PKKB.14.P.87590/1979; *Fővárosi Bíróság* 41.Pf.IX.27.007/1980); the court relied in part on the Hungarian law in the case of an accident suffered by a bus of Burgenland in Hungary, because the collision caused by the Hungarian tortfeasor had occurred in Budapest (PKKB.4.P.78.230/1981).

(b) *However, problems are and may be (and certainly will be) encountered* in some questions, as they have manifested themselves already and can be expected to emerge depending on the nature of cases that are growing in number. The reasons are various and arise partly from the condensed provisions of the Code, which are a significant source of international problems; this requires inventive interpretation by practice and presupposes greater assistance from theory. This holds true especially for matters on which the Code is silent and which will therefore present a need to search for the applicable law by the aid of comparative (see §84) and other analyses and then of analogy. Moreover, problems are posed by the fact that in certain fields (in contrast to cases of inheritance in the domain of torts), judicial practice is slow to adjust itself to the greater complexity of legal cases in private international law.

(ba) The uncertainty of practice in the interpretation of Art. 32 (2) follows from this fact as well as from the laconic wording of the Code. As was seen, the general rule (after postulating the *lex loci delicti commissi*) provides that "if it is more favourable to the injured party, the governing law shall be of the State in which the damage occurred". But *what does the place of occurrence mean*? The damage caused to a Yugoslav national who, in consequence of an unavoidable medical complication resulting from a course of injections at a Hungarian spa, suffered an impairment of health involving disability, the damage resulting therefrom really occurred or occurs in the country where he had and has to suffer that state of invalidity and its material consequences for the rest of his life, namely in Yugoslavia. The court nevertheless judged the liability of the hydropathic establishment under Hungarian law, apparently on the ground that the place of the tortious conduct was Hungary (District Court of Szombathely P.21. 170/1979). Similarly, Hungary was the place of the tortious conduct in the case of a foreign bus which was damaged in Budapest by a Hungarian motor car violating traffic regulations. Ordinarily Hungarian law was deemed to be the applicable law, under which the operator (as generally that of a vehicle in Hungary) could not have claimed compensation in addition to repairs. The court nevertheless held that, in view of the Austrian market conditions, the bus was to "experience" the damage in Austria and therefore awarded the deterioration in value under the Austrian law, for such damages can be claimed in that country in the case of vehicles as well (PKKB. 4.P.87.230/1981).

The place of occurrence lends itself to various interpretations even under the aforementioned judicial appraisals. Interpretation may be broad (extreme) and narrow. (1) As broadly conceived, this place includes any place where the material consequences of a wrongful act occur, regardless of the place of the tortious conduct and the damage, which in the above examples, is the country of the injured patient and, again, the country of the bus which suffered deterioration in value, but it is Hungary if a Hungarian national living in Hungary suffers an accident abroad. In short, the place in question is always the country in which the damage as a consequence occurs. There are many who maintain that the occurrence of damage cannot be understood so broadly [it should be construed to have the following (second) meaning], as it would entail the use of another connecting factor, namely the personal law of the injured party. However, this is usually not indicated in the legal systems, which reach that localizer at best indirectly, e.g., by using the concept of better law or government interest (§84). (2) The narrower concept refers in this respect to "distance torts" (*Distanzdelikten*). Here are some examples. (i) In a refreshment bar of country A the plaintiff eats his substandard hot dogs made somewhere, takes a train, and becomes unwell in country B. The damage occurred through eating, and becoming upset by, the hot dogs. The consequences to be suffered in country B or C are a different phenomenon, which is uncertain for the added reason that the plaintiff keeps changing the place where his state of invalidity or his damage is constantly experienced. (ii) Another plaintiff is given injections in country A, is let home, and the damaging side-effect of the injections is felt in country B, his own country. Here, too, the damage occurs upon that fact. Whatever occurs afterwards is the appearance of material consequences at changing places. (iii) The defendant has done something in a river crossing the border of countries A and B, causing damage to the plaintiff in country B on the other side of the river, because his water-driven sawmill does not work for lack of water. Here the place of occurrence is evident, namely the country of the sawmill (but a foreign court applied the law of country A, which it deemed to be more favourable; Makarov, p. 128). This category includes damage caused by emission of pollutants, which is covered by a separate provision in, e.g., the Swiss Code (Art. 138): claims for damages based on damaging effects produced by immovables (industrial or other activities like pollution of the environment by establishments) are to be judged according to the *lex situs* or the law of the place where the damage actually occurred, as the injured party may choose.

On the basis of the foregoing it may perhaps by stated in general that the cited "more favourable law" rule of the Code is to be applied carefully, having regard to all the circumstances of the case. A broader interpretation may be justified in cases where, for instance, the result in question is "supported" by some other relevant connecting factor under the Hungarian regulation.

(bb) International practice is witness to a widening sphere of *party autonomy* prevailing in respect to delictual relationships as well. Under Art. 132 of the Swiss Code mentioned above, the parties are free to choose the law of the forum. A court of Hamburg pronounced the freedom of party autonomy in the case of a collision between ships (Hamburg OLG, 6.4. 1961, Makarov, p. 129).

The Hungarian Code contains no direct provision on such freedom, but comes close to allowing it through other channels. In cases where domicile is shared by the injured person and the tortfeasor the law of that State is *ex lege* applicable, so it should not be chosen by the parties (para. 3 of Art. 32). Under Art. 9, the parties may request disregard of the otherwise applicable law, and in that case (with their request construed in a broad sense to be a choice-of-law situation) the legal system governing their dispute will be the law of the forum.

(bc) In the field of *minimum statutory requirements* described above, it may be questionable whether a legal consequence of an extent or a nature unknown in Hungary can be applied if such consequence would follow from the otherwise applicable law. If we reverse the above-cited example of a bus, a Hungarian tortfeasor causes a foreign bus deterioration in value in country A and the passengers suffer intangible damage as well, then they go to a Hungarian court, and the governing substantive law will be that of their own country under the Hungarian Code. The scope of intangible damage and (as was seen) the extent of deterioration in value of vehicles are more limited in Hungary than in country A. The property standards of which country's law are to apply? Can the provision of Hungarian law on "legal consequences unknown in Hungary" be construed in so broad a sense as to exclude anything outside the scope of Hungarian values (lump-sum compensation, grounds for claims) by resorting practically to the public policy clause? The appropriate solution will certainly be one which compares the legal-dogmatic purposes of similar institutions, their ethical and economic substance and functions, while having regard to the reasonable extent of compensation in terms of function. Such comparison may result in the court considering the particular legal consequence under the foreign law to be "unknown" wholly or in part and accordingly refusing to apply that consequence wholly or in part, or, conversely, in the court being unable to find anything to be essentially "unknown" and consequently applying the foreign institution under the corresponding practice.

(bd) The Code is silent, *inter alia*, on whether a more differentiated or special regulation is needed for aspects of delictual liability like *damage caused through products*, or *damage caused by violation of rules relating to unfair competition and economic competition*, which have already appeared in other modern laws (see §84). In practice it will certainly be necessary for the general rules of the Code to be interpreted with flexibility or perhaps to be complemented by the judge (see our earlier statement on the rules relating to "special protection needed" under item 4 of §83, as we have here largely similar phenomena). In solving cases of product liability in the field of delictual relationships, for instance, it may appear reasonable, as can be seen in our comparative survey (§84), to apply, in addition to the law of a product's manufacturer, the law of the place where the product is marketed (purchased) and the law of the injured party's domicile, if the product in question was not imported into these countries without the consent of the manufacturing company. Act X of 1993 on Product Liability states in this connection that "in case of imported products the provisions of this Act on manufacturers" (namely that the manufacturer is liable for damage caused by the defect of the product) "shall apply, *mutatis mutandis*, to importers as well". In situations controlled by the law of competition, a wrongful act may also worsen the competitive position with respect to several countries. It is obviously by considering all the circumstances present that it can be decided whether the court may or must decide a given case under as many applicable laws as there are such countries involved or whether it should, in cases where the injured person was caused damage in several countries, consider the damage to have occurred at the seat of the injured person. It is very likely that the forum of the injured person's country will judge the delictual relationship according to its own law.

§86. UNJUST ENRICHMENT

1. Unjust enrichment has a common feature with delictual liability, namely it is one of the phenomena not sanctioned, but opposed, by law. It is a case of unlawfulness in the broader sense, a wrongful fact of a rather general range at that, which occurs whenever material benefit is obtained at the expense of someone and at the same time in favour of another, having a causal relationship, but no recognized legal ground (*iusta causa*). Cases in point are payment of a non-existent debt or, in some laws (e.g. German), performance effected under an invalid contract. Often material gain cannot be settled under the legal cloak of the underlying contract and there remains no option but to restore the original situation on the ground of unjust enrichment. Here is where this institution as distinct from liability comes into play: in addition to the fact of material gain which occurred objectively and in a causal relationship there is not one aspect, the lack of *iusta causa*, to consider or to prove. This is why the conflict rules on liability cannot be applied to this case, the central question not being the conduct at all, but rather the material benefit unjustly obtained.

From all this it follows that *unjust enrichment is half an independent phenomenon of private international law, half not*. Lack of independence or preference for such status (as if unjust enrichment were, e.g., an external concomitant of a contractual relationship, or belonged to the realm of liability by reason of a wider interpretation of tort) would entail the following in private international law: the connecting factor would be chosen according to the contractual relationship whose settlement by this method is at issue or to an alternative conflict rule on delictual liability. Hence the governing law is the particular *lex causae*, the law otherwise applicable to the basic or underlying legal relationship.

2. For the reasons stated above, the new Hungarian regulation has established *a quasi-independent statute of private international law* to control unjust enrichment: "Unjust enrichment and its legal consequences shall be governed by the law of the State in which the enrichment occurred" (Art. 35 of the Code). This solution by Hungarian law is specific even in comparison to the private international laws of several countries and it is an option for a course of greater predictability and legal certainty. (While the Swiss Code has formulated a rule on this matter, it first goes back to the law applicable to the underlying legal relationship and opts for the Hungarian solution only in the absence of such law: Art. 132.) Practice will be the test of whether this benefit of seeking legal certainty will be a compensation for the disadvantage of thus establishing a double statute to govern a single concrete legal relationship. Under previous practice, the judge tried to solve a dispute arising from an originally contractual relationship by applying the substantive rules of the law of contracts. If he failed, because the contract had meanwhile "melted away" (e.g. had proved invalid) and material benefit been obtained, he switched to the institution of unjust enrichment within the scope of the same substantive law (*lex causae*) in

order to arrive at a judgment. Now he has to take this second step by switching to the realm of another substantive law, notably the law of the place where the enrichment took place.

3. If someone should not believe unjust enrichment to be a real-life phenomenon in the private international legal practice of Hungarian fora, let him think of a Hungarian tourist who suffered an accident in Rome, was taken unconscious by the ambulance to a hospital where he received treatment, and then, when back in Hungary, he is sued for the expenses incurred. As he was unconscious, he cannot be supposed to have made a contract (e.g. a contract for service) to which he could have been a party (customer). Even though the operation did not make him any richer, there was some material benefit gained by him at the expense of the other party (he recovered, received the necessary treatment and care of material value, while the other party was caused loss of remuneration and expenses). Material gain is illustrated even more clearly by a combination of this case with the sum of money paid out under the accident insurance policy. Thus, with another legal category to be found only with difficulty, the institution of unjust enrichment can also be used in private international legal practice.

TITLE 7

FOUNDATIONS OF THE INTERNATIONAL PROTECTION OF INTELLECTUAL PROPERTY

CHAPTER XXVII

THE FUNDAMENTALS OF INTERNATIONAL COPYRIGHT LAW

§87. SOURCES

There is hardly any class of facts of daily life, other than those of authors, that call for international protection and there are few areas of law as inevitably international in character as copyright. The possibility of making use of authors' works has always transcended national boundaries and has indeed been made universal by the advent of new means of technology (radio, television, sound and picture recording, etc.). It is understandable that parallel to the emergence of modern national copyright laws, initiatives were made to ensure international protection and that, after thorough preparation, an international convention was adopted on the subject by the late 19th century.

1. (a) The first international convention, the International Union for the *Protection of Literary and Artistic Works* (named the *Berne Union* after the venue of the preparatory conference), was adopted in 1886. Of course, it has since been amended and supplemented several times [in Paris (1896), in Berlin (1908), in Berne (1914), in Rome (1928), in Brussels (1948), in Stockholm (1967) and in Paris (1971)] to adjust legal protection to the requirements of technical and social change, namely to extend protection to the new forms of authors' creations and the new modes of their utilization. The Berne Union Convention (henceforth referred to as BUC) is open for accession by any State at any time (according to the latest Paris text). Up to 1 July 1996, 119 countries acceded to it.

A permanent body (the Berne Bureau) was set up to handle the administrative tasks connected with the application of the Convention. In 1967 these tasks were transferred to the World Intellectual Property Organization (WIPO or OMPI for the English and French designations, respectively), with headquarters in Geneva. A main concern of this Organization is to ensure harmony between the systems of protection provided by the various international conventions on copyright and industrial property.

(b) The main achievement of BUC was the internationalization of copyright protection rooted in European traditions. However, despite its undeniable success and broad acceptance, the regulation which resulted from efforts in this direction was not necessarily workable for States at other levels of development (chiefly the former colonial countries) or for States having established a different system of copyright protection (USA, some South American countries). This explains why in 1952, under the auspices of the United Nations, a new international convention on copyright protection – the so-called *Universal Copyright Convention* (henceforth referred to as UCC) – was concluded at Geneva (amended in Paris in 1971). This Convention is likewise open (and by 1 January 1992 had 84 adherents) but it has virtually lost its practical relevance during the 1990s because most of the States, having previously framed national copyright laws different from the continental system, have acceded to BUC (primarily the USA in 1989), while the successor States of the former Soviet Union (Russia, Belarus, Kazakhstan, Baltic States) have also become parties to BUC (after having codified their national copyright laws on the basis of European traditions).

(c) In 1961 there was adopted the *Rome Convention* for the protection of *performing artists*, producers of phonogrammes, and radio and television broadcasting companies. On 1 July 1996 this Convention had 51 adherents.

(d) Recent decades have witnessed a *new trend of development* in international copyright protection, with the principal emphasis being given to the *protection of users* parallel to, and to some extent even with priority over, the protection of authors and performers. (It is of interest to note a historical parallel here. The origins of copyright protection revealed a similar phenomenon: legal protection was first granted to publishers in the form of privileges, but the protection of authors themselves emerged only at a later stage!) Several conventions were concluded for the international protection of radio stations, or radio and television broadcasts and producers of phonogrammes (Geneva, 1971), etc.

Another noteworthy trend of development can be said to focus on the *commercial law approach*, chiefly under American influence, in international legal regulation as well. This approach has an obvious and ancient core: authors' works are articles of commerce which are, for all their peculiarities, marketed within the ambit of international commercial law. This change of outlook finds a concrete legal expression in the latest trade agreements concluded within the framework of GATT (General Agreement on Tariffs and Trade) and called TRIPS Convention [ratified in Hungary by Decision No. 72/1994. (XII.27.) of the Parliament]. Understandably, this legal regulation did not go beyond the substantive-law rules of BUC but opened up new avenues for the practical implementation of intellectual property rights.

(e) The foregoing makes clear that international protection for copyright and related rights is provided chiefly by multilateral agreements. Some role is nevertheless reserved for *bilateral treaties* because they may

– grant protection also in relation to States not party to multilateral conventions;

– guarantee wider rights and protection than those accorded by multilateral conventions;

– establish a longer period of protection in particular cases; and, last but not least,

– unfortunately facilitate exercise of commercial pressure (e.g. by threatening to withdraw the most-favoured-nation clause). (This tool is used particularly by the USA in its bilateral agreements on the protection of intellectual property.)

2. Among the *multilateral conventions* Hungary is a party to the Paris text of BUC (promulgated by Law-Decree No. 4 of 1975), to the Paris text of UCC (promulgated by Law-Decree No. 3 of 1974), to the Geneva Convention of 1971 for the Protection of Producers of Phonogrammes (gramophones, cassettes, etc.) against Unauthorized Duplication of their Phonogrammes (promulgated by Law-Decree No. 18 of 1975) and to the Rome Convention of 1961 for the Protection of Performing Artists, Producers of Phonogrammes, and Broadcasting Organizations [promulgated by Decision No. 4/1994. (II.11.) of the Parliament]. (The Hungarian Parliament also decided on accession to the Geneva Convention of 1989 on the Registration of Audiovisual Works, although accession did not formally take place until 1 January 1997.)

Among the *bilateral* copyright agreements we single out, by way of example, the treaty with the *United States of America* as far back as 1911 (promulgated by Act LXI of 1912). Mention is deserved by the fact that Hungary has also a more general agreement with the USA on the protection of intellectual property (published in *Magyar Közlöny*, No. 173 of 1993), which contains provisions (in Art. II) on copyright and related rights as well. Treaties with the *Soviet Union* on mutual copyright protection were first signed in 1967 (promulgated by Law-Decree No. 6 of 1968, prolonged by Law-Decree No. 15 of 1971, amended by Law-Decree No. 15 of 1974) and again, with additions, in 1977 (promulgated by Law-Decree No. 1 of 1978). [These still apply in relation to Russia.]

3. The *uniform international conflicts law and substantive law* codified by the aforementioned conventions cover a large part of the problems concerning international copyright law, but are far from complete on a worldwide basis. International copyright disputes are therefore bound to arise and inevitably cause the judge to rely on the *international law of conflicts* for solving them. It is in view of such cases that the Hungarian Code, too, offers a solution under conflicts law, adopting the principle of the *lex loci protectionis*: "Copyrights shall be governed by the law of the State in whose territory protection is claimed" (Art. 19). This rule is to be applied primarily to cases involving authors' – property and non-property – rights connected with works originating from *non-party* States.

The *lex loci protectionis* can be regarded as generally accepted in the practice of international codification concerning the protection of authors' rights under the law of conflicts. This principle was adopted by, e.g., the Berne Union Convention. The *lex loci protectionis* may be the *lex fori*: along with the rules of BUC, the Supreme Court (Pf.IV.20 841/1991, BH 1992/10, 631) had regard to the provisions of the Hungarian Copyright Act. It should be stressed, however, that in practice the application of the *lex loci protectionis* does not necessarily mean that of the *lex fori*, as it may occur that in a given lawsuit international copyright protection is claimed, not (or not exclusively) in the territory of the State of the proceeding forum, but (also) in the territory of other States. Such claims are not generally barred by the more recent rules on jurisdiction (including the provisions of the Hungarian Code in Arts. 54 *et seq.*). If, for instance, a Hungarian theatre presents in Slovakia a work of a French author in violation of the law, the author may request a Hungarian court (too) to extend protection to Slovakia, and the Hungarian judge will, on the basis of BUC, apply the rules of the Slovak copyright law (*lex loci protectionis*) rather than the provisions of the Hungarian Copyright Act (*lex fori*) (on related problems, see Ulmer: *op. cit.*, p. 16, in the List of Sources).

The international copyright conventions do not cover *contracts for the exploitation* of authors' works, a reason why the legal appraisal of such transactions always necessitates the use of conflict norms. [This problem was correctly recognized by the Supreme Court (Pf.IV.22 284/1994), which applied the Code provisions in determining the law applicable to an international contract of publishing.] The rule of the Hungarian Code on contracts also recognize party autonomy in determining the law applicable to contracts for the exploitation of authors' works. If the subjects of such contracts do not use their right to choose the applicable law as recognized by the Code, the following rule is to apply as the objective connecting factor: the applicable law of contracts for the exploitation of rights under copyright protection is the law of the State in which, at the time of contracting, the user has his domicile or habitual residence, or seat or business headquarters [para. (c) of Art. 25]. As can be seen, the Code does not apply the principle of "the law of the obligor of the typical performance" (see item 2 in §83) to contracts for the exploitation of authors' works. It should be emphasized in this respect that the legal system as defined by Art. 25 (c) is not necessarily identical with the law of the place of exploitation.

§88. THE ESSENCE OF INTERNATIONAL COPYRIGHT PROTECTION

1. The necessity for the international protection of copyrights and the peculiarity of such protection can be attributed to the fact that *national copyright laws*, owing to the distinctive features of their historical development, follow the principle of *territoriality*, under which the copyright laws of the different States accord protection only to works (either by national or by foreign authors) which were (first) published in the territory of the particular country, implying that under national copyright laws, authors are not protected against unauthorized

utilization of their works in countries other than their own. Consequently, international copyright protection (beyond national boundaries) was only possible under separate international conventions. (On principle it could naturally have been conceivable for the copyright law of every country to extend, within its own scope of applicability, protection against unauthorized utilization of works first published abroad, but this practice was adopted only by French legislation, only to be abandoned recently for lack of reciprocity.)

As regards the two, multilateral and open, international conventions for the international protection of authors' works, BUC grants a much wider protection than UCC, which is guided by the primary aim of "rather granting less but with the participation of more countries". Both Conventions contain *direct norms and conflict rules*, too, which constitute a uniform law.

2. The regime of protection under *BUC* is built on *three general principles.*

(a) The principle of *national treatment (régime nationale)* means that the work of an author who is a national of any of the Union States shall, irrespective of whether his work is not published or is first published in any Union States, enjoy in all Union States the same protection as that accorded to works of nationals of the given States. (Membership in the Union is, according to the Paris text, governed not only by nationality of, but also by domicile in, any of the Union States.) In other words, this principle practically means that the contracting States, disregarding the territoriality doctrine, grant to each other's nationals the same legal protection in their respective territories as to their own nationals. For instance, a Hungarian author, in respect of his work published or not yet published in Hungary or in any Union State, enjoys the same treatment in the Czech Republic as Czech authors, in Finland as Finnish authors, in Gabon as Gabonese authors, in Fiji as Fijian authors, etc., whereas the authors of these countries (or of any other Union State) enjoy the same rights in Hungary as Hungarian authors.

The principle of national or equal treatment means in practice *formal reciprocity* only. Such formal equality may conceal substantive inequality, because the copyright laws of the Union States are different in substance concerning the conditions of protection, the extent of guaranteed rights, or the period of protection. The *rules on minimum protection* established by BUC itself are intended to remove, at least in part, inequalities which may arise in this way. These rules (by virtue of the Brussels text) become *part of national laws* upon acceptance of the Convention and impose the minimum protection requirements which the Union States are obliged to meet in respect of foreign authors regardless of whether their national laws accord such protection to their own authors.

(b) Laying down another general principle, BUC provides that the enjoyment and exercise of the recognized rights are not subject to any formal requirement (*principle of informality*). This rule creates a conspicuous difference in protection accorded to authors' rights on the one hand and to other forms of intellectual property (patent, trademark, industrial design) on the other.

Originally the principle of informality derived its significance from a comparison with the copyright solution of the United States and with system of protection granted by some South American countries, since these subjected copyright protection to compliance with formal requirements. The new Copyright Act of the United States (adopted in 1976) follows the European approach.

(c) The enjoyment and exercise of the rights granted under the third principle of BUC are not conditional on protection of a given work in its country of "origin". (A *country of origin* is deemed to be the country of the author in the case of an unpublished work, or else the country of first publication. In the case of simultaneous publication in several of the Union States the country of origin is that which provides for the shortest period of protection, whereas in the case of simultaneous publication in a Union State and a non-Union State the country of origin is deemed to be the Union State.) The principle of independent *protection* can also be traced to the underlying concept of territoriality, according to which the laws and regulations of the country of origin do not apply beyond national boundaries, so any infringement of rights in a foreign country is to be determined by the law of that country rather than the country of origin.

There is, however, a *break in the operation* of the independent protection principle, because in some cases BUC itself counterbalances the principle of formal reciprocity with that of substantive reciprocity, which inevitably curtails the principle of independent protection. The most striking example of this is provided by the regulation of the *period of protection*. Since the Brussels text (1948), the minimum period of protection has, as a rule, been 50 years after the author's death. As against this, the earlier (Rome) text allows the States parties to grant a shorter period of protection. This possibility is balanced by the requirement of substantive reciprocity which, if one draws a comparison between the periods of protection, means the following: the period of protection is established by the law of the State in which protection is claimed, but the period of protection so granted must not be shorter than that determined in the country of origin. (This same principle applies in cases where a country grants more than 50 years of protection. A longer period of protection cannot be claimed when the country of origin establishes a shorter period of protection.)

This brief presentation of the general principles governing the regime of protection under BUC needs to be complemented with the following observations.

(a) The purpose of Union protection being to protect authors of foreign countries, such protection *does not extend to rights claimed in the country of origin*. For example, the protection of a work first published in Hungary is governed by BUC in all Union States except Hungary.

(b) Union protection normally extends to authors of the Union States only, but there is scope for the enjoyment of protection by *authors of non-Union States* if, for instance, the work of an author of a non-Union State is first published in any of the Union States. In that case the author enjoys the same rights in the country of first publication as national authors and may claim in the other Union States the rights granted by BUC.

(c) BUC applies to States *parties to the different texts* thereof always according to the earlier text. Thus, for instance, in relations between Hungary (Paris text), and Turkey (Brussels text), the Brussels text applies. (An exception to this rule is that newly-adhering States are bound by the latest – Paris – text only, while an older Union State may have to apply an earlier text in relation to them!)

The possibility of conflict situations arising from the various texts of BUC is reduced by the fact that each text is governed by the same principles, primarily the principle of equal treatment *(régime nationale)*. This leaves room for difference only with respect to the Union rules for minimum protection, and possible differences acquire practical relevance only if the internal law of a Union State grants less protection than the Union rules for minimum protection.

3. Since UCC has virtually lost its practical relevance [see item 1 (b) in §87], we will say but a few words about its regime of protection, which concurs anyway with that of BUC in some important aspects: both protect essentially the same range of works, provide for the obligation of protection, and are based on the *régime nationale*. The differing rules of UCC relate mainly to *formal requirements* and the *period of protection*. In the countries subjecting protection to formal requirements, a work first published in another State must bear the mark (C) and indicate the name of the person enjoying copyrights and the year of first publication. As a general rule, the period of protection is the author's lifetime and 25 years after his death, but there are several exceptions to this rule, including comparison of the periods of protection.

4. Membership in the two universal international conventions for copyright protection (BUC and UCC) shows numerous overlaps; a considerable number of signatory States are parties to both Conventions. It is therefore important to glance at the *relationship between the two instruments*. The main points are the following:

(a) UCC is of relevance only in relation to those States one of which at least is not a Union State (Berne Union), or else (if the country of origin and the country in which protection is claimed are parties to both Conventions) their *inter se* relations are governed by the provisions of BUC. (In its Ruling Pf.IV.22 284/1994 the Supreme Court failed to notice this hierarchy between the two multilateral conventions.)

Considering that, as was stressed above [see item 1 (b) in §87], the range of the State parties to BUC has been noticeably widened during the 1990s, the group of the State parties to both Conventions has been enlarged, with a resultant decisive increase in the hegemony of BUC.

(b) The author of a country withdrawing from the Berne Union enjoys no protection under UCC in another Union State even if both countries are parties to the latter Convention. The purpose of this provision is to ensure that the system of international copyright protection established by BUC is not upset by the conclusion of UCC. As a result of the Paris revision, the States belonging to the group of "developing countries" were granted the right, along with other privileges, to withdraw from BUC without the aforesaid sanction being applied.

5. There emerge practical problems even in the parallel application of *BUC* and *bilateral agreements*. BUC (in Art. 20 of its Paris text) accords priority to bilateral agreements on the same subject if they grant wider rights than those guaranteed by BUC, or if they are not contrary to the provisions of BUC. [The problems encountered in the joint application of BUC and Hungary's agreement with the United States of America are well illustrated by a judgment of the Supreme Court (Pf.IV.22 284/1994).]

6. The mainsprings of the *continued development* of international copyright law are to seek chiefly in technical advance and in the needs of developing countries. In addition to these general aspects, the European regional unification of law raises special requirements upon the development of international copyright law as well.

(a) Constant and rapid *technical change* poses successive challenges to legal regulation in the field of protecting authors' works and their utilization under private international law as there appear on the stage new carriers of works (computer programmes, etc.) and new forms and means of utilization (cable television, satellite broadcasting, etc.).

Preparations for refining the substantive-law system of BUC have got under way. Particularly important during the negotiations aimed at a revision is the fact that the *developing countries* are also largely in need of imports in the field of intellectual property under copyright protection, and it is therefore necessary to devote increased attention to their specific problems in the process of refining international regulations.

The *legal form* of the revision cannot as yet be foreseen with complete certainty, but it appears impossible to win all State parties to a wholesale revision. It is therefore probable that a group of States will conclude *supplementary agreements* on some partial problems such as the international protection of related rights.

In the course of negotiations for streamlining international copyright law, it is a similarly important endeavour of State parties to BUC (as well as of State parties to other intellectual property conventions under the auspices of WIPO) to find a more efficient *forum* for the settlement of their disputes about the interpretation and application of the Conventions. In recent years efforts in this direction have grown in importance on account of the fact, among others, that the *national economic value* of goods forming the object of copyright protection (e.g. computer programmes) is on the increase. A solution of this question is not facilitated by the possibility for the procedure of the Hague International Court of Justice, which has been vested with general jurisdiction over disputes between State parties to BUC, to be excluded at any time by way of reservation at the time of accession through bilateral agreement. Since that high forum has not yet judged any case involving international copyright law, it has not been

been possible to have recourse to joint jurisdiction leading to a uniform interpretation and application of the rules of the Conventions.

(b) Encouragement to the efforts at refinement is given by the *European Union*'s guidelines for the unification of copyright law, notably Guidelines 91/250 EC on the legal protection of software, Guidelines 92/100 EC on the leasing of carriers of works, Guidelines 93/83 EC on certain questions of satellite broadcasting and wire rebroadcasting, Guidelines 93/98 EC on the period of protection, and Guidelines 96/9 EC on the protection of data bases.

Our obligations relating to the harmonization of laws under the Association Agreement (Art. 68) with the European Union and its member-states (promulgated by Act I of 1994) and our prospective accession, make these Guidelines increasingly important for legal development in Hungary. It may be stated that today about 80% of the rules of the Hungarian copyright law is in keeping with the guidelines of the European Union. We should note that the legislation of the European Community brings a significant influence to bear on a worldwide unification of law as well, consequently playing an important role primarily in the efforts to revise BUC. (On the current problems of the international copyright law and its future, see Boytha, Ficsor, Gyertyánfy in the List of Sources.)

CHAPTER XXVIII

AN OUTLINE OF THE INTERNATIONAL PROTECTION OF INDUSTRIAL PROPERTY

§89. THE PARIS UNION CONVENTION FOR THE INTERNATIONAL PROTECTION OF INDUSTRIAL PROPERTY

1. As in the case of international copyright protection, the foundations for the international protection of industrial property were laid at the end of the last century; the Paris Union Convention, still the principal international treaty, was concluded in 1883 [revised in Brussels (1900), in Washington (1911), in The Hague (1925), in London (1934), in Lisbon (1958) and in Stockholm (1967)]. The Convention is open – the Union States numbered 140 on 1 February 1997. Hungary acceded to it in 1909 and at present is a party to the Stockholm text (promulgated by Law-Decree No. 18 of 1970).

As with copyright protection, the *main objective* of the Paris Union is to ensure that protection granted with *territorial* effect in any of the Union States is accorded in the other States parties as well. The attainment of this objective is sought chiefly *by three means*:

(a) by enunciating the principle of equal treatment *(régime nationale),* under which the Union States are to accord to nationals and organizations of all States parties the same rights as are granted to their own nationals and organizations;

(b) by the institution of *Union priority*, meaning that on the basis of first application in any of the Union States the person claiming protection may, within a specified time limit, obtain protection in all (any one) of the other contracting States with retroactive effect to the date of first (basic) application;

(c) by *rules common* to and binding upon the Union States, from which the internal laws of the States parties must not derogate. For example, a coercive measure because of failure to apply an invention must not be taken until after the lapse of a specified period of time.

On the whole, proceeding from the national protection of industrial property and its territorial effect, the Paris Union Convention does not affect the national regimes of protection. Thus, except for the aforesaid rules of binding force, it is left to the national legislation of the States parties to determine the scope and nature of, or the limitations on, legal protection, etc.

The scope of the Paris Union Convention embraces several fields of the international protection of industrial property, its rules governing protection for *inventions*, industrial and registered *designs, trademarks*, trade names, and indications and marks of origin as well as protection against unfair competition. *In partial aspects* of protection (trademarks, indications and marks of origin, industrial designs, specific issues of patent law), the comprehensive provisions of the Paris Union Convention are *supplemented by separate international agreements*, several of which are collateral to the Union Convention, are open accession by the Union States only and rest on the Union principles. The system of international conventions covering more narrow areas has significantly expanded over the past two decades. The more important special conventions will be dealt with in the following sections on the various forms of protection of industrial property.

A revision of the Paris Union Convention (by WIPO with over 160 Contracting States) was demanded mainly by the *developing countries*, which, as in the case of copyrights, are large or even larger importers of industrial property and therefore expect to receive facilities, preferences, legal and technical assistance from the industrialized countries through the international institutions of industrial property protection as well. Instead of a comprehensive revision, on which no broad consensus can be hoped for, efforts have recently been made to develop the system of the Paris Union, by conclusion of separate international treaties, *in partial areas* (chiefly in the interest of simplifying *procedural requirements*). As a result, the Trademark Law Treaty (TLT) was concluded in 1994 and preparations for a revision of the Patent Law Treaty (PLT) are under way.

2. The system of international conventions regulating the field of industrial property protection cannot be complete (despite the fact that the State parties to, e.g., the Paris Union Convention number as many as 140 today), just as the network of international copyright conventions is not (see §87), which makes it indispensable for the *national conflicts laws* to play a subsidiary role in this respect as well.

Under the Hungarian *Code* (Art. 20), an inventor and his successor in title shall be granted protection under the law and in the territory of the State in which the patent was issued or the patent application was filed. This rule is to be applied, *mutatis mutandis*, to other industrial property rights (industrial designs, trademarks, etc.).

§90. INTERNATIONAL PROTECTION OF PATENTS

1. The principal rules on the international protection of patents are contained in the *Paris Union Convention*. Accordingly the *régime nationale* is upheld and the *Union right of priority* is granted in this domain, too, to the inventor (who may claim it within 12 months of first application). Attention should be drawn

to the *independence of patents* principle, according to which a patent obtained within the scope of the Union is, e.g. in respect of expiration or destruction, to be considered independently of the additional (analogous) patents obtained by the inventor on the same invention either in a Union State or in a non-Union State. Several provisions are of mandatory application under the *national laws* of the Union States: e.g. a patent must not be denied or invalidated on the ground that trade in a patented product (or a product made by a protected process, such as firearms, poison) is prohibited or restricted by the laws and regulations of the particular State. Special rules refer to the temporary protection of patentable inventions used in products on public display *at international exhibitions* officially organized (or officially recognized) in the territories of State parties to the Convention.

2. In the field of international patent protection a new convention, the *Patent Cooperation Treaty* (PCT), was signed at Washington in 1970 and came into operation in 1978. It was revised in 1979 and 1984.

The aim of PCT is, on the one hand, to *simplify, speed up* and *reduce the cost of* the procedure for obtaining protection for inventions in case of parallel applications in several countries and, on the other, to facilitate the licensing of *"strong" patents* certain to meet the criteria of patentability. With a view to achieving these aims, the PCT

– permits *international application* (at one place, in one language) with a legal effect extending to all States in which the applicant seeks protection;

– allows scope for *international research and inquiry* by international organizations.

The PCT's tools will perhaps be able to redress the imbalance, which has resulted from the accelerated tempo of technical change in recent decades, between the long drawn-out patent procedure and the period of quickening amortization of inventions. The PCT was also ratified by the leading industrial countries, including Britain, the Federal Republic of Germany, France, Japan, Switzerland and the United States. It was signed by Hungary, too (ratified in 1980 and promulgated by Law-Decree No. 14 of 1980). The State parties to it numbered 89 on 1 February 1997. (In 1989 the total number of applications was 15,000 against more than 20,000 filed with Hungary alone on 1996.)

3. In addition, *several special agreements* were signed on the international protection of patents and scientific inventions: the Paris Convention of 1961 (amended at Geneva in 1972, 1978 and 1991) for the Protection of New Varieties of Plants (with 32 accessions by 1 February 1997; in Hungary promulgated by Law-Decree No. 14 of 1983); the Strasbourg Convention of 1971 for the International Classification of Patents (not ratified, but applied by Hungary); the Budapest Treaty of 1977 for the International Recognition of the Deposit of Micro-organisms for the Purposes of Patent Procedure (with 38 accessions by 1 February 1997; in Hungary promulgated by Law-Decree No. 1 of 1981); the Geneva Treaty of 1978 on the International Recording of Scientific Discoveries (it has as yet not entered into force).

The diplomatic conference held at Washington in 1989 drafted a new international treaty (not yet in force) for the protection of intellectual property relating to integrated circuits, and preparatory work is under way within the framework of WIPO concerning the harmonization of patent laws and the protection of biotechological inventions.

4. Europe has established a developed system of regional cooperation in the field of patents.

The Munich Convention of 1973 on the licensing of European patents entered into force in 1977. Its principal aim is to simplify and increase the efficiency of the procedure for obtaining patents for inventions in several countries. This aim is achieved by permitting a single European application, replacing the multitude of national applications of identical content for a particular invention, to be filed with effect in all State parties to the Convention and to be considered under uniform rules in a single procedure in place of a great many parallel national procedures.

The Convention, its implementing rules and annexed protocols constitute a common European law governing the licensing of patents and functioning as a "patent law choice" as a parallel alternative to national laws.

European patents granted according to uniform requirements under a single procedure do not mean legally unified, "unitary" patents extending to the territories of the States indicated therein, but essentially a set of national patents which are, after licensing, under the control of the same rules as relate to national patents directly granted by different countries, namely they are transformed into national patents. The legally uniform protection is intended to be accorded by the Luxembourg Convention of 1975 (which, however, did not enter into force until 1 February 1997).

The Munich Convention set up the European Patent Organization, the working bodies of which are

– the European Patent Office (based in Munich) attending to operative tasks connected with the licensing, according to uniform requirements, of European patents extending to the territories of the States parties;

– the Administrative Council exercising directive functions and composed of representatives of the States parties.

In addition, there were set up sub-offices of the European Patent Office in The Hague, Berlin, Berlin and Vienna, and a research and training centre for industrial property protection (EIPI) in Strasbourg.

Accordingly, until patents are granted, these countries "touch the same tone", herein lies the most profound effect of the European patent system.

In 1997 there are 18 States parties to the Convention. They are the following in chronological order from

– 1977: Belgium, France, Germany, Luxembourg, Netherlands, Switzerland, United Kingdom;

– 1978: Italy and Sweden;

– 1979: Austria;

– 1980: Liechtenstein;
– 1986: Greece and Spain;
– 1990: Denmark;
– 1991: Monaco;
– 1992: Portugal and Ireland;
– 1995: Finland.

As the listing shows, the Convention is open not only to the member-states of the European Union, but any European country may become a party to it at the request of the Administrative Council. At present, beside the EU member-states, Switzerland is a party to the Convention, and other countries of the European "economic area" (Turkey, Czech Republic, Slovakia, Hungary and Poland) similarly show interest in accession. In 1996 Hungary filed its application for accession (which can be expected to take place around the year 2000).

§91. INTERNATIONAL TRADEMARK PROTECTION

1. The basic legal framework for the international protection of trademarks is likewise provided by the Paris Union Convention, whose general principles of regulation (*régime nationale*, Union priority, etc.) mentioned above prevail in this field as well. The *régime nationale* here means that natural and legal persons of the Union States may, in any Union State, directly apply for trademark protection, subject to the substantive and procedural conditions applicable to nationals and to the formalities required by the trademark law of the particular State. In the case of trademarks, a Union priority date of application may be obtained within six months of first application.

2. The significance of international trademark protection is shown by the fact that by the time of the late 19th century a separate international agreement, the *Madrid Agreement* of 1891 for the International Registration of Marks, was signed within the framework of the Paris Union Convention [and was revised in Brussels (1900), in Washington (1911), in The Hague (1925), in London (1934), in Nice (1957), in Stockholm (1967)]. Hungary has also acceded to the Agreement (Stockholm text), which was promulgated by Law-Decree No. 29 of 1973. (On 1 February 1997, there were 52 States parties to the Agreement.)

The Madrid Agreement was initiated by the need to devise a simpler, speedier and cheaper procedure for organizing trademark protection in several countries. To meet that need the Madrid Agreement established the institution of "*international trademark*", the core and substance of which is that natural and legal persons of the States parties may, by a single application, obtain protection in the territories of all contracting States for their trademarks protected in the country of origin. The international trademark thus makes it possible to avoid filing several applications for international protection in a more complicated, more expensive and protracted procedure.

In 1989 there was attached to the Madrid Agreement a Protocol adopted within the framework of the Diplomatic Conference (signed by 28 States and operative from 1995). In 1997 it has 16 States parties and can be expected to be ratified by Hungary, too. The Protocol has a triple aim: to uphold the general principles of the Agreement, to respond to the needs of countries (including Britain) showing an interest in the Agreement, and to ensure that the European Union may, through its regional cooperation in the field of trademarks and in its own right, participate in the universal system of protection.

3. Also, with a view to simplifying trademark registration and ensuring its international uniformity, a separate agreement, the *Nice Agreement* of 1957 for the International Classification of Goods and Services for the Purposes of the Registration of Marks, was signed within the framework of the Paris Union Convention (and was revised in Stockholm in 1967 and in Geneva in 1977). On 1 February 1997 it had 50 States parties. Hungary acceded to the Agreement and promulgated the Geneva text in *Magyar Közlöny*, No. 5 of 1983.

§92. INTERNATIONAL PROTECTION OF INDICATIONS AND MARKS OF ORIGIN

The international protection of indications and marks of origin is also guided by the general *principles of the Paris Union Convention* (first of all the *régime nationale*). Protection is regulated in detail by separate agreements complementing the Paris Union Convention.

1. As early as 1891, the *Madrid Agreement for the Repression of False and Deceptive Indications of Origin on Goods* was signed [revised in Washington (1911), in The Hague (1925), in London (1934), in Lisbon (1958) and supplemented in Stockholm (1967)]. Hungary is a party to the Lisbon text (promulgated by Law-Decree No. 7 of 1967) and to the supplementary document of Stockholm (promulgated by Law-Decree No. 18 of 1970). (The Agreement had 31 States parties on 1 February 1997.) The substance of protection is that any merchandise bearing a false or deceptive indication which shows one of the contracting States (or a place in that State) to be the country (place) of origin must be seized, or its importation must be prohibited, or the indication of origin in question must be prevented in the State party (either of origin or of importation).

2. The *Lisbon Agreement for the Protection and International Registration of Marks of Origin* was signed in 1958 (it had 17 States parties on 1 February 1997). Hungary is a party to the Stockholm text of 1967 as revised in 1979 (promulgated by Law-Decree No. 1 of 1982). Under the Agreement the States parties accord protection to the marks of origin on one another's products, subject to compliance with the substantive and procedural requirements.

§93. INTERNATIONAL PROTECTION OF INDUSTRIAL DESIGNS

The basis for the international protection of industrial designs was likewise laid down by the *Paris Union Convention*, which, as in the case of patents and trademarks, grants *Union priority of date of application* (within six months of first application) and contains provisions on protection to be mandatorily incorporated into the internal laws of the States parties.

Under *The Hague Agreement* for the International Deposit of Industrial Designs [revised in London (1934), in The Hague (1960); supplemented in Monaco (1961), in Stockholm (1967); a Protocol attached in Geneva (1975); amended in 1979] protection for industrial designs may be obtained by a single application in several countries. The States parties numbered 26 on 1 February 1997. Hungary acceded to the Agreement in 1984 (promulgation by Law-Decree No. 29 of 1984).

Within the framework of the Paris Union Convention a supplementary agreement, the *Locarno Agreement for the International Classification of Industrial Designs*, was signed in 1968. (On 1 February 1997 it had 28 States parties, and was promulgated in Hungary by Law-Decree No. 29 of 1973.) (On related problems, see the studies by Bobrovszky in the List of Sources.)

TITLE 8

INTERNATIONAL LAW OF SUCCESSION

CHAPTER XXIX

INTERNATIONAL LAW OF SUCCESSION

§94. SUCCESSION IN PRIVATE INTERNATIONAL LAW; THE LAW OF SUCCESSION

1. Just as individuals are governed by their personal law (*lex personae*) and contracts by the law of obligations (*lex obligationis*), inheritance is subject to the law of succession (*lex successionis*), the commonly used term or institution which emerged historically to indicate the law governing inheritance relations. The law of succession controls not only inheritance in the narrow sense, in terms of the estate's status under the law of property, but inheritance relations in their entirety.

The law of succession is a complex unity of personal and property relations, which should be regarded as including the continuation of familial and other personal relations with respect to the decedent.

As regards the connecting factors by which the law of succession was determined in different historical periods, it may be stated that development started with the control of the law of the place where the assets of an estate were situate, and later the approach became "more personal" in that the personal law of the deceased person was considered to be in control of inheritance relations at least with respect to movable property, a tendency which led to the exclusive application of the deceased person's personal law in some States, perhaps in most European countries.

(a) *From the Middle Ages* down to the 18th century the dominant principle was the *lex rei sitae*, according to which inheritance relations were considered under the law of the country in which the assets of an estate were found at the time of the accrual of inheritance. In the 14th century Bartolus laid emphasis, in the domain of the law of succession, on the acquisition of property (*acquisitio*) rather than on personal aspects and held that normally the law of the place where the property was situate was the connecting factor to govern inheritance relations. This concept reflected the fact that during that period land was the most important object of property and that its fate was inseparable from the entire feudal system of land tenure prevalent in a particular country. For example, the pattern of land ownership was to develop according to whether the property, in case the owner went abroad, reverted to the feudal lord or passed on to the first born, who was always the first to succeed to property. It further expressed the fact that the international mobility of persons was on a relatively smaller scale at that time, one reason why the personal law and the *lex rei sitae* coincided anyway in most cases of inheritance.

(b) *In modern times*, during the period of the Renaissance, the growth of industry, trade and business increased the significance of movable property parallel to real estate. Particularly in the period of capitalism, a larger role came to be played by money, shares and securities, and other movables of great value. It was this circumstance and the growing volume of transactions that generated and bred the concept which placed the succession to movables under the control of the decedent's personal law, thus separating it from the oft fortuitous *situs*. This is how the *slicing of inheritance theory (Spaltungstheorie)* evolved: while succession to immovable property was subject to the *lex rei sitae*, movable property came to be governed by the decedent's personal law prevailing at the time of his death. In the 17th century Huber of the Dutch school, in his work *De conflictu legum in diversis imperiis*, clearly taught that it was reasonable to render land and buildings as immovable property subject to the *lex situs* only, while succession to movable should be governed by the decedent's personal law. This was also the teaching of Coccei of the German school who, in his work on private international law (*Disputatio*) published at the end of the 17th century, was more analytical and less equivocal in stating the position of private international law on inheritance relations: he favoured and argued for the control of the *lex rei sitae* over immovables, while with respect to movables he wrote that they should be considered not to be situate at a particular place but to follow the person (*eius quasi ossibus inherent, quia tempore mortis subiectus fuit domicilii*). It should be added that the personal law is determined by the domicile theory, which was also adopted by French law. A great representative of the French school in the 16th century, D'Argentré had stated, though in a less elaborate and less categorical manner than the aforesaid authors, that movable things (*mobilia*) had no permanent site, they negated, as it were, their location (*situm habere negantur*). Thus they could not derive their status from anything but the person of their owner, from his personal law, which in that period was, naturally with D'Argentré too, the domicile (*ideo legem ab domicilii loco capiunt*).

(c) *The 18th century saw the appearance of the unity of the estate doctrine*, while in countries such as France the dual concept of slicing the estate remained predominant. English law was developing along that line. At that stage of development the principle of unity of the estate did not imply the *lex situs* only, as was the case earlier, but gave prominence to the decedent's personal law as controlling the whole of inheritance relations in respect of both movable and immovable property. We find it first discussed, in scientific depth and in a way significantly influencing practice, by Mencken in his *Dissertatio* on the private international law of inheritance, which was published at Leipzig in the 18th century. His tenets and even his arguments were upheld and further elaborated by Savigny, who adapted them to the more modern conditions of the 19th century. His theory became prevalent in the law of inheritance, as in the elaboration of the modern bourgeois system of private international law in general, not only in legal science but also in German law. This theory advances the following main arguments. The law of inheritance is an artificial extension of the decedent's person after his death, either expressly (by testamentary succession) or tacitly (by intestate succession). This relationship concerns, entirely and directly, the person of the decedent and his personal relations. Practically, with Mencken, this appears to be a legal expression of the continuation of the fictitious relation between the deceased and the heirs. Savigny goes on to argue (pp. 295 *et seq.*) that the other solution could be nothing other than the law of the *situs* of the estate, but, given the specific features of the assets of the estate, it is likely to lead to arbitrary decisions. In modern conditions – and here he points out a most essential factor – the estate consists, in addition to landed property, mainly of movables comprising various rights, obligations and debts, assets and liabilities. Hence, an estate is the totality of assets, an ideal object with a content difficult to define which, as such, has no clearly definable location; such property is everywhere and nowhere at the same time. By this reason the *situs* of the estate theory stands, in point of fact, notionally in contrast to the character of the estate. If one is definitely to give preference to the *lex rei sitae*, it remains to be concluded that every object of property is subject to its own local law and that, consequently, the whole estate is governed by as many legal systems as there are places in which the various assets of it are situate and as there are systems of law controlling them. As this is clearly an irrational approach, the only course would be to subject the entire estate to the law of the country in which the larger part of the property is to be found. This in turn is an arbitrary choice which is, over and above, bound to lead to legal uncertainty hard to bridge in practice.

(d) *In earlier periods Hungarian law* first followed the unity of the estate principle under German and Austrian influence, but later *adopted the slicing of the estate doctrine, which prevailed until 1945.* The application of the slicing theory was nevertheless limited by a demarcation drawn between immovables and movables, with an immovable estate subjected to the law of the *situs* and a movable estate to the decedent's personal law. Full adoption of the slicing theory means not only a basic distinction between movable and immovable property, but also the fact that every asset of an estate is governed by the law of its *situs*, namely the applicability of several laws of succession to movable property.

2. The peculiarity of *present-day foreign solutions* lies in that they are actually the continuations of yesterday's solutions. The contemporary private international law of some countries adheres to the slicing theory, while the unity of the estate doctrine prevails in others. The picture is made more variegated by a

differentiation between domestic immovables and immovables in numerous countries where the principle of unity of the estate is generally extended to immovables, but domestic immovables are rendered subject to the internal law of inheritance. Another novel feature of development is found in the interstate regulation of inheritance matters, including aspects of both conflicts and substantive law, under bilateral agreements concluded by many countries. Noteworthy solutions were formulated in The Hague Conventions on the law of succession (see item 3).

(a) The *slicing of the estate* theory was adopted by the British and American as well as the French systems of law, which render immovable property subject to the *lex rei sitae* (Dicey, pp. 518 *et seq.;* Ehrenzweig, p. 282), and movable property to the law of the decedent's last domicile (pp. 598 and 287, respectively).

(b) The principle of *unity of the estate* was accepted by most countries in Europe, and it received general statutory expression in the enacting law of the German *BGB* (Arts. 24 and 25 of the *EGBGB*). Article 25 of the German PIL Code of 1986 upheld this approach with a notable change: it allows choice of law concerning immovables in the FRG, namely the testator may stipulate the application of the German law of succession in respect to such immovables. The unity of the estate appears also in the new Austrian PIL Code (Art. 28) and the Swiss Code of 1987 (Art. 90) as well as in the former Czechoslovak Code (Art. 17), the Yugoslav Code (Art. 30) and the Polish Code (Art. 34).

(c) The *situs* of immovable property has nevertheless retained a considerable weight, which is often perceivable even in the uniform approach of the countries adhering to the principle of unity of the estate: *the control of national law over domestic immovables cuts across the otherwise upheld principle of unity of the estate.* This is found to be motivated by the interest in having the legal situation of the overwhelming majority of national wealth controlled in every possible way by the legal policy objectives expressed in the domestic rules of law. The preference given by this approach to domestic immovables appears, as was seen, in the new German Code as well, albeit through choice of law only, but this tendency has recently been observed to be taking hold, as is the case in the domain of international agreements (see item 3).

(d) Where and to the extent it is applied, the slicing of the estate theory distinguishes between movables under the control of the *lex situs. Accordingly, the personal law governs all movable property* and the entire estate where its principle of unity is fully observed. There is a difference, however, in the content of personal law. While in the British and American legal systems the personal law is determined by the domicile, in Europe in general (including France which adheres to the slicing of the estate theory), the content of personal law is controlled by the law of nationality. Such was generally the case in Europe until very recently, while the domicile was predominant in Britain and the other common-law countries (USA, Australia). Nationality is the main connecting factor in the Codes of FRG (Art. 25), Greece (Arts. 29–31), Poland (Art. 34), former Czechoslovakia (Art. 17) and Austria (Art. 28). Yet there are some exceptions even in Europe. The Swiss PIL Code similarly ordains application of the law of last domicile (Art. 90). The principle of domicile is strongly upheld and is even accorded preference over the principle of nationality particularly in international agreements covering matters of inheritance, notably in agreements on legal assistance.

3. Matters of inheritance receive an ever greater coverage in interstate treaties.

(a) *Consular conventions and particularly agreements on legal assistance* often provide detailed regulations for inheritance relations on a bilateral basis. Regulation is partly of a conflict nature, but it also covers numerous questions of substantive law. Central to conflict situations are the provisions adopting the principle either of unity or of slicing the estate. On the evidence of agreements on legal assistance and of consular conventions, *the practice of countries* concerning this basic issue of private international law *is characterized by a pragmatic diversity*, as will be seen later in our discussion of the relevant agreements signed by Hungary. The substantive-law rules of such agreements regulate the obligations of the contracting States concerning the protection, administration and delivery of the estate, cover questions of jurisdiction, the enforcement of judgments and decisions in matters of inheritance, etc. Equal treatment is a general principle of these interstate agreements, which provide, mainly in preambular paragraphs, that either contracting party accords to nationals of the other contracting party the same treatment as is enjoyed by its own nationals in matters of inheritance.

(b) The *multilateral Hague Conventions* on the law of succession provided a new cast to regulation in many respects, chiefly by pursuing the goal of promoting the unification of law. At present the marked growth of two-way *migration* is leading to a high degree of internalization of inheritance relations. The diverse systems of substantive and conflicts law of the different countries are, *ab initio*, out of line with this trend. The Hague Conventions seek to eliminate the disadvantages stemming from such disintegration, from the systems of regulation differing by country. They do so in two ways: on the one hand, by directly or indirectly influencing, with their very existence (with the values they have created in international legislation), the development of national laws in the direction of harmonization and, on the other, by codifying a uniform law on the subject in relation to the State parties. Thus the uniform international regulation gives an adequate expression of the said trend, serving to meet the needs of the growing internationalization of inheritance relations.

To date the Hague Conference has adopted three international conventions, notably on the conflict rules governing the formal requirements of testamentary dispositions (1961), on the international administration of estates (1973) and on the private international law of estates (1988). Hungary contributed a share to the elaboration of these conventions, and its accession is obviously of topical interest, with the motives thereof already stated in legal literature.

Rather than seeking to be exhaustive, we deem it practicable to underline a few features of the aforementioned Convention of 1988 which point to the new elements manifested in this field of legal thinking and regulation. One such element is the integration of the alternative application of nationality and domicile into a flexible equilibrium between habitual residence (see item 5 in §29), conceived as constituting a strong link, and nationality (Art. 3). Another novelty allows choice of law (*professio iuris*), conferring on the testator the right to select the law of the country of which she/he is/was a national or in which she/he has/had her/his habitual residence either at the time of making her/his will or of her/his death (Art. 5). The testator may stipulate the laws of different countries in respect to specified assets of her/his estate, but such stipulation must not serve to avoid application of the *jus cogens* rules of the otherwise applicable law (Arts. 3, 5 and 6). As can be seen, by these provisions the Convention opened the way to a limited slicing of the estate as well, a trend further strengthened by placing specific assets of the estate (immovables, enterprises), which are governed by special rules of the *situs* on inheritance, under the control of the *lex rei sitae* (Art. 15). These novel principles of the Convention serve adequately to express and meet the demands of large-scale migration ("habitual residence"), a fuller manifestation of a person's autonomy ("choice of law") and the special considerations of the national systems of inheritance (mainly in respect of specific immovables).

§95. REGULATION OF INHERITANCE IN HUNGARIAN LAW

1. *Inheritance relations, including intestate succession*, are governed by the following main provision of the Hungarian Code of Private International Law: "Inheritance relations shall be subject to the personal law of the deceased person at the time of death" (para. 1 of Art. 36). We should add some comments on this score.

(a) As the quoted provision shows, *Hungarian law adheres to the principle of unity of the estate*, breaking with the pre-1945 practice. In line with the argument advanced in literature, legal development after 1945 in Hungary made a break with the previous concept which had given rise to numerous complications. In its Decision No. 4804/1952 the Supreme Court ruled that claims to inheritance must be adjudicated according to the law of the State of which the decedent was a national.

(b) The Hungarian law currently in force is thus based on the principle of full unity of the estate: the law of succession is, irrespective of the assets of the estate, the law of the State to which the decedent belonged under his personal law at the time of his death. *Consequently, the law of succession thereby determined applies to all assets of the estate and to all elements of the inheritance relation*, including intestate and testamentary succession, the State's right of inheritance, the conditions of succession (*ipso facto* succession, capacity to succeed grounds for elimination from succession, etc.), the legal status of heirs and their *inter se* relations, the effects of the law of inheritance, contracts of inheritance and so on.

By way of illustration we will refer to only a few of the many cases in which this general principle is applied in the practice of courts and notaries public: the proceeding Hungarian fora applied Swiss law in the case of a Swiss decedent (Bp. 10. Kjö. II.4915/1981), Mexican law in the case of a Mexican decedent (Bp. 22. Kjö. V.3115/1981), English customary law prevailing in the Sudan in the case of a Sudanese decedent (Bp. 6. Kjö. XI.7907/1981) and the Hungarian law in the case of a Hungarian decedent (County Court of Szolnok 2, Pf. 20498/1982).

(c) *The said general principle was not broken* by the request of, e.g., the two Brazilian heirs to the immovable estate in Hungary of a Brazilian decedent to have the estate considered under Hungarian law in accordance with Art. 9 of the Code rather than under Brazilian law (Bp. 9. Kjö. IX.5645/1980), nor was it contravened by the heir receiving the estate in Hungary of a Sudanese decedent under English law, because under Sudanese law invoked the Christian nationals of Sudan are subject to the customary rules of the English law of succession (Bp. 6. Kjö. XI.7907/1981).

(d) Considering that Art. 36 (1) quoted above refers to "inheritance relations" without giving a definition thereof and that certain institutions of the law of succession belong, wholly or in part, to a different category under some systems of law, the problem of qualification arises with great frequency especially in the domain of the law of succession.

Practical examples of qualification are also provided by cases adjudicated according to the Hungarian system of law (Baja 2. Kjö. 1910/1981). As indicated above, *contracts of inheritance* between foreign testators and Hungarian heirs are governed by the law of the State of the foreign testator's last nationality. Emerging questions are to be qualified in Hungary under Hungarian law in accordance with Art. 3 of the Code. Contracts of inheritance are regulated by the Civil Code in its section on the law of succession (Arts. 655–658), and such contracts can be regarded as an institution of the law of succession despite references in the Civil Code to the rules governing contracts of maintenance and life-annuity in certain aspects. Accordingly the case referred to above should have been judged under foreign law, but the proceeding forum, in view of the strong contractual element and the bearings of maintenance and life annuity in the case, considered that the legal relationship in question was one of the latter category, which in turn is governed, under Art. 26 (3) of the Code, by the law of the place of maintenance. Since that law was of Hungary, Hungarian law was applied. Even if there should be any argument in support of qualifying a contract of inheritance as an institution of the law of obligations (which is at least disputable), there is no ground for placing a contract of inheritance under the control of the law which, by virtue of the Code, governs the said category of maintenance and life annuity. If the contract of inheritance is not clearly regarded as a category of the law of succession, it remains to apply the law of the domicile of the obligor of the most characteristic performance or the law of the country "most closely connected with the essential elements of the particular contractual relationship" (Art. 29 of the Code), because such type of contract (one of inheritance) is unknown to the chapter of the Code on the law of inheritance. In the case at hand that law would also most certainly have been Hungarian law (which is not sure to be applicable to a different set of facts), as the testator's place of residence was Hungary, the heir was a Hungarian, the estate was in Hungary and maintenance in return for inheritance was to be provided in Hungary.

Another aspect of qualification under the law of inheritance concerns the *situation of the surviving spouse under the private international law of inheritance*, more specifically the question of whether it is controlled by the law of marital property, the *régime of common marital property*, or family law. If it is controlled by the law of inheritance, the problem is governed by the rules of private international law on inheritance, namely by the decedent's last personal law according to the Hungarian legal system. If it is a matter of family law, it should be governed by the rules of private international law on family law, which in turn is normally determined by the common personal law of the spouses. The two do not necessarily coincide. The régime of common marital property is but one aspect of the problem. The other aspect is the *widow's portion* which, under the law of some countries, is a category of the family law rather than the law of inheritance. As regards Hungarian regulation on these two institutions, régime of common marital property is a category of family law (Art. 27 of the Family Law), whereas succession of the *surviving spouse* to the estate in default of issue, and/or the *widow's or widower's portion as her/his right of usufruct* in the estate inherited by another person, is regarded as an institution of the law of inheritance, and both are covered by the provisions of the Civil Code on succession (Arts. 607 and 615). Since, according to Hungarian private international law, characterization must be accomplished primarily under the law of the forum, the Hungarian judge has to look to the Hungarian law to determine whether the institution of régime of common marital property or the status of the surviving spouse is a category of this or that branch of law. This is well illustrated by the right practice of Hungarian fora as reflected in the following case (Bp. 10. Kjö. II.4915/1981). There were two Swiss heirs to the immovable estate in Hungary of a decedent of Swiss nationality: the surviving spouse and a descendant. The nature of the immovable property and hence the question of whether only one half of that property was to be inherited was decided by establishing the nature of the property under the law applicable to the personal and property relations of the spouses. That law was, under Art. 39 of the Code, the last common personal law of the spouses, notably Swiss law. One might of course say that the law determined by the decedent's last nationality would also be Swiss law. Yet a different set of facts would indicate another law (e.g. there is only the last domicile, which is nothing other than the State of the decedent's last nationality), not to mention that Swiss law invoked to govern the personal and property relations of the spouses refers to the law of the spouses' first common domicile, which was Hungarian law. Since reference back is to be accepted under Art. 4 of the Hungarian Code, the proceeding forum finally relied on Hungarian law for determining the status of the particular immovable property under the family law. Reliance on the law of succession would not have led to this same result as reference back is not used by Swiss law. Thus the widow's right of usufruct in the other half of the immovable property subject to inheritance (as it is a category of the law of succession under Hungarian law) had to be determined, by virtue of Art. 36 of the Code on the law of inheritance, under Swiss law (the widow had to choose between full usufruct and succession to one quarter of the estate).

(e) In legal disputes involving inheritance, the judge is often faced with the need to decide the *preliminary question* of whether there was a *valid marriage* between the deceased and the surviving spouse or whether *paternity* was acknowledged by the deceased. These aspects that are known to be decisive in determining whether an inheritance relation between the spouses concerned has actually come into being at all. Although these questions arise mostly in connection with the acquisition of an inheritance, namely in legal disputes involving inheritance, one should be aware that these preliminary questions are not matters of inheritance and therefore are not subject to the rules of private international law on inheritance, but to those applying to the legal institution involved, namely, in our instance, to marriage or paternity (see §§98 and 101 below).

(f) Another question may be related to the *time factor of an inheritance relation* (this is the so-called intertemporal question of private law). An inheritance may have opened during the operation of the previous Civil Code, or before the completion of the codification of the Hungarian civil law in 1959, and the substantive law of the country invoked may now be different, in its general context, from that in force at the time of accrual of the inheritance. For instance, redemption by the heir of the widow's right of usufruct in her portion of the estate is a relatively new element of Hungarian civil law [the relevant provision was added to the Civil Code (para. 3 of Art. 616) when it was amended in 1977]. Therefore the status of heirs differs according to whether the dispute is governed by a regulation before or after its amendment. It is therefore necessary that, in the consideration of such matters, the inheritance situation should be tested against the temporal aspects of the appropriate substantive law, namely the system of inheritance governed by it at a specific point of time. Furthermore, changes may have occurred in the conflict rules of the particular country. An example is provided by Hungary where, as was seen, the slicing of the estate theory had persisted for a while after 1945 but was then replaced by the principle of unity of the estate. Thus, if the inheritance situation at hand concerns a legal dispute in which the decisive factor, namely the accrual of inheritance, occurred prior to World War Two, it will be governed by another rule of the applicable Hungarian private international law: formerly by the slicing of the estate theory and later by the principle of unity of the estate.

(g) The last question to consider – no longer a preliminary but rather a subsequent one, if there is any sense in making a comparison here – concerns the situation in which *inheritance by the State* occurs. Such is known to be the case when there is an estate but no heir. Failing statutory and testamentary heirs, the State appears as heir general. The status of the State in the law of inheritance is interpreted and hence regulated differently by the diverse systems of law. There are two prevalent views. According to one view, the State, for the purposes of the law of inheritance, becomes heir "within the ordinary meaning of civil law", whereas under the other concept it acquires an escheated estate on the strength of its sovereignty. The first view prevails in most European laws, and the second is held in, e.g., France, Belgium and Austria. The essential difference lies in probate proceedings and in the partially different rules on the acquisition of and liability for inheritance on the one hand and, on the other, in the application of the slicing of the estate theory to inheritance by the State in several countries where the principle of unity of the estate otherwise prevails. (In most of these countries it is generally spelt out on the strength of sovereignty that, by failure of heirs, immovable property reverts to the State of the place of the estate rather than of the nationality of the decedent.)

2. As was pointed out earlier, the law of inheritance, mainly the one determined by the law of the State of the decedent's last nationality, applies to an inheritance relation as a whole, including testamentary succession. Accordingly the law of the country of last nationality governs first and foremost the freedom of testamentary disposition, i.e. the possibility of testamentary succession along with statutory succession, the admissible types of testamentary disposition (e.g. the admissibility of making a will by a contract of inheritance in addition to a testament), the prerequisites for the validity of wills under substantive law, including the conditions for the making and revocation of a will, legal share, the consequences of failure to mention a person entitled to inheritance, the admissibility and limitation of appointing a reversionary heir, bequest and its revocation, the status of executor, etc.

As can be seen, most questions of testamentary succession are governed by the law of last nationality as the general connecting factor for the law of inheritance, whereas certain elements of testamentary succession may be subject to different conflict rules both in foreign laws and in Hungarian law, an aspect to be given special treatment below.

(a) Under *previous Hungarian law,* two questions related to testamentary succession – *testamentary capacity* and the *formal validity of testamentary dispositions* – were controlled by a law other than the law of inheritance. The first question was subject to the testator's domestic law, that is generally the law of nationality applicable at the time of making the will, while the second question was governed by the rules prevailing at the time and place of making the will.

(b) The *Code* renders a will generally subject to the law of the country of which the testator was a national at the time of his death, namely it places wills mostly under the control of the *law of succession* and formulates the necessary exceptions as special rules permitting departure from this general premise. By this regulation the Code follows international legislative practice and the theoretically correct solution in favouring a flexible application of the *principle of unity of the estate*. The essential exception bears on formal validity and implies a stronger support for the *favor testamenti*. These features of regulation are expressed in Art. 36, para. 2 of the Code. The first sentence reads: "Testamentary dispositions shall be under the control of the testator's personal law at the time of death", while the second provision states that "a testamentary disposition and its revocation shall be formally valid if they satisfy the requirements of Hungarian law; or the law in effect at the time and place of making or revocation; or the personal law of the testator at the time of making or revocation, or of his death; or the law in effect at the testator's domicile or habitual residence at the time of making or revocation, or of his death; or the law of the *situs* of immovables in the case of testamentary disposition of such property". This makes it clear that the Hungarian law of conflicts employs a variety of connecting factors in order to secure the foremost aim of upholding the validity of wills (*favor testamenti*), helping to attain goals of substantive law.

This is evidenced by practice as well. An Australian testamentary heir to an immovable estate in Hungary of a Swiss testator was not supported in his claim firmly enough by the will, which showed some irregularity. By a cumulative application of the Swiss and Hungarian substantive laws the *favor testamenti* rules allowed the will to be declared valid and the Australian heir to acquire ownership in the estate (Bp. Kjö. III.2741/1983).

3. The growth of international personal and economic transactions, which are of particular importance to Hungary, increasingly entailed the objective need for States to regulate by *interstate agreements* the status of their nationals under the law of inheritance in cases involving the other contracting State and/or its nationals. Over the past thirty years, this has resulted in a large number of international agreements (and in greater emphasis on bilateral regulation) concerning several aspects of international legal disputes involving inheritance. The relevant treaties include *agreements on legal assistance*, consular conventions covering matters of inheritance as well, and *interstate agreements relating* specifically *to matters of inheritance*, such as the Hungarian–Austrian interstate agreement on the "regulation of matters of inheritance" (promulgated by Law-Decree No. 25 of 1967) or the Hungarian–Austrian agreement for the avoidance of double taxation in the matter of taxes on estates and inheritances (promulgated by Law-Decree No. 1 of 1976).

Matters of inheritance are regulated by every agreement on legal assistance and by most of the consular conventions.

This field of international legislation is generally concerned with the following elements of the law of succession as a whole: equal treatment, conflict rules for the governing law of statutory succession, regulation of testamentary succession under private international law, jurisdiction, protection, administration and delivery of the estate, and avoidance of double taxation in certain respects.

As a result of bilateral regulations on matters of inheritance, pertinent issues in relations between the countries concerned are *governed by special norms rather than by the general rules of private international law*. In view of the differences between the regulations provided by the bilateral agreements themselves, the regulation of inheritance relations under private international law has grown somewhat in complexity by running on two planes in some countries. This becomes manifest when the above general picture of regulation by the Hungarian private international law of inheritance is broadened to include the principal features presented by the international treaties to which Hungary is signatory.

(a) The most general rule, which is part of the private international law of all the countries concerned, relates to *equal, or national treatment (régime nationale)*. As was seen in our discussion of persons (§§44–45), this means that each contracting party accords to nationals of the other contracting party equal status with its own nationals under the law of succession with respect to capacity to succeed and other matters of inheritance alike. Provisions to this effect are contained in, among others, Art. 30 of the Bulgarian–Hungarian Agreement on Legal Assistance (promulgated by Law-Decree No. 6 of 1967) and Art. 3 of the Austrian–Hungarian Agreement on the Regulation of Matters of Inheritance (promulgated by Law-Decree No. 25 of 1967). Furthermore, these agreements provide that if an object of property is subject to restrictions in respect of nationals in the countries of the contracting parties, the governing law of such matters is the *lex rei sitae*; in other words, if international transactions involving objects of property or rights deriving therefrom are subject to restrictive foreign exchange regulations, the States mutually take notice of them and even remove them from the general rule of the law applicable to the determination of the law of succession.

(b) As for the applicable law, the general rule as defined in interstate agreements ordinarily prescribes the application of the law of the decedent's last nationality or the control of the law of the decedent's last nationality over movable property and that of the *lex situs* over immovable property (as in, e.g., Art. 31 of the Bulgarian–Hungarian Agreement on Legal Assistance). Thus nationality as the general rule does not mean that certain provisions of the *lex rei sitae* (e.g. foreign exchange regulations) are not applicable to all cases. Since, however, these provisions also apply to the State's own nationals, they do not prejudice the principle of equal treatment.

Inheritance by the State is an important question of the applicable law, which is likewise covered by some of the agreements on legal assistance as follows: movables are inherited by the State of which the decedent was a national, whereas immovables revert to the State in which they are situate (Art. 32 of the Bulgarian–Hungarian Agreement on Legal Assistance).

Finally, the said agreements place the main questions of testamentary succession under the control of the applicable law by providing that the formalities of the will are normally governed by the law under whose jurisdiction the will was made. However, there is a strong tendency towards the application of the principle of *favor testamenti* inasmuch as the agreements spell out that a will is valid if so held under the law of the place where the will was made, or under the law of the State of which the testator was a national at the time of making the will or of her/his death; or under the law of the State in which the testator was domiciled at the time of making the will or of her/his death. Testamentary capacity is governed by the general rule subjecting it to the law of the State of which the testator was a national at the time of making the will (Art. 4 of the Austrian–Hungarian on the Regulation of Matters of Inheritance; Art. 33 of the Bulgarian–Hungarian Agreement on Legal Assistance).

(c) The question of *jurisdiction* is governed in a rather uniform manner by the slicing of the estate doctrine. Under the said agreements, proceedings in matters of succession to movables are within the jurisdiction of the State of which the testator was a national at the time of her/his death, whereas jurisdiction over proceedings in matters of succession to immovables is determined by the law of the State in the territory of which the immovable property is situate (Art. 6 of the Austrian–Hungarian Agreement on the Regulation of Matters of Inheritance; Art. 34 of the Bulgarian–Hungarian Agreement on Legal Assistance).

(d) Another set of problems covered by interstate agreements concerns the *rights and obligations of States as such in connection with opened estates* resulting from intervening succession. The State in whose territory the inheritance of a national of the other contracting State intervenes is obliged to give notice thereof to the competent organs, usually the diplomatic or consular mission of that other State. It is further obliged to take steps, according to its own law, for the protection and administration of the estate in order to ensure that the person entitled may take possession thereof. The authorized officers of the diplomatic or consular mission of the State concerned have the right to act in matters of inheritance by their nationals, to represent their interests, to accept, where necessary, the estate for temporary safekeeping and to surrender it to the person entitled thereto. If in one State the estate of a national of the other State was accepted for protection and administration, it must by surrendered in an appropriate proceeding. The diplomatic or consular mission of the State concerned must surrender such movables or the value of such movables and immovables (if sold) after satisfaction of creditors and payment of taxes and duties. The delivery of the estate (its repatriation to the country of the heir) is henceforward governed by the rules of foreign exchange law. Of course, the heirs too may, directly or through representatives, act in probate proceedings concerning the protection, administration and repatriation of the estate. In that case, logically, no consular action is taken by the State representing them, because such action is possible and necessary only in the event of safeguarding the interests of nationals who, though entitled to act, are absent. Where there is no need for such action, no legal possibility is open for representation either. [The corresponding provisions are contained in, e.g., Art. 18 of the French–Hungarian Consular Convention (promulgated by Law-Decree No. 33 of 1967), Arts. 43–46 of the USA–Hungarian Consular Convention (promulgated by Law-Decree No. 22 of 1973), Art. 9 of the Austrian–Hungarian Agreement on the Regulation of Matters of Inheritance, Arts. 35 and 38–39 of the Bulgarian–Hungarian Agreement on Legal Assistance).]

(e) Among several other provisions of interstate agreements mention is perhaps deserved of those concerning the *mutual enforcement of judgments* (Chapter XXXVII) or by the recent tendency for the *avoidance of double taxation* as expressed in the Austrian–Hungarian Agreement (promulgated by Law-Decree No. 1 of 1976). It is rather common for heirs to be taxed both in the country where the estate is situate and in their own, because the heir is deemed by both countries to have obtained a gratuitous increment in property. This is the element of economic and fiscal policies on which States rely for taxation. Such double taxation is contestable by itself, because what is really at issue is a material and economic problem of the heir, who inherits only once. The problem, namely the elimination of double taxation and justification for single taxation, may be seen in its full scope if one keeps in mind that inheritance taxes or duties (the denomination makes no difference at all) are on a progressive scale and at a relatively high rate in most countries. Consequently double taxation may place on the heir a greater financial burden than is intended by the very institution of inheritance, viz. the acquisition by the heir of the estate from which to satisfy the various obligations emanating from, among others, his relationship to the decedent or the decedent's family. This is the motive behind the provision of the aforementioned Austrian–Hungarian Agreement (Art. 10) that the State in which the heir is domiciled, levies no tax on the heir in respect of an estate which is situate in the territory of the other State and is therefore liable to taxation in that other State.

TITLE 9

INTERNATIONAL FAMILY LAW

CHAPTER XXX

THE SOURCES OF HUNGARIAN INTERNATIONAL FAMILY LAW

§96. THE CODE. INTERNATIONAL TREATIES

Although in the past the number of familial relations possessing foreign elements was not negligible because of marriage with foreigners and, less frequently, of other facts of family law such as adoption, the sources of Hungarian international family law were rather scattered and possessed many lacunae until the adoption of the current Code of Private International Law. The relevant sources of law were found in domestic norms on matters of detail, such as those governing jurisdiction and determining the applicable law (mainly Law-Decree No. 23 of 1952 enacting the Family Law) as well as in bilateral and multilateral international agreements.

The Code repealed these domestic norms (para. 4 of Art. 75) but, naturally, this did not affect the applicability of the international agreements in question (Art. 2). Consequently the sources of Hungarian international family law are currently in Chapter VII of the Code and in bilateral and multilateral agreements.

A) The *Code* (Arts. 37 to 50) gives a *wide coverage* of international family law, with its *conflicts norms* determining the law applicable to the basic institutions of family law in foreign element cases (marriage, family status, adoption, guardianship, etc.).

B) The *international treaties* dealing with family law are bilateral or multilateral.

1. Most of the international treaties dealing with family law are *bilateral*, especially so the *agreements on legal assistance*, which have the primary objective of regulating international familial relations by establishing special rules on jurisdiction and the determination of applicable law. (The jurisdictional rules of bilateral *consular conventions* may also be of relevance to matters of international family law.) Since the agreements on legal assistance lay down conflict rules, they employ the indirect method of legal regulation as does the Code itself. [The agreements on legal assistance and the consular conventions containing rules of international family law are listed under item 2 (ab) and (ac) of Sect. I in the List of Sources.]

2. By the beginning of the 20th century, the growing internationalization of familial relations led to the conclusion of *multilateral* conventions to resolve conflicts between national family laws.

(a) The Hague Conventions, which were concluded between 1902 and 1905, regulated the problems of applicable law concerning the validity, dissolution and legal effects of marriage as well as guardianship. Hungary (then part of the Austro-Hungarian Monarchy) ratified most of the Hague Conventions and kept them in force until recently [the Convention on guardianship over persons of full age and on similar measures of protection was the last to be denounced in 1977 by Decree No. 6/1977. (VII.27.) of the Minister of Justice].

Changes in social conditions and in national legislation had rendered one Hague Convention after the other outdated and, after the Second World War, had led to their revision within the framework of the Hague Conference on Private International Law. This elaborated conventions on the law applicable to maintenance obligations towards children (1956); on the recognition and enforcement of decisions relating to maintenance obligations towards children (1958); on the rules governing jurisdiction, the applicable law and the recognition of decisions relating to the protection of minors (1965); on the recognition of dissolution of marriage and judicial separation (1970); on the recognition and enforcement of decisions concerning maintenance (1973); on the law applicable to matrimonial property matters (1978, not yet in force); on marriage and the recognition of its validity (1978, not yet in force); on the civil-law aspects of child abduction (1980).

The main sources of international family law include, in addition to the Hague Conventions, the New York Conventions concluded under the auspices of the United Nations, and mention should also be made of the conventions (and recommendations) elaborated within the framework of the Council of Europe.

(b) We single out for special attention six of the multilateral conventions relating to family law, *to which Hungary is a party*:

– one containing provisions of principle in the nature of family law in the field of protection of human rights and fundamental freedoms;

– one on marriage;

– two affecting maintenance obligations and laying down chiefly procedural rules;

– one pertaining to the law of nationality; and

– one covering the civil-law aspects of abduction of children.

(ba) The Rome Convention of 4 November 1950 on the Protection of *Human Rights and Fundamental Freedoms* (and the eight Additional Protocols thereto) became part of the Hungarian legal system upon promulgation by Act XXXI of 1993. Under its Article 12, men and women of marriageable age have the right to marry and to found a family, this right to be exercised in accordance with *Hungarian law*. The Seventh Additional Protocol to the Convention provides (in Art. 5) that the spouses, both in relations *inter se* and with their children, have *equal rights* and *equal responsibility* in civil law with regard to marriage, during marriage and in case of its dissolution, this provision not preventing the States from taking such measures as may be necessary in the interest of children. The European Court of Human Rights (along with the competent organs of the State parties) is called upon to give effect to these provisions of principle.

(bb) Convention on *Consent to Marriage, Minimum Age for Marriage and Registration of Marriages*, done at New York on 10 December 1962 (promulgated in Hungary by Law-Decree No. 7 of 1976).

(bc) Convention on *Recovery Abroad of Maintenance*, done at New York on 20 June 1956 [promulgated in Hungary by Law-Decree No. 53 of 1957, and Decree No. 9/1957. (IX.13.) of the Minister of Justice on its execution as amended by Decree No. 7/1961. (XII.23.) of the Minister of Justice]. In relations between Hungary and the other States parties [Algeria, Argentina, Austria, Barbados, Belgium, Benin, Bosnia and Herzegovina, Brazil, Burkina Faso, Central African Republic, Chile, Croatia (Republic of), Czech Republic, Denmark, Ecuador, Finland, France, Germany (Federal Republic of), Great Britain, Greece, Guatemala, Haiti, Holy See, Israel, Italy, Liechtenstein, Luxembourg, Monaco, Morocco, Netherlands, Niger, Norway, Pakistan, Philippines, Poland, Portugal, Romania, Slovakia (Republic of), Slovenia (Republic of), Spain, Sri Lanka, Sweden, Tunisia, Turkey, Yugoslavia] this Convention accords facilities to persons entitled to maintenance in enforcing claims to maintenance (for the purposes of the Convention, "maintenance" means maintenance of children, relatives and spouse) by the aid of a competent *foreign authority* (ordinarily the Ministry of Justice or of Foreign Affairs) which summons the obligor to pay and may, where necessary, bring an action against him and even resort to levying execution on the amount in question [cf. item 3 (b) in §103]. In relations between Hungary and the component States of the USA (except for the State of Mississippi), the Convention is applied on the basis of reciprocity.

(bd) Convention concerning the *Recognition and Enforcement of Decisions* relating to *Maintenance Obligations towards Children*, done at The Hague on 15 April 1958 [promulgated in Hungary by Law-Decree No. 7 of 1965 and Decree No. 8/1965. (VII.4.) of the Minister of Justice on its enforcement]. Under it, *recovery of maintenance* established by a Hungarian court may be sought *abroad*, and decisions of Hungarian courts (final judgments and, in some countries, provisional measures) are admitted to execution in the other signatory States [in 1996: Austria, Belgium, Denmark, Finland, Germany (Federal Republic of), Italy, Liechtenstein, Netherlands, Norway, Portugal, Spain, Surinam, Sweden, Switzerland, Turkey] [cf. item 3 (a) in §103). Applications for the enforcement abroad of Hungarian decisions may be filed with the local court of competence by the place of residence (the Central District Court of Pest in the capital city). The claimant may apply for the enforcement of a final, recognized and enforceable decision. In case of a claim by a foreign person in need of maintenance (if the debtor fails to pay voluntarily), the court appoints for the rightful claimant an *ad hoc* person who is entitled to bring an action.

Similar facilities are generally provided by the bilateral agreements on legal assistance between Hungary and, for the most part, the neighbouring countries. Claims for maintenance of children in relations between Hungary and the component States of the USA may be enforced on the basis of reciprocity.

(be) Convention on the *Nationality of Married Women*, done at New York on 20 February 1957 (promulgated in Hungary by Law-Decree No. 2 of 1960).

(bf) Convention on the *civil-law aspects of unlawfully taking children abroad*, done at The Hague on 25 October 1980 (promulgated in Hungary by Law-Decree No. 14 of 1986). Under it, the States parties [in 1996: Australia, Austria, Canada, Denmark, France, Germany (Federal Republic of), Hungary, Ireland, Israel, Luxembourg, Netherlands (in the European territory of the Kingdom), New Zealand, Norway, Portugal, Spain, Sweden, Switzerland, United Kingdom, USA] are mutually to ensure, by supporting cooperation between their central organs established for this purpose, return of children under 16 years of age unlawfully taken from parental custody to their national territories. The nationality of the child is immaterial to the proceedings: the place of the child's habitual residence (seat of his upbringing) is of relevance. (Legal assistance in Hungary is provided by the International Law Department of the Ministry of Justice, and legal proceedings are within the exclusive jurisdiction of the Central District Court of Pest.) Under the Convention, a decision on the return of a child unlawfully taken from Hungary or hidden abroad is passed by the authority of the *foreign* State to the territory of which the child was taken. The foreign authority is to apply *Hungarian substantive law* in deciding whether a child was taken or is kept abroad unlawfully. In order that the foreign authorities (courts) concerned may correctly apply the relevant Hungarian regulations in a uniform manner, the Supreme Court has deemed it necessary to issue a statement of position (PK 284) which sums up, on the basis of the Family Law, the conditions under which a child is considered, in accordance with Hungarian law, to be unlawfully taken from Hungary or to be unlawfully taken from Hungary or to be unlawfully hidden abroad, and indicates the range of persons entitled to initiate proceedings for the return of the child (BH No. 2 of 1992).

§97. RELATIONSHIP BETWEEN THE SOURCES OF LAW

In the system of rules of international family law we will first examine the relationship between the Hungarian Code and international treaties and then the hierarchy between the latter.

1. The *hierarchy in the application of the Code and international treaties* is unambiguous: no matter governed by an international treaty is subject to the rules of the Code, as is stated in Art. 2 thereof.

Moreover, the primacy of international treaties implies the possibility for a Hungarian judge to use different connecting factors in dealing with cases based on the same facts, according to whether he is to consider the case under a bilateral agreement on legal assistance or a multilateral treaty and, failing rules formulated by an agreement or a treaty, under the relevant provisions of the Code. In elaborating the Code it was a definite aim of the legislature to avoid such *duplication of conflict norms*. That aim was largely achieved, full success being impossible for the very reason that, owing chiefly to the different legal traditions of the contracting States, the agreements on legal assistance themselves often use differing connecting factors for one and the same matter.

One example will suffice to illustrate the problems involved: under most agreements of Hungary on legal assistance, the intrinsic incidents of the validity of marriage are subject to the personal law of each of the intending spouses should they have different personal laws (consequently the marriage may be invalid in respect of one spouse but valid in respect to the other), whereas under the Code a marriage is valid only if the intrinsic incidents of its validity are present under the personal laws of both intending spouses (cf. item 3 in §98).

The following discussion of the major provisions of international family law (Chapters XXXI to XXXIII) will be generally confined to the rules of the Code, with brief references made to disparities between the Hungarian regulation and the agreements on legal assistance.

2. As regards the *relationship of international treaties inter se*, the general principle is that *bilateral* agreements normally have priority over multilateral conventions in the application of their rules relating to the same matter. Thus, for instance, the relevant provisions of the agreement on legal assistance between Hungary and the former Czechoslovakia (promulgated in Hungary by Law-Decree No. 15 of 1962 and Ordinance No. 111/1962 of the Minister of Justice on its execution) took precedence over the rules of the Hague Convention concerning the Recognition and Enforcement of Decisions relating to Maintenance Obligations towards Children (promulgated in Hungary by Law-Decree No. 7 of 1965 and Decree No. 8/1965 of the Minister of Justice on its Execution).

At the same time, the rules of bilateral agreements may be usefully *supplemented* by those of multilateral conventions relating to the same matter. Such a subsidiary role is played by, e.g., the New York Convention on Recovery Abroad of Maintenance (promulgated in Hungary by Law-Decree No. 53 of 1957 and Decree No. 9/1957 of the Minister of Justice on its execution as amended by Decree No. 7/1961 of the Minister of Justice) in relations between Hungary and Poland, for recourse to the procedure provided for in the New York Convention may be of advantage to Poland because Art. 35 of the Hungarian–Polish Agreement on Legal Assistance (promulgated by Law-Decree No. 5 of 1960, modified by Law-Decree No. 24 of 1981) establishes the jurisdiction of Polish courts in fixing the amount of maintenance, if the child is a Polish national resident in Hungary, but the person obliged to pay maintenance is resident in Poland.

CHAPTER XXXI

MARRIAGE

§98. CONCLUSION AND VALIDITY OF MARRIAGE

1. In Arts. 37 (3) and 38 the Code lays down some basic rules on jurisdiction (and competence) relating to the conclusion of marriage (for the general rules on jurisdiction, see §113). These are rather flexible in that they do not seek to raise unnecessary legal impediments to "international marriages" where there are no important interests to be invoked against them.

(a) A Hungarian national may contract a marriage abroad with a Hungarian or non-Hungarian national (foreigner or stateless person) before a competent authority. Conclusion of a marriage abroad by a Hungarian national (or a stateless person residing in Hungary) is subject to a certificate issued by the head of the metropolitan or county administrative organ with the relevant territorial jurisdiction, to the effect that under Hungarian law there is no impediment to the marriage: if the Hungarian national concerned is of foreign domicile, such a certificate is issued by the Hungarian Diplomatic Authority [paras. (3) and (4) of Art. 38].

If both intending spouses are Hungarian nationals, they may also celebrate a marriage abroad before a Hungarian *foreign representation*, provided that the Government has authorized such foreign representation; such marriages are considered to have been celebrated in Hungary (Art. 37). A marriage contracted abroad by a Hungarian national or a stateless person residing in Hungary must be registered by the metropolitan recorder of the Budapest municipality [Sect. 3 (2) of Government Decree No. 21/1992. (I.28.)].

(b) A *non-national* may celebrate *in Hungary* a valid marriage with a Hungarian or non-Hungarian national, subject to a certificate showing that under his/her *personal law* there is no impediment to the marriage (he/she is of marriageable age as required by the family law of his/her country, has no previously concluded valid marriage, etc.). The requirement for such a certificate may, in justified cases, be waived by the head of the metropolitan or county administrative organ with the territorial jurisdiction [para. (1) of Art. 38]. Being present together, the intending spouses may apply for a waiver to the registrar competent to solemnize marriages, the waiver to be valid for six months from the date of issue [Art. 20, paras. (1) and (2) of Law-Decree No. 17 of 1982].

Conclusion of a marriage by a non-Hungarian national in Hungary is nevertheless barred if there is an *unavoidable impediment thereto under Hungarian family law* [para. (2) of Art. 38]. Thus, for instance, the existing marriage of the intending spouse(s) prevents the celebration in Hungary of a marriage by non-Hungarian nationals even if multiple marriage happens to be permitted by the personal law (e.g. the Islamic law) of the party or parties. This holds for ties of kinship as stated by the Family Law which constitute an impediment to marriage (prohibition of marriage between relatives in the direct line of descent and between brothers and sisters). The Code considers these cases to come, as it were, under the *public policy clause*, imparting an *imperative* character to the pertinent provisions of the Family Law.

2. The Code [para. (2) of Art. 37] declares the *extrinsic incidents of the validity* of marriage to be governed by the law applicable at the time and place of the ceremony (*lex loci celebrationis*), a connecting factor which has been generally accepted in international practice for decades. If Hungarian nationals celebrate a marriage before a Hungarian representation abroad, their marriage must be deemed, also in respect of the formal prerequisites of its validity, to have been concluded in Hungary and must accordingly be tested against the formal requirements of validity under Hungarian family law.

It should be noted on this score that, like Hungarian family law, the rules of family law in most countries require the intending spouses to declare *in person* that they want to marry each other. Such is the case (apart from certain exceptional possibilities in times of war) in German law, French law (Art. 75 of the *Code Civil*), Austrian law [Art. 17 (1) of the *Ehegesetz*: Art. 16 (1) of the *IPR-Gesetz*], etc. On the other hand, the institution of "marriage by proxy" (proxy marriage, *Handschuhehe*) is known to and recognized by the family laws of quite a few States, such as the Spanish *Código civil* of 1981 (Art. 55), the Portuguese *Código civil* of 1978 (Arts. 1620–21), some Latin American family laws [the Brazilian *Código civil* of 1919 (Art. 194), the Mexican *Código civil* of 1952 (Art. 102), etc.], and the family laws in several constituent states of the USA.

3. The *intrinsic validity* of marriage is subject to the personal law of the intending spouses at the time of concluding the marriage. The case is simple if at that time the personal laws of the intending spouses are *identical* (i.e. are not based on the strength of nationality acquired by one of the parties perhaps upon marriage!) and is therefore governed by their *common personal law* [para. (1) of Art. 37].

If the personal laws of the intending spouses are different at the time of celebrating the marriage, there are in principle two options: *disjunctive* (separate) or *conjunctive* (cumulative) consideration of the matter. In the first case, intrinsic validity is to be judged separately with respect to each of the intending spouses under the personal law of each. It may be conceived that, owing to the diverse requirements of the different family laws for intrinsic validity, the marriage is held valid with respect to one spouse but invalid with respect to the other (this is usually called "limping marriage"). Marriage between cousins, for instance, is not barred by Hungarian law, but would be barred by the law of several constituent states in the United States. Accordingly, in the case of disjunctive consideration, a marriage between Hungarian and US cousins would be "limping" from the point of view of validity: it would be valid for the party subject to Hungarian law and invalid for the party subject to the law of the particular constituent state in the United States. As has been noted earlier (item 1 of §97), our agreements on legal assistance take a stand for disjunctive consideration, which was also favoured by the previous Hungarian law [Art. 16, para. (1) of the Law-Decree enacting the Family Law]. By contrast, the Code adopted the principle of *conjunctive* consideration (practically returning to the position of the Family Law previous to 1 January 1953): if the personal laws of the intending spouses differ at the time of the ceremony, the marriage can be held valid in respect of *both parties* only if the intrinsic incidents of validity are present under the personal laws of *both parties* [para. (1) of Art. 37]. This approach is aimed at preventing "limping marriages", or situations in which a marriage would be valid for one spouse and invalid for the other.

4. In the application of the provisions of the Code governing the validity of marriage there may be argument as to whether, in a particular case, resort should be had to the rules for formal validity or to those for essential validity. Thus, for instance, the question arises whether the competent authority (registrar, etc.) solemnizing the marriage at a place other than the official premises has transgressed the formal or essential requirements of validity. Since both cases are governed by different connecting factors, as was illustrated in the preceding paragraphs (items 2 and 3), the applicable law may also differ.

The question is this: to which system of law must the judge turn to determine whether the given circumstance regarding the validity of marriage is to be considered as a ground for extrinsic or intrinsic validity or invalidity. The problem should therefore be looked upon as presenting a case for classification (see Chapter V) and should consequently be subjected to the rule of the Code on classification (Art. 3) and be decided by the proceeding judge (other authority) under Hungarian law.

This same problem may recur in disputing the *existence* or *non-existence of a marriage*, since the Code subjects it to the application, *mutatis mutandis*, of the rules governing the validity of marriage [para. (4) of Art. 37]. Again, the question of whether it is more appropriate for the judge – when, for instance, one of the intending spouses makes a legal declaration but not in person – to resort to an analogous application of the rules on formal or essential validity (cf. the problem discussed under item 2) is one of classification and hence subject to the *lex fori* under Art. 3 of the Code.

§99. PERSONAL AND PROPERTY RELATIONS AS BETWEEN SPOUSES

1. Like the agreements of Hungary on legal assistance, the Code regards marital relations, *personal* as well as *proprietary*, *as a whole* and subjects both their aspects to the same law. This approach appears to be correct if to avoid classification problems and borderline cases. In some laws it is disputed, for instance, whether *alimony* is a personal or a property right. Should the Code use (as some foreign laws do) different connecting factors for determining the two kinds of relationship, there might arise difficult classification problems concerning alimony (see Chapter V).

It is specifically stated in the Code (Art. 39) that the law governing the relations of spouses *inter se* is also applicable to alimony and *matrimonial property settlements*. As can be seen, the Code removes alimony from the range of relatives' maintenance and, in view of a stronger connection, considers it as part of marital relations. Matrimonial property settlements are given the same systematic treatment although in the private international law of several countries, it is governed by a (contractual) connecting factor different from the general rules of matrimonial property law.

In addition, several foreign laws of more recent date [e.g. the Austrian Code (Art. 19), the German Code (para. 2 of Art. 15), the Swiss Code (Arts. 52–53)] allow the spouses to subject their proprietary relations to a law of their choice (perhaps to one selected from a specified range of laws). Thus these foreign private international laws recognize the *autonomy* of spouses (cf. §82), confined at least to specified legal systems, concerning their proprietary relations *inter se*. The Hungarian Code disallows such autonomy and uses *objective connecting factors*.

2. The law applicable to the personal and property relations of spouses, as outlined above, is determined by the connecting factors of the Code in a *step-by-step* approach (Art. 39). The point of departure is the *personal law*, which is often used in international family law [and is likewise determined by the Code (Art. 11) on a step-by-step basis]:

– in the first place, the applicable law is the *common personal law* of the spouses at the time of the adjudication of the case;

– if the spouses have different personal laws at the time of adjudication, the applicable law is their *last common personal law;*

– if the spouses never had a common personal law (e.g. were not nationals of the same State), the applicable law is that of the State in whose territory they had their *last common domicile*;

– lastly, if the spouses had neither a common personal law nor a common domicile, resort is had to the *lex fori* as the usual *ultima ratio* among the connecting factors used by private international law: the applicable law is that of the State of the proceeding court (other authority), namely *Hungarian law*.

3. In determining the applicable law, i.e. the *personal and property statutes*, it is important to establish the relevant point of time. In the case of the law ap-

plicable to the relations of spouses *inter se,* the private international law of some countries uses various means to establish the relevant point of time: the moment of relevance to the applicable law is deemed to be the time of the ceremony or of the adjudication of the case (whereas contracts controlled by property law are often subject to the law prevailing at the time of contracting). Each solution may have advantages and disadvantages.

If the connecting factor determines the applicable law by making it dependent on a point of time at which a fact of law occurred and *cannot be repeated* (e.g. conclusion of a marriage or of a contract involving matrimonial property), the given legal relationship (a marriage, a contract involving matrimonial property) is, together with any legal dispute arising therefrom, *invariably* placed under the control of a single legal system. For example, the common personal law of the spouses at the time of contracting the marriage will also apply to marital disputes, personal as well as proprietary, which occur subsequent to a change in the personal law of the spouses. This approach gives preference to *legal certainty* and predictability over flexibility.

If, on the other hand, the point of time relevant to the determination of the applicable law is linked by the law to a fact *variable* and perhaps *recurrent* (e.g. a legal dispute), any eventual disputes, which might be several, may in principle be subject to different legal systems. For example, there arise disputes between the spouses concerning, first, the choice of common domicile and years later, matters of property; if the common personal law of the spouses has changed during the period between the two actions, each action will be subject to a different law (even in the event that the second action turns on the choice of common domicile, which was the subject-matter of the first). This approach is *more flexible*, leaving room for disputes to be judged generally by the legal system most closely connected with the facts giving rise to them, and thereby allowing considerations for the predictability of the applicable law to slip into the background.

The Hungarian Code has adopted this latter approach, rendering the common personal law as the *primarily* applicable law dependent upon the *time of adjudication* [para. (1) of Art. 38]. This solution is, however, counteracted by a *subsidiary rule* intended to ensure that change in the applicable law does not affect the rights validly acquired under the earlier law: change in the personal law of the spouses does not affect the use of the husband's name authorized under the earlier law, nor the validly produced property law effects, including those of alimony and matrimonial property settlements [para. (4) of Art. 39].

§100. DISSOLUTION OF MARRIAGE

1. As has been repeatedly stated (primarily in §21), a question precedent to the solution of conflict situations always concerns the jurisdiction of the proceeding court (or other authority). This is of particular importance in proceedings for the ascertainment of personal status, including a divorce suit. While the

rules on jurisdiction will be discussed in detail at a later stage (in Chapter XXXV), particular attention is paid here, in view of their close interrelationship, to two special rules of the Code concerning *jurisdiction* in divorce cases.

(a) *Hungarian* courts have *exclusive* jurisdiction in divorce proceedings of Hungarian nationals (*even if only one of the spouses* is a Hungarian national!) unless the Hungarian national is domiciled abroad, in which case the decision of a foreign court (or other authority) is to be recognized [para. (a) of Art. 55]; exceptions are decisions offending Hungarian public policy and some other specified cases (Art. 73).

Under the Code, the decision of a foreign court in the divorce proceedings of a Hungarian national is to be recognized in Hungary only if he/she is (also) *domicile abroad* [para. (a) of Art. 71], (cf. BH No.12 of 1982, 516). In cases where only the non-Hungarian spouse is domiciled abroad, the divorce proceedings, even though conducted abroad, must also take place before the competent Hungarian court. That happened, among others, in Case BKKB. 11.P.I.34.330/1982, in which the spouse (of Hungarian nationality and domiciled in Hungary) of a Finnish respondent, who in the meantime had become a resident of Finland, had to sue for divorce despite the fact that the Finnish court had granted a valid order of divorce. We wonder whether it would not be more appropriate to allow, *de lege ferenda*, recognition of foreign orders of divorce in such cases as well. It would be all the more justified to do so since the rules of the Code safeguarding the interests of Hungarian nationals (Art. 73) preclude the possibility of abuse.

A special problem for the practice of registrars and courts was raised by cases in which a foreign court made a decision in the divorce suit of two Hungarian nationals, one of whom was domiciled abroad and the other in Hungary. The Hungarian courts refused to recognize a few similar decisions because, we believe, they interpreted the provision of Code Art. 71 (a) too rigidly (grammatically, in the literal sense). This practice is objectionable if only for the reason that it leads to "limping marriages" without sufficient cause: the decision will be valid (abroad) for the Hungarian national residing abroad but invalid for the other spouse residing in Hungary. Such a situation brings the spouse residing in Hungary unilaterally into a difficult position because until an obviously formal divorce case is decided, he/she cannot contract a new valid marriage, will receive no social benefits for the child, there may arise a paternity dispute concerning a new-born child, etc. Therefore, in its statement of position (PK. 443), the Supreme Court is correct in pointing out that the decision must be recognized of a foreign court made in the divorce proceedings of a Hungarian national domiciled abroad, regardless of whether the other spouse is domiciled in Hungary or abroad. In such cases too, the necessary guarantees are provided by Art. 73 of the Code.

Decisions of foreign courts on matrimonial bonds are in practice registered by the competent registrar after the Ministry of Justice has taken a stand on the recognition of such decisions. Should a problem concerning the recognition of a decision of a foreign court emerge in legal proceedings, the Hungarian court will suspend the proceedings and will continue it after the registration procedure for recognition has been completed.

Mention is deserved of the fact that the rule of the Code on the exclusive jurisdiction of Hungarian courts [para. (a) of Art. 55] may also be applied in a complementary way in cases which in other aspects are covered by a bilateral agreement on legal assistance. (The court correctly followed this way of deciding a Hungarian–Soviet divorce suit in Case PKKB. 16.P. 100.064/1982.)

(b) In divorce cases of non-Hungarian nationals (where *both* spouses are foreign nationals or stateless persons!), Hungarian courts may take jurisdiction only if at least one of the parties to the proceedings is domiciled in Hungary [para. (1) of Art. 58]. The court based itself on this rule in establishing its own jurisdiction in, e.g., divorce proceedings of German spouses, one of whom was domiciled in Hungary (PKKB. 16.P. 105.936/1981). (For a disputable wider interpretation, see §113.)

Like the Code, some of Hungary's agreements on legal assistance allow Hungarian courts to take jurisdiction in divorce proceedings of two foreign spouses. For instance, under Art. 33 (1) of the Hungarian–Polish Agreement on Legal Assistance (promulgated in Hungary by Law-Decree No. 5 of 1960, modified by Law-Decree No. 24 of 1981), Hungarian courts have jurisdiction in divorce proceedings of Polish nationals if the spouses reside in Hungary. (The court was correct in applying this rule in Case PKKB. 16.P. 100.032/1981.) The establishment of jurisdiction was based on this same rule in the divorce suit of two Zambian university students in Hungary (PKKB. 16.P. 104.478/1981): the ground for establishing jurisdiction in this case was provided by the fact that one of the spouses was staying in Hungary with the intent to settle and therefore the court found the requirements of the Code to have been met for the ascertainment of "domicile" (Art. 12).

2. In determining the *law applicable* to dissolution of marriage, the Code in fact employs the same step-by-step approach as in the use of the connecting factors governing the personal and property relations of spouses (Art. 40).

(a) Accordingly, the conditions for the dissolution of marriage are subject primarily to the *common personal law of the spouses* at the time of filing the action with the court. That law is rather often Hungarian law in divorce proceedings before Hungarian courts. For example, in cases where one of the spouses is domiciled abroad but retains his/her Hungarian nationality (perhaps along with a foreign nationality), the Hungarian judge correctly applies the Hungarian family law by virtue of the Code provision in Art. 40 (1). Of course, the common personal law of the spouses may also be a foreign law, which was the family law of FRG in, e.g., Case PKKB. 16.P. 105.936/1981.

(b) If, at the time of filing the action with the court, the spouses have different personal laws, the governing law is their *last common personal law* [para. (2) of Art. 40)]. In some of the cases occurring *in judicial practice,* that law may also be the Hungarian family law, naturally when both spouses were originally Hungarian nationals.

(c) Failing a common personal law, the applicable law is that of the State in whose territory the spouses had their *last common domicile* [para. (2) of Art. 40].

Under some of our agreements on legal assistance, e.g. that with the Soviet Union (promulgated by Law-Decree No. 38 of 1958, modified by Law-Decree No. 18 of 1972), in cases where both spouses are foreign nationals and, under Art. 33 (3) of the Agreement with Poland (promulgated by Law-Decree No. 5 of 1960, modified by Law-Decree No. 24 of 1981), in divorce proceedings of spouses of different nationality the applicable law is that of the State in whose territory "the spouses have their *common domicile* or had it for the last time". (The court was correct in applying the Agreement with Poland in Cases PKKB. 16.P. 103.463/1982.)

(d) If the spouses had no common domicile, resort is had to the *lex fori*, notably Hungarian law [para. (3) of Art. 40].

(e) This sequence of connecting factors is subject to one *exception*: if one of the spouses is a *Hungarian national*, the applicable law is – failing a common personal law – not the law of the last common domicile but the Hungarian law as the next succeeding step. Thus, in divorce proceedings of a Hungarian spouse, the *lex fori* comes into play a step earlier, as if both spouses were non-Hungarian nationals.

By taking this approach the legislator adjusted the provisions of the Code to the rules of agreements on legal assistance. In *judicial practice* the divorce rules of Hungarian family law are applied on such a "subsidiary" basis with relative frequency, because in most divorce cases before Hungarian courts one of the spouses is a Hungarian national (only that, unfortunately, judgments fail to refer to the Code, virtually deeming it natural to apply the Hungarian family law). Often the family law would otherwise be applicable if thc Code did not ordain the *lex fori* to precede the law of the State of the last common domicile. Thus, for instance, the spouse of foreign nationality [as in the case of a Soviet petitioner before the District Court of Szekszárd (9.P.21.453/1980) or of a Yugoslav petitioner before the same court (9.P.20.184/1981)], shortly after contracting the marriage, leaves for home to arrange for her settlement in Hungary, but the settlement does not take place, Hungarian law would be applied (if the spouses had no common personal law) for lack of common domicile. The same situation occurs in cases (PKKB. 15.P. 100.163/1980 or PKKB. 16.P. 104.726/1979, actions against German respondents) where the Hungarian spouse does not follow her spouse abroad and therefore the parties have no common domicile.

3. The *family law* (and, with it, the divorce law) of some States usually exhibit more and greater conceptual differences than do, for example, the rules of contract law. In this field one can perceive essential differences even between legal systems that have a similar economic basis and level of development and

are linked by closely allied cultural, religious and other traditions, and still more between divorce laws embedded in diverse economic, social, cultural and other environments.

Several (though increasingly fewer) systems of law still repudiate the dissolubility of marriage and often show widely varying degrees of stringency in the conditions for divorce, while other national family laws have established a set of absolute grounds for divorce or built their divorce laws on the principle of culpability, to mention but a few conceptual approaches adopted by family law in nearby European countries. The doctrinal difference may be so great as to induce the law of the forum to regard differing foreign norms as running counter to its public policy and therefore to disallow their application.

The Code (Art. 41) considers

– the dissolubility of matrimonial bonds,

– the exclusion of absolute grounds for divorce, and

– the inadmissibility of divorce based on culpability (fault), to be principles of *public policy* and therefore covers them by *special public policy rules* (cf. item 2 in §42).

Accordingly, in a judgment of a Hungarian court,

– a marriage may be dissolved even if dissolution is excluded by the applicable foreign law and if the conditions for divorce do not exist under the applicable foreign law but are present under the Hungarian law;

– even if absolute grounds for divorce are established by the foreign law, it should be examined whether marital life is completely and irretrievably ruined;

– a decree of divorce must not be granted on the ground of fault.

We think that these provisions of the Code leave too much room for the invocation of public policy. They go especially far by allowing a divorce decree even in cases where the grounds therefore do not exist under the applicable law but are present under the Hungarian law (Art. 18 of the Family Law). [It is worth noting here that the German PIL Code (Art. 17 Abs.1. S. 2 *EGBGB*) is much more restrained, yet it is rightly criticized in legal literature (Jayme, *IPRax* 1987, p. 167), albeit under the conditions defined by German family law the matrimonial bonds may only be dissolved in cases where one of the spouses had German nationality, if dissolution *in concreto* were not allowed by the otherwise applicable law.] This rule leads to the practical result that the principles of Hungarian family law should also apply in a divorce action of a foreign spouse (and even of two foreign spouses on the basis of jurisdiction allowed by Art. 58 of the Code), although such "bias" fails to promote implementation of the ideas embodied in private international law.

In other respects, the operation of the said special principles having the nature of public policy (Art. 41) does not necessarily lead to complete disregard of the applicable law except to the non-application of the rules affected by them and to their replacement by the appropriate rules of Hungarian family law. In such cases, therefore, instances may occur of a *combined application* of two laws, the applicable law and the *Hungarian law* complementing each other.

Cases will nevertheless be dominated by Hungarian law, because the important principles governing the prerequisites of divorce are to be determined by Hungarian law (owing to the strongly exaggerated assertion of the approach taken by Hungarian family law), with the otherwise applicable law controlling no more than partial aspects or important attendant legal relationships (custody of the child, right to see and meet the child, property disputes, etc.).

We are of the view that, among the aforementioned special public policy rules of the Code, there is ground to uphold only the rule allowing in principle the dissolubility of marriage, which (incidentally) could be deduced from the general public policy clause itself (Art. 7). Consequently we maintain that it should in no way be possible for foreign judgments, at least in divorce proceedings of Hungarian nationals residing abroad, to be denied recognition [para. (1) of Art. 71] on grounds of conflict with public policy [para. (a) of Art. 73] – if dissolution of marriage is based on an absolute ground for divorce or on the ground of culpability, nor in the absence of any ground for divorce under the foreign law applied, amounting to a reason why the foreign judge refused to grant an order of divorce, even though the prerequisites of divorce could have been stated to exist under Hungarian family law [for Hungarian practice concerning recognition of foreign orders of divorce (see Gehér, in the List of Sources)].

CHAPTER XXXII

RULES ON KINSHIP

§101. FAMILY STATUS

1. The problems likely to arise in connection with the family status of the child are subjected by the Code (as by the agreements on legal assistance) to the *personal law* of the child (Art. 42). This offers the absolute benefit of allowing all questions related to family status to be considered according to the family law rules of one and the same State.

In formulating the conflict rules, it is never possible to foresee the essential substantive-law consequences nor, therefore, whether the child would actually benefit, on the substance, more from his own personal law or perhaps from another system of law. At any rate, there may be an advantage in placing the family status as well as the familial relations with the parents (cf. §103) under the control of a single law.

The major problems of relevance here include establishment of paternity, contestation of the presumption of paternity, acknowledgement of paternity, and establishment of maternity.

2. *Establishment of paternity* or *maternity* as well as *contestation of the presumption* of paternity are governed by the child's personal law at the time of birth.

Acknowledgement of paternity is likewise subject to the child's personal law, naturally at the time of acknowledgement.

Further, most family laws allow acknowledgement of a child conceived but not yet born (foetus). Considering that the foetus has no personal law, which is acquired by birth, the Code places acknowledgement of the paternity of an unborn child under the control of the mother's personal law prevailing at the time of acknowledgement.

The *form of a declaration* of acknowledgement is likewise subjected to the said laws (the personal law of the child or the mother's personal law in the case of foetus). A declaration of acknowledgement, however, cannot be regarded as invalid on formal grounds if (though not meeting the requirements of the personal law of the child or the mother's personal law in the case of foetus) it was made in a valid form either under Hungarian law (*lex fori*) or under the law applicable at the time and place of acknowledgement (*lex loci actus*). This favourable rule of the Code follows the principle of *favor negotii*.

3. In the existing practice of applying the Code, most of the problems connected with lawsuits for settling the family status of the child and encountered in proceedings for establishing the personal status of Hungarian nationals have been posed by the provision [para. (a) of Art. 55] ordaining the *exclusive jurisdiction* of Hungarian courts. This rule has caused proceedings to be instituted before Hungarian courts by a great number of persons having Hungarian nationality, who have not been living in Hungary for decades or perhaps have never lived here. Rather often the very facts of law relevant to family status (conception, birth, acknowledgement of paternity) and arising in similar lawsuits have occurred abroad. Moreover, the litigants, too, live abroad, are usually not in a position to appear in person in the proceedings, and consequently the taking of evidence during the proceedings, often by the interposition of an *ad hoc* guardian, encounters great difficulties. The suits brought by the *ad hoc* guardians of minors of Hungarian nationality residing in Italy, the FRG and France to contest the presumption of paternity were conducted before the Central District Court of Pest (Cases 112.429/1983, 111.361/1983 and 110.321/1983, in which the domiciles of the mothers and the putative fathers were abroad or perhaps unknown). It appears justified to us to ordain, *de lege ferenda*, the exclusive jurisdiction of Hungarian courts in such cases.

§102. ADOPTION

1. Adoption is made by the Code *conditional* on the concurrent presence of the requirements determined by the legal systems involved (as is the case with the intrinsic validity of marriage; item 3 in §98). This means that the requirements must be considered *in conjunction with* the personal laws of the adopter and the prospective adoptee prevailing at the time of adoption. Accordingly, adoption is normally subject to the requirements of two laws, and if the adopters are husband and wife and their personal laws differ, consideration must be given to the requirements of three legal systems [para. (1) of Art. 43].

If in the legal relationship a *Hungarian national* is involved either as adopter or adoptee, the Code [para. (4) of Art. 43] requires compliance by both sides with the prerequisites designated by Hungarian law (Arts. 47–49 of the Family Law) concerning, among others, the infancy of the adoptee even if he/she is not a Hungarian national (but only the adopter is). This means in practice that the prerequisites determined by the Family Law for adoption involving Hungarian nationals are regarded by the Code as bearing the character of public policy. Compliance with the conditions prescribed by Hungarian family law is supervised by the guardianship authority, whose permission (approval) is required for adoption involving a Hungarian national either as adopter or adoptee [paras. (2) and (3) of Art. 43].

2. The *effects* of adoption under family, inheritance and any other law as well as the *termination* of adoption and its legal consequences are subject to the personal law of the adopter at the time of adoption (or its termination) [para. (1) of Art. 44, cf. PKKB. 112.620/1982].

The legal situation is more complicated if the adopters are *husband and wife* [para. (2) of Art. 44], because in that case the legal effects of adoption or its termination are controlled by the *common personal law* of the adoptive parents. If their personal laws differ at the time of adoption or its termination, the legal effects of adoption and of its termination are (unlike the conjunctive consideration of the conditions for adoption under the different personal laws of the adoptive parents and the personal law of the prospective adoptee, as noted under item 1 above) governed by

– the *last common personal law* of the adoptive spouses or, failing such a law,

– the law of the State in whose territory the spouses had their *common domicile* at the time of adoption or of its termination or, failing such a domicile,

– the *Hungarian* law (*lex fori*).

In this tier of localizers, the Code applies the same order of sequence as in marriage law: (last) common personal law, or, failing it, the law of common domicile, or, lastly, in default of both, the *lex fori*.

§103. LEGAL RELATIONS AS BETWEEN PARENTS AND CHILDREN

1. The family-law relations of parents and children are, just as the family status of children, placed by the Code under the control of the personal law of the *child*, the relevant point of time being the date at which enforcement of a particular claim is sought (Art. 45).

The enumeration by the Code of the most typical and most important legal relationships between parents and children (the child's name, custody, care, legal representation, maintenance, administration of his/her property, etc.) is illustrative rather than exhaustive.

In *judicial practice* most of the pertinent cases are related to the establishment of a *child's maintenance* and, the child being a Hungarian national, are usually judged according to Hungarian family law [in actions against, e.g., an Austrian, an Egyptian and a Swiss defendant (PKKB. 111.494/1983, 105.563/1981 and 105.484/1981, respectively)]. Actions for the *custody of the child* are usually antecedents to claims for maintenance and therefore the two problems are typically considered in one and the same proceedings. Cases of custody nevertheless occur without obligation for the child's maintenance (e.g. PKKB. 111.160/1983, or 105.538/1982 against an Ethiopian defendant). (In proceedings for custody some problems may be presented by the application of the "law more favourable to the child" (Art. 46; BH No. 7 of 1989, cf. §104).

The said illustrative enumeration indicates the advisability of approaching the questions of legal relevance from the angle of the child. For this reason the pertinent questions are subjected to the *child's personal law.*

The substance of relationship is different in the case of parents' maintenance, the parent claiming maintenance being of greater legal relevance, and the Code removes parents' maintenance from the range of parent-child relationship and considers it to be a part of relatives' maintenance (Art. 47).

2. The law applicable to legal relationships between parents and children, including custody and maintenance of children, is also determined by most of Hungary's *agreements on legal assistance.* It is therefore natural for the rules of the Code to be preceded by the provisions of those agreements in matters affecting nationals of the signatory States (Cases PKKB. 105.808/1981, 104.744/1981 and BP. XVII. ker. P. 20.005/1981 against GDR, Soviet and GDR defendants, respectively).

3. Finally we should state again that there are two multilateral international conventions seeking to secure recovery of children's maintenance, notably –

(a) the *Hague Convention of 1958* concerning the Recognition and Enforcement of Decisions relating to Maintenance Obligations towards Children (promulgated by Law-Decree No. 7 of 1965 and Decree No. 8/1965 of the Minister of Justice on its execution), to which the following countries were party on 1 October 1988: Austria, Belgium, Czechoslovakia, Denmark, Finland, France, Germany (Federal Republic of), Hungary, Italy, Liechtenstein, Netherlands, Portugal, Spain, Surinam, Sweden, Switzerland, Turkey (it was also signed but has not yet been promulgated by Greece and Luxembourg), and

(b) the *New York Convention of 1956* on Recovery Abroad of Maintenance (promulgated by Law-Decree No. 53 of 1957 and Decree No. 9/1957 of the Minister of Justice on its enforcement as modified by Decree No. 7/1961 of the Minister of Justice), to which all the State parties to the Hague Convention except France and Liechtenstein are signatory, together with Algeria, Argentina, Barbados, Brazil, Burkina Faso, Central African Republic, Chile, Ecuador, Guatemala, Haiti, Holy See, Israel, Luxembourg, Monaco, Morocco, Niger, Pakistan, Poland, Sri Lanka, Tunisia, United Kingdom and Yugoslavia.

§104. APPLICATION OF THE LAW MORE FAVOURABLE TO THE CHILD

1. As was seen, the Code renders the personal law of the child applicable to legal relationships between parents and children. In order to protect the *interests of the child* the Code, following the example of foreign laws, found it necessary to include an additional provision which allows choice of a law more favourable to the child to govern certain matters.

This is warranted by the fact that, as has been repeatedly noted, the conflict norm (with its remission) is "blind", does not "foresee" the substantive-law effects of future solutions, and hence the application of the child's personal law does not necessarily offer the substantive-law solution most favourable to the child. It is possible, for instance, that another system of law will guarantee the child's maintenance with greater ease (under a simpler procedure) or secure a larger amount of maintenance.

The Code recognizes the possibility of *alternative connection*, leading to the application of a substantive law more favourable to the child, by endeavouring to ensure by all means the benefit of *Hungarian family law as a minimum* for children who are nationals or residents of Hungary.

This purpose cannot, even in the case of a child who is a national of Hungary, be secured merely by directing the application of the child's personal law, because at the time a claim is enforced the child may happen to be a Hungarian national, although he was not one at the time of birth (the point of time relevant to personal law concerning, e.g., the presumption of paternity). Not infrequently, the child domiciled in Hungary is a foreigner and therefore his personal law is other than Hungarian. In both cases (namely when the applicable personal law of a Hungarian child is not Hungarian law, or when a child domiciled in Hungary is non-Hungarian and hence his personal law is a foreign law), the application of the rules of Hungarian family law should be ordained by a separate provision.

This is why the Code (Art. 46) directs that Hungarian law must be applied, *whenever it is more favourable to the child*, to the family status of a child who is a *national* or *resident of Hungary*, to the family-law relations between him and his parents, and to maintenance obligations towards him (a similar provision has been added to the Law-Decree enacting the FamilyAct).

Even logically, the minimum requirement of determining a more favourable law is for the child's personal law (a foreign law) to be compared with Hungarian law. The existing judicial practice has not always been correct in applying this provision of the Code. Much more detectable is the "homeward trend" of the judge who, for instance, in a judgment passed in a case for changing the custody of a child having Yugoslav and French nationality and residing in Hungary, failed to compare the essential aspects of possible substantive-law solutions and applied the rules of Hungarian family law by invoking Art. 46 of the Code (Legf.Bír.P.törv. II.20. 642/1988, BH No. 7 of 1989, 274).

It may be stated in principle that under Art. 46 of the Code the rules of Hungarian family law may be applied, if the otherwise applicable law (e.g. the child's personal law) were to secure less protection for the child than the substantive rules of Hungarian family law do.

2. Again, the said provision motivates in part the rule of the Code (Art. 50) directing the application of *Hungarian law* whenever an *immediate measure* is deemed necessary concerning the custody, maintenance or care of a non-Hungarian national domiciled in Hungary. Nevertheless, the foremost reason

for applying the *lex fori* (i.e. the Hungarian law) to the solution of similar problems lies in allowing recourse to a prompt procedure. By a special provision [para. (2) of Art. 60] the Code confers jurisdiction on the Hungarian guardianship authority to deal with such cases.

3. Like Art. 46 of the Code, several bilateral agreements of Hungary on *legal assistance* prescribe application of the "law more favourable to the child". Of course, this benefit is mutually secured by the signatory States for each other's nationals. Thus, for instance, under Art. 34 of the Hungarian–Polish Agreement (promulgated in Hungary by Law-Decree No. 5 of 1960, modified by Law-Decree No. 24 of 1981) the court found Polish law to be more favourable to the child in a case contesting the presumption of paternity (PKKB. 111.338/1982). In like manner, in an action for the custody of the child (P. 20.405/1982), the District Court of Miskolc applied the GDR law under Art. 31 of the Hungarian–GDR Agreement on Legal Assistance (promulgated in Hungary by Law-Decree No. 20 of 1958, modified by Law-Decree No. 26 of 1977), which ordained the applicable law to be that more favourable to the child.

§105. MAINTENANCE OF RELATIVES

The Code places maintenance of relatives under the control of the *personal law of the individual entitled to maintenance* (Art. 47). This approach is motivated essentially by the same considerations guiding the application of the child's personal law to the child's family status and to questions affecting legal relationships between parents and children. The privileged "protagonist" is the child in the former case and the person entitled to maintenance in the latter.

As was seen, the maintenance of consorts and that of children (as part of the relations of spouses *inter se* and of the relationship between parents and children) are governed by different provisions of the Code. Therefore the connecting factor controlling relatives' maintenance refers practically to parents' maintenance as well as to *possible* maintenance of *more distant ascendant and collateral relatives.*

The *point of time* relevant to the personal law of the individual entitled to maintenance is when he attempts to enforce a claim for maintenance. Thus *the conditions for entitlement to and the extent and mode of maintenance* (in kind or in money) as well as the order of *other* potential *persons* entitled and the relationships between them are determined by the personal law, prevailing at that point of time, of the individual entitled to maintenance.

CHAPTER XXXIII

GUARDIANSHIP AND CURATORSHIP

§106. GUARDIANSHIP

1. The institution of guardianship in Hungarian law is designed to fill the role, where necessary, of taking care of the legal representation of minors. This is not so clear in foreign legal systems, many of which draw a dividing line, different from that in Hungarian law, between guardianship and curatorship (devising guardianship for minors under family law and curatorship for adults under civil law). At any rate, persons under guardianship or curatorship are in need of special administrative support under every legal system, so the need may also arise for foreigners staying in Hungary to be placed under guardianship or curatorship.

2. The *conflict* rules of the Code (Art. 48) for guardianship are the following:

(a) the appointment of a guardian and the conditions for the termination of guardianship are subject to the *personal law of the ward*;

(b) the guardian's obligation to accept guardianship is subject to *his own personal law*;

(c) the substance of the legal relationship between guardian and ward (rights and obligations, including the guardian's duty to administer property and to give account thereof) is subject to the law of the State whose authority appointed the guardian (*lex fori*), namely *Hungarian law*.

§107. CURATORSHIP

1. The great affinity between the functions of guardianship and curatorship and the different lines of demarcation drawn by the various systems of law between the two institutions both permit and warrant a similar regulation thereof in private international law.

Therefore the Code, too, directs the application, *mutatis mutandis*, of the rules on guardianship to curatorship *affecting disposing capacity* (Art. 49). This means the following:

(a) placement under, and termination of, curatorship affecting disposing capacity are governed by the *personal law of the individual under curatorship*;

(b) the curator's obligation to accept curatorship is governed by *his own personal law*;

(c) the substance of the legal relationship between curator and ward is governed by the *lex fori*, notably the Hungarian law.

2. Curatorship *not affecting disposing capacity* is of a different character and therefore calls for different treatment. There are two forms of such curatorship known to Hungarian civil law: representation of a person prevented from managing his own affairs and *ad hoc* curatorship (Arts. 224–225 of the Civil Code). Both cases involve appointment of a temporary curator, usually for a short period, with a function not affecting disposing capacity but relating to administration of property. Accordingly the Code renders the *lex fori*, namely the rules of Hungarian civil law, applicable to cases of curatorship not affecting disposing capacity [para. (2) of Art. 49].

3. The Code (Arts. 59–60) recognizes the *jurisdiction* of a Hungarian court or guardianship authority over placement under curatorship, termination of curatorship, appointment of a curator and his release from office, and appointment of an *ad hoc* curator also in respect of a non-Hungarian national domiciled in Hungary (cf. §113).

TITLE 10

INTERNATIONAL LABOUR LAW

CHAPTER XXXIV

INTERNATIONAL LABOUR LAW

§108. SOME GENERAL ASPECTS OF INTERNATIONAL LABOUR LAW

1. The large-scale international mobility of labour in our time is a *significant new phenomenon in both practice and theory*. It is known that the advanced countries of Western Europe employ millions of migrant workers. Moreover, free movement of labour is a general principle of economic policy in the European Communities, as is stated in a separate Chapter of the Treaty of Rome (Title III, Chap. I, Arts. 48 *et seq.*). This is, of course, merely an attendant phenomenon of the international mobility of capital and of the internationalization of economic processes, including the appearance of a large volume of labour relations which possess international elements and therefore call for, and become the subject of, some sort of special regulation.

However, Hungary is also witness to a significant new phenomenon: questions of employment in various international organizations and multinational economic organizations; workers in other countries under agreements with EU countries (e.g. the FRG in 1989 and under the Hungarian–EU Association Agreement of 1991) concerning employment abroad; and the transactions of specialists and Hungarian undertakings abroad necessitating the movement of the labour force, all combine to cause international labour law to acquire relevance for Hungary as well. There is also a voluminous literature on the subject, dealing, as does legislation, with conflict problems and substantive-law regulation alike. A few decades ago these problems occupied a modest chapter of classical private international law. Seeing international labour law against this background, we will hereafter *take a complex approach to it as a whole*, and will discuss conflict as well as substantive rules.

2. Taking a complex approach is further warranted because the *concept of labour law in the law of conflicts* was *previously* subject to a variety of interpretations, to say the least.

Under the classical concept, the general contractual elements of labour law (conclusion, form, content, validity, termination of labour contract, etc.), which were subject largely to the autonomy of the parties (who had the right to designate the law applicable to their legal relationship), were treated as part of civil law, notably the law of obligations. By contrast, with the growth of social legislation and of the economic function of the modern State, there emerged an increasing number of norms which, being in the nature of public law, were intended to give expression to labour safety and to labour protection (labour safety, social insurance, labour disputes, professional training and conditions of work). Since these questions could not be allowed to depend on party autonomy, the law of the State of employment subjected them to its norms of mandatory application. Where there was no stipulation of law these aspects generally came under the control of the *lex loci laboris*, viz. the law of the State of employment.

Legal literature was also not exempt from uncertainties in the conflict area. For a long time it was the firmly held view, almost prevalent, that the applicable law should always be that of the place of employment (*lex loci laboris*), and the possibility for stipulation of law was hardly ever raised. There was hesitation in confronting the said interests of substantive law. This was due, among others, to the insignificant mobility of the labour force. On the other hand, the view was widely held and is still accepted that the *lex bandi* should apply to means of international transport, and that labour relations involving employment abroad should be subject to different rules. These aspects will be discussed below in connection with the current regulation.

3. Today the sources of international labour law present a more differentiated and clearer picture of labour relations with foreign elements. (a) In the first place, there have appeared general codes of private international law, including the Hungarian Code, which devote large sections to labour law. (b) Internal legislation lays down substantive rules to govern the major aspects of employment abroad. As will be seen, the Hungarian regulation has lost its previous restrictive character. (c) In addition, there is a considerable body of international legislation which forms part of international labour law and, of course, has a bearing on Hungary as well. Next we will discuss the major aspects of international labour law on the basis of these regulations. (d) Regulation concerning the employment of foreigners in Hungary has entered into this differentiated picture, but it has been treated above in connection with the domestic status of foreigners (Art. 47).

§109. REGULATION IN PRIVATE INTERNATIONAL LAW

1. Regulation in private international law (through conflicts norms) controls any employment relation or any of its elements in respect of which the appropriate conflict rule is not overridden by a peremptory norm of internal substantive law, or an international treaty which takes precedence in accordance with Art. 2 of the Code and operates as *ius speciale* against the *ius generale* (conflict rule). The *general rules* are consequently laid down in the *law of conflicts*, in our instance in the Code of Private International Law. Thus the fact that in-

ternational labour law is conceived by literature in its broader sense (too) does not imply that the conflict rules should not be regarded as part of the codes of private international law.

2. When viewed *in a comparative approach*, this aspect of international labour law calls for the following comments. Differentiation in the statutes of labour relations can be seen as a general tendency, meaning that some elements of labour relations are controlled by different laws. This is manifested chiefly in the areas mentioned below.

(a) While labour contracts are more and more subject to the law stipulated by the parties, there is an increasingly generalized exception that the applicable peremptory rules relating to and protecting the employee in a particular country are those of the place of employment. On a tacit assumption of the control of the restrictive rules here mentioned, stipulation of law is allowed by Art. 32 of the Polish Code and Art. 16 of the former Czechoslovak Code. The same is provided for in the Austrian Code (Art. 44) and the EC Convention on the international private law of contracts (Art. 6), except that the said assumption (precedence of peremptory norms protecting the employee in the State of employment) is formulated *expressis verbis* instead of being tacitly understood.

(b) A different rule, the application of the *lex bandi* (see, e.g., Art. 16 of the former Czechoslovak Code), is being extended to workers engaged in international transport.

(c) The *lex loci laboris* is not always used as the general rule even in the absence of a stipulated law. The Polish Code gives preference to the common domestic law, applying the law of the place of employment in the second place (Art. 33). Where work is to be performed in the territories of several countries the law of the employer's seat is made applicable, in another context, by the Austrian Code (Art. 44). The said EC Convention admits the alternative application of the employer's law or the law of another country if the link to it is so close as to justify its use as a connecting factor (Art. 6).

(d) The principle of the *lex loci laboris* is also superseded by rules according to which a given case is normally governed by the law of the foreign place of employment, while specific domestic aspects of the labour relation (suspension, social insurance and other benefits, etc.) remain controlled by the pertinent norms of domestic law.

3. The Hungarian regulation is contained in Chapter VIII of the Code (Arts. 51–53). The main aspects of regulation are as follows.

(a) The *principle of the law of the place where work is performed* is set out in Art. 51 (1): "Unless otherwise provided by law, employment relations shall be governed by the law of the State in whose territory the work is to be performed". This has two important consequences. (i) First, stipulation of law is disallowed by the Hungarian private international law in the field of labour law, including labour contracts. Given the general contractual nature and, in some aspects the permissive nature of labour law regulation, this could be advanced in favour of party autonomy, which is allowed in some countries. By contrast, as can be seen, the Hungarian regulation is unambiguous: exception to the *lex loci laboris* can only be made by law. (ii) The other aspect lies precisely in such exception. It is known that numerous labour relations are controlled by a double statute. For instance, a Hungarian national taking up employment abroad comes under the control of the labour law of the place where the work is performed, which is to say that in this respect he is subject to the general rule but, on the other hand, certain elements of his domestic labour relation continue to prevail, as will be seen presently.

(b) The *Code itself has devised numerous exceptions* to the *lex loci laboris* as the general rule, thus giving an appropriate expression of the distinctive feature of particular labour relations. Foreign enactments rely on similar rules to govern specific cases. (i) Labour relations of an international character established *by appointment* or *election* are subject to the personal law of the appointing authority or the electing body [para. (2) of Art. 51]. Such is the case, for instance, with some fields of employment in the United Nations or other international organizations, which have detailed staff regulations of their own and (several of them like the United Nations) even a separate administrative tribunal. (ii) If the employer is a foreign State, state organ or administrative agency, a diplomatic representative in Hungary or any other foreign national enjoying immunity from Hungarian jurisdiction, and if the contracting parties have the same personal law, labour relations are subject to that law [para. (3) of Art. 51; similar provisions are contained in Art. 1 (3) of the Labour Code (Act XXII of 1992)]. (iii) If under the terms of a labour contract work is to be performed *in the territories of several States*, labour relations are governed by the personal law of the employer [para. (1) of Art. 52]. (iv) "Employment relations shall be subject to Hungarian law, if an employee of a *Hungarian employer* is working abroad on assignment or in long-term foreign service" [para. (2) of Art. 52; Art. 1 (1) of the Labour Code]. Under the stress of real-life situations, however, this provision should be interpreted in a somewhat broader sense, because even if the Hungarian law generally applies to, e.g., the long-term foreign assignment of an employee of a Hungarian enterprise, the worker is also perforce controlled by the norms of a foreign labour law during his lasting employment abroad, with respect to certain elements of the work to be performed in a foreign country (except where he is assigned to a foreign organizational unit of a domestic enterprise): such as his remuneration and its charges levied abroad, his rights and duties implied in his employment, leave, non-working days, etc. Thus the duality mentioned in connection with the general rule in Art. 51 (1) prevails in this respect as well. (v) The labour relations of workers employed *on a vessel or aircraft of a carrier* are subject to the law of the State under whose flag or insignia the vehicle is sailing or flying, whereas the labour relations of employees of other carriers are governed by the personal law of the carrier [para. (3) of Art. 53; essentially the same provisions are contained in Art. 1 (2) of the Labour Code].

(c) The closing question concerning the conflict rules is this: *What falls within the scope of the law thus applicable to labour relations*? The answer may be given by stating the following. (i) All matters of employment, that is labour relations in their entirety, are controlled by the applicable law except when otherwise provided for in a peremptory rule or a norm of international origin. Accordingly the labour relations of persons taking up employment abroad are normally governed in their complexity (in respect not only of the labour contract, but also of sickness and accident insurance, for instance) by the law of the country concerned. This notwithstanding, numerous aspects of the labour-law status of the persons under consideration, fundamental questions such as suspension of employment relations, or crediting workers and employees with the time spent abroad for purposes of subsequent eligibility for domestic benefits (e.g. inclusion of such period in the computation of the total number of years spent in service), are controlled by other provisions to be discussed in the next section. (ii) Separate consideration should be given to workers' and employees' disposing capacity under labour law, for disposing capacity and contract in civil-law relations are governed by a different statute in the domain of private international law. This latter aspect, which is covered by Art. 53 of the Code, does not generally hold for labour law: "Workers' disposing capacity, the substantive and formal validity of a labour contract, the consequences of its invalidity, and the content and termination of employment relations shall likewise be subject to the law controlling employment relations".

§110. PEREMPTORY RULES OF SUBSTANTIVE LAW ON EMPLOYMENT ABROAD

1. The set of the relevant peremptory substantive rules was formerly embodied in extensive and differentiated partial regulations of an administrative nature. One of the first economic policy measures aimed at remodelling the economy was the *liberalization by regulations of employment abroad*. This aim was largely achieved by Decree No. 105/1989. (X.25.) of the Council of Ministers, which required no permission for taking up employment abroad. The other elements covered by the earlier set of related norms – general rules and those governing specific occupations and forms of employment abroad – have likewise undergone several stages of deregulation. To give an example, the provisions of Decree No. 157/1989. (XII.30.) of the Council of Ministers concerning certain emoluments of persons engaged in lasting employment abroad were consigned to the past by Government Decree No. 29/1992. (II.13.) repealing them.

2. *Restrictions by foreign exchange law* were similarly phased out in parallel with the lifting of limitations imposed by internal substantive law. No permit of the foreign exchange authority is required for making a labour contract with a foreigner, workers and employees are no longer obliged to offer their foreign

earnings to the State for purchase, and, furthermore, Art. 12 of Act XCV of 1995 provides that persons working abroad are not under obligation to remit to Hungary their income (remuneration or scholarship).

3. As regards the aspects of *social insurance coverage*, it may be stated in brief that the security associated with social insurance is preserved in case of taking up employment abroad in an institutional setting; the social insurance status of workers abroad is essentially governed, by reason of the employer being in Hungary, by the rules of Hungarian law, along with the *lex loci laboris*, in respect of obligations and of entitlement to services. On the other hand, individual workers abroad do not continue to be insured by the State in Hungary and are not therefore required to pay a contribution to the health and social insurance fund unless they make a related contract with the social insurance institute. As of 1 March 1992, such contractual social insurance coverage is a possibility open to individual workers abroad, who may consequently become independent of the Hungarian social insurance scheme.

4. Of course, the *system of authorization of employment in the host country* is controlled by the law of the place of employment. This aspect (especially contingents, if any) is generally also covered by bilateral agreements between Hungary and foreign States (see §111).

§111. INTERNATIONAL REGULATIONS OF RELEVANCE TO HUNGARY

1. Labour legislation takes *several international forms* today and has certain bearings on Hungary as well.

We have already referred to the *special staff rules of the United Nations and its specialized agencies*. They have implications for Hungary in that Hungarian nationals may also become subjects of labour relations with these organizations. It is on record that this category of labour relations is not without significance. Legal regulations adopted by the United Nations as an international organization bear upon member-states in this area as well; their application is taken for granted and accepted within the United Nations family. The same holds for the international economic organizations (WTO, IMF, IBRD, EBRD etc.), the special staff regulations of which naturally apply to Hungarian employees as well. This principle will prevail in respect to the relatively large number of Hungarian employees in the European Union as soon as Hungary becomes a member of the Union, and many Hungarians will also be employed in the large organization of the EU Commission.

2. It is pertinent to add that the *forms of international legislation* do not always cover all aspects of labour relations, but only those specific matters whose regulation is warranted by employment with a particular institution. Some matters (e.g. non-working days) are controlled by the local labour law (of the seat), while the domestic labour laws of employees continue to prevail in the

aspects referred to above. Therefore this type of labour relation is in practice governed by three sets of rules. It should be stressed that such diversity of regulation serves the interests of workers. For instance, the domestic regulation normally counts the length of employment abroad towards the total period of service for purposes of eligibility for benefits (leave, pension), but the pension rules of the particular international organization are also in control, and the two sets of rules may and actually do compete for consideration, with benefit to the employees.

3. A *special field* of international regulation is represented by *EU integration*. The free movement of labour among member-states is known to be an essential element thereof [Art. 48 of the Treaty of Rome; see Király: *Az EU belsőpiac szabályozása* (The Regulation of the EU' s Internal Market), pp. 60–67]. This question respecting the associate States is governed by the association agreements. There are two elements of the EU–Hungarian Association Agreement which need to be emphasized here. One provision refers to the movement of labour, stating that the opportunities extended to the employment of Hungarians should be preserved and be improved so far as possible and that the other member-states (with which no such bilateral agreements are concluded) will favourably consider the possibility of signing similar agreements (Art. 41). The other provision spells out that the senior employees ("key personnel") of the beneficiaries of settlement rights (of the domestic interests of the other country) are exempt from the otherwise prevailing restrictions on employment (Art. 52). From these provisions it becomes clear that, given the difficulties in the manpower situation within EU, this area is controlled by a strongly protectionist policy, which will certainly be relaxed by accession in substantive terms.

CHAPTER XXXV

JURISDICTION

§112. THE QUESTION OF JURISDICTION IN INTERNATIONAL LITIGATION

1. On the practical plane, the first question concerning legal disputes with international elements is always one of *who has the right to decide the case.* This question is asked by the party intending to assert his right, because he brings his action before the court indicated by the answer given. On the other hand, this is also the first question asked by the court: can it take jurisdiction over the case? Nor is the question of where to initiate action indifferent to the party, because the judge is bound by his own law of conflicts, whose differing provisions may result in a judgment different from that of the forum of another country. The choice of forum in such situations has led to the phenomenon of "forum shopping", which some legal systems find it hard to rule out all by themselves, for they cannot generally deny jurisdiction except under an express prohibitive rule, mainly by reliance on the institution of excluded jurisdiction to be noted below.

The problems of jurisdiction are diverse and multiple in both practice and jurisprudence. One of them is presented by the *concept of jurisdiction.* Jurisdiction in international legal relationships is only partly identical with its equivalent category in internal law, or with its counterpart in it, i.e. competence. True, competence is also meant to indicate which court has jurisdiction in a particular case, but here there is an essential element added to it, namely how the competence of its fora is viewed by the State in its relations with other States in the light of the fact that the given legal dispute affects the legal systems of several States. Some States apportion cases between courts not only within the State, partly by subject-matter (domestic jurisdiction), partly by territory (domestic competence), but also internationally, by adopting appropriate rules to govern the division of relevant matters between different fora of the States concerned. Such *international division of cases, on the basis of domestic law or of international legislation, between the authorities of States is called international jurisdiction*, which stems from state sovereignty, namely from the sovereign right of a State (expressed in domestic rules or in norms of international origin shared by the State) to adjudicate foreign element cases by reliance on a state procedure, administrative or judicial.

2. On the basis of legislation and legal practice, legal literature has worked out several categories and classifications of jurisdiction, the main elements of which are expressed by the following *types of jurisdiction*:

(a) *general jurisdiction*, meaning that the fora of the State may deal with any matters except those specifically removed by law from their powers;

(b) *excluded jurisdiction*, meaning that a State totally refuses to take jurisdiction in specified cases;

(c) *exclusive jurisdiction*, meaning the opposite of the preceding, namely that a State claims or reserves jurisdiction in specified cases for its own authorities;

(d) *jurisdiction stipulated by the parties*, meaning the right of the parties to designate the forum of competent jurisdiction in their case;

(e) *jurisdiction fixed by an international treaty*, meaning that States define, by a bilateral or multilateral treaty, the mandatory jurisdiction of authorities or courts in a specified range of matters;

(f) *parallel* (alternative, optional or cumulative) *jurisdiction*, meaning that, as is usually the case, two or more States have jurisdiction in specified matters, that is to say that adjudication of the case by a forum depends on the decision of the parties (and on "forum shopping" as noted above).

3. As regards the *mode of regulation*, the relevant *sources of law* are found, with respect to Hungary, in Chapter IX of the Code of Private International Law, Act LXXI of 1994 on Arbitration, and agreements on legal assistance and other legislation and international conventions referred to in the next section. By virtue of these sources, Hungary exercises its function as defined in the concept of jurisdiction, namely it proceeds in an international legal dispute on the strength of its sovereignty in accordance with the provisions of the said legislative sources.

4. As can be seen, the institution of jurisdiction also concerns the question paramount to private international law, notably the fact that a legal dispute of a civil-law nature (i.e. in the field of private international law and international economic relations) possesses an international element, creating a conflict situation between the legal systems involved, the solution of which is governed by jurisdictional rules. The answer given by these rules relates here to jurisdiction as a procedural element of the law of conflicts. The decisive conflict aspect pertains to regulation by substantive law, which in turn is controlled by the relevant rules of private international law. Although the question concerns a specific, internally coherent legal relationship and dispute, it should be stressed that the *problems of jurisdiction and the applicable substantive law in private international law are independent of each other both in principle and in general*. In this context we should refer to three aspects.

(a) Save as otherwise provided in the governing source of law, jurisdiction is not by itself a general connecting factor of the law of conflicts. The jurisdiction of a forum in a legal dispute does not entail the application of the substantive law of the country of the forum. This follows from the legal substance of private international law itself, whose rules have their legal function precisely in that, by virtue of them, the legislator allows the application of a law other than that of his own forum, thus permitting an exception to the general rule, namely to the application of his own law. This could be exemplified by many decisions of Hungarian fora (in all of which the foreign element was observed to bear on private international law and hence the laws of FRG, Mexico, Austria, Switzerland and other countries were applied, although jurisdiction was exercised by Hungary: see Cases PKKB. 4.P. 89.579/1982, PKKB. 4.P. 86.327/1978, Bp. 10.Kjö.II. 4915/1981, Bp.22. Kjö.V. 3115/799). To illustrate how consciously jurisdiction and the applicable law are separated in the practice connected with foreign trade contracts, we refer to the legal relationship-contract complex mentioned earlier and involving several stipulated jurisdictions and laws as well as Hungarian substantive law and a foreign-based arbitration court (see 83. 1.8., Vb./83.069. This is not contradicted by the coincidence, precisely in the cited case as well, of jurisdiction and the applicable law in some aspects. Similarly, the practice of ordinary courts presents numerous cases which illustrate that the "homeward trend" (*Heimwärtsstreben*) is not alien to Hungarian fora either. This term is used by international practice and literature to refer to the phenomenon that the proceeding fora are strongly inclined to apply their own substantive law, at times even in disregard of their own conflict rules. Although, since the entry into force of the Code of Private International Law (1980), Hungarian judicial practice has greatly refined its conflicts law culture (i.e. has detected the foreign elements of cases and has acted accordingly in pursuance of the Code provisions), the courts often pass over the foreign elements present and simply apply the Hungarian law even to matters governed by foreign law. Let it be said in its defence that this error happens to be committed even in countries with greater traditions in private international law, but it does not alter the fact that what we have here are cases of unlawful "oversight".

(b) The contrary is also true. The applicability of a foreign substantive law to a given legal dispute does not entail the jurisdiction of the country involved. The reasons for this are, *mutatis mutandis*, the same. Should the rules for jurisdiction and for the applicable law mutually and generally determine each other, the result would be a situation possible in both theory and practice: either everyone should turn to the forum of the country as determined by the applicable substantive law (which is, in a large number of cases, difficult to determine in advance) or resort would be had to a single connecting factor of private international law, the *lex fori*, which would amount to elimination of private international law.

(c) It should nevertheless be taken into account that (i) the *lex fori* is an important connecting factor of private international law; (ii) the courts exhibit some propensity to the application of their own law even if a concrete legal relationship is subject to a conflict rule other than the *lex fori*; (iii) where jurisdiction was stipulated by parties who, however, failed to designate the applicable substantive law, the fora are inclined to think (as they judge all other links to be less close) that their own law has thereby been determined.

§113. THE TYPES OF JURISDICTION

1. Jurisdiction in every State is most commonly determined by the internal rules on international jurisdiction in the form of *general jurisdiction*. This implies three sets of factors. (a) The jurisdictional powers of States are naturally expressed through their internal legislative powers, the primary form of which is domestic legislation. It is through their internal legislative powers that States participate in international legislation, also in respect of jurisdiction, but such participation is always partial in principle, even if it encompasses a broad range of cases, a wide variety of jurisdictional aspects. (b) The internal law similarly recognizes several types of international jurisdiction, so domestic regulation displays a differentiated picture, but it will therefore precisely confer some sort of a general international jurisdiction on the domestic fora, one that allows the adjudication of any international legal dispute which need not be subjected to a special rule differing on account of some peculiar aspect. (c) This is so much the case that the laws of some countries (pertinent legislative sources and customary law) introduce their provisions on other types of jurisdiction with general jurisdiction (as does the Hungarian Code), or do not specifically name any other type of jurisdiction. The forms may vary, though they are not entirely irrelevant in this context, but both approaches retain the same substance.

In Art. 54 the Hungarian Code of Private International Law defines the *general jurisdiction of Hungarian courts* in these terms: "Hungarian courts or other authorities may take jurisdiction over any case in which their jurisdiction is not excluded by this Law-Decree". This formulation denotes the following. (a) The jurisdiction so defined implies general powers in the absence of contrary provisions of law. Such "contrary" provisions are presupposed by the general power themselves as implied in the phrase "over any case in which (their) jurisdiction is not excluded by this Law-Decree". (b) The picture is complete when this is viewed in the context of the entire chapter on jurisdiction: the Hungarian law establishes special types of jurisdiction delimiting general jurisdiction and prescribing the application of the rules thereon (*ius speciale derogat iuri generali*). (c) The Article providing for general jurisdiction does not refer to possible contrary provisions of international treaties. But this, being natural in itself, follows from the general rule of the Code, which is of relevance to this aspect as well, that international treaties take precedence over the provisions of the Code, to wit, exclude their application from matters covered by the international treaty concerned (Art. 2).

Especially in recent years the practice of the Supreme Court has exploited general jurisdiction to the utmost (Art. 54) as it has established its existence, without any particular examination of the linkage of cases to the Hungarian forum, if it is not explicitly excluded by Art. 56 of the Code (e.g. Legf. B. Pf. III.20. 163/1993; Legf. B. Pf. VI.20. 927/1996). The numerous legal cases referred to in this book go to show that the Hungarian fora do exercise the general jurisdiction in question.

[The Supreme Court (e.g. Legf. B. Pf.III.21. 741/1994) is guided by this spirit in overruling the erroneous decision of the court of first instance by stating that "under Art. 54 (of the Code) a Hungarian court may take jurisdiction over any case not covered by Art. 56".]

Performance of this international function of law enforcement is a matter of course for the added reason that the cases generally possess a Hungarian element (defendant, plaintiff, immovable property, estate, etc.) which would make denial of law enforcement unnatural. The question may rather be put this way: Can law enforcement be denied by a Hungarian forum if the case is linked to Hungary by a very thin or no relationship other than the plaintiff initiating the action in this country? Can the Hungarian forum refuse to hear a case in the absence of excluded jurisdiction or in the presence of other jurisdictions fixed by an international treaty or stipulated by the parties in an earlier agreement of theirs (see items 2, 4 and 5)? For instance, a former Hungarian national residing abroad brings an action involving personal status (establishment of paternity, maintenance, custody of the child) against a foreign national who was but temporarily staying in Hungary; since this case is not subject to excluded jurisdiction, does general jurisdiction extend to the extreme limits implied in the example?

The question could be answered in the negative on the ground, among others, that the Code uses the phrase "may take jurisdiction", which includes the possibility for the Hungarian forum to deny jurisdiction if the case is not linked to Hungary by any element. It may appear unlikely in the facts of life, for someone to turn to a completely alien forum on the one hand and for such act to be a real-life phenomenon at all on the other.

The answer may also be in the affirmative, and it is supported by more arguments of greater weight. International practice testifies to this being a lifelike phenomenon, and Hungarian practice has also met with such "un-Hungarian" cases possessing no Hungarian element.

By the Code's wording "may take jurisdiction over any case", the legislator conferred general jurisdiction with no restriction over the given range of matters (except those explicitly removed from such jurisdiction). The relevant part of the motivation to the Law-Decree similarly states that "Hungarian organs may proceed *in all other cases*" (my emphasis – F.M.). Viewed from the angle of civil procedure, the situation is this: an action filed with the court may, without summons, be dismissed in this context only if "the Hungarian court can be stated to have no jurisdiction over it" [Art. 130, para. 1 (a) of the Code of Civil Procedure]. This, however, cannot be stated because the said provision of the Code of PIL would be hard to interpret with such a content. It should be further noted that the agreements on legal assistance generally provide, as does, e.g., the Yugoslav–Hungarian Agreement (promulgated in Hungary by Law-Decree No. 1 of 1969), that nationals of one Contracting Party may take action before the courts of the other Contracting Party on an equal footing with nationals of this Contracting Party (Art. 1). A range of cases, more closed but supporting the affirmative approach, is that submitted to arbitral jurisdiction. Even in such disputes as present no Hungarian element, the Arbitration Tribunal of the Chamber of Commerce offers its jurisdiction to foreign parties external to the Chamber (see §117). It is known that at the arbitral tribunals of some countries, e.g., Switzerland, it is an everyday occurrence that the country concerned (Switzerland) has absolutely nothing to do with a large part of the cases heard by those fora. In international practice the jurisdiction of the fora is understood rather broadly even on the general plane. In American law this phenomenon is called "long arm jurisdiction" (*longa manu jurisdictio*), in which reasonableness is the ultimate limit of flexibility itself (Restatement 27; see Gábor in the List of Sources). In this respect the Swiss Code of PIL refers to "jurisdiction of necessity" (*for de nécessité, Notzuständigkeit*), which is admitted if the Code does not provide for Swiss jurisdiction over a particular case, but proceedings abroad are impossible, or the plaintiff cannot be expected to litigate abroad ("*sieht dieses Gesetz keine Zuständigkeit vor und ist ein Verfahren im Ausland nicht möglich oder zumutbar...*"), as inadmissibility of jurisdiction would amount to denial of justice or law in the given case ("*déni de justice ... Rechtsverweigerung bedeuten würde*": Draft Art. 4 and Art. 3 of the Code). The range of such stop-gap arrangements is narrowed (or eliminated) by efforts to have the problems of forum covered as fully as possible by international agreements or conventions [see item 5 (d) in §113).

2. *Excluded jurisdiction* means that the authorities of the State are explicitly barred from adjudicating certain specified disputes, cannot take jurisdiction over them. It must be said that, again at first sight, there appear to be numerous such cases covered by Hungarian law (Arts. 56–61 of the Code), but a closer look at the relevant provisions modifies the picture somewhat.

(a) The justification for the great number of facts relating to *personal status* covered by legislation is questionable, for it appears as if the Code had already covered them by a general or principal rule excluding the jurisdiction of Hungarian fora in legal disputes concerning the personal status of foreigners (but there is no such general rule: there was one though but only in the draft) and as if the special rules consequently referred to the exceptions. The common core of these sets of facts as defined in Arts. 58–60 is precisely that the said legal disputes concerning personal status may still be considered by a Hungarian authority. Since the general rule with the opposite meaning was left out of the Code at a later stage of codification, but the exceptions thus "having no purpose to serve" were included, these may now be regarded as exemplifying the facts covered by the general rule under which Hungarian jurisdiction over disputes concerning the personal status of foreigners is not excluded at all. True, in Hungarian legal practice, too, the principle prevailed that a Hungarian court or other authority should not take jurisdiction over cases involving the personal status of persons whose personal law is other than Hungarian. Although there was no written rule to this effect, this position followed *a contrario*, as it were, from Art. 15 of Law-Decree No. 22 of 1952 enacting the Code of Civil Procedure, which, considered to be such a rule, subjected proceedings on the personal status of Hungarian nationals to the exclusive jurisdiction of Hungarian authorities. This *a contrario* reasoning, however, may now be disregarded in view of the rules of the Code, which under the caption of "Excluded Jurisdiction" does not, in this respect, provide for excluded jurisdiction, although some hold (see §100) that Art. 58 (1), namely that the requirement for at least one of the parties to be domiciled in Hungary, is of a general restrictive nature, and the principle of general jurisdiction as discussed in the preceding item comes into play. While this is self-evident, it remains to be added that the absoluteness of exclusive Hungarian jurisdiction has also been relaxed somewhat with respect to legal disputes involving the personal status of Hungarian nationals (the said *a contrario* reasoning thereby losing some of its relevance on this ground as well). Nevertheless, as will be seen below, the action of foreign fora on the personal status of Hungarian nationals is honoured indirectly, through the recognition of foreign judgments, in a significant number of cases.

As regards now the class of cases enumerated by way of illustration of admitted jurisdiction in Arts. 58–60 of the Code, the jurisdiction of the Hungarian forum may be summarized briefly as follows: (a) "A Hungarian court may proceed in a lawsuit between non-Hungarian nationals concerning their personal status, with the exception of a lawsuit relating to curatorship, if one of the parties is domiciled in Hungary" (Art. 58, para. 1); (ii) where so required by a domestic legal interest, a Hungarian court may declare a person legally dead even if he is a foreigner (Art. 58, para. 2); (iii) in matters of curatorship and (iv) guardianship a Hungarian authority may assume jurisdiction irrespective of whether or not its decision is subject to recognition by the country of personal law, provided that the person concerned is otherwise resident in Hungary; (v) if the person involved is a foreigner prevented from managing his own affairs; (vi) if a measure of pressing necessity must be taken for the placement, maintenance or care of a foreign national residing in Hungary (Arts. 59–60). Although such measures must be notified to the competent foreign authority of the person concerned, they remain in effect pending other measures by the said authority (Art. 61).

(b) The jurisdiction of Hungarian fora is generally excluded in proceedings against a *foreign State* (a State as such, its authority or administrative organ) and against persons enjoying *diplomatic immunity* (Art. 56 (a) and (b); Art. 57), but this rule, too, is subject to several exceptions, as was indicated in connection with immunity in general and in practice (§§35–37 in Chapter X).

(c) The Code excludes Hungarian jurisdiction *in proceedings concerning the granting, extent and termination of foreign industrial property rights* [para. (c) of Art. 56].

(d) Lastly, the Code leaves open a *general possibility* of recourse to excluded jurisdiction in cases defined by "special provisions of law" [para. (d) of Art. 56].

3. By the notion of *exclusive jurisdiction* the law expresses the fact that the State claims and reserves the right exclusively for its own organs to proceed in matters subject to exclusive jurisdiction. This might be said to be close to *lex imperfecta per definitionem*, for a State will employ its own law by virtue of its relevant provisions, with no regard to exclusive jurisdiction reserved by another State for itself in a particular case. In the United States, for instance, the authorities of that country will not refuse to proceed in cases concerning the personal status of Hungarian nationals domiciled there just because such suits were subjected by Hungarian law exclusively to Hungarian jurisdiction (if they refuse to proceed, they do so on other grounds specified by American law). It is partly for this consideration that, among others, the former Czechoslovak and Polish Codes of PIL and Codes of Civil Procedure use the terms "Czechoslovak" and "Polish" jurisdiction rather than "exclusive" jurisdiction (barring proceedings before foreign fora even on principle); a special group of cases is subject to excluded jurisdiction, whereas in domestic aspects of other cases recognition is extended to decisions of domestic fora only. The relevant provisions are less assertive on the one hand and, on the other, create no separate group of specified cases generally subject to exclusive jurisdiction, they do not suppose the absoluteness of domestic jurisdiction to be honoured in every foreign country.

The approach may vary but the essential point is that, by the rules on exclusive jurisdiction the State can achieve one goal, that of accepting the decisions of no forum other than its own on the domestic aspects of such cases.

Under Art. 55 of the Hungarian Code of PIL, the relevant classes of cases are these:

(a) proceedings on the personal status of Hungarian nationals, except where judgments rendered by foreign courts or other authorities are recognizable under the Code (to be discussed in Chapter XXXVII of this book on Foreign Judgments);

(b) proceedings concerning immovables situate in Hungary;

(c) probate proceedings concerning the estate in Hungary of a deceased Hungarian national;

(d) proceedings against the Hungarian State, its authorities or administrative organs;

(e) proceedings abroad against a Hungarian national acting as a diplomatic representative or otherwise enjoying immunity from foreign jurisdiction, proceedings which in pursuance of an international treaty or of reciprocity cannot be initiated against such person abroad. As is known, this implies one aspect of immunity (for full coverage see §§35 to 37 in Chapter X of this book);

(f) proceedings for the cancellation of securities and deeds issued in Hungary;

(g) proceedings concerning the granting, extent and termination of industrial property rights in Hungary.

This "wish list" is obviously rational in general, also in its "external" effect, even if, as said, it does not bind foreign States (we refer only to foreign cases adjudicated in judicial practice under the rules covering subitems (d) and (e) and discussed earlier in connection with state immunity in §§35 to 37. With respect to certain personal status cases, this is indicated by the Code which, after all, recognizes foreign jurisdiction over some matters). A smaller group of cases subject to exclusive jurisdiction can also be illustrated by another example: a deceased Hungarian national was domiciled in State A, left part of his estate in States A and B (where his children also live) as well as a small portion of it in Hungary. It might appear reasonable for the situation of the whole estate to be settled in probate proceedings conducted in State A, for the purposes of which the inventory of the estate in Hungary could be made available to the proceeding forum through international legal assistance. While a solution is also offered by the current regulation, the heirs living in Australia would not find it so simple to act their "part" in a proceeding taking place in Veszprém County of Hungary.

4. *Stipulation of jurisdiction* concerning arbitration was formerly permitted by Art. 360 (1) of the Code of Civil Procedure, but is now admissible under Act LXXI of 1994 on Arbitration (Arts. 3–5 and 46–47). The Code of PIL allows the stipulation of the jurisdiction of any forum in general, including ordinary courts and arbitral tribunals, by providing in Art. 62 that "the parties may, by written stipulation, determine the jurisdiction of a foreign or domestic ordinary court or arbitral tribunal with respect to legal disputes arising from international economic contracts". Thus, while jurisdiction may be stipulated in respect of any judicial forum, and reference is made to "parties" in general, the subject-matter is limited to disputes arising out of international economic relations. As can be seen, stipulation of jurisdiction is allowed in respect of either ordinary courts or arbitral tribunals, but is limited to international economic contracts, and the parties may stipulate the jurisdiction of an *ad hoc* or a permanent arbitration court (see §117).

A contract concluded by the parties concerning "exclusive jurisdiction" is of binding force: jurisdiction may not be assumed by any other court of law or arbitral tribunal in the particular case (Art. 62, para. 2). This provision on exclusive jurisdiction amounts in effect to "overinsurance", because the rule that in the case of stipulation of the jurisdiction no other court of law or arbitral tribunal may take jurisdiction is applicable even if the term "exclusive" is not used in the stipulation. This wording of Art. 62 (2) should therefore be construed to mean that the parties may rely on the unambiguity of their stipulation of jurisdiction even if they failed to accentuate it by adding the attributive "exclusive". On this point Art. 8 of the cited Act on Arbitration is indeed unambiguous, and also reflective of an unambiguous international practice, by providing that the (ordinary) court before which an action was filed in a matter constituting the object of a contract of submission to arbitration must, without summons, dismiss the action (save annulment of an arbitral award) or discontinue it except when it finds that no such contract was made or the contract is invalid, inoperative or incapable of fulfillment. It should nevertheless be noted that in respect of disputants covered by the European Convention on International Commercial Arbitration (done at Geneva on 21 April 1961 and promulgated in Hungary by Law-Decree No. 8 of 1964), exceptions barring litigation before the court on the basis of a contract of submission to arbitration must, under pain of loss of right, be taken before or simultaneously with the plea of defence on the merits of the case, according to whether such exceptions are deemed to be in the nature of procedural or substantive law under the law of the proceeding ordinary court [Art. VI (1) of the Convention]. [It was for such omission that the Supreme Court turned down the defendant's submission concerning the non-existence of jurisdiction (Pf.VI. 21 140/1994).]

The following remarks should be added to complete the picture of stipulated jurisdiction.

The Hungarian Code of PIL refers to stipulated jurisdiction only in the international arena. The Arbitration Act, which was framed under a new and more up-to-date concept (see Horváth, Pfaff), lays down more general provisions which, guided by the spirit of party autonomy, allow recourse to arbitration in domestic cases as well, if one of the parties is an economic subject and the dispute is connected with his economic activity, or if the parties are free to make stipulations on the object of proceedings (Art. 3). As regards stipulation of jurisdiction, there has also appeared a variant of jurisdiction stipulated by domestic law, such as the jurisdiction of a stock exchange arbitration tribunal: the law provides for binding jurisdiction over specified disputes of the parties about legal relationships involving securities and stock exchange transactions (Art. 202 of Act CXI of 1996 concerning the Negotiation of Securities, Investment Services, and the Stock Exchange). The subjects of possible legal disputes involving negotiation of securities may be natural as well as legal persons, while legal disputes may either have foreign elements or remain domestic in all their aspects.

Stipulation by the parties of a particular forum to adjudicate their international legal disputes is allowed, in addition to domestic sources of law, by international treaties, notably

– the 1961 Geneva European Convention on Arbitration;

– the New York Convention of 1958 on the Recognition and Enforcement of Foreign Arbitral Awards;

– agreements on investment protection (see §§117 and 120).

The 1965 Hague Convention (No. XV) on the Choice of Court came out in favour of the freedom of choice of forum, including ordinary courts, to deal with international commercial and civil litigations, though allowing certain exceptions (lawsuits involving, e.g., personal status, inheritance, maintenance, immovables), but it has met with a marginal response. This is certainly because it seeks to extend party autonomy to a broad field embracing not only international commercial disputes but also all civil controversies, albeit with some exceptions. A global need for such a wide scope of autonomy appears not to be compelling enough for now.

5. *Jurisdiction determined by international treaties* in respect of Hungary is formulated in several groups of agreements.

(a) A *forum for interstate dispute settlement* was set up by the Convention on "Conciliation and Arbitration within the Framework of the Conference on Security and Cooperation in Europe" (done at Stockholm on 15 December 1992 and promulgated in Hungary by Act XIII of 1996). Similar bilateral treaties have also been signed by some countries (see, e.g., Act XVIII of 1996 promulgating the Treaty between the Republic of Hungary and the Swiss Confederation on Arbitration and Conciliation signed at Budapest on 17 December 1992). These instruments establish or provide for the operation of fora of conciliation and arbitration between States. The dispute settlement fora thus established by law function on the basis of voluntary and mutual submission by the parties concerned. With their aims defined and their procedures precisely outlined, they are called upon to adjudicate on disputes that arise primarily between States and are in the nature of public international law, but interstate controversies may also be of an economic nature. This is why it is necessary to mention this new system of institutions at this juncture as well. Even with their interstate character, these fora of jurisdiction have a complementary (quasi-subsidiary) role to play in the peaceful settlement of disputes. As is strongly emphasized in the Preamble to the said CSCE Convention, the States parties in no way intend to weaken the other existing institutions or mechanisms, including the International Court of Justice, the European Court of Human Rights, the Court of the Justice of European Communities and the Permanent Court of Arbitration.

(b) The second group of *international treaties*, those *on investment protection*, covers specifically stipulated fora of arbitration which serve to settle disputes between States and private persons (investors) in addition to those concerning interpretation of interstate treaties (see item 4 in §117).

(c) Jurisdictional rules established by international treaties for private persons, generally with respect to transactions and legal disputes other than those in the field of commerce or the external economy, are also found in *agreements on legal assistance* forming the third group of relevant international treaties. Thus, for instance, Hungary's agreements on legal assistance in matters of inheritance provide that probate proceedings involving movables are subject to the jurisdiction of the State of which the deceased person was a national at the time of his death, while jurisdiction in proceedings involving immovables is governed by the law of the State in which such property is situate (Art. 6 of the Austrian–Hungarian Agreement on the Regulation of Matters of Inheritance. It was on this basis that in a supplementary probate proceeding, a Hungarian forum dealt with the case of a Hungarian decedent who had had his place of permanent residence abroad, in a country other than Austria where, however, he had had assets in foreign currency at an Austrian bank, and so it was possible to enforce the pertinent decision of a Hungarian notary public through the appropriate channel of legal assistance: Bp. 22. Kjö.VIII. 9295/1981). Similar arrangements are contained in other agreements (e.g. Art. 34 of the Bulgarian–Hungarian Agreement on Legal Assistance). Under this same Agreement, divorce proceedings are subject to the jurisdiction of both countries, legal disputes between parents and children to the jurisdiction of the country of the child's residence, and matters of adoption to the jurisdiction of the adopter's country (Arts. 20 and 22).

These examples are sufficient to show that the agreements on legal assistance contain different provisions on these matters as well. Since, however, the said agreements take precedence over domestic law, in concrete cases it should be examined whether the countries concerned have a relevant agreement in force and what provisions it contains on the particular case.

(d) Those provisions of agreements on legal assistance forming a special (fourth) group of jurisdictional rules ensure that subjects at law of both contracting parties may have free and unfettered access to courts to settle their civil, family and commercial disputes and may act before the courts on an equal footing with nationals of the other contracting party [see Italian–Hungarian Agreement on Legal Assistance promulgated in Hungary by Law-Decree No. 11 of 1981; Finnish–Hungarian Agreement on Legal Assistance promulgated in Hungary by Law-Decree No. 25 of 1982; Greek–Hungarian Agreement on Legal Assistance promulgated in Hungary by Law-Decree No. 21 of 1981 (Art. 1)]. What we have here is a bilateral guarantee of *access to justice*.

Mention is deserved at this point, in view of its significance and nature as well as of Hungary's desirable and expected accession, by the *Hague Convention of 1980 on International Access to Justice*, to which numerous European countries have acceded within a short period of time and which can also be expected to become part of the legal infrastructure of Europe. Its substance is in ensuring, under the principle of national treatment, that parties domiciled in the Contracting States may seek justice, institute actions, etc. in every State party (Art. 1) and regulating all elements of the provision of legal assistance (mode of serving actions filed and documents submitted, legal costs, issue of copies of registers, conditions for taking coercive measures, etc.).

(e) It is certainly more than interesting to refer to the *Brussels Convention of 1968 on Jurisdiction and the Enforcement of Judgments in Civil and Commercial Matters*, which is of outstanding importance in the international regulation of the jurisdiction of fora, in a uniform European solution of this question even in a longer-term perspective. This Convention, which naturally also applies to the States that have since acceded to it (see Lasok-Stone in the List of Sources) and is in force for 15 countries of Europe, marks a decisive step toward implementing Art. 220 of the Treaty of Rome. This latter Article is simplification of the formal legal requirements for the mutual recognition and enforcement of judicial decisions, strengthening the legal protection of subjects at law in the European Union, and creating and defining the international jurisdiction of the courts of the States parties, as is stated in the Convention. With respect to *jurisdiction*, this Convention of the European Union has indeed devised a uniform structure for the entire area of integration, by determining the scope of court jurisdiction and regulating in detail questions of where (subjects at law) EU nationals may litigate in commercial and civil matters and where the courts have the right and obligation to proceed in their disputes (on questions of recognition and enforcement, see §120). The principal rules of relevance, in addition to the general principle of domicile, are these: a person domiciled in any State party may be sued, irrespective of his nationality, before the court of that State; if the person sued is not a national of the particular State, that State proceeds on his jurisdictional status under the jurisdictional rules applicable to its own nationals (Art. 2); if the defendant has no domicile in any of the States parties, every State party applies its own rules on internal jurisdiction (Art. 4); in matters enumerated in the Convention the relevant rules allow the defendant domiciled in the EU to sue in a State party other than that of his domicile (e.g. in the State of the place of performance in contractual disputes, in the State of the place of the wrongful act in case of torts, in the State of the beneficiary's domicile in matters of maintenance; Art. 5); special detailed rules on jurisdiction apply to contracts of insurance (Arts. 7–12) and consumer contracts (Arts. 13–15), exclusive jurisdiction (Art. 16), stipulation of jurisdiction by the parties (Art. 17), effect of litigation giving rise to jurisdiction (Art. 18), grounds for pending at law and other causes permitting the approached court to deny jurisdiction (Arts. 19–23), emergency measures (Art. 24), etc.

This brief review makes it sufficiently clear that by this Convention the European Union has really framed a comprehensive and uniform set of norms governing jurisdiction over commercial and civil cases. Already today, though its general applicability to Hungary is expected only in the future, this set of norms is of relevance for this country inasmuch as it provides a guide to plaintiffs of third countries concerning the forum they can file an action with against a defendant in the European Union. Further the choice of forum is of special interest as the parties, one of whom may be a Hungarian, are free to agree, with regard to be had to exclusive jurisdiction, on the forum of a country other than a State party.

(f) The *Lugano Convention on Jurisdiction and the Enforcement of Judgements in Civil and Commercial Matters* (adopted on 16 September 1988) is a closer reality for Hungary than the aforesaid EU Convention is, because, by virtue of its Art. 62, non-signatory States may also accede to it upon invitation, at the initiative of any signatory State, by the Swiss Confederation as the depositary of the Convention. This possibility is open to us now, and the preparations for accession are under way. The Lugano Convention was brought about by the member-states of EU and EFTA in order to create a uniform law and practice concerning this important question in those countries, thereby contributing to strengthening the integration of the entire European Economic Area. Although the Brussels Convention will naturally remain in effect with respect to matters bearing exclusively on EU (as is provided for in Art. 64/B of the Lugano Convention), these two Conventions have codified a law of the same content with respect to the EFTA and EC countries, because the substantive provisions of the Lugano Convention are essentially identical to those of the Brussels Convention. This is symbolically expressed in exactly the same designation of the two Conventions. The same holds for the jurisdictional rules of the Lugano Convention.

6. *Parallel jurisdiction* is exercised: (a) in any case determined by international treaty; (b) in cases not governed otherwise by international treaty and not subject to any of the said rules on the types of jurisdiction, namely in matters which are not exempted from general jurisdiction as discussed under item 1 above, but which are or may also be within the jurisdiction of the competent organ of a foreign State by virtue of the law of that State.

Parallel jurisdiction is not regulated explicitly by Hungarian law. The Code, like the legal systems of most foreign States, takes cognizance of the jurisdiction of other fora (parallel jurisdiction) in any case not rendered by domestic or international law subject to some special type of jurisdiction (exclusive, excluded, stipulated, or internationally determined). It takes cognizance of the considerations for which parties going to law turn to a Hungarian forum, even though their case would also be heard by the court of another country (and its judgment would be recognized in Hungary).

Here are some examples in illustration of practice. An Austrian expert acting in Austria on an assignment by a Hungarian contractor in matters of construction could have sued for his fee in Vienna, but he sued in Hungary (perhaps he had more confidence in an expeditious procedure, easier execution, lower legal costs in Budapest, which is a beautiful city, and he could have several other reasons to commend a trip here, where even the applicable law was that of Austria, since the Hungarian conflict rule directed the application of the Austrian law; PKKB 4.P. 86. 327/1978). Selecting onc of parallel fora (called "forum shopping" for short) is sometimes motivated by the greater likelihood of a more favourable result under substantive law. An injured Hungarian person (he was caused injury in Italy by a car insured and operated in Switzerland) counted, under the Italian conflicts law, on a more open-handed court attitude under the Italian substantive law than under that of, say, Hungary or Switzerland concerning the amount of damages, so it is understandable that he should choose to sue in Italy. It is the advantage of turning to lawyers' offices experienced in such matters, the large amounts of compensation that are taken for granted, of a greater "understanding" that can be expected in the jury system, and the size of accumulated assets held by enterprises and insurance companies that have led, e.g., to the forum shopping which cause claims of persons damaged by air accidents capable of linkage to America on some ground to be brought before American fora. [On the bases of favourable judgments obtained in America for a few injured persons, the American corporations *McDonnell* and *General Dynamics* paid an agreed amount of US$ 68 million in compensation after the 333 passenger victims of the air crash near Paris in 1974. The aircraft was owned by the Turkish Airlines, the accident occurred in France, and the great majority of the passengers were not Americans, but nationals of 24 countries. Relying on these aspects, notably the hopes pinned on establishing the liability of the manufacturing company, even the British lawyers of the British victims sued in America, where the aircraft had been manufactured and manufacturers' liability is governed by more stringent conditions and, in case of defect, larger amounts of compensation can be expected (see Juenger's article, discussing this case, in the List of Sources).]

CHAPTER XXXVI

PROCEDURE

§114. ON PROCEDURE IN GENERAL

1. Once a court or other authority takes jurisdiction over an international legal dispute, the next essential question is that of deciding *what special rules of procedure should be applied* to non-standard disputes presenting other than domestic elements, because the general rules of procedure are ordained by the legislator for application to internal civil (commercial or economic) litigation. Nevertheless, throughout the history of legal development, the legislator has increasingly relied on more and more differentiated rules to express the actual specificity that characterizes several aspects of foreign element proceedings and therefore calls for specific solutions in procedural law. The law of international civil procedure has grown into a far-flung system of institutions, on which Hungarian literature is fairly elaborated, i.e. on international legal assistance, judicial and extrajudicial, the role to be fulfilled by the Minister of Justice in private international litigation, etc. It should be pointed out that the Hungarian Code is comprehensive in this respect as well and has few rivals in international practice. A legal text covering procedural law in greater detail than the Hungarian Code is to be found, among others, in the Swiss Code, which governs matters of jurisdiction and procedure in respect of each institution, but devotes a separate chapter to arbitration (Arts. 176–194).

3. The relevant *sources of law* are found partly in Hungarian domestic law, primarily in the Code of Civil Procedure, the Code of PIL and the Act of 1994 on Arbitration, and partly in international agreements on procedural aspects to which Hungary is a party, chiefly those on legal assistance and arbitration.

§115. THE MAIN RULES OF PROCEDURE IN DOMESTIC AND INTERNATIONAL LEGISLATION

The main general rules of procedure governing international litigation may be said, by way of theoretical generalization, to be basically of two kinds. On the one hand, they generally include the domestic rules of procedure which are applied regardless of the international character of litigation, precisely because specified matters and *international legal disputes in general are subjected* by rules of international civil procedure *to the domestic law of procedure*. It is so provided by Art. 63 of the Hungarian Code: save as otherwise provided for therein, proceedings before Hungarian courts or other authorities are, even in matters of international litigation, subject to Hungarian law. Embracing the entire material of Hungarian procedural law [see Petrik (ed.): *Polgári eljárásjog-kommentár* (Commentary on the Law of Civil Procedure)], this is then the *general rule* which does not, of course, transform the domestic law of civil procedure. In fact, this is the only general provision which can be judged by its nature to be a rule of international civil procedure because it serves as a guide to a fictitious conflict situation in the procedural area, namely to the application of the *lex fori* as the general rule. The *lex fori* means the general rules of procedure (both civil and administrative) as well as the special rules of procedure (e.g. on bankruptcy).

2. On the other hand, the principal rules of international procedural law are made up of the sum of procedural norms different from the domestic rules of procedural law, representing exceptions allowed by the Code to the above general rule, in view of the international character of the litigation. *These are strictly speaking the rules of international procedural law.* They take certain procedural conditions or acts out of the generally applicable domestic law of procedure and give them a different regulation, with the maxim of *ius speciale derogat ius generale* again coming into operation. The most important of these rules in the Code are the following:

(a) The legal and disposing capacity of litigants are governed by their personal law (nationality, domicile), not by Hungarian law (Art. 64, para. 1).

(b) Nevertheless, a foreign national who has no disposing capacity under his personal law, but would have disposing capacity under Hungarian law, is deemed capable of action in proceedings before Hungarian courts. This, however, does not preclude the possibility of his legal representative acting on his behalf (Art. 64, paras. 2 and 3).

(c) Where, between the parties, proceedings based on the same facts is instituted before a foreign court or other authority and the resulting decision is recognizable in Hungary under the Code, the Hungarian court or other authority terminates proceedings subsequently instituted before it, or it dismisses the action without issuing a summons (Art. 65).

(d) The Minister of Justice issues a certificate of Hungarian law and legal practice to a person who is in need thereof to assert his right abroad (Art. 66).

3. As can be seen, the Code may allow exceptions to the general applicability of the domestic law of procedure. Such exceptions include those relating to legal assistance and arbitration to be discussed hereafter. Added to them are the *general rules* established by international agreements and, under Art. 2 of the

Code, taking precedence over domestic law with respect to jurisdiction or any other matter.

(a) Provisions establishing general rules of international procedural law are usually found in *agreements on legal assistance and in consular conventions.* The general rules laid down in these agreements are practically in harmony with the aforementioned general rule, since most agreements on legal assistance provide that nationals of either contracting party may assert their rights in civil proceedings under equal conditions with nationals of the other contracting party (see, e.g., Bulgarian–Hungarian Agreement on Legal Assistance; Art. 14 of the Austrian–Hungarian Agreement on the Regulation of Matters of Inheritance). True, there are also instances of a rarely employed solution, according to which the applicant contracting party may, in matters of legal assistance, request that the contracting party applied to also employ the procedural law of the applicant party with respect to acts of procedural law (Polish–Hungarian Agreement on Legal Assistance promulgated in Hungary by Law-Decree No. 5 of 1960).

In addition, international treaties contain several other special provisions on procedure concerning, among others, the use of language or consular action in matters of succession (protection and delivery of the estate, etc.) as regulated by agreements on legal assistance and consular conventions. (A great number of such provisions are included in every agreement on legal assistance and every consular convention.)

(b) Among other treaties, special mention should be made of the Hague Convention of 1954 on the Law of Procedure, to which Hungary acceded in 1966 (Law-Decree No. 8 of 1966). It is one of the most comprehensive Hague Conventions which have been ratified by a great number of States, including almost all European countries (see Mádl: *Ius Commune Europae*), so it may be regarded as constituting a rather uniform set of norms in this field. It is comprehensive in terms of subject-matter as well, but it contains few procedural rules in the narrow sense. As it actually covers different forms of legal assistance, we will discuss it hereunder (see §§116 and 120).

§116. INTERNATIONAL LEGAL ASSISTANCE

In the law of international civil procedure, by international legal assistance are meant those *legal acts which a court or other authority of a State performs, mostly upon application, for a court or other authority of another State.*

1. The *main rules*, condensed and comprehensive, *of domestic law* on the provision of legal assistance are contained in the Code. The most important rule is found in Art. 67: "(1) In applying for legal assistance a Hungarian court shall contact a foreign court or other authority through the Minister of Justice, while other authorities shall do so through the Minister of Foreign Affairs with the intervention of the supervising minister. (2) In executing an application for le-

gal assistance the proceeding authority shall follow Hungarian law. However, at the request of the applicant authority, it may employ foreign procedures, provided that such procedures do not offend Hungarian public policy."

We may add the following rules (Art. 68): legal assistance is rendered by Hungarian courts or other authorities by virtue of an international treaty or of reciprocity; legal assistance must be denied, even in case of reciprocity, where execution of an application would violate public policy; in the absence of reciprocity, the decision on the provision of legal assistance lies with the Minister of Justice.

It remains to be mentioned that for the purposes of legal proceedings abroad extrajudicial affidavits may be made or oaths taken before a Hungarian notary public, who issues certificates thereof (Art. 69).

The practical aspects of providing international legal assistance call for further regulation by the above general or additional rules. Service of documents summoning witnesses, registration of immovables, expert opinions, language of documents and applications, legal costs, etc. are all matters that need coverage by appropriate norms. These aspects are governed by the sources of law cited above (see item 3 in §114).

2. International legal assistance is naturally governed in the first place by *international treaties*.

(a) Of special relevance are, in view of their general character, the Hague Conventions, first of all the abovementioned *Hague Convention of 1954 on the Law of Procedure*, to which Hungary is also a party and which is applied to a large number of cases involving legal assistance between Hungary and other countries. While the Convention is designated as one on procedural law, in fact it gives a uniform regulation of various forms of international legal assistance in civil and commercial matters, such as service abroad of judicial and extrajudicial documents (Arts. 1–7), applications for performance of legal acts abroad (Arts. 8–16), payment and recovery of legal costs (Arts. 17–19), conditions for legal assistance *ex gratia* (Arts. 20–24), access to registers of civil (personal) status (births, marriages and deaths) and certificates thereof (Art. 25), taking of coercive measures (Art. 26), etc. While the first two categories of cases are handled, as a general rule, through consular or diplomatic channels (including direct contact as may be regulated by the contracting parties on a bilateral basis), the other categories are generally subject to the principle of national treatment.

In order to respond on (more) modern lines to the changed set of conditions, the requirements of fresh experience, and new demands, the Hague Conference on the Law of Procedure elaborated additional conventions on legal assistance to govern separately each of the subject-matter covered by the Convention on the Law of Procedure. These are, in chronological order, the Convention of 1961 on Abolishing the Requirement of Legislation for Foreign Public Documents (to which Hungary acceded by Law-Decree No. 11 of 1973), the Convention of 1965 on the Service Abroad of Judicial and Extrajudicial Documents in Civil and Commercial Matters, the Convention of 1970 on the Taking of Evidence Abroad in Civil and Commercial Matters, and the Convention of 1980 on International Access to Justice. The last three Conventions are equally in force (on the reasons for ratification by Hungary, see Mádl: *Ius Commune Europae*).

(b) A significant role is played, as is also suggested by their name, by international agreements on *legal assistance* (and partly, e.g. in matters of inheritance, by consular conventions). While these treaties are generally called agreements on legal assistance, a large part of their provisions refers to legal assistance in the narrow sense as indicated above and regulates matters such as the provision of general legal assistance, the forms of application for legal assistance, the method of communication, transmission of material evidence, hearing of experts and witnesses, service of documents, etc. The substance of these provisions is that in providing legal assistance, the courts and other authorities of the contracting parties normally communicate with one another through the intermediary of their central organs, except, of course, when otherwise provided for in an agreement, instances of which are not lacking. In executing an application for legal assistance, every State normally follows its own law of procedure.

§117. INTERNATIONAL ARBITRATION AND CONCILIATION

1. As was seen above, international arbitration – a procedure before an international court of arbitration exercising jurisdiction – can be used in two cases: where jurisdiction is so stipulated and where jurisdiction is internationally determined (the exercise of jurisdiction by an arbitration tribunal is provided for in an international treaty). Arbitration has a long history, and today it serves international economic relations with a large differentiated system (see, in the List of Sources, the series "Yearbook of Commercial Arbitration" and the volume edited by Sarsevic, which are published annually on arbitral legislation and practice in different countries and international organizations). At present international arbitration has essentially *two forms*.

(a) *Ad hoc arbitration*, to which the parties decide, by virtue of the permissive rules of law, to submit their dispute, while designating their arbitrators *in concreto*. This form of arbitration is created by a contractual agreement and ceases upon the rendering of an award. It is employed with great frequency in international trade.

(b) *Institutional arbitration*, a form by which arbitral tribunals are set up on an institutional basis within national chambers of commerce or similar bodies. Such a tribunal is made up of a president and other officers (normally secretary and the administrative staff) as well as of a list of eligible arbitrators. It has a statute and rules of procedure, or regulations of its own. It exists in all countries to consider foreign trade disputes in general and, increasingly today, to settle economic disputes between domestic partners. Such tribunals also function within the framework of international cooperation (pursuant to an agreement or in international organizations) (see item 4 below). The main point is that the institutional arbitration tribunals derive their institutional character from their organizational set-up as described above, but only function in cases which the parties submit to their jurisdiction. Institutional courts of arbitration are attached to the chambers of commerce in some countries, including the Chamber of Commerce and Industry of Hungary, and in some others, e.g. the United States, they are attached to arbitration associations. While handling a considerable volume of international trade disputes, they are extensively used in domestic litigation (they happened to decide 27,000 matters in a single year: see Cohn–Domke–Eisemann (eds.): *Institutional Arbitration*, p. 252).

2. As regards now the *recent past* and the *sources of law*, the following brief points can be made.

(a) A great need had long been felt for the *unification of law* in this field, and this need called forth several conventions over the years. Considerable works of codification are under way even today. Of direct relevance to Hungary are the New York Convention of 10 June 1958 on the Recognition and Enforcement of Foreign Arbitral Awards (promulgated in Hungary by Law-Decree No. 25 of 1962) and the European Convention on International Commercial Arbitration done at Geneva on 21 April 1961 (drafted within the framework of the United Nations Economic Commission for Europe and promulgated in Hungary by Law-Decree No. 8 of 1964). Prior to these Conventions international codification had produced conventions on arbitration, e.g. in 1923 and 1927, but Hungary did not become a party to them. Mention should also be made of the Arbitration Rules adopted by ECE in 1966. This, originally a draft prepared by delegates of various countries, was meant to be a convention, but, since some of the delegates wanted to regard it merely as model rules, it remained a draft which may nevertheless be stipulated by contract as the governing rule of arbitration procedure. Finally, it remains to note UNCITRAL's Uniform Arbitration Rules, which were recommended by United Nations General Assembly Resolution No. 39/98 of 15 December 1976 for stipulation in international trade contracts. Also a product of international codification, but merely a normative instrument in the sociological sense as it derives its legal character from practical application, is the one called the Arbitration Rules of the International Chamber of Commerce (ICC). These Rules have been in force since 1 July 1975 (reworded with effect from 1 June 1988, see *New ICC Rules*), and are often stipulated by Hungarian enterprises as well (see, e.g., Case Vb. 83.069, in which only one sub-issue was adjudicated by the Arbitration Tribunal of the Hungarian Chamber of Commerce as the Hungarian enterprise and the Kuwaiti party subjected the particular contract of representation as such to the jurisdiction and procedure of the ICC Court of Arbitration; the same occurred in Case 5617/GAA/C.I. of a Hungarian party against a Swedish company; between 1980 and 1988 the ICC Court of Arbitration dealt with 56 cases involving Hungarian and foreign parties and has, since its establishment in 1923, adjudicated a total of over 6,000 cases – *New ICC Rules*, p. 4).

(b) The rules of *Hungarian domestic law* on arbitration are laid down in Act LXXI of 1994 on Arbitration. Referring the reader to literature (Horváth, Pfaff) for a comprehensive discussion, we will single out the following main provisions, in addition to what has been stated in connection with jurisdiction. One of the Act's most special provisions is contained in Art. 58, which spells out that an arbitral award has the same effect as a final judicial judgment and its enforcement is governed by the rules on judicial execution. Other significant and detailed provisions are stated in Chapter IV on Procedure: the arbitration tribunal shall hear the parties, accord them equal treatment, keep a *procès verbal* of the proceedings and state the reasons for its decision; otherwise, in default of a special agreement, it shall define its own rules of procedure within the limits set by law, but shall not impose fines or take other coercive measures (Arts. 27, 28, 34 and 41). This points to a wide scope of procedural freedom in all forms of arbitration. In the case of institutional arbitration, however, such freedom is considerably limited by the rules of procedure of the institutional arbitration tribunal.

Another important procedural rule of the Arbitration Act is that the competent local or district court must, upon the application of the arbitration tribunal, render legal assistance by the taking of evidence and by the adoption of coercive measures as may be necessary for the taking of evidence by the arbitration tribunal (Art. 37). The emphasis here is on the adoption of coercive measures. Obviously, an arbitration tribunal cannot employ such means, which may only be provided, where necessary, by an ordinary court in the form of legal assistance.

An arbitral award (and a settlement) is final in itself and cannot be appealed against nor protested on legal grounds (Arts. 39 and 58). At the most, an arbitral award may, in specified cases (Arts. 54–55), be referred for an annulment to a law court, which, according to Arts. 51–52, is the county court or the Metropolitan Court of Budapest. This recourse is available when, for instance, the contract of arbitration did not cover the dispute decided by the judgement, the losing party was not heard, the rules on setting up the arbitration tribunal were violated, or the judgment offends public policy.

The Act renders, as a rule, its own general provisions (Art. 46) applicable to international arbitration procedures before the Permanent Arbitration Tribunal attached to the Hungarian Chamber of Commerce and Industry (see item 5 below).

3. Among the rules of the major *international conventions and normative instruments,* we have referred to the provisions of the abovementioned Geneva Convention, the Arbitration Rules of the International Chamber of Commerce, the UNCITRAL Uniform Arbitration Rules and Model Law on International Commercial Arbitration, and the arbitration systems relating to international investments, which may be given a brief treatment here (for a detailed exposi-

tion of the subject in its theoretical and practical aspects, see the volume edited by Sarcevic in the List of Sources). In contrast, the New York Convention is concerned with the recognition and enforcement of arbitral awards, not with procedure in general (it will therefore be discussed hereafter in connection with the recognition and enforcement of foreign arbitral awards). Accordingly the Geneva Convention is the most important of the relevant international treaties because it is one of general applicability and Hungary is also a party to it. (For an extensive list of conventions and other instruments on arbitration, see the List of Sources.)

(a) Among the international instruments of general applicability the *Geneva Convention* deals with the following main questions. In the first place, Art. 1 provides that the rules of the Convention are applicable to contracts with submission to arbitration concluded for the settlement of foreign trade disputes between natural or legal persons whose domiciles or seats are in the territories of different States at the time of contracting, as well as to arbitral procedures and awards based on contracts subject to the preceding provision. This means that any arbitration procedure which takes place under an arbitration agreement concluded by Hungarian parties with foreign parties, in the field of foreign trade is to be governed by the rules of the Geneva Convention.

It is worth noting that pursuant to Art. 2 of the Convention, legal entities under public law may also resort to arbitration and use the forms of procedure provided for therein.

Long Articles of the Convention are devoted to questions like designation of foreigners as arbitrators (a possibility commended by Art. 3); constitution of an arbitration tribunal; complaints about the powers of an arbitration tribunal; certain aspects of the powers of ordinary courts; problems of the applicable law; statement of reasons for decisions; annulment of arbitral awards within a rather narrow scope of cases: if the parties to the contract of arbitration had no legal or disposing capacity; if the contract of arbitration is invalid; if the losing party was unable to affirm his procedural rights (e.g. to submit his declarations); if the composition or proceedings of the arbitration court were not in accord with the agreement of the parties (Art. 9).

Mention is deserved of the provision of Art. 7 concerning the applicable law that, as has been noted above, jurisdiction – in our case the stipulated jurisdiction of a stipulated arbitral tribunal – does not also imply designation of the applicable law. On this point Art. 7 states that the parties may, by agreement, freely determine the law which is to be applied by the arbitrators in deciding the dispute on its merits. Where the parties failed to designate the applicable law the arbitrators must apply the law which, in their judgment, is determined by the conflict rule governing the case before them. In either case, the arbitrators must take into account the stipulations of contract and the commercial usages. The arbitrators decide the dispute as amicable mediators (*amiables compositeurs*) if such settlement accords with the will of the parties and is permitted by the law governing arbitration. In the latter case, the arbitrators are not bound either by a specified substantive law or by a specified procedure, but adopt a decision based on their own judgment. This is also suggested by the term amicable mediators (see Loguin: *L'amiable composition*).

(b) The Arbitration Rules of the International Chamber of Commerce deserve the attention of Hungary in view of its great practical relevance [see item 2 (a) in §117]. The organic structure of the Arbitration Court is constituted by three bodies: the Court itself, the proceeding arbitrator or panel of arbitrators, and the Secretariat. The Court (in its narrow sense) is elected by the ICC Council for a term of 3 years, with the President and the 8 Vice-Presidents, the General Secretary, one or more technical advisers, and a member of the Court designated by each national committee (Arts. 1–2 of the Statute: see *New ICC Rules*).

The main rules of procedure are these: the individual arbitrator is designated jointly by the parties or a member of the panel of three is designated by each party, with the President elected by two members: if the parties fail to designate them, the arbitrators and the President are appointed by the Court, after consultation with the appropriate national committees of ICC; the arbitrators designated by the parties and the President are confirmed by the Court; prior to confirmation or appointment, each arbitrator must notify the General Secretary of any circumstance that might cause the parties to have doubts about his independence, each party may challenge an arbitrator on a specified ground, the challenge to be accepted or rejected by the Court; the Court's decisions (on appointment, confirmation and challenge) are final (Art. 2). In addition the Rules regulate in such detail the process of considering cases, including matters like initiation of action (Art. 5), exchange of documents (Art. 6), effect of the arbitration clause in the contract of the parties (Arts. 7–8), advance payment of arbitration fees (Art. 9), handing over of the file (by the Secretariat) to the proceeding arbitrators (Art. 10), procedural rules and the seat of arbitration (Arts. 11–12), conduct of proceedings on the merits of the case and the mechanisms of the arbitral procedure (Arts. 14–16), arbitral award (Art. 20), special role of the Court in finalizing the award (Art. 21), final award, its legal effect and service to the parties, etc. (Arts. 23–26). The Annexes to the Rules contain the Statute of the Court (I), its Order of Business (II), and the arbitration fees (III).

(c) *UNCITRAL's Model Law on International Commercial Arbitration* was adopted in 1985, was approved by UNCITRAL at its session on 21 June, and was confirmed by Resolution 40/72 of the United Nations General Assembly. It derives its importance from the following major facts: it is a modern synopsis of national and international experience; it regulates the entire arbitration process with a theoretical grounding, in a coherent system and in operative depth; while not an international convention, it is enabled by its said values as a model law to give substance to national legislative frameworks of arbitration either through full adaptation or through national legislation drafted along its lines, thereby strengthening the unification of the conduct of the international commercial arbitration procedure; it is able by its reception into national laws, by an insignificant technical adaptation of its text, to lead to simplifying or eliminating the duality (in the national arbitration systems) of the international and domestic norms of arbitration. The desirable effect of the Model Law on legislation on arbitration cannot be disputed in respect of Hungary either (see item 5 below). It is certainly worth noting that the Model Law was codified in UNCITRAL under the presidency of Hungary and that it constitutes a UN-born legal instrument, which serves by itself to increase the chances of its global application, as is already indicated by existing experience.

The said operative depth of regulation by the Model Law may be described in brief as follows.

Consisting of 36 – generally long – articles in all, the Model Law covers all essential aspects of international arbitration in 8 chapters: I. General Provisions, II. Agreement to Arbitrate, III. Composition of the Arbitration Court, IV. Jurisdiction of the Arbitration Court, V. Arbitration Procedure – Rules of Procedure, VI. Award and Termination of Procedure, VII. Legal Remedy (Annulment of Award), and VIII. Recognition and Enforcement of Arbitral Awards.

In theoretical aspects the Model Law goes a long way to respect party autonomy in the settlement of disputes (establishment of procedural rules in the narrow sense, determination of the applicable law), the right of the parties to equal treatment, and the broad competence of the court to adjudicate disputes at its discretion within the limits of stipulations by the parties. At the same time, it is still able to meet the fundamental requirements of justice and the applicable norms (for a detailed analysis, see Hermann).

(d) UNCITRAL's Arbitration Rules preceded by the Model Law by many years: in Resolution No. 31/98 of 15 December 1976, the United Nations General Assembly recommended the use of the Rules for the settlement of disputes arising in international economic relations, in particular the stipulation by the parties in their trade contracts of the application of the Arbitration Rules, in the conviction that adoption of rules on *ad hoc* arbitration that are acceptable for States with different legal, social and economic systems would contribute significantly to the unhampered development of international economic relations (Preamble). Experience shows, further, that this undertaking has been a success as UNCITRAL's Arbitration Rules are stipulated in ever more international trade contracts and also became the established Rules of a growing number of permanent arbitration tribunals (see Hermann, p. 11). The reason lies in the specifics as stated in the Preamble and in the fact that the Rules have formed a synthesis derived from decades of practical experience in the use of arbitral procedure and of the efforts of legal science to achieve such a synthesis. The natural value of the Rules consists in covering, by 41 articles, the entire process of arbitration with all its essential elements like the agreement to arbitrate, the institution of actions, the constitution of the arbitration court, the rules of procedure (on seat, language, documents, objections to the jurisdiction of the court, the taking of evidence, experts, etc.), awards, the termination of proceedings, costs, etc. It is clearly seen that UNCITRAL's Model Law and Arbitration Rules coincide on numerous points of regulation, although originally each had a different function to fulfill. The former was aimed, as was observed, at a harmonization of national legislation on arbitration and the latter constituted the procedure before an arbitration court set up by arbitration agreements in concrete international trade contracts. However, the drafters of the Model Law did not conceal their assumption that, failing stipulation of any rules of procedure, the role of unstipulated arbitration rules could also be played, in many respects and rather fully, by a regulation adjusted to the Model Law (see Hermann, p. 11).

4. A growing role in international arbitration has been assumed by *special arbitration fora and rules of arbitration procedure concerning foreign investments*, which further play an outstanding part in the protection and expansion of foreign investments (see Chapter XVII).

The difference lies in them dealing with disputes, under the law of investment (i.e. association), between persons other than foreign investors and their domestic partners. In other words, between private persons who, also in the past, routinely arbitrated their controversies before arbitration fora in every country with ample experience in foreign investment activities. The separate standing of the special arbitration fora derives from their resolving legal disputes arising between the State where the investment is effected and the private investor from acts of the State damaging the investment. More recently, national legislation on arbitration have similarly indicated and thereby institutionalized, as it were, the role which "traditional" (*ad hoc* or institutional) arbitration courts can play in such disputes (see, e.g., Art. 177 of the Swiss Code of PIL, it being understood that in such cases the State may not, by invoking its own law, challenge the procedure of the arbitration court once it has become a party to the arbitration agreement). This is nevertheless a new phenomenon which is being allowed to spread because the other party opposing a commercially private party should still be in the position of a sovereign. It is not accidental that a more marked breakthrough was bound to be produced by international conventions, since a system of arbitration and the availability of arbitration procedure under international conventions hold out the promise of a more efficient conflict settlement mechanism than the earlier practice did. Such previous practice could not rely except on possibilities offered by the fora and procedures based on diplomatic efforts and on the domestic regulation of the host country, which were often doubtful as to a genuine protection of investors who justifiably presumed that an arbitration procedure would afford a real opportunity to consider and establish the lawfulness or unlawfulness of the acts of States as well. An arbitration procedure accepted under an international treaty places a constraint even on sovereign States which they cannot evade. In order to use the language of physics, it creates a force field which holds captive even the strongest "elementary particle", notably States; without such a force field or with its disintegration, there would be nothing but hopeless litigation between unequal parties (for a fuller exposition, see Giardin; Király–Mádl).

(a) The most important convention by reason of its being a general international legislative instrument (with over 100 accessions) is the *Washington Convention on the International Centre for Settlement of Investment Disputes* (ICSID), which was promulgated in Hungary by Law-Decree No. 27 of 1987.

The Convention first establishes the organic structure of the Centre (Board of Directors, with the President of the World Bank as its Chairman, Secretariat, General Secretary, Body of Conciliators and Arbitrators), its status and financing (Arts. 1 to 24).

A most important article deals with the Centre's functions and jurisdiction (Art. 25), stating in para. 1 that the jurisdiction of the Centre extends to all legal disputes, directly arising out of an investment project, in which one of the parties is a contracting State (or its agency as notified to the Centre) and the other party is a national of another contracting State, provided that the litigants agree in writing to submit their dispute to the Centre. Once the parties have so agreed, neither of them may unilaterally withdraw the agreement. Thus the essential point is that the dispute involves (a) a said matter (investment), (b) a State and a private person (national) as parties thereto, and (c) voluntary submission. Paragraph 2 clearly provides that the concept of "national" must include both a national of a contracting State and a legal person having the nationality of the particular State.

The next provisions deal in essence with conciliation (see item 6 in §117) and arbitration procedures. The Convention regulates all important elements of arbitration procedure, which include in part the usual ones (institution of action, constitution of the arbitration court, its powers and function, award, its interpretation and enforcement, costs and seat of procedure: Arts. 36 to 62), but, given the peculiarities of disputes and parties, several elements of regulation differ from the usual or general norms of arbitration. The major ones are these: if the court acts in a panel, the majority of its members may not be nationals of the States of the parties to the action (Art. 39); in case of a dispute, the parties may request the court to interpret the award and even to revise (a sort of a new trial) if there have emerged new facts affecting the merits of the case; in that event the same court must deal with the case or, should it be impossible, a panel must be formed; an award is likewise annulled by arbitrators, through forming an *ad hoc* committee, appointed by the Centre's President from its list of the Body of Arbitrators (Arts. 50–53; for the general rules differing from these, see item 6 in §117); if the parties disagree on the interpretation of the Convention, the dispute is to be referred to the International Court of Justice at The Hague (Art. 64). The growing importance of the Centre may be indicated, besides the above aspects, by the fact that, as will be seen below, submission to the Centre is provided for in an increasing number of bilateral interstate agreements on investment protection and that the Centre practises a considerable volume of arbitration even by virtue of subsequent submission (see the corresponding chapters in the volumes of the *Yearbook of Commercial Arbitration*). Hungary, too, has signed an agreement with a foreign investor in which the Government subjected itself to the Centre's jurisdiction over a possible dispute which the parties (the Government and the investor) might be unable to settle amicably.

(b) Recent years have witnessed a growing significance assumed by *bilateral agreements on investment protection* (see Chapter XVII), which create arbitration fora and procedures for the settlement of disputes between the contracting States and their subjects at law, disputes connected with investments in their respective countries. Hungary has concluded several such agreements over the years.

(ba) These agreements serve to settle disputes between contracting States, namely those which arise between the parties in connection with the interpretation and application of the particular agreement. The agreements provide for *ad hoc* arbitration procedures where an amicable settlement proves impossible: each contracting State appoints a member of the arbitration court and the president of the court is elected by the arbitrators thus appointed, nonetheless subject to the consent of the contracting States; if the arbitrators and/or the president are not/is not designated/elected in due course, each party may request designations to be made by the President of the International Court of Justice or the Secretary-General of the United Nations, depending on the provision of the particular agreement; the court decides by a majority of votes and adopts its own rules of procedure; the costs are borne in the same proportion by the Governments involved; interpretation of an award, if deemed necessary by the parties, is also within the competence of the proceeding arbitration court [see Art. 10 of the Swedish–Hungarian Agreement (promulgated by Decree No. 25/1987 of the Council of Ministers), Art. 11 of the French–Hungarian Agreement (promulgated by Decree No. 59/1987 of the Council of Ministers), Art. 10 of the FRG–Hungarian Agreement (promulgated by Law-Decree No. 5 of 1988), Art. 9 of the British–Hungarian Agreement (promulgated by Decree No. 5/1988 of the Council of Ministers)].

(bb) Another type of dispute concerns a controversy between a contracting State and an investor (a natural or legal person) of the other contracting State about an act of State of the place of investment and damaging to the project of the investing party, against which the particular agreement seeks to provide protection. Where an amicable settlement proves impossible, the agreements normally provide for the following system of arbitration: (i) an *ad hoc* arbitration procedure, with reference to, e.g., UNCITRAL's Arbitration Rules; (ii) consent of the contracting States to proceedings before the International Centre for Settlement of Investment Disputes under its own rules of conciliation or arbitration procedure if both contracting States are or will be party to the Washington Convention on the Centre [see item 4 (a) in §117]. Such consent implies mandatory submission to the Centre in relations between the particular States, as is also shown by the agreements cited above (Art. 11 of the Swedish–

Hungarian Agreement, Art. 9 of the French–Hungarian Agreement, Art. 8 of the British–Hungarian Agreement).

(c) In order to give a relatively complete picture and considering that arbitration procedure indirectly concerns foreign investments, mention is warranted here of the fact that the International Investment Guarantee Agency (MIGA, see Chapter XVII), in Arts. 56–57 of and Annex II to the relevant Convention (promulgated in Hungary by Law-Decree No. 7 of 1989), set up a similar disputes settlement mechanism based on conciliation and arbitration.

5. Under Arbitration Act LXI of 1994 as well, proceedings before the *Permanent Arbitration Tribunal of the Hungarian Chamber of Commerce and Industry* are, as noted earlier, subject to the (new) Rules of Arbitration Procedure of that Tribunal (Arts. 28 and 46) established and adopted by Decision 168/1/Vb/1995 of the Chamber's Presidium in conformity with the said Act.

(a) By taking account of the fact that our international trade contracts are dominated by relations with the market economy countries, that such contracts satisfy the clear requirements of contractual freedom and party autonomy and that the demands of arbitration guided by this approach are also taking hold in domestic economic relations, the new Arbitration Rules respond emphatically to the need for Hungary to rise to the European and world standards. It is rightly stated in the Preamble to the new Rules that, for all these reasons, the Rules have drawn heavily upon UNCITRAL's Model Law as well as upon the internationally known conventions and agreements [partly discussed under items (3) and (4) in §117] and other international normative instruments (for a general treatment of the *Rules of Procedure of the Arbitration Tribunal attached to the Hungarian Chamber of Commerce and Industry*, see Horváth: *The New Arbitration Act in Hungary*, Budapest, 1995).

(b) As regards now the substance of the Rules, we will consider the following main elements thereof. The body of rules gives a full coverage of related matters both in detail and in scope and is adjusted to international standards. It consists of 45 articles in all, supplemented by 10 provisions of the same date covering the fees and costs of arbitration and the expenses of parties. Among the general provisions the Rules state (in Art. 1) that the jurisdiction and the operational character of the Chamber's Arbitration Tribunal are dual: (i) the Tribunal exercises jurisdiction as a court of institutional arbitration if that forum is stipulated in the contract of the parties or the parties agree on subsequent submission to it, such agreement to be in writing. Under para. (4), the jurisdiction of the Tribunal is also established if it is contained in the documents relating to the claims and defence filed in such a way that one of the parties alleges the existence of the agreement thereon and the other party does not deny it. To give an example in support of adjustment to international standards, this provision is also literally transplanted from the pertinent rule of UNCITRAL's Model Law (Art. 7); and (ii) the Tribunal functions as a court of mandatory institutional treaty.

An examination of the Tribunals's jurisdiction from the aspect of potential subjects and matters reveals a modern open-ended nature of the Rules; subjects may include national and foreign natural and legal persons, while matters may involve legal disputes arising out of contractual or non-contractual relationships except where domestic laws and regulations exclude consideration of a particular case under an arbitration procedure [see paras. (2) and (3) of Art. 1].

In addition, the general provisions deal with the organization and functioning of the Arbitration Tribunal as well as with the applicable law (Arts. 2 to 14).

The procedure in the narrow sense comprises questions (covered by Chapter II) like the principles of procedure, designation of arbitrators, filing of action, documents and replies, constitution of the proceeding panel, hearing, cross-action, evidence, conclusion of proceedings, award and its enforcement, conciliation procedure, etc. (Arts. 17 *et seq.*).

In dealing with the jurisdiction of the Chamber's Arbitration Tribunal, we have referred to it as an important element in the effort to adopt international standards and models. This is supported by further similar features of regulation: the list of arbitrators may also include foreigners and is of an informative nature (Art. 4); the language of proceedings may be determined by the parties (Art. 9); conciliation procedure follows modern lines (Art. 45); procedural autonomy is of broad scope (Art. 17); awards are classified as confidential, with rather narrow public access thereto (Arts. 15 and 31); the Tribunal has a decisive role in establishing its own jurisdiction [para. (6) of Art. 1].

6. With all essential elements of arbitration reviewed, we will now subject *some* questions to closer scrutiny.

(a) One of them concerns the *scope of the rules of arbitration procedure stricto sensu.*

The practice of countries differs widely in respect of the extent to which matters not covered by the special rules of arbitration procedure are subject e.g., to the general rules of procedural law, which refer back to the former (e.g. in respect of recourse to a new trial) in some countries but do not in others (as is evidenced by *Handbook of Institutional Arbitration in International Trade*, see Cohn–Dornke–Eisemann (eds.) in the List of Sources).

As noted earlier in connection with the domestic sources of law of general applicability [item 2 (b)], the Arbitration Act provides that, in default of a separate agreement, the Arbitration Tribunal has a discretion to adopt its own rules of procedure "within the limits set by law" (Art. 28). What does the phrase "within the limits set by law" mean? Does it mean that the Tribunal may take jurisdiction only in cases covered by an explicit permissive provision of the Act (Art. 61) or that questions not so covered are "free for all", or discretion may not be exercised or may only be exercised by interpretation *per analogiam*? What is the limit here to procedure based on "free agreement" or "discretion"? There emerge many questions and the answers are just as varied (see Szászy; van Houtte in the List of Sources). On this point the following may be stated in brief: cases differ by *ad hoc* and institutional arbitration.

(aa) On the basis of evidence offered by the general rules of different countries on *ad hoc* arbitration (see *International Handbook on Commercial Arbitration*, Chapters on Switzerland, US and FRG) and by international treaties, the following general statements can be made: (1) National legislation and international treaties provide that the rules of procedure are determined – so to say, within the limits set by the relevant laws – by the parties or the arbitration court. (2) This may be done, among others, in accordance with the rules of arbitration procedure established by a domestic law or by stipulation of some international rules (e.g. the Arbitration Rules of UNCITRAL). Of course, the sources of law and the rules so determined are applicable in case of such stipulation. (3) Concerning questions not regulated, the solutions vary. (i) One is furnished by, e.g., the Swiss Intercantonal Convention on Arbitration, Switzerland's internal law of arbitration procedure, which provides in Art. 24 that the Procedural Act of the Confederation is to be applied *per analogiam* to the cases in question. A similar principle prevails in the law of FRG – according to the sources cited above, the governing rules are those of the seat of the arbitration court; (ii) another solution is that the domestic sources of law (e.g. the Hungarian law in force) prescribe the application of no particular law, thus leaving room for the said freedom of action as an otherwise general principle of arbitration. In such cases, where international treaty norms are lacking, there remain but two paths (rather broad in fact) to follow in both theory and practice: the arbitration court tacitly relies on, e.g., the procedural law of the country of the seat, simply employing its rules in concrete procedural matters, as its freedom allows it to do so, or, being independent of any national or international rules of procedure, it determines, in an autogenerative way, how to act on a particular procedural matter, as its freedom also allows it to do so; broad (iii) the third solution relates to cases not covered by the rules of procedure of stipulated international arbitration. Here again we have the two broad paths of freedom mentioned in subitem (ii). On this aspect UNCITRAL's Arbitration Rules, for instance, state among the general provisions on procedure that the arbitration court shall, within the framework of the rules, conduct the proceedings in the form it deems to be the most appropriate (Art. 15). The said freedom is formulated here in the phrase "in the form it deems to be the most appropriate". A similar formulation is found in UNCITRAL's Model Law (Art. 19).

(ab) In the case of *institutional arbitration*, which is governed by its rules of procedure (or rules covering procedural matters as well), the pertinent matters are naturally subject to the corresponding provisions of those rules, which (may) also provide a guide as to how to proceed on matters not covered by them. The Arbitration Rules of ICC state this: the rules of procedure to be followed in matters not covered by the Rules are determined by the parties or (if they did not stipulate any rules on them) by the arbitration court, either by referring or by failing to refer to a national law of procedure (Art. 11). Thus, here again, we see the principle of freedom come into play along the paths indicated above.

The same holds essentially true for the Rules of Procedure of the Arbitration Tribunal attached to the Hungarian Chamber of Commerce and Industry, with the added element, however, that the freedom conferred in matters not regulated is kept, as it were, within the bounds of some general principles: "In procedural matters not covered by the Rules of Procedure, and failing concurrent stipulations by the parties, the Arbitration Tribunal shall act as it thinks fit, having regard to the general principles of procedure corresponding to the domestic or international character of the legal relationship between the parties. During the proceedings the Tribunal shall observe the principle of the parties' equality, of equal treatment, and the right of each party to become acquainted with the material of the arbitration procedure, the submissions of the parties, the evidence presented by them and the acts performed by the Tribunal, and to state his position, by word of mouth or in writing, in the course of proceedings" (Art. 17). Thus, within these limits, we see the manifestations of freedom as indicated under item (aa), 3 (ii) and (iii).

With regard to the practice of the Chamber's Arbitration Tribunal, over the years it may be stated that the proceeding arbitrators and the parties have kept in mind and even expressly employed the provisions of the Code of Civil Procedure. True, they might (also) be said to have the right to do precisely by virtue of the said procedural autonomy, thus no problem was presented by the need to apply the rules of the Code of Civil Procedure relating to interpleading or intervention unknown to the earlier Rules (in Art. 30 of the current text) (Vb. 82.104; Vb. 83.023) or by the competition, also unknown to the Rules, of declaratory and condemnatory action under the Code of Civil Procedure (Vb. 83.191). However, problems may be encountered with respect to aspects of procedural law in which such implied choice of a rule of the Code of Civil Procedure is not so simple, but gives rise to more essential problems like the doubtful possibility of a new trial which, as noted, has found its way into the general procedural approach of some countries. Moreover, similar solutions are recognized in respect of special arbitral institutions such as the International Centre for Settlement of Investment Disputes [see item 4 (a)] covered by Art. 51 of the pertinent Convention. A rule or principle of general applicability is difficult or impossible to formulate in the light of Hungarian arbitration practice. The decisive criterion can only be the freedom and judgment of the proceeding panel of arbitrators within the said limits of the Rules of Procedure.

(b) The *jurisdiction* of the Arbitration Tribunal has repeatedly been the focus of debates by reason of the fact, among others, that one of the parties questions its unambiguous stipulation or denies its very existence, or alleges modification of the arbitration clause and thereby the competence of the arbitration forum other than the one with which the plaintiff filed his action, or alleges that the original stipulation has lost effect or is no longer valid. In a case taken from real life, for example, the defendant (and enterprise of a foreign country) claims that the Arbitration Tribunal of the Hungarian Chamber of Commerce has no jurisdiction over the dispute because the original relevant arbitration clause was modified in the meantime and that a high court of the country in question was stipulated as the new forum; the defendant – appearing as plaintiff in this aspect – brings proceedings before this forum against the original plaintiff because he also has a ground for action. Meanwhile this original plaintiff contests before the forum of country X the modification of the original arbitration agreement, the result being the conduct of proceedings before both fora, which have to examine the existence of their jurisdiction in the first place. It is often the case that one of the parties turns to an ordinary court for it to establish the invalidity of the arbitration agreement or commences proceedings at that forum despite the existence of an arbitration agreement. Again, it frequently occurs that the parties invoke the invalidity of the stipulation of arbitration and, with it, the jurisdiction of the stipulated forum. In a concrete case, for example, the German plaintiff alleged before the arbitration forum of country X that the stipulation of the forum was invalid, the forum had no jurisdiction because the underlying contract of licence, which contained the arbitration clause, was invalid on account of violating the prohibition stated in the German anti-trust law, but the arbitration court pointed out that the validity of the arbitration clause was not affected by the complaint about the invalidity of the basic contract and that the case was to be considered by it (*Yearbook of Commercial Arbitration*, Vol. 4, 1979, pp. 197–199).

Generalizing the variants of the dispute, we are faced here with the following main issues: (i) Which forum is competent to determine the challenged competence of the arbitration court (question of the competence of competence)? (ii) What role can be played in this respect by an ordinary court? (iii) Is the arbitration clause valid in itself, or does the invalidity of the basic contract "drag down" the former's validity with it as Titus Dugovich dragged down the Turk with him from the bulwark during the siege of today's Belgrade (question of separability)?

(ba) Instead of going into detail (Mádl: *Competence*) we can state the situation under the current law to be the following *in respect of Hungary*.

The legal material covering *ad hoc arbitration* consists of the Arbitration Act (Arts. 24–25), the Code of PIL (Art. 62) and the European (Geneva) Convention on Arbitration (Arts. V–VI), under which decision on the competence of the arbitration court is primarily within the competence of that court, with the ordinary court playing but a subsidiary role, and separability is definitely acceptable.

As regards *institutional arbitration* (by the Arbitration Tribunal of the Chamber of Commerce), the following explicit provision of the Tribunal's Rules of Procedure is to be added: "The Arbitration Tribunal shall examine *ex officio* the existence of its jurisdiction. Its jurisdiction shall extend to decision on the existence or non-existence of its own competence and to consideration of complaints about the existence or validity of the arbitration agreement. For these purposes, the arbitration agreement forming part of the contract shall be regarded as one independent of any other stipulations of the contract. A decision of the Arbitration Tribunal to the effect that the contract is invalid shall not entail *ipso iure* the invalidity of the arbitration agreement. Any complaint about the jurisdiction of the Arbitration Tribunal shall be lodged simultaneously with the filing of defence at the latest... The Arbitration Tribunal shall consider separately any complaints against its competence as a preliminary question, but shall also be entitled to conduct the proceedings and to settle the complaint in its decision on the case" (paras. 6 to 8 of Art. 1).

(bb) As concerns *international practice*, the situation is essentially the same as is indicated by Hungarian positive law, with the added remark that the reason lies in the Hungarian legislator's having regard to the international processes and seeking to follow the modern trend in adjusting the regulation to the current status of or changes in those processes. The answers given to the questions outlined above are clearly identical or similar in the Arbitration Rules of ICC (Art. 8), the UNCITRAL Model Law (Art. 16), the European Convention (Arts. V–VI), which is also in force with regard to Hungary, and several national laws (see, e.g., Art. 178 of the Swiss Code of PIL).

(c) A special institution of arbitration procedure was devised by Art. 13 of the Arbitration rules of ICC under the title of Terms of Reference (a quasi *order of business* governing proceedings on the merits of cases). Its substance consists in the task of the arbitration court, to be accomplished during the preparations for proceedings, to compile a document – with the participation and signatures of the parties and on the basis of papers and the parties' declarations – in which the parties determine or state, beside the essential data relating to the case, the substance of the action, the main elements of defence and evidence, the place of the proceedings (hearing), the rules of procedure, the applicable law and all those matters that need to be decided in order for the future award to be enforceable. This document will serve as the decisive "script" for the proceedings which the court will adhere to. This is why the Rules of Procedure are emphatic about the requirement of that document to be signed by both the arbitration court and the parties. The document is a kind of mini-code of proceedings and hearings tailored to a concrete dispute. Hungarian enterprises should consider seriously participating in drawing up the Terms of Reference, because several matters may be brought to an issue already at this stage, matters that one might think would be decided in the award following upon the proceedings (e.g. the scope of taking evidence, the applicable rules of procedure). There is an instructive body of experience available in this respect, and it calls for a greater measure of care to be exercised.

(d) As regards the *applicable substantive law,* the *lex obligationis*, we might practically bring upon the carpet the entire private international law of obligations (Titles 5 and 6 of the Code; Lando). The relevant provisions of the Code as well as the various arbitration rules [the European (Convention on Arbitration (Art. VII), ICC Rules (Art. 13), paras. 3 to 5), the UNCITRAL Model Law (Art. 28), UNCITRAL's Uniform Arbitration Rules (Art. 33), the Washington Convention (Art. 41)] – when seen, as it were, from the angle of the arbitration court – contain the following tenets in almost identical wordings, this comparison also revealing an identical codification of the Rules of Procedure of the Arbitration Tribunal attached to the Hungarian Chamber of Commerce and Industry, including the pertinent Art. 14 on Applicable Law. So, the tenets are these: (i) the stipulation and the seat of the arbitration court do not imply stipulation of the substantive law under the *lex fori*; (ii) the arbitration court applies the substantive law stipulated by the parties; (iii) stipulation of law is to be construed as referring directly to the substantive law of a particular State rather than to its conflict norms and as consequently excluding the *renvoi*; (iv) where the parties choose no law, the arbitration court has a large freedom of action: under each of the said sources of law the arbitration court is to apply the law which it deems appropriate [Art. 23, para. (3) of ICC Rules], which it finds to be determined by the governing conflict rule in the particular case [Art. VII, para. (1) of the European Convention], which it considers applicable determined by the conflict of laws rules [Art. 28, para (2) of UNCITRAL's Model Law]. On this point the Rules of Procedure of the Hungarian Chamber of Commerce are somewhat "more limitative" as they provide for the application of the law in control under the Hungarian Code of PIL [para. (2) of Art. 14]; (v) along with the contractual stipulations, the relevant commercial usages are to be taken into account under all of the said sources of law, including Art. 14 (4) of the Hungarian Rules of Arbitration Procedure; (vi) an important provision of each of the cited instruments, contained also in the Rules of Procedure of the Hungarian Chamber of Commerce, is that the arbitrators are to decide a dispute on the bases of *ex aequo et bono* or as *amiables compositeurs* only if expressly authorized thereto by the parties [para. (3) of Art. 14] (for the related significant practice, see Loguin, Lando); (vii) finally, the tenet is obviously operative that the ways of action open to the arbitration court along the lines described above are preceded by the pertinent legal material of the binding international conventions on substantive law or of the *lex mercatoria* discussed earlier in this book (Titles 5 and 6).

(e) As a general rule, an arbitral award takes immediate and full *effect* pursuant to Art. 58 of the Arbitration Act. Under the Rules of Procedure of the Hungarian Chamber of Commerce, "the award of the Arbitration Tribunal shall be final and binding, ... the parties shall comply with it voluntarily" (Art. 46). The same general rule is contained in UNCITRAL's Model Law (Art. 35). There is no question, of course, that none of the ordinary remedies are available, for one-instance settlement is a *raison d'être* of arbitration.

Nonetheless there exist certain kinds of recourse (*exceptional remedies*) which defer final effect till the end of the process or bar it altogether. Not speaking now of the quasi natural availability of interpretation, completion and correction of awards as institutions of a technical character (see, e.g., Art. 42 of the Rules of Arbitration Procedure of the Hungarian Chamber of Commerce, Art. 33 of UNCITRAL's Model Law, Arts. 35–37 of UNCITRAL's Arbitration

Rules, Art. 51 of the Washington Convention), the major exceptional remedies are the following.

(ea) *Reversal* (*annulment*) of arbitral awards is a known remedy (see Sarcevic). As is provided for in Arts. 54–55 of the Arbitration Act, the county court or the Metropolitan Court may be requested to establish invalidity on any of the specified grounds [see item 2 (b) in §117]. In keeping with the principles of UNCITRAL's Model Law, the most important grounds expressly enumerated are these: the parties to the arbitration contract had no legal or disposing capacity; the party applying for annulment was unable to exercise his procedural rights; the arbitration court exceeded the scope of its jurisdiction; the composition of the arbitration court did not conform to the parties' agreement; the matter involved in the case was not capable of being submitted to arbitration; the award offends public policy. The forum to which an application for such remedy is to be submitted is, even under UNCITRAL's Model Law (Arts. 6 and 34), naturally determined by domestic law. As was just noted, this forum in Hungary is the county court or the Metropolitan Court of Budapest.

(eb) The institution of a new trial is also known to and regulated *expressis verbis* by the Washington Convention on the International Centre for Settlement of Investment Disputes [Art. 51; see item 4 (a) in §117].

(ec) The available remedies include *waiver of a claim for or a right to annulment* as covered by some sources of law and legal instruments. This is explicitly presumed ("if such waiver can be validly made") by the Arbitration Rules of ICC (Art. 24) and is regulated in detail by the Swiss Code of PIL (Art. 192), which states that the New York Convention on the Recognition and Enforcement of Foreign Arbitral Awards (also operative in Switzerland) is applicable, *mutatis mutandis*, to such cases, as that Convention likewise specifies, in connection with enforcement, the criteria of or grounds for annulment (see §120).

Although not covered specifically by legal regulations, waiver is also possible in Hungarian practice within the aforesaid limits, naturally "if waiver can be validly made", and the New York Convention is to be applied, *mutatis mutandis*, to such cases in Hungary as well. It is more than interesting that a few years ago, a Hungarian enterprise succeeded before the Federal (supreme) Court of Switzerland in its complaint of nullity and unconstitutionality against an award granted obviously in violation of law by a court of arbitration (with its seat in Switzerland) under the ICC Rules. In its Ruling P.1409/84 of 15 October 1984 the highest judicial forum of Switzerland sustained the Hungarian plaintiff's complaint under constitutional law and confirmed the position that in accordance with the Swiss Intercantonal Convention (Concordat) of 1969 on Arbitration the parties may not waive with legal effect the remedies specified by the Concordat. This is a *ius cogens* rule, which is not changed at all by the parties waiving in advance all remedies under the ICC Rules. The question of what would be the situation today, after the entry into force (in 1987) of the Swiss Code of PIL, which in Art. 192 allows exclusion by contract of remedies in the said manner, is a different matter, the solution certainly depending on the outcome of the competition between the two sources of law and ultimately on choice of the priority of either.

(f) The institution of *conciliation*, now also covered by positive law, is a relatively new phenomenon in the sphere of arbitration, implying peaceful settlement of disputes without litigation. The term's variants of Latin origin are used in the different legal instruments.

Conciliation has been established by three normative instruments of direct relevance to Hungary: the Arbitration Rules of ICC under the heading "Rules of Optional Conciliation" (the term "conciliation" has been omitted in our previous references for the length of the instrument's full designation); the Washington Convention on the International Centre for Settlement of Investment Disputes under the heading "Conciliation" in Chapter III, and the Rules of Procedure of the Arbitration Tribunal attached to the Hungarian Chamber of Commerce and Industry under the heading "Conciliation Procedure" (Art. 45). The three legal instruments give essentially identical regulations, which naturally show substantial differences as well. Taking the Chamber's conciliation procedure for a guide, the major elements include these: (i) What we have here is not that "the Arbitration Tribunal seeks to achieve a peaceful settlement of a dispute between the parties under an arbitration procedure", as is provided for in Art. 17. (ii) Conciliation as regulated by Art. 45 has its notional substance in that the parties first try, in a kind of choreographed order, to achieve a peaceful settlement of their dispute, with the interposition of a conciliator acting as a good catalyst, before it "degenerates" into the stage of arbitration. (iii) Conciliation is arranged for by the Arbitration Tribunal at the initiative of one of the parties (with his application transmitted to the other party). (iv) If the parties agree to the conciliation procedure, the Arbitration Tribunal designates a conciliator from the list of arbitrators. (v) The conciliator examines the dispute and invites the parties to an oral hearing, proposing a peaceful settlement. (vi) A settlement reached is entered on the conciliator. (vii) Upon application by the parties the Arbitration Tribunal may designate the conciliator as an individual arbitrator, who in this case must incorporate the settlement in an arbitral award. (viii) If no settlement is reached, the procedure is to be regarded as terminated, with the declarations made by the parties during the conciliation procedure no longer binding on them (e.g. in a future dispute submitted to arbitration). (ix) The costs of procedure are borne by the parties in the same proportion.

CHAPTER XXXVII

RECOGNITION AND ENFORCEMENT OF FOREIGN DECISIONS

§118. ON THE RECOGNITION AND ENFORCEMENT OF FOREIGN DECISIONS IN GENERAL

1. Recognition and enforcement of foreign judgments and decisions are, just as in the case of domestic judgments, *at least the "omega" of any legal dispute* before a court or other authority. A court judgment is, of course, not the only guarantee of realizing in a reasonable manner a legal relationship with international elements or of giving effect to the solution of such a relationship under domestic or international law. Most of the transactions within the ambit of private international law and of international economic relations are effected by voluntary compliance with law. The role of law in this context is that of defining the conditions, the forms of procedure and the norms of conduct that the subjects at law are expected to observe. What the law does then is that it organizes the pertinent forms of international contacts and assists in their operation. The coercive measures of the State – adoption of a decision by the court or other authority and enforcement thereof – is but the *ultima ratio*, as is the *ultima ratio regis*, the fine Latin term for the use of force in international politics. It is in this sense that recognition and enforcement of foreign judgments should be understood to be at least the omega of legal disputes before the courts. Without recognition and enforcement of foreign judgments the entire legal mechanism would become inoperative.

In addition to the general phenomenon of voluntary compliance with law, mention should be made of the high moral standards of voluntary execution of awards in legal disputes connected with international trade law. This results from economic pressure itself, for those who fail to fulfill their obligations, especially when a court order makes them liable to comply, face hardships on the international market. Yet even here there is a not insignificant number of cases of non-compliance, a reason why it is natural for coercive measures taken to enforce decisions to be institutionalized, even by permitting, where necessary, preliminary recourse to security of claims. Such security is also resorted to by Hungarian fora in the case of, e.g., mature pecuniary claims precisely in the face of a probable bankruptcy (insolvency). A Hungarian enterprise enforced such a claim before the Supreme Court (Pf. IV. 20.222/1983). A plaintiff estimated the probability that he had a mature claim for a specified amount of money from his foreign partner. The case was amenable for submission to arbitration but, as bankruptcy proceedings were being conducted against the debtor, the creditor turned to the competent ordinary court to secure his claim. Such a recourse is permitted by the Geneva Convention on Arbitration, which is also in force in Hungary, through the Hungarian enactment promulgating it. The debtor had a proven claim against another Hungarian enterprise. The claiming creditor applied for and was granted security for that claim. The current Hungarian law has devised a differentiated system of enforcing security (see Chapter X on Execution of Security Measures in Act LIII of 1994 on Judicial Enforcement).

So, where coercive measures by Hungarian fora are warranted by important practical interests as well as by pertinent laws and regulations, there is also an evident need for the other side of the matter, viz. recognition and enforcement of foreign decisions in Hungary, to be viewed in this context. This is likewise important in other cases (matters of family law, maintenance, custody and support of children), where judicial measures and their execution are more frequent than in the field of foreign trade contracts.

Clearly enough, foreign judgments and decisions cannot be regarded as matters of domestic law only. The reason is obvious, for the impossibility of enforcing, here necessary, court orders and administrative decisions would lead to bankruptcy of economic and personal transactions in the international arena. Although, as we shall see in relation to Hungary, there is considerable domestic legislation in favour of recognition and enforcement, it is not out of place to recall the significant process of international codification being conducted in this sphere (see §120).

2. Both theory and practice (and, as will be seen, the Hungarian codification) make a *distinction between recognition and enforcement of foreign judgments or decisions*. Although recognition is a prerequisite for enforcement, the latter presupposing the former, it is an important institution in itself. A large part of foreign judgments, as judgments in general, are executed without enforcement. In respect of domestic bearings this holds for foreign judgments only if their effect is also recognized in Hungary. Foreign declaratory judgments (establishment of paternity), judgments and foreign awards concerning personal status (divorce decree, adoption order, etc.), decisions concerning the liquidation of commercial companies (enterprises), that is to say, the so-called constitutive decisions effecting an essential change in legal status, are carried out on the basis of recognition, without the need for enforcement. A great number, perhaps most, of the judgments and decisions relating to property and material obligations are also executed without enforcement, usually by voluntary compliance. Further, no enforcement is needed for judgments which may arise in respect of legal cost. Recognition of such foreign judgments means that their *res judicate*

effect is recognized and accepted for the domestic aspects of the legal situation stated therein. Thus, for instance, if agreements on legal assistance provide (as they do) that a divorce decree of either country is to be recognized by both parties, then the foreign decree dissolving the marriage of the Hungarian party to the divorce case cannot be disputed in Hungary (meaning for practical purposes that he or she need not obtain another divorce decree in Hungary) and the Hungarian organs (registry offices) must recognize his/her capacity to marry in this respect. That the registry office may request the competent Hungarian authority (Ministry of Justice or other competent organ) to declare that the recognition of the judgment is in keeping with the requirements of the particular agreement on legal assistance, is quite another matter not affecting recognition.

Enforcement means more than that, however. It implies considering, in part, whether the judgment is capable of recognition under the internal law or an international agreement and, in part, whether the domestic organ applied to, will also take the necessary coercive measures for enforcement as envisaged by the domestic law or an international agreement. Action in the latter respect is clearly warranted in case of decisions which notionally call for proper measures when, for example, the obligor refuses to effect payment voluntarily. In this sense, the need for enforcement arises mostly in legal disputes involving property and other material-financial claims.

Since enforcement means the taking of coercive measures by the State, its régime of conditions differs from that of recognition. This is one of several indications that the two institutions are of a different nature. Whereas the only condition of recognition is normally the absence of exclusive jurisdiction of the domestic forum in the particular legal dispute (Art. 70 of the Code), enforcement may presuppose the existence of an international agreement or the practical application of reciprocity (Art. 74).

§119. NATIONAL REGULATION

1. The national regulation concerning the *recognition* of foreign decisions and judgments is contained in Arts. 70–73 of the Code under the heading "Recognition and Enforcement of Foreign Judgments". The main provisions may be summarized as follows.

(a) The general rule is this: "Unless otherwise provided by this Law-Decree, the decision of a foreign court or other authority *shall be recognized* in cases not subject to the exclusive jurisdiction of the Hungarian court or other authority" (Art. 70, para. 1), meaning that in matters subject to the exclusive jurisdiction of a Hungarian forum (as noted earlier in §113), foreign judgments cannot be recognized in Hungary. This is not to say, of course, that such judgments are not effective abroad, but that in respect of their Hungarian aspects they are regarded as irrelevant under the Code.

In situations such as this the only avenue generally open to achieving the purposes sought in respect of the Hungarian aspects, is for the parties to institute another set of proceedings in Hungary, where the judgment so pronounced will be deemed to be effective.

As can be seen, the cited provision does not specifically refer to settlement, which should nonetheless be regarded as a decision as a matter of course, since under Art. 148 (3) of the Code of Civil Procedure a settlement approved by the court has the same effect as a court order, whereas recognition is governed by the *lex fori*, i.e. the Hungarian law, which similarly determines what is to be considered a decision or an administrative act covered by the notion of decision.

(b) Considering that exclusive jurisdiction may produce such two-way solutions (a foreign and a domestic judgment) and that the growing volume of international transactions serves to reinforce the tendency for possible legal simplification, the majority of countries extend *recognition to foreign decisions and judgments in several categories of cases which the law would, in principle, refer to domestic jurisdiction.* The number and significance of exceptions to the general rule tend to increase, as is also reflected in the Hungarian Code, which states, in para. (2) of Art. 70, that, with the specified conditions prevailing, foreign judgments passed in cases subject to exclusive Hungarian jurisdiction may also be recognized in Hungary. A specification follows in Arts. 71 *et seq.*

(ba) It is with respect to personal status that Art. 71 provides for the recognition of a decision (i) passed in a divorce case of a Hungarian national domiciled abroad, naturally also in the event that only one of the spouses is domiciled in a foreign country (see §100), (ii) placing a Hungarian national domiciled abroad under curatorship or terminating such curatorship, (iii) by which a foreign court or other authority authorized, approved or terminated the adoption of a Hungarian national, provided that the adoptive parent is a foreign national and the adoption was approved by the Hungarian guardianship authority.

(bb) Recognition is likewise to be granted to a decision passed by a foreign court or other authority in a proceeding instituted abroad by or against the *Hungarian State* or a Hungarian national acting abroad as a diplomatic representative or otherwise enjoying immunity from foreign jurisdiction, provided that the Hungarian State has expressly waived immunity or the foreign court or other authority may also proceed by virtue of an international agreement or of reciprocity. In case of recognition of a decision, the judgment rendered by a foreign court or other authority in a counterclaim arising from the same legal relationship must also be recognized. However, the enforcement of a decision passed in such an action is subject to a separate express waiver by the Hungarian State of immunity from enforcement. As can be seen, these rules, too, reflect an aspect of immunity, which was given full treatment in §§35–37 under Chapter X of this book.

(c) Nevertheless, under Art. 73 of the Code, *decisions recognizable in accordance with the foregoing must be denied recognition* in cases where "(a) recognition would violate Hungarian public policy; (b) the foreign court or other authority proceeded against the person involved on a ground of jurisdiction which, under the law of the foreign State, cannot be invoked against its own nationals (legal persons) either; (c) the person against whom the decision or judgment was passed had not participated in the proceedings, either personally or through his representative, because of some irregularity in the conduct of the proceedings or because the summons had not been served on him at his place of residence (seat) in Hungary or on his agent named by him at the place of the proceedings; (d) with respect to the same right based on the same facts, a Hungarian court or other authority has already passed a final decision on the merits of the same case involving the same parties; (e) prior to the institution of the foreign proceedings, proceedings had been instituted before a Hungarian court or other authority in a case of the same parties concerning the same right based on the same facts".

2. The main provisions concerning the *enforcement* of foreign decisions and judgments are contained in the Code of Private International Law, Act LIII of 1994 on Judicial Enforcement, and Act LXXI of 1994 on Arbitration.

Now, what is expressed in the Code of PIL? In fact, the Code lays down clearly defined conditions for enforcement, as is also stated in the motivation to the Code, Art. 74 of which reads: "Final decisions passed by a foreign court or other authority in matters relating to claims under property law and under the law of other material obligations or to the custody of children shall be enforced by virtue of an international treaty or of reciprocity"; and para. (3) extends this provision contained in the Act on Judicial Enforcement: "Foreign court orders and arbitral awards may be enforced by virtue of a provision of law, an international treaty or of reciprocity" (Art. 205). These regulations make clear that foreign decisions cannot be enforced in Hungary without the presence of a further procedural element, by reliance on which Hungarian law follows general international practice. However, this does not mean that Hungarian law attaches no importance to the enforcement of foreign decisions in Hungary. There is no need to refer to material reasons here; they were discussed earlier. And as to the conditions, they are determined by the provisions quoted above. Accordingly, with those conditions prevailing, the Hungarian State and its authorities resort, where appropriate, to coercive measures, without any formal proceedings, in order to give effect to the legal settlement awarded under substantive law, notably, (a) a decision must settle a claim under property law and the law of other material obligations, the only exception to legal disputes other than such claims being provided by decisions concerning the custody of children (although the cited article of the Judicial Enforcement Act establishes no such restriction, it is stated in Art. 210 that enforcement of foreign decisions is also subject to "separate provisions of law", such law being the Code, which is expressly referred to in the aforesaid motivation to Art. 113 of the former Judicial Enforcement Law (Law-Decree No. 18 of 1979); (b) a decision must be recognizable and (c) final; (d) the ordering and effecting of enforcement must be prescribed by an international agreement with the State of the foreign court rendering the decisions; or (e) failing an international agreement, reciprocity must be declared by the Hungarian Minister of Justice to be prevailing in respect to the enforcement of decisions (as para. 2 of Art. 74 requires the existence of reciprocity instead of its presumption, the text reading: "...On the existence of reciprocity the Minister of Justice shall issue a declaration binding upon the courts and other authorities."). The other sentence of this same paragraph, which reads: "No enforcement shall lie, even in case of reciprocity, where the judgment of a foreign court or other authority is incapable of recognition on some ground specified by this Law-Decree", amounts in effect to "overinsurance", since, evidently, the enforcement of non-recognizable decisions is notionally excluded, as was mentioned in connection with recognition.

§120. INTERNATIONAL TREATIES

1. Among the *multilateral international treaties* reference should be made to several conventions.

(a) As was seen (§117), international arbitration is a very frequent recourse in foreign trade transactions and is therefore equally associated with the concepts of recognition and enforcement. This area is covered by the *New York Convention on the Recognition and Enforcement of Foreign Arbitral Awards*, which was promulgated in Hungary by Law-Decree No. 25 of 1962. The main provisions of the Convention are these: (i) all Contracting States recognize the right of the parties to arbitration; (ii) all Contracting States are to recognize arbitral awards as binding and to enforce them in accordance with the rules of procedure applicable in the territory where recognition and enforcement are sought (Art. III); (iii) the various grounds on which recognition and enforcement of a foreign award may be denied essentially coincide with those for exceptional remedies [available for application for establishment of invalidity; see item 6 (e) in §117] and include lack of disposing capacity; invalidity of the arbitration agreement; failure to give notice of the proceedings for the appointment of the arbitrator; rendering of an award on matters not falling within the terms of submission to arbitration; non-conformity of the composition or procedure of the arbitral tribunal with the agreement of the parties; pleading of circumstances to the effect that the arbitral award has not yet become binding on the parties, or the award was annulled or its enforcement suspended by the competent authority, under the law, of the State in which the award has been made; the object of the dispute is incapable of submission to arbitration; recognition or enforcement of the award would offend the public policy of the country in which it is applied for (Art. V).

A case which was before four fora on the ground of the validity or invalidity of an arbitration agreement (for the practice concerning the application of the New York Convention see the respective chapters in the volumes of *Yearbook of Commercial Arbitration*) is well illustrative of how important an oft-emerging problem is. Considered by two lower courts of Austria, an objection to the enforcement in Austria of an award granted by the Arbitration Court of Belgrade (attached to the Yugoslav Chamber of Commerce) caused the dispute to be brought before the Supreme Court of Austria. There the party against whom the award was to be enforced pleaded that enforcement was to be denied by virtue of Art. V of the New York Convention on the ground of the invalidity of the arbitration agreement because it contained, along with the clear stipulation of the said arbitration forum of Belgrade, a clause to the effect that "the next forum ("*Instanz*") for the settlement of disputes is the competent court of international law", a stage which the case had not reached by that time, so the award had as of that moment no legal force. The Supreme Court upheld the decisions of the lower courts and declared the arbitration agreement to be valid because the stipulation of the arbitration court of Belgrade was unambiguous, only the reference to the next forum being vague, but that was irrelevant as it did not affect the validity and enforceability of the award rendered by the clearly stipulated arbitration court (*IPRax* 1989, Heft 5, pp. 302–303).

(b) A significant role was played in the past (and may still be played until the expiration of the relevant treaties of an older date) by the CMEA (COMECON) Arbitration Agreement of 1973 (promulgated in Hungary by Law-Decree No. 23 of 1973), which regulated arbitration of legal disputes between enterprises of the member-states and stated that arbitral awards "shall be deemed recognized without further proceedings" and be enforceable in the same manner as domestic judgments are enforced. Such awards may continue to be rendered in accordance with the Rules of Procedure of the Arbitration Tribunal attached to the Hungarian Chamber of Commerce and Industry (p. 6).

(c) Mutual enforcement of awards in the sphere of international economic transactions is also required by Art. 52 of the *Berne Convention* of 1970 on the Carriage of Goods, Persons and Luggage by Rail, as it was promulgated in Hungary by Law-Decree No. 9 of 1975.

(d) Mention is deserved of the *Hague Convention on Civil Procedure* [see item 4 (b) in §115), which was promulgated in Hungary by Law-Decree No. 8 of 1966. Most of the rules in this multilateral treaty provide for the recognition and enforcement of decisions against the defending party with respect to the costs of litigation. On application made through diplomatic channels, the competent authorities of the Contracting States declare the costs of litigation to be capable of enforcement without charge and order the execution of enforcement.

(e) We should also refer to the *Hague Convention concerning Maintenance Obligations Towards Children* (promulgated in Hungary by Law-Decree No. 7 of 1965), which seeks to ensure mutual recognition and enforcement in the Contracting States of judgments which, on international or domestic application, were passed in respect of claims for maintenance for children who are under 21 years of age, whether born in or out of wedlock, or have been adopted and are unmarried. Such judgments may or must be recognized and enforced in the Contracting States without a review procedure on their merits, if (i) the authority passing the decision was, under the Convention, competent to render the decision; (ii) the summons conformed to the requirements; (iii) the decision is final; (iv) the matter involved is not *res judicata*; and (v) the decision is not contrary to the public policy of the State in which it is to be relied upon.

There is no need to emphasize the particular importance of this multilateral Convention in view of the growing volume of international personal transactions. This explains the accession to it by so many countries, including Hungary (cf. §96). It is easy to realize without any documentary evidence adduced, that our judicial practice handles a considerable volume of cases in this category.

(f) Finally, mention should be made of the *Hague Convention* concerning the unlawful taking of children abroad, which covers civil-law aspects and was promulgated in Hungary by Law-Decree No. 14 of 1986. The Convention assumes that judicial decisions concerning the custody of or parental supervision over children will be mutually recognized and enforced by the States parties without a review procedure on their merits by ordering the return of children unlawfully taken or withheld abroad. It was on this basis that the Metropolitan Court of Budapest upheld the order of the court of first instance to take the child back to France without delay, the country from where the mother, owing to the problems of her ruined marriage, had brought the child to Hungary in defiance of the order of the court of Neuilly-sur-Seine (50.Pf.24.548/1988–3, BH No. 6 of 1989:233).

2. The recognition and enforcement of foreign judgments and administrative decisions are also regulated by numerous *bilateral* agreements.

(a) The first to mention are the *agreements on legal assistance*. Hungary's agreements regulate in detail the conditions for the mutual recognition and enforcement of decisions under property law and the law of other material obligations. While considerably differing in wording and in some aspects of substance, they are in accord on one point, namely in stating that decisions passed on matters of civil and family law are capable of recognition and enforcement without a review procedure on their merits. Such provision is contained in, e.g., Art. 45 of the Romanian–Hungarian Agreement on Legal Assistance (promulgated in Hungary by Law-Decree No. 19 of 1959). The Metropolitan Court of Budapest invoked that provision in overturning, in appellate procedure, the judgment of the court of first instance in which the court contested the tie of kindred between the plaintiff and the testator and thereby the right of the former to contest the oral will. The decision of second instance was based on the fact that the tie of kindred had been stated in the final judgment of the competent Romanian court, as the case involved Romanian nationals, and that judgment had to be recognized by virtue of the above Agreement (*Fővárosi Bíróság*, 44.Pf. 23605/1983). In relation to some countries, however, resort is also had to a kind of review procedure on the merits of certain cases: a judgment concerning personal status is recognizable only if it is not contrary to the domestic law of the country in which recognition is sought (on this subject theme, see Martiny, Várady). Enforcement is normally subject to the law of the State of the organ ordering it. The Agreements extensively cover the procedure for ordering enforcement (e.g. the documents to be enclosed with the application), the objections that may be raised to enforcement, and the exceptional cases in which recognition and enforcement of a foreign court judgment may be denied. Such cases, already known in connection with the exceptional remedies against arbitral awards [see item 6 (e) in §117] include these: the judgment is not final, the debtor failed to participate in the proceedings through no fault of his own, *res judicata*, etc.

From the 1980s onwards Hungary has signed agreements on legal assistance with ever more countries, including member-states of the European Community. These agreements uphold the philosophy guiding the content of earlier ones: they formulate essentially the same principles governing the recognition and enforcement of ordinary court decisions and arbitral awards [see, e.g., Arts. 21–26 of the French–Hungarian Agreement by Law-Decree No. 3 of 1982: Arts. 24–28 of the Greek–Hungarian Agreement on Legal Assistance (promulgated in Hungary by Law-Decree No. 21 of 1981)].

(b) Other bilateral agreements regulate the enforcement of decisions concerning payment of the costs of procedure, of decisions passed and settlements reached in probate proceedings, and of decisions pronounced in other legal disputes. (Hungary has concluded such bilateral agreements with several countries.)

3. As for the perspectives, it is worth making a brief inquiry into the legal instruments which, though Hungary is not a party to them, *form part of the legal infrastructure of the advanced countries, including the European Communities*, notably into those to which Hungary has to adjust its regulations with a view to catching up with Europe (for details see Mádl: *Ius Commune Europae*).

(a) The more distant perspective may be presented by the *1968 Brussels Convention of the European Communities on Jurisdiction and the Enforcement of Judgments in Civil and Commercial Matters*. Its importance with respect to jurisdiction was discussed under item 5 (e) of §113. No lengthy explanation is needed to highlight the significance of a uniform European system of norms governing the recognition and enforcement of judgments. The Convention has consolidated the laws of 12 – now 15 – countries into a single system, which has become an important factor of consummating European unity. It represents an unparallelled development in this field of law, all the more so since it is both comprehensive and exhaustive, thus being a Convention functioning with an operative norm potential. Its uniform character is also protected against phenomena of disintegration by the fact that the Luxembourg Court of Justice of the European Communities was vested with jurisdiction to interpret the Convention in accordance with the Protocol thereto.

Instead of continuing with a general appraisal and analysis of the Convention (on related details see Lasok–Stone) we will refer to its main elements embodied in over 100 articles, including those contained in the Annexes: court judgments of all member-states must, on application by the interested party, be recognized in the EC without a review procedure on their merits (Art. 26); recognition may be denied on the known grounds (public policy, *res judicata*, errors of representation in the basic procedure, etc.: Art. 27); on application by the interested party, the appropriate court of member-states is to order enforcement if the judgment was enforceable in the State where it was pronounced (Arts. 31–32); proceedings are subject to the law of the State of enforcement (Art. 33); the party against whom enforcement is sought may, under a procedure regulated by the Convention, appeal against the decision ordering enforcement (Art. 36); other provisions cover application and the documents to accompany it, the relationship of the Convention to the bilateral agreements of member-states (in fact, the former's priority) and other matters relating to the scope of application of the Convention.

(b) A nearer reality for Hungary is represented by the *Lugano Convention on Jurisdiction and the Enforcement of Judgments in Civil and Commercial Matters* concluded between the EC and EFTA member-states in September 1988 [see item 5 (f) in §113]. This Convention is equally applicable in respect of recognition and enforcement as in respect of jurisdiction. Its provisions on recognition and enforcement are similar to or identical with those of the Brussels Convention as was outlined above, so, with regard to their substance, we can refer to the said elements of the Brussels Convention.

(c) The relevant *Hague Conventions* appear in a shorter-term perspective. One of them is the *Convention of 1965 on the Recognition of Decisions concerning Adoption*. Though in force, it has so far only been acceded to by a few countries. By contrast, nearly 20 countries, chiefly in Europe, have acceded to the *Convention of 1970 on the Recognition and Enforcement of Divorce Decrees and Decisions Recognizing Separation.*

Of particular relevance is the *Convention of 1971* (with the Protocol thereto) *on the Recognition and Enforcement of Foreign Judgments in Civil and Commercial Matters*, because it embraces almost the whole spectrum of judgments indicated in its designation (with the exceptions expressly enumerated in Art. 1) and forms a synthesis of international and national legislative experiences and solutions as well as of the considerations of legal science in favour of their harmonization. This Convention is also in force, although with few accessions since the EU countries have created their own legal infrastructure in the EC Convention discussed in subitem (a) above. For non-member-states, however, it may be the path to harmonization. In terms of object the Convention comprises all essential elements of recognition and enforcement, those covered by the aforesaid legal instruments, including the EC Convention and, *inter alia*, Hungary's bilateral agreements on legal assistance.

The "shorter-term perspective" in regard to the Hague Conventions is offered by the fact that accession to them is open to Hungary as well without further consideration. Hungary is a member of the Hague Conference, has participated and participates in the elaboration of the European infrastructure and those of a more general nature which are already completed or in the process of completion, and has also received repeated invitations to accede. All these areas are of importance to our catching up with Europe. As is indicated by this entire review, our positions taken in our agreements are not, in principle, contrary to the said endeavour, but out accession could also authentically serve, by the international and foreign legislative regulations, our desirable purpose of catching up with Europe as well as our national practical interests. The *ius commune* is within reach in this respect (see Mádl: *Ius Commune Europae*). So is, of course, conclusion by Hungary of a series of bilateral agreements with different countries. One should be aware, however, that ever since the Hague Convention of 1971 was elaborated by the Hague Conference and entered into force, the bilateral agreements of the advanced Western countries essentially coincide with the Hague Convention, most of them even in identical wording.

§121. ENFORCEMENT IN HUNGARY

1. The enforcement of foreign judgments and decisions, once admitted in the cases as discussed in §§119 and 120, will be carried out according to the relevant rules of Hungarian law. The *general rules* are contained in the Judicial Enforcement Act, the Arbitration Act, and the Code of Private International Law providing as follows: (a) the procedure for enforcement is governed by Hungarian law except where otherwise provided by law or an international treaty (Art. 63 of the Code; Arts. 1, 208 and 210 of the Judicial Enforcement Act); (b) the application for enforcement must be accompanied by the foreign decision to be enforced and, at the instance of the court (definitely in the case of an arbitral award) by a Hungarian translation thereof (Art. 207 of the Judicial Enforcement Act; Art. 60 of the Arbitration Act); (c) the local court of competence by the debtor's domicile (seat) or, failing it, by the place of his distrainable assets of property, and in the case of an arbitral award the county court (the Metropolitan Court of Budapest) writes its enforcement order on the enforceable foreign decision [see item 2 in §119, item (a) in §120, Art. 206 of the Judicial Enforcement Act]. Thereby it certifies that the decision is enforceable under Hungarian law in the same manner as a judgment of a domestic court (or an award of a domestic arbitration court) (Art. 208); (d) once the order of enforcement passed has become final, the court issues a warrant or a writ of execution treated as such on the basis of the foreign decision certified by the enforcement order in the said manner (Art. 209). In other aspects, enforcement follows its normal course under the domestic law (see Vida–Balogh; Hegedűs–Loibl); (e) although covered by the foregoing [see item 2 (b) in §119 and item 1 (a) in §120], it is stated in the Arbitration Act that an arbitral award has the same effect as a final court judgment and its enforcement is subject to the rules of judicial enforcement; the court may deny the enforcement of an arbitral award if it holds that the object of the dispute is incapable of arbitration under

Hungarian law, or the award offends Hungarian public policy (Arts. 58–59 of Act LXXI of 1994).

2. As concerns the requirements of the foreign exchange law for the enforcement of judgments relating to claims, largely pecuniary, under property law and the law of other material obligations, Act XCV of 1995 on Foreign Exchange has lifted the earlier restrictions, practically introducing the convertibility of the forint with respect to current payment operations in this field as well. Payments by domestic residents to aliens under the Foreign Exchange Act, to be made by virtue of final court decisions either voluntarily or pursuant to a procedure for enforcement, are deemed to be a legal ground as indicated in para. 41 entitled "Other Unsatisfied Current Transfers" among the current payment operations covered by Annex I, which was inserted by Government Decree No. 222/1996. (XII.26.) in execution of Act XCV of 1995, and as such they are not subject to any restriction.

3. Although the aforementioned mechanisms (conventions, bilateral agreements, and enactments) for the recognition and enforcement of foreign judgments and decisions relate to the possibilities for the *recognition and enforcement abroad of Hungarian judgments* as well, it appears justified to make the following brief statements in general.

(a) The legal conditions for the recognition and enforcement abroad of Hungarian judgments and decisions are governed by the bilateral or multilateral treaties in force and the domestic law of the foreign State concerned (including, e.g., its practice of reciprocity).

(b) Applications for enforcement can be transmitted through the Hungarian courts under the pertinent interstate agreement on international legal assistance (see §116) in relation to countries with which Hungary has signed such agreements.

(c) The actual procedure for enforcement will then be subject to the internal law rules of the particular State.

APPENDIX

LAW-DECREE No. 13 OF 1979 ON PRIVATE INTERNATIONAL LAW

CHAPTER I

GENERAL RULES

PURPOSE AND OPERATION OF THE LAW-DECREE

Art. 1. The purpose of this Law-Decree is to determine, with a view to development of peaceful international relations,

– the law of the State which shall apply to civil, family or labour relations involving a foreign person, property or law (hereinafter referred to as a foreign element) and are subject to the control of the law of several States;

– the jurisdictional and procedural rules which shall govern a legal dispute containing a foreign element.

Art. 2. This Law-Decree shall not apply to matters governed by international treaty.

LEGAL CHARACTERIZATION

Art. 3. (1) Any dispute arising in an action as to the legal characterization of facts or relationships affecting the determination of applicable law shall be resolved by interpretation of the rules and concepts of Hungarian law.

(2) If a legal institution is unknown to Hungarian law, or is known with a different content or by a different name, and cannot be defined by interpreting the rules of Hungarian law, the foreign law governing the legal institution shall also be consulted for the purposes of characterization.

RENVOI

Art. 4. Where this Law-Decree ordains the application of foreign law, the adjudication of the case shall be subject to the directly controlling rules of the applicable foreign law. If, however, the foreign law refers back to Hungarian law, the particular matter shall, by virtue of such reference, be decided under Hungarian law.

DETERMINATION OF THE CONTENT OF FOREIGN LAW

Art. 5. (1) The court or other authority shall ascertain *ex officio* the foreign law unfamiliar to it and, where necessary, shall obtain expert opinion, and it may also consider evidence of foreign law submitted by the parties.

(2) The Minister of Justice shall, upon inquiry by the court or other authority, furnish information about the foreign law.

(3) If the content of foreign law cannot be ascertained, Hungarian law shall apply.

RECIPROCITY

Art. 6. (1) Unless otherwise provided by law, the application of foreign law shall not depend upon reciprocity.

(2) If a rule of law makes the application of foreign law subject to reciprocity, the existence of reciprocity shall be presumed until the contrary is proved. In cases where law requires the proof of reciprocity, the Minister of Justice shall give a declaration to that effect, such declaration to be binding upon the court or other authority.

NON-APPLICATION OF FOREIGN LAW

Art. 7. (1) The application of foreign law shall be disregarded where it would violate Hungarian public policy.

(2) The application of foreign law shall not be disregarded solely on the ground that the socio-economic system of a particular foreign State differs from that of Hungary.

(3) Hungarian law shall be applied instead of the disregarded foreign law.

Art. 8. (1) The foreign law shall not be applied where a foreign element is artificially or fraudulently created by the parties (fraud), with a view to avoiding the otherwise applicable law.

(2) In the event of fraud (fraud *à la loi*), the controlling law shall be that which is otherwise applicable under this Law-Decree.

Art. 9. If the parties request, by agreement, to disregard the foreign law applicable under this Law-Decree, the governing law shall be Hungarian law or, in choice-of-law situations, the law selected by the parties.

CHAPTER II

PERSONS

MAN AS A SUBJECT AT LAW

Art. 10. (1) The legal capacity, disposing capacity, personal status in general and personal rights of the individual shall be governed by his/her personal law.

(2) Claims arising from the infringement of personal rights shall be decided under the law of the place and time of the injury; if, however, Hungarian law provides more favourable compensation for the person injured, the claim shall be judged according to Hungarian law.

Art. 11. (1) The personal law of the individual shall be the law of the State of which he is a national. A change in nationality shall affect neither the former personal status nor the rights and obligations created pursuant to it.

(2) If an individual has several nationalities, one of which is Hungarian, his personal law shall be Hungarian law.

(3) The personal law of individuals having several nationalities, none of which is Hungarian, as well as of stateless persons shall be the law of the State of their domicile or, if they are also domiciled in Hungary, Hungarian law. With respect to such individuals having several foreign domiciles, the personal law shall be the law of the State with which they have the closest relationship.

(4) Where the personal law of an individual cannot be determined according to the provisions of the preceding paragraphs and such person has no domicile, his personal law shall be the law of the place of his habitual residence. If one of his habitual residences is in Hungary, his personal law shall be Hungarian law.

Art. 12. (1) Domicile is the place where an individual resides permanently or with the intent to settle.

(2) Habitual residence is the place where an individual lives for an extended period of time without the intent to settle.

Art. 13. The personal status of an individual enjoying asylum in Hungary shall be governed by Hungarian law. This provision shall affect neither his former personal status nor his rights and obligations created pursuant to it.

Art. 14. (1) The economic, producing or commercial activity (hereinafter referred to as economic status) of a private person shall be governed by the law of the State in which the licence for such economic activity was granted.

(2) If no licence for economic activity is required or such licence was granted in several countries, the economic status of a private person shall be controlled by the law of the State in which he has his business headquarters.

Art. 15. (1) Unless otherwise provided by law, the legal capacity, disposing capacity, personal and other rights under property law and the law of obligations as well as the obligations of foreign nationals and stateless persons shall be governed by the same law as is applicable to Hungarian nationals.

(2) A foreign national who, under his personal law, has limited or no disposing capacity shall be considered capable of action in respect of economic transactions effected for the purpose of meeting the usual needs of everyday life, provided he would have disposing capacity under Hungarian law.

(3) A foreign national who, under his personal law, has limited or no disposing capacity, but would have disposing capacity under Hungarian law, shall be considered to have disposing capacity also in respect of other economic transactions, provided that the legal consequences of his transactions are destined to occur in Hungary.

Art. 16. (1) Declaration of death or disappearance and proof of death shall be subject to the last personal law of a missing person.

(2) Hungarian law shall apply in cases where, on behalf of a domestic legal interest, the Hungarian court declares a non-Hungarian national to be dead or missing, or determines the proof of death of such person.

THE STATE AS A SUBJECT AT LAW

Art. 17. (1) Within the ambit of this Law-Decree, the legal relationships of the Hungarian State shall be governed by its own law, except where:

(a) the State has expressly consented to the application of foreign law; or

(b) the legal relationship concerns foreign real property owned or intended to be acquired by the State; or

(c) the legal relationship concerns participation in an economic organization involving foreign interests.

(2) Paragraph (1) shall not apply to a foreign State except in case of reciprocity.

LEGAL PERSONS

Art. 18. (1) The legal capacity, economic status and personal rights of a legal person as well as the relationships *inter se* of its members shall be governed by its personal law.

(2) The personal law of a legal person shall be the law of the State in whose territory the legal person was incorporated.

(3) If a legal person was incorporated according to the law of several States, or if incorporation is not required by the controlling law of its seat as stated in its charter, the personal law shall be the law of the seat so stated in the charter.

(4) If, according to its charter, the legal person has no seat, or has several seats but was not incorporated under the law of either State, its personal law shall be the law of the State in whose territory its central management is located.

(5) The personal law of a separately incorporated branch or subsidiary of the legal person shall be the law of the incorporating State of such branch or subsidiary.

CHAPTER III

LAW OF INTELLECTUAL PROPERTY

COPYRIGHTS

Art. 19. Copyrights shall be governed by the law of the State in whose territory protection is claimed.

INDUSTRIAL PROPERTY RIGHTS

Art. 20. (1) An inventor and his successor in title shall be granted protection under the law and in the territory of the State in which the patent was issued or the patent application was filed.

(2) The provision of paragraph (1) shall apply, *mutatis mutandis*, to other industrial property rights (protection of industrial designs, trademarks, etc.) as well.

CHAPTER IV

PROPERTY LAW AND RELATED RIGHTS

Art. 21. (1) Unless otherwise provided by this Law-Decree, property rights and other rights *in rem* as well as mortgage and possession shall be governed by the law of the place where the property is situate.

(2) The governing law of the place where the property is situate shall be the law of the State where the property is located at the time of the occurrence of the legally relevant fact.

Art. 22. (1) Prescription of movable property shall be subject to the law of the State in whose territory the property was located at the expiration of the period of prescription.

(2) A change in the place where the property is situate shall not by itself interrupt the period of prescription.

Art. 23. (1) The creation, existence and termination of property rights relating to registered vessels or aircraft shall be controlled by the law of the State under whose flag or other insignia the vehicle is operating.

(2) Property rights relating to goods under transportation shall be controlled by the law of the State of destination. However, the property-law effects of forced sale, storage or mortgage of such property shall be subject to the controlling law of the place where the property is situate.

(3) Property rights relating to the personal effects of a passenger carried with him shall be subject to his personal law.

(4) If enterprise (business) assets devolve as a whole upon the successor in title, the property-law changes shall, with the exception of such changes concerning immovable property, be under the control of the personal law of the predecessor in title.

(5) If rights of ownership in a thing are transferred by a court order or by way of execution, acquisition of property shall be governed by the law of the State whose court issues the order or whose authority proceeds in the matter of execution.

CHAPTER V

LAW OF OBLIGATIONS

CONTRACTS

Art. 24. The law chosen by the parties at the time of contracting or later shall be applied to their contract. In the absence of such a stipulation of law, the law applicable to the various types of contracts shall be determined in accordance with Arts. 25 to 29 of this Chapter.

Art. 25. The applicable law of contracts shall be the law of the State in which, at the time of contracting –

(a) the seller, with respect to contracts of sale;

(b) the lessor, with respect to contracts of lease and tenancy;

(c) the licensee, with respect to contracts for the exploitation of rights under copyright protection;

(d) the licensor, with respect to contracts for the exploitation of industrial property rights and other rights representing material value;

(e) the bailee, with respect to contracts of deposit (storage);

(f) the agent with respect to contracts of agency;

(g) the commission agent (consignee), with respect to contracts of commission;

(h) the representative (agent), with respect to contracts of commercial representation;

(i) the carrier or the forwarding agent, with respect to contracts of carriage or forwarding;

(j) the bank or credit institution rendering service, with respect to contracts for banking and credit transactions;

(k) the insurer, with respect to insurance contracts;

(l) the lender, with respect to contracts for the use of money and contracts for the use of goods;

(m) the donor, with respect to contracts concerning gifts,

– has his domicile or habitual residence, or seat or business headquarters.

Art. 26. (1) Contracts concerning immovables shall be governed by the *lex situs* of immovables, whereas contracts concerning registered vessels or aircraft shall be governed by the law of the State under whose flag or other insignia the vehicle is operating.

(2) Contracts of *locatio conductio operis* (designing, installation, work for hire, etc.) shall be subject to the law of the State in whose territory the activities of the undertaking shall be performed or the results shall be accomplished under the terms of the contract.

(3) Contracts for support and for life annuities shall be under the control of the law of the State in whose territory the corresponding services shall be rendered.

Art. 27. (1) Contracts concluded through stock exchange, competitive bidding or auction shall be governed by the law of the State in whose territory the stock exchange is located, or the competitive bidding or the auction takes place.

(2) Company contracts shall be subject to the law of the State in whose territory the company is operating. Company contracts constitutive of legal persons shall be governed by the personal law of the legal person.

Art. 28. (1) The existence and extent of an obligation deriving from securities shall be subject to the law applicable at the place of performance.

(2) The creation, transfer, termination and enforcement of contractual rights and obligations involving bonds issued as loans to the public shall be governed by the personal law of the issuer.

(3) If a security involves a right to dispose of merchandise, the ensuing property-law effects shall be governed by the provisions of this Law-Decree concerning property-law relationships.

(4) If a security involves membership rights, the creation, transfer, termination and enforcement of rights and obligations deriving from such security shall be governed by the personal law of the legal person concerned.

Art. 28/A (1) The laws of the country in which the consumer has his domicile or habitual residence shall apply to a consumer contract provided that:

(a) in that country the conclusion of the contract was preceded by a specific invitation addressed to him or by advertising, and he had taken in that country all the steps necessary on his part for the conclusion of the contract; or

(b) the other party or his agent received the consumer's order in that country; or

(c) the contract is for the sale of goods and the consumer travelled from that country to another country and there gave his order, provided that the consumer's journey was arranged by the seller for the purpose of inducing the consumer to buy.

(2) In the application of this Article, a consumer contract is a contract directed at the supply of goods or services or a contract for the provision of credit

or loan for that object, concluded with a person for a purpose which can be regarded as being outside of his trade or profession.

(3) The provisions of paragraphs (1)–(2) shall not apply to:

(a) a contract for the carriage of goods or persons;

(b) a contract for the supply of services where the services are to be supplied to the consumer exclusively in a country other than that in which he has his domicile or habitual residence; notwithstanding this provision, this Article shall apply to a contract which, for an inclusive price, provides for a combination of travel and accommodation.[1]

Art. 29. If the applicable law cannot be determined within the framework of Arts. 24 to 28, contracts shall be governed by the law of the domicile, habitual residence or business headquarters (place of business) of the obligor of the most characteristic performance. The law most closely connected with the essential elements of the particular contractual relationship shall apply in cases were the applicable law cannot be determined in the aforesaid way either.

Art. 30. (1) The governing law of contracts extends to all elements of the contractual relationship, particularly to the formation of the contract, its material and formal validity, its effects under the law of obligations and, unless otherwise agreed by the parties or otherwise mandated by this Law-Decree, to any agreement securing the contract (mortgage, suretyship, etc.) as well as to any set off, assignment and assumption of claims related to the contract.

(2) Unless otherwise agreed upon between the parties, the existence of the obligee's duty to inspect the performance stipulated by the contract, the method of inspection, the time-limit for complaints and the legal effects of all these elements shall be governed by the law of the place of destination, or delivery.

(3) A contract which is formally invalid under its governing law (Arts. 24 to 29) shall be considered by the court to be valid, provided that it is valid under the law of the State in which it was made or the intended legal effects shall occur.

(4) The statute of limitation for a claim shall be governed by the law otherwise applicable to the claim.

Art. 31. Unless otherwise provided by this Law-Decree, unilateral declarations shall be subject, *mutatis mutandis,* to the rules for contracts.

LIABILITY FOR NON-CONTRACTUAL DAMAGE; UNJUST ENRICHMENT

Art. 32. (1) Unless otherwise mandated by this Law-Decree, liability for non-contractual damage shall be subject to the law prevailing at the time and place of the tortious act or omission.

(2) If it is more favourable to the injured party, the governing law shall be of the State in which the damage occurred.

---

[1] Introduced by Art. 11(3)(c) of Act CXLIX of 1997

(3) If the tortfeasor and the injured party are domiciled in the same State, the applicable law shall be that of the State concerned.

(4) If, under the law of the place of the tortious act or omission, liability is subject to fault, the existence of culpability may be determined either by the personal law of the tortfeasor or by the law of the place of tortious act.

Art. 33. (1) Whether the tortious conduct consisted in violation of traffic or other safety regulations shall be determined according to the law of the place of the tortious conduct.

(2) If the tortious act or omission occurred on a registered vessel or aircraft, the infliction of damage and its consequences outside of national jurisdiction shall be governed by the law of the State under whose flag or other insignia the vehicle was operating at the time of injury.

Art. 34. (1) A Hungarian court shall not establish liability for conduct not considered unlawful under Hungarian law.

(2) A Hungarian court shall not, on the ground of liability for damage, establish legal consequences unknown to Hungarian law.

Art. 35. Unjust enrichment and its legal consequences shall be governed by the law of the State in which the enrichment occurred.

CHAPTER VI

LAW OF INHERITANCE

Art. 36. (1) Inheritance relations shall be subject to the personal law of the deceased person at the time of death. This law shall also govern the extent to which acquisition of an estate and disposition of an expected estate shall be admissible.

(2) To testamentary dispositions, the last personal law of the testator shall apply. A testamentary disposition and its revocation shall be formally valid if they satisfy the requirements of Hungarian law, or

(a) the law in effect at the time and place of making or revocation; or

(b) the personal law of the testator at the time of making or revocation, or of his death; or

(c) the law in effect at the testator's domicile or habitual residence at the time of making or revocation, or of his death; or

(d) the law of the *situs* of immovables in the case of testamentary dispositions of such property.

CHAPTER VII

FAMILY LAW

MARRIAGE AND ITS VALIDITY

Art. 37. (1) The substantive requirements of a valid marriage shall be subject to the common personal law of the parties to be married at the time of celebrating the marriage. If, at the time of marriage, the parties to be married have different personal laws, the marriage, to be valid, shall comply with the substantive requirements of validity under the personal law of both parties to the marriage.

(2) The formal validity of marriage shall be subject to the law in effect at the time and place of celebration.

(3) Subject to authorization by the Council of Ministers, a Hungarian Diplomatic Authority may also solemnize a marriage if both parties thereto are Hungarian nationals. Such marriage shall be considered to have been celebrated in Hungary.

(4) The provisions concerning the conclusion and validity of marriage shall also apply, *mutatis mutandis*, to matters involving determination of the existence or non-existence of marriage.

Art. 38. (1) A non-Hungarian national desiring to marry in Hungary shall prove that under his/her personal law there is no impediment to the marriage. This requirement may, in justified cases, be waived by the head of the metropolitan or of county administrative agency having territorial competence.[2]

(2) A marriage shall not be celebrated in Hungary if, under Hungarian law, there is an unavoidable impediment thereto.

(3) If a Hungarian national or a stateless person residing in Hungary intends to marry abroad, the lack of impediment to the marriage under Hungarian law shall be certified by the head of the metropolitan or county administrative agency having territorial competence.[3]

(4) If the Hungarian national concerned is of foreign domicile, such a certificate shall be issued by the Hungarian Diplomatic Authority.

PERSONAL AND PROPERTY RELATIONS OF THE SPOUSES

Art. 39. (1) The personal and property relations of the spouses, including marital name, support and property settlement, shall be governed by the common personal law of the spouses at the time of the action.

(2) If at the time of the action the spouses have different personal laws, the applicable law shall be their last common personal law or, failing such a law, the law of the State in which they had their last common domicile.

---

[2] The text of the second sentence was established by Art. 1 (1) of Act CVIII of 1995.

[3] The text of this paragraph was established by Art. 1 (2) of Act CVIII of 1995.

(3) If the spouses had no common domicile, the applicable law shall be of the State of the proceeding court or other authority.

(4) A change in the personal law of spouses shall not affect the use of the marital name as arranged and the property-law effects, including support and matrimonial property settlement, as validly prevailing under the former personal law.

DISSOLUTION OF MARRIAGE

Art. 40. (1) The conditions of divorce shall be controlled by the common personal law of the spouses at the time of filing the petition with the court.

(2) If, at the time the petition is filed, the spouses have different personal laws, the applicable law shall be their last common personal law or, failing such a law, Hungarian law where one of the spouses is a Hungarian national, or else the law of the State in which they had their last common domicile.

(3) If the spouses had no common domicile, the applicable law shall be of the State of the proceeding court or other authority.

Art. 41. The foreign law governing the dissolution of marriage shall be applied with the following deviations:

(a) A marriage may be dissolved even if its dissolution is excluded by the foreign law, or if the conditions of divorce are absent according to the foreign law, but are present according to Hungarian law.

(b) The question of whether marital life has been completely and irreparably ruined shall be considered even in cases where absolute grounds for divorce are present according to the foreign law.

(c) A marriage shall not be dissolved on the ground of fault.

FAMILY STATUS

Art. 42. (1) Establishment of paternity or maternity and challenging of the presumption of paternity shall be subject to the personal law of the child at the time of birth.

(2) Recognition of paternity shall be subject to the personal law of the child at the time of recognition or, in the case of a child conceived but not yet born, to the personal law of the mother at the time of recognition.

(3) Recognition shall not be considered invalid according either to Hungarian law or to the law in effect at the time and place of recognition.

ADOPTION

Art. 43. (1) The conditions of adoption shall be under the joint control of the personal law of the adoptive parent(s) and that of the person to be adopted in effect at the time of adoption.

(2) Adoption of a non-Hungarian national by a Hungarian national shall be subject to permission by the Hungarian guardianship authority.

(3) Adoption of a Hungarian national by a non-Hungarian national shall be subject to permission by the Hungarian guardianship authority.

(4) Adoption shall not be permitted or approved by the guardianship authority except when it satisfies the requirements of Hungarian law.

Art. 44. (1) The legal effects of adoption as well as the termination of adoption and its legal effects shall be governed by the adopter's personal law at the time of adoption or its termination.

(2) If, at the time of adoption or its termination, the adoptive parents have different personal laws, the legal effects of adoption and its termination shall be governed:

(a) by the last common personal law of the spouses; or, failing such a law,

(b) by the law of the State in which the spouses had their common domicile at the time of adoption or its termination; or, failing such a domicile,

(c) by the law of the State of the proceeding court or other authority.

LEGAL RELATIONSHIPS BETWEEN PARENT AND CHILD

Art. 45. (1) Family-law relationships between parent and child, particularly the child's name, custody, care, legal representation, support, and administration of his property, shall, with the exception of parent's maintenance, be governed by the personal law of the child.[4]

(2) [5]

APPLICATION OF THE LAW MORE FAVOURABLE TO THE CHILD

Art. 46. If it is more favourable to the child, Hungarian law shall be applied to the family status of a child who is a national or a resident of Hungary, to the family-law relationships between him and his parents, and to the maintenance obligations towards him.

MAINTENANCE OF RELATIVES

Art. 47. The conditions for maintenance obligations of relatives towards one another as well as the extent and mode of support shall be governed by the personal law of the individual entitled to maintenance.

GUARDIANSHIP

Art. 48. (1) The conditions for the appointment of a guardian and for the termination of a guardianship shall be governed by the personal law of the ward.

[4] The text of this paragraph was established by Art. 52 of Act IV of 1986.

[5] Repealed by Art. 39 (2) of Act IV of 1986.

(2) The extent of the guardian's obligation to exercise the guardianship shall be governed by his personal law.

(3) Legal relationships between guardian and ward, including the guardian's duty to administer property and to render account thereof, shall be subject to the law of the State whose authority appointed the guardian. However, if it is more favourable to the ward, the Hungarian law shall apply when the ward is resident in Hungary.

CURATORSHIP

Art. 49. (1) The rules on guardianship shall apply accordingly to curatorship.

(2) Representation of a person prevented from attending to his affairs and *ad hoc* guardianship shall be governed by the law of the State whose authority appointed the curator.

TEMPORARY MEASURES

Art. 50. The Hungarian law shall apply where the need arises to take immediate measures in the interests of the custody, support or care of a non-Hungarian national resident in Hungary.

CHAPTER VIII

LABOUR LAW

Art. 51. (1) Unless otherwise provided by law, employment relationships shall be subject to the law of the State in which the work is to be performed.

(2) Employment relationships established by appointment or election shall be subject to the personal law of the appointing authority or the electing body.

(3) Where the employer is a foreign State, State authority or administrative agency, or a foreign national acting as a diplomatic representative in Hungary or otherwise enjoying immunity from Hungarian jurisdiction, and the parties have the same personal law, employment relationships shall be subject to that law.

Art. 52. (1) If, under a labour contract, work is to be performed in the territories of several States, employment relationships shall be subject to the personal law of the employer.

(2) Employment relationships shall be subject to Hungarian law if a worker of a Hungarian employer is working abroad on assignment or on long-term foreign service.

(3) The employment relationships of workers on board of vessel or aircraft shall be subject to the law of the State under whose flag or other insignia the

vehicle is operating; the employment relations of workers of other carriers shall be governed by the personal law of the carrier concerned.

Art. 53. The substantive and formal validity of a labour contract, the consequences of its invalidity, and the content and termination of employment relationships shall likewise be subject to the law applicable to employment relationships.

CHAPTER IX

JURISDICTION

Art. 54. Hungarian courts or other authorities may take jurisdiction over any case in which their jurisdiction is not excluded by this Law-Decree.

EXCLUSIVE JURISDICTION

Art. 55. Hungarian courts or other authorities shall have exclusive jurisdiction:

(a) in proceedings concerning the personal status of a Hungarian national, except when decisions of a foreign court or other authority on such matters are recognizable under this Law-Decree;

(b) in proceedings concerning immovables in Hungary;

(c) in probate proceedings concerning the estate in Hungary of a deceased Hungarian national;

(d) in proceedings against the Hungarian State, a Hungarian State authority or administrative organ;

(e) in proceedings against a Hungarian national acting as a diplomatic representative abroad or otherwise enjoying immunity from foreign jurisdiction, in cases where, by virtue of an international agreement or of reciprocity, no proceedings against such person may be instituted abroad;

(f) in proceedings for cancellation of a security or a deed issued in Hungary;

(g) in proceedings concerning the granting, extent and termination of industrial property rights in Hungary.

EXCLUDED JURISDICTION

Art. 56. Unless otherwise provided by this Law-Decree, the jurisdiction of Hungarian courts or other authorities shall be excluded:

(a) in proceedings against a foreign State, a foreign State authority or administrative organ;

(b) in proceedings against a foreign national acting as a diplomatic representative in Hungary or otherwise enjoying immunity from Hungarian jurisdiction, in cases where, by virtue of an international agreement or of reciprocity, no proceedings against such person may be instituted in Hungary;

(c) in proceedings concerning the granting, extent and termination of foreign industrial property rights;

(d) in cases where the jurisdiction of Hungarian courts or other authorities is excluded by special provisions of law.

Art. 57. (1) A Hungarian court or other authority may proceed against a foreign State, a foreign State authority or administrative organ, or a foreign national acting as a diplomatic representative in Hungary or otherwise enjoying immunity from Hungarian jurisdiction, if the foreign State has expressly waived immunity.

(2) In cases where immunity is waived, the jurisdiction of Hungarian courts or other authorities shall also extend to a counterclaim arising from the same legal relationship.

(3) A judgment rendered against a foreign party in such proceedings shall not be enforced except when the foreign State has expressly waived immunity from execution as well.

Art. 58. (1) A Hungarian court may proceed in lawsuits between non-Hungarian nationals concerning their personal status, with the exception of lawsuits relating to curatorship, if one of the parties is domiciled in Hungary.

(2) Where so required by a domestic legal interest, a Hungarian court may declare a person legally dead or missing, or may establish the fact of his death, even if his personal law is other than Hungarian.

Art. 59. (1) A Hungarian court may place under curatorship a non-Hungarian national domiciled in Hungary and may terminate the curatorship, while the Hungarian guardianship authority may appoint a curator for him and may release the curator.

(2) A Hungarian court may place a non-Hungarian national under guardianship or curatorship, if his domicile or habitual residence is in Hungary, while the Hungarian guardianship authority may take the necessary measures to secure his custody, support and care.

Art. 60. (1) The Hungarian guardianship authority may appoint a legal representative or an *ad hoc* guardian for a non-Hungarian national incapable of taking care of his own affairs.

(2) The Hungarian guardianship authority may take immediate measures to secure the custody, support or care of a non-Hungarian national resident in Hungary.

Art. 61. The court or the guardianship authority shall immediately notify the measures taken to the competent foreign authority of the person concerned; such measures shall remain in effect pending other measures by the said authority.

STIPULATION OF JURISDICTION

Art. 62. (1) The parties may, by written stipulation, determine the jurisdiction of a foreign or domestic ordinary court or arbitral tribunal with respect to legal disputes arising from international economic contracts.

(2) Where exclusive jurisdiction was so stipulated, no other ordinary court or arbitral tribunal shall proceed in such matters.

CHAPTER X

RULES OF PROCEDURAL LAW

GENERAL RULES

Art. 63. Unless otherwise provided by this Law-Decree, the procedure of Hungarian courts or other authorities shall be governed by Hungarian law.

Art. 64. (1) The legal and disposing capacity of a party in respect of legal proceedings shall be controlled by his personal law.

(2) A non-Hungarian national who has limited or no disposing capacity under his personal law, but would be capable of action under Hungarian law, shall be considered to have disposing capacity in proceedings before a Hungarian court or other authority.

(3) This provision shall not prevent a person who has limited or no disposing capacity under his personal law from using the services of his legal representative entitled thereto under his personal law to act on his behalf.

Art. 65. Where, between the parties, proceedings based on the same facts and on the same claim are instituted before a foreign court or other authority and the resulting decision is to be recognized as valid and enforceable in Hungary by virtue of this Law-Decree, the Hungarian court or other authority shall terminate proceedings subsequently instituted before it, or the court shall dismiss the action without issuing a summons.

Art. 66. The Minister of Justice shall issue a certificate of Hungarian law and legal practice for a person who is in need thereof to assert his right abroad.

INTERNATIONAL LEGAL ASSISTANCE AND LETTER OF REQUEST

Art. 67. (1) In applying for legal assistance a Hungarian court shall contact a foreign court or other authority through the Minister of Justice, while other authorities shall do so through the Minister of Foreign Affairs with the intervention of the supervising minister.

(2) In executing a request for legal assistance the proceeding authority shall follow Hungarian law. However, at the request of the applicant authority, it

may employ foreign procedures, provided that such procedures do not offend Hungarian public policy.

Art. 68. (1) A Hungarian court or other authority shall provide legal assistance at the request of a foreign court or other authority on the basis of an international treaty or of reciprocity.

(2) Regarding the existence of reciprocity, the Minister of Justice shall give a declaration binding upon the court or other authority.

(3) In the absence of reciprocity, the Minister of Justice shall decide, in concurrence with the Minister of Foreign Affairs and the minister competent by the subject-matter of the case, on the execution of a request for legal assistance.

(4) Legal assistance shall be denied where execution of the request would violate Hungarian public policy.

Art. 69. For the purposes of legal proceedings abroad extrajudicial affidavits may be made or oaths taken before a Hungarian notary public, who shall issue certificates thereof.

CHAPTER XI

RECOGNITION AND ENFORCEMENT OF FOREIGN JUDGMENTS

Art. 70. (1) Unless otherwise provided by this Law-Decree, the judgment of a foreign court or other authority shall be recognized in cases not subject to the exclusive jurisdiction of the Hungarian court or other authority.

(2) The judgment of a foreign court or other authority on matters subject to the exclusive jurisdiction of the Hungarian court or other authority shall not be recognized except in cases specified by this Law-Decree.

Art. 71. Recognition shall be granted to judgments:

(a) passed in a divorce case of a Hungarian national domiciled abroad;

(b) placing under curatorship a Hungarian national domiciled abroad or terminating such curatorship;

(c) by which a foreign court or other authority permitted, approved or terminated the adoption of a Hungarian national, provided that the adoptive parent is a foreign national and the adoption was approved by the Hungarian guardianship authority.

Art. 72. (1) Recognition shall be granted to a judgment passed by a foreign court or other authority in proceedings instituted abroad by or against the Hungarian State, a Hungarian State authority or administrative organ, or a Hungarian national acting abroad as a diplomatic representative or otherwise enjoying immunity from foreign jurisdiction, provided that the Hungarian State has expressly waived immunity, or the foreign court or other authority may also proceed by virtue of an international treaty or of reciprocity.

(2) Where a judgment is recognized, recognition shall extend to the judgment rendered by a foreign court or other authority in a counterclaim originating in the same legal relationship.

(3) The enforcement of a judgment passed in such proceedings shall be subject to a separate express waiver by the Hungarian State of immunity from enforcement.

Art. 73. Nevertheless, with the conditions as stated in the preceding provisions otherwise prevailing, a foreign judgment shall not be recognizable in cases where:

(a) recognition would violate Hungarian public policy;

(b) the foreign court or other authority proceeded against the person involved on a ground of jurisdiction which, under the law of the foreign State, cannot be invoked against its own nationals (legal persons) either;

(c) the person against whom the judgment was entered had not participated in the proceedings, either personally or through his representative, because of some irregularity in the conduct of the proceedings or because the summons had not been served on him at his place of residence (seat) in Hungary or on his agent named by him at the place of the proceedings;

(d) with respect to the same right based on the same facts, a Hungarian court or other authority has already passed a final judgment on the merits of the same case involving the same parties;

(e) prior to the institution of the foreign proceedings, proceedings had been instituted before a Hungarian court or other authority in a case of the same parties, concerning the same right, based on the same facts.

Art. 74. (1) Final judgments passed by a foreign court or other authority in matters relating to claims under property law and the law of other material obligations as well as relating to the custody of a child shall be enforced by virtue of an international treaty or of reciprocity.

(2) No enforcement shall lie, even in case of reciprocity, where the judgment of a foreign court or other authority is incapable of recognition on some ground specified by this Law-Decree. On the existence of reciprocity the Minister of Justice shall issue a declaration binding upon the courts and other authorities.

(3) These provisions shall apply also to the enforcement of foreign arbitral awards.

FINAL PROVISIONS

Art. 75. (1) This Law-Decree shall enter into force on 1 July 1979.

(2) The provisions herein shall also be applied to legal disputes arising from legal relationships prior to the entry into force of this Law-Decree and not yet

decided by final judgments. This provision shall not be invoked to change the chosen law applied in ongoing proceedings or the jurisdiction of the court or other authority dealing with the case.

(3) A judgment rendered in accordance with Art. 71 shall be recognizable even if it predates the entry into force of this Law-Decree, except when a Hungarian court or other authority has already passed a judgment in the same case.

(4) At the same time as this Law-Decree comes into force:

(a) it shall supersede Art. 34 of Act XVI of 1876 *(sic);* Art. 200 of Act III of 1952 on Civil Procedure; Arts. 5 and 6 and the second sentence in Art. 47, para. 3 of Act I of 1974 on the Amendment and the Integrated Text of Act IV of 1952 on Marriage, the Family and Guardianship; Arts. 14–16 of Law-Decree No. 22 of 1952 on the Entry into Force and the Execution of Act III of 1952 on Civil Procedure; Arts. 15–20, 42, 44 and 45 of Law-Decree No. 23 of 1952 on the Entry into Force and the Execution of Act IV of 1952 on Marriage, the Family and Guardianship as well as on the Regulation of Some Questions Concerning the Personal Law; Art. 209 of Law-Decree No. 21 of 1955 on Judicial Execution; and Art. 29 of Decree No. 6/1958 (II. 4) of the Minister of Justice on Probate Proceedings;

(b) [6]

[6] Repealed by Art. 203, para. 3 (a) of Act XXII of 1992.

LIST OF SOURCES

I. MAJOR SOURCES OF LAW

1. INTERNAL LAWS AND REGULATIONS

(a) *Laws of general coverage*

Consitution: Constitution of the Republic of Hungary, with amendments and the integrated text in *Magyar Közlöny* No. 84 of 1990; Act LVIII of 1991; Act CVII of 1993; Act LXI of 1994; Act LXXIII of 1994

Code of Private International Law: Law-Decree No. 13 of 1979 as amended by Act IV of 1986; Act XXII of 1992; Act CVIII of 1995

Decree No. 50/1990. (II.21.) of the Council of Ministers promulgating the European Convention concerning Information about Foreign Law, signed in London on 7 June 1968, and the Additional Protocol to the Convention signed in Strasbourg on 15 March 1978; Bulletin No. 8001/1995. (XI.8.) of the Ministry of Justice

Civil Code: Act IV of 1959 as amended by, and with the integrated text in, Act IV of 1977 (recent major amendments: Act XIV of 1991; Act IL of 1991; LXV of 1991; Act XCII of 1993; Act LXXI of 1994; Act XXVI of 1996; Act CXI of 1996)

Law-Decree No. 8 of 1978 on the Application of the Civil Code in External Economic Relations

Code of Civil Procedure: Act III of 1952 as amended by Act VI of 1954; Act VIII of 1957; Law-Decree No. 12 of 1960; Law-Decree No. 14 of 1961; Law-Decree No. 26 of 1972 (integrated text) (recent major amendments: Act XXVI of 1991; Act LXVIII of 1992; Act LII of 1994; Act LX of 1995)

Family law: Act I of 1974 on the Amendment and Integrated Text of Act IV of 1952 on Marriage, Family and Guardianship as revised by, *inter alia*, Act IV of 1986; Act XV of 1990; Act XXXI of 1995

Execution of judgments: Act LIII of 1994; Decree No. 11/1994 (IX.8.) of the Minister of Justice

(b) *Economy related sources of law*

Economic associations: Act VI of 1988, with amendments and the integrated text in *Magyar Közlöny* No. 143 of 1991; Decision No. 59/1991. (XI.19.) of the Constitutional Court (recent major amendments: Act LXV of 1991; Act LV of 1992; Act LXXXI of 1993; Act CXI of 1996)

Act I of 1992 on *Cooperatives* (as amended by Act LV of 1992; Act XLIV of 1994; Act C of 1994; Act XXXII of 1996)

Act II of 1992 bringing into force Act I of 1992 on Cooperatives and laying down transitional rules, as amended

Investments by foreigners in Hungary: Act XXIV of 1988 as amended by Act XCVIII of 1990; Act VI of 1991; Act LXV of 1991; Act LXIX of 1991; Act LXXXVI of 1991; Act LV of 1994; Act LXXIX of 1994; Act XCV of 1995; Act CXXI of 1995

Act V of 1990 on *Individual Undertakings*, as amended

Act CXI of 1996 on the *Marketing of Securities, Investment Services and the Stock Exchange*

Act XLIV of 1992 on the *Programme for Worker's Part-Ownership*, as amended

Act XXXIX of 1995 on the *Sale of State-Owned Business Property*

Act LV of 1992 *amending enactments relating to laws on the State's business property* (important amendment: Act XXXI of 1995)

Act LXXIV of 1990 on the *privatization of the property of state enterprises engaged in retail trade and public catering and providing consumer services*, as amended

Act LVII of 1996 *prohibition of unfair conduct on the market and restriction of competition*

Act XCIII of 1990 on *Duty*, as amended

Act C of 1990 on *Local Taxes*, as amended

Act XVI of 1991 on *Concessions*, as amended

Act XXV of 1991 on *partial compensation, with a view to the settlement of property relations, for damage unjustly caused by the State to citizens' property by the application of laws and regulations adopted in the period from 1 May 1939 to 8 June 1949*; Government Decree No. 92/1992. (VI.10.) on its Execution

Act XXXI of 1992 on *Conversion of Compensations Bonds into Life Annuity;* Government Decree No. 87/1992. (V.29.) on its Execution

Act XXXII of 1992 on *compensation to persons unlawfully deprived of their lives and property for political reasons;* Government Decree No. 111/1992. (VII.1.) on its Execution

Act IL of 1991 on *Bankruptcy Procedures, Winding-up Procedures, and Final Adjustments*, as amended

Act LX of 1991 on the *Hungarian National Bank* as amended (by Act IV of 1994)

Act LXIII of 1991 on *Investment Funds*, as amended (by Act XXXI of 1994)

Act CXII of 1996 on *Credit Institutions [Banks] and Financial Businesses*

Act LXXIV of 1992 on *General Sales Tax*, as amended by Government Decree No. 2/1993. (I.13.) on *refund of general sales tax for taxpayers registered abroad*

Act LXXXVI of 1991 on *Corporate Tax*, as amended

Act CVII of 1995 on *Personal Income Tax*, as amended

Act XCI of 1990 on the *Procedure for Taxation*, as amended

Decision No. 62/1991. (XI.22.) of the Constitutional Court *annulling the legislation on corporate tax and special corporate tax*

Act XVI of 1994 on the *Chambers of Commerce*

Act LXXI of 1994 on *Arbitration and the Rules of Procedure of the Arbitration Court*

(c) *Stay in Hungary. Legal status of foreigners and other foreign trade related regulations*

Act LXXXVI of 1993 on *Foreigners' Entry into, Residence in and Immigration into Hungary*; Government Decree No. 64/1994. (V.4.) on its Execution

United Nations Convention of 1951 and Protocol of 1967 relating to the *Status of Refugees*, promulgated by Law-Decree No. 15 of 1989

Law-Decree No. 19 of 1989 on the *Status of Persons recognized as Refugees*

Decree No. 7/1991. (X.17.) of the Minister of Labour on the *Authorization of Foreigners' Employment in Hungary*, as amended

Act XXII of 199 on the *Labour Code*, as amended

Social insurance: Act II of 1975 as amended; Decree No. 89/1990. (V.1.) of the Council of Ministers on its Execution, as amended

Government Decree No. 7/1996. (I.18.) on the *Acquisition of Immovable Property by Foreigners*

Decree No. 3/1989. (II.26.) of the Minister of Trade on *Foreigners' Trade Representations as well as Information and Service Offices*

Foreign Trade Law: Act III of 1974 enforced by Decision No. 1053/1974. (X.17.) of the Council of Miniters as amended and Decree No. 7/1974. (X.17.) of the Minister of Foreign Trade as amended

Decree No. 1/1982. (I.16.) of the Minister of Foreign Trade on the *General Rules of Procedure for Foreign Trade Administration* as amended by Decree No. 9/1991. (XI.22.) of the Minister of International Economic Relations

Government Decree No. 112/1990. (XII.23.) on the *Importation and Exportation of Goods, Services and Intangible Assets*, enforced by Decree No. 6/1990. (XII.9.) of the Minister of International Economic Relations

Anti-Dumping procedure: Government Decree No. 69/1994. (V.4.) on the *Rules for Anti-Dumping and Value-Equalizing Customs Duties*

Government Decree No. 113/1990. (XII.23.) on *market protection measures applicable to the importation of goods, services and intangible assets*, as amended

Government Decree No. 61/1990. (X.1.) on the *authorization of trade in Certain Kinds of War Material* and *Military Technological Services under International Control*, as amended

Government Decree No. 48/1991. (II.27.) on the *exportation, importation and re-exportation of war material and military technological services*, as amended by Government Decrees No. 66/1991. (V.21.) and No. 1/1995. (I.20.)

Act XLII of 1994 on *Hungarian Export–Import Bank Corp. and Hungarian Export Credit Insurance Corp.*

Government Decree No. 105/1995. (IX.8.) on the *Interest-Equalizing System Associated with Export Credits*

Act CI of 1995 on *Customs Duties*

Customs Code: Act C of 1995 on *Customs Law, Customs Procedure and Customs Administration*; Government Decree No. 45/1996. (III.25.) on its Execution, as amended

Act XXIV of 1994 on the *Prevention of Money Laundering*

Act VI of 1993 on the *Agricultural Market Regulations*

Act LV of 1994 on *Arable Land*

Government Decree No. 177/1995. (XII.29.) on *Budgetary Support for the Attainment of Certain Agricultural Objectives*

Government Decree No. 55/1996. (IV.12.) on *Support for Particular Economic Organizations in 1996*

2. MAJOR INTERNATIONAL TREATIES, AGREEMENTS AND CONVENTIONS

(For complete and authentic sources hereof, see the corresponding volumes of *Magyar Közlöny* (Hungarian [Official] Gazette) and *Hatályos Jogszabályok Gyűjteménye* (Collection of Laws and Regulations in Force))

(a) *Bilateral treaties*

(aa) *Treaties of general coverage*

Act XLVII of 1995 promulgating the Treaty on Friendly Relations and Cooperation between the Republic of Hungary and the Republic of *Croatia*, signed at Budapest on 16 December 1992

Act LXXIV of 1995 promulgating the Treaty on the Foundations of Friendly Relations and Cooperation between the Republic of Hungary and the Republic of *Estonia*, signed at Tallinn on 8 August 1992

Act LXXV of 1995 promulgating the Treaty of Understanding and Friendship between the Republic of Hungary and the *French* Republic, signed at Paris on 11 September 1991

Act LXXIX of 1995 promulgating the Treaty on the Foundations of Friendly Relations and Cooperation beween the Republic of Hungary and the Federal Republic of *Germany*, signed at Budapest on 6 February 1992

Decision No. 28/1994. (IV.13.) of the National Assembly ratifying the Treaty of Friendship and Cooperation between the Republic of Hungary and the *Hellenic* Republic

Decision No. 13/1994. (III.10.) of the National Assembly ratifying the Treaty of Friendship and Cooperation between the Republic of Hungary and the *Italian* Republic

Act LXXVII of 1995 promulgating the Treaty on the Foundations of Friendly Relations and Cooperation between the Republic of Hungary and the Republic of *Latvia*, signed at Riga on 7 August 1992

Act LXXVIII of 1995 promulgating the Treaty on the Foundations of Friendly Relations and Cooperation between the Republic of Hungary and the Republic of *Lithuania,* signed at Vilnius on 12 August 1992

Act LXXVI of 1995 promulgating the Treaty of Friendly and Good Neighbourly Cooperation between the Republic of Hungary and the Republic of *Poland*, signed at Cracow on 6 October 1991

Act XLVI of 1995 promulgating the Treaty of Friendship and Cooperation between the Republic of Hungary and the Republic of *Slovenia*, signed at Budapest on 1 December 1992

Act LXXX of 1995 promulgating the Treaty of Friendship and Cooperation between the Republic of Hungary and the *Spanish* State, signed at Madrid on 6 February 1992

Decision No. 23/1996. (III.28.) of the National Assembly ratifying the Treaty of Friendship and Cooperation between the Republic of Hungary and Republic of *Turkey*, signed at Budapest on 7 September 1994

Act XLV of 1995 promulgating the Treaty on the Foundations of Good Neighbourhood and Cooperation between the Republic of Hungary and *Ukraine*, signed at Kiev on 6 December 1991

(ab) *Agreements on investment protection*

Argentina: Decision No. 97/1996. (XI.26.) of the National Assembly
Australia: Act XXXVII of 1993

Austria: Government Decree No. 12/1990. (VII.24.)
Belgian–Luxembourg Economic Union: Decree No. 7/1989. (I.15.) of the Council of Ministers
Bulgaria: Act CIV of 1996
Canada: Act XXIII of 1995
China: Act XCIV of 1994
Cyprus: Government Decree No. 33/1990. (VIII.30.)
Czech Republic: Act CV of 1996
Denmark: Decree No. 6/1989. (I.15.) of the Council of Ministers
Egypt: Decision No. 98/1996. (XI.26.) of the National Assembly
Finland: Decree No. 91/1989. (VIII.17.) of the Council of Ministers
France: Decree No. 59/1987. (XI.29.) of the Council of Ministers
Germany, Federal Republic of: Law-Decree No. 5 of 1988
Greece: Act XXXVIII of 1993
Indonesia: Decision No. 104/1995. (X.13.) of the National Assembly
Israel: Act LXIV of 1993
Italy: Government Decree No. 30/1990. (VIII.21.)
Kazakhstan: Decision No. 2/1996. (II.9.) of the National Assembly
Korea, Republic of: Decree No. 46/1989. (V.31.) of the Council of Ministers
Kuwait: Act XCV of 1994
Netherlands: Decree No. 63/1988. (VIII.1.) of the Council of Ministers
Malaysia: Act XCVI of 1996
Moldova: Decision No. 9/1996. (II.9.) of the National Assembly
Mongolia: Decision No. 3/1996. (II.9.) of the National Assembly
Norway: Act LXI of 1993
Paraguay: Act XCVIII of 1996
Poland: Act XCVI of 1996
Portugal: Decision No. 103/1996. (XI.26.) of the National Assembly
Romania: Decision No. 4/1996. (II.9.) of the National Assembly
Russian Federation: Decision No. 10/1996. (II.9.) of the National Assembly
Slovakia: Decision No. 39/1995. (IV.7.) of the National Assembly
Spain: Act LXV of 1993
Sweden: Decree No. 25/1987. (VII.28.) of the Council of Ministers
Switzerland: Decree No. 89/1989. (VIII.5.) of the Council of Ministers
Thailand: Government Decree No. 135/1992. (X.1.)
Ukraine: Decision No. 104/1996. (XI.26.) of the National Assembly
United Kingdom: Decree No. 5/1988. (II.12.) of the Council of Ministers
United States of America: (Investment Guarantee Agreement) Decree No. 74/1990. (IV.25.) of the Council of Ministers
Uruguay: Act XXXIX of 1993
Vietnam: Act CIII of 1996

(ac) *Agreements on legal assistance*

Albania: Law-Decree No. 25 of 1960; Enforcement Ordinance No. 114/1960. (IK.20.) of the Minister of Justice
Algeria: Law-Decree No. 15 of 1985
Australia: Act XIII of 1936

Austria: Law-Decree No. 24 of 1967; Enforcement Ordinance No. 115/1976. (IK.15.) of the Minister of Justice; (on the regulation of inheritance matters) Law-Decree No. 25 of 1967; Enforcement Ordinance No. 2/1967. (X.27.) of the Minister of Justice

Belgium: Decree No. 64/1984. (XII.21.) of the Council of Ministers promulgating the Agreement (Brussels, 11 May 1983) to facilitate the application of the Hague Convention on Civil Procedure (1 March 1954)

Bulgaria: Law-Decree No. 6 of 1967 (as amended and supplemented by Law-Decree No. 2 of 1983); Enforcement Ordinance No. 103/1967. (IK.5.) of the Minister of Justice

Canada: Act XIII of 1936

China: Decision No. 15/1996. (III.1.) of the National Assembly

Cuba: Law-Decree No. 4 of 1984

Cyprus: Law-Decree No. 19 of 1983

Czechoslovakia (both the Czech Republic and the Republic of Slovakia as successor States): Act LXI of 1991

Fiji Islands: Act XIII of 1936 [upheld by Decision No. 28/1974. (IX.29.) of the Presidential Council]

Finland: Law-Decree No. 25 of 1982

France: Law-Decree No. 3 of 1982

Great Britain: Act XIII of 1936

Greece: Law-Decree No. 21 of 1981

Iraq: Law-Decree No. 11 of 1978

Italy: Law-Decree No.11 of 1981

Kenya: Act XIII of 1936 [upheld by Decision No. 14/1967. (V.16.) of the Presidential Council]

Kcrea, Democratic People's Republic of: Law-Decree No. 12 of 1971; Enforcement Ordinance No. 3/1971. (IX.9.) of the Minister of Justice

Lesotho: Act XIII of 1936 [upheld by Decision No. 29/1974. (IX.29.) of the Presidential Council]

Mongolia: Law-Decree No. 11 of 1969; Enforcement Ordinance No. 8/1969. (XI.16.) of the Minister of Justice

New Zealand: Act XIII of 1936

Poland: Law-Decree No. 5 of 1960 [as amended and supplemented by Law-Decree No. 24 of 1981]; enforcement Ordinance No. 102/1960. (IK.4.) of the Minister of Justice

Romania: Law-Decree No. 19 of 1959; Enforcement Ordinance No. 5/1959 (V.6.) of the Minister of Justice and Bulletin No. 310/1967. (IK.11.) II.1. of the Ministry of Justice

Soviet Union (of the successor States, ratified by Belarus, Moldova, Russia, Armenia and Ukraine): Law-Decree No. 38 of 1958 (as amended and supplemented by Law-Decree No. 18 of 1972); Enforcement Ordinance No. 10/1958. (XII.20.) of the Minister of Justice

Swaziland: Act XIII of 1936 [upheld by Decision No. 28/1973. (XI.28.) of the Presidential Council)

Syria: Law-Decree No. 9 of 1988

Tonga: Act XIII of 1936 [upheld by Decision No. 30/1974. (IX.29.) of the Presidential Council]

Tunisia: Law-Decree No. 2 of 1985

Turkey: Act LVII of 1992

Vietnam: Law-Decree No. 8 of 1986

Yugoslavia (of the successor States, ratified by Bosnia and Herzegovina, Croatia, Macedonia, Slovenia): Law-Decree No. 1 of 1969 (as amended and supplemented by Law-Decree No. 1 of 1988); Enforcement Ordinance No. 102/1969. (IK.3.) of the Minister of Justice

(ad) *Consular conventions*

Austria: Law-Decree No. 18 of 1977
Belgium: Law-Decree No. 25 of 1978
Bolivia: Law-Decree No. 7 of 1987
Bulgaria: Law-Decree No. 14 of 1972
Cambodia: Law-Decree No. 12 of 1981
China: Law-Decree No. 32 of 1986
Cuba: Law-Decree No. 22 of 1972
Czechoslovakia: Law-Decree No. 4 of 1974
Ecuador: Law-Decree No. 6 of 1983
Finland: Law-Decree No. 2 of 1973
France: Law-Decree No. 33 of 1967
Great Britain: Law-Decree No. 37 of 1971
Greece: Law-Decree No. 14 of 1979
Iraq: Law-Decree No. 10 of 1975
Kazakhstan: Decision No. 37/1995. (IX.28.) of the National Assembly
Korea, Democratic People's Republic of: Law-Decree No. 5 of 1971
Laos: Law-Decree No. 10 of 1984
Libya: Law-Decree No. 5 of 1982
Mongolia: Law-Decree No. 1 of 1975
Nicaragua: Law-Decree No. 42 of 1982
Romania: Law-Decree No. 2 of 1975
Soviet Union: Law-Decree No. 6 of 1972 (as applying according to the relevant Russian and other rules on state succession)
Spain: Law-Decree No. 14 of 1984
Syria: Law-Decree No. 14 of 1988
Tunisia: Law-Decree No. 28 of 1984
Turkey: Act XXV of 1940
Ukraine: Decision No. 34/1992. (VI.12.) of the National Assembly
United States of America: Law-Decree No. 22 of 1973
Vietnam: Law-Decree No. 8 of 1980
Yugoslavia: Law-Decree No. 3 of 1964 (as supplemented by Law-Decree No. 2 of 1981)

(ae) *Trade agreements*

Argentina: Act XLVIII of 1871
Chile: Act L of 1871
Czechoslovakia: Law-Decree No. 25 of 1964 (as applying according to the relevant rules of state succession)
Denmark: Act XXXVI of 1887
Ethiopia: Act X of 1910
Finland: Decree No. 2860/1926 of the Prime Minister
France: Act V of 1926

Great Britain: Act XVIII of 1927
Greece: Act XXV of 1931
Guatemala: Act XXVII of 1871
Israel: published in *Magyar Közlöny*, No. 84 of 1991
Japan: Law-Decree No. 10 of 1977
Korea, Republic of: published in *Magyar Közlöny*, No. 12 of 1989
Netherlands: Decree No. 132/1926 of the Prime Minister
Norway: Decree No. 2250/1925 of the Prime Minister
Peru: Act XLIX of 1871
Poland: Act XLI of 1948
Portugal: Act XXXI of 1930
Soviet Union: Act XXVIII of 1947 (as applying according to the relevant rules of state succession)
Spain: Act IX of 1926
Sweden: Decree No. 1750/1929 of the Prime Minister
Switzerland: Act VII of 1906
Tanzania: Law-Decree No. 15 of 1967
United States of America: Act XII of 1978
Uruguay: published in *Magyar Közlöny*, No. 45 of 1983
Zimbabwe: published in *Magyar Közlöny*, No. 20 of 1988

Act LXXXIII of 1993 promulgating the Free Trade Agreement between the Republic of Hungary and the Member States of the European Free Trade Association, signed at Geneva on 29 March 1993

Act I of 1994 promulgating the European Agreement on Association between the Republic of Hungary and the European Communities as well as Its Member States, signed at Brussels on 16 December 1991

Act XCIX of 1994 repealing the Agreement of 2 May 1974 on the Removal of Trade Barriers between the Republic of Hungary and the Republic of Finland and Law-Decree No. 1 of 1982 promulgating it, as amended by Law-Decree No. 5 of 1975, as well as the Protocol on the Treatment of Products in Chapters I to XXIV of the Harmonized régime between the Republic of Hungary and the Republic of Finland and Act VIII of 1994 promulgating it

Act XIII of 1995 promulgating the Agreement on Free Trade in Central Europe between the Czech Republic, the Republic of Hungary, the Republic of Poland and the Republic of Slovakia

(af) *Further Agreements published*

Agreement on *Changeover to a New Mechanism of Mutual Economic Relations* between the Government of the Republic of Hungary and the Government of the Union of Soviet Socialist Republics

Agreement of 1991 *on Commercial and Economic Cooperation* between the Government of the Republic of Hungary and the Government of the Union of Soviet Socialist Republics

Agreement on *Commercial and Economic as well as Scientific-Technical Cooperation* between the Government of the Republic of Hungary and the Government of the Russian Soviet Federal Socialist Republic

Agreement on *Mutual Trade and Payments* after 1 January 1991 between the Government of the Republic of Hungary and the Government of the Republic of Poland

Agreement on *Mutual Trade and Payments* after 1 January 1991 between the Government of the Republic of Hungary and the Government of the Socialist People's Republic of Albania

Agreement on *Trade and Payments* after 1 January 1991 between the Government of the Republic of Hungary and the Government of Romania

(The above Agreements are published in *Magyar Közlöny*, No. 91 of 1991.)

European Economic Community: Agreement on Trade as well as Commercial and Economic Cooperation, published in *Magyar Közlöny*, No. 4 of 1989

Agreement on Commercial and Economic Relations as well as Scientific-Technical Cooperation between the Government of Hungary and the Government of the Ukrainian Soviet Socialist Republic (1992)

Agreement on Commercial and Economic Relations as well as Scientific-Technical Cooperation between the Government of the Republic of Hungary and the Government of the Republic of Belarus (1992)

Agreement on Commercial and Economic Relations between the Government of the Republic of Hungary and the Government of the Republic of Lithuania (1992)

Agreement on Commercial and Economic Relations as well as Scientific-Technical Cooperation between the Government of the Republic of Hungary and the Government of the Komi Soviet Socialist Republic (1992)

Agreement on Commercial and Economic Relations between the Government of the Republic of Hungary and the Government of the Republic of Moldova (1993)

Agreement on Commercial and Economic Relations between the Government of the Republic of Hungary and the Government of the Republic of Croatia (1993)

Agreement on Commercial and Economic Relations between the Government of the Republic of Hungary and the Government of the Republic of Armenia (1996)

Government Decree No. 178/1995. (XII.29.) promulgating the Agreement on Economic, Technical and Other Related Assistance between the Government of the Republic of Hungary and the Government of the United States of America

(ag) *Agreements for the avoidance of double taxation*

Albania: Act XCI of 1996
Australia: Act XXXVI of 1993
Austria: Law-Decree No. 2 of 1976
Belgium: Decree No. 20/1984. (IV.18.) of the Council of Ministers
Bulgaria: Act XCII of 1996
Brazil: Act XXVII of 1992
Canada: Act XVI of 1995
China: Decision No. 57/1994. (XI.17.) of the National Assembly
Cyprus: Decree No. 82/1982. (XII.29.) of the Council of Ministers
Czech Republic: Act XCIII of 1996
Denmark: Decree No. 45/1979. (XI.10.) of the Council of Ministers
Egypt: Act XVII of 1995
Finland: Decree No. 66/1981. (XII.16.) of the Council of Ministers
France: Decree No. 65/1981. (XII.16.) of the Council of Ministers
Greece: Decree No. 33/1985. (VII.1.) of the Council of Ministers
India: Decree No. 11/1988. (III.10.) of the Council of Ministers
Ireland: Decision No. 99/1996. (XI.26.) of the National Assembly

Israel: Act LXIII of 1993
Italy: Decree No. 53/1980. (XII.12.) of the Council of Ministers
Japan: Law-Decree No. 18 of 1980
Kazakhstan: Decision No. 7/1996. (II.9.) of the National Assembly
Korea, Republic of: Act XXVIII of 1992
Kuwait: Decision No. 58/1994. (XI.17.) of the National Assembly
Luxembourg: Act XCV of 1990
Malaysia: Act LX of 1993
Malta: Act LXVII of 1993
Moldova: Decision No. 6/1996. (II.9.) of the National Assembly
Mongolia: Decision No. 100/1996. (XI.26.) of the National Assembly
Netherlands: Decree No. 10/1988. (III.10.) of the Council of Ministers and Act V of 1940
Norway: Decree No. 67/1981. (XII.16.) of the Council of Ministers
Russia: Decision No. 101/1996. (XI.26.) of the National Assembly
Pakistan: Act II of 1996
Poland: Act XCV of 1996
Portugal: Decision No. 102/1996. (XI.26.) of the National Assembly
Romania: Law-Decree No. 16 of 1994 and Act XCIX of 1996
Slovakia: Act C of 1996
South Africa: Decision No. 5/1996. (II.9.) of the National Assembly
Spain: Decree No. 12/1988. (III.10.) of the Council of Ministers
Sweden: Decree No. 55/1982. (X.22.) of the Council of Ministers and Act XVI of 1937
Switzerland: Law-Decree No. 23 of 1982
Thailand: Government Decree No. 13/1990. (VII.25.)
Turkey: Act CI of 1996
Ukraine: Decision No. 8/1996. (II.9.) of the National Assembly
United Kingdom: Law-Decree No. 15 of 1978
United States of America: Decree No. 49/1979. (XII.16.) of the Council of Ministers
Vietnam: Act CII of 1996
Yugoslavia: Law-Decree No. 6 of 1988

(ah) *Agreements on the protection of industrial property*

Law-Decree No. 18 of 1973 promulgating the Agreement on the *Protection of the Indications of Origin on Agricultural and Industrial Products and of Other Indications of Origin* between the Hungarian People's Republic and the Republic of Austria, signed at Vienna on 21 July 1972

Law-Decree No. 27 of 1981 promulgating the Agreement on the *Protection of Indications of Origin and Other Geographical Designations* between the Hungarian People's Republic and the Swiss Confederation

(ai) *Agreements on copyright*

Soviet Union: Law-Decree No. 6 of 1968; prolonged by Law-Decree No. 15 of 1971 (as amended by Law-Decree No. 15 of 1974 and Law-Decree No. 1 of 1978)

United States of America: Act LXI of 1912

(b) *Multilateral conventions* (with Hungary adhering)

(ba) *International sale of goods and services*

Law-Decree No. 20 of 1987 promulgating the United Nations Convention on *International Contracts for the Sale of Goods*, done at Vienna on 11 April 1980

Law-Decree No. 1 of 1989 promulgating the Convention on the *Period of Limitation for International Contracts for the Sale of Goods*, done at Vienna on 11 April 1980

Bulletin No. 8001/1990. (VII.17.) of the Ministry of International Economic Relations concerning the application of the United Nations Convention on *International Contracts for the Sale of Goods*, done at Vienna on 11 April 1980, as promulgated by Law-Decree No. 20 of 1987

Bulletin No. 8002/1990. (VII.17.) of the Ministry of International Economic Relations concerning the application of the Convention on the *Period of Limitation for International Contracts for the Sale of Goods*, done at New York on 14 June 1974, and of the Protocol Amending the Convention on the Period of Limitation for International Contracts for the Sale of Goods, done at Vienna on 11 April 1980

Bulletin No. 8002/1991. (MK.60.) of the Ministry of International Economic Relations concerning the application of the United Nations Convention on *International Contracts for the Sale of Goods*, done at Vienna on 11 April 1980, as promulgated by Law-Decree No. 20 of 1987

Bulletin No. 8003/1991. (MK.60.) of the Minisry of International Economic Relations of the Convention on the *Period of Limitation for International Contracts for the Sale of Goods*, done at New York on 14 June 1974, and of the Protocol Amending the Convention on the Period of Limitation for International Contracts for the Sale of Goods, done at Vienna on 11 April 1980

Law-Decree No. 4 of 1989 promulgating the General Conditions of *Delivery of Goods between Organizations of the CMEA Member States* in 1968/1988

Government Decree No. 13/1990. (XII.30.) on the Application of the General Conditions of *Delivery of Goods between Organizations of the CMEA Member States* in 1968/1988

Law-Decree No. 5 of 1977 promulgating the *Fifth International Tin Convention*

Decree No. 35/1980. (IX.1.) of the Council of Ministers promulgating the *International Beef Convention* done at Geneva on 12 April 1979

Decree No. 36/1980. (IX.3.) of the Council of Ministers promulgating the *International Convention on Dairy Products*, done at Geneva on 12 April 1979

(bb) *Carriage*

Act VI of 1931 ratifying the Convention on *Bills of Lading*, done at Brussels on 25 August 1924

Act XXVIII of 1936 ratifying the Warsaw Convention of 1929 on International Carriage by Air; Law-Decree No. 19 of 1964 promulgating the Hague Protocol of 28 September 1955 amending the Warsaw Convention of 12 October 1929 on the Unification of Certain Enactments concerning *International Carriage by Air*

Law-Decree No. 3 of 1971 promulgating the Convention on *Contracts for the International Carriage of Goods by Road*, done at Geneva on 19 May 1956

Law-Decree No. 16 of 1978 promulgating the Tariff Convention relating to *International Carriage of Goods under Cover of TIR Carnets*

Law-Decree No. 2 of 1986 (Annexes amended by Decree No. 11/1991. (V.23.) of the Minister of Transport, Telecommunications and Water Conservancy) promulgating the Convention on *International Carriage by Rail* (COTIF), done at Berne on 9 May 1980, as amended by Decree No. 4/1987. (V.13.) of the Minister of Transport [modified by Sect. 1 of Decree No.7/1988. (VIII.11.) of the Minister of Transport and supplement I; Order No. 1/1990. (IV.30.) KÖHÉM; Ordinance No. 45/1986. (MÁVÉRT 28) of MÁV] executing Act II of 1995

(bc) *Industrial property protection*

Law-Decree No. 18 of 1970 (amended by Law-Decree No. 20 of 1986) promulgating the texts of the Berne Union Conventions on the *Protection of Industrial Property*, as revised at Stockholm on 14 July 1967

Paris Union Convention on the Protection of Industrial Property, done on 20 March 1883, as revised at Brussels on 14 December 1900, at Washington on 2 June 1911, at The Hague on 6 November 1925, at London on 2 January 1934, at Lisbon on 31 October 1958, and at Stockholm on 14 July 1967

Stockholm Instrument of 14 July 1967 Complementary to the *Madrid Agreement for the Repression of False or Deceptive Indications of Origin on Goods*, signed on 14 April 1891, as revised at Washington on 2 June 1911, at The Hague on 6 November 1925, at London on 2 June 1934 and at Lisbon on 31 October 1958

Stockholm Convention of 14 July 1967 establishing the *World Intellectual Property Organization*

Nice Agreement of 15 June 1957 for the *International Classification of Goods and Services Capable of Distinction with Seals or Trademarks*, as revised at Stockholm on 14 July 1967

Law-Decree No. 29 of 1973 (amended by Law-Decree No 21 of 1986) promulgating the *Madrid Agreement* of 14 April 1891 *for the International Registration of Marks*, as revised at Brussels on 14 December 1900, at Washington on 2 June 1911, at The Hague on 6 November 1925, at London on 2 June 1934, at Nice on 15 June 1957 and at Stockholm on 14 July 1967; and the *Locarno Agreement* of 8 October 1968 *for the International Classification of Industrial Designs*

Law-Decree No. 8 of 1975 promulgating the Agreement for the *Legal Protection of Inventions, Industrial and Registered Designs and Trademarks in the Process of Economic and Technical Cooperation*

Decree No. 22/1977. (VI.27.) of the Council of Ministers promulgating the Agreement on the *Uniform Requirements for the Preparation and Submission of Applications for Patent Protection*

Decree No. 3/1978. (I.18.) of the Council of Ministers promulgating the Agreement on the *Mutual Recognition of Authors' Certificates and Other Documents of Patent Protection*

Law-Decree No. 14 of 1980 (amended by Law-Decree No. 30 of 1984; Law-Decree No. 22 of 1986) promulgating the *Treaty of Cooperation in Patent Protection*: Decree No. 29/1980. (VII.29.) of the Council of Ministers on its Execution (amended by Decree No. 56/1984. (XII.8.) of the Council of Ministers)

Law-Decree No. 1 of 1981 (amended by Law-Decree No. 23 of 1986) promulgating the Budapest Union for the International Recognition of the *Deposit of Micro-Organisms for the Purposes of Patent Protection*

Law-Decree No. 1 of 1982 (amended by Law-Decree No. 24 of 1986) promulgating the Lisbon Agreement for the *Protection and International Registration of Marks of Origin* (Stockholm text of 14 July 1967)

Law-Decree No. 14 of 1983 promulgating the International Convention for the *Protection of New Varieties of Plants*

Law-Decree No. 29 of 1984 promulgating the Hague Agreement for the *International Deposit of Industrial Designs*

(bd) *Copyright*

Law-Decree No. 3 of 1975 promulgating the *Universal Copyright Convention* (Paris text of 24 July 1971)

Law-Decree No. 4 of 1975 promulgating the Berne Convention of 9 September 1886 for the *Protection of Literary and Artistic Works* (Paris text of 24 July 1971)

Law-Decree No. 18 of 1975 promulgating the Geneva Convention for the *Protection of Producers of Phonogrammes against Unauthorized Duplication of their Phonogrammes*, concluded on 29 October 1971

Act XXXI of 1931 ratifying the Convention on *Literary and Artistic Property*, concluded at *Montevideo* on 11 January 1899

(be) *Family law*

Law-Decree No. 53 of 1957 promulgating the Convention on *Recovery Abroad of Maintenance*, done at New York on 20 June 1956; Decree No. 9/1957. (IX.13.) of the Minister of Justice (as amended by Decree No. 7/1961. (XII.23.) of the Minister of Justice)

Law-Decree No. 2 of 1960 promulgating the Convention on the *Nationality of Married Women*, done at New York on 20 February 1957

Law Decree No. 7 of 1965 promulgating the Convention concerning the Recognition and Enforcement of Decisions relating to *Maintenance Obligations towards Children*, done at The Hague on 15 April 1958; Decree No. 8/1965. (VII.4.) of the Minister of Justice on its enforcement

Law-Decree No. 7 of 1976 promulgating the Convention on *Consent to Marriage, Minimum Age for Marriage and Registration of Marriages*, done at New York on 10 December 1962

Law-Decree No. 14 of 1986 promulgating the Treaty on the *Civil-Law Aspects of Unlawfully Taking Children Abroad*, concluded at The Hague on 25 October 1980

(bf) *Law of civil procedure*

Law-Decree No. 8 of 1966 promulgating the Hague Convention of 1 March 1954 relating to *Civil Procedure*; Decree No. 4/1966. (VI.15.) of the Minister of Justice on its Execution

Law-Decree No. 8 of 1964 promulgating the European Convention on *International Courts of Commercial Arbitration*, done at Geneva on 21 April 1961

Law-Decree No. 25 of 1962 promulgating the Convention on the *Recognition and Execution of Foreign Arbitral Awards*, done at New York on 10 June 1958; Decree No. 12/196. (X.31.) of the Minister of Justice on its Execution

Law-Decree No. 11 of 1973 promulgating the Convention *Abolishing the Requirement for Diplomatic or Consular Certification (Legalization) of Official Documents to be Used*

Abroad, done at The Hague on 5 October 1961; Execution Decree No. 9/1973. (XII.29.) of the Minister of Justice and the Minister of Foreign Affairs

Act XXXVI of 1995 repealing Law-Decree No. 23 of 1973 promulgating the Agreement on *Submission to Arbitration of Civil Disputes Arising out of Economic and Scientific-Technical Cooperation*

Bulletin No. 8003/1990. (VII.17.) of the Ministry of International Economic Relations concerning the application of the Convention on the *Recognition and Execution of Foreign Arbitral Awards*, done at New York on 10 June 1958

Bulletin No. 8001/1995. (IK.8.) of the Ministry of Justice on the *existence of reciprocity or the execution of applications in the absence of reciprocity*

(bg) *Other international treaties*

Act XVIII of 1947 ratifying the *Peace Treaty* signed at Paris on 10 February 1947

United Nations International Covenant of 1966 on Civil and Political Rights (promulgated by Law-Decree No. 8 of 1976 as amended by Law-Decree No. 25 of 1988)

United Nations International Covenant of 1966 on Economic, Social and Cultural Rights (promulgated by Law-Decree No. 9 of 1976)

Optional Protocol to the International Covenant on Civil and Political Rights (promulgated by Law-Decree No. 24 of 1988)

Act II of 1995 promulgating the *Second Optional Protocol to the International Covenant on Civil and Political Rights*, adopted by the United Nations General Assembly at its 44th Session on 15 December 1989

Law-Decree No. 22 of 1965 promulgating the Convention on *Diplomatic Relations*, done at Vienna on 24 April 1963

Act XXXV of 1991 abrogating the *Charter of CMEA and the Agreement on the Legal Capacity, Privileges and Immunities of CMEA*

Act LXXI of 1991 promulgating the Statute of the Council of Europe signed at London on 5 May 1949 and amended in accordance with the records of the Council's Secretary-General of 11 May 1951, 18 December 1951, 4 May 1953, 30 May 1958, 3 November 1961, 6 May 1963, 24 May 1965, 14 October 1970, 17 February 1971, 9 December 1974, 2 October 1976, 9 January 1978, 20 January 1978 and 27 November 1978

Act LXXII of 1991 promulgating the General Agreement on the *Privileges and Immunities of the Council of Europe* signed at Paris on 2 Sepember 1949 and complemented by the Strasbourg Protocol of 6 November 1952

Act XXXI of 1993 promulgating the Rome Convention of 4 November 1950 for the Protection of Human Rights and Fundamental Freedoms and the eight Additional Protocols thereto

Act LXXXVI of 1994 promulgating the Ninth Protocol to the European Agreement concerning Persons Participating in Proceedings before the European Commission and Court of Human Rights

Law-Decree No. 6 of 1982 promulgating the Statute of the *International Monetary Fund*

Decision No. 1/1991. (IV.13.) of the National Assembly on *raising the quota for the Republic of Hungary in the International Monetary Fund and amending the Statute thereof*

Law-Decree No. 21 of 1989 *raising the quota of the Republic of Hungary in the International Monetary Fund and promulgating the amendment to the Statute hereof*

Law-Decree No. 15 of 1982 promulgating the Statute of the *International Bank for Reconstruction and Development*

Law-Decree No. 19 of 1985 promulgating the Statute of the *International Development Association* (IDA)

Law-Decree No. 20 of 1985 promulgating the Statute of the *International Financial Corporation* (IFC)

Act LV of 1991 promulgating the Agreement on the *Establishment of the European Bank for Reconstruction and Development*

Decision No. 78/1990. (XI.17.) of the National Assembly on the Acceptance of Membership in the *European Bank for Reconstruction and Development* (as complemented by Decision No. 61/1991. (X.19.) of the National Assembly)

Act III of 1996 promulgating the *Framework Agreement on Financial Cooperation between the Republic of Hungary and the European Investment Bank*

Decree No. 23/1973. (IX.9.) of the Council of Ministers promulgating the Geneva Convention of 12 April 1979 on *Technical Barriers to Trade*

Government Decree No. 83/1996. (VI.14.) promulgating the Convention on *Uniform Procedure for the Dispatch of Goods*

Government Decree No. 84/1996. (VI.14.) promulgating the Convention on the *Simplification of Customs Formalities*

Decree No. 40/1980. (X.27.) of the Council of Ministers promulgating the Convention relating to the *Implementation of Article VI of the General Agreement on Tariffs and Trade*

Law-Decree No. 1 of 1965 promulgating the *Conventions on Bills of Exchange*, done at Geneva on 7 June 1930; Decree No. 1/1965. (I.24.) of the Minister of Justice on its execution (as amended by Decree No. 10/1974. (IX.25.) of the Minister of Justice

Law-Decree No. 27 of 1987 promulgating the Washington Convention of 18 March 1965 on the *Settlement of Investment Disputes between States and Natural and Legal Persons of Other States*

Law-decree No. 7 of 1989 promulgating the Convention on the *Establishment of the International Investment Insurance Agency*, done at Seoul on 11 October 1985

Act XIII of 1996 promulgating the *Stockholm Convention of 15 December 1992 on Conciliation and Arbitration, concluded within the framework of the Conference on Security and Cooperation in Europe, and the Financial Protocol adopted pursuant to Art. 13 of the Convention*

Act XVIII of 1996 promulgating the *Treaty on Arbitration and Conciliation between the Republic of Hungary and the Swiss Confederation*, signed at Budapest on 17 December 1992

Act LXXXV of 1994 *extending the privileges, immunities and facilities recognized in the Vienna Convention of 18 April 1961 on Diplomatic Relations to the institutions, officers and employees of the Conference on Security and Cooperation in Europe, to representatives of the participating States, and to the staff members of CSCE Missions*

Act LXVII of 1995 *ratifying the Framework Document on the Programme of "Partnership for Peace", signed with the North Atlantic Treaty Organization, and enforcing it on the part of the Republic of Hungary*

Act CII of 1995 ratifying and promulgating the *Agreement on the Legal Status of Armed Forces between the States Party to the North Atlantic Treaty and Other States Participating in the "Partnership for Peace"*

3. OTHER INTERNATIONAL CONVENTIONS AND SOURCES

(a) *International conventions*

(to which Hungary is not a party)

Hague Convention of 1955 on the *Law Applicable to International Sale of Goods*

Hague Convention of 1956 on the *Legal Status of Legal Persons in Private International Law*

Hague Convention of 1956 on the *Law Applicable to Maintenance Obligations towards Children*

Hague Convention of 1961 on the *Law of Conflicts Governing the Formal Requirements of Testamentary Dispositions*

Hague Convention of 1964 relating to a *Uniform Law on the International Sale of Goods*

Hague Convention of 1965 on the *Law Applicable to Jurisdiction over Judgments on Adoption and on the Recognition of Judgments on Adoption*

Hague Convention of 1965 concerning *Service Abroad of Judicial and Other Administrative Documents in Civil and Commercial Cases*

Hague Convention of 1965 on *Choice of Forum*

Hague Convention of 1970 on the *Recognition of Divorce Decrees and Judgments on Separation*

Hague Convention of 1970 on the *Taking of Evidence Abroad in Civil and Commercial Cases*

Hague Convention of 1971 on the *Law Applicable to Road Accidents*

Hague Convention of 1971 on the *Recognition and Enforcement of Foreign Judgments in Civil and Commercial Cases*

Hague Convention of 1973 on the *Law Applicable to Liability for Products*

Hague Convention of 1973 on the *International Administration of Estates*

Hague Convention of 1986 on the *Law Applicable to International Contracts for the Sale of Goods*

Hague Convention of 1988 on the *Private International Law of Succession*

(b) *Other international sources*

Universal Declaration of Human Rights, 10 December 1948

Final Act of the Conference on Security and Cooperation in Europe (Helsinki, 1975), Part II on Economic Cooperation

Charter of Economic Rights and Duties of States (United Nations, 1974)

Charter of Paris for a New Europe, 1991

Incoterms 1990, with Hungarian, English, French and German texts, *MGK Külkereskedelmi Jogi Dokumentációk 17*

Convention on International Financial Leasing (UNIDROIT Convention, Ottawa, 1988, Hungary deposited its declaration of accession with the Canadian government on 6 May 1996)

European Economic Community – Treaty of EEC (Rome) Establishing the European Economic Community signed in Rome on 25 March 1957

Single European Act adopted in Luxembourg on 17 February 1986 and in The Hague on 28 February 1986

European Union – EU Treaty (Treaty on European Union signed in Maastricht on 7 February 1992; it entered into force on 1 November 1993)

Agreement on the European Economic Area (EEA) signed in Oporto on 2 May 1992
International Monetary Fund Articles of Agreement as amended (effective 11 November 1992), Washington, D.C., 1992

IBRD Articles of Agreement (as amended through 28 April, 1993), Washington, D.C., 1993

4. PRINCIPAL FOREIGN CODES AND PUBLISHED DRAFTS OF PRIVATE INTERNATIONAL LAW

(a) *Foreign codifications*

USA: Restatement of the Law -- Conflict of Laws, Second, 1969

Austria: Federal Act on Private International Law, 15 June 1978, in: *RabelsZ* 1979, pp. 375 *et seq.*

Czechoslovakia: Act of 4 December 1963 on Private and Procedural International Law

France: *Code civil* of 1804; draft of 1967 (*Project de loi complétant le code civil en matière de droit international privé*)

Germany, Federal Republic of: Act of 25 July 1986 Reregulating Private International Law

Greece: Civil Code of 1940/1946, Book I, Chap. II

Italy: Act 218 of 31 May 1995 Reforming the Italian System of Private International Law

Japan: Act of 21 June 1898 on the Application of Law (*Horei*)

Poland: Act of 12 November 1965 on Private International Law

Portugal: Law-Decree No. 47.344 of 25 November 1966 (as amended by Law-Decree No. 496/77) on the Civil Code, Book I, Title I, Chap. III

Romania: Act 105 of 22 September 1992 Regulating Private International Relations

Spain: Civil Code of 1889 (as amended on 31 May 1974), Introductory Title and Chap. IV

Switzerland: Act of 18 December 1987 on Private International Law

Turkey: Act of 1982 (*RablesZ* 1983, pp. 131 *et seq.*)

Yugoslavia: Law of 23 July 1982 (Official Gazette No. 43)

(b) *International codifications*

Code Bustamante (the Uniform Code of Private International Law in some Latin-American countries), Havana, 1928

Rome Convention of EC on the Determination of the Law Applicable to Contracts, 1980 (*RablesZ* 1982, pp. 196 *et seq.*)

Brussels Convention of EC on Jurisdiction and the Enforcement of Judgments in Civil and Commercial Cases, 1968 [29. I.L.M. 1413 (1990)]

Lugano Convention of EC-EFTA on Jurisdiction and the Enforcement of Judgments in Civil and Commercial Cases, 1988 [28. I.L.M. 620 (1989)]

Arbitration Rules of the United Nations Economic Commission for Europe (Draft Convention), 1966

Arbitration Rules (UNCITRAL Uniform Arbitration Rules, 1985, recommendation of the United Nations)

Arbitration Rules of the International Chamber of Commerce: New ICC Conciliation Rules and Amended Arbitration Rules in Force as from 1 January, 1988. ICC Publication No. 447, Paris, 1987

II. BIBLIOGRAPHY

1. MONOGRAPHS, TEXTBOOKS, HANDBOOKS

Bán, Ch.–Mádl, F.: *A külgazdaság jogi alapintézményeinek fejlődése (a külkereskedelmi monopólium)* [Main Legal Institutions of the External Economy (Foreign Trade Monopoly)]. Budapest 1988

Bar, von Ch.: *Internationales Privatrecht I: Allgemeine Lehren, II: Besonderer Teil.* München 1987, 1991

Batiffol, H.–Lagarde, P: *Droit international privé, I–II.* Paris 1981, 1983

Beale, J.H.: *The Conflict of Laws, I–III.* New York 1935

Bergmann, A.–Ferid, M. (eds.): *Internationales Ehe- und Kindschaftsrecht.* Frankfurt 1969 ff.

Bianca, C.M.–Bonell, M.J. (eds.): *Commentary on International Sales Law.* Milan 1987

Bónis, Gy.: *Középkori jogunk elemei* (Institutions of Medieval Law in Hungary). Budapest 1972

Bucher, A: *Grundfragen der Anknüpfungsgerechtigkeit im internationalen Privatrecht.* Basel–Stuttgart 1975

Buxbaum, M.R.–Mádl, F. (eds.): *State and Economy.* Vol. XVII of the International Encyclopedia of Comparative Law. Tübingen–Dordrecht–Boston–Lancaster (with individual chapters continuously published since 1975)

Caemmerer, von E.–Schlechtriem, P. (eds.): *Kommentar zum Einheitlichen UN-Kaufrecht.* 2nd ed. München 1995

Cavers, D.F.: *The Choice-of-Law Process.* Ann Arbor 1965

Cheshire, G.C.–North, P.M.: *Private International Law.* London 1979

Clarke, M.A.: *International Carriage of Goods by Road:* CMR. London 1991

Cohn, E.J.–Domke, M.–Eisemann, F. (eds.): *Handbook of Institutional Arbitration in International Trade. Facts, Figures and Rules.* Amsterdam–New York–Oxford 1977

Currie, B.: *Selected Essays on the Conflict of Laws.* Durham N.C. 1963

Dicey, A.V.–Morris, J.H.C.: *The Conflict of Laws.* London 1987

Dölle, H. (ed.): *Kommentar zum Einheitlichen Kaufrecht.* München 1976

Ehrenzweig, A.A.: *A Treatise on the Conflict of Laws.* St. Paul, Minn. 1962

Ehrenzweig, A.A.: *Private International Law. General Part.* Leyden–New York 1967

Ehrenzweig, A.A.: *Private International Law.* A Comparative Treatise on American International Conflicts Law. I–III (II–III: Ehrenzweig, A.A.–Jayme, E.), Leiden–New York 1972, 1973, 1977

Ehrenzweig, A.A.: *Conflicts in a Nutshell.* St. Paul, Minn. 1974

Enderlein, F.–Maskow, D.–Stargardt, M.: *Kommentar zur Kaufrechtskonvention der UNO.* Berlin 1985

Ernst, E.: *Nemzetközi áruegyezmények* (International Commodity Conventions). Budapest 1977

Ferid, M.: *Internationales Privatrecht.* Frankfurt 1986

Ferid, M.–Firsching, K. (Eds.): *Internationales Erbrecht.* Quellensammlung mit systematischen Darstellungen des materiellen Erbrechts, sowie des Kollisionsrechts der wichtigsten Staaten. München-Berlin 1975 ff.

Filipescu, I.–Jacota, M.: *Drept international privat.* Bucharest 1968

Fischer, G.: *Verkehrsschutz im Internationalen Vertragsrecht.* Köln 1990

Firsching, K.–v. Hoffmann, B.: *Internationales Privatrecht, 4. Auflage.* München 1995

Flessner, A.: *Interessenjurisprudenz im IPR.* Tübingen 1990

Francescakis, Ph.: *La théorie du renvoi; les conflicts de systemes en droit international privé.* Paris 1958

Fulda, C.M.–Schwartz, W.F.: *Regulation of International Trade and Investment.* New York 1970

Gamillscheg, F.: *Der Einfluss Dumoulins auf die Entwicklung des Kollisionsrechts.* Berlin-Tübingen 1955

Gamillscheg, F.: *Internationales Arbeitsrecht.* Berlin–Tübingen 1959

Gamillscheg, F.: Art. 13–17 EGBGB, in: *von Staudinger: Kommentar zum BGB, EGBG* Teil 3, Berlin 1973

Graveson, R.H.: *Conflict of Laws. Private International Law.* London 1974

Gutzwiller, M.: *Der Einfluss Savignys auf die Entwicklung des Internationalprivatrechts.* Friburg (Schweiz) 1923

Gutzwiller, M.: *Geschichte des Internationalprivatrechts.* Basel–Stuttgart 1977

Hamza, G.: *Jogösszehasonlítás és antikvitás* (Comparison of Laws and Antiquity). Budapest 1985

Hegyi, A.–Törzsök, É.–Gulyás, I.–Metz, Zs.–Sipos, Z.: *A külkereskedelem technikája és szervezése* (Technique and Organization of Foreign Trade). Budapest 1991

Heldrich, A.: Art. 3–38 EGBGB, in: *Palandt: Kommentar zum BGB.* München 1991

Herbert, R.–Czerwenka, B.: *Internationales Kaufrecht (Kommentar).* München 1991

Hontvári, M.: *Felelősség a minőségért a nemzetközi adásvétel körében* (Liability for Quality in International Business Transactions). Budapest 1979

Internationales Privatrecht: *Kommentar zum Rechtsanwendungsgesetz* (Hrsg.: Ministerium der Justiz der DDR). Berlin 1989

Ipsen, H.P.: *Europäisches Gemeinschaftsrecht.* Tübingen 1972

Jackson, D.C.: *The "Conflicts" Process.* Jurisdiction and Choice in Private International Law. New York 1975

Jayme, E.: *Pasquale Stanislao Mancini.* Ebelsbach 1980

Jayme, E.: *Methoden der Konkretisierung des ordre public im Internationalen Privatrecht.* Heidelberg 1989

Jayme, E.–Hausmann, R. (eds.): *Internationales Privat- und Verfahrensrecht.* Textaufgabe. München 1990

Joerges, Ch.: *Zum Funktionswandel des Kollisionsrechts* – Die "Governmental Interest Analysis" und die "Krise des Internationalen Privatrechts". Berlin–Tübingen 1971

Juenger, F.K.: *Zum Wandel des Internationalen Privatrechts.* Karlsruhe 1974

Kahn, F.: *Abhandlungen zum internationalen Privatrecht.* München–Leipzig 1928

Kalensky, P.: *Trends of Private International Law.* Prague 1971

Kegel, G.: *EGBGB, in: Soergel–Siebert: Kommentar zum BGB VII.* Stuttgart 1970

Kegel, G.: *Internationales Privatrecht.* 7. Auflage. München 1995

Keller, M.–Siehr, K.: *Allgemeine Lehren des internationalen Privatrechts.* Zürich 1986

Király, M.–Mádl, F.: *A külföldi beruházások jogi védelme* (Legal Protection of Foreign Investments). Budapest 1989

Koerner, D.: *Fakultatives Kollisionsrecht in Frankreich und Deutschland.* Tübingen 1995

Kornfol, Z.A.: *Protection of Foreign Investment.* Leiden 1972

Kropholler, J.: *Internationales Einheitsrecht.* Allgemeine Lehren. Tübingen 1975

Kropholler, J.: *Europäisches Zivilprozessrecht.* Heidelberg 1991

Kropholler, J.: *Internationales Privatrecht,* 2nd ed. Tübingen 1994

Lagarde, P.: *La nationalité française.* Paris 1989

Langen, E.: *Transnational Commercial Law.* Leiden 1973

Lasok, D.–Stone, P.A.: *Civil Jurisdiction and Judgements in the EC, in: Conflict of Laws in the European Community*. Oxon–Worcester 1987, pp. 149–325

Leflar, R.A.: *American Conflicts Law*. Indianapolis–New York–Charlottesville 1977

Lipstein, K. (eds.): *International Encyclopedia of Comparative Law*. Vol. III. Private International Law. Tübingen–Paris (with individual chapters continuously published since 1972)

Loeber, D.A.: *East-West Trade*. Vols. 1–4. Dobbs Ferry, New York 1976–1977

Loewe, R. (eds.): *Internationales Kaufrecht*. Wien 1989

Loewenfeld, F.A.: *International Economic Law*. Vol. II. International Private Investment. New York 1976

Loewenfeld, F.A.: *International Economic Law*. Vol. IV. The International Monetary System. New York 1977

Loquin, E.: *L'amiable composition en droit comparé et international*. Paris 1980

Lorenz, E.: *Zur Struktur des internationalen Privatrechts – ein Beitrag zur Reformdiskussion*. Berlin 1977

Loussouarn, Y.–Bredin, J.D.: *Droit du commerce international*. Paris 1969

Lunts, L.–Marusheva, N.J.: *Kurs mezhdunarodnovo chastnovo prava*. Mezhdunarodny grazhdanskiy protsess. Moscow 1976

Lunz, L.: *Internationales Privatrecht*. Besonderer Teil. Berlin 1962

Lunz, L.: *Internationales Privatrecht*. Allgemeiner Teil. Berlin 1971

Lübchen, G.A.–Posch, M.: *Zivilrechtsverhältnisse mit Ausländsberührung*. Berlin 1978

Lüderitz, A.: *Internationales Privatrecht*, 2nd ed. Berlin 1992

Majoros, F.: *Les conventions internationales en matière de droit privé*. Abrégé théorique et traité pratique. I, II. Paris 1976, 1980

Makarov, A.N. (eds.): *Quellen des Internationalen Privatrechts*. Tübingen 1978

Mancini, P.S.: *Diritto internationale, Prelezioni*. Napoli 1873

Maresceau, M. (ed.): *The Political and Legal Framework* of Trade Relations between the European Community and the Eastern Countries. Dordrecht–Boston–London 1989

Martonyi, J.–Vattay, Gy. (eds.): *A külkereskedelmi tevékenység jogi kézikönyve* (Legal Manual Of Foreign Trade Activity). Budapest 1991

Mádl, F.: *Az Európai Gazdasági Közösség Joga* (The Law of the European Economic Community). Budapest 1974

Mádl, F.: *Összehasonlító nemzetközi magánjog*. A nemzetközi gazdasági kapcsolatok joga (Comparative Private International Law. The Law of International Economic Relations). Budapest 1978

Mádl, F.: *A külgazdaság és a nemzetközi beruházások joga* (The External Economy and the Law of International Investment). Budapest 1988

Mádl, F.: *Az Európai Gazdasági Közösség és Magyarország* (The European Economic Community and Hungary). Budapest 1988

Mádl, F.–Vékás, L.: *Magyar nemzetközi magánjog – a nemzetközi gazdasági kapcsolatok jogának főbb elemeivel* (Hungarian Private International Law, with the Main Elements of the Law of International Economic Relations). Budapest 1981, 2nd ed. 1985, 3rd ed. 1992, 4th ed. 1997

Messmann, S.: *Die rechtliche Stellung ausländischer Direktinvestitionen*. Zürich 1978

Mestmäcker, E.J.: *Recht und ökonomisches Gesetz*. Über die Grenzen von Staat, Gesellschaft und Privatautonomie. 2nd ed. Baden–Baden 1984

Mohi, Cs.–Dienes-Oehm, E.–Bajor, S. (eds.): *Magyarország külkereskedelmi tárgyú kétoldalú nemzetközi szerződései* (Hungary's Bilateral International Treaties on Foreign Trade). Budapest 1979

Neuhaus, P.H.: *Die Grundbegriffe des internationalen Privatrechts*. Tübingen 1976

New ICC Conciliation Rules and Amended Arbitration Rules in Force as from 1 January 1988. ICC Publication No. 447, Paris 1987

Niboyet, J–P.: *Cours de droit international privé français.* Paris 1949

Niederer, W.: *Einführung in die allgemeinen Lehren des internationalen Privatrechts.* Zürich 1961

Nussbaum, A.: *Principles of Private International Law.* New York–London–Toronto 1943

Pescatore, P.: *Le droit de l'integration. Emergence d'un phénomene nouveau dans les relations internationales selon l'expérience des Communautés Européennes.* Leiden–Géneve 1972

Pillet, A.: *Traité pratique de droit international privé.* I–II, Grenoble–Paris 1923–1924

Pisar, S.: *Transaction entre l'Est et l'Ouest.* Paris 1972

Plender, R.: *The European Contracts Convention* (The Rome Convention on the Choice of Law for Contracts). London 1991

Pusztai, Gy. (eds.): *Iparjogvédelmi kézikönyv* (A Manual of the Protection of Industrial Property). Budapest 1986

Raape, L.: *Internationales Privatrecht.* Berlin–Frankfurt 1961

Raape, L.–Sturm, F.: *Internationales Privatrecht.* Allgemeine Lehren. München 1977

Rabel, E.: *The Conflict of Laws.* I–II, Ann Arbor 1958, 1960

Reichert–Facilides, D.: *Fakultatives und zwingendes Kollisionsrecht.* Tübingen 1995

Reinhart, G.: *UN-Kaufrecht. Kommentar.* Heidelberg 1991

Reithmann, Ch.–Martiny, D.: *Internationales Vertragsrecht.* 4th ed., Köln 1988

Restatement of the Law (Second). Conflict of Laws 2d. I–III, St. Paul, Minn. 1971

Réczei, L.: *Nemzetközi magánjog* (Private International Law). Budapest 1960

Rieber, H.: *EFTA Übereinkommen zur Errichtung der Europäischen Freihandelsassoziation.* Baden–Baden 1967

Rigaux, F.: *Droit international privé.* I–II, Bruxelles 1977, 1979

Sajko, K.: *Medunarodno privatno pravo.* Zagreb 1982

Samtleben, J.: *Internationales Privatrecht in Lateinamerika, Der Código Bustamante in Theorie und Praxis. I. Bd.* Tübingen 1979

Sándor, T.: *A nemzetközi adásvétel. (Az áruk nemzetközi adásvételéről szóló 1980. évi ENSZ-Egyezmény magyarázata)* [International Sale. (Comments on the United Nations Convention of 1980 on the International Sale of Goods)]. Budapest 1990

Sarcevic, P. (ed.).: *Essays on International Commercial Arbitration.* London–Dordrecht–Boston 1989

Savigny, von C.: *System des heutigen Römischen Rechts.* VIII, Berlin 1849 (Unveränderter Nachdruck. Darmstadt 1956)

Schlecht, O.: *Grundlagen und Perspektiven der Sozialen Marktwirt*schaft. Tübingen 1990

Schlechtriem, P.: *Einheitliches UN-Kaufrecht.* (Das Übereinkommen der Vereinten Nationen über internationale Warenkaufverträge. Darstellung und Texte.) Tübingen 1981

Schlechtriem, P.: *Internationales UN-Kaufrecht.* Tübingen 1996

Schmitthoff, C.M.: *The Export Trade.* The Law and Practice of International Trade. London 1969

Schnitzer, A.F.: *Handbuch des internationalen Privatrechts.* I–II. Basel 1957, 1958

Schnyder, A.K.: *Das neue IPR-Gesetz. Eine Einführung in das Bundesgesetz vom 18. Dezember 1987 über das Internationale Privatrecht (IPRG).* 2nd ed., Zürich 1990

Schurig, K.: *Kollisionsnorm und Sachrecht.* Berlin 1981

Schwander, I.: *Lois d'application immédiate, Sonderenknüpfung, IPR-Sachnormen und andere Ausnahmen von der gewöhnlichen Anknüpfung im international Privatrecht.* Zürich 1975

Schwarzenberger, G.: *Foreign Investments and International Law*. London 1979

Schwimann, M.: *Grundriss des international Privatrechts*. Wien 1982

Schwind, F.: *Handbuch des Österreichischen Internationalen Privatrechts*. Wien–New York 1975

Schwind, F.: *Internationales Privatrecht*. Wien 1990

Shihata: *MIGA and Foreign Investment*. Dordrecht–Boston–Lancaster 1988

Starr, R. (ed.): *East-West Business Transactions*. New York–Washington–London 1974

Steindorff, E.: *Sachnormen im internationalen Privatrecht*. Frankfurt/M. 1958

Steiner, J.: *EGK-jog. Az Európai Gazdasági Közösség jogrendszere* (EEC Law. The Legal System of the European Economic Community). Budapest 1990

Story, J.: *Commentaries on the Conflict of Laws*. Boston 1834 (Reprint: New York 1972)

Szászy, I.: *Az európai népi demokráciák nemzetközi magánjoga* (Private International Law in the European People's Democracies). Budapest 1962

Szászy, I.: *Nemzetközi polgári eljárásjog* (International Law of Civil Procedure). Budapest 1963

Szászy, I.: *Jogszabály-összeütközések* (Conflicts of Laws). Budapest 1973

Trutmann, V.: *Das internationale Privatrecht der Deliktsobligationen*. Basel–Stuttgart 1973

Ulmer, E.: *Die Immaterialgüterrechte im internationalen Privatrecht*. Köln–Berlin–Bonn–München 1975

Várady, T.: *Medunarodno Privatno Pravo*. Novi Sad 1990

Vékás, L.: *A nemzetközi magánjog elméleti alapjai* (The Theoretical Foundations of Private International Law). Budapest 1988

Világhy, M.: *Bevezetés a nemzetközi magánjogba* (Introduction to Private International Law). Budapest 1966

Vogel, K.: *Der räumliche Anwendungsbereich der Verwaltungsrechtsnorm*. Frankfurt/M.–Berlin 1965

Volker, P.: *Konventionskonflikte im IPR*. Zürich 1977

Walker, G.: *Internationales Privatrecht*. Wien 1934

Wengler, W.: *Internationales Privatrecht*. I–II, Berlin–New York 1981

Wiethölter, R.: *Einseitige Kollisionsnormen als Grundlage des Internationalen Privatrechts*. Berlin 1956

Will, M.R.: *International Sales Law under CISG*, International Bibliography 1980–1995, *The First 150 or so Decisions 1988–1995*. Geneva 1995

Will, M.R.: *International Sales Law under CISG, The First 284 or so Decisions 1988–1995*. Geneva 1996

Wolff, M.: *Das internationale Privatrecht Deutschlands*. Berlin–Göttingen–Heidelberg 1954

2. TREATISES

Balázs, P.: *Az EGK kívülálló országokhoz fűződő kapcsolatainak jellege és rendszerezése* (Nature and Systematization of EEC's Relations with Non-Member States). Külpolitika, June 1988

Bán Ch.: Mádl–Vékás: *Magyar nemzetközi magánjog. A nemzetközi gazdasági kapcsolatok jogának főbb elemeivel című könyvéről* (On Mádl's and Vékás's Book Entitled Hungarian Private International Law, with the Main Elements of the Law of International Economic Relations). Állam- és Jogtudomány XXV (1982), pp. 179–191

Barry, N.: *The Vienna Convention on International Sales Law*. Law Quarterly Review 105 (1989), pp. 201–243

Behrens, P.: *Voraussetzungen und Grenzen der Rechtsfortbildung durch Rechtsvereinheitlichung*. RabelsZ 50 (1986)

Beitzke, G.: *Les obligations délictuelles en droit international privé*. Recueil des Cours 1965 II, pp. 63–145

Bennett, T.W.: *Choice of Law Rules in Claims of Unjust Enrichment*. International Comparative Law Quarterly 39 (1990), pp. 136–168

Best, M.–Winsconsin, F.: *CISG: To Use, or Not to Use?* International Business Lawyer, January 1993, pp. 10–14

Binder, H.: *Zur Auflockerung des Deliktsstatus*. RabelsZ 20 (1955), pp. 401–499

Bobrovszky, J.: *Nemzetközi iparjogvédelemi kapcsolataink jogi szabályozása* (Legal Regulation of Hungary's Relations in the Field of International Industrial Property Protection). Jogtudományi Közlöny XXXVI (1981), pp. 1015–1025

Bobrovszky, J.: *Nemzetközi iparjogvédelmi együttműködés, in:* Pusztai, Gy. (főszerk.): *Iparjogvédelmi kézikönyv* (International Cooperation in Industrial Property Protection, in: Pusztai, Gy. (gen. ed.): Manual on the Protection of Industrial Property). Budapest 1989, pp. 265–307

Bobrovszky, J.: *Iparjogvédelem a külkereskedelmi kapcsolatok területén*, in: Martonyi–Vattay (szerk.): A külkereskedelmi tevékenység jogi kézikönyve (Protection of Industrial Property in the Field of Foreign Trade Relations, in: Martonyi–Vattay (eds.): Legal Manual on Foreign Trade Activities). Budapest 1991, pp. 293–324

Bogsch, Á.: *A Szellemi Tulajdon Világszervezete* (The World Intellectual Property Organization). Jogtudományi Közlöny XXXVI (1981), pp. 973–983

Bonell, M.J.: *Vertragsverhandlungen und culpa in contrahendo nach dem Wiener Kaufrechtsübereinkommen*. Recht der Internationalen Wirtschaft, 1994/9

Boytha, Gy.: *A nemzetközi szerzői jogi és szomszédjogi egyezmények összefüggései* (Interrelationships of International Conventions on Copyright and Related Rights). Jogtudományi Közlöny XXXVI (1981), pp. 994–1007

Boytha, Gy.: *Nemzetközi szerzői jog,* in: Petrik, F. (szerk.): *A szerzői jog* (International Copyright, in: Petrik, F. (ed.): Copyright). Budapest 1990, pp. 313–373

Broches, A.: The World Bank, in: Rendell, R.S. (ed.): International Financial Law. London 1983, Vol. II, pp. 83–96

Burián, L.: *A jogi személyek honossága, különös tekintettel az amerikai embargó extraterritoriális hatályára* (The Nationality of Legal Persons, with Particular Emphasis on the Extraterritorial Effect of the American Embargo). Jogtudományi Közlöny XXXIX (1984), pp. 199–205

Burián, L.: *A deliktuális felelősség nemzetközi magánjogi szabályozásának kialakulása* (Evolution of the Regulation of Delictual Liability in Private International Law). Jogtudományi Közlöny XLI (1986), pp. 78–84

Burián, L.: *A deliktuális felelősség kapcsoló szabályai az angol nemzetközi magánjogban* (The Delictual Liability in English Private International Law). Jogtudományi Közlöny XLI (1986), pp. 278–284

Burián, L.: *A deliktuális felelősség kollíziós szabályainak fejlődése az Amerikai Egyesült Államokban* (Evolution of the Conflict Rules of Delictual Liability in the United States of America). Állam- és Jogtudomány XXIX (1986), pp. 632–650

Burián, L.: *A deliktuális felelősség a francia nemzetközi magánjogban* (Delictual Liability in French Private International Law). Jogtudományi Közlöny XLIII (1988), pp. 415–421

Burián, L.: *A deliktuális felelősség a német nemzetközi magánjogban* (Delictual Liability in German Private International Law). Állam- és Jogtudomány XXXI (1989), pp. 57–96

Burián, L.: *A deliktuális felelősség a magyar nemzetközi magánjogban* (Delictual Liability in Hungarian Private International Law). Jogtudományi Közlöny XLV (1990), pp. 150–161

Burián L.: *A szerződésen kívüli károkozásért fennálló felelősség nemzetközi szabályainak gyakorlati és elméleti kérdései néhány európai ország jogában* (Practical and Theoretical Questions of the International Rules on Liability for Non-Contractual Damage in the Laws of Some European Countries). Állam- és Jogtudomány XXXII (1990), pp. 143–168

Burián, L.: *Az Incoterms*, in: Martonyi-Vattay (szerk.): *A külkereskedelmi tevékenység kézikönyve* (Incoterms, in: Martonyi-Vattay (ed.): Manual on Foreign Trade Activities). Budapest, 1991. pp. 43–55

Burián, L.: *A lex mercatoria alkalmazása nemzetközi kereskedelmi jogvitákban* (Application of the lex mercatoria in International Commercial Litigation). Magyar Jog 43 (1996), pp. 490–503

Camacho, J.E.: *The International Finance Corporation*, in: Rendell, R.S. (eds.): *International Financial Law*. London 1983, Vol. II, pp. 97–104

Cavers, D.F.: *Contemporary Conflicts Law in American Perspective*. Recueil des Cours 1970 III, pp. 75–308

Conetti, G.: *Die internationale Adoption Minderjähriger: Einführung einseitiger Kollisionsnormen in ein zweiseitiges System des Internationalen Privatrechts*. ZfRV 29 (1988), pp. 162–166

Csaba, L.: *Kis országok a KGST-ben: merre tovább?* (Small Countries in CMEA: Which Way to Proceed?). Közgazdasági Szemle 37 (1990), No. 1, pp. 1–18

Csehi, Z.: A *nemzetközi kereskedelmi választottbíróság eljárására alkalmazandó szabályok meghatározása* (Determination of the Rules Applicable to the International Commercial Arbitration Procedure). Magyar Jog 42 (1995), pp. 431–448

Deák, F.: *Organs of States in Their External Relations: Immunities and Privileges of State Organs and of the State, in: Manual of Public International law*. London-Melbourne-Toronto 1968, pp. 381–468

Dienes–Oehm, E.: *Az Európai Közösségek külső kapcsolatainak jogi alapja és gyakorlata* (The Legal Basis and Practice of the External Relations of the European Communities). Külgazdaság, No. 4 of 1987

Dienes–Oehm, E.: *A külföldi tőke magyarországi beruházásainak elősegítése a nemzetközi jog eszközeivel* (Promotion of Foreign Capital Investments in Hungary by Means of International Law). Külgazdaság XXXII (1988), No. 2, pp. 17–27

Droz, A.L.–Dyer, A.: *International Conventions Viewed in Terms of the Work Accomplished by the Hague Conference on Private International Law,* in: Annario Juridico Interamericano 1984, pp. 223–261

Edler, R.: *Verjährung und Res Iudicata im englischen internationalen Privatrecht*. RabelsZ 40 (1976), pp. 43–55

Einsele, D.: *Rechtswahlfreiheit im Internationalen Privatrecht*. RabelsZ 60 (1996), pp. 417–447

Flessner, A.: *Fakultatives Kollisionsrecht*. RabelsZ 34 (1970), pp. 547–584

Gábor, F.: *Új korszak az Egyesült Államok nemzetközi magánjogában* (A New Period in the Private International Law of the United States). Jogtudományi Közlöny XXXVIII (1983), pp. 167–172

Gehér, J.: *A külföldön kötött házasságot felbontó határozatok elismerése Magyarországon* (Recognition in Hungary of Divorce Decrees Dissolving Marriages Contracted Abroad). Magyar Jog XXXIII (1986), pp. 149–156

Giardina, A.: *The International Center for Settlement of Investment Disputes between States and Nationals of other States (ICSID)*, in: Sarcevic (ed.): pp. 214–222

Goed, J.: *Balance of Payment Transactions of the International Monetary Fund, in: Rendell, R.S. (ed.): International Financial Law.* London 1983, Vol. II, pp. 65–82

Gutzviller, P.M.: *Von Ziel und Methode des IPR.* Schweizerisches Jahrbuch für internationales Recht 25 (1968), pp. 161–196

Gyertyánfy, P.: *A számítógépes eljárási rendszer (szoftver) összehasonlító szerzői jogi vizsgálata* (An Analysis of Computerized Processing (Software) in Comparative Copyright Law). Jogtudományi Közlöny XXXVII (1982), pp. 491–499

Gyertyánfy P.: *Ellentmondások és változások korunk szerzői jogában* (Contradictions and Change in Contemporary Copyright Law). Jogtudományi Közlöny XXXIX (1984), pp. 55–59

Gyertyánfy, P.: *Szerzői jogunk és az európai integráció* (Hungarian Copyright Law and the European Integration). Magyar Jog XXXVII (1991), pp. 344–350, 534–540, 594–600

Hahn, H.J.–Gramlich, L.: *Foreign Commerce and Investment in Market Economy Countries,* in: *International Encyclopedia of Comparative Law,* see Buxbaum, M.R.–Mádl, F. (eds.): Chapter 22

Hamza, G.: *Nemzetközi magánjog és a római jog* (Private International Law and Roman Law). Acta Fac. Pol.–Iur. Univ. Budapest XXIV (1982), pp. 260–283

Harmathy, A.: *A tartós gazdasági kapcsolatokból eredő jogviták a választottbíróság gyakorlatában* (Legal Disputes Arising out of Lasting Economic Relations in the Practice of Arbitration). Jogtudományi Közlöny XXXVIII (1983), pp. 216–222

Harmathy, A.: *A Bécsi Vételi Konvenció alkalmazásának kizárása* (Exclusion of the Application of the Vienna Sales Convention). Friss Hírek 4/1991, pp. 8–10

Hay, P.: *Die Qualifikation der Verjährung im US-amerikanischen Recht.* IPRax 9 (1989), pp. 197–202

Heini, A.: *Neuere Strömungen im amerikanischen internationalen Privatrecht.* Schweizerisches Jahrbuch für internationales Recht 19 (1962), pp. 31–70

Hellner, J.: *Einheitliches Kaufrecht und internationales Privatrecht,* in: Gedächnisschrift Ehrenzweig. Karlsruhe-Heidelberg 1976, pp. 21–34

Hermnann, G.: *The UNCITRAL Model Law on International Commercial Arbitration,* in: Sarcevic (ed.): pp. 3–26

Hoffmann, von B.: *Über den Schutz des Schwächeren bei internationalen Schuldverträgen.* RabelsZ 38 (1974), pp. 396–420

Hontte, H. van: *Conduct of Arbitral Proceedings,* in: Sarcevic (ed.): pp. 113–128

Horváth, É.: *Incoterms 1990.* Friss Hírek 4/1991, pp. 3–8

Hoyer, H.: *Die gemeinsamen Bestimmungen des schweizerischen IPR-Gesetzentwurfs.* Schweizerisches Jahrbuch für internationales Recht 35 (1979), pp. 35–56

Jayme, E.: *Zur Krise des "Governmental-Interest-Approach".* Festschrift Kegel, Frankfurt 1977, pp. 359–366

Jayme, E.: *Allgemeine Geschäftsbedingungen und internationeles Privatrecht.* ZHR 1978, pp. 105–123

Joerges, Ch.: *Die klassische Konzeption des internationalen Privatrechts und das Recht des unlauteren Wettbewerbs.* RabelsZ 36 (1972), pp. 421–491

Joerges, Ch.: *Vorüberlegungen zu einer Theorie des internationalen Wirtschftsrechts.* RabelsZ 43 (1979), pp. 6–79

Juenger, F.K.: *Der Kampf ums Forum.* RabelsZ 46 (1982), pp. 709–716

Juenger, F.K.: *A Page of History.* Mercer Law Review 35 (1984), pp. 429–460

Kappus, A.: *Rechtsvergleichende Aspekte zur Vertragsaufhebung wegen Sachmangels nach UN-Kaufrecht.* Recht der Internationalen Wirtschaft (1992), No. 7,.

Karollus, M.: *UN-Kaufrecht: Hinweise für die Vertragspraxis.* Juristische Blätter 115 (1993), pp. 23–33

Kecskés, L.: *Az állam immunitása a nemzetközi magánjogban* (The Immunity of the State in Private International Law). Magyar Jog XXXIII (1986), pp. 157–162

Kecskés, L.: *A külföldi jog alkalmazása Angliában, az Amerikai Egyesült Államokban* (Application of Foreign Law in England and the United States of America). Magyar Jog XXXVII (1990), pp. 775–780, 866–875

Kegel, G.: *The Crisis of Conflict of Laws.* Recueil des Cours 1964, II, pp. 91–268

Kegel, G.: *Joseph Story.* RabelsZ 43 (1979), pp. 609–631

Kegel, G.: *Story und Savigny.* Festschrift für die Rechtswissenschaftliche Fakultät Köln, 1988, pp. 65 et seq.

Király, M.: *Beszámoló egy megifjodott könyv vitájáról* (Mádl, F.–Vékás, L.: Nemzetközi magánjog és a nemzetközi gazdasági kapcsolatok joga) [An Account of the Debate on an Updated Book (Mádl, F.–Vékás, L.: *Private International Law and the Law of International Economic Relations*).] Jogtudományi Közlöny XLI (1986), pp. 304–305

Korkisch, F.: *Neues IPR in Ostmitteleuropa*, RabelsZ 32 (1968), pp. 601–650

Koschucharoff, A.: *Das internationale Eherecht im bulgarischen Familiengesetzbuch.* RabelsZ 36 (1972), pp. 492–509

König, D.: *Vereinheitlichung des internationalen Schuldrechts in der Europäischen Gemeinschaft.* Europarecht 1975, pp. 289–318

Kötz, H.: *Rechtsvereinheitlichung – Nutzen, Kosten, Methoden, Ziele.* RabelsZ 50 (1986), pp. 1 et. seq.

Kramer, E.A.: *Uniforme Interpretation von Einheitsprivatı echt – mit besonderer Berücksichtigung von Art. 7 UNKR.* Juristische Blätter 118 (1996), pp. 137–151

Kropholler, J.: *Das kollisionsrechtliche System des Schutzes der schwächeren Vertragspartei.* RabelsZ 42 (1978), pp. 634–661

Lalive, P.: *Tendances et méthodes en droit international privé.* Recueil des Cours 1977, II, pp. 1–424

Lando, O.: *The Law Applicable to the Merits of the Dispute*, in: Sarcevic (eds.): pp. 129–159

Laursen, F.: *The Community's Policy towards EFTA*: Regime Formation in the European Economic Space (EES). Journal of Common Market Studies 28 (1990), pp. 303–325

Leloczky, K.: *Az exporthitel-biztosítás továbbfejlesztése* (Further Development of Export Credit Insurance). Külgazdaság XXII (1978), pp. 55–58

Leloczky, K.: *A politikai kockázatok elleni biztosítás aktuális kérdései* (Topical Issues of Insurance against Political Risks). Külgazdaság XXIII (1979), Jogi Melléklet, pp. 1–7

Lewald, H.: *Regles générales des conflits de lois.* Recueil des Cours 1939, III, pp. 1–147

Lontai, E.: *Aktuális tendenciák a nemzetközi iparjogvédelem területén* (Current Trends in the International Protection of Industrial Property). Jogtudományi Közlöny XXXVI (1981), pp. 1007–1015

Lüderitz; A.: *Anknüpfung im Parteiinteresse.* Festschrift Kegel, Frankfurt 1977, pp. 31–54

Mádl, F.: *Új szakasz a magyar nemzetközi magánjogban?* (A New Stage in Hungarian Private International Law?). Állam- és Jogtudomány XI (1968), pp. 285–317

Mádl, F.: *Elméleti megfontolások gyakorlati célra nemzetközi magánjogi norma alkotásához* (Theoretical Considerations for Practical Purposes in Formulating Private International Norms). Jogtudományi Közlöny XXIV (1969), pp. 451–463

Mádl, F.: *Az állam a gazdaságban és az immunitás problémái, különös tekintettel a gazdasági integrációkra* (The State in the Economy and the Problems of Immunity, with Particular Emphasis on Economic Integration). Jogtudományi Közlöny XXIX (1974), pp. 265–274

Mádl, F.: *Újabb szakaszban egy korszerű magyar nemzetközi magánjogi kódexért* (A New Stage of Efforts for a Modern Hungarian Code of Private International Law). Jogtudományi Közlöny XXXIII (1978), pp. 639–655

Mádl, F.: *Beruházások és gazdasági társulások külföldiek részvételével Magyarországon* (Investments and Joint Ventures with Foreign Participation in Hungary). Állam- és Jogtudomány XXV (1982), pp. 270–320

Mádl, F.: *Political Risks within the Sphere of Foreign Trade Transactions.* Annal. Univ. Budapestiensis 26 (1984), pp. 138–147

Mádl, F.: *Érték vagy jogbiztonság a nemzetközi magánjogban,* in: Németh J.–Vékás L. (szerk.): Emlékkönyv Beck Salamon születésének 100. évfordulójára (Value or Legal Security in Private International Law, in: Németh, J.–Vékás, L. (eds.): *Memorial Volume on the 100th Anniversary of the Birth of Salamon Beck*), Budapest, 1985, pp. 105–119

Mádl, F.: *Competence of Arbitral Tribunals in International Commercial Arbitration,* in: Sarcevic (ed.): pp. 92–112

Mádl, F.: *Az akarati autonómia a magyar nemzetközi magánjogban* (Party Autonomy in Hungarian Private International Law). Állam- és Jogtudomány XXX (1987–88), pp. 633–644 [in German: Acta Juridica XXXI (1989), pp. 289–305]

Mádl, F.: *On the Legal Regulation of the Integrating Market of the European Community,* in: Trends in World Economy – The Single European Market 1992, Changes and Tasks for Hungary. Budapest 1989, pp. 103 et seq.

Mádl, F.: *Ius Commune Europaea.* Jogtudományi Közlöny XLV (1990), pp. 117–132 (in English in: *Conflicts et harmonisations.* Mélanges en l'honneur d'Alfred E. von Overbeck. Fribourg 1990, pp. 287–319)

Magnus, U.: *Währungsfragen im Einheitlichen Kaufrecht.* RabelsZ 53 (1989), pp. 116–143

Magnus, U.: *Aktuelle Fragen des UN-Kaufrechts.* ZEuP 1 (1993), pp. 79–99

Martiny, D.: *Anerkennung ausländischer Entscheidungen nach autonomen Recht,* in: Handbuch des Internationalen Zivilverfahrensrecht Bd. III/1 (1984), Kap. I

Martonyi, J.: *Az EGK hatásköre a nemzetközi gazdasági kapcsolatok terén* (The Jurisdiction of the EEC within the Sphere of International Economic Relations). Külgazdaság XXVI (1982), Jogi Melléklet, pp. 33–45

Martonyi, J.: *A külföldi beruházások jogi kérdései* (Legal Issues of Foreign Investments). Külgazdaság XXXI (1987), pp. 113–122

McCaffrey, St.C.: *The Thirty-Fourth Session of the International Law Commission.* American Journal of Comparative Law 77 (1983), pp. 323–338

Mehren, von A.T.: *Une esquisse de l'évolution du droit international privé aux États-Unis.* Cluent 100 (1973), pp. 116–157

Meyer–Grimberg, Ch.: *Rechtswahl im internationalen Bereicherungsrecht.* IPRax 12 (1992), pp. 153–154

Mohi, Cs.: *A dömpingjog néhány összefüggéséről* (On Some Aspects of Dumping Law). Jogtudományi Közlöny XXXVIII (1983), pp. 278–284

Nadelmann, K.H.: *Some Historical Notes on the Doctrinal Sources of American Conflicts Law.* Festgabe Gutzwiller, Basel 1959, pp. 263–281

Náray, P.: *A GATT Tokiói Fordulójának hatása a nemzetközi kereskedelem szabályaira* (The Impact of the Tokyo Round of GATT on the Regulation of International Trade). Gazdaság és Jogtudomány XV (1981), pp. 129–155

Nestor, I.–Capatina, O.: *Chronique de jurisprudence roumaine relative au droit international privé 1967–1970.* Clunet 98 (1971), pp. 618–640

Neuhaus, P.H.: *Savigny und dir Rechtsfindung aus der Natur der Sache.* RabelsZ 15 (1949–50), pp. 364–381

Neuhaus, P.H.: *Neue Wege im europäischen internationalen Privatrecht?* RabelsZ 35 (1971), pp. 40–428

Neuhaus, P.H.: *Der Schweizer IPR-Entwurf – Ein internationales Modell?* RabelsZ 43 (1979), pp. 277–289

Neuhaus, P.H.: *Abschied von Savigny?* RabelsZ 46 (1982), pp. 4–25

Nicolaysen, G.: *Az Európai Gazdasági Közösség autonóm kereskedelempolitikája* (The Autonomous Trade Policy of the European Economic Community). Jogtudományi Közlöny XXXVIII (1983), pp. 254–260

de Nova, R.: *Historical and Comparative Introduction to Conflict of Law.* Recueil des Cours 1966, II, pp. 435–621

Puttfarken, H.-J.: *Droit commun législatif und die Einheit der Profession.* RabelsZ 45 (1981), pp. 91–105

Rabel, E.: *Das Problem der Qualifikation.* RabelsZ 5 (1931), pp. 241–288

Rajski, J.: *The New Polish Private International Law.* International Comparative Law Quarterly 15 (1966), pp. 457–469

Réczei, L.: *A visszautalás* (Reference Back). Jogtudományi Közlöny XXV (1970), pp. 151–160

Reese, W.L.M.: *Choice of Law Rules or Approach.* Cornell Law Review 57 (1972), pp. 315–334

Reinhart, G.: *Az egységesített nemzetközi magánjogi normák egységes értelmezéséhez az EGBGB 36. cikke szerint* (On the Uniform Interpretation of Unified Private International Norms under Art. 36 of EGBGB). Magyar Jog 42 (1995), pp. 542–547

Reisch, G.: *The EFTA Dimensions in the Relations EC-Eastern Europe.* A summary manuscript for the colloquium of the Europe Institute of Geneva University (The Political and Legal Framework of Trade and Economic Relations between EC and Eastern Europe, Geneva, 10–11 May 1990)

Reus, A.: *Die "forum non conveniens-doctrine" in Großbritannien und den USA in Zukunft auch im deutschen Prozeß?* "Recht der internationalen Wirtschaft 1991/7, p.

Rheim, E.: *Auf dem Weg zu einem westeuropäischen Wirtschaftsraum.* Europa-Archiv 14 (1985), pp. 417–424

Sarcevic, P.: *The Setting Aside and Enforcement of Arbitral Awards under the UNCITRAL Model Law*, in: Sarcevic, P. (ed.), pp. 176–196

Schlechtriem, P.: *Internationales Bereicherungsrecht.* Ein Beitrag zur Anknüpfung vom Bereicherungsansprüchen im deutschen IPR. IPRax 14 (1994), pp. 65–71

Schmitthoff, C.M.: *International Trade and Private International Law.* Festschrift Dölle, Tübingen 1963, II, pp. 254–272

Schmitthoff, C.M.: *The Unification or Harmonisation of Law by Means of Standard Contracts and General Conditions.* International and Comparative Law Quarterly 17 (1968), pp. 551–570

Schwind, F.: *Die Rechtswahl im IPR-Gesetz und nach der Resolution des Institut de Droit International vom 1991.* ZfRV 33 (1992), pp. 101–108

Schwung, S.: *Das Ersatzrecht bei einem Verstoss des ausländischen Rechts gegen den ordre public.* RabelsZ 49 (1985), pp. 407–425

Siehr, K.: *Ehrenzweigs lex-fori-Theorie und ihre Bedeutung für das amerikanische und deutsche Kollisionsrecht.* RabelsZ 34 (1970), pp. 585–635

Sinclair, I.M.: *The European Convention on State Immunity.* International and Comparative Law Quarterly 22 (1973), pp. 256–281

Sturm, F.: *Fakultatives Kollisionsrecht: Notwendigkeit und Grenzen.* Festschrift Zweigert, Tübingen 1981, pp. 329–351

Székely, K.: *A fizetés pénznemének kérdései a Bécsi Vételi Egyezményben* (Questions of the Currency of Payment in the Vienna Sales Convention). Friss Hírek 3/92, pp. 24–28

Takáts, P.: *Általános szerződési feltételek – kollíziós jogi problémák* (General Conditions of Contract – Problems of Conflicts Law). Jogtudományi Közlöny XXXVI (1981), pp. 762–771

Váli, F.: *A magyar-csehszlovák vegyes döntőbíróság és az Állandó Nemzetközi Bíróságok ítélete a Pázmány Péter Egyetem perében* (The Award of the Hungarian-Czechoslovak Mixed Court of Arbitration and the Judgement of the Permanent Court of International Justice in the Lawsuit of Péter Pázmány University). Budapest 1934

Várady, T.: *Anerkennung und Vollstreckung ausländischer Entscheidungen in Jugoslavien.* RabelsZ 57 (1987), pp. 632–680

Várady, T.: *Választottbíráskodás a felek ellenére?* (Arbitration against the Will of the Parties?). Magyar Jog 42 (1995), pp. 51–64

Vékás, L.: *A kollíziós jog kodifikációjának elveihez* (On the Principles of the Codification of Conflicts Law). Jogtudományi Közlöny XXV (1970), pp. 651–661

Vékás, L.: *Zur Kodifikation des ungarischen Internationalen Privatrechts.* Jahrbuch für Ostrecht XX/2 (1979), pp. 297–331

Vékás, L.: *Tervezetek az NSZK nemzetközi magánjogának kodifikálására* (Drafts for the Codification of FRG Private International Law). Magyar Jog XXVIII (1981), pp. 561–566

Vékás, L.: *Elméleti tanulságok a nemzetközi magánjog újabb nyugati kodifikációiban* (Theoretical Lessons in More Recent Western Codifications of Private International Law). Jogtudományi Közlöny XXXVII (1982), pp. 38–45

Vékás, L.: *Zur Sonderanknüpfung von Drittstaaten-Eingriffsnormen.* Annal. Univ. Budapest 27 (1985), pp. 263–272

Vékás, L.: *Wertorientierung und ihre Grenzen im IPR*, in: Holl, W-Klinke, U. (ed.): Internationales Privatrecht – Internationales Wirtschaftsrecht, Köln 1985, pp. 145–159

Vékás, L.: *Zum persönlichen und räumlichen Anwendungsbereich des UN-Einheitskaufrechts.* IPRax 7 (1987), pp. 342–346

Vékás, L.: *Az áruk nemzetközi adásvételére vonatkozó ENSZ-Egyezmény hatálybalépése elé* (In Anticipation of the Entry into Force of the United Nations Convention on the International Sale of Goods). Magyar Jog XXXIV (1987), pp. 385–500

Vékás, L.: *Das Internationale Kaufrecht im "Ostgeschäft"*, in: Hoyer, Posch, (eds.): Das Einheitliche Wiener Kaufrecht. Wien 1992, pp. 215–228

Vida, S.: *A szellemi alkotások és a nemzetközi magánjogi kódex* (Intellectual Works and the Code of Private International Law). Jogtudományi Közlöny XXXVI (1981), pp. 1040–1048

Vida, S.: *Alapvető szerződésszegés a nemzetközi adásvételnél: Német bírói gyakorlat* (Fundamental Breach of Contract in International Sales: German Judicial Practice). Jogtudományi Közlöny XLVIII (1993), pp. 169–176

Vischer, F.: *Die Kritik an der herkömmlichen Methode des Internationalen Privatrechts. Festschrift Germann*, Bern 1969, pp. 287–307

Vischer, F.: *Das Problem der Kodifikation des schweizerischen internationalen Privatrechts.* Zeitschrift für Schweizerisches Recht 90 (1971), pp. 1–106

Wächter, von C.G.: *Über die Kollision der Privatrechtsgesetze verschiedener Staaten.* AcP 24 (1841), pp. 230–311; AcP (1842), pp. 161–200, 361–419

Weber, R.H.: *Parteiautonomie im Internationalen Sachenrecht?* RabelsZ 44 (1980), pp. 510–530

Weiss, E: *Droit de la famille et des successions*, in: Legislation comparée, 2, 1993, Hongrie

Wengler, W.: *The General Principles of Private International Law*. Recueil des Cours 1961, III, pp. 273–469

Wiethölter, R.: *Begriffs- oder Interessenjurisprudenz – falsche Fronten im IPR und Wirtschaftsverfassungsrecht*. Festschrift Kegel, Frankfurt 1977, pp. 213–263

Will, M.R.: *Verwirkung im internationalen Privatrecht*. RabelsZ 42 (1978), pp. 211–226

Yntema, H.E.: *Die historischen Grundlagen des internationalen Privatrechts*. Festschrift Rabel, Tübingen 1953, I, pp. 513–537

Yntema, H.E.: *The Comity Doctrine*. Festschrift Dölle, Tübingen 1963, II, pp. 65–86

Zlinszky, J.: *A nemzetközi magánjog kezdetei Magyarországon* (The Beginnings of Private International Law in Hungary). Jogtudományi Közlöny XXVI (1981), pp. 941–949

Zweigert, K.: *Die dritte Schule im internationalen Privatrecht*. Festschrift Raape, Hamburg 1948, pp. 35–52

Zweigert, K.: *Internationales Privatrecht und öffentliches Recht*, in: Fünzing Jahre Institut für internationales Recht an der Universität Kiel. Hamburg 1965, pp. 124–141

Zweigert, K.–Drobnig, U.: *Einheitliches Kaufgesetz und internationales Privatrecht*. RabelsZ 29 (1965), pp. 146–165